The Elephant and the Tiger

The Full Story of the Vietnam War

The Elephant
and
the Tiger

The Full Story
Of the Vietnam War

Wilbur H. Morrison

Hellgate Press
Central Point, Oregon

The Elephant and the Tiger
© 1990, 2001
Published by Hellgate Press

Hellgate Press, an imprint of PSI Research

P.O. Box 3727
Central Point, Oregon 97502

Email: info@psi-research.com
Web: psi-research.com

Library of Congress Cataloging-in-Publication Data
Morrison, Wilbur H. 1915—
    The elephant and the tiger: full story of the Vietnam War/Wilbur H.
Morrison
    Originally published: New York: Hippocrene Books, 1990.
    Includes biographical references and index.
    ISBN 1-55571-612-1 (paper)
    1. Vietnamese Conflict, 1961-1975. I. Title.

DS557.7 .M65 2001
959.704'3--dc21

                                                                2001016788

Printed and bound in the United States of America

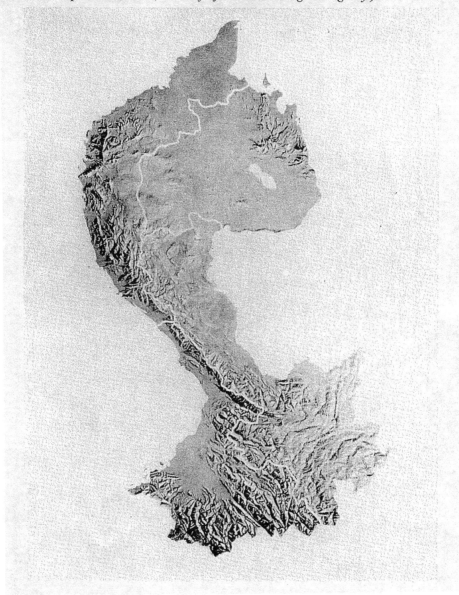

Relief map of Indochina. *(Courtesy of Central Intelligence Agency.)*

Contents

Acknowledgments   xi

Introduction   xv

Prologue   xix

PART I. A TROUBLED ERA

Chapter 1. The Elephant and the Tiger   3

Chapter 2. French Underestimate Vietminh   15

Chapter 3. Fall of Dien Bien Phu   27

Chapter 4. A New Type of Warfare   41

Chapter 5. The Human Factor   55

Chapter 6. The Heart of the Matter   73

Chapter 7. "What Is the Attitude of the United
            States?"   87

Chapter 8. End of a Troubled Era   105

PART II. WAR ESCALATION

Chapter 9. Political Instability Affects War Effort   119

Chapter 10. The Big Lie 137

Chapter 11. Open American Combat 149

Chapter 12. Rolling Thunder 159

Chapter 13. An Old Play with New Actors 173

Chapter 14. Search and Destroy 187

Chapter 15. "Hey, Hey, L.B.J., How Many Kids Did You Kill Today?" 201

Chapter 16. "Without Reinforcements, Kiss Us Goodbye!" 215

Chapter 17. "General, We Will Die Together!" 229

Chapter 18. Bouncing Bettys 243

Chapter 19. It Was a New Day—and They Still Held. 261

Chapter 20. "You No Warn VC No More." 277

Chapter 21. All Targets Must Be Struck 299

Chapter 22. "What Will I Tell the President?" 313

Chapter 23. A Hammer and Anvil Operation 327

Chapter 24. "God, I've Got It." 345

Chapter 25. Enemy Buildup 363

PART III. A REDISCOVERED FAITH

Chapter 26. Tet Offensive 389

Chapter 27. Khe Sanh 405

Chapter 28. A Disastrous Defeat for the Communists 419

Chapter 29. Vietnamization   437

Chapter 30. Fear and Uncertainty at Home   451

Chapter 31. Agent Orange   465

Chapter 32. A Tidal Wave of Refugees   479

Chapter 33. To the Last Man   495

Chapter 34. The Siege of An Loc   511

Chapter 35. A Time for Action   527

Chapter 36. Linebacker II   545

Chapter 37. A Blunt, Emphatic Message   559

Chapter 38. Ceasefire   573

Chapter 39. "Don't Curse the Darkness. Light a
             Candle."   589

PART IV. THE FINAL COLLAPSE

Chapter 40. Ceasefire Violations   603

Chapter 41. Battles for Key Terrain   613

Chapter 42. Fall of Phuoc Long   625

Chapter 43. Ban Me Thuot Falls   635

Chapter 44. Exodus from the Highlands   645

Chapter 45. Americans Flee Nha Trang   655

Chapter 46. The Final Stand   663

Epilogue   677

Bibliography 683

Index 687

MAPS

Corps Area xxiv

North Vietnam's Sanctuaries 246

Cedar Falls Operation and the Iron Triangle 328

Northern Quang Tri Province 376

The Enemy Plan 378

The Battle of Hue 394

The Final Days 628

Acknowledgments

IN MY RESEARCH FOR *THE ELEPHANT AND THE TIGER*, I READ OVER TEN million words of text about the war in Indochina, most of it in highly detailed reports by members of all branches of the United States armed services, and in specially written documents by former officials of both Vietnams, Laos and Cambodia. Without the extraordinary efforts of hundreds of men and women who prepared these narratives, often using material that was gained first hand on the battlefields or within their respective governments, this book would have been almost impossible to write. I owe each of them a debt of gratitude that, I hope, will be repaid by giving greater distribution to their thoughtful and honest critiques.

In addition to this basic research material, I interviewed a great many people who fought in Indochina, from those at the highest levels to those in the front lines.

In acknowledging those who aided me most in my research, I would like to give credit to General Curtis E. LeMay, A.F. Ret., Admiral James S. Russell, U.S.N. Ret.; Admiral Ulysses S. G. Sharp, U.S.N. Ret.; Vice Admiral David C. Richardson, U.S.N. Ret.; Major General Kenneth J. Houghton, U.S.M.C. Ret., Rear Admiral James D. Ramage, U.S.N. Ret., Army Colonel Harry G. Summers, Jr.; Colonel William E. Le Gro, U.S.A. Ret.; Captain Robert Arnold, U.S.N. Ret.; Captain R. G. Hanecak, U.S.N. Ret.; Gunnery Sergeant Bradley Spencer, U.S.M.C. Ret.; Raul Fernandez, Jr., library director of the Naval Training Center at San Diego; Patrick J. Carney, library director at Camp Pendleton; William Z. Slany, historian, Department of State; Paul Marr, Central Intelligence Agency; Congressman Ron Packard and Senator Alan Cranston.

The historians at the United States Department of State provided me with a valuable off-the-record briefing that was most helpful in resolving certain pertinent facts in my possession. Mr. Slany was most cooperative and his assistance is appreciated. In other dealings with the Department of

State—in which I used the Freedom of Information Act to secure further documentation of the role of the late President John F. Kennedy and the late Ambassador Henry Cabot Lodge in President Diem's overthrow—I was stonewalled for months. This bureaucratic procrastination makes a mockery of the United States Congress's intent for the Freedom of Information Act. Forty-three documents—mostly classified as secret—were finally identified and all but one was made available to me. Release of this document was denied for security reasons. The released material is included in Chapters 7 and 8.

Wilbur H. Morrison
Fallbrook, CA 92028

"If the tiger ever stands still, the elephant will crush him with his mighty tusks. But the tiger will not stand still. He will leap upon the back of the elephant, tearing huge chunks from his side, and then he will leap back into the dark jungle. And slowly the elephant will bleed to death. Such will be the war in Indochina."

—Ho Chi Minh

Introduction

PRIOR TO AMERICA'S ENTRY IN WORLD WAR II, PRESIDENT FRANKLIN D. Roosevelt ordered a defense buildup in the United States to meet the threat posed by Adolf Hitler and Germany's Third Reich. In opposition, former Roosevelt supporter General Hugh Johnson denounced the president's so-called warlike acts as "a kind of reckless shooting craps with destiny for the sake of democracy." Later events proved the fallacy of Johnson's isolationism, but his words might well be applied to the war in Indochina as the free world's soldiers, sailors and airmen were used as pawns in a war without definite political or military goals.

This book was written for those men and women who fought bravely and honorably in that war. It is not limited to one service but involves the actions of land, sea and air forces of the United States, both Vietnams and their allies. Like my previous books it uses basic research material but relies heavily on eyewitness accounts by those who were there.

The book seeks to portray the truth behind the war's initiation, and describes in detail how the United States lost the war. After extensive interviews, the book explores the actions of the war's political, social and military leaders from December 13, 1954—the date when the United States first signed a formal agreement with France to assume more responsibility for equipping and training the South Vietnamese armed forces—until 1975 when South Vietnam's army was swept aside by the North Vietnamese Army and the last Americans were forced to flee the country in ignominious defeat.

There are several basic reasons for Indochina's loss to the communists. President Lyndon B. Johnson's indecision is not fully understood because it involves his attempts to further President John F. Kennedy's hardline goals to contain communism in the Far East by taking a stand in Vietnam. There were others equally responsible, some of whom gave President Johnson inexpert advice. Chief among them were Secretary of Defense

Robert S. McNamara whose inept attempts to control war operations contributed later to America's defeat, and General William G. Westmoreland who kept insisting that the best way to win the war was to involve more and more American ground troops in a war of attrition. It is my belief that if Westmoreland had limited the United States Army's role to training South Vietnam's ground forces, letting them fight the war assisted only by American air and sea power, that the armed forces of the Republic of Vietnam would have been better prepared after extensive combat experience—including some defeats on the battlefields—to defend themselves when they faced the North Vietnamese on their own.

Through the years the armed forces of the United States, and those of every other nation, have each had to learn that there comes a time when they must stand and fight their own battles. Westmoreland's decision to use American and Allied troops to fight South Vietnam's tough battles tended to make that nation's armed forces weaker and brought them to a state of near impotence even though properly led members often fought well and heroically in the defense of their homeland.

Five American presidents—Truman, Eisenhower, Kennedy, Johnson and Nixon—must share a measure of responsibility for the war's outcome, along with congressional leaders who abrogated their responsibilities to the American people. Dishonest actions were repeatedly taken by escalating the United States' involvement under the guise of containment of communism. But I believe the United States cannot be faulted for its moral responsibility to assist another nation when that nation is threatened by forces outside its control and requests assistance. However, the actions taken by United States political leaders, without concurrence by the majority of the American people, cannot be condoned. These leaders must be held accountable. If the issue of war had been brought before the Congress, and the question of war or peace decided on the merits of the case, few people would have had cause for objection.

It is the author's belief that the fighting abilities of America's men and women, and those of her allies, are not sufficiently appreciated. Almost all members of the United States military establishment acted honorably. As I have demonstrated in this book, Americans never fought better despite incredible restrictions on their activities. They deserved far better leadership than they received at the political and military levels in Washington.

I believe that the United States should have declared war to get the American people committed to the war or, barring that, it should not have become involved.

In any war the main purpose of military action is to convince the enemy that he is defeated. In Indochina we did not even convince the North

Vietnamese that we *wanted* to defeat them. Our military actions served only to convince the North Vietnamese that we were not so tough a foe after all. President Johnson's statements that we did not want to change their government and that we would not consider invading North Vietnam left military people wondering, "Why are we here?"

I have nothing but admiration for the men and women of all nations who fought in Indochina and served their countries so unselfishly. It is my hope that *The Elephant and the Tiger* will contribute to a greater understanding of the war and its tragic outcome.

Wilbur H. Morrison
Fallbrook, CA 92028

Prologue

SAIGON'S SULTRY NIGHT AIR INCREASED CAPTAIN ARTHUR MALLANO'S feeling of uneasiness as he sat in the pilot's seat of his United States Air Force C-130 Hercules. He had flown to Tan Son Nhut air base from Clark Air Force Base in the Philippines less than an hour earlier; his fifth such one-thousand-mile flight to evacuate Americans, third country nationals and South Vietnamese leaving their doomed country. The long hours in the air, and the tenseness of the situation in South Vietnam, had brought him close to a state of exhaustion. Vivid lights, stabbing at the dark sky to the north, momentarily highlighted the tight lines around his eyes.

Mallano glanced anxiously out of his side window at the long line of people approaching his plane's rear loading ramp. Vietnamese women, many with babies in their arms, and clutching other youngsters by their hands, struggled to suppress their emotions. Their babies, instinctively sensing their mothers' fears, were quiet although their dark eyes were staring, while a touch of terror lingered in their depths. The deep-rooted fears of their mothers were quickly transmitted to the children through their mothers' clutching hands and the tremors that shook their arms. The scene made Mallano wince, and he concentrated on preparations for takeoff.

Before he had left Clark, his flight had been set up, cancelled and then finally approved shortly after midnight April 29, 1975. United States A-37 aircraft, now in the hands of the North Vietnamese, had bombed Tan Son Nhut the evening before and temporarily closed the field.

The military situation was rapidly approaching a critical phase, and the status of Tan Son Nhut as the major air base for evacuation from South Vietnam was grim. The government-imposed twenty-four hour curfew had maintained a shaky calm, but Mallano knew the situation would last only as long as security forces maintained their posts. He had no illusions. The American involvement in Vietnam was about to end. At least fourteen

North Vietnamese Army divisions, totaling close to 200,000 battle-hardened combat troops, were poised to make their final attack. They had swept from the north in human waves with large numbers of tanks and heavy guns. South Vietnamese government troops had often fought well, but they had been no match for the well-led communist troops who fought with a ferocity that few armies had ever displayed.

Saigon's population had swelled to more than 4 million people—more than two-and-a-half times its normal population—as refugees from the northern provinces flocked to the city, along with thousands of panic-stricken members of South Vietnam's armed forces.

Mallano glanced up, noting that a third transport from Clark Air Base was taxiing to a nearby loading ramp.

Streaks of light that he had earlier assumed were bolts of lightning (this was the start of the monsoon season) appeared again. Mallano turned to his co-pilot. "That thunderstorm is getting a little closer. It is moving toward the field."

The darkness quickly disappeared as different-colored rocket bursts and mortars erupted on the field. Mallano realized that those bright flashes he had mistaken for lightning were a concentrated barrage of mortars and rockets. The tower was hit, and a fuel truck exploded with a blinding flash. Rockets fell all over Tan Son Nhut, and one landed just under the wing of a C-130, setting it on fire. Miraculously, the crew escaped.

Mallano knew they had to get away quickly or they would meet the same fate. He glanced at his watch. It was 3:58 A.M. He yelled to his loadmaster, "Get the last passengers on. We're leaving. Forget the baggage."

The evacuees needed no urging and they clambered aboard and sat on the floor while the ramp was raised and Mallano taxied the overloaded C-130. He learned later that he had more than 260 people on board—far more than the seventy-five specified for normal operations. With the rocket attack increasing in severity, and accurately hitting targets, he taxied faster than was prudent because rockets were exploding on all sides, trying to stop his transport before it could become airborne. He headed for a taxiway in lieu of the damaged runway but, at the last moment, he recalled that there was an anti-aircraft battery at the end of the strip and the barrels of its big guns were sticking straight up. He knew that, in his overloaded condition, he would be barely off the ground at this point and the C-130 transport would crash into the battery. Despite the condition of the runway he headed for it. In the rear he could hear his loadmaster screaming, without understanding his words. He hoped someone had not died. He taxied even faster with his four engines at power settings normally used only in flight until he got to the end of the runway. There, he quickly went to full power and the four props chewed at the air trying to force the heavily laden transport to gain takeoff speed.

He caught a quick glimpse of the C-130 that had been hit on the ramp as it blew up with a blinding flash. He learned later that this was Captain Lawrence Wessel's plane.

When a rocket had landed beneath the wing of Wessel's plane he had yelled to his crew, "This is it. We're getting out!" They had left the burning plane and hurried to Captain Gregory Chase's nearby plane and boarded it just as it was hurriedly getting ready to embark even though it was not fully loaded.

Mallano, meanwhile, fought to keep his C-130 in the air. It was so overloaded that Captain Chase's airplane, with Wessel's crew on board, beat Mallano's plane to cruise altitude because of its lighter weight. Chase's plane was the last United States Air Force fixed-wing aircraft to leave Tan Son Nhut.

President Gerald R. Ford had sought $327 million from the United States Congress for humanitarian aid, but the request included a provision giving Ford authority to send American combat troops into South Vietnam to protect the evacuation. Due to his request for commitment of American troops the House of Representatives turned down the authorization by a vote of 245 to 162.

President Ford sent a letter to the Congress saying their action "was not worthy of a people which has lived by the philosophy symbolized by the Statue of Liberty."

There were 5,000 American troops on ships at sea who could have been used, but the end came so suddenly that there was no need for them even if Congress had authorized their participation.

The Congress later did authorize the $327 million to bring the refugees to this country and to get them established in their adopted land.

This frantic evacuation had not been foreseen. For months, plans had been made to leave South Vietnam in an orderly fashion if the South Vietnamese government should fall to the North Vietnamese Army. The United States embassy in Saigon and its Defense Attaché Office at Tan Son Nhut had worked out evacuation plans in December, 1974, with Ambassador Graham Martin in charge. At the time, most Americans in the Defense Attaché Office, established after the ceasefire in late January, 1973, to handle United States' interests in South Vietnam, knew that such an evacuation was a foregone conclusion. With the continued infiltration of North Vietnamese Army units in the South, American officers believed that it no longer was a question of whether an evacuation would be necessary, but when it would be needed. But few thought collapse of South Vietnam's armed forces would be so sudden, and this proved to be a major flaw in the plan, and the primary reason why the actual evacuation failed to resemble the original plan.

At the start of 1975 American planners figured 8,000 Americans and third country nationals would need to be evacuated. A firm figure for South Vietnamese evacuees was never achieved for various reasons. There were estimates that ranged from fifteen hundred to a million people. Included in these totals were those considered most endangered by a communist takeover of South Vietnam.

One of the problems that was only partially solved was the matter of ground communications to alert potential evacuees. No such reliable system was ever devised. Actually, ground evacuation was feasible only in a few areas. It was agreed that sealift would be more practical than airlift of some of their people while millions of others awaited an uncertain fate at the hands of the communists.

Russian SA-7 hand-held, heat-seeking missiles were available to the North Vietnamese Army and they had proved deadly as anti-aircraft missiles. Helicopters were most vulnerable because of their slow speed, low-altitude environment.

The United States had long since withdrawn its large military transports so the only reliable aircraft were operated by the Central Intelligence Agency's Air America whose helicopters and small aircraft were unable to fly outside South Vietnam. Evacuation planners knew that, if needed, Military Airlift Command planes and commercial jetliners could be brought to South Vietnam quickly for an emergency airlift. Actually, there were 30,000 people and planes of the Seventh Air Force at Nakhon Phanom, Thailand—both airlift and combat—that could be used in an emergency.

Although ground communications problems were never solved, personnel of the Defense Attaché Office requested a satellite communications unit. With remarkable foresight, the unit was installed in a secure place accessible to the Defense Attaché Office and was ready for use March 30. It was completely independent of all other communications systems, and it worked well throughout the evacuation.

By the date of its installation, the military situation throughout South Vietnam had deteriorated drastically, and Saigon itself was close to anarchy. The Central Highlands had fallen earlier, and so had the great airport and sea terminal at Da Nang. Even worse for the fate of the South Vietnamese government, the United States Congress had made it clear that no additional emergency appropriations would be approved. Compounding the problems in South Vietnam, the crisis in neighboring

Cambodia was at its peak, and the situation there was competing with Saigon for American resources and attention.

Ambassador Graham Martin and members of the Defense Attaché Office had no illusions about the reliability of South Vietnam's security forces. They had seen the chaos earlier that had enveloped Pleiku, Da Nang and the abandoned cities north of Saigon under the relentless advance of the North Vietnamese Army. Martin therefore ordered that American security forces provide for their own defense at American installations.

First, it was clear that South Vietnamese dependents of American personnel, and those on an earlier list of non-essential United States citizens, should be evacuated as soon as possible. A major problem developed when South Vietnam's citizens had to obtain exit visas before they could depart regardless of whether they were dependents of citizens of the United States. Despite the best of intentions, all sorts of delays prevented the departure of Americans who refused to leave without their wives and children. No one had foreseen the red tape that was now encountered by government departments and non-official agencies. The bureaucracy of the United States Civil Service Commission, with its built-in procedures and safeguards, now posed other substantial problems in obtaining permission to evacuate United States Civil Service employees, even though only weeks remained before the country was overrun. Civil Service rules called for gathering large numbers of official personnel folders for shipment to Travis Air Force Base in California to reconstruct individual files before requests for transfer could be processed. Maintaining such files in Vietnam was a questionable procedure. It would have made more sense to maintain them in the Philippines or in Hawaii.

The Evacuation Control Center started operations April 1 in the Defense Attaché Office's annex. It was manned by twelve United States officers representing each of the military services.

Initially, operations centered around refugee sealift from corps I and II that were now largely overrun. So chaotic were conditions along the coast in the northern provinces that the matter became a nightmare for United States and South Vietnamese officials. Originally, plans called for the evacuation of a million people from I Corps. This proved impossible because the pressure of the North Vietnamese Army proved too great.

Major General Homer D. Smith, United States defense attaché, said later, "In retrospect, had the one million refugees been successfully evacuated south, the Republic of Vietnam would have had an insurmountable problem with their relocation. As it was, they experienced great difficulties in assimilating the less than 100,000 that did escape."

As one area after another fell to the communists, American transports

Map of Vietnam showing corps areas. *(Drawn by Master Sergeant Bradley A. Spencer, M.C., Ret.)*

arrived with greater frequency. By late March, two or three landed each day bringing in military supplies.

The airlift of Vietnamese orphans—or Babylift—continued in April and on the 4th thirty-seven secretaries and analysts who worked for the Defense Attaché Office were selected to help serve as escorts for about two hundred and fifty orphans. A huge C-5 departed on this day from Tan Son Nhut. At 23,000 feet during climbout and while flying ten miles off the Vietnamese coast near Vung Tau, a latch on the rear cargo doors suffered a major structural failure and the sudden explosive decompression created pandemonium inside the huge transport with its improvised crates strapped to the floor that served as bassinets for the babies. Captain Dennis Traynor and his crew nursed the crippled transport back over Saigon. The explosive decompression had blown out a huge section of the cargo ramp and cut all control wires to the rudder and elevator. Using only ailerons and all the power of the four engines for pitch control, Traynor kept the plane in the air. With only limited control Traynor was unable to prevent the plane from touching down momentarily on the ground along the east side of the Saigon River. Incredibly it bounced back into the air and, after flying another half mile, crashed in rice paddies five miles short of Tan Son Nhut's runway, breaking into four sections, and spilling screaming babies and adults into the rice paddies over a wide area and killing 206 of them, including Air Force nurse Captain Mary T. Klinker. A column of black smoke billowed skyward from the scene where the massive fuselage lay twisted and burning in the mud. Eyewitnesses stared as 175 mud-splattered survivors exited from the remnants of the fuselage. Some were white-faced and quiet while others screamed in pain or fright. With great efficiency, some survivors hurried back to the wrecked airplane and began to pull out the dead and injured. Within minutes Vietnamese Air Force helicopters, and those from Air America, were on the scene to help. Later, these helicopters evacuated the living and the dead.

The South Vietnamese province chief, who offered to guard the wrecked airplane, joined his villagers in pilfering the baggage of the dead and the survivors. Although it was never determined, sabotage was suspected. On future flights all baggage was checked for explosive devices.

Evacuation planners knew that difficulty would be experienced in bussing evacuees through Saigon's crowded streets. On April 6, thirty-seven buildings were selected as possible evacuation centers. The number later was reduced to thirteen. Those selected were at least four stories high with roofs that could withstand helicopter operations. Some modifications were needed to clear the rooftops of obstacles and to beef up their structures. Initially, the evacuation job was given to Air America which removed extra helicopters from storage so they could put twenty-four helicopters in the air at a given time. There was a shortage of Air America pilots so each UH-1 had to be flown by only one pilot. This was risky but necessary under the circumstances. Rooftop modifications were completed April 13, and ground transportation was limited to buses that were prepositioned each night at forty-two designated parking locations. Cars were eliminated because the streets were already too congested and buses, with their larger loads, were more efficient.

The Military Sealift Command simultaneously arranged for evacuation down the Saigon River, and it was hoped that 30,000 people could be taken out in merchant ships. It was realized that river security would be a problem and that snipers and mines would be hazards against ships.

After evacuees were moved down the river, they had another seventy road miles to travel before they reached the seaport of Vung Tau where they could be taken on board ships of the Seventh Fleet. The sealift evacuation, like the airlift, was complicated by the evacuation of Americans from Phnom Penh after the Cambodian government was overthrown April 17 by the communist Khmer Rouge.

During the middle of the month Admiral Noel Gaylor, commander-in-chief, Pacific, met with Ambassador Martin to determine how South Vietnamese dependents of United States citizens should be processed to leave South Vietnam. Martin suggested that a single piece of paper be used whereby a sponsor could sign an affidavit certifying that the people on his list were dependents, and that he would be responsible for them after their departure. This suggestion was approved so Americans no longer had any excuse for delaying their departure.

Ambassador Martin had been in a difficult position because he did not want to provoke a mass evacuation that would immediately topple the shaky South Vietnamese government. He had done everything in his power to convince Americans that they should leave, but he had no authority to force United States citizens with legal passports to leave the country. As a result, by April 19 only 2,535 of an estimated ten thousand Americans had left South Vietnam.

As the growing collapse of South Vietnam's ground forces became more apparent, estimated evacuation figures escalated from the original figure of 200,000 to more than a million. Now, control over Vietnam's panicky citizens caused increasing problems at evacuation points. Many who were not authorized to leave got out because of the chaotic conditions that had developed. President Ferdinand Marcos of the Philippines caused additional problems April 23 by limiting the number of evacuees in his country at any one time to 200. Plans were hastily put into effect to move thousands of evacuees to Guam, Wake Island and Yokota Air Force Base in Japan while the Saigon airlift expanded.

Wealthy Vietnamese families arrived at Tan Son Nhut in chauffeur-driven Mercedes limousines and waited for hours under the broiling sun alongside bar girls who clung protectively to their half-American children.

Early in the evacuation, thieves mingled with crowds trying to escape, taking advantage of the congestion. Many evacuees lost their valuables, especially jewelry. To prevent thefts from their luggage, women came through the lines wearing six or eight bracelets on each arm, a couple of rings on each finger, and a dozen or more necklaces. The sight would have been comic except that their jewelry often involved their only negotiable assets.

The South Vietnamese government still refused to permit active duty military personnel and draft-age youths to leave. Many such youths were turned back, causing great anguish to their departing parents.

Some American military personnel assigned to bases in the western Pacific came to Vietnam to rescue their families. While waiting for their dependents' authorizations to leave, these men volunteered their services and were of great help to the over-burdened fifty officers and men of the Defense Attaché Office.

Unfortunately not all American sponsors were honorable. Some evacuated family groups that were unrelated to them after receiving payoffs to pose as their sponsors. They would then return on commercial airlines and take out another family—for a price. Some military deserters tried to get out, and notes were attached to manifests that those who were suspected should be checked upon their arrival outside of South Vietnam.

Earlier evacuees were more routinely processed. Cuong Nhieu, a thirty-four-year-old Vietnamese employee of the United States embassy's security office, left April 23 with his nineteen-year-old pregnant wife Ai. There were more than 1,000 people still waiting to leave when this couple boarded a C-130 at 3:00 A.M. at Tan Son Nhut. On board were American civilians and Vietnamese embassy employees. The full impact of the collapse of South Vietnam's northern province had not registered as the Nhieus departed for the Philippines. To them the flight was a temporary leave-taking and they expected to return to rejoin their families. Up front, the pilot's cockpit was locked, and a Marine guard stood in front of the door with an M-16 rifle. He was a reassuring sight and they felt safe for the first time in weeks.

A week later, during the early hours of Tuesday, April 29, when the last fixed-wing transports were leaving Tan Son Nhut, Lieutenant Colonel

Arthur E. Laehr, the United States Air Force's staff operations officer for the Defense Attaché Office, was jarred out of bed as rockets landed near his trailer in the complex. He learned later that one of the first rockets killed two United States Marines—the only Americans who died on South Vietnamese soil during the evacuation, although two Marine helicopter pilots were killed in a crash at sea. Laehr got up hastily as more rockets exploded.

Lieutenant Colonel John F. Hilgenberg, Air Force chief of the training management branch of the Defense Attaché Office, dove for cover with other workers and evacuees as a rocket hit the top of the gymnasium, scattering metal roofing in all directions, and setting the building on fire. To the east, a huge fireball erupted at the Pacific Architects and Engineers warehouse that had been built by a contractor who managed the last United States facilities in Vietnam. The blaze cast a flickering light over the whole area.

To Hilgenberg the rockets sounded like heavy artillery as they increased to a rate of forty rounds per hour after 4:30 A.M. He was much too preoccupied to be concerned even when the rockets concentrated on the flight line and fuel and ammunition storage areas. He, and the others, kept the crowds under cover and, to keep them occupied, placed them in groups for rapid movement once the airlift was resumed. He quickly learned that an American in uniform was a more powerful and reassuring force than an American in civilian clothes.

Throughout April 29's daylight hours it was apparent to Hilgenberg and other officers of the Defense Attaché Office that flights by fixed-wing aircraft were too hazardous due to the heavy rocket impacts. Captain William O'Brien, a United States officer temporarily assigned to Tan Son Nhut from Clark Air Force Base, was a tower of strength. When the true status of Tan Son Nhut was needed, "Obie" usually volunteered to go out despite the rocket attacks. Often he took his jeep without being asked and went cruising the runways to determine their condition. During the day his radio was the only worthwhile contact officials had of the flight line's status. In the thick of this chaotic mess, with rocket attacks increasing by the hour, "Obie" remained on the field calmly reporting conditions until he was ordered out by Hilgenberg. The order was not given until Hilgenberg was convinced that all hope of continuing the fixed-wing airlift was gone. When "Obie" finally returned rockets and artillery shells were bursting all around him. Of equal danger was the mob of uncontrollable Vietnamese who swarmed all over the flight line, looking for any reason to shoot someone—particularly an American. In the worst of this crisis O'Brien walked slowly away from his jeep to pick up his enlisted men, and then with the same casual air that belied his inner turmoil he drove back to the operations building of the Flying Tigers Airlines to join the rest of the Americans.

During the night, after the last American transport had left for the Philippines, members of the South Vietnamese Air Force began their own evacuation to U-Tapao, Thailand. The dark sky was stained a blotchy red, even though the sun had gone down, due to the fires that ringed Saigon. First Lieutenant Richard Coleman, assistant officer in charge of the Clark Air Force Base detachment that had been flown in to protect American operations, was on the flight line when the rockets started to hit. He watched with horror as the scene got ugly and Vietnamese fought to board their aircraft as they taxied away from the ramps. Some Vietnamese women, children and men were roughly brushed off the aircraft loading ramps as they prepared for a hasty departure. Many of them fell to their death because they clung stubbornly to the ramps until the planes' doors were slammed in their faces as the aircraft taxied rapidly away from the loading areas. Their screams of agony were lost in the hysterical cries of hundreds of people trying desperately to get away. Coleman was shocked as crowded buses were hit by rockets, and he felt a sense of helplessness. One South Vietnamese transport took off on a taxiway, barely clearing the old airfield tower as it staggered off the ground in its overloaded condition. A C-47 tried to take off on one engine, but it spun off the runway into the grass infield where it exploded. While Coleman watched the burning plane a number of survivors dashed to safety. No one checked to see if others were trapped in the plane. This was a time when survivors thought only of themselves.

Air Vice Marshal Nguyen Cao Ky, former vice-president and earlier commander of the Vietnamese Air Force, collected some of his pilots and personally flew them in his helicopter to the carrier *Midway*.

At dawn April 29 South Vietnamese fighters and bombers fired up and took off, not to continue the fight against the North Vietnamese but to fly to Thailand. Many of these planes jettisoned their external fuel tanks, bombs and rockets on the runway, posing an additional problem for all remaining airplanes waiting to take off.

One abandoned fighter blocked the entrance taxiway to the Flying Tigers' passenger loading area. About forty vehicles and several hundred South Vietnamese crowded the area scrambling to board the transports trying to get away.

Not all South Vietnamese were trying to escape before the war ended. At least one gunship spent most of the night dropping flares to light up North Vietnamese Army positions around the airfield, and firing at their exposed positions. This plane refueled time and time again and went back to its lonely and dangerous job of offering resistance to the communists.

At daybreak, two A-1 Skyraiders also took to the air and remained there to attack North Vietnamese Army positions. One supposedly was hit by an SA-7 missile.

At the Evacuation Processing Center John Hilgenberg pondered what to do with several bus loads of evacuees who had been returned to the ramp after their plane had been destroyed in the middle of the night. Although he did not believe that fixed-wing operations could start up again from Tan Son Nhut, shut down since the massive rocket attacks, he ordered members of the United States Navy's Shore Patrol, Marines and civilian volunteers to keep groups in line in case the airlift was resumed. The crowd was tense, he noted, but still controllable and hopeful of getting away. Some of their confidence was reduced, however, when a gunship was shot down at 7:00 A.M., and there was a noticeable increase in depression. With the North Vietnamese Army on the perimeter of Tan Son Nhut, and evidently well equipped with missiles, Hilgenberg now had serious doubts about a resumption of the airlift even if helicopters were used. He believed that any such attempt would be hazardous and costly to crews and evacuees.

When the crowd became more restive, Hilgenberg directed that all remaining evacuees be assigned to plane-size groups, ready to board if the airlift was resumed. This was a token gesture, but it reduced some of their fears.

In Washington, D.C., President Gerald R. Ford convened an emergency meeting of the National Security Council. After discussing the tense situation in South Vietnam, and particularly at Tan Son Nhut, word was sent to Ambassador Martin that if the shelling by the North Vietnamese Army stopped by dawn, fixed-wing aircraft should continue the airlift for one more day. The president and his advisers agreed that only high-risk South Vietnamese, members of the Defense Attaché Office and a substantial portion of the remaining American personnel should be flown out.

When General Smith received the order from Ambassador Martin he asked airlift supervisor Colonel Earl Mickler to evaluate the situation at Tan Son Nhut.

Mickler contacted his men on the field who advised him that the airfield was no longer usable because of ordnance on the runways, and the possibility of rioting South Vietnamese Army and Air Force troops who were streaming onto the runways, ramps and taxiways.

General Smith overruled Colonel Mickler's recommendation to close the field and he was advised to resume the airlift and to start loading people.

Convoys, each with seven buses, now brought Defense Attaché Office personnel, plus Vietnamese civilians who had been approved for evacuation, to the compound. All went well until rockets and artillery shells again started to fall on the airfield and there was panic to get inside the Defense Attaché Office building.

Hilgenberg realized that the walls of the building were a blessing in disguise. They automatically marshaled the people into controllable columns, and the two-story building provided more than enough halls to prevent overcrowding.

General Smith's original doubts about restarting the airlift were reinforced when his associates insisted that it was not humanly possible in the face of consistent artillery barrages and rocket attacks. He called Ambassador Martin to tell him that Tan Son Nhut was no longer usable for aircraft other than helicopters. The ambassador went to the airport personally to check the situation, and he even drove to the flight line for a first-hand look. This was dangerous with bands of Vietnamese roaming the base, many of them heavily armed. For the first time Martin realized the gravity of the situation but he insisted that the airlift should be resumed because he wanted to evacuate a significant number of Vietnamese and he believed that heavy airlift was the only way to do it.

General Smith reported his concern to Admiral Gayler who agreed that it was foolhardy to resume fixed-wing flying from Tan Son Nhut. The commander-in-chief, Pacific, reported Smith's views to the Joint Chiefs of Staff in Washington and he recommended that alternate means of evacuation should be used. The Joint Chiefs concurred and immediately informed Ambassador Martin that he should not try to resume evacuation with heavy aircraft.

At Tan Son Nhut there were approximately twenty-eight hundred evacuees in the area who now believed they would be abandoned, including twelve Americans with their Vietnamese dependents—with an average of ten in each family group.

At 8:00 A.M. April 29 Lieutenant General Tran Van Minh, commander-in-chief of South Vietnam's Air Force, and thirty of his staff entered the Defense Attaché Office compound and demanded evacuation by American aircraft. Lieutenant Colonel Laehr was in the Evacuation Control Center and he sent a message to General Smith in the Readiness Room that senior South Vietnamese Air Force officers were demanding evacuation, and that they were heavily armed.

Smith turned to Lieutenant Colonel Richard Mitchell, assistant air attaché and coordinator for Vietnamese Air Force evacuations. "Tell them I will have them shot if they refuse to give up their arms."

Mitchell looked at the general with dismay. "Just me?"

Smith nodded curtly.

Fortunately the Vietnamese officers offered no resistance. Mitchell escorted them to the Intelligence briefing room so as not to excite others in the building. They were later successfully evacuated.

With top members of the South Vietnamese Air Force at the compound, it was clear to General Smith and his staff that total breakdown of South Vietnam's armed forces was only hours away.

At the Flying Tigers' operations building a group of forty to fifty South Vietnamese, including more Air Force officers and other officials, came in at 9.30 A.M. and demanded evacuation. Major Dale Hensley, supervisor of airlift personnel, remained calm even when two South Vietnamese pilots took him and two others hostage. He convinced them that American planes would arrive from the Philippines as soon as things quieted down. He promised them a seat on one of the first planes. Quietly, Hensley asked for their guns and they were handed over. Any wrong move would have gotten someone killed. Later, they were all evacuated.

By the morning of April 29 most Vietnamese air units had departed Tan Son Nhut because of the artillery and rocket attacks. Major Thanh Tran and a few others remained. Tran's wife Loan and their three children had left earlier by air for Con Son, a small island off South Vietnam's southern coast while he elected to remain behind and continue to fight.

Tran, an assistant commander of a Vietnamese helicopter squadron, had been called in March 22 by his 62nd Wing Commander at Nha Trang. "Da Lat has been lost to the communists," he was told, "but we hope to retake it." This defense bastion was close to Nha Trang and north of the city.

Six days later it was apparent that the South Vietnamese could not hold, and the 2nd Air Division moved its base closer to Nha Trang from its headquarters south of the city. All Air Force units now were ordered to evacuate the area and transfer to Tan Son Nhut at Saigon. Tran, a veteran pilot with 4,000 combat hours who had been shot down five times and hospitalized with injuries several times, joined the exodus for Tan Son Nhut. While he served earlier with the 1st Air Division it had been given a Presidential Unit Citation for valor in combat. Many of Tran's missions had been in support of the Green Berets during 1965–1971.

With the departure of South Vietnam's Air Force leaders, Tran quickly sought a helicopter on the ramp April 29 with sufficient fuel to fly to the southern part of his country. He selected one machine in flyable condition but it had less than 400 pounds of fuel—sufficient for thirty minutes flying time. This was inadquate to reach their refueling stop so he and other members of his squadron drained fuel by hand from the other helicopters. It was an agonizingly slow process, and it took them four hours to transfer fuel in small ammunition cans.

At noon, Tran dropped to the ground when he heard a rocket impact on the runway near his helicopter. He knew that if it exploded they would all be killed. For a tense five minutes they hugged the pavement, rising only when they realized the rocket would not go off.

Tran ordered his men to prepare for a quick takeoff and he checked the helicopter to assure it was still in flyable condition. He glanced up when he heard a car approaching the flight ramp at a high rate of speed. He was relieved to see his operations officer, Major Thu Huynh, with his wife and three children. Now he had a co-pilot. He had been resigned to taking off with just a crew chief in the right seat.

Tran ordered everyone aboard the helicopter and he took off as rockets and artillery shells fell around the field, igniting the remaining aircraft and helicopters. At the time, he believed he flew out the last Vietnamese helicopter to take off from Tan Son Nhut. Although Tran had a responsible position, he was completely ignorant of the true status of what was happening to his country. All he knew was that he had to get away from the Saigon area, and hopefully have another chance at fighting the North Vietnamese who were quickly taking over his country. With his family safely out of the combat zone, he thought of nothing but resuming the fight against the communists.

Nearing Can Tho, he heard voices on the radio that he identified as his squadron mates calling the American aircraft carrier *Midway* fifty miles at sea off the South Vietnamese coast. He had no idea where the carrier was located because there was a jumble of voices on the emergency frequency they had been ordered not to use for routine information calls. He knew the pilots were desperate, and that many of them were short on fuel. He heard one pilot identify himself and request permission to land on the carrier. By its number he knew it was Air Vice Marshal Ky's plane.

Before landing at Can Tho, Tran called the *Midway* and requested the coordinates so he could locate it. They were given, and he studied his map until he could pinpoint the carrier's position at sea.

He knew he had insufficient fuel to fly to Con Son to pick up his wife and three children and then fly to the *Midway*, so he landed at Can Tho to refuel.

After refueling at Can Tho, Tran flew to the island of Con Son where he rejoined his family. The next morning Tran gathered his family and five pilots with their wives and children to make the flight to the *Midway*. Once the helicopter was loaded, Tran quickly counted heads. He was appalled to find that his helicopter—designed for eleven people—had thirty-nine on board! This was three times the weight for which the helicopter was designed.

Tran ordered the cabin doors removed, along with all items not necessary to fly the helicopter. He refused to consider leaving any of his friends behind to an uncertain fate with the communists.

Grimly, Tran went to maximum power and slid the helicopter's skids for 300 feet before the overloaded machine took to the air in a running takeoff. Over his radio he heard pilots calling American bases in Thailand as Vietnamese fighters and tranports fled to the south. He still hoped that he and the others could return in a few days to continue the fight against the communists.

En route to the *Midway*, the helicopter's engine quit and Tran's passengers began to scream and cry, believing they were going to die. Until that moment they had been quiet, although their staring eyes had mirrored the fear that possessed them. Tran immediately went to auto rotation while he tried to relight the engine. He was not successful until they were 1,500 feet above the ocean because the aircraft was so overburdened. Everyone quieted down as the engine started and they proceeded towards the carrier. Only Tran's extensive flying experience brought them out of the emergency.

Tran listened closely to his radio as it was announced that Saigon had fallen to the communists. He realized for the first time there would be no going back. He sought the *Midway* in vain but he could not spot the carrier. Over the radio he asked the *Midway* to give him a heading.

This was done and he was asked, "How many people on board?"

"Thirty nine," Tran replied.

"How many?"

"Three niner."

"What kind of a helicopter are you flying?"

"Huey. U-1H."

Tran's contact evidently thought he had heard wrong because he knew the capacity of the Iroquois. With complete incredulity, he called Tran again, "How many?"

"Three niner."

Tran knew the American still did not believe him. When he set the copter down on the crowded deck and thirty-nine people crawled out, there were expressions of disbelief that so many people could have crowded into such a small space.

Tran was told by a lieutenant that one of the ship's top officers wanted to question him to determine the situation at Tan Son Nhut at the time he had left.

Tran expressed concern for the large number of refugees at Con Son, explaining that the island had long been used to incarcerate Vietcong and North Vietnamese prisoners. He told the American officer that once the prisoners were released, he feared there would be a massacre of the South Vietnamese still there, many of whom were pilots and airmen with their families.

The officer promised to send a ship to Con Son to pick up the remaining South Vietnamese. He was a good as his word and Major Tran was shortly advised over the loudspeaker that an American ship had been dispatched to Con Son to pick up those left behind.

While Major Tran and his fellow pilots with their families were escaping that April 29, the situation for the American evacuation of Tan Son Nhut became worse.

General Smith sent six armed Marines to Marine Operations and all remaining United States personnel were removed from that building.

At the Evacuation Processing Center in the Defense Attaché Office annex, Lieutenant Colonel Hilgenberg waited anxiously for word whether the evacuation would continue. Hundreds of people, some of whom had waited for forty-eight hours, clamored for information. He requested shore police and Marine guards at 9:00 A.M. because his own guards had left for the United States embassy an hour earlier. To make matters worse, South Vietnamese Army paratroopers, billeted next to the evacuation center, had cut a hole in the cyclone security fence behind the bowling alley, and they threatened to further disrupt operations.

Hilgenberg could not move around the center without eight or ten people grabbing him, pleading to be the first out. "Don't leave me," they cried, "for surely we will die when the VC take over." He kept calling for help to control the mobs of people, but none was forthcoming because they were needed elsewhere. At this stage, he was convinced that the evacuees would never permit the Americans to leave without them.

Earlier, in metropolitan Saigon, air and surface evacuation had started at 8:10 A.M. that morning. One serious mistake was made when rooftop controllers were evacuated to Tan Son Nhut becuase they were assigned to the Defense Attaché Office. Fortunately, when it was realized that a mistake had been made, may of them were returned to their rooftop positions.

Air America had twenty helicopters available to get evacuees out of the city, but when their fuel supply was destroyed at Tan Son Nhut they had to refuel from American ships at sea and that procedure was time consuming. They flew throughout the twenty-ninth of April, using agreed-upon landing sites, and despite the lack of ground controllers on some rooftops they did a remarkable job. Throughout the day they picked up Americans wherever they found them, regardless of whether or not these were designated evacuation sites.

On Saigon's streets the number of buses dwindled to thirty, and evacuation sites were reduced from ten to four. Some measure of control was lost when embassy personnel commandered buses but they were all driven by American drivers with convoy escorts. Prior to 5:45 P.M. nine bus convoys had carried over 2,500 evacuees from metropolitan Saigon to the Defense Attaché Office compound at Tan Son Nhut. Only one convoy was broken up by dissident South Vietnamese Army units. Originally, it had been planned to load forty passengers and their luggage on each bus. Loads increased to sixty to seventy passengers without luggage before the day ended. Vietnamese were forced to remove thick wads of money from their suitcases and to stuff them into shirts, blouses and pants. For most, this money was their life's savings.

Due to the delay in getting helicopters launched from Seventh Fleet carriers with supporting Navy fighters, it was not until shortly after noon April 29 that the evacuation from downtown Saigon could be initiated. The first American fighters were fired on by South Vietnamese ground units who, knowing their own aircraft were no longer flying, shot at anything that flew.

In Saigon, bus convoys continued to be harassed, and the scene outside the United States embassy was chaotic. Most Vietnamese looked at the departing buses with blank stares. There were no smiles or waves. Despite earlier plans no coordinated scheme had seemed feasible to prevent congestion and to maintain crowd control. The last convoy left the embassy for Tan Son Nhut at 3:30 P.M. amid such disorder that it was feared that none of the evacuees would get through alive. The convoy was rushed by mobs of Vietnamese downtown who smashed bus doors and forced their way on board. Marine security guards fired shots into the air, and the buses were used as slow-moving bulldozers to forcibly gain headway and free them from the mobs. This last convoy had almost eight hundred people when it tried to enter Tan Son Nhut's Gate 1 at 5:45 P.M. but was turned back. The buses had to continue moving along the gate's traffic triangle to prevent being overrun.

A Marine officer, Captain Anthony Wood, and a member of the Special Planning Group, braved small arms fire to talk to the guards about permission for the buses to pass through the gate. Wood threatened to call for attack aircraft overhead to direct suppressive fire against them.

Vietnamese guards continued to fire their rifles in the air and at the buses with their helpless loads of evacuees. They shouted, "We want to go, too."

Wood directed the bus convoy to try and go through Gate 1 again but the Vietnamese guards prevented its passage. Wood called the control center for instructions. Brigadier General Carey, ground support commander, told Wood to instruct the buses to fall back and to stand by. Carey then called for air cover above the gate. When the American planes appeared, Carey told Wood to tell the South Vietnamese Army guards to look up. "Tell them that if passage is not permitted, the entire area will be destroyed."

Simultaneously Major General Smith told Lieutenant Colonel Nguu, deputy base commander and security chief, that if the buses were not permitted through Gate 1, his chances of leaving Vietnam were nil.

Nguu ordered the buses in, but that was the end of surface evacuation from downtown Saigon to Tan Son Nhut.

Air America now was forced to close down its command post in the Defense Attaché Office area and thereafter controlled its helicopters from the command and control aircraft flying overhead.

By noon, Hilgenberg had started covertly to move the remaining Americans and their Vietnamese dependents from the annex to the Defense Attaché Office compound. He formed them quietly in the gymnasium, and walked them out the back door because it was screened from other evacuees. Simultaneously he ordered the wounded to be moved to the landing zone.

In one of the groups being readied for departure were thirty South Koreans: contractor personnel and their families. Such people were given preference for evacuation. Their leader approached Hilgenberg and asked point blank if he thought that the remaining evacuees would have a chance to get out. The lieutenant colonel responded truthfully that he did not know. With rare courage, the Korean leader asked him to provide weapons and ammunition for his group because they were determined not to be captured. Hilgenberg deferred his decision, saying that he still hoped to get everybody out. He appreciated the Korean leader's offer because his assistance might be important if the Americans had to take a determined stand against unauthorized South Vietnamese who were trying to get away by any means.

Hilgenberg's earlier call for reinforcements was answered at 2:00 P.M. when First Lieutenanct Dick Coleman and nine military police members from Clark Air Force Base returned to the annex. Their arrival steadied the crowd. Hilgenberg and Coleman now went to the bowling alley where South Vietnamese paratroopers were reported to be inside the building harassing evacuees and looting their baggage. Hilgenberg quickly sized up the situation. He ordered Coleman and Master Sergeant Taylor to stop a dozen or more South Vietnamese soldiers armed with rifles from going through luggage. With only two carbines and a handgun between them, Coleman yelled, "Get the hell out!" Fortunately, the soldiers retreated through the hole they had made in the fence. Coleman stationed two SPs there to prevent further entry.

Most of the people, evacuees and Americans, had not eaten in twenty-four hours and Hilgenberg was relieved to see a truck full of C-rations pull up in front of the annex.

The first troop carrier helicopters from amphibious ships offshore arrived at 3:06 P.M. Hilgenberg had not seen them arrive because they had deposited the first of an 840-man ground security force on the airfield before coming to the compound six minutes later as Marine CH-53s roared overhead fifty feet above the ground.

Loading the helicopters began immediately and they quickly took off for the waiting ships off-shore. For the first time that day Hilgenberg had hopes that the evacuation might be completed as the crowd of waiting refugees broke into a cheer and clapped their hands. These were the first smiles Hilgenberg had seen in two days.

When the helicopters passed over the dependent housing area to the southwest they were fired upon by South Vietnamese paratroopers. Hilgenberg radioed that future departures should fly higher and by different routes. Evidently the firing of rifles and grenades was done by dissident South Vietnamese soldiers who knew they had no chance to get out.

Hilgenberg grew more concerned as sporadic sniping took place when South Vietnamese paratroopers in their cantonment area started to fire at huddled evacuee groups. A sniper on a water tower's catwalk was driven off by rifle shots. Hilgenberg feared that this new outbreak might create panic, but the evacuees bore this new outrage with stoical calm.

Once the helicopter evacuation was underway, aircraft shuttled routinely back and forth from the compound to the ships. By 4:30 P.M. helicopters were flying in ninety-minute cycles between the ships and the Defense Attaché Office compound, and Hilgenberg noted that there was a definite thinning of the crowd of refugees. Huge piles of luggage covered the area. Each person was permitted to take just one bag on board so more people could get out. Hilgenberg shrugged helplessly as he watched South Vietnamese civilians and paratroopers swarm over the piles of baggage, tearing them open to look for valuables.

Artillery and rocket firings from North Vietnamese positions ended during the afternoon, and Hilgenberg suspected that the North Vietnamese leaders in Hanoi deliberately permitted the evacuation to continue in large part unmolested. This was true, as Ambassador Martin later told the Special Investigating Subcommittee of the United States House of Representatives. In his testimony he revealed that officials of the Soviet

Union had informed the United States that the North Vietnamese had agreed not to interfere with the final stages of the evacuation from Tan Son Nhut and the embassy in Saigon.

At 6:00 P.M. the North Vietnamese bombardment of Tan Son Nhut, a quarter of a mile from the Defense Attaché Office compound, began again. It started to rain and low black clouds rolled in from the south. Navy fighter cover ceased as night fell but Marine Corps gunships continued to fly in near darkness while flashing beacons appeared to the south of the field as the helicopter gunships started to maneuver for approaches to the baseball park and the compound's landing zones. These zones were difficult to land in during daylight because they required near vertical approaches over buildings and trees. At night such landings appeared impossible. Although the compound was well lit by floodlights, the ball park was dark. Ground security personnel tried to light the ball park with headlights by ringing it with vehicles. That didn't work, and only one helicopter landed. Several others tried but they were not successful. During landing attempts two aircraft, one flying level across the field, with the other climbing up after a missed approach, almost collided. They were less than fifty feet apart when the pilot in the lower helicopter saw the higher one and maneuvered violently to his right. Hilgenberg watched the maneuvering helicopters, piloted by United States Marine and Air Force pilots, with awe. Despite his many worries, he marveled at their airmanship in flying into this hazardous environment not only at night, but in pouring rain as they carefully sought paths between radio and water towers before setting down on the tennis courts.

United States Air Force tactical fighters and gunships were now called in from Thailand by Cricket, the Airborne Command and Control plane orbiting above the field. The controller on board Cricket called, "Karen lead, rendezvous with the choppers at Point Hope and provide escort." Night escort had never been flown before at low level but, as the Karen leader said to himself, we've never evacuated Saigon before. By now the adrenaline level of the pilots was so high that no one thought of caution. Vulnerability can be a heady emotion.

The night was pitch dark so the pilots over Point Hope could see few distinguishing characteristics of the land below them. Marine chopper pilots realized their predicament and turned on their exterior lights, knowing they were exposing themselves to ground fire. They hoped the sound of the fighter planes would discourage ground fire. From Point Hope just off the south coast they followed the river to Saigon and to the United States embassy building. Vung Tau, apparently a city under siege, had been clearly visible as they passed it en route to Saigon as flares went off and artillery shells set ground fires. Some radio transmissions were eerie. Voice tones of the pilots, although their words were not distinguishable, told of their deep desperation more clearly than intelligible words.

When the planes arrived over Saigon the pilots at times could not recognize it due to the heavy cloud cover, while lightning flashes added a witch's brew character to the ghostly, blacked-out city. They could spot Tan Son Nhut only when the lightning flashed. During breaks in the clouds several fires could be seen scattered throughout Saigon. Ground flashes intensified as the North Vietnamese stepped up their artillery and mortar fire. The voices of the pilots over their radios grew more desperate as the city they had known died beneath their wings. One pilot glanced north toward Bien Hoa eighteen miles away where he had once spent a year, and where the Vietcong undoubtedly now were sleeping in his old hootch. His jaw quivered with frustration, and the tears welled up in his eyes. He realized more fully that the sacrifices by so many had all been in vain.

At the Defense Attaché Office compound, Staff Operations Officer Laehr was called upon to witness the burning of approximately $3,624,800 in United States currency and 85,344,000 Vietnamese piastres, or $113,787. The money was placed in barrels in the open courtyard between layers of thermite. General Smith ordered a hold on the burning by mid-afternoon and told all witnesses to leave the courtyard and the door was locked. Evidently someone had expressed concern that if the barrels were ignited the building might also be destroyed. Laehr, inasmuch as he had already signed a document that he had seen the money destroyed to keep it from falling into the hands of the North Vietnamese, kept checking the locked door to the courtyard throughout the day.

Except for security personnel the evacuation from the Defense Attaché Office compound and Tan Son Nhut had to be terminated about 6:30 P.M. and the Vietnamese airlift ceased an hour later when the last helicopter was recovered by a carrier at sea. The evacuees had been moved to ships in nearly twelve hours of continuous operations. Cool heads and flying skill paid off, but it was much too close for comfort.

Brigadier General Carey, commander of the Marine Ground Security Force, ordered all personnel, other than Marines, to leave between 8:00 P.M. and 11:00 P.M. One reason for the end of the evacuation was a power failure due to sabotage in the Evacuation Control Center at 7:15 P.M. Emergency power was used but it was inadequate to handle the increasing communications problems. Only the Marine ground security force plus two United States Air Force communicators were allowed to remain. Carey advised General Smith, "Let's clear this place so we can work on embassy problems."

In downtown Saigon embassy officials had reported that morning that 1,000 people still needed to be evacuated but another 1,000 were reported later. It seemed to General Carey that no matter how many people were evacuated from the embassy during the day that the number always remained the same—2,000. This was still true that evening at 7:30 P.M., and, with the constant influx of new people, the figure probably would have remained the same for days.

At Tan Son Nhut all remaining Defense Attaché Office staff members were ordered to embark on two helicopters at 8:00 P.M. Hilgenberg and Laehr were assigned to leave on these aircraft. Before Laehr departed he checked all rooms and locked them. He made one final check that the metal screens still were locked in place on the money barrels, and he noted approvingly that the Marine destruction team had wired the barrels for automatic burning when the rest of the Defense Attaché Office building was destroyed. Later, the building did burn, and the compound was destroyed.

General Smith now joined the others for departure. After all personnel were on board, about forty Vietnamese came through the hole in the fence and requested evacuation. They sat between the legs of the Americans, on their laps and on the floor. One helicopter had more than ninety people on board and literally staggered off the ground.

At 11:12 P.M. the last contingent of the Ground Security Force lifted clear of the compound amidst spreading smoke and flames from the satellite communications unit and the Defense Attaché Office's headquarters building. The Marines had done an efficient job of destroying the compound with thermite grenades.

During the early hours of April 29 an evacuation down the Saigon River had started with three tugs, four barges and an LST (Landing Ship, Tank.) At first, calm had prevailed along this front. By noon, however, a bus convoy from the United States embassy guarded by South Vietnamese security forces was forced back temporarily by hostile crowds as it tried to reach the docks. Captain Neil Carmody, United States Navy Chief of the American Legation, authorized the loading of the LST, and it sailed that afternoon at 3:00 P.M. under the protective cover of American planes. A tug and a barge that tried to tie up at the docks were driven off by unruly crowds of Vietnamese who threatened to overwhelm them. Their crews eventually drove them off and the evacuees were boarded in an orderly fashion and the ships were permitted to depart at 5:15 P.M. Despite some minor small arms fire from one section of the city, all remaining river craft made the trip safely.

Although a policy had been previously established that South Vietnamese citizens would be embarked in or transferred to Military Sealift Command or its contract ships, a large number of refugees arrived in small boats. It was necessary, therefore, to reverse this policy. All ships, including Seventh Fleet units, were advised to take on refugees and to remain in the holding area off Vung Tau until those who desired evacuation were on board.

Another group of about one hundred, including a number of Americans, was also evacuated by sea. These were members of the Consul General's staff from Can Tho in IV Corps. They had been unable to get out any other way.

In downtown Saigon, markets were looted and mobs broke into the American base exchange by tearing away the barbed wire defenses with their bare hands. Spectators gaped as refrigerators were loaded into trishaws, while other Vietnamese carried boxes of food and cartons of cigarettes. Boxes of soap flakes, many split open, were tossed aside and their contents littered the streets. Some Vietnamese soldiers had wrist watches up their arms as far as their elbows. Others had expensive cameras draped over their shoulders.

Outside the United States embassy a huge mob of desperate people thronged the streets, trying to claw their way inside by climbing over the fences and by rushing the gates whenever they were opened briefly to permit approved evacuees to enter. Marines stamped on their fingers and clubbed them with rifle butts.

Inside the 15-foot concrete fence of the embassy compound Marines sawed down the giant tamarind tree in the rear parking lot to clear the landing zone for the big transport helicopters. Two weeks earlier, Admiral Noel Gayler, commander-in-chief, Pacific, had urged Ambassador Martin to remove the tree but he had refused. He told Gayler that he would not take any step that might indicate the Americans were preparing to leave. Without his knowledge some members of his staff had been chopping down parts of the tree that were not visible to the ambassador.

Behind the parking lot, in the swimming pool area, several thousand Vietnamese waited amidst piles of suitcases and bundles of clothing for evacuation. There were three generals in uniform, several South Vietnamese senators, a former Saigon mayor and dozens of others with their families. While they waited impatiently for the helicopters, hundreds rushed into the embassy's cafeteria and grabbed candy bars and bottles of wine.

The embassy's tall white gates were constantly besieged by hundreds of people who were desperate to get inside the compound. A few were permitted to enter through a side gate, and this action caused a small riot. Bui Diem, former South Vietnamese ambassador to Washington, was told quietly to go around to the front entrance where Marine guards would let him in. General Dang Van Quang, a former IV Corps commander who had once been fired for corruption, showed up at a side gate. The portly Quang was allowed to squeeze through the gate while his two suitcases were passed over the fence. Meanwhile, four Americans tried to get to the rear gate but their cars were turned back at gunpoint by South Vietnamese soldiers.

Ambassador Martin asked to be driven home so he could pack his bags' and pick up his black poodle Nitnoy. When the chauffeured car could not get out the gate, Martin went out the back way and walked the three blocks to his house. He returned an hour-and-a-half later with his cook and two security men with a suitcase and a briefcase while one of the men led his dog on a leash.

A squad of Marines with fixed bayonets stood inside the side gate to keep the Vietnamese from climbing over the fence. At the back gate, Marines repeatedly had to use their rifle butts to force back Vietnamese attempting to scale the fence.

At nightfall cars and a fire engine were lined up in the square so headlights could illuminate the helipad. An explosion in front of the embassy brought everyone to shocked alert. A passerby on a bicycle had thrown a grenade into the crowd. Then another explosion was heard but this one was caused by members of the Central Intelligence Agency who were detonating a device to destroy the embassy's communications equipment.

By mid-evening, there were few United States civilians left in the embassy. Three days earlier the embassy's most sensitive electronic gear had been loaded aboard a freighter in Saigon and sent downriver with most of the technicians.

Ambassador Martin came outside his third-floor office to say goodbye to a few close aides. There were hesitant pats on the back, and controlled emotions.

The original evacuation plan had been unrealistically optimistic: that only 150 people would have to be evacuated from the embassy. Now, no one really had a precise count of those awaiting departure. Some people were airlifted from the parking lot and the rooftop during the day but by 4:30 P.M. the small Marine guard was helpless to maintain control even after they were joined by some American civilians. A measure of control had been established when three platoons of 130 Marines were helicoptered from the Defense Attaché Office at Tan Son Nhut, but that had left that area desperately short of security guards. Earlier, Colonel John Massion, the Air Force chief of the United States delegation assigned to the Four-Party Military Team, had been told to report to the embassy. He and his staff had been directed to remain in Saigon after the evacuation to form the nucleus of a four-powered joint military team. Instead, they became an integral part of the evacuation from the embassy. In many cases they directed it while the augmented Marine contingent attempted to maintain order.

As helicopters continued to lift off, yellow flares arched up and hung in the sky coloring the city a ghastly yellow. To the east, the Long Binh ammunition dump exploded and rattled windows throughout the city, as red fireballs shot high into the night sky.

By 9:00 P.M. the embassy evacuation was still far from complete despite continuous helicopter airlifts from the two landing zones.

A temporary lull in the airlift at 11:00 P.M., while the helicopters refueled from ships at sea, caused near panic among the Vietnamese. But the growing discontent was calmed by efforts of the United States military men. This lasted only a brief time. With chaos and tension mounting after midnight, the embassy communications site was closed at 3:00 A.M. during the early hours of April 30. The airlift continued, however, as some helicopters used the parking lot and others the rooftop to fly in and out despite substantial ground fire.

The landing zones were difficult to locate and approach in daylight. In the dark, pilots faced almost insurmountable problems that were compounded by the chaos inside and outside the grounds. The fires and explosions throughout the city and at Tan Son Nhut added to the confusion. Some crews had been flying eighteen hours by the time the parking lot was cleared and sealed off. Inside the buildings another 1,200 evacuees still milled about, including Marine guards and other Americans awaiting evacuation.

At 4:00 A.M. helicopters were no longer able to land on the roof so the lower landing pad on the parking lot was reopened. Despite almost continuous flights, at 4:20 A.M. there were still hundreds of people who needed to be moved out. This number included approximately six more loads of Vietnamese.

For the first time communications broke down completely. American members of the Four-Party Joint Team informed the embassy staff of the remaining airlift requirements, and they assumed that the request for a definite number of helicopters would be transmitted to the fleet. It was not.

With dawn only hours away, some areas of Saigon still had street lights. Fires burned throughout the city, but the greatest number were in the Tan Son Nhut area. In the northern section of the city ground-to-ground and ground-to-air tracer fire increased in intensity.

Cricket, the command plane orbiting Saigon, now transmitted a message from President Ford in Washington, D.C., on a frequency monitored by all units. "The following message is from the President of the United States and should be passed on by the first helicopter in contact with Ambassador Martin. Only twenty-one lifts remain. Americans only will be transported. Ambassador Martin will board the first available helicopter and that helicopter will broadcast 'Tiger, Tiger, Tiger' once it is airborne and en route."

At 4:45 A.M. Ambassador Martin and members of his staff departed on Lady Ace. The commander of the Marine contingent now advised that further sorties would carry only members of the Four-Party Team, records, and the remaining Marine guards.

When Martin's helicopter landed on board an American ship he was the last to emerge. His eyes were masked by dark glasses and his silver-gray hair blew in the wash from the helicopter's rotor blades. To bystanders he appeared to be an old, beaten man.

In Saigon, at 7:53 the final group from the Marine security force was ready for a hasty evacuation as eleven Marines stood on the embassy's flat roof with their M-16s ready while shots rang out from below and thousands of Vietnamese milled angrily in the embassy's courtyard while others stormed through the six-story building. When the helicopter touched down the Marines scrambled aboard with the embassy's American flag neatly folded and stuffed inside a brown paper bag.

In the final evacuation, 420 authorized evacuees, including members of the Korean embassy, Vietnamese employees who worked for the embassy's fire department and other employees of the United States government were left behind. This was a sad anticlimax to the desperate evacuation of Saigon, and the end of the United States presence in the former Republic of Vietnam.

Over 73,000 Vietnamese fled their homeland by sea in small sampans, fishing boats and deep-draft freighters that had been given to South Vietnam's Navy as part of the Vietnamization project. Some were large ships, with thousands of refugees that sailed on their own to Subic Bay in the Philippines, and then on to Guam in the Marianas. Others sailed to Hong Kong, Malaysia, Singapore and Thailand. Many ships capsized and their occupants were drowned. Pirates preyed upon the smaller vessels and the women were raped and all were robbed of their possessions. Many were brutally murdered. Some Vietnamese ships, after transferring their human cargo, were later scuttled to avoid endangering international shipping.

The United States Consul General's staff fled from Can Tho in the delta region to the sea via the Bassac River. The adjoining Vietnamese Air Force base at Binh Thuy had been bypassed by the North Vietnamese in their rush to Saigon. Some artillery guns and rockets were fired, but there were no large assaults. The airfield remained open all day April 29 and until the morning of April 30. The South Vietnamese actually launched air strikes against North Vietnamese Army tanks as they entered the outskirts of Saigon, and several were destroyed. About this time President Duong Van "Big" Minh announced the surrender of all South Vietnamese armed forces. South Vietnamese pilots now stripped the remaining A-37 aircrafts to their basic necessities and flew them to Thailand. Most aircraft carried three pilots, some even four. In Thailand they joined a large number of other South Vietnamese Air Force personnel who had fled during the early hours of April 29 from Tan Son Nhut. Most of those earlier aircraft had been fixed-wing transports and fighters. A few helicopters from Tan Son Nhut made it to Thailand, although some were forced to land along the coast in Cambodia. Most Vietnamese helicopters flew east to land on or near American ships. On board ships of the Seventh Fleet at least forty-five of these helicopters were dumped overboard because there was no room to store them.

At mid-morning April 30 United States helicopters transferred hundreds of evacuees from the carrier *Midway* to ships of the Military Sealift Command scattered nearby on the ocean's surface.

At one point, while the carrier *Midway* had a deck full of helicopters working on the transfer, a South Vietnamese O-1 "Birddog" appeared overhead and set up a holding pattern around the ship. The captain of the carrier refused to permit the O-1 to land, and ordered a zigzag course to prevent an approach. These maneuvers refused to discourage the Vietnamese pilot so attempts were made to convince him to ditch in the water while a rescue helicopter hovered overhead. The pilot refused. He dropped a message for the carrier, but it failed to land on the deck. A second message was recovered. It said, "Low on fuel and have wife and four young children aboard." He insisted that he was going to land, even if the helicopters were in the way. The *Midway*'s captain ordered the deck cleared, the carrier's course straightened, and its speed increased to 30 knots. Deck hands gaped as the O-1 came in for a landing. This was the first time that such an airplane had tried to land on a carrier. The O-1 made an excellent landing, although it came to a stop almost at the end of the carrier's deck.

Shortly after noon, with an estimated twenty-five hundred Vietnamese still on board the *Midway*, an armada of Vietnamese aircraft—thirty-one helicopters and another O-1—flew out of the West. To some of the men it looked like a scene from the movie "Tora! Tora! Tora!" depicting the Japanese attack on Pearl Harbor at the start of World War II.

Lieutenant Colonel Laehr, former chief of the Air Operations Desk of the Defense Attaché Office at Tan Son Nhut, watched with amazement and pride as the ship's captain ordered the new arrivals to orbit the *Midway* in wide holding patterns. In the next hour, United States helicopters were positioned on the launch deck, and the area forward of the carrier's island was cleared to store the South Vietnamese aircraft. Working with a precision and energy that astonished Laehr, *Midway* crewmen safely recovered all the new aircraft and their passengers. At one time there were seven helicopters sitting on the landing deck with their rotors turning. Only one aircraft—the second O-1—was tossed over the side after landing safely.

President Minh surrendered his country to the North Vietnamese by saying over Radio Saigon that he was doing so to avoid unnecessary shedding of Vietnamese blood. "I ask the soldiers of the Republic of Vietnam to cease hostilities, be calm and to stay where you are."

Jubilant North Vietnamese soldiers, their rifles spiked with flowers, rode into Saigon. White flags flew from government buildings as long convoys of Russian-made trucks loaded with regular soldiers in jungle fatigues and pith helmets rolled through the city. The soldiers were smiling and polite, chatting amiably with some of the Saigonese.

Nguyen Huu Cu, political instructor for the First Battalion of the People's Liberation Armed Forces, ordered his men at 11:00 A.M. to break into the Presidential Palace. A tank was moved up and it broke down the iron gates at the main entrance. One of their first acts was to run up the tri-colored flag of the Provisional Revolutionary Government.

Inside the palace General Duong Van Minh, South Vietnam's last president and leading elements of his regime sat in two rows of chairs. Minh stood up when the North Vietnamese strode in. "The revolution has come, and you have come," he said. It was 11:05 A.M., April 30, 1975.

The North Vietnamese immediately initiated an iron discipline throughout the countryside, and Saigon was named Ho Chi Minh City. They announced that all large businesses would be nationalized and decrees ended dancing, prostitution, and "acting like Americans." There were few acts of resistance. A French diplomat said roughly one-third of the people in Saigon greeted the communists with genuine enthusiasm, another third with indifference while the remainder appeared to have deep apprehension. For those in sympathy with the invaders there were smiles and handshakes for the soldiers. Some South Vietnamese soldiers rode their motorcycles alongside trucks loaded with armed communist soldiers, while others attempted to trade their uniforms for civilian clothes. Some South Vietnamese soldiers shed their uniforms and walked around in their shorts.

For months after the start of the final offensive Lieutenant Phat Dang, a platoon leader with the 93rd Artillery Battalion based at Dao Phu Quoc Island south of Cambodia, had directed his guns at the communists as they closed in on the city. This small island, ten miles off the Cambodian coast, had been under constant attack since the Cambodian government fell to the communists, and the danger of their position grew more acute. The battalion was part of Division 9 headquartered at Vinh Long Airport, but it took its orders directly from the city's mayor who was a lieutenant colonel.

With the fall of Cambodia, refugees flocked to the island, hoping to escape the communists. Dang asked one who spoke Vietnamese, "What happened to your country?"

"The communists have taken over, so we have to leave our country." Dang was informed that the communists would soon control everything in the area. The Cambodian warned that Dang should profit from their experience.

After all of Cambodia was taken over by the communists in mid-April, attacks increased against the island of Dao Phu Quoc. Although the South Vietnamese had two infantry battalions, Dang's artillery battalion was not up to full strength, and it became a desperate battle to support the infantry as attacks increased night and day.

Dang's wife Hai visited him April 23 from their home in Vinh Long to spend a week with her husband. She had their youngest son Phi while four older children remained at home with their grandparents. Hai told her husband that life was very difficult in Vinh Long because the communists were attacking the airport every night. Hai was anxious to rejoin the rest of her children in Vinh Long but her husband said, "Better stay with me a couple of weeks until we see what happens."

With the communists drawing ever closer to the city, they went to see the mayor April 30. "Why are you still here?" the mayor said.

"What's wrong?" Dang said.

"Is your wife here?"

Dang pointed to Hai.

"You and your wife better go out with me."

"Where will we go?" Dang said.

"The communists will soon take over, so we have to leave the country." Dang was deeply troubled. "Where will we go?"

The mayor was impatient. "To the ship to find out," he said sharply.

Dang and his wife wanted no part of leaving at this time. They had four children on the mainland, and such a precipitate departure was not pleasing to them. Dang said, "No way. I'll wait for awhile."

A short time later a friend of the mayor's arrived by plane from Saigon and they left the island.

Dang was desperate, believing now he had no choice but to leave. He turned to his diminutive wife. "We'd better get out of here."

"Where will we go?" she said, fear and uncertainty in her eyes.

Dang talked with a higher ranking officer in one of the infantry battalions. He was told that with the mayor's departure they had to find a way to leave the island.

Hai pleaded, "Better we go home." She was deeply concerned for their four children at Vinh Long.

"No way," her husband replied, although he was just as concerned for his children. "If we stay the communists will kill me."

Dang informed his men that they had to leave, and urged them to join some Chinese civilians in a small boat. He said he and his wife would go with them.

As they started to push the boat away from the beach, Dang asked, "Do we have enough fuel to go to Thailand?"

He was informed that they did not. The fishing boat was only thirty feet long and when 145 men, women and children tried to board her the strong surf almost swamped the boat and they had to give up the attempt.

They spotted an inter-coastal ship about sixty feet long that normally carried merchandise throughout the area. They commandeered it and set sail for Thailand. When they arrived at a small village in that country they were given food and water but they were refused permission to land.

They set sail for Malaysia and arrived at Pulau Bidong Island where they had to wait until they received American approval to fly to the United States August 13 from Kuala Lumpur. Unlike many other refugees they were not molested by pirates, a fate that fell to thousands in the coming months and years.

When the American carrier *Midway* departed May 2 at least forty-five South Vietnamese and Air American helicopters were stored beneath her decks.

The evacuation had brought out 57,507 people by air, including 2,678 orphans, and more than 73,000 by sea. Of the Americans evacuated, over 99 percent came out by air. It was an incredible rescue effort under the circumstances, and airmen of all services and their counterparts on the ground and at sea can be proud of their efforts. In all, 130,000 refugees were taken to the United States and to other free nations to start a new life. They would continue to flee Vietnam for years to come.

Great Britain, Australia, New Zealand, Canada, Italy, Thailand and

Laos shut down their embassies. The British left in such haste that many of their Vietnamese employees were left behind, including some with British passports.

In the United States as refugees like Phat Dang and Thanh Tran and their families began to arrive a Gallup poll revealed that 54 percent of the American people believed that the Vietnamese should be resettled elsewhere. There was some racism involved in their beliefs but the preponderant view was that these refugees would take jobs from American workers.

More typical views prevailed as the plight of these bewildered people became evident and more compassionate Americans stepped forward by the tens of thousands to offer help. The early treatment of these refugees at times was sordid, and hardly in keeping with a nation founded by immigrants and refugees who had fled religious and political persecution.

President Ford spoke for most Americans when he said, "This action closes a chapter in the American experience. I ask all Americans to close ranks, to look ahead to the many goals we share and to work together on the great tasks that remain to be accomplished."

The loss of the Republic of Vietnam to the communists seemed almost unreal to most Americans, many of whom were too embarrassed to discuss the war and to admit that it had been a defeat for their country.

At Berkeley, the cradle of student radicalism in northern California, some 1,000 demonstrators marched the city's streets carrying Vietcong flags in honor of the communist victory. Activist Tom Hayden called Saigon's fall "the rise of Indochina."

California's former governor, Ronald Reagan, while lecturing at Georgia Tech, was cheered when he blamed the fall of South Vietnam on "the most irresponsible Congress in our history."

Actress Jane Fonda, a political activist, said, "What happened is what happened to us 200 years ago—a revolution for independence, playing itself out in Vietnam. To say Saigon has fallen is to say that the thirteen colonies fell two centuries ago."

Hayden, who founded the Students for a Democratic Society, and a peace-movement advocate, said, in part, "This is the first time in over one hundred years that that country has not been occupied in one form or another by either French or American troops. Now they are able to try and put their house in order. But ending the war is only half the goal. The other half is learning the lessons of the war so it doesn't happen again."

Commander Richard Stratton, who had been incarcerated as a prisoner in North Vietnam for six years and two months, spoke for the majority of Vietnam veterans when he said upon release, "American disengagement from Vietnam was inevitable, but the manner in which we did it was embarrassing. I certainly thought we owed it to the Vietnamese to show a little more class than that. We led them down the primrose path and left them hanging on the end of the limb. Then we sawed it off. So why should we be surprised when we see them fall? As for me, I did everything I could. I can face myself in the mirror. I don't know how many other Americans like Jane Fonda can say the same thing."

As thousands of South Vietnamese fled their country, choosing freedom like the 400,000 eastern European refugees who were admitted to the United States after World War II, the 30,000 who fled after the Hungarian revolution in 1956, and the 650,000 mostly middle class Cubans who escaped or left Castro's Cuba, they soon became part of the mainstream of American life like the 50 million people from other lands who are known to have come to the United States since the government first started to keep immigration records in 1820. As in the past, these new refugees are America's gain and Indochina's loss of invaluable people.

The impact of the loss of Indochina to the communists was quickly evident among responsible men and women in and out of government. Defense Secretary James Schlesinger said, "A consequence of the events in Southeast Asia has been to shake the confidence of many countries in American power, and particularly in American steadfastness."

Greece and Thailand ordered the United States to reduce its military presence. The Philippines considered abrogation of its defense treaty with the United States. There was concern in Washington that the communists in North Korea might attack South Korea. There were some who believed that the United States was now free to deal with more important foreign policy problems.

While the communists were taking over South Vietnam, there were reports of a bloodbath in Cambodia. There was relief when 590 foreigners were permitted to leave and arrived in Thailand. Still, there were persistent reports that all former officers in the Cambodian armed forces would be killed along with their families. At first there was disbelief about these reports but in the coming years up to 2 million Cambodians were murdered in one of the world's most savage blood baths.

Kissinger, who had represented the United States at the peace table, and who had been responsible for the treaty signed with North Vietnam, now warned, "We must be very careful in the commitments we make." Such a belief should have been paramount in his negotiations with the North Vietnamese.

Former Defense Secretary Clark Clifford, a Democrat, called on President Ford to replace Kissinger as secretary of state. Even a Republican National Committeeman said, "He has to go."

President Ford refused to act.

In retrospect, American participation in the Vietnam war could have been ended in 1963 after President Ngo Dinh Diem was assassinated, without undue loss of American prestige, or even in 1965 when there was a lack of cohesiveness in South Vietnam's political structure and the country was gripped by chaos.

At the end of the war the United States failed to live up to the promise made by President Richard M. Nixon to intervene if North Vietnam violated the terms of the Paris Ceasefire Agreement that was signed January 28, 1973, and even failed to replace all of the expended South Vietnamese arms and equipment that it was authorized under terms of the agreement. As elements of the North Vietnamese Army fought their way southward in early 1975, the United States Congress reduced the amount of funds to the point where South Vietnam could no longer defend itself. Eventually all increases in funds were denied. Senator Mike Mansfield expressed the feelings of the majority of American congressmen when he said, "Additional aid means more killing, and more fighting. This has got to stop sometime."

Could the war have been resolved differently, or was the United States' military intervention doomed to fail from the start of its involvement? There were mistakes on all sides—civilian and military. Only a thorough examination of all factors dating back to the presidency of Harry S. Truman—and four subsequent presidential administrations—can provide the answer.

PART I

A TROUBLED ERA

CHAPTER 1

The Elephant and the Tiger

ONE OF THE TRAGEDIES OF THE TWENTIETH CENTURY IS THE FAILURE of the United States, through its presidents and elected representatives in Congress, to understand the legitimate aspirations of the people of Asia. Instead of seeking the truth on its own, the United States relied upon two of its western allies—France and Great Britain—to determine its policies toward the region. Despite its good intentions, the events following World War II were predictable because the United States became a part of the problem, and was tarred by the hated brush of colonialism. The people of the Far East, who had hoped for more consideration from a once-oppressed people who had earlier thrown off the yoke of colonialism, deserved better treatment.

With the United States government rejecting their pleas, communism, distrusted by most of the deeply religious people of Asia, now began to gain adherents through the efforts of two charismatic communist leaders—Mao Tse-tung of China and Ho Chi Minh of Vietnam.

The United States made senseless mistakes in the years after World War II and paid a price that cannot be measured in dollars or even in lives lost during the Korean War and the Indochina War. For a nation that prides itself on its democracy and humanity, the American military involvement in Asia created deep wounds that will take generations to heal. Something fundamentally good and decent in American life was temporarily lost and it behooves everyone to determine why it occurred so it can never happen again.

In a military sense, one of the greatest errors was made by some politicians who were convinced that the People's Republic of China would intervene with its armed forces if the war escalated into North Vietnam. There is no evidence that the Chinese ever had any such intention—despite their earlier intervention in the Korean War—and privately they decided to restrict their aid to North Vietnam to military hardware and technical assistance. China not only decided not to intervene militarily but if it had done so it would have been opposed strongly by North Vietnam's communist officials.

Vietnam's history is a continuing story of resisting invasion—mostly by armies from China. In between periods of domination there has been a surface politeness between officials of the two nations. Underneath there is a distrust that dates back two thousand years that may never be overcome.

The people of Vietnam have lived for centuries under threats of subjugation. In 208 B.C. Trieu Da, a renegade Chinese general, conquered Au Lac in the northern mountains of present-day Vietnam and established a capital. He proclaimed himself emperor of Nam Viet. Later, in 111 B.C., the Han dynasty incorporated Nam Viet into the Chinese empire as the province of Giao Chi. Thus, for the next thousand years, the Vietnamese were subjugated by China.

During the Chinese domination there were three Vietnamese insurrections in A.D. 39, 248 and 542. The Trung sisters, Trieu An and Ly Bon, tried to set up an independent state in A.D. 39 but they failed to overthrow their country's rulers.

Despite these years the Vietnamese people resisted assimilation even though the Chinese imposed their own political system, customs, education and language.

Independence was not achieved until A.D. 939 under the Ngo dynasty. It is surprising that the Vietnamese emerged after 1,050 years of domination by China as a free and independent nation with its culture largely intact.

During the next six centuries, the forefathers of the Le, Ly and Tran dynasties expanded the national territory during years of prosperity. In 967 Emperor Dinh Bo Linh ascended the throne, naming his country Dai Co Viet. This was 99 years before the Norman invasion of England and 640 years prior to the first permanent English settlement on American soil in Virginia.

Under the leadership of Tran Hung Dao huge Mongol invasions from the north were repulsed by the Vietnamese in 1257, 1284 and 1287. Such actions were unparalleled, coming during a period when the Mongols had annexed China.

The Vietnamese people's affinity for disunity was apparent in 1527 when Mac Dang Dung tried to usurp power from the Le, but his attempt at secession was defeated. The second attempt began in 1620 and intermittent warfare lasted for almost 200 years as the Trinh, who occupied the north, fought the Nguyen who lived in the south. A unified nation did not become a reality again until 1802 when a pretender to the throne—Nguyen Anh—installed himself as emperor with the assistance of France.

A permanent French fleet was deployed in Asian waters in 1843, a year after Great Britain defeated China in the first Opium War, and gained valuable trade concessions from the Chinese.

Although the French had reneged in 1787 on most of their promises to support Nguyen Anh as pretender to the Vietnamese throne in exchange for exclusive commercial privileges, France continued to expand its efforts to Christianize the Vietnamese and to exploit its trade advantages. With the spread of French influence in Vietnam there were frequent clashes—particularly in 1847 after Emperor Tu Duc ascended the throne and announced that he would eliminate Christianity in his country. French forces and Vietnamese mandarins in the city of Tourane—present-day Da Nang—clashed repeatedly in bitter battles.

When Napoleon III assumed power in France in 1852, he approved Vietnam expeditions to protect French missionaries and to expand trade. French forces captured Saigon in 1861, the year Civil War erupted in the United States. The following year, Tu Duc signed a treaty with France that gave the French broad religious, economic and political concessions. In 1863 France extended its control to Cambodia.

There were many insurrections during the 94 years of French rule. Monarchists like Phan Dinh Phung and Phan Boi Chau, who tried to restore the old monarchy, and thirteen nationalists of the Vietnam Kuomintang Party led by Nguyen Thai Hock, died on the French guillotine in 1930 for seeking independence.

Vietnamese resistance to outside domination of their country has always been strong. Unfortunately, a basic weakness of their society is divisiveness and a predilection for fighting among themselves. A Chinese historian once said, "The Vietnamese are disdainful, belligerent, astute in military matters, and not afraid to die. They live in the mountains yet move about on water, using boats as vehicles and carts as horses. When they come, it is like a gentle breeze; when they go, it is hard to catch up with them."

Through the centuries religious beliefs influenced many Vietnamese, inducing a dangerous kind of lethargy when they faced the highly motivated communists of the twentieth century. Confucianism, Buddhism and Taoism produced a steadfast adherence to fatalism, or the belief that everything is predestined or preordained by mysterious forces.

Confucianism left one of the few indelible Chinese marks on Vietnamese society. The religion was founded 500 years before the birth of Christ. The teachings of Confucius are based on the concept of natural law that, in practical terms, translates into a social order with specific rules of conduct. Under Confucianism a nation was an extended family in which the emperor was the father and the subjects his children. "The ruler is like the wind," Confucius taught, "and the commoners the grass blades. When the wind blows, the grass blades have to bend under it."

Buddhism arrived in Vietnam at the end of the second century before the birth of Christ, and evolved through three periods. Its philosophy is that human beings are continually beset by suffering from one life to the next, and that sufferings endured in this life are caused by actions in a previous life, and the cause for sufferings in the next life. Buddha taught that the real cause of suffering is man's greed and that it must be eliminated. From the seventh to the fourteenth century Buddhism gained ascendancy and remained almost a national religion in Indochina because it was the primary religion for 80 percent of the people.

Taoism, founded by a Chinese named Lao-tzu, arrived in Vietnam about the same time as Confucianism. It had a broad following although few understood it. Its essence lies in passivism. Taoists must give up all desire and ignore the bodily self to achieve spiritual purity and tranquility. Its proponents must adhere to a rigid state of mind that is devoid of all wishes and actions. The possibility of abuse inherent in such a rigid control of one's life inevitably degraded the Taoist philosophy to a super-stitious belief in which magic and sorcery were widely practiced by the common people under the guise of religion.

Ho Chi Minh's father had been a minor mandarin, or public official, in the imperial administration. He had joined with Emperor Nam-Nghi against the French in 1884, but the rebellion was crushed four years later. Ho's father then joined the French resistance movement.

His son, Ho Chi Minh—one of several pseudonyms he used during his lifetime—and the one for which he is best remembered, was originally named Nguyen That Thanh (who will be victorious). As a young man he was expelled from school at Vinh because of his political activities. He had carried messages for the anti-French underground, and he gave speeches denouncing the French. His father had sufficient influence to get him enrolled in the prestigious high school in the imperial capital of Hué—the Lycée Quôc-Hoc. There he acquired a sound French education and a thorough exposure to Vietnamese culture and history. The school was a hotbed of resistance to the French administration and Ho Chi Minh was one of its most active members. He graduated from the school, although he left without a diploma in 1910, along with Vo Nguyen Giap—later General Giap—and Pham Van Dong who became North Vietnam's prime minister.

Although he was educated as a teacher, he went to a cook's and baker's school in Saigon because such jobs paid better than a teacher's position.

In 1912 Ho Chi Minh left home—not returning for thirty years—aboard the French liner *Latouche-Trevalle* where he served as a mess boy.

Far from the colonial restrictions of his homeland Ho Chi Minh acquired a knowledge of democratic ideals. He settled in England shortly before the start of World War I and he worked in the pastry division of the Carlton Hotel.

After service at sea during the early part of the war Ho Chi Minh moved to France in 1917 where he gained an appreciation of the merits of communism—particularly after the Russian revolution in October, 1917. He now considered himself a communist and worked as a photo retoucher under the name of Nguyen Ai Quoc.

The Vietnamese communist movement gained impetus among some of the 80,000 whom France had brought to Europe to work in her factories and to serve in her armies. When they were sent home following the war these communists formed the nucleus of the party.

In 1919, Ho Chi Minh tried unsuccessfully to petition American President Woodrow Wilson at the Versailles peace conference to consider self-determination for Vietnam.

Ho Chi Minh's proficiency in English and French was a valuable asset to the French communist party when it was formed in December, 1920. When they rejected his appeal that Vietnam should be free, he became disillusioned with the French party. In 1924, he left Paris for Moscow where he became a fulltime communist agent before returning to the Far East where he was assigned as assistant to Mikhail Borodin, the Soviet representative in China.

In 1925 the French colonial government divided what is now Vietnam into three parts. The countryside comprising Saigon and the Mekong delta was named the colony of Cochin China; the central area with its imperial capital at Hué was designated the protectorate of Annan. In the north, the area with its capital at Hanoi was made the separate protectorate of Tonkin. Despite the terminology, all sections were ruled as colonies of France even though the two northern regions were supposedly ruled by the Annamese emperor, Kah Khai Dinh, while the Cochin China region was governed directly from Paris.

French rule was demanding, and the country's resources were used to enrich European shareholders. The Vietnamese were dominated at all levels of society by a harsh regime that brooked no rebellion from re-calcitrant workers. The few Annamese who collaborated with the French became enriched by their association, but for the vast majority life was a drudgery with few rewards.

The great colonial empires were not only weakened by the huge cost of fighting World War I but the formation of the Communist International in 1919 posed a deeper threat, dedicated as it was to the overthrow of capitalism. Throughout the 1920s Comintern agents worked secretly to enlist the millions who had been denied the right to live as free human beings. They found fertile ground in some parts of the Far East.

In Vietnam, discontent reached a new high, particularly in Annam, following the premature death at age forty-three of Emperor Khai Dinh in the late fall of 1925. Resistance accelerated when the French announced that the emperor would be succeeded by his twelve-year-old son Bao Dai who was going to school in Paris. The French hoped to gain even greater control over the Annamese by keeping the boy in school in France for another seven years and to give France's Résident Supérieur in Hué total authority over the populace. Anti-French feeling reached a new peak and Annamese nationalists and communists joined forces to resist the succession.

The Far East was in a ferment with the attempts of Sun Yat-sen and Mao Tse-tung to eliminate foreign control of China. And, the world-wide depression of 1929 proved a catastrophe for Indochina when the sharp drop in the price of rice brought misery and starvation to millions.

Ho Chi Minh was assigned to unify the Vietnamese communists in 1930 by including Cambodian and Laotian sections. Learning of the attempt, the French arrested him, Pham Van Dong, Giap and the party's first secretary general Tran Phu. The latter died in prison. Ho Chi Minh escaped in the guise of a Chinese businessman, but he was later arrested in Singapore and given a six-month sentence. He was smuggled to Moscow in 1934 with other Vietnamese communists for further training on communist ideology and tactics. During Premier Stalin's purges he escaped prosecution, but he received a lesson about the harshness of communist disciplinary tactics that were meted out to those who did not adhere strictly to the party line.

He returned to China in 1937 but the Russians made him publicly renounce most of his treasured views about Vietnamese independence.

Annamese resistance to French rule was crushed in 1932, aided in part by a period of greater economic stability. A deep hatred remained because 50,000 Annamese nationalists and communists were imprisoned or deported and the rebellion was brutally put down. It is believed that more than 10,000 Annamese were killed. There was excessive brutality and torture on both sides during 1930 and 1931 but the world outside Indochina knew little of this struggle for independence. Ho Chi Minh's communists modeled their tactics after those developed by Mao Tse-tung in southern China and "self defense" forces murdered peasants who would not cooperate, and publicly hanged pro-French mandarins and Annamese landlords. Some, in weighted bamboo cages, were thrown into lakes. Those who were particularly hated had their noses chopped off, their teeth brutally yanked out and their beards set on fire before they were murdered.

Ho Chi Minh, the communist leader who headed the insurgency, was sentenced to death in absentia by the French but he continued to evade capture by the Sûreté Générale, although he spent a brief time in a British prison in Hong Kong. He fled the country in 1932 once the French gained the upper hand and went to Moscow where it was reported that he had died.

The other leaders of the movement that he had founded were arrested and held in the Paulo Condore prison off the coast of Cochin China. Together they trained for another attempt to wrest their country from the French. They might have remained there for the rest of their lives if, with the rise of Adolf Hitler to power in Germany, the French Communist Party had not joined forces with the socialists and centrists in an anti-fascist coalition in Paris. This Popular Front Government legalized the Communist Party in Indochina and an amnesty in 1936 freed the men from Paulo Condore. The Sûreté Générale kept a watchful eye on them as they dispersed to their communities.

Now that Nazism was gaining ground in Germany under Adolf Hitler's Third Reich, communist parties were ordered in 1936 to follow a détente policy with Western democracies. For Ho Chi Minh and his Vietnamese communists this meant there would be no support for their dream of a free Vietnam. He expressed his bitterness—in private—and was particularly upset when Hitler and Stalin reached an agreement just prior to Germany's invasion of Poland September 1, 1939. Many dedicated communists left their parties around the world, but Ho Chi Minh bided his time.

German armies overran Denmark, Norway, Holland and Belgium in the spring of 1940, and France's military situation quickly became acute.

By June it appeared to the Vietnamese communists that the United States had written off Indochina. This was true because Under Secretary of State Sumner Welles told the French ambassador in Washington June 30 after France had requested an armistice that "considering the general situation the government of the United States could not enter into conflict with Japan and that, should the latter attack Indochina, the United States would not oppose such an action." With typical lack of understanding of the situation in Indochina the United States State Department did not believe that part of the world was in danger of occupation, believing the Japanese would not try to take over another nation in the near future because they had been unable to fully subjugate China. It was a serious miscalculation.

After France surrendered to the Germans the French governor general of

Indochina gave control of the Annamese territory to the Japanese Imperial Army on the orders of the collaborationist Vichy government. For the remainder of the war French authorities cooperated with the Japanese and supplied Japan with rice, rubber, coal and other raw materials. France thus lost all credibility with the Vietnamese people, and the communist party took advantage of this loss of prestige by joining other anti-French groups not only in Annam but in Cochin China and Tonkin to seek independence after the war.

A year later, after Hitler abrogated the two-year-old treaty he had signed with Marshal Stalin of Soviet Russia, he ordered an invasion of the Soviet Union. For Ho Chi Minh and his communist party this invasion was a godsend. His party, and all other communist parties throughout the world, now were allied with the Western democracies. This alliance gained stronger credibility when the Japanese attacked Pearl Harbor December 7, 1941, and brought the United States into the conflict.

Prior to the attack on Pearl Harbor by the Japanese, Ho Chi Minh had served with Mao Tse-tung's Communist Eighth Route Army against the Japanese in China. He returned to his own country in 1941 after an absence of thirty years. He immediately set out to organize the communist party, telling comrades that the French had been defeated by the Axis powers and he stressed that Japan would later be defeated by the Western Allies. At the age of fifty-one he formed the League for Revolution and Independence May 19, 1941. The acronym for the Vietnamese title of this organization became Vietminh. He also changed his name to Ho Chi Minh because the name he had used in France and China—Nguyen Ai Quoc—identified him as a Comintern agent. Inasmuch as he wanted to solicit support from the Nationalist Chinese government he knew that his former name would identify him as a communist, and that would be anathema to Chiang Kai-shek's government.

Vo Nguyen Giap became particularly embittered when his young wife, a militant feminist for Vietnam's freedom, died in a French jail in 1941. Her sister, who had been arrested for terrorism, was guillotined in Saigon at the same time. His selection by Ho Chi Minh to shape the Vietminh army shortly afterwards proved ideal for this dedicated communist who now had more than a cause to fight.

Ho Chi Minh was arrested August 28, 1942, by a Chinese war lord when he refused to pack his organization with pro-Chinese Nationalists. He was held in jail until September 16, 1943, and when he was released he was a sick man. He desperately sought allies to help the Vietnamese communist party because he needed military equipment and trainers to convert his guerrilla force into a professional army. The United States, through the Office of Strategic Services, offered military assistance if he would help to rescue downed American airmen, and provide intelligence information about the Japanese. Ho Chi Minh agreed. He established a good relationship with the Americans who contacted him, always careful not to reveal his true political status, and he never tried to sell them on the communist party line. He stressed only his hatred of the French, and his hope to achieve national independence for his country. The Office of Strategic Services detachment was withdrawn in October, 1945, and an opportunity was lost to establish a direct relationship with Ho Chi Minh that might have saved the United States a long and agonizing war.

President Franklin D. Roosevelt held strong anti-colonial views so his policy makers expected that, after the war, he would strive to free Indochina from French hegemony. He believed Indochina should be turned over to a trusteeship instead of permitting France to assume control of its former colonies. His death in the spring of 1945 ended any possibility that his views would prevail.

During World War II, and later, United States officials were ambiguous in their views of Indochina. United States relations with France appeared to support the latter's request for return of its colonial possessions even though the United States was committed to the Atlantic Charter which specified self-determination for all countries.

At the Potsdam Conference in July, Allied leaders authorized Great Britain to disarm the Japanese in the southern part of Vietnam, while the Chinese Nationalists were made responsible for the same thing north of the 16th parallel.

With Japan's capitulation August 15 to the Allies, Ho Chi Minh convened a national congress at Tan Trac, north of Hanoi, and urged his followers to take control of Vietnam from the defeated Japanese occupiers before the Allied troops arrived. During the occupation the Japanese had backed a figurehead government under Emperor Bao Dai.

The Japanese command in Indochina willingly transferred power to the Vietminh August 18, and Bao Dai, last member of the Vietnamese royal family, abdicated five days later. Ho Chi Minh and his communist followers quickly consolidated their gains by proclaiming a provisional government in Hanoi. On August 25 the emperor formally handed over his Great Seal to the communist representatives.

After Saigon was taken over by the communists, Ho Chi Minh announced independence for the Democratic Republic of Vietnam effective September 2. In asserting independence he borrowed some of the words from the American Declaration of Independence. "We hold the truth that all men are created equal, that they are endowed by their Creator with certain unalienable rights, among them life, liberty and the pursuit of happiness." Although Ho Chi Minh borrowed these American words, the country he created never lived up to their spirit.

British forces under General Douglas Gracey landed in Saigon September 13, and the Chinese Nationalists occupied Hanoi. The Allied force faced a communist army under Ho Chi Minh that had acquired the weapons of the 50,000 members of the 39th Imperial Japanese Area Army, plus military stocks in the former French arsenals. In a series of skirmishes, 2,000 Vietnamese were killed by British forces and control was restored to France.

As a foretaste of what lay in store for the Americans an Office of Strategic Services officer, Lieutenant Colonel A. Peter Dewey, was killed September 26 in Saigon, the first American casualty in that part of the world following World War II.

At first the Vietnamese people welcomed the Vietminh. They knew little of communism, and the Vietminh was considered merely another nationalist group. With the long-awaited quest for independence gained initially by the Vietminh, much enthusiasm was expressed for the party. Ho Chi Minh's ability to channel the Vietnamese hatred of French colonialism towards support for his party was successful until French rule was re-established. In late 1945, however, knowing he would need popular support to achieve his goal of independence now that the French were back in power, Ho Chi Minh disbanded the Indochinese Communist Party—although he and his followers remained dedicated communists—and replaced it by an Association for Marxist Studies.

With authority for Indochina returned to the French there was a period of discord as to who controlled the country. Due to the ravages of war, and the lack of a clear line of authority, over 2 million Vietnamese died of famine in the northern part of the country.

Through negotiations in early 1946 China agreed to withdraw its forces from Vietnam, and France agreed to drop its extra-territorial rights in China.

At a communist cabinet meeting in March, Ho Chi Minh argued for an agreement to permit 15,000 French troops to return to North Vietnam. There was sharp disagreement among some of his followers who argued that France's left-wing government would be more inclined to give Vietnam independence while members of the party's right wing—mostly Chinese Nationalists—called for closer ties with China whom they called a "blood brother."

Ho Chi Minh was incensed. "You fools! Don't you realize what it means if the Chinese stay? Don't you remember our history? The last time the Chinese came they stayed a thousand years!

"The French are foreigners," he said. "They are weak. Colonialism is dying out. Nothing will be able to withstand world pressure for independence. They may stay for a while, but they will have to go because the white man is finished in Asia. But if the Chinese stay now, they will never leave.

"As for me, I prefer to smell French shit for five years, rather than Chinese shit for the rest of my life."

Ho Chi Minh won them over and the Vietminh reached an agreement with the French. France agreed to recognize Vietnam as a "free state" within the French union. It was agreed that French troops would be permitted to return to the north for five years to replace the Chinese. And it was resolved that the issue of whether Tonkin, Annam and Cochin China should be reunited would be determined by a referendum.

Ho Chi Minh and other party officials went to France May 31 to negotiate with Admiral Thierry d'Argenlieu, Indochina's high commissioner. The admiral violated the March agreement and in June proclaimed a separate government for Cochin China.

Negotiations broke down September 14 at Fontainebleau when the French refused to grant unification of Vietnam. Before he returned home Ho Chi Minh made a practical compromise that covered economic issues, and he agreed to a cessation of hostilities. Of the agreement that he and France's Overseas Minister Marius Moutet signed, Ho Chi Minh said, "I'm signing my death warrant." He no longer had any illusions but that full-scale war would soon come to his country.

During a period of growing tension, Ho Chi Minh misjudged the power of his communist and socialist friends in France, and he had doubts that they were even interested in granting independence to his country.

General Giap's communist army retaliated against the French December 19, 1946, when all French electrical plants were blown up that night and Vietminh shock troops attacked French garrisons from south of Saigon to the Chinese border.

After these attacks Giap's army was forced to evacuate Hanoi and retreat into the rural areas to prepare for a protracted guerrilla war against the French.

Meanwhile, Ho Chi Minh sought vainly for any kind of support, knowing that Soviet Russia was preoccupied with problems in Europe and that the Chinese Nationalists would have strings attached to any aid they offered. As for the United States, Ho Chi Minh had appealed to President Harry S. Truman for help but he had failed to reply to his letters. Ho Chi Minh was convinced that the United States government had little interest in Asian problems now that World War II had ended.

While some officials of the Truman administration sympathized with the aspirations of the nationalists in Vietnam for independence, and were reluctant to see the French gain control of the country by force, greatest concern was voiced that with Vietnamese independence might come control by the communist Vietminh. State Department officials urged France to seek an end to guerrilla warfare by agreeing to a political solution that was acceptable to both sides. At this time, the United States prohibited export of war materiel to the French in Vietnam, although munitions were regularly sent to metropolitan France and undoubtedly many of these shipments were diverted to Vietnam.

Ho Chi Minh knew that General Giap's army needed professionals to train it and he sought the assistance of renegade Japanese officers who were trying to avoid war crimes at home, and even some former Germans and French Foreign Legionnaires. These men, he knew, would be invaluable to teach the use of American, French and Japanese weapons, of which they had an abundance.

To intimates Ho Chi Minh described what he believed would be the character of the coming guerrilla war, likening it to a contest between an elephant and a tiger, with the Vietminh as the tiger. "If the tiger ever stands still," he said, "the elephant will crush him with his mighty tusks. But the tiger will not stand still. He will leap upon the back of the elephant, tearing huge chunks from his side, and then he will leap back into the dark jungle. And slowly the elephant will bleed to death. Such will be the war in Indochina."

In retrospect, his words were prophetic.

CHAPTER 2

French Underestimate Vietminh

THE ARMIES OF FRANCE BY MAY, 1947, APPEARED TO BE SUCCESSFUL throughout Vietnam, so the French government dispatched Professor Paul Mus, a Vietnam specialist who had been raised in that country's northern section, to discuss an armistice. Although militarily successful, the war was a serious economic drain on France. Mus was an ideal choice to deal with Ho Chi Minh because he had always counseled independence for Vietnam. As a result, the talks at first quickly agreed on an exchange of prisoners, and the resumption of political talks, but Ho Chi Minh objected to the surrender of foreign specialists.

"Monsieur le professeur," he said, "you know us very well. If I were to accept this [the clause] I would be a coward. The French Union is an assemblage of free men, and there can be no place in it for cowards."

They could not agree because the Vietnamese leader was adamant that he had to retain foreign specialists for the development of his country and he was not about to give them up. He walked out of the meeting, and the war continued. He was convinced not only that the French had betrayed him but also the Chinese and the Russians, because they had offered only lip-service to his pleas for help in freeing his country from the French.

Ho Chi Minh had long since written off any hope of assistance from the United States. At the time, the United States government was more interested in aiding Greece and Turkey to combat communist insurgencies and demonstrated its interest when funds were voted by Congress May 15, 1947, to aid these two nations. On June 5, Secretary of State George C. Marshall outlined the details of what later became the Marshall Plan—the single largest economic aid plan for Europe in history. This was the year also that Great Britain granted independence to India and Pakistan.

The year closed on a more hopeful note when former emperor Bao Dai, living in Hong Kong, offered to negotiate with France to achieve Vietnam's independence. He actually initiated an understanding with French High Commissioner Emile Bollaert in December that recognized Vietnamese independence within certain limits.

In North Vietnam, middle-class revolutionaries like Ho Chi Minh continued to lead the Vietminh in their war against the French. Their constitution, created a year earlier, may have sounded liberal but it established a dictatorial government.

The Vietminh received support initially from poor farmers because they were able to rise to leadership positions in their villages, districts and provinces. Often they used their influence to get even with members of the upper classes who had long ruled them.

Still, the majority of the Vietnamese people were united in their desire to oust the French, but the Vietminh had other intentions such as destroying all vestiges of monarchy in Vietnam and the elimination of the former ruling class.

Although popular sentiment among the lower and middle classes for the Vietminh was not strong, they were eager to fight for independence. Many of these people became battalion and regimental commanders under General Giap. Later, as the communists moved toward a stronger brand of socialism, some of them were eliminated and they felt betrayed. They had never considered themselves enemies of the Vietminh.

A number of disaffected nationalists left the Vietminh and joined forces with ex-Emperor Bao Dai although he had little backing because of his pro-French views.

One of the most significant evolutions in Vietnam's culture was the changed status among women of the Vietminh. They were made equal partners with men, and their long-standing role of dependency on men was eliminated.

Ninety-eight percent of North Vietnam's farmers owned small plots. The reverse was true in the South where 6 percent of the landowners held 45 percent of the land. As a result, when the land rent reduction program was initiated in 1950 by the Vietminh the greatest alienation occurred in the South between landowners and poor farmers.

With full-scale war the Vietminh army was no match for France's army so Ho Chi Minh ordered his government to retreat to the limestone caves in Tonkin which had been their earlier refuge. Since he had served as head of the Vietminh government, Ho Chi Minh had urged his followers to plant quick-growing crops and a severe famine in the North had been overcome. Elections in Annam and Tonkin were won by the Vietminh League although communist elements often used terror tactics against the nationalists who opposed them, and most prominent members were assassinated.

Hatred of the French was so intense that most Vietnamese still approved of the Vietminh and France's 150,000 troops were able to control only the cities and their lines of communications. The French achieved small victories against the Vietminh but a stalemate resulted that was extremely costly to the occupiers.

As the cold war intensified with the civil war in Greece, a coup d'etat in Czechoslovakia and the Berlin blockade, the Truman administration became more inclined to accept French control over Indochina. American officials now were almost totally preoccupied with the rehabilitation of Western Europe in preparation for possible Russian aggression.

President Vincent Auriol of France now initiated negotiations with anti-communist parties and in April, 1949, former Emperor Bao Dai returned to Vietnam and was named chief of state of an association that included Tonkin, Annam and Cochin China. France, however, retained control over the armed forces, finances and foreign policy of these states.

The success of Mao Tse-tung's communist army in driving the Chinese Nationalists from the mainland to the island of Formosa in October, thereby completing the conquest of China, strengthened views in Washington that Ho Chi Minh's drive to communize Indochina had to be stopped. The United States Congress passed the Mutual Defense Assistance Act to deal with the cold war and the president was empowered to dispense funds to those nations—particularly those in the general area of China who were resisting communist expansion. In other words, he was given authority to assist Vietnam and other nations of Southeast Asia.

United States officials were particularly concerned that the guerrilla war in Vietnam would weaken French support for the North Atlantic Treaty Organization that was formed August 24 for the defense of Europe.

Ho Chi Minh further complicated the international situation by declaring January 14, 1950, that the Democratic Republic of Vietnam was the sole legal government. A certain legitimacy was given to it when China and the Soviet Union recognized the new Vietnamese government.

Secretary of State Dean Acheson spoke for the United States publicly February 1. He told the American people that China's and Soviet Russia's support of the Vietminh should remove any "illusions as to the 'nationalist' nature of Ho Chi Minh's aims and reveals Ho in his true colors as the mortal enemy of native independence in Indochina."

A State Department report was kept secret that Ho Chi Minh controlled two-thirds of Vietnam, and recommended that the United States support the French in Indochina, "or face the extension of communists over the remainder of the continental areas of Southeast Asia and, possibly, farther westward." The report further recommended that the United States furnish military aid, but not troops, to the anti-communist governments of Indochina.

Acheson formalized his views to President Harry S. Truman February 2 by recommending that Vietnam, Laos and Cambodia be recognized as independent states, to encourage the national aspirations of the people of those countries under non-communist governments. He also urged support for France as a friendly country and a signatory to the North Atlantic Treaty Organization. He said the United States should demonstrate its displeasure of communist tactics that, he charged, were aimed at the eventual domination of Asia, while working under the guise of indigenous nationalism.

At a cabinet meeting the following day Acheson sought recognition for the states of Indochina and most cabinet members agreed, and President Truman approved the recommendation.

Maurice Couvé de Murville of the French Ministry of Foreign Affairs advised Charles A. Bohlen at the United States embassy that France would find it difficult to go it alone in Indochina. With Soviet Russia's recognition of the Ho Chi Minh government, he stressed that the threat to French forces in Indochina was serious and that the region was an American and British concern as well as French.

Bao Dai, the chief of state for the French-sponsored government in Saigon, added a personal appeal and told the American consul general that Vietnam needed American military assistance.

In Washington, French Ambassador George Bonnet met with Secretary of State Dean Acheson and formally requested military assistance for Indochina and joint military staff talks.

When Chinese troops appeared on Vietnam's northern border following formal recognition of Ho Chi Minh's government by the People's Republic of China and the Soviet Union in January, 1950, the Truman administration was convinced that it had no recourse but to adopt the French plan of limited sovereignty for Vietnam's three states under Bao Dai. However, the policy of the United States prevented military assistance to countries unless they were evolving toward self-government and independence. After the French Parliament ratified agreements that granted a degree of autonomy to the associated states of Indochina the United States acted. On February 7, 1950, the United States extended diplomatic recognition to these states and to the kingdoms of Laos and Cambodia. Great Britain promptly followed suit.

The decision was tragic because it supported the hated French rule. But Truman was convinced—and with some justification—that the partnership of China and Russia in the Far East, and the communization of all of Indochina, was a threat to the interests of the United States.

Nine days after United States recognition of the Indochinese states France requested American economic and military support to continue prosecution of the war, saying bluntly that, if Ho Chi Minh continued to receive supplies from China and the Soviet Union, France would be forced to withdraw from the region. The French had particularly urgent need for ammunition, napalm and barbed wire to defend its perimeter defenses around Hanoi and Haiphong against Vietminh attacks. Its airplanes were obsolete, and technicians were in extremely short supply. The American Joint Chiefs of Staff had already recommended spending $75 million to resist communist infiltrations in these countries.

The American diplomatic position was reviewed again by the National Security Council February 27, and a policy paper advised that all practicable steps should be taken to prevent further communist expansion in Southeast Asia. It stressed that Indochina was the key area and under immediate threat. "The neighboring countries of Thailand and Burma can be expected to fall under communist domination if Indochina were controlled by a communist-dominated government."

President Truman later approved the resolution.

For Truman, the problems of Indochina were of deep concern. Should he intervene in Indochina as he had in Greece and Turkey under his Truman doctrine? His decision was firm. "Absolutely not!" He told his cabinet that he wanted a different approach because he was concerned about the instability of the French government. He cautioned Undersecretary of State Webb "to be most careful in the handling of the situation."

Truman did approve an allocation of $10 million May 1 for military assistance to Indochina.

Secretary of State Acheson said publicly May 8, following a meeting with French officials in Paris, that the United States would give economic aid and military equipment to Laos, Cambodia and Vietnam "in order to assist them in restoring stability and permitting these states to pursue their peaceful and democratic development."

An economic mission was established to carry out the aid plan. For the first time the United States became directly involved in aid to those countries opposing the Vietminh in Indochina.

Meanwhile, France continued to insist that the United States should make a substantial and long-term commitment. Such action was opposed by President Truman because many officials of his administration believed that Southeast Asia was already lost to the communists. Despite these views authorization was given to provide $164 million in military aid for France to use in Indochina during fiscal year 1951.

The People's Republic of China thereupon increased its aid to the Vietminh. When the Republic of Korea invaded South Korea June 25,

1950, President Truman and his cabinet had no doubt about communist intentions in the Far East. The president spoke to the American people June 22, saying that communism "had passed beyond the use of subversion to conquer independent nations and will now be used for armed invasion and war." He promised to resist aggression in Korea, and to accelerate military assistance to France for Indochina.

As United Nations forces countered the communist invasion of South Korea, and French armed forces resisted Vietminh attacks in Tonkin, Donald H. Heath was named United States Minister to the Associated States of Indochina. He took office July 6. Less than a month later a Military Assistance Advisory Group was formed in Saigon, and $30.5 million in additional defense funds were granted. Two years later the United States was bearing a third to one-half of France's costs to fight the Vietminh. Actually, since the start of 1950 the United States had given France $1.1 billion in military aid funds, including $740 million worth of United States Army materiel delivered directly to the French Expeditionary Corps in Indochina.

In its new role, American officials hoped to deal directly with the Vietnamese. They met immediate resistance from the French who said that the Bao Dai government and its military forces were incapable of dealing with assistance matters. This was partly true because there were few Vietnamese military units, and most of the fighting was done by French units.

American assistance was expanded December 23 when a Mutual Defense Assistance Agreement was signed by France, Laos, Cambodia and the Vietnamese associated states. It directed that all American supplies to these countries pass first through French hands.

Two months earlier, forty United States Navy F6F Hellcat fighters had been delivered to Vietnam by a French aircraft carrier. Early in 1951 ninety F8F Bearcat fighters were also sent to the French in Indochina. With an even later delivery of B-26 bombers, the Americans completed their airplane deliveries under the terms of the Mutual Defense Treaty. Although these airplanes were of World War II vintage, they gave the French armed forces superiority in the air against the almost non-existent Vietminh air force.

The French authorized the training of some Vietnamese pilots, but the three squadrons that were formed did not see action until 1952.

With the effective use of airpower, and the addition of more artillery guns, a major Vietminh offensive was defeated. Ho Chi Minh's army was forced again to return to guerrilla operations. A stalemate resulted, but the French armed forces and their government in Paris were appalled by the daily casualties and expenditures that rose dramatically as guerrilla warfare escalated.

After Mao Tse-tung's communist armed forces gained control of China, Ho Chi Minh's guerrillas had a sanctuary that could be reached by merely crossing the border. More importantly, the Chinese now provided training for General Vo Nguyen Giap's army, and armed it with substantial numbers of American artillery weapons that had been acquired when the Nationalists fled to Formosa.

Forty-three fully trained and equipped Vietminh battalions crossed into Vietnam in late 1950 and defeated the French by killing 6,000 troops. Quickly, the Vietminh consolidated their gains after capturing huge stocks of weapons and military vehicles. Now completely dominated by its communist leaders, and allied with the People's Republic of China and Soviet Russia, the Vietminh soon controlled most of Vietnam from the Chinese border to within a hundred miles of Saigon except for an area around the Red River delta and Hanoi in the North that the French still held behind extensive fortification.

In September, 1951, a Japanese Peace Treaty was signed in San Francisco officially ending World War II. It was negotiated on a non-partisan basis that called for non-punitive terms against Japan. President Truman spoke before the fifty-two nation conference. "At the present time the Pacific area is gravely affected by outright aggression and by the threat of further armed attack. One of our primary concerns in making peace with Japan, therefore, is to make Japan secure against aggression and to provide that Japan will so conduct itself as not to endanger the security of other nations."

Separate treaties were signed by Japan with the Philippines, Australia and New Zealand. The United States also reached agreement with Japan to permit the stationing of American armed forces there.

The Korean War was extended by intervention of the Chinese in late 1950, but United Nations forces were successful after an initial precipitate withdrawal from North Korea in driving the Chinese and North Koreans out of the south.

Meanwhile in Vietnam Ho Chi Minh in February, 1951, created the Lao Dong, or Workers Party, to replace the communist party that he had supposedly dissolved in 1945.

While the war dragged on in Korea President Truman on April 11 dismissed the United Nations Commander Douglas MacArthur for unauthorized statements the general made about escalating the war. Although cease-fire talks began in July, fighting continued for two more years.

With the Korean War still stalemated through the election year of 1952, and the French apparently unable to defeat the Vietminh in Indochina, Dwight D. Eisenhower was elected president of the United States in November. The popular World War II general had made a strong case that he would end the war in Korea and his Democratic opponent Adlai Stevenson was soundly defeated.

Truman's Secretary of State Dean Acheson briefed the president-elect shortly afterwards that the French both at home and in Vietnam were wavering in their support of the war. He told Eisenhower that France wanted international backing and additional assistance. Eisenhower listened but made no commitments.

Once Eisenhower took office in January, 1953 he decided that his administration would support Vietnamese aspirations for greater independence from French rule. He told his cabinet that such a proposal would help to destroy some of the credibility of the Vietminh who claimed to be the sole organization seeking self-rule. As a former professional officer he said that the French should use more Vietnamese nationals in its armed forces, and provide better equipment and training for them. It was his belief, Eisenhower said, that France was carrying the burden of resistance in an international struggle, and that free world nations should provide more assistance.

In March Eisenhower's Secretary of State John Foster Dulles promised the French that the United States would increase its financial support if France would develop an acceptable plan for ending the war in Indochina.

Before such aid could be implemented, the Vietminh launched an offensive into western Tonkin, and sent its army into Laos and even threatened Thailand.

At the North Atlantic Treaty Organization meeting in Paris the French sought the loan of transports from the United states to airlift tanks and other heavy equipment into Laos. Dulles passed along the request to Eisenhower but the president refused to permit United States Air Force crews to participate in Vietnamese combat missions. Eisenhower did agree to lend the transports if civil air transport crews from Taiwan flew them. The missions were flown and the civilian crews completed their assignment in July.

General Henri-Eugène Navarre, who replaced General Jean de Lattre de Tassigny as French military commander and high commissioner for Indochina in May, 1953, following the latter's death in January, was instructed by the French government to defeat the Vietminh and to end the war. He used mobile strike forces against main enemy units, and achieved a greater cooperation among all elements of his command—including its Vietnamese units. His plan was to lure the Vietminh into open battles and to break up their main forces. Once this was achieved Navarre hoped by 1955 to reduce the Vietminh to minor guerrilla activity that he believed the nationalist Vietnamese could contain without French support.

Such plans received the approval of the American government and a joint military mission headed by United States Army Lieutenant General John W. O'Daniel was sent to Saigon June 20 to observe operations and to report to Washington what assistance would be needed to help the French. O'Daniel was impressed by what Navarre had accomplished and he forwarded the French general's request for more transport aircraft, and it was approved. O'Daniel's suggestion that American advisers be permitted with French troops was politely but firmly turned down. Navarre said the war in Vietnam was French business.

After an armistice agreement was signed July 27 to end the Korean War, the United States government held out hope that more aid to the French in Indochina might be forthcoming.

The French government now promised eventual independence for Vietnam and further helped their cause in October by granting independence to Laos as a member of the French Union, and a majority of the French National Assembly expressed hope that a settlement would soon be negotiated to end the Indochina war.

In a related development, Norodom Sihanouk assumed command of the Cambodian army November 9, and declared independence from France. On this fateful date, acting under orders from Paris to block a communist advance into Laos, General Navarre ordered French forces to re-occupy Dien Bien Phu.

The United States assured France it would increase its aid beyond the $305 million it had already committed for the period ending March, 1954, by reimbursing France up to $785 million for expenditures in 1953.

That fall Navarre put his plan into operation for ending the war by re-occupying Dien Bien Phu in northwest Tonkin, twenty miles from the Laotian border. This site controlled the main road between the two countries. Navarre believed that with the establishment of a strong air and ground base at Dien Bien Phu that Vietminh intrusions into neighboring Laos would be prevented.

French paratroopers dropped on the airstrip at Dien Bien Phu November 20, and started to fortify the place. Supplies were brought in by French or contract civilian fliers from Hanoi and Haiphong. Unfortunately for the French, military supplies were limited in both cities and necessary supplies transferred to Dien Bien Phu drastically reduced the defenses of these key cities. General Giap's army made repeated attacks against Hanoi and Haiphong in late 1953 and early 1954 while enlarging the attacking force around the French at Dien Bien Phu.

General Navarre's decision to expose his men in a long valley dominated by hills was incredibly stupid. At the time he calculated that he could set up an impregnable defense and lure General Giap's communist army to attack so that they could be destroyed in the process. He believed that French air superiority and greater firepower could easily destroy an enemy that had no aircraft or tanks, and only limited means of transport. The French had been successful once before by fortifying a fixed position behind Vietminh lines at Na Son where the communists had lost a battalion against French fixed positions. Navarre was so positive of his reasoning that he purposely placed no men on the high ground surrounding Dien Bien Phu and the local French commander Brigadier General Christian de Castries did not even send regular patrols out to the ridge lines.

For three months after the French landed at Dien Bien Phu General Giap directed Vietminh plans to lay siege to the base. He established a camouflaged command post so it had a line-of-sight view of de Castries' headquarters.

General de Castries' force soon numbered 16,000 men—all from elite French battalions—including units from the Foreign Legion. The general was convinced that the Vietminh had no heavy artillery and could not supply a strong force far from their main bases, but he was wrong on both counts.

De Castries was well trained in mobile warfare, but ill-informed about siege conditions. He did set up three artillery strongpoints, reportedly named for his current mistresses: Gabrielle and Beatrice to the north and Isabelle to the south.

The general badly underestimated the ability of the Vietminh. They did bring up artillery and ammunition and occupied the hills that surrounded the valley. Meanwhile, they prepared to start a series of attacks against each of the French strongpoints.

While the communist forces built up in the surrounding hills, French planes tried to check the communist convoys that carried food and ammunition to Giap's army on an around-the-clock basis. Despite hardships that would have defeated a less-determined army, the Vietminh built up their forces until they soon surpassed the numbers of men in the French garrison. They were well equipped with artillery and anti-aircraft guns. Weapons had been disassembled and brought in on the backs of thousands of Vietminh, then re-assembled and placed in position in the hills where they were concealed under heavy vegetation overlooking the French position. A 100-mile road had been opened to a major depot on the Chinese border, and a fleet of 10,000 trucks brought supplies and weapons, including sufficient artillery shells to permit days of rapid firing.

February 18, 1954, the United States, Great Britain, France and the Soviet Union agreed to a Berlin conference to discuss political solutions for Korea and Indochina. They scheduled their next meeting for April 26 at Geneva.

Secretary of State Dulles opposed a specific date for further international negotiations. He said setting a fixed time would tempt Ho Chi Minh to make some spectacular move.

For weeks President Eisenhower had been concerned by reports of the Vietminh buildup around Dien Bien Phu and instructed Defense Secretary Charles E. Wilson to give the highest priority to the Mutual Assistance Program without regard to funding limits. He made it clear, however, that United States armed forces would not be committed to combat in Vietnam without congressional approval. He did authorize additional airplanes for the French. And when Eisenhower was advised that French air units had only 25 percent of their necessary strength, he approved transfer of some airplane mechanics to Haiphong. He assured an anxious public that these mechanics "would not get touched by combat."

General Otto P. Weyland, commander of the Far East Air Force, expressed his concern at the transfer of American Air Force personnel to Haiphong because, he said, their loss hampered his Air Force's combat readiness. He said that he would prefer that American funds be used to hire civilian mechanics to do the job. Weyland's officers in Vietnam told him that Vietnamese hatred of the French was causing political and psychological problems. He was told, further, that Vietnamese laborers who worked at French airfields outside of Hanoi and Haiphong by day might well be Vietminh sympathizers at night.

It soon became apparent to General Navarre that the Vietminh were able to cut surface routes to Dien Bien Phu and that his garrison would soon be isolated. In response he ordered new French and Vietnamese troops to be airlifted into the area. Some planes were fired upon by 37 mm. anti-aircraft guns, but two American Air Force officers who flew in for a visit were not fired upon, so they believed that the French had exaggerated the threat to their troops.

President Eisenhower grew more apprehensive of the French position, but General Navarre remained confident that his men could overwhelm the large Vietminh force now preparing to attack, although he did consider the situation critical.

Intelligence reports from Vietnam were further distorted when the United States Directorate of Intelligence said Ho Chi Minh would be "stupid" to attack and to take heavy losses when "hit and run" tactics were so much more effective.

By early March, the Vietminh had built up their forces in the surrounding hills to 60,000 troops, almost four times the number of French defenders in the valley below. They had been well trained by the Chinese, and they were supremely confident they could win an all-out victory.

CHAPTER 3

Fall of Dien Bien Phu

WHILE OPPOSING FORCES AT DIEN BIEN PHU WAITED FOR THE FINAL showdown, other Vietminh guerrillas struck airfields in the Hanoi-Haiphong area. Extensive damage was caused to planes and installations.

The morning of March 13 Giap ordered a massive artillery barrage against strongpoint Beatrice. The French were shocked, disbelieving at first that so many guns were arrayed against them. They were even more dismayed when, after several hours of bloody fighting, the Vietnamese overran the strongpoint and wiped out one of the best battalions of the Foreign Legion. The Vietminh suffered terrible losses—probably three thousand men—when they ignored heavy French fire and kept attacking.

Bad news followed in rapid succession as strongpoint Gabrielle fell to the Vietminh the following day. This was the position that was farthest to the north. Its fall forced closure of the airstrip the French had relied on to bring in supplies.

Supposedly loyal Vietnamese fighting alongside the French at strongpoint Anne deserted their positions March 15 at the northwestern corner of the defense perimeter.

Although two French parachute battalions were dropped to assist the defenders, with the airfield closed all future supplies had to be airdropped.

Captain James McGovern, known as Earthquake McGoon, was one of two Americans killed at Dien Bien Phu. He and his co-pilot Wallace Buford were shot down while flying supplies to the French garrison in an unmarked American transport. McGovern's nickname was derived from a comic strip character in Li'l Abner.

The French artillery commander had assured General de Castries that his guns would silence any Vietnamese artillery in the hills. When this proved impossible he killed himself March 17 with a hand grenade.

The Vietminh now dug trenches between the remaining French positions and soon isolated each of them while other troops slowly worked their way towards the remaining French positions.

In the United States, Eisenhower considered direct military intervention but he was reluctant to take such a step unless a coalition of nations, including Great Britain, offered at least moral support. He ordered plans drawn up for all contingencies.

With the situation worsening daily at Dien Bien Phu, the French government asked the United States to fly two battalions of French paratroopers and some naval personnel from France to Vietnam. Eisenhower agreed but Prime Minister Jawaharlal Nehru refused permission for the planes to overfly India so they had to be sent by a longer and more indirect route.

French Premier Joseph Laniel talked to American Ambassador C. Douglas Dillon at midnight April 4 and requested United States Navy carrier strikes against Vietminh artillery positions around Dien Bien Phu. As an alternative, if such a request was turned down, Laniel sought the immediate loan of ten to twenty B-29s that would be flown by French crews but maintained by the United States Air Force.

Secretary of State Dulles was in a difficult position. He had told the Overseas Press Club in Washington March 29 that the United States government was determined to resist Chinese aggression and the extension of communist power in Southeast Asia.

After his speech, British Foreign Secretary Anthony Eden sought clarification, wanting to know precisely what Dulles meant by his remarks. Eden believed it was useless to encourage the French unless the United States was ready to provide more than limited military assistance. Eden requested that the British ambassador to Washington, Roger M. Makins, inform Dulles that the British government believed the French situation in Indochina was beyond salvage. He was advised to stress to the Americans that it was important to refrain from any step that might endanger the upcoming Geneva conference.

Secretary of State Dulles and Admiral Arthur W. Radford, chairman of the Joint Chiefs of Staff, held a briefing April 3 for a select group of congressional leaders. It was later revealed that these members of Congress had made it clear there would be no support for unilateral United States intervention in Indochina unless there was unified action by non-communist nations in Southeast Asia and the United Kingdom. It was also stressed that complete independence must be granted to the Associated States of Vietnam, and that the French must continue their military activities on the same scale after other nations joined the conflict.

It seemed obvious to Eisenhower and Dulles that the British held the key if France was to receive further air and naval assistance. Eisenhower wrote Prime Minister Winston Churchill a personal letter April 4 to seek his advice, but Churchill had no enthusiasm for military activities in Indochina.

In testifying before the House Foreign Affairs Committee April 5, Secretary of State Dulles said that the Chinese were "coming awfully close" to overt military intervention. He stressed that Eisenhower would not countenance such action.

Despite Dulles' words, Eisenhower agreed to the British position, and France was notified April 6 that other circumstances would have to be necessary before the United States took a direct role.

Brigadier General Joseph D. Caldara, commander of the Far East Air Force Bomber Command, was requested by General Navarre to fly over Dien Bien Phu to ascertain whether B-29 Superfortress bombers would be helpful. Caldara made the flight, and recommended against their use, saying there were no worthwhile targets.

General Nathan F. Twining, the Air Force's chief of staff, also recommended that no B-29s be loaned to France for use in Vietnam. He gave two reasons. One, that France had little ability to operate the planes, and could not support them. He also said that suitable targets did not exist for such large bombers.

The French government dropped their request for B-29s when General Navarre informed officials that he did not have French flight crews who could fly the Superfortresses, and that without fighter escorts the B-29s might be shot down if the Chinese intervened with jet fighters.

With the situation worsening, President Eisenhower told a press conference in Washington April 7 that surrender of any free people to communism was inimical to freedom everywhere. He said that the loss of Vietnam would expose other nations in Southeast Asia to communist aggression. "You have a row of dominoes set up," the American president said. "You knock over the first one, and what will happen to the last one is the certainty it will go over quickly."

Eisenhower's reluctance to intercede with American combat forces on behalf of the French in Vietnam was based on military studies within the Defense Department that stressed that France still followed an arrogant colonial policy that had so alienated the Vietnamese people that victory was impossible. Military strategists were critical of the French commander's failure to interdict Vietminh supply lines to Dien Bien Phu and to use air strikes against concentrations around the beleaguered bastion.

Major General James M. Gavin, who headed a fact-finding team that was sent to Vietnam by Army Chief of Staff Matthew B. Ridgway, reached the conclusion that eight United States divisions, plus thirty-five engineer battalions, would be necessary in the Hanoi delta, and that Hainan Island (a part of the People's Republic of China) would have to be seized if the situation were to be reversed. Gavin's team reported that support requirements for such a large force would pose enormous problems because Southeast Asia had no good seaports, airfields and land communications.

Ridgway sent the report to President Eisenhower. As a former military man the president was aware of the enormity of supply and logistics problems.

Gavin said later, "We finally decided when we were all through that what we were talking about doing was going to war with Red China under conditions that were appallingly disadvantageous."

Although Eisenhower refused to commit American combat forces, he did order Far East commanders to furnish all-out logistics support to the French even when it meant removing vital equipment from American units. Sizable numbers of aircraft were involved, plus missiles and ammunition.

Actually, the French had more fighter-bombers and light bombers in the Hanoi area than they could keep in commission due to personnel and maintenance problems.

Secretary of State Dulles learned in Paris April 19 that French government officials considered the situation so desperate that Dien Bien Phu could be saved only by United States airpower. Dulles discussed the matter with Chairman of the Joint Chiefs of Staff Admiral Radford who said it was too late for intervention to save Dien Bien Phu, and Dulles agreed with him. This viewpoint was strengthened the following evening when Sir Anthony Eden, Great Britain's foreign secretary, told Dulles that the United Kingdom would oppose direct air involvement.

Luong Dinh Chinh was a platoon leader during the assault on strongpoint Elaine. In early May he had helped to surround it as troops tunneled 325 feet beneath it. Two hundred thousand and two hundred pounds of explosives were detonated May 7 below the French position and the final attack began against Elaine. Many French defenders were killed by the explosive charge and others soon were overwhelmed by Vietminh soldiers with grenades and bayonets.

That afternoon, fifty-five days after the attack began, General de Castries and his staff surrendered in their bunker. The French had lost 5,000 troops, including colonials. Eleven thousand men surrendered and most were severely debilitated by wounds, malaria and malnutrition. After a formal peace treaty was signed four months later at Geneva, only 4,000 were still alive for repatriation. For Ho Chi Minh and the Vietminh it was a decisive victory that permitted the movement of troops and weapons toward the vital Hanoi-Haiphong perimeter.

Five days later 500 Vietnamese regular troops deserted the Hanoi garrison, increasing doubts among the French command that the Red River delta could be held. For Navarre, the situation was perilous and his first consideration was to save the remainder of his Expeditionary Corps. When he made his position clear to Paris officials, Navarre was directed to withdraw his troops and retire as far as the 18th parallel to safeguard the southern part of Vietnam.

Throughout the battle for Dien Bien Phu the American Joint Chiefs of Staff had been reluctant to recommend the use of American combat troops in Vietnam. They believed it was mandatory for the United States to avoid another Korea-type situation, and instead they preferred action against the People's Republic of China but only if such a step were absolutely necessary. The Joint Chiefs seriously considered attacks against Chinese war-making facilities and even "employing atomic weapons whenever necessary."

General Paul H. R. Ely, who was preparing to go to Vietnam as Commander-in-Chief and High Commissioner for France, met in Paris at the end of May with General Thomas H. Trapnell whom Eisenhower had appointed as head of the military advisory group to discuss plans on a cooperative basis. Trapnell was candid with Ely, saying that he should not hope for American combat troops even if the communist Chinese joined the war against the French. Ely, who had hoped for more than token assistance as a show of good faith, now realized that France was on its own in Indochina.

Discussions to seek an armistice in Vietnam began May 8 with Great Britain and the Soviet Union serving as co-chairmen. The Vietminh sensed overwhelming victory over the French so its delegate was not anxious to compromise. Ho Chi Minh was convinced the French were defeated and that it was just a question of time until all of Vietnam fell to the Vietminh. By now they were establishing control over South Vietnam's Central Highlands. They virtually destroyed 3,600 men of French Mobile Group 100 in Mang Yang Pass while it was attempting to withdraw towards Pleiku along Route 19.

The Geneva conference had convened in April to seek a solution and formally end the Korean War. Now it also sought a compromise settlement for Indochina. A spokesman for the Vietminh insisted that the French had to withdraw from all parts of Vietnam. For the present, he said, the country should be partitioned at the 13th parallel and elections should be held six months after an armistice. The Vietminh spokesman was chagrined by an apparently conciliatory attitude towards France by representatives of the Soviet Union and the People's Republic of China. He suspected their main concern was not victory for the Vietminh but a settlement that would preclude United States intervention in Indochina.

France's problems at home were intensified when the government of Prime Minister Joseph Laniel fell, and Pierre Mendès-France was named in his place on June 17. The new prime minister pledged to achieve a ceasefire in Indochina within a month.

Eisenhower and Prime Minister Winston Churchill of Great Britain in late June agreed on terms and offered them to France to serve as the basis for a Vietnamese armistice. They pledged to seek collective defense in Southeast Asia and they warned that the international situation would be "seriously aggravated if the French government refused to accept an agreement."

The Soviet Union made a proposal through Foreign Minister Vyacheslav Molotov to Premier Mendès-France that it would seek a favorable settlement in Indochina if the French refused to participate in an European Defense Community.

Chinese Foreign Minister Chou En-lai also pressed for an early agreement because he feared the atomic power of the United States, and he was most anxious that Indochina be demilitarized to keep the Americans from establishing bases on the Asian mainland.

With such power plays the negotiations moved more rapidly and the 17th parallel in Vietnam was approved as the demarcation line between South and North Vietnam. Two states thus were formed, with a demilitarized zone on each side of the line. The ceasefire agreement of July 20 called for withdrawal of all French troops from the North, and of the Vietminh from the South. Article 16 of the agreement had far-reaching effects. It prohibited introduction into South Vietnam of troops and military support personnel who had not been there at the time of the ceasefire. The number of assistance advisers was set at 888—the total number of French and Americans there at the time of the armistice. Other articles restricted weapons and military hardware except on a piece-by-piece replacement basis. All new materiel was prohibited, and no new military bases could be built. An International Control Commission composed of representatives from Canada, India and Poland was established to supervise the terms of the agreement. It was agreed that in 1956 an election would be held to unify the country.

The agreement also called for a cessation of hostilities in Cambodia and Laos.

American officials refused to sign the agreement but they affirmed that the United States would abide by its terms although they would view any new aggression with the gravest concern.

Bao Dai's South Vietnamese government denounced the agreement and also refused to sign it.

Before the agreement was approved the United States, acting under orders of Defense Secretary Charles Wilson, on July 13 ordered the immediate suspension of all materiel shipments to Indochina.

After the armistice was signed an exodus of Vietnamese from the North started as 880,000 people announced their determination to flee communist domination. French air operations quickly proved inadequate to support its 182,000 troops and to move this mass of refugees from the North. So, the United States Navy provided ships for the evacuation.

In addition to this exodus from North Vietnam, more than 100,000 Vietminh soldiers and civilians were permitted to relocate in the North.

Although the Eisenhower administration did not approve of the agreement reached at Geneva because it believed that it enhanced the chances of communist exploitation, the president was relieved. He had opposed American combat assistance to the French, saying that such assistance could never cure an "unsound relationship between the Asiatics and the French," and that such help would have been of "only limited value."

There was considerable congressional opposition to the agreement when it was signed in August without the United States. Some of it was expressed by Senator Jenner on August 14. "The United States has been outthought, outtraded and outgeneraled. It does no good to say we did not physically sign the Geneva agreement. That is the old excuse of Pontius Pilate who washed his hands to keep his conscience clean."

Colonel Edward G. Lansdale had been sent to Saigon by the American Central Intelligence Agency in May. He now was placed in charge of a team of agents to conduct paramilitary operations, and to wage psychological warfare against the Vietminh.

With the division of Vietnam, two of the world's most densely populated and richest rice-producing regions became separate countries. In the North was the Red River delta and in the South was the delta formed by the Mekong River as it heads towards the sea. The narrow central portion of South Vietnam was covered mostly with mountainous jungles with a fertile coastal strip. The dividing line separating north from south was roughly at the center of the narrow strip along the 17th parallel with a demilitarized zone extending eight miles on each side of the demarcation line. South Vietnam was approximately the same length as the state of California but only half as wide. About 80 percent of its people lived on 40 percent of the land in the lowlands between the mountains and the sea, while another 40 percent was largely uninhabited and covered with jungle or scrub growth, ideal for guerrilla warfare.

The strip of arable lowland along the coast extended almost South

Vietnam's entire length. South of the former imperial city of Hué, however, a precipitous chain of mountains—the Annamites—dip into the sea. Access from the North into South Vietnam's two northernmost provinces of Quang Tri and Thua Thien to Hué and Quang Tri was by a single road that hugged the coast and crossed the high Hai Van Pass. The northern provinces, therefore, were practically cut off from the rest of South Vietnam. The communists had tried to get these two provinces ceded to them in the peace negotiations, but they had failed. In the northwest, the Annamite Mountains reach to 8,000 feet. They are covered with thick growth and the mountains form a backbone southward across two thirds of the country, reducing in height below Da Lat. In this town, the French had developed a mountain resort with expensive hotels and villas. In the center of the country, the mountains are broken by the Kontum Plateau. This area, called the High Plateau, extends farther south and forms the Darlac Plateau. This region of South Vietnam is called the Central Highlands. Another chain—the Seven Mountains—rises to the southwest along the Cambodian border.

South Vietnam was divided into forty-four provinces, smaller than most American states, and each was headed by a chief. Each province was divided into 246 districts, somewhat resembling American counties, with each district governed by a district town. Local mandarins wielded authority at the district level instead of officials of the central government. Most Vietnamese opposed a strong central government because it reminded them of domination by foreigners, or Vietnamese who acted like foreigners. Throughout South Vietnam there were 2,500 villages and 16,000 hamlets that had loose and ineffectual ties with the government at Saigon. Such a situation was understandable to those who knew Vietnam's long history of domination by foreigners, but it made the country virtually indefensible against those seeking to control it from North Vietnam.

Communications were poor everywhere with such an ineffective central government. There were few major highways. Route 1 followed the coast from Saigon to the demilitarized zone and Route 14 went north from Saigon over the Darlac and High Plateaus. Route 20 was the principal avenue to carry produce from the Central Highlands to Saigon while Route 4 was the lifeline to transport rice from the Mekong Delta to the capital. Across the nation's midsection there were few major roads. The principal railroad was a narrow-gauge single track that generally paralleled Route 1. There were more than thirty-five hundred miles of navigable canals and rivers, but these were mostly in the Mekong Delta and were that area's primary means of transportation. There was only one major port at Saigon that connected the capital with the sea by the Saigon River. Da Nang had some port facilities. South Vietnam had only one major airfield and that was Tan Son Nhut.

In the North there were 21.3 million people ruled by a communist dictatorship and controlled by a battle-trained army. The harsh collectivization of land and factories in 1954 and 1955 had reduced the popularity of the communist regime, but its leaders expected to win the 1956 plebiscite that was supposed to decide the unification of the country. There were 16.5 million people in the South, including refugees who had fled the North. Under French colonialism few Vietnamese leaders were developed. With Bao Dai in France, control of the government was handled by Ngo Dinh Diem who became head of the South Vietnamese cabinet June 18, 1954. A few weeks later Diem—son of a Hué Mandarin family—was invested as president of the Council of Ministers. A bachelor, and a member of the Catholic minority, Diem was not widely known. His aloofness, and his dependence on his brother Ngo Dinh Nhu for counsel, alienated many officials of the government.

Ho Chi Minh now called upon his followers to wage a long and arduous struggle to take over the southern half of Vietnam. He called this area "territories of ours." He authorized cadres to be sent south—in violation of the Geneva agreement—to prepare for future infiltrations. These cadres became known as Vietcong, an acronym for the name of Vietnamese communists.

President Eisenhower retained the United States embassy in Saigon, and ordered its officials to help strengthen the government by aiding the French who had agreed to remain until the election to unify the country.

The Vietminh victory over the French had worldwide significance, particularly throughout the Far East, and Ho Chi Minh moved quickly to extend his country's influence by exploiting internal political differences in neighboring countries.

The United States now recommended joint action in the Far East with Great Britain, France, Australia, New Zealand, Pakistan, Thailand and the Philippines to counter the growing threat posed not only by North Vietnam but by the People's Republic of China and the Soviet Union. The result was a Southeast Asia defense agreement that was signed in Manila September 8, 1954. Its goal was to act promptly against armed aggression by supporting legitimate governments who needed assistance to insure their internal security against foreign aggression. Collective military action was not contemplated but the organization would serve as a clearing house for the exchange of information. Under terms of the pact, external armed aggression against any member would be recognized as a common danger and members were pledged to meet collectively to discuss it.

The Geneva agreement prevented South Vietnam, Laos and Cambodia from joining the organization, but the Southeast Asia Treaty Organization (SEATO) agreed to offer them protection. The United States agreed to continue working through the French to maintain whatever military forces were needed for South Vietnam's internal security. Further, the United States committed itself to the rapid deployment of mobile forces to a threatened area instead of maintaining on-site military units. The Southeast Asia Treaty Organization became effective in February, 1955. Secretary of State Dulles hoped that the new organization would be an effective shield against internal aggression and that South Vietnam would need military forces only for such aggression. The treaty was not as strong as he would have wished. He was particularly disturbed that Article IV did not pledge automatic response to aggression with force. The article was weasel worded, saying, in part, each signatory agrees to "act to meet the common danger in accordance with its constitutional processes."

The American Joint Chiefs of Staff disagreed. They believed that military assistance should provide not only internal security, but limited defense against external attack. With money scarce to build up the armed forces of the United States, the Joint Chiefs did not recommend the expenditure of funds for South Vietnam until a stable government was formed.

Dulles understood the views of Defense Department officials, but he believed that well-trained Vietnamese armed forces would strengthen Diem's government. At the time, the Vietnamese army was a collection of former French colonial troops with little command experience and with little or no support forces. Therefore, the secretary of state insisted that the Joint Chiefs provide funds to establish five Vietnamese divisions for internal security that could also be used to provide a limited response to external attack. He was aware that such a force would take two to three years to train. Three Air Force squadrons had been created, but they were equipped mostly with liaison planes although there was a squadron of light bombers. Most Vietnamese pilots still flew with French squadrons. Few officers had gained sufficient rank for high positions, and most were inexperienced. The enlisted ranks were demoralized and desertions were frequent. After the Geneva agreement the French changed their mind about permitting the United States to train the Vietnamese. President Eisenhower warned Prime Minister Diem that for such assistance he would expect Diem to reform his government and to make it more responsive to the national aspirations of the Vietnamese people. The president said Vietnam must have a representative and democratic government if it was to expect American military and economic assistance.

Diem agreed and South Vietnam's armed forces were modeled along the lines of the American services.

Lieutenant General John W. "Iron Mike" O'Daniel, chief of the Military Assistance Advisory Group for Indochina, had reached an agreement in June with the French commander for United States participation to train Vietnamese units, and he had sent a request to Washington for more advisers. After the ceasefire July 20, O'Daniel drew up plans for a comprehensive assistance program for the Vietnamese Army, but the American Joint Chiefs of Staff said that it was "hopeless to expect a United States training mission to achieve success unless the nation considered is able effectively to perform those governmental functions essential to the raising and maintenance of armed forces."

Secretary of State Dulles disagreed. He said it was necessary "to bolster that government by strengthening the army which supports it."

The National Security Council backed him up and political considerations were allowed to override military objections.

United States Ambassador Donald R. Heath and General O'Daniel were authorized to "collaborate in setting in motion a crash program designed to bring about an improvement in the loyalty and effectiveness of the free Vietnamese forces."

Eisenhower sent General J. Lawton Collins to Saigon November 3 as his special United States representative to determine the loyalty of the Vietnamese Army to Diem's government. Collins had broad powers to negotiate with French High Commissioner General Paul Ely who had replaced General Navarre. After January 1, 1955, when the Union of Associated States agreement with France was terminated, Collins dealt directly with Diem's government. An agreement was reached for a Vietnamese Army of 94,000, and the United States agreed to assume full responsibility for assisting the Vietnamese government to train its armed forces. The United States took formal control of Vietnamese military training February 12, although French control of military operations in Indochina remained in effect. This agreement drastically changed the United States' role from one of materiel supply and delivery to a truly military assistance and advisory role in support of the French government. Specifically, for the first time the United States became fully involved in South Vietnam's future.

The United States split the Indochinese Military Assistance Advisory Group into two parts—one for South Vietnam and the other for Cambodia. This reorganization was necessary to adjust to political realities because May 16 the United States and Cambodia signed an agreement for direct military aid. This move gained additional significance in September of 1955 when Cambodia announced it was a free and independent state.

In South Vietnam the Military Assistance Advisory Group was given two objectives—to create a conventional army of divisional units and supporting forces by January 1, 1956, and to establish programs to maintain the efficiency of this force.

The American training mission in South Vietnam found its work limited by South Vietnam's internal military and political situation. Also, South Vietnam's Army was organized into small units, and it lacked trained leaders, equipment and logistical capabilities at all levels. Units were scattered throughout the country and a large proportion was still fighting remnants of religious sects and other dissident factions. The chronic American problem was lack of personnel. However, the establishment of a separate Military Assistance Advisory Group in Cambodia in June, 1955, and a Programs Evaluation Office for Laos in December relieved the situation somewhat.

At the close of the French involvement in the Indochina war its Expeditionary Corps totaled approximately one hundred forty thousand men. With the signing of the American defense agreement in December, 1954, the United States agreed to support a combined French and Vietnamese force of 150,000, but this figure was never achieved. By the middle of the following year the French corps was reduced to 35,000. The weak political status of French forces in South Vietnam, plus the fact that the French defense military budget for calendar year 1956 made no provision for Indochina, was a sure indication to Americans that France's military presence in Vietnam was coming to a close.

The American Defense Department's reluctance to commit funds to support the Saigon regime is understandable because the Diem government was finding it difficult to form a stable regime. In the view of many Vietnamese Diem appeared to be the only leader who could unify the nation. His position remained precarious although he took several positive steps to consolidate his control of the government. He replaced General Nguyen Van Hinh, son of Bao Dai's former Prime Minister Nguyen Van Xuan, as commander of the National Army. Hinh had been a major in the French Air Force and held French nationality. He also was married to a French woman. Diem met stiff opposition at first but the general of the Cao Dai religious sect rallied his troops around Diem despite French opposition to Hinh's removal. American support for Diem proved crucial.

The internal situation in Saigon was tense because the Binh Xuyen had control of the city's police. Gambling casinos, brothels and opium dens operated openly under their control. Outside the capital, armies of the Cao Dai and Hoa Hao religious sects controlled the provinces north and southwest of Saigon where the majority of the people lived under feudal conditions and suffered as a result.

Once Diem gained control of the armed forces he worked to create dissension among the feudal lords. When two Hoa Hao groups supported

Diem he felt strong enough to crack down on the Binh Xuyen. There was no question of allegiance with this group and in late March, 1955, Diem's security forces clashed with the Binh Xuyen. French High Commissioner General Paul Ely intervened to prevent use of the National Army against the Binh Xuyen. His action created a major crisis as the French supported the anti-government group. Several cabinet ministers resigned, including Foreign Minister Tran Van Do and Defense Minister Ho Thon Minh.

Diem courageously fought back and on April 28 he sent army units against the Binh Xuyen and, after two days of fighting, they were driven out of the city. Some went into hiding in a mangrove swamp but surrendered several months later. With this forthright action Diem liquidated the Binh Xuyen and drove them from control of Saigon.

Chief of State Bao Dai, who spent most of his time on the French Riviera, summoned Prime Minister Diem and his chief of the General Staff, General Le Van Ty, to France for consultation. They refused, and they were backed by the United States. In effect, Bao Dai's action destroyed any possibility that he could control the government.

Religious sects soon lost influence. Even the Cao Dai sect that had rallied in support of Diem and generals Trinh Minh The and Nguyen Thanh Puong lost strength among the people. The Hoa Hao remnants were now reduced to small guerrilla bands.

Prime Minister Diem moved to unify his nation and formally asked the French to leave his country. The United States urged France to do so and return all sovereign power to South Vietnam, as she had pledged in the Geneva agreement.

The American Joint Chiefs continued to express private concern that defense of South Vietnam from external aggression, without the use of atomic weapons, would be costly and well-nigh impossible. Studies indicated that to counter an invasion from the North four American Army divisions would be required in addition to South Vietnamese divisions. If the decision was made to invade and occupy North Vietnam, it was predicted that a force of at least eight United States divisions would be required.

When Ho Chi Minh called upon Prime Minister Diem to open negotiations for a national plebiscite, Diem said that an honest election would be impossible because the totalitarian regime in the North would not permit a free election in North Vietnam. Dulles publicly agreed with Diem's stand and on August 9, 1955, Diem rejected elections unless North Vietnam granted democratic freedoms and fundamental rights to its people.

Diem instead announced that a popular referendum would be held in October for the people of South Vietnam to choose their own form of government. This was primarily a choice between Chief of State Bao Dai, who continued to live in France, and Ngo Dinh Diem. The prime minister easily won the election October 26, and Diem declared South Vietnam a republic and officially became its first president. The United States quickly extended recognition.

A constitutional assembly was convened the following year on March 4. On the first anniversary of Diem's election as president of the Republic of Vietnam a Constitution was proclaimed October 26, 1956. It gave Diem and the executive branch more powers than were allotted to the legislative or judiciary branches of the South Vietnamese government. Diem defended such action as necessary in order to have a strong head of state because South Vietnam's economy had been ravaged by war, and his political forces were still divided and immature.

The American Military Assistance Advisory Group in Saigon recommended that the Diem government concentrate its armed forces against attempts by the Vietminh to infiltrate the South. Diem agreed, and Civil Guard and Self-Defense Corps training was stepped up.

In Washington, meanwhile, the Joint Chiefs approved an increase in South Vietnam's armed forces from 94,000 to 150,000. Lieutenant General Samuel T. Williams was appointed to head the Military Assistance Advisory Group in Saigon. He arrived November 15, and soon was immersed in the problems of assisting the withdrawal of French forces which were needed to meet the revolt against French sovereignty in Algeria.

Williams tried to obtain approval of the International Control Commission to increase the number of personnel under the allowable 342 under his command but his request was denied. He was permitted to enlarge his group on a temporary basis, and 350 Americans were approved for inventory purposes and to remove surplus equipment.

The French High Command left Saigon by the end of 1955, and officials were given six months to decide on French or Vietnamese citizenship. The last French forces departed April 28, 1956, ending ninety-four troubled years that had brought frustration and tragedy to both countries.

CHAPTER 4

A New Type of Warfare

THE UNITED STATES HAD NOT HAD A COHERENT FOREIGN POLICY FOR Indochina in years, and as its involvement in South Vietnam's survival intensified it still had no long-range plan of what precisely it would do in the event of a communist invasion. By the middle of 1956 there was still no agreement among American political and military officials as to whether subversion or invasion posed the greatest threat. They were all in agreement that scattered Vietnamese units must be organized into a strong field force and brought up quickly to combat effectiveness.

A step in the right direction was taken in July when Eisenhower, the National Security Council and the Joint Chiefs directed Commander-in-Chief, Pacific, Admiral Felix B. Stump, to prepare contingency plans for defending South Vietnam from invasion. Stump believed that a United States-South Vietnam defense command should be set up, and the Joint Chiefs accepted his viewpoint. His greatest concern was control of airpower due to the proliferation of separate commands. Consolidation of United States Far East and Pacific Commands had been under study for more than a year. Secretary of Defense Charles E. Wilson had objected that the worldwide command structure was too large, unwieldy and expensive. He insisted that the entire airpower system be simplified and reduced in size. He referred his views to the Joint Chiefs and, after much argument, a single commander directly responsible to the Joint Chiefs was appointed with the United States Navy as executive agent. Under him three component commanders representing the Air Force, Army and Navy units of the Pacific Fleet were established in the Pacific Ocean area.

In North Vietnam the massive land reforms that began the previous December continued as landlords were tried before "people's tribunals."

Other changes around the world were affecting Indochina. Prince Sihanouk, now Cambodia's prime minister, stated in the spring of 1956 that his country would follow a neutralist policy. Later that year, in October, the Soviet Union brutally crushed uprisings involving rebellions in Hungary and Poland. The following month Great Britain, France and Israel launched what became known as the Suez War.

The Soviet Union in January, 1957, proposed that North and South Vietnam be admitted to the United Nations as separate states. For reasons of its own the Soviet Union favored a permanent division of the two nations.

President Diem arrived in the United States May 8 seeking support for a ten-division army. Ambassador Eldridge Durbrow had already recommended a lesser force, saying that large an army would be too much of a drain on South Vietnam's economy. President Eisenhower, however, appeared to give tacit approval to Diem's request in their joint communique. The two presidents agreed that they would continue to work for the peaceful unification of Vietnam and Eisenhower promised Diem that the United States would support South Vietnam against communist aggression. The United States tour was a triumph for Diem who was hailed as the savior of his country. *Life* magazine called him a tough miracle man. Mayor Robert Wagner of New York City said he was a "man history may judge as one of the great figures of the twentieth century."

Meanwhile, in North Vietnam, plans were set in motion by Ho Chi Minh's government to organize thirty-seven armed companies in the Mekong Delta in South Vietnam. They were so successful the rest of the year that a great many minor South Vietnamese officials were assassinated.

In Laos, Prince Souvanna Phouma dissolved his government. His neutralist regime was replaced July 22 with one headed by Phoui Sananikone and, with American support, it agreed to take an anti-communist position in the Far East.

The Army of the Republic of Vietnam reached a total of 150,000 by 1958. To permit more intensive field training, Diem released the Army from internal security duties.

Cambodia's Prince Sihanouk was almost overthrown in February, 1959, but the plot was unsuccessful and the United States relations reached a new low when it was learned that an American Central Intelligence Agency operative was involved in the plot.

In May, North Vietnam formed a group known simply as 559 that was charged with infiltrating soldiers and weapons into South Vietnam over what soon became known as the Ho Chi Minh Trail. Another group— 759—was organized in July to send supplies to the South via sea routes.

Although one American was killed earlier in Vietnam prior to increased United States involvement, two more Americans were killed by guerrillas at Bien Hoa on July 8. They were Major Dale Buis and Sergeant Chester Ovnand.

President Diem cracked down on communist suspects and dissidents in August as the infiltration of communist cadres from the North began to exert control of outlying communities.

In Laos a coalition government was negotiated that would include the communist Pathet Lao group. An accord was finalized on August 5, 1959, and a new American Military Assistance Advisory Group was organized for Laos. The groups in Laos and Cambodia were significantly different from the one in Saigon as they were confined primarily to logistical support.

The North Vietnamese thereupon increased their military activities in Laos by creating Group 959 to supply insurgents with weapons and supplies.

In September the North Vietnamese government proposed to South Vietnam that the two governments reach an understanding guaranteeing peaceful relations. Diem declined because communist guerrillas had kidnapped 236 South Vietnamese and assassinated 193 already that year.

At a secret session of North Vietnam's Central Committee of the Lao Dong Party in May, 1959, it was agreed to continue the revolution in South Vietnam, and to use force to overthrow the "feudalist imperialist regime in order to establish a revolutionary democratic situation and create conditions for peaceful reunification of the Fatherland." Committee action not only called for a resumption of warfare in South Vietnam—totally contrary to the Geneva armistice agreement—but also in Laos.

The army of the People's Republic of China was causing American concern also by making probes across the border into India. Incursions into Laos by North Vietnamese involved combat units driving Laotian military units from the border between Laos and South Vietnam. Once achieved, transportation units set up relay stations so supplies could be transported in support of communist infiltrations into both countries.

In September, 1959, the Vietcong began guerrilla activity against two South Vietnamese army companies in the marshy region southwest of Saigon known as the Plain of Reeds. A month later the Vietcong attacked a small force in Kien Phong Province, proclaiming, "The armed struggle has been launched." These illegal incursions into South Vietnam were directed by the Politburo in Hanoi, and manifested the Vietminh's commitment to achieve its political goals in the South through military action.

The real threat was not immediately apparent to American officials in Saigon, primarily because President Diem kept making optimistic assessments of his control of the countryside. With his government in control of intelligence activities he frequently used information gained by his operatives in the field for his own political purposes.

The Military Assistance Advisory Group, therefore, had little knowledge of the true state of affairs as its assistance programs were used to counter the communist threat in Laos and in sparsely populated areas of Vietnam's Central Highlands adjacent to the Laotian border. This area had been of particular interest to President Diem since 1957 when he authorized the building of agrovilles or new agricultural communities around Pleiku. Settlers were used to establish control of the area and by February, 1959, there were twenty-eight outposts. Five months later Diem expanded the settlements program and formed Vietnamese Ranger units with a projected strength of ten thousand men to protect them. The Rangers were needed because the area had been infiltrated by at least five thousand Vietcong and regular North Vietnamese troops plus communist political agents.

Once the American Joint Chiefs realized the extent of communist guerrilla infiltration in the South, officials of the advisory group in Saigon were directed to produce a counter-insurgency plan, and the group's authority was increased. Under direct orders from President Diem the Civil Guard was transferred to the Ministry of Defense in November, and the following month the Military Assistance Advisory Group was given responsibility to train and equip it.

Although the Army of the Republic of Vietnam was approaching its authorized strength, the Vietnamese Air Force was still using obsolete airplanes, and most of its officers were young and still with little command experience.

An important change occurred in France as Charles de Gaulle assumed office in December as head of the Fifth Republic.

In 1960 the United States still considered that internal subversion was a relatively minor problem that the South Vietnamese could keep under control. Officials believed that the aggressive attitude of the People's Republic of China was the most threatening problem in the Far East. They were convinced, however, that the Southeast Asia Treaty Organization would act as a deterrent to Chinese aggression. North Vietnam imposed universal military conscription in April, and its dedication to the goal of a military takeover of the South became more evident.

The ever-changing scene in Laos brought power back to Souvanna Phouma after Captain Kong Le staged a coup d'etat. With CIA backing, General Phoumi Nosavan headed an opposition group in southern Laos.

Nikita Krushchev, who replaced Joseph Stalin as premier of the Soviet

Union following Stalin's death March 5, 1953, spoke to the United Nations General Assembly in September, 1960, about the danger of colonial wars escalating into a new world war. There evidently had been a growing debate between officials of the People's Republic of China and the Soviet Union about such a danger. Apparently their divergent views resulted in a compromise that was not revealed until January 6, 1961. Krushchev said that world wars and local wars that might end in a world thermonuclear war must be avoided. This was not an important statement by itself but he made a significant addition, that national liberation wars to permit colonial peoples to attain independence were not only "admissable but inevitable." He said such wars should receive full communist support.

The same month that Krushchev was speaking to the United Nations Assembly the Lao Dong Party in Hanoi revealed September 10 that it had formed in South Vietnam "a broad national, united front" of workers, peasants and soldiers to overthrow the Diem government.

From then on North Vietnamese infiltration of the South increased rapidly, and President Diem's government was soon unable to contain the Vietcong and the infiltrating communists from the North.

North Vietnam's Constitution, dating back to November, 1945, was replaced in 1960 by a new document that was full of denunciations of the West, and praised President Ho Chi Minh for his "far-sighted" leadership. Ho Chi Minh was given almost unlimited powers, and he used them to place associates in key jobs. Ton Duc Thang was named vice president, and Pham Van Dong was appointed prime minister. Dong was an able administrator and he held Ho Chi Minh's confidence. General Vo Nguyen Giap, who defeated the French at Dien Bien Phu, was named vice premier and minister of defense. However, most of the power continued to be invested in North Vietnam's communist party.

Ngo Dinh Nhu, President Diem's brother, now introduced some reforms that had long been demanded by the United States but he refused to decentralize tight authoritarian controls, and unrest among South Vietnamese reached new heights. One of Diem's worst faults as president was his failure to delegate authority, and he kept his armed forces fragmented in small commands controlled by thirty-three provincial chiefs. Actually, forty-two armed forces leaders reported directly to President Diem.

Diem and his brother Nhu suspected that American officials favored officers of South Vietnam's Army who waged a coup November 11 that failed, although there is no concrete evidence that such was in fact the case. But relations with American Ambassador Durbrow were strained as discontent among Vietnamese officers continued to interfere with the fight against the communists. Officers were particularly disappointed when Diem, who had promised to liberalize his government, failed to do so.

In the United States, Democrat John F. Kennedy narrowly defeated Republican Richard M. Nixon for the presidency in November, 1960.

Communist leaders on December 20 formed an organization called the National Liberation Front for South Vietnam, and Diem's officials named its members Vietcong or communist Vietnamese.

After Commander-in-Chief, Pacific, Admiral Harry D. Felt, was alerted to a new outbreak of war in Laos, he reported the facts to Washington. Eisenhower believed that the Southeast Asia Treaty Organization should take action, but on January 5, 1961, Charles de Gaulle flatly refused French participation. As a result, the CINCPAC alert was reduced the next day on orders from Washington. On January 7, however, the State Department announced that the United States would work with other free nations to pursue "whatever measures seem most promising."

President Eisenhower decided that he would make no major commitment in the closing days of his administration because that might obligate his successor, John F. Kennedy, to a predetermined course. He briefed the president-elect on January 19 and emphasized that he considered that Laos was the key to all of Southeast Asia and that it must be defended. "If the Allies failed to do so," he told Kennedy, "our unilateral intervention would be our last desperate hope." He said what happened in Laos had meaning for the future because Laos was along the northwestern frontier of South Vietnam and along the entire western frontier of North Vietnam. He stressed that Laos was geographically vulnerable, largely because it had a politically fragile government and was an obvious avenue of approach for infiltrators from North Vietnam to South Vietnam's northern provinces and its Central Highlands. He described Laos as the crossroads of the area: the corridor from North Vietnam and China to South Vietnam, Cambodia, Thailand, Burma and Malaya, and possibly even Indonesia. He stressed the domino theory that the loss of Laos would mean the loss of the entire region.

One Laotian government after another had failed to make its will prevail in the face of infiltrations from the People's Republic of China and North Vietnam. Due to the constant instability of the Laotian government, American officials had long realized that a neutral Laos was almost as much a danger to South Vietnam as one controlled by the communists.

In his farewell address to the nation Dwight D. Eisenhower warned that the military-industrial complex had the potential for a disastrous use of misplaced power. "Public policy could itself become the captive of the scientific technological elite." He stressed that the subversion of the nation's scholars by federal employment, project allocations, and the power of money was a distinct threat to democratic institutions. "American leadership and prestige depend," he said, "not merely upon our unmatched material progress, riches and military strength, but on how we use our power in the interests of world peace and human betterment."

Eisenhower's words had a profound effect on the nation because they were so unexpected, coming from a man who had spent most of his life as part of the complex about which he now warned the American people.

In his inaugural address January 20, 1961, John F. Kennedy's words were equally eloquent. "Let every nation know, whether it wishes us well or ill, that we shall pay any price, bear any burden, meet any hardship, support any friend, oppose any foe to assure the survival and the success of liberty." His ringing words, "Let us never negotiate out of fear, but let us never fear to negotiate," struck a responsive chord, particularly on the nation's youth who at first rallied to his call for the defense of freedom.

In retrospect, Eisenhower's words are more meaningful, despite Kennedy's expressive play on words.

Soviet Premier Krushchev's support for wars of national liberation, revealed in early January, was recognized by President Kennedy as a threat to the United States. He ordered Secretary of Defense Robert S. McNamara February 1 to train and equip more United States troops for counter-insurgency operations. The new president's concern was heightened by the increase in fighting in Laos between Phoumi Nosavan's pro-American government forces and those of the pro-communist Pathet Lao. Much of Kennedy's first two months in office was directed to this crisis. He considered use of American military forces, but rejected the idea because the Joint Chiefs expressed their adamant opposition.

In March, President Kennedy announced that the United States would support Laotian sovereignty, but Great Britain and the Soviet Union instead proposed an international conference to be held in May to resolve the crisis rapidly building up in Indochina.

With his new administration, Kennedy replaced Ambassador Durbrow in Saigon with Frederick W. Nolting.

A Joint Chiefs of Staff meeting was scheduled in early April, 1961, and Vice Chief of Staff of the Air Force, General Curtis E. LeMay, attended on behalf of the chief, General Thomas White, who was off on a trip. They sat there for fifteen minutes waiting for Chairman Lemnitzer to start the meeting. Finally, a man in civilian clothes came in, whispered into Lemnitzer's ear and the general said, "Okay, we can start now."

LeMay quickly realized that this man was a Central Intelligence Agency representative and he was attending a meeting for which he was not cleared; only the Air Force chief of staff was authorized.

Without any introduction, the CIA representative pulled a curtain back from a map of Cuba and announced that an air strip would be needed on a suitable beach, and he sought their recommendation. He explained that the CIA had organized an air force equipped with World War II-type planes.

LeMay spoke up. "I'm a little cold on this. I presume you have an invasion of Cuba planned. How many men?"

"About 700."

"Morgan took Panama with 700 once," LeMay said, "but this is a little different. I presume this will be a signal to set off an uprising throughout the country?"

The CIA representative eyed LeMay coldly. "That's none of your business." Actually, the representative was either ill-informed or evasive because 1,400 were scheduled for the invasion, involving dissident Cubans under CIA auspices.

They inspected the photographs of several beaches, noting there was not much choice, and selected one.

LeMay was alerted April 15 that there would be a special meeting at 8 o'clock the next morning of the Joint Chiefs. He went in an hour earlier to try and learn what it was about. All he was told was that the meeting would discuss the invasion of Cuba.

At the meeting, the Joint Chiefs were advised that the invaders would be provided with CIA air cover and by planes from the United States Navy's Atlantic Fleet ships, including the carrier *Independence* that was in the area. The first CIA air strike was flown from staging areas in Nicaragua but the number of planes was reduced from sixteen to six. As a result, only six of Castro's fifty-five Cuban air force planes were destroyed.

That night at 10:00 P.M. Secretary of State Dean Rusk cancelled the second air strike. LeMay braced General Charles Pearre Cabel, deputy director of the Central Intelligence Agency, and was told that he had objected to Rusk about pulling the air cover but that he was told, "President Kennedy had already made the decision. You can go and see him if you want to but I advise against it. He's dressing to go to a party." Cabel told LeMay that he had decided against appealing to the president.

The following morning LeMay went to see McNamara but he had to talk to Deputy Defense Secretary Roswell I. Gilpatric instead. He told him, "You've just cut the throat of everybody on the beach down there."

"What do you mean?"

"They've cut off the air cover and you can't be successful without it."

It was too late. The invaders ran out of ammunition after Castro's air force sank the invasion ships with their reserve supplies.

The "Bay of Pigs" invasion April 17 by 1,400 Cuban refugees under the

American Central Intelligence Agency ended in failure when most of the men were captured or killed.

Soon after, President Kennedy referred to the similarity of events in Cuba and Indochina, saying there was a new type of warfare being waged that used subversion and infiltration to achieve victory without the firing of a single missile or the crossing of a single border. In linking Laos and Cuba as identical problems for the free world, Kennedy said, "We dare not fail to grasp the new concept, the new tools, the new sense of urgency we will need to combat it, whether in Cuba or South Vietnam. We face a relentless struggle in every corner of the globe that goes far beyond the clash of armies or even nuclear armaments."

Richard Nixon, who had opposed Kennedy in the election as the Republican candidate, told the new president that he would support "positive actions" to the hilt.

Kennedy, after a review of military and economic plans for South Vietnam, approved an increase in funds. He also signed a Treaty of Amity and Economic Relations between the United States and South Vietnam that was approved April 3, 1961.

When Kennedy was urged by some advisers to commit United States airpower in support of the pro-American government in Laos, he responded, "I just don't think we ought to be involved in Laos, particularly where we might find ourselves fighting millions of Chinese troops in the jungles. In any event, I don't see how we can make any move in Laos, which is ten thousand miles away, if we don't make a move in Cuba, which is only ninety miles away."

The deteriorating military situation in Laos prompted Kennedy April 20 to change the military advisory board there to a Military Assistance Advisory Group that would use American military men in uniform to work closely with Laotian troops. Such action would have been an open commitment by the United States to intervene in Laos and it would have happened if Great Britain and the Soviet Union had not appealed for a ceasefire April 24 and called for an international conference at Geneva.

Kennedy was now receiving a variety of recommendations from various political and military people. General Douglas MacArthur advised against using American ground forces on the mainland of Asia. He told the president that if the United States did intervene in Asia that it must be ready to use nuclear weapons if the People's Republic of China entered the conflict.

The Joint Chiefs of Staff informed Secretary of Defense Robert S. McNamara that "any intervention with United States forces in Laos, either unilaterally or under Southeast Asia Treaty Organization auspices, should be taken only after firm United States governmental decisions were approved, that the nation was committed to succeed in its military intervention regardless of the extent of possible consequent communist escalation; this is an unequivocal position which is fundamental to United States military actions."

McNamara expressed his conviction to the president that the United States soon had to decide whether or not to stand and fight.

Army Chief of Staff General George H. Decker told McNamara that he did not believe that the United States could win a conventional war in Southeast Asia. He suggested that it might be appropriate to move troops into Thailand and South Vietnam to see if their presence would produce a ceasefire in Laos. He warned that if the United States moved combat troops into Laos "we should go in to win, and that means Hanoi, China, and maybe even using nuclear bombs."

Later, he clarified his remarks saying that this was the last place in the world where he would like to see the United States commit forces unless it was absolutely necessary. He said that if only the Pathet Lao were involved, there would be no problem. But he added that he believed the North Vietnamese would intervene, and probably the Chinese communists, and that if they did come in it would be difficult to predict where the matter would end.

General Emmett O'Donnell, commander of the Pacific Air Forces, said his air forces could prosecute a small war in Laos with conventional weapons but that an enlarged conflict involving North Vietnam and/or China would require a massive increase in United States ground and air strength.

In South Vietnam, only six Vietnamese Air Force squadrons were combat ready. The Army had seven infantry divisions, an airborne group and nineteen separate battalions. There were now urgent steps taken by the Military Assistance Advisory Group in Saigon to train and arm paramilitary forces like the Civil Guard—later called Regional Forces—and the Self-Defense Force to free the Vietnamese Army for major war responsibilities.

Such action was necessary. During the early part of 1961 the Vietcong had redoubled its terror campaign, particularly to disrupt the presidential election. Assassinations rose to new heights as the Vietcong killed more than 4,000 civil officers, 2,000 state employees and 2,000 police.

The United States government through its ambassador again officially pressed President Diem for reforms, particularly changes in South Vietnam's chaotic field command, and for improvements in the gathering and dissemination of intelligence information. Diem tried to correct discrepancies but with only modest success.

Kennedy, meanwhile, talked to Senator J. William Fulbright, chairman of the Senate Foreign Relations Committee, on May 4 about the possibility of sending United States combat troops to South Vietnam. This was an option that he kept under active consideration although he considered such a step inappropriate without prior discussions with South Vietnam's leaders. Fulbright agreed to support moves in South Vietnam and Thailand if such actions were necessary, but only if those nations requested them. The Air Force Plans Division had approved such a step, but opposed premature commitment of United States armed forces because it "might reduce pressure on Vietnam for initiative and forceful action." Also under consideration by the planning division was the possibility that such action might provoke the Chinese into intervening, and might also have a bad political effect on allied governments and their relations with the United States.

General Lyman J. Lemnitzer, chairman of the Joint Chiefs of Staff, said that he felt a sense of urgency. He deplored the "tendency of the United States government to waste time in quibbling over policy."

President Kennedy wrote a letter to Diem May 8, 1961, and asked Vice President Lyndon B. Johnson to deliver it in person. In the letter, Kennedy said he was "ready to join with you in an intensified endeavor to win the struggle against communism and to further the social and economic advancement of Vietnam.

"If such an expanded joint effort meets with your approval, we are prepared to initiate in collaboration with your government a series of joint, mutually supporting actions in the military, political, economic and other fields. We would propose to extend and build on our existing programs, including the Counter Insurgency Plan, and infuse into our actions a high sense of urgency and dedication."

The letter further spelled out support for 20,000 additional regular Vietnamese troops under the Military Assistance Program, to enlarge the size and mission of the advisory group, support the 69,000-man Civil Guard, strengthen the Vietnamese Junk Fleet, and cooperate on other programs.

Johnson departed Washington May 9, and met with President Diem the next morning. After reading Kennedy's letter Diem said he agreed to everything the president said.

At an embassy reception, Johnson called Diem "the Churchill of Southeast Asia," and he said that the United States would stand "shoulder to shoulder" with South Vietnam against the communists.

Upon his return from South Vietnam Johnson said he saw no need for American troops except to help the Vietnamese to train their armed forces. He stressed that the nations of Southeast Asia had to make decided efforts, with stronger American support, to develop their economic and political systems and to provide their own defense. The vice president passed on to Kennedy Diem's concern that the communists would employ the same strategy they had used in Laos—infiltration, aerial resupply and the establishment of a recognizable government. "Any help," Johnson said, "economic as well as military, we give less-developed nations to secure and maintain their freedom must be part of a mutual effort. These nations cannot be saved by the United States alone. To the extent that the Southeast Asia nations are prepared to take the necessary measures to make our assistance effective, we can be—and must be—unstinting in our acceptance."

The Special Forces of the United States Army, first started in 1942 during World War II, had been training and advising the Army of the Republic of Vietnam since 1957. Such men were double volunteers—first for airborne training and then for Special Forces. That first year, only fifty-eight Vietnamese soldiers were trained. Ten years later over 40,000 paramilitary troops, plus another 40,000 Regional and Popular Forces, had undergone training by the American Army's Special Forces.

Until 1961 the South Vietnamese government and the United States mission in Saigon had placed primary emphasis on developing regular military forces, excluding ethnic and religious minority groups. Now the program was broadened to provide training and advisory assistance to organizations that collectively became known as the Civilian Irregular Defense Group. The primary mission of the Special Forces now was directed to the development of such paramilitary forces among minorities.

The Montagnards in the strategic Central Highlands were the first to prevent the Vietcong from gaining control in their region. In the first Special Forces effort, a village self-defense program was created with one medical non-commissioned officer assigned to it.

Initially, the counter-insurgency effort was supervised by the Central Intelligence Agency as the Civilian Irregular Defense Group. The first Special Forces unit numbered about two thousand men, and they were highly trained combat specialists. Specifically they were assigned to Vietnamese units to train and advise them about operations against the Vietcong. Such a procedure soon proved impractical because the advisers went along on combat patrols and, through necessity, became directly involved in the fighting.

Special Forces programs used area development centers in remote areas where there was little government control. Each base included a South Vietnamese detachment and its American advisers. They assisted in village defense with small arms and mortars. The program extended South Vietnam's control into areas where it had been lacking, and initially such control was resented by provincial officials because the project was essentially American. However, the danger of Vietcong domination in the Central Highlands was strong in 1961, and efforts by the Vietnamese Army had been ineffective. The Montagnards often were alienated by the South Vietnamese, but there were other ethnic groups that were equally turned off including Nung tribesmen, Cambodians and members of the Cao Dai and Hoa Hao religious sects.

Admiral Felt as Commander-in-Chief, Pacific called for introduction of American troops by recommending that an Army Infantry Division be dispatched with supporting troops and a small number of fighters and bombers. President Kennedy was not ready for such a major escalation of the war. He asked McNamara and the Department of Defense May 11 to assess the value and cost of increasing South Vietnam's armed forces from 170,000 to 200,000. The same day he committed an Army Special Forces group of 400 to help clear and hold Vietcong areas, mainly along the Cambodian and Laotian borders.

Step-by-step President Kennedy was getting the United States further involved in the war in Indochina but still without clear and definite goals.

CHAPTER 5

The Human Factor

ONE OF THE GREAT SIDE BATTLES IN THE EARLY 1960S WAS WAGED between the United States Air Force and the Navy on one side and Secretary of Defense McNamara's team on the other. There had been a long-term requirement in both services for a new fighter-bomber, but McNamara was cutting the defense budget and he wouldn't listen to their pleas. Finally, he said, if you get together on one airplane I might consider that, stressing that a common airplane for both services would save a billion dollars. In the past, Air Force and Navy officials had tried to combine their missions in one airplane but it never worked out. Each service ended up spending more money than if they had developed separate airplanes.

Admiral James S. Russell, vice chief of naval operations in the spring of 1961, discussed such a proposed fighter-bomber—now known as the TFX—with Dr. Harold Brown, director of the Defense Department's research and engineering section. He argued that a first-line fighter for the Air Force should not be penalized in performance by those features required by the Navy for shipboard operation. As one example, he cited that the landing gear of a Navy plane had to be two and a half times as strong. Such strength, he said, was needed for arresting and catapulting and added weight to the airframe, but permitted a reasonably low approach speed in landing, plus a low takeoff speed for catapulting. Russell explained that a Navy plane landing on a carrier used an optical glide path and did not flare but actually flew into the deck until it was stopped by the ship's arresting gear. He said that a Navy pilot immediately upon touchdown opened his throttle wide so that the engine's turbine would be up to speed if he missed an engagement with the arresting gear and had to go around for another try.

Dr. Brown, as the number two man under McNamara, kept insisting

55

that a common aircraft had to be approved. He handed Russell some specifications. "Why can't you accept this launching speed and this weight?"

Russell replied, "There is not a catapult in the fleet that will throw that mass, at that velocity, into the air."

Brown said, "Next time you replace your carriers you can have some that will."

"Harold," Russell said patiently, "there is not an airplane that somewhere along the line does not add weight. If you start with a negative margin, you are really going to have a lemon."

Russell was frustrated when Brown refused to accept the views of Navy engineers as to what they needed aboard carriers.

General Curtis E. LeMay became chief of staff of the Air Force June 3, 1961, and Admiral George Anderson was named chief of naval operations a month later.

Shortly afterwards members of the Air Force staff approached LeMay and said that a common fighter-bomber might be developed to satisfy both Navy and Air Force requirements. They agreed this was not the way to proceed but that a new airplane was desperately needed by both services and this approach would be a compromise, but would at least give them a reasonably good airplane. From long experience they knew that they always had to fight with airplanes that the Congress would agree to, and not necessarily those that the services truly needed.

LeMay was convinced and he talked to George Anderson. "Why don't you have your boys listen to what my staff have to say and let's talk it over again?"

Anderson agreed and the two staffs presented a common proposal to McNamara. The Defense Secretary reluctantly agreed and the Air Force was assigned responsibility to develop the new airplane.

After a thorough evaluation, using a numerical score to rate the two final contestants—Boeing and General Dynamics—Boeing easily won the competition and the Navy agreed to go along, although it was still concerned about the airplane's weight. The evaluation was sent to McNamara who returned it, saying, "We think you've made a mistake here. Reevaluate. Do it over again."

The Air Force and the Navy were not averse to a new evaluation because now there were two engines available, and they were anxious to see how Boeing's airplane would perform with a different engine. This time General Dynamics did better but Boeing still handily won the competition.

This new recommendation was sent to McNamara but he returned it as still unacceptable and the services were advised to reevaluate the proposal again.

There were three separate evaluations by the services who put in 600,000 manhours of the best technical brains in the country—civilian and military—and Boeing's proposal was still considered best.

LeMay was presiding over a staff meeting one morning when Air Force Secretary Eugene Zuckert came in. Everybody stood up, surprised by his visit because he seldom attended their meetings. Zuckert apologized for breaking up the meeting. "I have taken a look at the last evaluation," he said, "and I have decided on General Dynamics."

LeMay glanced at his staff, noting that Zuckert had immediately lost all credibility with them. They knew that the Air Force Secretary had not made a decision on a single program since McNamara took office.

The Boeing airplane would have satisfied most of the requirements for both services, whereas the General Dynamics airplane did not. The Navy version of the newly designated F-111 had to be cancelled because its suitability for carrier operations was sharply limited due to overweight and minimum-speed problems.

The program failed to fulfill McNamara's exaggerated claims although the Air Force used it as the F-111A. Billions of dollars were wasted instead of the billion dollar savings that McNamara had so confidently predicted. So blatant was McNamara's arbitrary action in overruling Air Force and Navy technical evaluators that Senator McClelland conducted Senate hearings but nothing changed despite huge cost overruns.

A week after the disastrous "Bay of Pigs" invasion of Cuba, Deputy Defense Secretary Roswell I. Gilpatric was appointed to head a Vietnam task force. He was supported by Brigadier General Edward Lansdale, assistant to the Secretary of Defense for Special Operations, who was well known for his work in the Philippines during the communist Huk insurgency, and who had been a key American figure in covert operations in Saigon. Gilpatric's committee coordinated its plans for Vietnam with the State and Defense Departments and proposed objectives May 19 for American forces that might be deployed in Vietnam. They should be used, he said, to deter North Vietnam and the Chinese and release Vietnamese forces for fuller use against major North Vietnamese Army units, and for training local troops. He said such an initial force would form a nucleus for a future United States buildup, and demonstrate American firmness. Gilpatric said his committee favored setting up two training centers, each run by a reinforced United States infantry battalion, with deployment of minimal air and naval forces to stop infiltration and to act against Vietcong insurgents. He said that the United States Army urged the deployment of an infantry division plus Special Forces. Gilpatric acknowledged that the United States Air Force was reluctant to place combat squadrons in a country where the major threat appeared to be an insurgency, and where the Vietnamese Air Force could offer only limited air support.

President Kennedy sent a list of thirty separate actions that he wanted carried out to Admiral Harry D. Felt, Commander-in-Chief, Pacific, and to Ambassador Nolting. The president called for political activities to buttress Diem's confidence in the United States and to enhance his popular support, steps to improve relations with Cambodia and economic measures to permit the Vietnamese to support larger military forces. The president suggested the installation of a radar surveillance system, a 20,000 expansion of Vietnam's armed forces, more support for the Civil Guard and the Self-Defense Corps, and an augmented Military Assistance Advisory Group in Saigon. Kennedy insisted that South Vietnam take steps to stop the infiltration from North Vietnam.

After being informed of Kennedy's desires, President Diem issued decrees to carry out the counter-insurgency measures proposed by the American president. He took no serious action to correct abuses in his military command relationship that relied on political cronyism for posts in the Intelligence command and the provincial commands. Nothing changed and most senior officers continued to compete for political favor and power.

Meanwhile, the conference that had been proposed by the Soviet Union and Great Britain opened in Geneva to discuss the Laotian situation. While the conference could not agree on steps to be taken to assure a ceasefire, Kennedy procrastinated about whether the United States should send troops to Laos. He continued to offer assurances of American support to Thailand and to South Vietnam.

En route to a summit meeting with Russian Premier Nikita Krushchev in Vienna President Kennedy stopped in Paris. There he met French President Charles de Gaulle who cautioned him about direct involvement in Indochina. Such a step, he said, would be unwise and would bring entanglement without end. "Once a nation has been roused no foreign power, however strong, can impose its will upon it." He reminded Kennedy, "The more you commit yourself there against communism the more the communists will appear to be the champions of national independence." He correctly predicted, "You will, step by step, become sucked into a bottomless military and political quagmire, despite the losses and expenditures that you may squander."

Kennedy learned a hard lesson in international politics when he met with Krushchev June 4, 1961, in Vienna. Due to his inexperience Kennedy was completely out-maneuvered during sessions with the tough-talking communist leader. Kennedy's proposal that "we all get out of Laos" and the formation of a "neutral and independent Laos under a government chosen by the Laotians" was accepted by Krushchev. Kennedy agreed to a neutral coalition headed by Souvanna Phouma but this step only delayed the final showdown. At a time when the United States had a forty to one superiority over the Soviet Union in nuclear weapons Kennedy should have insisted that both countries get out of Indochina.

After the conference Kennedy told James Reston of the New York *Times*, "Now we have a problem in making our power credible, and Vietnam looks like the place."

Two months later the Soviet Union started to erect a wall of concrete and barbed wire between East and West Berlin, plugging a hole in the Iron Curtain through which millions had fled to the West. President Kennedy mobilized American forces in retaliation, calling up 158,000 reservists and national guardsmen. Forty thousand men were sent to Europe. Later, on a trip to Berlin, President Kennedy electrified a huge crowd by declaiming in German, "I am a Berliner!"

In regard to Indochina, Air Force Chief of Staff LeMay urged the Joint Chiefs to suggest to President Kennedy that he "press for a high-level accord," with a "clear statement of United States objectives in the area." He said McNamara should be told that "timely, positive military actions are essential." LeMay said he envisaged no open engagement with the North Vietnamese, but that he could not rule out such contact. "Enemy military actions," the general said, "would not alter the political objective, but such actions may compel a military response which would not necessarily be confined to South Vietnam." He added that there was "no feasible military alternative of lesser magnitude that would prevent the loss of South Vietnam and ultimately Southeast Asia."

LeMay pointed out to the Joint Chiefs that during this period there were minor North Vietnamese troop intrusions into Laos and Cambodia that a small number of Air Force reconnaissance aircraft with a limited attack capability could easily destroy.

Although the Joint Chiefs were in agreement, McNamara was not convinced. He told President Kennedy, "I am not prepared to endorse the views of the Chiefs until we have had more experience with our present progress in South Vietnam." The president agreed.

LeMay privately told intimates that he doubted that the administration had a firm and definite Vietnam policy. He said later that none of the military chiefs really believed "that the United States was undertaking anything except [having] some diplomatic fiddling around with a little more aid program."

Kennedy's indecision about whether to use combat troops in Indochina was due to his habit of using ad hoc committees in lieu of the Joint Chiefs of Staff. Air Force Chief of Staff LeMay said later that these committees had too many people who were trying to make decisions about matters for which they had no competence. "Going to war is a very serious business," LeMay said long afterwards. "Once you make a decision that you are going to do that, you ought to be prepared to do just that."

Tension between the United States and the Soviet Union increased when the Russians broke the ban on exploding nuclear bombs in the atmosphere September 1, and Kennedy instructed McNamara to resume American nuclear tests.

In July, Dr. Eugene Staley was sent by Kennedy to Saigon to survey the Vietnamese economy. He reported to the president that he favored further aid for Vietnam but he warned against expecting military operations to achieve lasting results without economic progress. He said a free society and a self-sustaining economy in Vietnam was the best basis of hope for the future.

Military planners agreed so the Joint Chiefs recommended a ceiling of 200,000 men for the Vietnamese armed forces with priority given to train the Self-Defense Corps and the Civil Guard.

Vietcong attacks increased to such an extent by September, 1961, that South Vietnam's military situation seemed to be imperiled. On the 19th the Vietcong overran Phuoc Vinh, capital of Phuoc Thanh Province. They publicly beheaded the province chief, and held the city most of the day but left before South Vietnamese troops arrived. Diem now was thoroughly alarmed because infiltrators were operating at battalion strength.

Diem asked Ambassador Nolting September 29 for a bilateral peace treaty, and appealed to Admiral Felt for a "large increase in advisers of all types." He specifically requested tactical air squadrons.

President Kennedy approved additional military and economic aid on September 21 and the 5th Special Forces Group was activated in the United States. The president believed this group had great potential as a counter-insurgency force, and he gave permission for them to wear a distinctive green beret that became their symbol.

President Diem spoke to his National Assembly on October 2. "It is no longer a guerrilla war. It is a war waged by an enemy who attacks us with regular units fully and heavily equipped and who seeks a strategic decision in Southeast Asia in conformity with the order of the Communist International."

Communist infiltration into South Vietnam from the west was extremely difficult to counteract because its borders were 900 miles long adjoining Cambodia and Laos, and there were no distinctive markings. Roving patrols found it difficult to harass the North Vietnamese from these adjoining countries even though they were resupplied by C-47s. To aid in the fight against infiltrators, Ranger training was moved from Da Nang to Nha Trang and Montagnard scouts were brought into the program. The 400 new Special Forces men authorized by Kennedy helped immeasurably to control the border as they stepped up their training of the Vietnamese.

McNamara had directed the Department of Defense in September to create a Combat Development and Test Center in Vietnam. One of the first priorities given to the Research Projects Agency was to develop a chemical agent to kill tapioca plants. Tapioca was a food source for communist guerrillas. Also under consideration was the use of dogs, and the possible employment of chemicals to defoliate the jungles to deprive the Vietcong of assembly and ambush areas. There was also a sharp increase in the use of radar, and aerial reconnaissance was stepped up. But these were all defensive efforts that accomplished little to defeat the communists.

On October 11 Kennedy recalled his old friend General Maxwell D. Taylor from retirement, to join Dr. Walt W. Rostow, chairman of the State Department's Policy Planning Council, to go to Vietnam as members of his White House Staff to make recommendations as to actions the United States should take.

That afternoon another project was set in motion that had been developed in secret during the late 1950s when General LeMay was vice chief of staff of the Air Force. In March, 1961, LeMay had responded to Kennedy's instructions to examine how each service could best contribute to counter-insurgency. LeMay favored a direct and open American response but with the necessary strength to do the job. He stressed that overwhelming strength should be applied in Vietnam to avoid stretching out the war over an extended period. LeMay therefore directed the Tactical Air Command to form a small, elite volunteer unit for air operations using older aircraft in support of ground forces.

The 4400th Combat Crew Training Squadron—nicknamed Jungle Jim—came into being at Eglin Air Force Base, Florida, April 14, 1961. Its commander was Colonel Benjamin H. King and his squadron included sixteen C-47s, eight B-26s and eight T-28s. Equal numbers of aircraft were available in storage. The men wore a picturesque air commando uniform—personally picked by LeMay—that featured an Australian-type bush hat with turned-up brim, fatigues and combat boots. The transport aircraft were modified to carry bombs, rockets and machine guns.

In August, the Joint Chiefs suggested to McNamara that this unit be used for air interdiction of inland trails and, if not permitted openly, it should institute unconventional guerrilla operations. McNamara liked the idea and "Jungle Jim" was scheduled for Vietnam duty in November to fight—and not train Vietnamese.

En route to Saigon as President Kennedy's personal emissaries, Taylor and Rostow stopped in Hawaii to talk to Admiral Felt before they moved on to Saigon. The Commander-in-Chief, Pacific, pinpointed two serious weaknesses in South Vietnam. He said there was a tendency of province chiefs to meddle in military matters, and that South Vietnam's military commanders had a penchant for remaining in static defense positions. Felt endorsed the "Jungle Jim" project, but he said that he foresaw no further need for American combat units although he did recommend a continuation of American reconnaissance flights.

Taylor and Rostow were upset by Felt's words but they were even more disturbed by conditions in Saigon during their six-day visit. They detected an acute crisis of confidence at every social level, and doubts among the South Vietnamese people that the United States was seriously committed to resisting communist aggression. There was not only concern about recent Vietcong successes, but recent floods had devastated large parts of South Vietnam. The Americans believed that the military crisis mirrored a political weakness of the government. They considered President Diem an old-fashioned Asian ruler who sought to maintain the strings of power in his own hands, while fragmenting authority and responsibility beneath him. Taylor was convinced that the South Vietnamese armed forces suffered from poor intelligence, scant command control and inadequate mobility. It seemed obvious to General Taylor that the South Vietnamese Air Force was making no significant contribution. For example, there was little reconnaissance. Among the Americans in Saigon almost all were military men and they preferred to remain in the capital and not get out to the various provincial commands for a cross-check on the true state of affairs. Some American officers told Taylor they thought it was improper to criticize President Diem.

In his meetings with Diem, Taylor recommended that a military task force of 6,000 to 8,000 men, including combat troops for protection, should be sent from the United States to South Vietnam to aid flood relief efforts in the Mekong Delta that had suffered heavily from recent rain. Such a stated purpose, he told Diem, would disguise the real purpose of the task force that would free some South Vietnamese Army units to fight the Vietcong. This proposal was an underhanded approach that was beneath the dignity of a great nation.

Before Taylor and Rostow left Saigon they agreed that United States Air Force reconnaissance flights should continue, and that a United States tactical/ground system should be established, partly as a training program. They were convinced that "Jungle Jim" should have fewer restrictions than initially proposed. They believed that there was no reason to commit United States Army forces in a direct role at the moment. Success hinged on Diem's willingness to undertake political and social reforms. Both officials leaned toward bolstering the American military and advisory support for broadly conceived counter-guerrilla operations. The alternative, they were convinced, was to deploy up to ten thousand United States ground troops for defense to release the Vietnamese Army for counter-insurgency. They believed that there should be no more United States reinforcements until the nature of the final settlement in Laos was reached, and how North Vietnam reacted to that situation. These were negative viewpoints by officials without the courage to recommend worthwhile air strikes against North Vietnam or suggest to President Kennedy that the United States should disengage from the war.

Such indecision upset General LeMay. Taylor was one of the crosses that the Air Force Chief of Staff had to bear. While Taylor served later as chairman of the Joint Chiefs he repeatedly insulted LeMay by saying, "Your airplanes are no damn good. Don't bother me with your bombing recommendations. Hand-held missiles will shoot all your airplanes down. They are worthless. Obsolete. Over North Vietnam, your B-52s would be shot down like flies."

The error of Taylor's views was demonstrated during the December, 1972, bombing campaign against strategic targets in North Vietnam when less than 2 percent of the heavy bombers were lost.

Before he departed Saigon for Washington Taylor said that many Americans would be reluctant to send troops to South Vietnam "unless such action was absolutely necessary."

After six days of consultation with President Diem and other government officials Taylor and Rostow returned to Washington. They told Kennedy that troops should be sent to Vietnam only as a last resort. Taylor recommended, however, that an 8,000-man American self-defense task force be organized to use against North Vietnam if the infiltration continued from that country into the South. He said South Vietnam's basic problem was Diem's lack of faith that the United States would support his nation after its inconclusive policies in Laos. They both admitted to the president that they had reservations about Diem's government and its ability to defeat the Vietcong because it was so inefficient and unpopular among the people. In recommending a military commitment to South Vietnam, they said American military men should be inserted in each element of the government and the Army. Taylor said more support should be given to paramilitary groups, and that helicopter squadrons should be sent. Taylor added that the Military Assistance Advisory Group in Saigon should be increased, and that American combat troops might be needed, but on a limited basis. He stressed to the president that prompt and urgent military and economic steps should be taken to bolster Diem's government.

Rostow argued for a contingency plan of retaliation against North Vietnam. In other words, he recommended a program graduated to match the intensity of North Vietnam's support of the Vietcong.

Taylor warned President Kennedy of the possibility of more global tension, and he said that the "present guerrilla activity could escalate into a major war."

The Joint Chiefs did not approve of the Taylor-Rostow report. They wanted a positive "American commitment with a clear objective to prevent the fall of South Vietnam, even if that meant United States military forces would have to fight." They suggested that North Vietnam be warned that such action would be taken if Vietcong aggression continued. The Joint Chiefs said they envisioned a long war if China intervened that would necessitate an army of 205,000 in Vietnam.

Secretary of Defense McNamara sent a memorandum to President Kennedy November 8, 1961, saying, "The basic issue framed by the Taylor Report is whether the United States shall:

"a. Commit itself to the clear objective of preventing the fall of South Vietnam to communism, and

"b. Support this commitment by necessary immediate military actions and preparations for possible later actions.

"The Joint Chiefs, Mr. Gilpatric, and I have reached the following conclusions:

"1. The fall of South Vietnam to Communism would lead to the fairly rapid extension of Communist control, or complete accomodation to Communism, in the rest of mainland Southeast Asia and in Indonesia. The strategic implications worldwide, particularly in the Orient, would be extremely serious.

"2. The chances are against, probably sharply against, preventing that fall by any measures short of the introduction of U.S. forces on a substantial scale. We accept General Taylor's judgment that the various measures proposed by him short of this are useful but will not in themselves do the job of restoring confidence and setting Diem on the way to winning his fight.

"3. The introduction of a U.S. force of the magnitude of an initial 8,000 men in a flood relief context will be of great help to Diem. However, it will not convince the other side (whether the shots are called from Moscow, Peiping, or Hanoi) that we mean business. Moreover, it probably will not tip the scales decisively. We would be almost certain to get increasingly mired down in an inconclusive struggle.

"4. The other side can be convinced we mean business only if we accompany the initial force introduction by a clear commitment to the full objective stated above, accompanied by a warning through some channel to Hanoi that continued support of the Viet Cong will lead to punitive retaliation against North Vietnam.

"5. If we act in this way, the ultimate possible extent of our military commitment must be faced. The struggle may be prolonged and Hanoi and Peiping may intervene overtly. In view of the logistic difficulties faced by the other side, I believe we can assume that the maximum U.S. forces required on the ground in Southeast Asia will not exceed six divisions, or about two hundred and five thousand men (CINCPAC Plan 32-59, Phase IV). Our military posture is, or, with the addition of more National Guard or regular Army divisions, can be made adequate to furnish these forces without serious interference with our present Berlin plans.

"6. To accept the stated objective is of course a most serious decision. Military force is not the only element of what must be a most carefully coordinated set of actions. Success will depend on factors many of which are not within our control—notably the conduct of Diem himself and other leaders in the area. Laos will remain a major problem. The domestic political implications of accepting the objective are also grave, although it is our feeling that the country will respond better to a firm initial position than to courses of action that lead us in only gradually, and that in the meantime are sure to involve casualties. The overall effect on Moscow and Peiping will need careful weighing and may well be mixed; however, permitting South Vietnam to fall can only strengthen and encourage them greatly.

"7. In sum:

"a. We do not believe major units of U.S. forces should be introduced in South Vietnam unless we are willing to make an affirmative decision on the issue stated at the start of this memorandum.

"b. We are inclined to recommend that we do commit the U.S. in the clear objective of preventing the fall of South Vietnam to Communism and that we can support this commitment by the necessary military actions.

"c. If such a commitment is agreed upon, we support the recommendations of General Taylor as the first steps toward its fulfillment."

Secretary of State Dean Rusk, who had little confidence in President Diem, warned Kennedy not to tie American prestige to a "losing horse."

Deputy Undersecretary of State George Ball, a noted lawyer and banker who had recently been appointed, was deeply concerned by the Taylor-Rostow recommendations. He said if they were granted they would lead, within five years, to a request for 300,000 men.

President Kennedy refused to believe his estimate, but Ball's words were prophetic, and his figure proved to be on the low side five years later.

President Kennedy did not accept all of McNamara's recommendations. Instead, he agreed to send a thousand advisers instead of a large combat task force.

The "Jungle Jim" organization of air commandos was sent to Vietnam ostensibly to train South Vietnamese air crews. Due to emergencies, some of these pilots actually performed combat missions.

Instead of the Eisenhower doctrine of non-military involvement in Indochina, Kennedy now approved a policy of flexible but limited response to communist aggression. It was a decision that had a disastrous impact on all aspects of American life, including relations between the United States and its allies, and led later to consequences that few people at the time could foresee.

The secretaries of State and Defense submitted a joint memorandum to the president November 11 recommending prompt deployment of support troops and equipment, including helicopters, transport aircraft and maritime equipment. The memorandum stressed that the United States should have clear objectives for preventing the fall of South Vietnam to communism, and that it should be prepared to send combat troops and even to consider striking at the source of aggression in North Vietnam.

General LeMay's relations with McNamara became more strained with each passing day. He was particularly frustrated by the small Air Force influence in Southeast Asia. He believed there were too few and too-junior Air Force officers in the Military Assistance Advisory Group and that the Pacific Air Force had too restricted a voice in Vietnam affairs. So tight was McNamara's control of the war in Vietnam that his permission was required in mid-November for the transfer of three single-engine liaison aircraft to South Vietnam.

LeMay repeatedly voiced his concerns to the Joint Chiefs, and Admiral Felt also warned that General Lionel C. McGarr, the Military Assistance Advisory Group's chief in Saigon, and Sir Robert G. K. Thompson, who had figured prominently in subduing guerrillas in Malaysia and who was now head of the British advisory mission in Saigon, were both uneasy because the situation in South Vietnam was "more than serious. It is critical, with the peak of the crisis possible at any moment."

The North Vietnamese now believed that victory was within their grasp. The Vietcong had surrounded Saigon and other urban centers and they had blocked many highways.

The acceptance by President Kennedy of some of the Taylor–Rostow recommendations marked a shift in American policy from "advice to limited partnership and working collaboration" with the South Vietnamese. It was now evident that more material assistance would accompany an increase in American participation in the war. American advisers were viewed as friends and partners who would show the Vietnamese how the job should be done but not do it for them.

A compromise was worked out in December, 1961, between McNamara and Secretary of State Rusk to resolve some of the problems of command and control. A Military Assistance Command was approved under Commander-in-Chief, Pacific, that was modeled somewhat on the United States-Taiwan Defense Command, and placed under Lieutenant General Paul D. Harkins whom McNamara called an "imaginative officer, fully qualified to fill what I consider to be the most difficult job in the United States Army."

President Kennedy met Harkins briefly in Florida and was pleased that the general spoke French. He told him to assist President Diem and the South Vietnamese people, and wished him well in his new job. His appointment was set to take effect February 8, 1962. The Joint Chiefs recommended that General Harkins be made co-equal with Ambassador Nolting but this recommendation was turned down.

After he assumed office General Harkins shifted the former Military Assistance Advisory Group's operations and intelligence functions to the new Military Assistance Command and appointed Army Major General Charles T. Timmes as chief of the Army, Navy and Air Force sections.

At a Joint Chiefs meeting attended by McNamara, General LeMay charged that air planning was often omitted from field operations but Admiral Felt said that General Rollin H. Anthis, commander of the air component in South Vietnam and Thailand under the Military Assistance Command, had the privilege of participating anytime in such plans. Harkins was angered by what he considered was LeMay's "preferring charges" against him in Washington. He said that the Air Force Chief of Staff seemed to be thinking of command and control of large numbers of aircraft like in World War II, whereas there were essentially limited tactical opportunities for relatively few United States aircraft in Vietnam.

During a visit to Saigon the president's brother, and United States attorney general, Robert F. Kennedy, told a press conference on February 18, 1962, "We are going to win in Vietnam. We will remain here until we do win." He said that Vietnam's struggle to preserve its independence against communist aggression was a grave one that affects free countries everywhere.

In late 1961 the North Vietnamese had renamed the southern branch of the Lao Dong Party the People's Revolutionary Party. And on December 7 the Provincial Committee of the party in South Vietnam's Ba Xueyen Province declared, "The People's Revolutionary Party has only the appearance of an independent existence: actually our party is nothing but the Lao Dong Party in Vietnam, unified from North to South, under the direction of the Central Executive Committee of the North, the Chief of which is President Ho."

South Vietnam's President Diem secured a copy of the statement and sent it to President Kennedy, saying, "Here at last is a public admission of what has always been clear—the Vietcong campaign against my people is led by communists."

This was not new, but the question still remained how best to combat the situation. Diem had resisted the formation of an unbroken military command chain that would give confidence and authority to the military chief of the Field Command. Such a step had long been advocated by United States advisers, but most Vietnamese officers were convinced that American ideas and methods would not work in South Vietnam. Diem's intransigence was due, in large part, to his fear of a coup by army generals.

Diem earlier had been drawn to the ideas for defending Vietnamese villages proposed by Sir Robert G. K. Thompson, former secretary of defense for the Federation of Malaya. Thompson had arrived in September, 1961, as head of a British advisory mission. He had suggested a program of strategic hamlets that could be defended to clear the communists from the Mekong Delta. Diem agreed to establish a Strategic Hamlet Program under his brother's sponsorship because he knew it was necessary to restore the people's faith in their government. The strategic hamlet idea dated back to the days of Chinese domination of Vietnam. It was also similar to the "combat village" defense system that was established during the years of resistance to the French. Such a concept was needed because the Vietcong had turned every village under their control into a resistance pocket, and to justify their control they used the popular saying, "When bandits break into a house, even a woman fights back."

In north and central Vietnam the corral-like configuration of a typical village lent itself to defense against penetration with its high, thorny and dense bamboo hedge that was an almost impenetrable fortress. There was only one opening for access, and it could be easily defended.

In the South, the Vietnamese had a more difficult problem to keep their hamlets secure. Villages were much larger than in the northern regions so regrouping was forced upon the South Vietnamese despite their resentment at being removed from their homes and relocated to unfamiliar areas.

The program failed because of Diem's insistence on top-level control. The Americans proved too naive and, for some time, they were unaware of the program's failure.

In 1962, however, the Americans continued to press for a centralized, counter-insurgency strategy on a national basis, not only to secure Saigon and South Vietnam's other major cities, but to keep the Vietcong off-balance in the countryside by tactics that would seize and hold vital areas.

During the early months of the new year Diem gradually conceded such a plan of action was needed. The American advisory group thereupon devised strategic guidelines for a massive counter-insurgency plan but again Diem's fears of a coup prevented him from agreeing to an overall military commander to assure the operation's success.

While these steps to counter the North Vietnamese were underway Premier Chou En-lai of the People's Republic of China warned the United States publicly that his country could scarcely "be indifferent to the increasingly grave situation caused by United States imperialism in South Vietnam."

The Soviet Union also charged that Taylor's mission to South Vietnam was the result of flagging diplomatic discussions at Geneva, and a spokesman charged that the United States planned to send troops to Vietnam to bring pressure to bear on the situation in Laos.

President Kennedy had hesitated about approving the extension of an open-ended commitment to South Vietnam. "They want a force of American troops," he said, and he likened that force to the units sent to Germany in 1961 when Soviet Russia threatened to close the Allied corridor to Berlin. "They say it is necessary in order to restore confidence and maintain morale. But it will be just like Berlin. The troops will march in, the bands will play, the crowds will cheer; and in four days everyone will have forgotten. Then we will be told we have to send in more troops. It's like taking a drink. The effect wears off, and you have to take another."

Kennedy was convinced the war could be won only so long as it remained Vietnam's war. Otherwise, he said, the Americans would lose like the French.

In retrospect, it is regrettable that Kennedy did not follow his instincts. Instead, he continued to send combat advisers without seeking a share in South Vietnam's decision-making.

President Kennedy had agreed with McNamara's recommendation to send modest support units to South Vietnam and to study all aspects of the situation before resolving to send large organized units for actual or potential combat. The president had officially approved this policy November 13, 1961. It called for more airlift along with Air Force planes and personnel for reconnaissance and defoliation of jungle hideaways. President Diem was informed of Kennedy's decision and was advised to put South Vietnam on a firm war footing and to mobilize his nation's resources, give his government adequate authority and to overhaul the military establishment and its command structure.

That same date the Thirteenth Air Force in the Philippines organized an advance echelon of its 2nd Air Division at Tan Son Nhut on Saigon's outskirts. Other detachments were organized at Da Nang and Nha Trang. Control of these units was turned over to the Military Assistance Command.

A few months after General Paul D. Harkins assumed command of the Military Assistance Command in Saigon, he was permitted to increase his command to 2,395 persons. Although this increase was in violation of the agreement signed between North Vietnam and the French in 1954—an agreement never signed by the United States and certainly not honored by North Vietnam—such a step had long been requested by President Diem and members of the United States Department of Defense.

During a McNamara visit, General Harkins was asked, "How long will it take to pacify this country?"

"Mr. Secretary, I believe we can do it in six months. If I am given command of the Vietnamese we can reverse this thing immediately." Harkins had been General George S. Patton's deputy chief of staff in World War II, but this was a different war that he did not fully understand.

The Joint Chiefs of Staff now proposed that a unified American command be established that would report directly to them. Such a command would control all United States forces employed in the combined effort against the Vietcong. Admiral Felt, Commander-in-Chief, Pacific (CINCPAC), objected. He said the communists were threatening all of Southeast Asia, not just South Vietnam, and that it was one war against them. Felt's argument prevailed and the newly named Military Assistance Command ended up as a subordinate command under Admiral Felt's control. This command was envisaged as a temporary headquarters that would be withdrawn once the Vietcong insurgency was brought under control. General Harkins, head of the Military Assistance Command, was made responsible under Admiral Felt for all United States military policy, operations and assistance in Vietnam although command and control of Vietnamese forces remained under South Vietnamese commanders with Harkins as senior United States adviser. Felt named Harkins head of a similar command in Thailand.

Military and economic assistance for South Vietnam was not confined to the United States. Eventually more than forty nations made economic, technical, education or humanitarian contributions. Hundreds of free world civilians worked in Vietnam as doctors, teachers and technical specialists. Military assistance was later furnished by the Republic of Korea, Thailand, Australia, New Zealand and Spain. Discussions with nations requesting some kind of participation had started in 1961. In May, an ad hoc force had been appointed by Assistant Secretary of Defense Dr. Roswell L. Gilpatric who recommended to the National Security Council that the United States be prepared to fulfill its obligations under treaties, unilaterally if necessary. At the time the State Department agreed.

In the absence of presidential decisions, memorandums continued to be issued by Rostow who in October suggested that a 25,000-man Southeast Asia Treaty Organization force be sent to guard the South Vietnam-Laos border. The Joint Chiefs did not agree, recommending instead that a force be used to secure the Central Highlands.

Basically, United States military strategy was influenced by the war in Korea from 1950 to 1953 and recommendations called for the deployment of conventional infantry forces in depth from the demilitarized zone south to counter North Vietnamese aggression. As conceived, the primary mission of the Vietnamese national army was to fight a delaying action in the event of an invasion pending direct intervention by SEATO forces. South Vietnam's military commanders agreed to this assessment, but they also recommended territorial or area defense as a complement to conventional forces. They believed that areas of defense should be established under control of a territorial command whose responsibility was to coordinate all military activities to maintain security within its area of responsibility. Each territorial command should be given authority over all military and police forces. The Americans first agreed but later rejected such a command set up, recommending instead a conventional, anti-invasion military force.

What American military advisers did not comprehend was that the North Vietnamese had long ago discounted the Korean experience as not applicable to this war. After their experience fighting the French, the North Vietnamese decided to wage a people's or insurgency war to seize control of South Vietnam. Therefore, the Hanoi government had reactivated the local Vietminh infrastructure that had remained in the South after Vietnam's division in 1954. It had strengthened it with guerrillas trained in the North and then infiltrated into the South. They placed major emphasis on controlling the rich and populous rural areas that were not well defended.

It was not until 1961, therefore, that the Americans realized that security had to be maintained within South Vietnam's national borders, and not just to prepare to resist invasion. Unfortunately, by this time more than six vital years had been lost and much of the rural area of South Vietnam was irretrievably taken over by the communists.

The Korean War had provided an important warning that the national will in the United States should be mobilized, and the war legitimized through a declaration. Too many people in the United States government believed that a declaration of war was out of date. It was more important than ever. The support and commitment of the American people was needed as never before. A declaration of war at this stage would have given legitimacy to the United States' growing involvement in war actions that were clearly outside the law. Such a declaration would have been like a marriage certificate, that the relationship was genuine in the eyes of the world, and that it had the support of a majority of the American people. A war declaration would have focused national attention and provided certain responsibilities on all the nation's citizens. A rejection by members of the Congress would have given the president a chance to pull out of Indochina without loss of prestige. While neither a marriage certificate nor a declaration of war will guarantee success, these legal steps are morally of great benefit to society.

By refusing to sign the Paris peace accords between the French and the North Vietnamese in 1954 the South Vietnamese president was able to avoid elections two years later that he believed would have meant surrendering control of his country to the communists. In a separate declaration at the signing of the accord, the United States also refused to approve the terms of the agreement. Therefore, in 1962 it was able to argue that its military commitment in behalf of South Vietnam was in response to North Vietnamese "renewal of the aggression in violation of the aforesaid agreements."

Secretary of Defense McNamara could say in all seriousness in the early 1960s that the greatest contribution the government was making—right or wrong was beside the point—was the development of an ability in the United States "to fight a limited war, and to go to war without the necessity of arousing the public ire."

Right or wrong was *not* beside the point, nor was the intangible of public ire. Vietnam reinforced the lessons of Korea that there was more to war, even limited war, than those things that could be measured, quantified and computerized. Somehow the human factor had been forgotten.

CHAPTER 6

The Heart of the Matter

PRESIDENT DIEM IN 1961 ASKED THE UNITED STATES GOVERNMENT TO conduct aerial herbicide spraying in his country. Herbicides, or weed-killing chemicals, had long been used in American agriculture. After World War I many nations realized the potential for herbicides in war operations to deny cover and concealment to an enemy, and to destroy his food supply. Techniques were worked out to spray large areas by aircraft. Herbicides were considered during World War II but rejected because it was feared their use would invite retaliation. The British used herbicides to destroy crops during the post-war communist insurgency in Malaya, but on a limited basis.

Diem's request to the United States launched a policy debate in the White House and within the State and Defense Departments between those who viewed herbicides as an economical and efficient means of stripping the Vietcong of jungle cover and food, and those who doubted their effectiveness. The latter worried that such operations would alienate friendly Vietnamese and expose the United States to charges of barbarism for waging a form of chemical warfare. Both sides agreed about the propaganda risks.

Deputy Secretary of Defense Gilpatric submitted a memorandum to President Kennedy that contained proposals for a multi-faceted program designed to prevent a Vietcong victory in South Vietnam. The series of events that led to the president's decision to send C-123s to South Vietnam for spraying herbicides apparently began April 21, 1961. Walt W. Rostow, a State Department foreign affairs adviser, forwarded a memo on Vietnam to the president. He proposed a high-level meeting in the near future to consider measures to improve the war effort. He said that President Diem should now undertake reforms that had been proposed earlier before broader American help was approved. Among nine of the proposed techniques recommended by Rostow was aerial defoliation.

After Vice President Johnson went to Vietnam to deliver personally a Kennedy letter and assure Diem of the president's strong support, a May 11 meeting of the National Security Council approved several decisions to prevent communist domination of South Vietnam. To achieve a viable and increasingly democratic society a series of mutually supporting actions of a military, political, economic, psychological and covert character were recommended. Defoliation was one of these actions.

President Kennedy approved their recommendations.

A South Vietnamese helicopter equipped with a spraying system made its first defoliation mission along a road north of Kontum on August 10, 1961. Diem was impressed with the results and he became a staunch supporter of the program although initial results were actually disappointing to the Americans.

As the program expanded, General Lyman L. Lemnitzer, chairman of the Joint Chiefs, voiced doubts about crop destruction operations in Vietnam. McNamara also was concerned but he went along with the plans. Gilpatric now had serious reservations, and the Department of Defense urged that defoliants should be closely controlled by Washington. Secretary of State Dean Rusk expressed the views of his department, saying, "The use of defoliants does not violate any rule of international law concerning the conduct of chemical warfare and is an accepted tactic of war." He warned, however, that the United States might become the target of an intense germ warfare campaign initiated by communist nations, and some neutrals. "Successful plant-killing operations in Vietnam, carefully coordinated with and incidental to large operations, can be of substantial assistance in the control and defeat of the Vietcong," Rusk said. He went along with Gilpatric's recommendation for a limited defoliation program that would be restricted to transportation routes, with close control and supervision by Washington officials. President Kennedy agreed November 30 with the views expressed by his top advisers and accepted their recommendations. His approval was based, however, on a mission-by-mission basis.

The Tactical Air Command was given the job of aerial spraying. Initially it was agreed that the job would be done by volunteers wearing civilian clothes with no United States Air Force identification on the aircraft. If captured, the fliers would not be acknowledged as members of the United States military services. Early crew members found it frustrating to maintain contact with their families once they were assigned to Vietnam due to the program's secrecy, but most wives and parents soon learned what they were doing.

A McNamara adviser, Brigadier General Edward Lansdale, warned him December 1 of the potential adverse publicity inherent in the planned defoliation program. He was concerned about the secrecy of the operation and the resulting lack of support by the American people. He pointed out that the United States would sooner or later have to admit it was spraying a chemical from the air that kills something—in other words plants—and would therefore be vulnerable to serious psychological attack, very likely accompanied by unfavorable reaction from the United States media. He believed that the plan for President Diem and his government to announce they had asked the United States to spray defoliants was not strong enough. He urged effective psychological support for the program. He said he was convinced there were good reasons for using defoliants but that they should be publicly presented.

Air Force Secretary Eugene M. Zuckert wrote three days later saying much the same thing. On December 14 he said that use of United States crews and aircraft should not be disguised.

Two days later Secretary of Defense McNamara held a press conference in Hawaii and explained that defoliants would be used initially in road clearing because chemicals presented a "ticklish" problem and road clearance offered the least potential trouble.

McNamara sought President Kennedy's concurrence before he gave final approval to the use of herbicides by American aircraft. He submitted a proposal to the president January 3, 1962, and Kennedy authorized limited operations of an experimental nature against separate targets that together comprised about sixteen of the almost sixty miles of Route 15 between Bien Hoa and Vung Tau. Thus the last barrier to defoliant operations was removed.

It was agreed by American officials that the first flight January 10 would not be publicized, but President Diem sent a story to the press the next day. "The Republic of Vietnam today announced plans to conduct an experiment to rid certain key communications routes of thick, tropical vegetation. United States assistance has been sought to aid Vietnamese personnel in this undertaking." He acknowledged that commercial weed-killing chemicals would be used, including those widely used throughout the world.

Captain Carl Marshall and Captain William F. Robinson, Jr. flew the first two official missions on January 13, 1962.

A team headed by Air Force Chief of Staff LeMay was in Vietnam April 16 through 21 and flew over a sprayed area along Route 1. LeMay was not overly impressed by the results but he suggested further testing. Some complaints by South Vietnamese were registered but a few of them may have been instigated by the Vietcong. Defoliants proved to be 90 to 95 percent effective against mangrove forests, and 60 percent against tropical shrubs.

The Department of Defense soon relaxed its controls and ordered the use of chemicals to destroy crops. President Kennedy at first was opposed but later he agreed. There was some opposition in Congress, and in all departments of the government, but none of it was strong enough to kill the program. Opponents were disturbed when it was revealed that some crops of loyal South Vietnamese were destroyed when mistakes were made during spraying operations.

By the time Operation Ranch Hand ended nine years later 18 million gallons of chemicals had been sprayed on an estimated 20 percent of South Vietnam's jungles, including 36 percent of its mangrove forests. The United States Air Force also carried out herbicide operations in Laos from December 1965 to September 1969 with the permission of the Laotian government.

Air operations were hazardous for crews because their planes had to fly low and slowly over territory that was often heavily defended. UC-123 Providers sustained more than seven thousand hits from ground fire but only a few of their aircraft were lost.

Vietnamese territorial organizations had been realigned during 1961-62 and corps headquarters were established with a commander responsible for each area. Some problems of command and control were alleviated by these actions but the duties of area commanders inhibited the mobility of infantry divisions that were designed to operate as strike forces over much broader areas. Without an overall command, movement in and out of these corps areas to threatened areas proved extremely difficult in an emergency. Under the corps' command set-up, there was no overall top authority to respond forcefully when an emergency arose, and there was little uniform planning and coordination among the Vietnamese commands. A regional organization, with authority to move divisions from one territory to another, and to mass military strength where it was most needed, not only would have given South Vietnam a sound military structure, but would have created a sense of pride and self-assurance. Politically, President Diem could not or did not want to establish such a structure, despite strong American prodding to do so. Among his considerations Diem was always fearful—and with good reason as was proved later—of a plot by some of his generals to overthrow him.

Village defense had been under a self-defense corps. Beyond each village the Civil Guard had responsibility. Both were under the control of village and province chiefs and their activities were coordinated with the police to maintain local security. This was the age-old "citizens in peacetime, soldiers in wartime" type of defense. It had value because the soldiers were motivated to protect their homes and families. Ideally, such defenders were members of the village they were assigned to protect. Prior to 1961, they did not receive military aid directly from the United States so they had an assortment of obsolete weapons, many left behind when the French departed. Their training was poor and they were ineffective as counter-insurgents. The Civil Guard quite often had to fight like a regular army, but they were unable to do so because they lacked proper training and equipment. When the United States extended assistance in 1961, American advisers were assigned to the villages and an immediate improvement was noted. What was most needed, however, were regular battalions because they had the capability and organization to meet the fluid nature of tactical counter-insurgency warfare. A battalion could provide small units to conduct saturation patrol activities to keep the pressure on the enemy, or to mount a strong full battalion attack. Until replacement of their equipment could be completed, and better radio communications established between villages, such battalions could not be set up.

In each of the first four months of 1962 a thousand communists entered South Vietnam while Soviet aircraft stood ready to support two North Vietnamese regiments poised in the Laotian panhandle for a possible thrust across the border. The North Vietnamese evidently planned to move through South Vietnam's Central Highlands to cut the nation in half, or to forge an infantry division for attacks on Saigon. Both were considered likely alternatives by American intelligence officers.

Since his election President Kennedy had repeatedly ordered the military services to come up with special measures for countering insurgencies. He was still dissatisfied with the results. In early 1962 he directed the Joint Chiefs and the Central Intelligence Agency to create a single authority in Washington that would come up with an organizational plan. A special group was created January 18 under the chairmanship of General Taylor on the premise that subversive insurgency was a valid form of military/political conflict that should have equal status with conventional warfare. This group ran into opposition from Kennedy because it called for more Vietnamese involvement and less American. Kennedy wanted United States armed forces to use Vietnam as a laboratory for studying and testing counter-insurgency techniques and equipment. By fall, the Joint Chiefs won the argument and American counter-insurgency forces remained limited and merely supplemented Vietnamese military efforts. General LeMay publicly revealed the existence of one of these units— "Jungle Jim"—on April 27. He said it was instructing allied crews in all areas of air operations. "This is a realistic training program," LeMay said in Los Angeles. "Those people, the Vietnamese, are at war. Our instructors occasionally accompany them on combat missions. Our pilots are armed. They will protect themselves if fired upon."

Throughout 1962 staff deficiencies of the Military Assistance Command became more apparent. The Air Force sought to unite air and ground units in a cooperative effort against North Vietnamese insurgents. McNamara made it clear, however, that the Army was running the show. "If you have two or three men engaged in an operation," he said, "one has to be primary. The Army has to be primary in land war. The Air Force is there to serve the Army in the airlift role and the close support role, and the Air Force must tailor its activities to the Army." Such a statement appalled Air Force strategists who had long waged a bitter battle against such a philosophy.

As the American military command built up in South Vietnam, there were 6,419 Americans there by June 3, and planes were being sent in ever-increasing quantities. For the latter, it was evident that an air control system was badly needed. It was slow in coming although the Advance Research Projects Agency had been conducting small-scale defoliant tests in South Vietnam since the previous summer. President Diem liked this idea and most of the Joint Chiefs approved the spraying to reduce jungle cover over communist positions. Kennedy had approved this limited effort but he refused to give blanket authority saying that he did not wish it to appear to the world that Americans were making war upon Vietnamese peasants. Therefore, he approved every crop destruction target through the State Department.

McNamara held monthly conferences in Hawaii or Saigon to review war activities. He usually met with the chairman of the Joint Chiefs, members of the Pacific command, the ambassador to Vietnam and members of the Military Assistance Command. Lieutenant General Emmett O'Donnell, Jr., commander of the Pacific Air Force, at first was impressed by McNamara's statements of American determination to keep South Vietnam from falling to the communists but he quickly learned that strong talk did not necessarily mean strong action. He deplored the overcontrol from the Washington level but as a soldier he complied with the spirit of the policy to be ultra cautious. CINCPAC Admiral Felt believed that policies curbing airpower were scarcely in America's best interest. General LeMay was impatient with what he termed "our own military rules to handicap ourselves." The Air Force Chief of Staff said later that "if Krushchev had been running it [the war], he couldn't have done any better as far as handicapping us than what we did to ourselves all through the thing from start to finish."

After a Cambodian village was hit by accident on January 21, 1962, and several civilians were killed, McNamara ordered the Air Force not to engage in strikes on Cambodian territory. He said they were to balance risk against gain. For example, a mission was probably unacceptable if eight Americans were training a single Vietnamese, or if there was a chance of killing innocent people to get a few Vietcong. With new restrictions more than half of the T-29s in 1962 returned to base with their bombs. As a result air operations were almost totally ineffective.

Vietcong ground fire against aircraft caused increasing concern by September because losses escalated to unacceptable levels.

South Vietnam was still in existence although control over large areas was shaky. Taking cognizance of this unexpected state of affairs the National Liberation Front, North Vietnam's political organization in South Vietnam, said that it should create a neutral state in the South much like Laos. Of special interest was Ho Chi Minh's statement praising Diem's patriotism. Three years earlier Ho Chi Minh had predicted South Vietnam's defeat within a year. By September, 1962, he was saying that victory might take fifteen to twenty years.

In May of that year McNamara had looked ahead to an end to counter-insurgency. In Honolulu at CINCPAC Headquarters it was hoped that the war could soon be phased out, and major United States combat, advisory and logistical personnel could be sent home. Military assistance for Vietnam then could be reduced to less than $75 million a year. McNamara therefore directed General Harkins to draw up a program to prepare the Vietnamese armed forces to defeat the communists on their own.

"Six months ago," McNamara said, "we had practically nothing and we have made tremendous progress to date. However, we have been con-centrating on short-term crash-type actions and now must look ahead to carefully conceived long-range programs." When he was asked how long he believed it would take to defeat the Vietcong, Harkins replied, "About one year from the time we are able to get the Vietnamese fully operational and really processing VC in all areas." It was assumed that three years would be needed, and Harkins was directed to plan on that basis. McNamara said, "The objective is to give South Vietnam an adequate military capability without the need for special United States military assistance."

Optimism was high in the United States by mid-August, 1962, and a formal plan was budgeted for the phased withdrawal of American troops. Such a program had been approved July 23, with the concurrence of President Kennedy, at the July Honolulu conference. By this time Amer-ican military strength in South Vietnam had risen to 11,412. McNamara set 1965 as the planning date for ending United States military involvement in Vietnam and Harkins was told to base his plans on that date. Air Force and Navy officials were skeptical.

Former President Dwight D. Eisenhower complimented President Kennedy by saying that he had done the right thing by increasing the number of advisers in Vietnam.

There was wide disagreement on college campuses. Students for a Democratic Society called for "participatory democracy," and acclaimed themselves members of the new left. They started out with 200 members and initially were involved in community work, notably in Newark where one founder, Tom Hayden, concerned himself with slum poverty among blacks. The group at first was idealistic but as the Vietnam War escalated they turned more and more to radicalism. Two professors of psychology at Harvard, Timothy Leary and Richard Alpert, experimented with hallucinogenic drugs to "liberate the young." They tried various drugs but mostly used lysergic acid diethylamide (LSD). It caused the mind to divert to a fantasy world, and distorted and terrorized some individuals although Leary claimed that LSD opened the door of the mind. It was Alpert who coined the word psychodelic.

With the situation in Laos rapidly deteriorating in the spring of 1962 with the communist Pathet Lao close to taking over all of Laos, President Kennedy sent air units to Thailand for possible use against the North Vietnam-supported Pathet Lao. Joint Task Force 116 was deployed May 12 with Marine, Army and Air Force units. The Air Force was concerned by the muddled command structure. South Vietnamese units were responsible to the 2nd Air Division, while Thailand units were under the Thirteenth Air Force and elements of the Tactical Air Force were under the jurisdiction of Joint Task Force 116.

Before the task force could get into action, the communists decided they had more to gain by discussing a peace treaty in Geneva July 23 and agreed to abide by the 1954 accord.

American officials who supported such a treaty were naive to believe that it would be honored by the communists. North Vietnam ignored it and continued to support their forces in Laos and in South Vietnam.

For the rest of the year and into 1963 the North Vietnamese continued to infiltrate personnel and equipment to the South. They supplied the most modern weapons they could get from China and the Soviet Union. Although McNamara still considered South Vietnam a test case for the new communist strategy, to Americans on the fighting front it began to look more and more like a conventional war and not an insurgency.

In mid-August, 1962, the Military Assistance Command had recommended a plan for the formation of nine regular Vietnamese divisions, plus other units. They would operate under four autonomous corps commanders. These troops, it was hoped, would decimate local Vietcong elements, cut off replacements, and destroy lines of communication with North Vietnam and hem the communists into specific areas. And finally, it was hoped that a general offensive would annihilate them during simultaneous operations in the four corps areas. Such an effort was supposed to drive the Vietcong out of the country within a year. One staff officer thought this grandiose plan was reminiscent of what happened in Korea when General Douglas MacArthur made his famous statement "out of the trenches by Christmas." It wasn't true in Korea and it proved untrue in Vietnam.

Kennedy admired toughness and he suited his actions to his words. When the Russians later precipitated a crisis in October, 1962, by placing nuclear missiles in Cuba, the president was inclined to use air strikes, or even to authorize an invasion of the islands. Actually, the United States Navy had invasion forces capable of striking Cuba whose commander only awaited the president's word to invade. Kennedy was talked out of it, particularly by Secretary of Defense McNamara, who argued against it. Kennedy did impose a naval and air blockade of Cuba. The Soviets backed down and withdrew their missiles because they were in no position to oppose the American invasion. The United States had such an overwhelming nuclear superiority that the communists knew they would lose a nuclear war with the United States.

At the time, few Americans disagreed with President Kennedy's reported assessment of the struggle the United States faced against the forces of communism. His warnings were largely accepted that communism was a disease of ideas, and that nations could fall before it like dominoes. Most Americans agreed when he said, "Each day America draws near the hour of maximum danger." He called upon the American people to be freedom's "sentinel at the gate."

The South Vietnamese suffered their first serious setback near the village of Ap Bac in the IV Corps. The 7th South Vietnamese Division, that had wrested control of the Plain of Reeds from the Vietcong in the Mekong Delta earlier, was reputed to have killed more Vietcong than any other division. In late December, 1962, intelligence information pinpointed a Vietcong radio team in a relatively isolated area near Ap Bac, thirty-five miles southwest of Saigon. Officers of the 7th were confident they had the situation in the area under control because the enemy appeared to be pulling back its regular units to sanctuary bases. The 7th's commander issued orders to attack and ten helicopters of the United States Army's 93rd Helicopter Company agreed to land South Vietnamese troops and to provide four helicopter gunships to protect them. The Vietnamese company landed in the midst of a well-dug-in Vietcong battalion. The first three helicopters landed safely but the fourth was shot down and the gunships immediately moved in with suppressive fire. Another helicopter was shot down trying to rescue the crew of the fourth helicopter along with one of the gunships. Two other helicopters were damaged and barely made it back to base. Air Force Skyraiders were called in but they failed to dislodge the Vietcong. More bombers were summoned and they managed to rout the enemy.

The commander of IV Corps ordered a paratroop drop east of Ap Bac to block the Vietcong's escape route. Three companies dropped west rather than east of the village so they were in no position to stem the Vietcong retreat. That night, all of the Vietcong escaped. It was a costly battle with sixty-five South Vietnamese killed and three Americans. It was announced at the time that 100 Vietcong were killed but this number probably is much too high. They admitted later losing eighteen men.

The battle cost the Americans and the South Vietnamese much prestige because it soon became obvious that there had been no prior air-ground planning, and no fighter escort to cover the operation had been sought. When the Vietnamese Air Force was asked for support, they were not informed of the true situation.

In reviewing the situation, Admiral Felt was convinced that unescorted helicopter operations at Ap Bac were wrong. He told his staff that experience should have taught that the Vietcong are not surprised by helicopter landings, and are able to ambush helicopters. Felt said he could not understand how commanders could ignore the fundamentals of warfare by failing to prepare the landing area.

Brigadier General Rollen H. Anthis, head of the 2nd Air Division, later said after reviewing the operation that the failure at Ap Bac was due to the Army's concept for the use of airpower. He called the Army "a customer that is also a competitor." Much later he recalled that in some ways it would have been better if the Army had suffered a few relatively minor reverses at this time. He said it would have been better if their concept of close air support had been discredited in a relatively inexpensive way than to wait for the ultimate catastrophe.

North Vietnam became increasingly concerned by the United States' escalation of its involvement and called upon the International Control Commission February 2, 1963, to eject United States Air Force units from Vietnam that were "playing a key role" and causing widespread damage.

Secretary of State Rusk was concerned by widespread newspaper and television reports of the escalation, but the media had every right to report news of combat activities involving Americans that was officially being withheld from the American people. For example, American newspapers publicized the authorization of American helicopters to fire on the enemy. But spokesmen for the Military Assistance Command kept saying in Saigon that helicopters only fired their guns when they were fired upon. Rusk reiterated the official position, "Our policy remains that the American role in Vietnam be strictly limited to advisory, logistic and training functions." Those three Americans who died at Ap Bac hardly fit this stated policy.

General Wheeler, chairman of the Joint Chiefs of Staff, assessed the situation in January, 1963, by saying that in the past year and a half the military situation had improved from a point of near desperation to a condition where "victory is now a hopeful prospect." It wasn't long before he regretted those words.

Late that month a meeting was held at the Chinese embassy in Phnom Penh, Cambodia. It was agreed by representatives of North Vietnam, the National Liberation Front and the Soviet Union that twelve battalions should be added to the Vietcong's strength, eight of which would come from Laos and the other four to be recruited in North Vietnam.

The Vietcong's ability to fight against American helicopters and armored vehicles at Ap Bac gave them confidence and marked a major turning point in the conflict. From now on they often deliberately invited battle.

After this battle, there was a lull in the fighting on both sides. Admiral Felt urged President Diem to launch operations to exploit what he considered was an opportunity to overwhelm the Vietcong, but Diem was not anxious to involve his troops in other than defensive actions.

Diem resented American press coverage about the fiasco at Ap Bac, particularly allegations that American advisers were dying because of the reluctance of South Vietnamese troops to fight. Some reports charged that American advisers tried to lead South Vietnamese troops but that they would neither follow nor fight.

President Kennedy acted to repair what he correctly viewed as an eroding trust between the two countries. In a State of the Union address to Congress January 14, 1963, the president said that the "spearhead of aggression had been blunted in Vietnam." The reports he was receiving from Vietnam hardly justified such a statement.

Admiral Felt began to receive increasing reports that President Diem was withdrawing into seclusion, and leaving many decisions to his brother. There were reports from Saigon that both Diem and his brother believed that the growing number of American advisers was an encroachment on Vietnamese sovereignty. They were particularly upset by Senate Majority Leader Mike Mansfield's report in February that after seven years and $4 billion in American aid some difficulties still remain, "if indeed they have not been confounded." Mansfield said that South Vietnam was now less stable and more removed from properly responsible and responsive government.

In April, Ngo Dinh Nhu issued a series of private and public statements that dwelt on United States infringements of Vietnamese sovereignty. Aid came, he said, with too many strings attached. He told the Saigon bureau chief of the Central Intelligence Agency, John H. Richardson, that the situation would be helped if the American presence was reduced by several thousand men. He said he feared that his country was being turned into an American protectorate. He did not request that any official action be taken, so his words were not taken seriously. It would have been a blessing for the United States if he had done so.

Admiral Felt now passed to the Joint Chiefs a proposed psychological ploy that recommended: "If things go right by the end of 1963, we should take one thousand military personnel out of the Republic of Vietnam at one time, make a big proclamation out of this and publicize it widely. This would show: 1. The Republic of Vietnam is winning; 2. Take the steam out of the anti-Diemites; and 3. Dramatically illustrate the honesty of United States intentions."

Although Sir Robert Thompson with the British mission had said in March that the South Vietnamese government was "beginning to win the shooting war against the Vietcong, due chiefly to the American helicopters," the following month there were persuasive signs that the Vietcong had not been grievously hurt. The relationship between the American and Vietnamese governments remained tenuous but an excellent rice crop had brightened prospects for an improved economy. By April, 50 percent of the hamlet program had been completed, and sheltered 60 percent of the people. And, despite doubts about the fighting will of the South Vietnamese, there were over 900 offensive operations that month.

At the May 6 commanders' conference in Honolulu, McNamara announced that by the end of 1963 he would remove one thousand Americans from Vietnam to show that the military situation was improving. He said he would try to remove units instead of individuals and turn their equipment over to the South Vietnamese. He stressed that the conflict was not a United States war, and that it did not intend to fight it. While he made this statement even more Americans were en route to South Vietnam—under his orders.

Ambassador Nolting told the participants that President Diem kept intimating that the United States was infringing on Vietnam's sovereignty.

He said Diem's brother Nhu had suggested that the American advisory effort appeared to be hampering Diem's political base. He said both were suspicious of the strength of the American commitment and the thrust of American policy. The ambassador said that Nhu was "efficient and continues to accumulate power." Nolting stressed, however, that it was the unanimous opinion of the Americans in Saigon that the "current leadership is the best the United States can get. It is sincere, albeit not particularly adept, but it is better than most in Southeast Asia."

Two days later, demonstrators celebrating Buddha's birthday paraded in Saigon with religious flags, banners and devotional images. The procession violated a 1950 ordinance forbidding the flying of any flag in public without the national emblem beside it. A monk delivered a sermon protesting the Diem government's discrimination against Buddhists. When Civil Guard troops moved to break up the rally, an explosion killed several people, including children. The press was told by Buddhist leaders that the government must admit responsibility for the loss of life, rescind the flag regulation, and give Buddhists equality with Catholics. This was the heart of the problem. There were more than eight million Buddhists, compared to one-and-a-half million Catholics, and Diem, Nhu and most prominent families were members of the Catholic faith.

CHAPTER 7

"What Is the Attitude of the United States?"

WITH GROWING UNREST AMONG RELIGIOUS MINORITIES, NHU CRACKED down, increasing the tension while he strove to restore law and order.

In Washington, a newspaper published an anti-American statement attributed to Ngo Dinh Nhu. Representative Otto Passman, chairman of the subcommittee on appropriations, wrote McNamara, "Certainly, the Diem government ought to be made to understand that the American people have no interest in propping up an unpopular regime if it is more concerned with the pursuit of personal aims than with the protection of the country from communism."

President Kennedy was embarrassed by the situation and told the press that the United States hoped to withdraw some Americans by the end of the year.

Meanwhile, Diem still offered no redress to Buddhists and they demonstrated again in early June at Hué. When they refused to disperse, nine were killed. Disturbances now spread to all of the northern provinces.

The Department of Defense ordered that no United States aircraft be used to transport Vietnamese troops on anti-Buddhist missions, and General Harkins personally ordered Americans to remain aloof from the demonstrations.

After their demands were not met, a saffron-robed Buddhist monk had himself soaked with gasoline June 11 and the aged man committed sacrificial suicide by fire at a busy road junction. Six more immolated themselves. Madame Nhu shocked the world when she said, "I would clap my hands at seeing another monk barbecue show."

The clash between South Vietnamese government forces and the Buddhists was viewed by members of the National Security Council in

Washington with extreme gravity. They were particularly concerned by the effect it might have on the large number of Buddhists in the South Vietnamese armed forces, and feared that they might defect.

To review the situation, the Department of Defense sent Marine Major General Victor Krulak, on duty with the Joint Chiefs, to South Vietnam with State Department Vietnamese expert Joseph Mendenhall. They returned with such opposing views that President Kennedy said, "You two did visit the same country, didn't you?"

Krulak responded, "Mr. President, I think I can answer your question. I went to the countryside and my State Department colleague went to the cities, but the war is in the countryside."

Mendenhall admitted that he had visited only three cities, and that he had not gone into the country.

Krulak said later that they were sent to South Vietnam primarily to review the matter of Buddhist defections from the armed forces. He reported that he found no evidence throughout South Vietnam to support such a possibility. Mendenhall had given a pessimistic view about South Vietnam's hope of victory over the communists.

President Kennedy directed McNamara and General Taylor, now chairman of the Joint Chiefs, to make a personal assessment in South Vietnam. They left September 26 and returned six days later. They reported to Kennedy that the South was winning the war, and that it would be successfully concluded in three of the four military geographical regions by the end of 1964, and in the fourth or delta region by 1965. By then, they said, American advisers could be withdrawn. They admitted that political considerations were adversely affecting the war. They also strongly recommended that Ambassador Nolting keep aloof of the Diem regime.

In retrospect, it is obvious that McNamara and Taylor relied too much on American personnel in South Vietnam because their information was much too optimistic.

South Vietnam's Joint General Staff ordered all ground force units to operate a minimum of twenty days every month starting July 1. This was to be the start of a general offensive to attain "complete annihilation of the enemy," and to "saturate the countryside" in order to "complete Vietnamese control."

General Harkins voiced his enthusiasm for the Vietnamese plan, saying that the plan to "saturate the countryside" with small and large military actions was correct and would fragment and destroy the Vietcong. Unfortunately for this grandiose plan the Vietcong were now ready to launch their own offensive.

Although some American units were scheduled to leave South Vietnam by the end of 1963, the Joint Chiefs suggested and McNamara approved an additional C-123 Provider Squadron for Da Nang to augment the twenty-nine C-123s at Tan Son Nhut. In addition, approval was granted for more helicopter and observation planes to support tactical zones and American Special Forces. Much of this new airlift capability was used for tactical operations, particularly to supply and reinforce remote stations.

Although American planes flew nearly all reconnaissance flights in 1963, not much intelligence information was obtained. The jungle terrain effectively hid small and fleeing enemy targets. Air defense radar control centers—three in Vietnam and one in Thailand—provided high-altitude surveillance.

In early February, 1963, General LeMay had pressed for putting United States markings on counter-insurgency aircraft, claiming their operations were well known throughout South Vietnam. He said it was common knowledge that American airmen were flying combat missions. Such knowledge became more apparent when Captains John P. Bartley and John F. Shaughnessy, Jr. were shot down by the Vietcong on February 3. Three days later Major James E. O'Neill was lost. LeMay was overruled, and Secretary of State Rusk continued to insist that the American role was "strictly limited to advisory, logistic and training functions."

LeMay pressed the issue again in March, but Ambassador Nolting said, "We are winning without such overt United States action."

The Military Assistance Command reached a strength of 16,652 people in June, and roughly one-third of them were Air Force, but McNamara froze the command's strength on June 28.

Despite this action United States Air Force units continued to be formed outside of Saigon. On July 8 the 1st Air Commando Squadron was converted at Bien Hoa from a counter-insurgency squadron. This date also saw activation of the 33rd and 34th Tactical Groups at Tan Son Nhut, plus formation of more airlift squadrons.

South Vietnamese probes into Vietcong areas during February and March had made good use of pre-planned air interdiction strikes, and Vietnamese Rangers swept into the area later and destroyed enemy head-quarters and camps along the Ma Da River.

The Vietcong had been biding their time and in July they struck hamlets south of Ban Me Thuot and ambushed the roads leading to the area. The same type of activity now spread to other areas.

The Buddhists demonstrated again July 16 and monks and nuns milled in front of Ambassador Nolting's residence in Saigon demanding that the United States compel the Diem government to keep its promises. Violence broke out again the following day.

Diem addressed the nation by radio July 19 but his address was uncompromising. Despite criticism from religious minorities, Diem still enjoyed the support of many of the Vietnamese people, but his brother and his wife were mostly disliked.

President Kennedy replaced Ambassador Nolting with the aristocratic Henry Cabot Lodge whose urbane manner and fluent French endeared him to the Vietnamese leaders. Lodge made many changes after his appointment in June, and he refused to play North Vietnam's propaganda line. For example, he would not use such terms as the People's Army of Vietnam and the Democratic Republic of North Vietnam. Instead he always referred to them as the North Vietnamese Army and the state as merely North Vietnam.

After his appointment, and during a visit to Washington, Lodge talked to a "distinguished" Vietnamese who told him that "unless they left the country, no power on earth could prevent the assassination of Mr. Diem, his brother Mr. Nhu and Mr. Nhu's wife. Their deaths were inevitable."

In mid-August there were more immolations. Madame Nhu, who believed that self-immolations should be ignored, further charged the United States embassy with pressuring the Diem government to silence her.

Ambassador Lodge was given broad authority by Kennedy to make recommendations directly to him as president, and Lodge was expected to suggest drastic changes in United States policies that would alter relations between the two governments.

In anticipation of a change in United States–South Vietnam relations President Diem called an emergency meeting of his Joint General Staff for August 20. Diem appointed Tran Van Don as chief of staff of South Vietnam's armed forces, and his brother Nhu invited senior generals to sign a paper calling upon the government to seize and silence Buddhist leaders. At midnight, Diem declared martial law and a state of siege. Under his authority Vietnamese Special Forces and the police stormed Buddhist pagodas in Saigon and in Hué before dawn. Monks, nuns and students were rounded up but Buddhist leaders escaped and took refuge in the American embassy.

The following day Acting Secretary of State George W. Ball released an official statement that the United States deplored repressive actions against the Buddhists.

Ambassador Lodge arrived in Saigon August 22. He was briefed by embassy officials who told him that Vietnamese generals could depose Diem, although they admitted the new Chief of Staff General Tran Van Don had told embassy officials that they were too weak to do so. Lodge was advised that the Vietnamese generals were anxious to end martial law and hoped the United States would continue to support Diem while forcing him to liberalize his regime and to delegate authority. The generals suggested that it would be advisable to create an interim cabinet of officers and civilians.

Lodge briefed President Kennedy on the state of affairs he found in Saigon, and the president told Lodge that the United States could no longer tolerate the systematic suppression of the Buddhists, or Nhu's domination of the government. In a phone message, Kennedy told Lodge, "We wish to give Diem reasonable opportunity to remove the Nhus, but if he remains obdurate, then we are prepared to accept the obvious implication that we can no longer support Diem." Lodge was instructed by President Kennedy to tell the Vietnamese generals that the United States would renounce Diem unless he righted the Buddhists' wrongs and formed a more responsive and representative government. He said that the United States would take no part in any ouster of Diem, but would recognize an interim anti-communist military regime as the successor to the Diem government.

A Voice of America broadcast, certainly approved at the highest level, was beamed to the Vietnamese people in their language. It blamed Nhu for the pagoda attacks and the mass arrests of monks and students. The broadcast said that if these incidents continued to occur that the United States might sharply curtail its aid unless President Diem rid himself of certain associates.

This broadcast was a classic case of one nation—the United States—openly trying to interfere in the governing of another nation—a supposedly friendly power.

The following day a spokesman for the Vietnamese Joint General Staff refuted the broadcast, saying that responsible military commanders had unanimously proposed to President Diem that martial law be initiated and that necessary steps be taken against the Buddhists.

During his first week in office, Ambassador Lodge believed that the Diem government was in danger of collapse because the police had abused their power and were causing resentment. He was convinced that the well-publicized Buddhist immolations had turned the American people against Diem.

The State Department advised Lodge that Diem must remove Nhu and his wife otherwise the United States could no longer support President Diem. A department spokesman said that appropriate military commanders could be given a pledge of "direct support" in any interim period of breakdown in the central government's mechanism. Lodge was authorized to threaten Diem with a cut-off of American aid unless the jailed Buddhists were released.

Lodge replied that chances of "Diem's meeting our demands are virtually nil." By making them, he said, we give Nhu a chance to forestall a coup, and Lodge suggested that we "go straight to the generals with our demands."

Lucien Conein, a veteran Central Intelligence Agency operative, now a lieutenant colonel, was authorized to meet General Tran Van Don, the figurehead commander of South Vietnam's Army. They met in a Saigon night club July 4, 1963, and Don hinted that a coup against Diem was in the making. "What will the American reaction be if we go all the way?" the general asked Conein.

Conein had no authority to respond to Don's query. President Kennedy still hoped that Diem might be persuaded to reach a compromise with the Buddhists. Now was the time for the United States to make clear that it would not countenance such action, but its officials did not do so. Conein, in constant danger of his life if his part in the coup reached officials of the South Vietnamese government, had been placed in an impossible position when he was ordered to maintain contact with the rebel generals. This situation prevailed until late August and the generals continued to refuse to divulge their plans to Conein or any other Central Intelligence Agency operative. They feared betrayal but they desperately needed American endorsement of their plan.

In response to a query from President Kennedy about the situation, Ambassador Lodge replied that "United States prestige was publicly committed. There is no turning back."

After the National Security Council reaffirmed the United States' basic course that a coup would be supported if it had a good chance of succeeding, President Kennedy sent a private message to Lodge. He pledged "everything possible to help you conclude this operation successfully." He asked to be given continuing reports in case he wished to reverse his decision.

During discussions before the National Security Council in Washington, former Ambassador Nolting had pointed out that refusal to support President Diem and Nhu would renege on past commitments. Undersecretary of State Ball argued, however, that continued support for them risked losing the war against the Vietcong. He was emphatic in saying that Diem and Nhu had been profoundly wrong for quite some time.

In response to further instructions from Washington, Ambassador Lodge suggested that the Vietnamese generals who were hostile to Diem should be told that the United States had grave reservations about the Nhus.

The State Department agreed August 28 that the Nhus would have to be removed and that "a coup will be needed."

The next day Ambassador Lodge said, "We are launched on a course from which there is no respectable turning back: the overthrow of the Diem government."

President Kennedy weighed conflicting recommendations. He finally ordered Lodge and General Harkins to support a coup if it had a good chance of success but to avoid any direct American involvement. He further authorized them to suspend American air support to Diem whenever they thought it was prudent.

On the 29th, Secretary of State Rusk authorized Lodge to explore General Harkins' suggestion that a threat to withdraw United States assistance might force Diem to drop the Nhus. Lodge was somewhat puzzled because this new communication seemed to cancel the earlier message to "make detailed plans as to how we might bring about Diem's replacement." He realized that the president wanted him not to thwart a coup, nor to help plan one, but rather to keep in close touch with the plotters so he could be kept informed for future decision making. By now, Lodge was convinced that Diem's overthrow was imminent, so he avoided seeing him.

In a Central Intelligence Agency telegram to Secretary of State Rusk that same day, with copies to McNamara and others in the Defense Department, the probable loyalties of key South Vietnamese military units and their commanders were evaluated in the event of a coup against President Diem. The commander of the Presidential Guard, Lt. Col. Nguyen Ngoc Khoi, was said to be loyal to the Diem regime and would continue to support it. It was noted that the guard numbered about twenty-five hundred men, some of whom were billeted on the palace grounds, while others were at a camp in front. The CIA evaluation said the Guard was well-equipped with armored units permanently assigned to it without loyalties to any particular branch of the services.*

It was also noted that the armored forces in I, II and IV Corps were under control of their respective corps commanders, and not the Joint General Staff. III Corps, a key command in any coup d'etat, had its armored units assigned to the Joint General Staff because its commander had little interest in armor forces. The CIA report said that 70 to 80 percent of armor personnel were Buddhists and that, among the rank and file, "it is believed the regime enjoys little sympathy." There is "further evidence to indicate that armor officers not trusted by the regime are assigned to the armor branch,"* evidently to isolate them.

The CIA sent another telegram to Secretary Rusk two days later,

*This material, as well as that marked elsewhere in Chapters 7 and 8, was released to the author under the Freedom of Information Act.

downgrading the possibility of a coup against Diem, saying, "This particular coup is finished." As justification for this conclusion, General Harkins was quoted following a conversation he had with General Khiem who told him, in effect, "The generals do not feel ready and do not have sufficient balance of forces." Harkins was told that the dissident generals had talked with Nhu the day before and that he had assured them that South Vietnam would be able to continue the war, finding the means to do so where it could. Khiem told Harkins that the generals were thinking of proposing to President Diem that he bring senior officers into certain cabinet positions with Nhu in charge of the cabinet. In effect, this would establish a kind of prime minister role for him. Rusk was advised that in General Harkins' judgment the generals were not ready for a coup, and could not achieve a balance of forces favorable to them.*

With the deepening political crisis, the Commander-in-Chief, Pacific, established plans for the air evacuation of Saigon and Hué to bring home American military dependents and civilian employees.

A further complication for South Vietnam had developed a few days earlier when Cambodia broke relations August 27, citing border violations and the ill-treatment of Buddhists.

President Charles de Gaulle of France now offered to help restore peace in Indochina by seeking the unification of North and South as a neutral and independent country. How he would talk the communists into such an unrealistic acceptance was not clear.

At the request of some Asian and African nations U Thant, Secretary General of the United Nations, wrote President Diem on August 31 to "insure the exercise of fundamental human rights to all actions" of his country.

Chiang Kai-shek, head of the Republic of China on Taiwan, stated to Pacific Air Force Commander General Jacob E. Smart that it was essential to win the war because the Asian states were closely watching the United States in Indochina.

Smart was also told by influential Thailand officials that they doubted that the United States could be depended upon in a crisis.

With these conflicting signals coming from many parts of the world President Kennedy went on television September 2 to say that the government of Vietnam could win the war only if it had popular support. He claimed that the Vietnamese government was out of touch with its people, and he said that suppression of the Buddhists was unwise. Could the government regain the affection of its people? "With changes in policy, and perhaps with personnel," Kennedy said, "I think it can. If it doesn't make those changes, I would think that the chances of winning would not be good."

It was later revealed that De Gaulle's scheme to unify and neutralize Vietnam was explored, in part at least, by Ngo Dinh Nhu who admitted contact with Vietcong leaders of the National Liberation Front. Apparently he had also been in contact with communist officials in Hanoi. He told Ambassador Lodge September 2 of a discussion he had had with the Polish member of the International Control Commission. The Polish member had sought Mr. Nhu's reaction to De Gaulle's proposal so that he could forward it to the North Vietnamese foreign minister. At this time many South Vietnamese officers were convinced that Nhu would make a deal with the communist government in North Vietnam if he believed it would be in his, Nhu's, best interest.

President Diem replied September 5 to the letter from the Secretary General of the United Nations. He invited U Thant to send a fact-finding mission to Saigon. Eventually such a group was sent but it reached no conclusions. The Costa Rican member said he personally found no religious persecution. He said he believed South Vietnam's problems were political and involved only a small part of the Buddhist community.

When Kennedy privately sought advice about Diem's prospects from his White House advisers he was told, "Our best judgment is that he can't be successful on this basis."

Kennedy replied, "I don't agree with those who say we should withdraw. That would be a great mistake." He repeated for emphasis, "That would be a great mistake."

On another occasion Kennedy said, "It is their war. They are the ones who have to win or lose it. We can help them, we can give them equipment, but they have to win it."

Admiral George Anderson, whom Kennedy had appointed as Chief of Naval Operations in June, 1961, to replace Admiral Arleigh Burke, had quickly aroused McNamara's ire with his outspoken views. During the Cuban missile crisis McNamara tried to control Navy ships around Cuba by giving "left and right rudder" orders for which he had no expertise. Anderson resisted McNamara's instructions not only because he disagreed with them regarding the precise positioning of Navy ships, but also because they bypassed the chain of command and responsibility, with resultant confusion. When Anderson persisted, McNamara was furious. In addition, Anderson's objections to the joint Air Force and Navy experimental fighter program, with which he had disagreed from the program's inception, further aggravated their relationship. Anderson was particularly upset with McNamara's arbitrary award of the TFX contract to General Dynamics against the advice of a service advisory board.

In early September, 1963, Anderson was scheduled to appear before

Senator John L. McClelland's investigating committee. McNamara sent one of his aides to talk to Anderson the day before. "We want a copy of what you are going to say tomorrow."

"I don't have any prepared remarks," Anderson said. "I am going to tell the truth and that's that."

McNamara sent Navy Secretary Korth to Anderson's quarters on Sunday morning to tell him he was fired. Anderson was preparing for a reception that afternoon on the front lawn of his headquarters at Observatory House when the word was delivered. He immediately phoned President Kennedy to tell of the firing but the president felt he could not override his Secretary of Defense. As an alternative, Kennedy offered Anderson the position of ambassador to Portugal. Anderson asked for time to consider.

Anderson was advised by Arleigh Burke, former Chief of Naval Operations and his predecessor, "Tell him, hell no. I'm fired, and that's it." The Vice Chief of Naval Operations, Admiral Claude V. Ricketts, advised acceptance since the appointment would show confidence on the part of the president in the naval officer whom he had appointed to head the Navy. Anderson accepted.

Admiral Anderson went to see McNamara the next morning and the secretary got up with a sheepish grin and walked across the floor of his office with his hand out. Anderson put his hand behind his back.

"No, Mr. Secretary," he said, "I want you to know that I am deeply hurt over this. We have done our best to give you proper advice and I am very disappointed that you would consider my performance of duty such that I had to be relieved."

Anderson became ambassador to Portugal and was sworn in September 13, 1963.

Before Anderson reported to his new job he addressed the National Press Club in Washington. "I question neither the motivation, patriotism, dedication or ability of anyone." He said he did question the system imposed upon the Department of Defense by McNamara. "Over-centralized strictures are conducive to the abuse of power and compounding of mistakes. Monolithic structured organizations can kill imagination, stultify initiative, completely eliminate the effectiveness of those in the officer corps who have gained wisdom and experience."

He said he was disturbed that now "in the Department of Defense the operations analyst, properly concerned with cost effectiveness, seems to be working in the wrong echelon, above the professional military level rather than in an advisory capacity to the military who should thoroughly appreciate his assistance. Unfortunately, an unhealthy imbalance has resulted because at times specialists are used as experts in areas outside their fields. This has resulted in a tendency to draw conclusions before all the evidence has been examined."

Anderson assailed the modern fallacy that theories, or computers, or economics, or numbers of weapons win wars. "Alone they do not," he said. "Man, his wits and his will are still the key to war and peace, victory and defeat. Morale is the business of every leader in our defense establishment. Do all else right, and do this wrong—the product, in a crisis, is disaster."

It was not realized at the time but Admiral Anderson's indictment of McNamara's philosophy of running the military establishment should have been a warning that unless his policies were drastically changed the United States faced certain defeat in Southeast Asia.

Pacific Air Force Commander General Smart radioed Air Force Chief of Staff LeMay September 8, "My own feeling is that if we intend to remain committed to Vietnam—and I believe that it is strongly in the national interest we do so—then we must support Diem. Whether we like him or his family is not germane. My conclusion is that we must stick with him and that we must quickly demonstrate this by positive action even though we may have to pay some price in terms of embarrassment. We are probably going to have to swallow the fact that Diem will not exile his brother. . . . and from my discussions I am not at all convinced that this should be our objective. I get distinct impressions from Vietnamese that he is valuable and important to Diem, just as Diem is important to the nation."

In a secret "eyes only" telegram to Secretary of State Rusk dated September 20, Ambassador Lodge summarized the statements made by General "Big" Minh to an American officer two days earlier when Minh's evaluation of the Vietcong situation was sought.*

Minh said he thought the Vietcong were gaining steadily in strength and that 80 percent of the population "now have no basis for choice *between GVN and VC.*" He said Diem's lifting of martial law was simply eyewash for the Americans but that the situation remains the same and that arrests are continuing. Minh told the officer (not identified in the telegram) that the two guardhouses outside his headquarters were full of prisoners.*

The Vietnamese general said the student problem was by no means resolved and that it was, in fact, very grave. He said he knew that students were going over to the Vietcong but he cited no numbers or facts to support his allegation.*

In discussing the middle ranks of the South Vietnamese Army, Minh said they were badly disaffected and were asking for a coup. According to Minh, officers were not fighting aggressively because they did not have their heart in it. With the proper government, he said, they would fight "four times harder."*

Minh said he felt sure that Nhu was in charge of the South Vietnamese government. He said when he took military problems to Diem, he was either referred to Nhu or Diem called Nhu in.*

Minh told the American officer that he believed every district and province chief was a Can Lao Party member, and he charged that these officials were demanding and receiving kickbacks from the rural population who were receiving United States aid. He claimed the proceeds were going into the party's coffers. According to Minh, Archbishop Thuc was "attending to everything but church business."*

Lodge said that Minh gave the impression of having thought very carefully about the possibilities of a coup, although he gave no indication whether he was actively planning one. Speaking in hypothetical terms, Minh said that a "coup would have to be carried out suddenly, and with complete success, so as to leave no opportunity for Vietcong exploitation and to avoid the risk of civil war."*

The American officer asked Minh whether his visit was an embarrassment, but Minh replied in the negative. He said he had been told, like everyone else, to stay away from Americans but that the order was not in writing and he made it clear that he would not sacrifice his old friendships. He said the officer would be welcome to see him at any time.*

Minh's comments had a few grains of truth but most of his comments were so self-serving that they should not have been taken seriously in Washington, although apparently they were.

Unlike former Ambassador Nolting, who had used all Americans to secure policy consensus, Lodge was ordered by Kennedy to closely guard the cables they exchanged. Even the head of the Military Assistance Command—General Harkins—was kept in the dark about some of their communications. General Smart confided in LeMay that the United States Military Assistance Command in reality "was a one-man operation, conducted in total secrecy," by Ambassador Lodge. "The American team left me with the impression of a divided house," he said, "and divergent directions."

Lodge's recommendation that the threat of American aid suspension be used to pressure President Diem was opposed by McNamara and Rusk who believed such action would threaten the war effort. In an attempt to resolve conflicting recommendations, President Kennedy decided to send McNamara and Joint Chiefs Chairman General Maxwell Taylor to Saigon September 21 to gather information and to encourage Diem to solve his problems.

After a Diem visit, McNamara and Rusk told Lodge that they believed that Diem was consolidating his control throughout the country and that the military effort was gaining momentum. McNamara had stressed to President Diem that there should be more action against the Vietcong, and he cautioned him that he should change his policies to build a better case with the American people. They told Lodge that the war could be ended favorably in 1965, and that they would recommend a recall of a thousand advisers by the end of the year.

After their briefing of President Kennedy in Washington, the American president said the United States would continue working with the Vietnamese people to resolve their conflicts.

Meanwhile, Vietnamese-language broadcasts of the Voice of America continued to express American opposition to repressive actions by the Diem regime.

American newsmen were assaulted October 3 by Vietnamese plainclothesmen, and Ambassador Lodge filed a stern protest. Next day, another Buddhist monk burned himself—the sixth and most publicized.

Mr. Nhu told the press on October 17 that he failed to understand why the United States had "initiated the process of disintegration in Vietnam." President Diem's personal counselor accused the Central Intelligence Agency of inciting a coup.

Five days later, the United States government announced it was ending support of Vietnamese forces unless they were shifted from police duties to field operations or related training programs.

The CIA office in Saigon sent a telegram October 24 to Rusk citing intelligence information that a coup against Diem was imminent. The target was supposed to be the Gia Long Palace. The report said that in the event the initial assault failed troops would withdraw from the palace. Then, the classified report said the Vietnamese Air Force, led by Lt. Col. Nguyen Cao Ky, would bomb the palace and a renewed troop assault would be launched.*

The telegram makes it clear that CIA station officials in Saigon believed that plans for the coup were insufficient to achieve success, but cautioned that this action might trigger other units to take part.*

While these actions and counter-actions were underway, the plot against President Diem and his brother was in fact brewing under the leadership of Generals Duong Van Minh, Tran Van Don and Le Van Kim. They represented a coalition of older officers who wanted a neutralist solution to the war and young men who sought a military victory and believed they could secure it once they were in charge. Commanders of the first three corps areas were united in their opposition to President Diem but the IV Corps commander, who was also military governor of Saigon, remained loyal to Diem while the three other commanders plotted to remove him.

Although American military officials were careful to avoid taking any part in the coup, most were aware of the conspiracy to overthrow the Diem government. In the event that an evacuation of Americans might be necessary, the American Joint Chiefs October 28 directed the Commander-in-Chief, Pacific, to position a naval force off Vietnam. Three United States Air Force jet interceptors flew to Tan Son Nhut that same day. General Harkins was concerned when these moves were revealed because until now he had no idea that President Diem's overthrow was imminent.

Meanwhile, White House messages to Ambassador Lodge continued to stress "surveillance and readiness" but not active promotion of a coup. They stressed the need for plausibility if it became necessary to deny United States involvement.

Just when the coup seemed about to take place, it was canceled. General Harkins, head of the Military Assistance Command, had announced privately that he was strongly opposed.

Ambassador Lodge disagreed, opposing any move to "pour cold water" on the plot of the Vietnamese generals.

President Kennedy, in messages from the White House to Ambassador Lodge, told him that he should "discourage" the plot if quick success seemed unlikely.

Lodge replied that the United States was unable to "delay or discourage a coup."

At 1:30 P.M. November 1 the Vietnamese generals sent troops loyal to them to seize police headquarters, the radio stations, the airport and other installations while attacks against the Presidential Palace and the Special Forces barracks were set in motion. Loyal officers promptly alerted Mr. Nhu but he did not at first take their reports seriously. It was a typical, sunny siesta hour in Saigon when sporadic firing was heard in various parts of the city. Fighter-bombers appeared over the city amidst bursts of anti-aircraft fire. Radio stations went dead at 2:15 P.M. They were back on the air at 4:50 and the voice of Maj. Gen. Duong Van Minh was heard warning Diem and Nhu that they had five minutes to turn over the government or a massive air attack would be directed against the palace. It was also revealed that Special Forces commander Le Quang Tung had declared himself a prisoner, and that Vietnamese Marines were blocking routes out of Saigon toward Cholon. It was also announced that Special Forces soldiers were guarding the southern edge of Tan Son Nhut that was now in the hands of the dissidents. Saigon residents cowered in doorways, all civilian vehicular traffic ceased and their occupants lay down in the streets during periods of intense fire.*

Radio stations at five-minute intervals broadcast, "Countrymen, from this moment the Army has risen to lead the people. During the past nine years we have lived under a cruel dictatorship and lost all freedoms. The Army has decided to do away with the Diem regime. The Army appeals to all classes of people to cooperate and maintain order so that the fight against the Vietcong can continue." The appeal was made on behalf of the military committee's chairman Duong Van Minh.*

Then, at half-hour intervals, another message was broadcast. "Fellow soldiers, during the past nine years we have sacrificed. Who knows how many have been lost? Diem used the cadres for the benefit of a small clique and has lost the faith of the people. Through oppressive actions the people have turned against the family dictatorship. The Army was used in cruel acts against the people. Who knows how many students and people have been arrested? We felt bitter over being used against the people. We established a revolution to save the people. The leaders appeal to our fellow soldiers to continue the fight against the Vietcong. We will be victorious! From this date you will be better and more effectively commanded."*

This broadcast was followed by voices who identified themselves as supporters of the coup including major generals Tran Don, Duong Van Minh, Nguyen Ngoc and Tran Van Minh. The list included the names of ten brigadier generals and ten colonels and lieutenant colonels.*

Secretary of State Rusk wired Lodge at 10:50 A.M. Washington time: "1. If coup succeeds, recognition problem will be urgent. Of course, you would expect to deal in friendly and cooperative fashion with effective authorities from the outset but timing of our announcement of formal recognition might be delayed for brief period. Since coup is wholly Vietnamese, generals should understand that flash recognition by the United States in advance of other governments would falsely brand their action as American-inspired and manipulated. Since generals plan to establish a government within two or three days, formal recognition might better await that action."*

In regards to Tri Quang, the Buddhist critic, Rusk advised that he was free to come and go as he pleased but he said he was uneasy about his political orientation and as to the effects of his strong anti-Catholic views on the political stance of the new government. The Secretary of State advised that he was inclined to believe that it was the intention of the generals to designate Tri Quang as Buddhist adviser to the new government. Such an action, he said, made better sense than his inclusion in the cabinet as a minister with a significant portfolio. "Giving him specific responsibilities limited to Buddhists has two advantages in our view," Rusk said. "(a) It reassures Buddhists; and (b) it does not frighten Catholics or other groups which would be concerned by prospect over-zealous Buddhist reaction to Diem-Nhu repression. At same time, advisory position for Tri Quang with new government would avail generals Tri Quang's considerable talents without prejudicing non-denominational stance new government.*

"5. Regarding reftel, we assume generals leading coup will not call on you in large group, thus giving false impression they were reporting to headquarters. A certain formality and correctness is greatly in their interest in preserving Vietnamese character their action.*

"6. Assuming your departure Washington temporarily postponed."*

General Harkins contacted General Taylor and Admiral Felt to report that instead of getting four hours' or two days' notice, he got approximately four minutes. Harkins said he had just returned from Tan Son Nhut where, in the company of General Don and others, they had said goodbye to Admiral Felt, had lunch, and returned to his office. At 1:45 P.M., a telephone call was received at his office from Don saying that he had "decided to move and was notifying General Harkins and his American friends." Lt. Gen. Richard G. Stilwell, who took the call, asked him when they were going to move and Don said "immediately." At this time firing was reported in the vicinity of Tan Son Nhut. Don told Stilwell that Big Minh had told Ambassador Lodge that he and Don were trying to get in touch with President Diem to ask him to resign and that they had promised him and Mr. Nhu safe conduct out of the country if they would resign.

Within three hours all resistance in Saigon was crushed, except at the palace. The generals now demanded the resignation of the Ngo brothers. In reply, Diem invited the generals to visit him at the palace but they refused.

President Diem telephoned Ambassador Lodge to ask where the United States stood. "Some units have made a rebellion," he said, "and I want to know what is the attitude of the United States."

Lodge was aware of the United States attitude, having been personally briefed by President Kennedy. Therefore he was not truthful when he replied, "I do not feel enough informed to be able to tell you. I have heard this shooting, but I am not acquainted with all the facts. Also, it is 4:30 A.M. in Washington and the United States government cannot possibly have a view."

Diem persisted. "But you have general ideas. After all, I am a chief of state. I have tried to do my duty. I want to do now what duty and good sense require. I believe in duty above all."

"You have certainly done your duty," Lodge said. "As I told you only this morning, I admire your courage and your great contributions to your country. No one can take away from you the credit for all you have done. Now I am worried about your physical safety. I have a report that those in charge of the current activity offer you and your brother safe conduct out of the country if you resign. Have you heard this?"

"No," Diem replied. He paused, "You have my telephone number?"

"Yes. If I can do anything for your physical safety, please call me."

"I am trying to re-establish order," Diem said.

When the president of South Vietnam hung up he and his brother escaped through a secret tunnel while the fighting for the palace continued outside. They hid in the Chinese section of the capital until shortly after dawn the following day.

Throughout the night Diem had kept in touch with the dissident generals, but refused to reveal his hiding place. The generals urged him to surrender, offering guarantees of safe conduct to the airport so he could leave South Vietnam.

Diem telephoned General Duong Van Minh at 6:00 A.M. saying that he would resign but he refused to disclose his whereabouts. He made his recognition conditional that authority be transferred to the vice president or speaker of the legislature in accordance with the constitution. Minh rejected this approach.

A half hour later Diem called back. The leader of the dissident generals, General Don, suggested that Diem and his brother leave the country.

Diem replied, "I am the elected president of the nation. I am ready to resign publicly, and I am also ready to leave the country. But I ask you to reserve for me the honors due a departing president."

General Don hesitated. Then he said, "Really, I must say that we cannot satisfy you on that point."

"It's all right," Diem said. "Thank you."

Diem hung up. He called back a few minutes later saying that he would surrender unconditionally. He disclosed that he and Nhu were at Saint Francis Xavier, a French church in Cholon.

Diem and his brother were picked up by armored units and they were murdered in the car carrying them to the Joint General Staff's headquarters although General Don had guaranteed their security. The assignment to pick up the two men had been given to General Mai Huu Xuan, a former French secret police agent who had served Diem in a similar capacity. He detested Diem after the president had shunted him into a position that he considered beneath him.

President Kennedy was meeting with Maxwell Taylor and aides when word of Diem's death was transmitted to Washington. Kennedy leaped to his feet and rushed from the room with a look on his face of shock and dismay.

When Conein sought details of the murders from Minh the general claimed that the president and his brother had committed suicide.

"Where?" Conein demanded.

"Well, he was at a Catholic church, and . . ."

"Listen, this is your affair, but I'll tell you something as a Catholic. If a priest holds mass for him tonight, everybody is going to know that he didn't commit suicide. Therefore, your story doesn't sound right."

"Would you like to see him? We have him here."

"No," Conein replied hastily. "There's a one-in-a-million chance that people will believe your story. But if the truth gets out, I don't want to be blamed for leaking it."

CHAPTER 8

End of a Troubled Era

GENERAL HARKINS WIRED THE STATE DEPARTMENT NOVEMBER 2, 1963, "We are no longer a republic as you now know. . . . My summary evaluation, DTG 012200Z, reflected the remarkable cohesion of the RVNAF, once the coup started. Let's hope it will continue. . . . I shall push the generals hard to make good their stated intention to relinguish, as soon as possible, the ministerial posts they have assumed. The non-appearance of Big Minh in the cabinet was, of course, expected.*

"The big job now, and the entire interest of my people and me, is to get the new team focused on the VC immediately. We buckle down to this at once."*

Rusk sent a telegram to Lodge the following day with an information copy to CINCPAC suggesting that he see Maj. Gen. Duong Van Minh to discuss the manner of Diem's and Nhu's deaths. (The press had reported that both had been shot and stabbed with "gory" details.) Rusk stressed that press headlines had caused considerable shock in Washington. He said that when pictures of the bodies reached the United States that the reaction would be even worse. He advised an urgent and prompt clarifying statement with a full accounting of the plans that had been arranged for Diem's and Nhu's safe removal from the palace prior to their deaths. He said, "We do not think there should be any suggestion that this is just the sort of thing you have to expect in a coup. On the contrary, the generals should emphasize the extensive efforts we understand they made to prevent this result."*

Rusk said Madame Nhu had issued a long, bitter statement in effect holding the United States responsible for the coup, using such phrases as

---

*This material, as well as that marked elsewhere in Chapters 7 and 8, was released to the author under the Freedom of Information Act.

"cruel treachery," "treason," and "dirty crime." He said a statement and reaction to the Diem/Nhu deaths should accentuate the importance of assuring safety of the Nhu children. "We trust intentions expressed to you by Don re children and other members Ngo family will be carried out. Prompt and chivalrous treatment of children will be particularly helpful here in context of death of father." The wire closed with Rusk's concern about the arrests of people not guilty of any crimes plus the other developments. He suggested that Lodge point out to the generals that their activities "at minimum give appearance military not in full control of situation and unless promptly corrected will produce strong adverse international reaction contrary to regime's desire attract international sympathy."*

Rusk advised Lodge further that adverse American and world public opinion was sufficiently serious that points should be clarified before public announcement of full resumption of aid. "It is not rept not our intention to use delay in resuming aid as summary leverage on generals, but you should emphasize importance of immediate action to ensure as favorable international image as possible. Public here would not understand resumption of aid before clarification these points."*

Lodge wired Rusk November 3 that he had met with General Don and General Kim at 3 o'clock. "After my congratulations on their masterful performance and my offer of assistance they asked me if I had any questions.*

"1. I asked whether they were planning a statement which would absolve themselves from the assassination of Diem and Nhu. They had not thought of making statement, but obviously agreed that they should make it clear that they had offered Diem safe passage out of the country if he would resign; that they deeply deplored the assassination, that the assassination had not only not been in any way ordered by them but was contrary to their wishes and was, unfortunately, the kind of thing which will happen in a coup d'etat when order cannot be guaranteed everywhere. I am sure assassination was not at their direction. For your information, I believe this is the most that you can expect of them and that when they make a statement like this it ought to be welcome in Washington. Burial and funeral of Deim and Nhu would be family matters. Bodies would be in vault of cemetery and would be taken to family vault in Hué later.*

"2. I asked whether they had any ideas in mind concerning the relations between the United States and the government of Vietnam. Don said that for psychological reasons they planned to lift immediately restrictions on sale of milk in cafes, etc., which were recently instituted by Diem regime."*

Lodge said he queried generals about what kind of government they planned to establish and that General Kim, who did most of the talking, said they would form a government in which military had only a slight interest with a military committee presided over by General Minh with a prime minister and a ministerial cabinet of fifteen of whom four or five would be military. Mr. Tho would be prime minister. Title of president would be reserved for General Minh. Kim said the provisional government would last six months.*

Lodge said he then asked if the generals were going to stay united and win the war. He said this question moved them. They told him that they had been divided a long time and they knew from bitter experience what it cost to be divided. He said Kim told him that with Minh as their leader, they would do everything possible to be united. "The Army needs a much more aggressive morale than it has. Even Nhu had said the Army did not have as much drive as it should have, and he was responsible for many of the troubles."*

Don told Lodge that he was vice president of the committee and that Khiem was second vice president. Lodge was informed that safe passage into exile of the Nhu family had been promised and that there would be humane treatment for those arrested, including Tri Quang. (Tri Quang was later released from custody.) The generals promised Lodge that there would be no wholesale purges or reprisals.*

Lodge concluded his wire to Rusk by saying, "They were extremely frank and forthcoming in all their answers and we did more business in fifteen minutes than we used to be able to do at the palace in four hours. They expressed warm thanks to me for not thwarting, for not giving up Tri Quang, for my general attitude; and it was clear throughout that the withholding of commercial imports had a tremendous psychological effect. They said their coup was organized without a single piece of paper having been kept. All papers were burned; everything was memorized."*

Rusk forwarded the message to President Kennedy at the White House.*

General Harkins wired a message to the State Department and to General Taylor, chairman of the Joint Chiefs, November 5 with copies to Admiral Felt at CINCPAC and the United States embassy in Saigon. He said that "Gen Don called on me this morning. This is the first time I've seen him since Admiral Felt's departure last Friday. We discussed the recent past and future plans. I said I had heard so many conflicting stories on the coup and the demise of Diem and Nhu I would like to get his version.*

"He said as far as he could tell, Diem and Nhu left the palace Friday evening about 2200. They went in some Chinese civilian's car to a house in Cholon. Though the generals had talked to Diem and Nhu during the evening, neither of the brothers let on they were no longer in the palace. JGS intelligence knew the house in Cholon and the two were arrested there, Saturday, A.M.*

"They were placed in an M-113 for security and for delivery to the JGS compound. Upon arrival at the compound it was discovered they were dead. The generals were truly grievous over this because they had promised safe conduct. Don did not explain what happened, whether it was suicide or someone had not got the word. . . .*

"Don went on to say he received a call from Los Angeles from Mrs. Nhu this morning. That the madame went into a tirade, saying they were all fools-murders [sic] and bought by the Americans. That the people would never follow Big Minh or the military. Don disclaimed any connection with the demise of Diem and Nhu—also that he was not bought off. He told the madame if she were here she would see for herself the changed attitude of the people. She asked about her children. Don told her they departed last night, but could not tell her when they would arrive in Rome. Incidentally, they must be there by now as they made good connections with a jet flight out of Bangkok last night.*

"As to the present—they were still making changes in command—also in some province chiefs (I'll report them when firm.) I reminded him many of the province chiefs had done well and suggested not changing them all just for change' sake. . . .*

"All in all, if, I repeat, if things work out, we'll have a more orderly setup and a more streamlined chain of command, fewer para-military organizations under arms and not as much concern with political interference which cause delays and in some cases changed missions and orders.*

"I reminded Don that the courage and determination shown by the coup's battalions in overcoming the presidential brigade of 1,500 men, if displayed in fighting a VC battalion of three to four hundred men, could make short order of the remaining VC in SVN. All this might add up to a much earlier ETA for getting counter-insurgency in SVN under control.*

"I feel sure this will be true if I can get the show on the road."*

The United States resumed relations with the new government November 8, Saigon time, citing its determination to fight communism and honor all agreements with other nations. This was announced after the generals promised freedom of the press, expression and religion and the transfer of political power to a popularly elected government when the situation permitted.

Neither the American government, nor the dissident generals, ever conducted a public hearing into Diem's death because such an inquiry would have disclosed their own culpability.

President Kennedy said later that he had been "reluctant to intervene on behalf of Diem and Nhu for fear of appearing to offer support to them or reneging on our pledges of non-interference to the generals." This was an implausible excuse once the truth emerged long after the event.

Ambassador Lodge reported to President Kennedy November 4 that the change in regime would shorten the war against the Vietcong because of improved morale in South Vietnam. Within weeks his assessment would prove to be tragically wrong.

President Diem had worked hard to regain independence for his country. The shy and reclusive president had wanted to build a free and democratic system, but his regime was rightly criticized for its police-state methods, its discrimination against the Buddhists, his failure to include members of prominent nationalist parties and his tolerance of corruption. He was well known for his devotion to Catholicism and he had close ties with priests and enjoyed their support. Many people believed the Christians were too much a part of his administration, particularly because 80 percent of the people were Buddhists, and that they wielded excessive influence. This was true but, despite Diem's faults, he was the best president South Vietnam ever had. He had initiated land reform and he had put fallow land to work—over three million acres—that had been left uncultivated during the war with France. As a result, under Diem South Vietnam became a rice exporter. He never understood that a United States president could not do what he could do in South Vietnam. He ignored the fact that the American Congress limited the powers of its presidents.

Political in-fighting in South Vietnam served to aid the communists. Many of those opposed to Diem, constantly demanding more democratic rights, did not understand that some of these rights did not exist in democratic societies even in times of peace.

South Vietnam's society was composed of two vastly different groups—those who lived in the cities in relative affluence—and those who tried to make a precarious living on farms. The latter were in the majority: hardworking, basically submissive people who distrusted those in the cities and in the central government.

Diem had instituted a limited democracy, giving himself vast executive powers. As a result, the National Assembly assumed a symbolic role of democracy's watchdog, while the judicial branch felt it had an obligation to serve the people. Diem envisioned a democratic state, but one whose progress required time and patience under his strong leadership.

Diem was more successful with the people in rural areas and inspired their respect. He was not as successful in the cities. Urbanites regarded his methods of resolving national security as despotic, and some of his principal associates committed grave errors.

The First Republic was criticized for three main reasons: family rule or nepotism, a monolithic party rule, and discrimination on regional and religious grounds. His reliance on family members for counsel led to discontent.

Catholic and Buddhist groups were the only organizations capable of rallying the masses of people. Both were handicapped by their own excesses. In contrast, no political party had a significant popular following.

Most of Diem's critics did not understand that a democracy is a complex form of government that is difficult to operate effectively and requires knowledge, maturity and goodwill on the part of the common people, as well as the politicans, to make it work.

The growing American involvement in almost every aspect of South Vietnam's life gave the impression of a "big brother" who would somehow solve the nation's problems. After Diem's death no leader appeared who could shed this image. Therefore, no government was ever considered truly independent.

At times Diem's rule was despotic but his control of a single-party system created a strong national authority. This had a beneficial effect on a nation trying to survive in a war environment. Although Diem's strong mindedness sometimes verged on vanity and intransigence—and was resented by President Kennedy and many others in the United States government—the majority of South Vietnam's people admired Diem's strong leadership.

With his death, South Vietnam's political scene was splintered into small power groups with too many parties seeking supremacy and destroying one another in the process. To this power struggle were added the discords and rivalry of South Vietnam's leading groups. As a result, government authority was destroyed and there soon was no national unity or purpose.

One of the most maligned members of Diem's inner circle was Madame Nhu, his brother's wife, who was elevated to the position of First Lady because Diem was a bachelor. Always controversial, she was an intelligent, quick-minded and progressive woman who fought to get legislation enacted to change age-old habits and thereby improve the status of Vietnamese women. While she promoted women's rights, many of her successors participated in business and bought and sold influence to enrich themselves and their spouses. There is no doubt she carried her excessive zeal too far. Her imperiousness showed as she verbally dominated and abused her colleagues in the National Assembly as she tried to push through legislation to change age-old habits and to improve the lot of Veitnamese women.

Although Diem's government maintained a high degree of stability, it

had failed to achieve national unity. However, none of the nine governments that followed enjoyed the popularity necessary to assure the nation's
survival. After the demise of Diem's First Republic, South Vietnam had
sixty-two political groups vying for power. Although operating under a
single name, many of these parties were split into irreconcilable splinter
groups. As the war escalated, the cities sank deeper into decadence. Urban
society gradually decomposed with its worship of money and influence and
its tolerance of injustice and corruption. Worst of all, the nation's youth
turned to drugs and prostitution as an easy way to achieve wealth.

In dividing the spoils of power following Diem's death, the ruling
Duong Van Minh group that had overthrown him created enemies of its
own. Meanwhile, another clique controlled by General Nguyen Khanh
soon was conspiring to overthrow the new leader. To add to the problem,
Buddhist clerics became arrogant power brokers while university student
groups and Dai Viet activists pressed their demands on the government.

Along with the Khanh group, young turks like Nguyen Chang Thi,
Nguyen Cao Ky and Nguyen Huu Co made their debut on the political
scene. The Catholics turned defensive, refusing to take part in the government and the Cao Dai and Hoa Hao sects were content with their small
power niches while returned political exiles emerged to vie for power.

President Kennedy announced November 14 that Secretary of State
Rusk and Secretary of Defense McNamara would go to Honolulu for a
meeting on the 20th. He said they would review the situation in South
Vietnam and determine how to intensify the Vietnamese war and to
determine ways to end the American involvement. "Now," he said, "this is
our objective, to bring the Americans home, permit the South Vietnamese
to maintain themselves as a free and independent country, and permit
democratic forces within the country to operate."

McNamara told the group at Honolulu that "a certain euphoria had set
in since the coup, but actually the generals headed a fragile government."
Rusk posed a question of increased financial aid. Lodge replied that he
thought the Vietnamese had enough dollars and that what they needed
was "greater motivation." McNamara argued for more funds. He was
resolved to adhere to present plans for increasing the effectiveness of
Vietnamese military power, and thus be able to reduce American personnel in Vietnam. He urged that the withdrawal of one thousand American
military advisers be carried out as planned in December.

The day before, Prince Norodom Sihanouk had convened a special
national congress in Cambodia. At its conclusion, he renounced United
States aid, apparently in an attempt to avoid American interference in the
Khmer nation's domestic affairs. Two days later, Sihanouk tried without

success to initiate a limited international conference, with the participation of the United States, South Vietnam and other countries involved in Cambodia's security to grant his nation sovereignty within its current borders. Sihanouk was disturbed by United States duplicity, and the uncertainty of South Vietnam's future following President Diem's assassination. He was Cambodia's dominant personality, first as its reigning king in 1941, and then as chief of state where he held nearly absolute power in a tiny kingdom that shared over half its boundaries with South Vietnam.

Sihanouk had faced two great problems since World War II. First was the political struggle with France for complete independence while he was king of Cambodia. He had the almost total support of the Cambodian people during this period. His second problem was the danger inherent in the expansion of Vietminh forces who carried out guerrilla warfare in Cambodia against the French. Under the pretext of providing military assistance for Cambodian independence, Vietminh forces established themselves more and more deeply. The communists tried to facilitate their takeover of particular areas in the interior of Cambodia prior to the Paris Peace Accords in 1954. The warring parties were a confusing combination of French-Cambodian or purely Cambodian forces, the Vietminh and the Khmer Issarak or Free Khmer forces that were both anti-Sihanouk and anti-Vietminh. Most Cambodians survived this period convinced that nationhood must be achieved to prevent the expansionist tendencies of their neighbors.

At first, the Geneva accords presaged a durable peace guaranteed by such major powers as Great Britain, the Soviet Union and the People's Republic of China. The United States, which had refused to sign the accords, was temporarily left out of consideration as a protector.

The evacuation by the French of 3,000 Cambodians affiliated with the Vietminh later led to the start of the Khmer Communist Party. Once Cambodia was awarded independence by France a pro-communist bloc of North Vietnamese and Pathet Lao emerged in opposition to the pro–free world bloc of Cambodians, South Vietnamese and Laotians.

With this difficult situation the Cambodian government had tried to remain neutral, and attempted to keep its distance from South Vietnam and Laos who were allied with the United States.

The People's Republic of China, acting as discreetly as possible, equipped and trained North Vietnamese and the Pathet Lao and urged them to wage a struggle without mercy against their countrymen. Acts of armed rebellion soon became more and more serious and widespread.

Cambodian government officials tried to keep on good terms with South Vietnam, although opposition developed against Sihanouk as chief of state. One group accused him of being pro—free world while others criticized him for his dictatorial methods. While the Cambodian communist movement expanded, the Khmer Serei or Free Khmer, was created under Son Ngoc Thanh in the 1960s and was supported by the American Central Intelligence Agency. Cambodia faced two immediate dangers. The first was from the Khmer Serei movement and the expansion of North Vietnamese communism from the north, while the outlawed Khmer Communist Party—those opposed to Sihanouk and those who considered themselves persecuted by the Sihanouk regime—formed the second threat.

With the coup against South Vietnam's President Diem, Sihanouk was faced with a political decision of choosing between two alternatives—the communist or the free world. Neither alternative seemed to hold much assurance for the continuation of his regime, and for Cambodia's future as an independent nation.

In early 1963, Sihanouk had warned the Chinese during a visit to Peking of the growing danger of United States aid and the presence of the CIA-supported Khmer Serei troops. The communist Chinese expressed their concern about the increasing American presence in Cambodia.

Sihanouk cut off his country from United States aid primarily because he believed that Cambodia's interests would not be served by dealing with the West because it represented the present, but not the future of Asia. He believed that in ten years Thailand, which to him always had responded to the dominant wind, would have a pro-Chinese neutralist government and that South Vietnam would be taken over by Ho Chi Minh's northern armies. His decision to break with the United States was made because Cambodia's best interests would be served by dealing with the nation that he believed would soon dominate the whole of Asia. By coming to terms with the Chinese communists he hoped that Cambodia would get the best terms.

Privately, Sihanouk was convinced that the communists were his real enemies. But his persistent derogatory comments about the United States aggravated American officials, and promoted Secretary of State Rusk to tell the Cambodian ambassador in his office, "Mr. Ambassador, you've got to remember that small countries are not the only ones capable of outrage. Big countries can get mad, too."

President Kennedy spoke to a breakfast meeting of the Fort Worth Chamber of Commerce November 22 while on a political trip to Texas. In his last major speech he recalled the nation's pledges and alliances. "So this country [Vietnam], which desires only to be free, which desired to live at peace for eighteen years under three different administrations, has borne more than its share of the burden, has stood watch for more than its number of years. I don't think we are fatigued or tired. We would like to live as we once lived. But history will not permit it. The communist balance of power is still strong. The balance of power is still on the side of freedom. We are still the keystone of the arch of freedom, and I think we will continue to do as we have done in our past, our duty. . . ."

Later that day, during a motorcade through the streets of Dallas, President Kennedy was assassinated by a professed communist and former United States Marine—Lee Harvey Oswald.

Lyndon B. Johnson was sworn in as president on the plane returning him to a grieving capital.

It has been popular among some groups since then to speculate that if John F. Kennedy had not been assassinated that he would have withdrawn American support from the South Vietnamese government, an effort that he had intensified during the early years of his administration by sending more than sixteen thousand so-called advisers to South Vietnam, including helicopter pilots who flew combat missions. His last public words belie such talk.

Supposedly, as early as the spring of 1963, President Kennedy had decided to get out of Vietnam after the 1964 election. He is reported to have said privately to Senator Mike Mansfield, "In 1965 I'll be damned everywhere as communist appeaser, but I don't care. If I tried to pull out now we'd have another Joe McCarthy red scare on our hands, but I can do it after I am re-elected. So we had better make damned sure I am re-elected." At a time when most of his advisers were counseling just the opposite course, such a statement is almost unbelievable. There is no documentary evidence that President Kennedy had any such intention. In fact, his defenders do his memory an injustice by implying that he would have maintained United States armed forces in Vietnam solely for his own political expediency to get himself re-elected. These people evidently have no consideration for the hundreds of American servicemen who might have died as a result of such an extension, or the needless sacrifice of the South Vietnamese people and their allies.

Kennedy's actions as president were not those of a man of peace. The Bay of Pigs invasion of Cuba three months after he took office in 1961, in which he authorized the use of 1,400 Cuban refugees under the Central Intelligence Agency in an attempt to overthrow Fidel Castro's communist government, is just one instance. Like the others, this affair ended in failure with most of the Cubans either captured or killed. There were other instances, including the secret war of sabotage and paramilitary raids against Cuba authorized by the Kennedy administration through the CIA and alleged attempts to kill Castro. They all demonstrate a hard-line president in action.

The attempt to create an image of President Kennedy greater in death than he was in life is unfortunate. There are events during his presidency for which he must bear sole responsibility. His tacit approval during the latter part of 1963 that the Vietnamese generals could overthrow President Ngo Dinh Diem is just one case in point. Diem's murder in the coup that took place November 1 is a serious blot on Kennedy's memory despite the fact that he had not anticipated the tragedy of Diem's death, although he certainly should have done so. The abrupt change in South Vietnam's leadership threw South Vietnam into chaos, and led later to some of their major problems.

To view these years in perspective it should be remembered that John F. Kennedy was first of all a consummate politician and he should not be judged, despite the tragedy of his assassination, by some utopian Camelot standard that never existed.

President Kennedy's assassination signaled the end of a troubled era, and Lyndon B. Johnson's ascendancy to the presidency marked the beginning of another era that would end even more disastrously.

PART II

WAR ESCALATION

CHAPTER 9

Political Instability Affects
War Effort

FOUR DAYS AFTER TAKING OFFICE PRESIDENT LYNDON B. JOHNSON
reaffirmed American objectives in Indochina. He reiterated that "this is a
Vietnamese war and the country and the war must in the end be run solely
by the Vietnamese." He renewed Kennedy's pledge to withdraw some
American armed forces, but at the same time he instructed the State
Department to prepare a "white paper" documenting the Democratic
Republic of Vietnam's control of the Vietcong and its continued supply of
their forces in the South through Laos. The president further solicited
plans from the Joint Chiefs of Staff for increased clandestine warfare
against North Vietnam, and for cross-border incursions into Laos to check
infiltration.

With the deaths of President Diem and his brother/counselor Ngo Dinh
Nhu, South Vietnam's political situation rapidly deteriorated. Diem had
been the only South Vietnamese leader with sufficient stature to oppose
Ho Chi Minh, and his death was a disaster for the Republic of Vietnam.
The years of political instability that followed brought South Vietnam to
the brink of collapse, averted only by the United States' later decision to
commit combat troops to fight the ground war. With collapse of Diem's
First Republic went most of the accomplishments of the past nine years in
areas of nation-building and development of the strength to fight the
communists. The strategic hamlet program, core of South Vietnam's
defense effort, suffered almost a death blow when young people deserted
the program out of fear their association with the Diem regime would lead
to reprisals.

Diem's death ushered in a two-and-a-half-year period of political instability as civilian and military governments surfaced and then disap-

peared in rapid succession while religious and political groups jockeyed for power. General Duong Van Minh, who had led the Diem coup, was toppled two months later. Military leaders in the armed forces were affected by the national malaise, and the war against the Vietcong suffered as a result. Meanwhile, political disturbances and power struggles continued to tear apart the fabric of South Vietnam's society. The North Vietnamese took full advantage of the situation and stepped up subversive efforts while they infiltrated regular forces to join in the fight for control of South Vietnam.

Although United States officials were appalled by the brutality of Diem's death, President Johnson recognized the newly formed government in Saigon on November 24 in order to maintain diplomatic relations. But it soon became evident that South Vietnam's faltering economy, adverse military situation and the failure of the strategic hamlet program called for a full reappraisal of United States actions.

Prior to his assassination, President Kennedy had directed that a conference be held starting November 20 at Honolulu to review all aspects of the war in Indochina. The conference included the Secretary of State and the Secretary of Defense with forty-three other participants. Vietnam Ambassador Lodge told the group that the situation in South Vietnam was hopeful, and that the new military government showed promise, but that the United States should maintain plans for an eventual withdrawal.

Following Kennedy's death, President Johnson imposed a freeze on all military actions until new appraisals could be completed. At this Honolulu conference, an accelerated military assistance program had been proposed but Secretary of Defense McNamara cut it back.

President Johnson addressed a joint session of Congress November 27 and solemnly pledged, "We will keep our commitments from South Vietnam to West Berlin."

Privately, Johnson was disturbed when he learned that the Vietnamese leaders who had carried out the coup against Diem were having difficulties organizing their government. Johnson told Ambassador Lodge and cabinet members that he had serious misgivings about the new South Vietnamese government. He said many people were critical of Diem's removal and were shocked by his murder. He made it clear that he believed the American policy of failing to support Diem was a mistake. He also told Lodge there was too much internal dissension in Saigon among the Americans assigned there. As a first step to counter weaknesses in the embassy's staff he assigned new deputies to Lodge. Johnson continued to be upset about the events in Saigon and the role American officials had played in Diem's removal. He told cabinet officials that too much time and energy had been expended in trying to shape other countries in "our own image." He said they expected too much of young and under-developed countries who were trying to establish peace and law and order against well-trained and disciplined guerrillas. He said the United States' main objective should be to help these nations resist those using force against them. Johnson said the Vietnamese, the people of Thailand and other Asian peoples knew far better than we did what sort of countries they wanted to build. He sternly warned cabinet members that they should not be too critical of attempts by officials of these nations to achieve twentieth century democracies quickly. He flatly stated that Diem's death caused more problems than it solved.

The President received a number of suggestions. Senate Democratic Majority Leader Mike Mansfield recommended that South Vietnam be partitioned between the government-controlled area and those areas controlled by the Vietcong. McNamara argued against such a step, pointing out such an action would have an extremely serious effect on the rest of Southeast Asia and on the United States' position in the world.

President Johnson informed Joint Chiefs of Staff Chairman Taylor December 2 that Vietnam was "the most critical military area" for the United States, and he requested that the Joint Chiefs assign their best officers to General Harkins in Saigon. He said he wanted "blue ribbon" men at every level.

The president next sent Secretary of Defense McNamara to Vietnam December 19–20 on a fact-finding trip. When McNamara reported back to the president, Johnson's worst fears were realized. The Secretary of Defense told him that the situation in Vietnam was "fragile" and that General Duong Van Minh's government "was indecisive and drifting." McNamara also said that the military-political team in Saigon lacked leadership and was poorly informed. He blamed them for failing to keep the administration fully informed about the true state of affairs. He said that unless current trends were reversed in the next two or three months the situation at best would lead to neutralization, but more likely to a communist-controlled area. The president was faced with a dilemma of whether to increase the number of American combat personnel or withdraw American assistance. He was concerned that an escalation of the American presence might hinder rather than help the Vietnamese to stand on their own feet.

Meanwhile, Vietcong activity in the countryside increased and the situation throughout South Vietnam rapidly worsened.

So chaotic were conditions in South Vietnam that it would have been sensible on the part of the United States government to adopt either a policy of winning the war, or end completely its participation in the conflict. Every American president since World War II had stressed that the South Vietnamese must establish a viable government to preserve their nation. Too many leaders of the Republic of Vietnam had demonstrated they were more interested in favoritism for their friends and more inclined to participate in internal conflicts for their own aggrandizement than in fighting the Vietcong. It was a no-win position for the United States, but President Johnson made the biggest error of his administration by escalating the American involvement instead of insisting that South Vietnam's armed forces take over responsibility for defending their country.

The plan by the Commander-in-Chief, Pacific (CINCPAC), to use covert actions against North Vietnam with South Vietnamese troops was formally presented to McNamara. The Secretary of Defense doubted its effectiveness, but he approved American high-altitude U-2 photographic reconnaissance flights to obtain more accurate data about enemy infiltration routes into the South.

At McNamara's suggestion, President Johnson, on December 31, assured General Minh of lasting American support, and final approval was given to clandestine U-2 flights over North Vietnam. These flights revealed extensive supply networks in North Vietnam and Laos that were capable of infiltrating large numbers of trucks, men and materiel into South Vietnam.

In Saigon, General Harkins had expressed hope that Vietcong attacks had peaked after the Diem coup, but his optimism was short-lived. Vietcong ambushes not only continued but the South Vietnamese 21st Divison suffered grievous losses in An Xuyen Province.

By the end of 1963 American combat deaths reached their highest level: 409 during the year, compared to 109 in 1962.

In early 1964, the Joint Chiefs recommended that the United States take over the fighting in South Vietnam. Earlier they had directed CINCPAC Admiral Felt to update contingency plans and to propose a strategy for an air campaign against North Vietnam. Felt proposed that North Vietnam's harbors be mined, and that American planes attack shipping and selected lines of communication. Air Force officials agreed, adding that North Vietnam should be bombed to cut off supplies to the Vietcong in the South. They disagreed with Felt's plan to attack lines of communication, saying such attacks would be ineffective because of jungle growth, and the primitive means of transport used by the North Vietnamese. Felt refused to change his plan, citing Department of Defense policy that called for a graduated response to communist provocations. Limited air strikes were approved that would start against targets close to the demilitarized zone and work north, although the most important targets remained off-limits.

The Joint Chiefs agreed that such American intervention was necessary to save South Vietnam but Air Force Chief of Staff General Curtis E. LeMay argued instead for concentrated attacks against targets in the heart of North Vietnam. He said indirect attacks in South Vietnam and Laos would not be decisive. He recommended that a limited number of troops be sent to South Vietnam immediately to secure main airfields and other strategic areas. Then he called for a devastating air offensive against North Vietnam's strategic targets. He said that he would only recommend that a large ground force be sent to Southeast Asia if the air offensive failed to stop the South's infiltration.

Army Chief of Staff General Earle G. Wheeler continued to insist that United States troops were needed to take over the combat role and that an air campaign should be used against lines of communication near South Vietnam's borders, but not against North Vietnam. He emphasized air interdiction of the Ho Chi Minh Trail, and the communist supply network south of Vinh. Most Army officers agreed and they believed that the Air Force would be most useful in close support of Army troops. This was the classic argument that had been going on since World War I. Wheeler's views prevailed when he was supported by Secretary of Defense McNamara.

The Joint Chiefs responded January 22 to President Johnson's earlier request for war recommendations by presenting a ten-point program of "bolder actions to arrest South Vietnam's military/political decline."

LeMay opposed most of these recommendations, saying he had little confidence in the "very limited" actions and studies recommended by the Joint Chiefs. "We are swatting flies," he said, "when we ought to be going after the manure pile." The Air Force chief called for more positive and bolder actions to include bombing targets in North Vietnam. He recommended more interdiction, crop destruction, and attacks on guerrillas in Laos, along with destruction of dams and dikes in North Vietnam to flood their croplands. He said power sources should be disrupted by bombing, military centers should be attacked and that North Vietnam's ports should be mined to cut off outside materiel support. LeMay's own recommendations included the dispatch of more aircraft, including jets, to enlarge air-dropped and air-landed operations, plus the bombing of targets beyond the reach of ground forces. He recommended that barriers to cross-border actions should be relaxed. LeMay said the United States' only hope to keep from getting bogged down in a ground war on the Asian mainland was to use massive air operations against North Vietnam.

President Johnson's displeasure with the military-political team in Saigon was somewhat alleviated when General William C. Westmoreland, former commander of XVIII Airborne Corps, was appointed the Military

Assistance Command's first deputy, and this command and the former Military Assistance Advisory Group were later united May 15. Four days later, Major General Joseph H. Moore, one of Westmoreland's closest friends, also replaced General Anthis as 2nd Air Division commander.

The political situation in South Vietnam continued to deteriorate in early January, 1964, when the provisional government of General Minh was brought down by Major General Nguyen Khanh. The Minh government had floundered from the time it took office, and it was removed without popular protest. Politicians loyal to President Diem had high hopes that Khanh, once known as Diem's adopted son, would vindicate him. A three-man military junta was now appointed to run the government. It consisted of Major General Duong Van "Big" Minh, Major General Tran Van Don and Major General Le Van Kim. Twenty-three days later Khanh assumed the junta's leadership as chairman of the Revolutionary Military Council while Minh remained as nominal chief of state.

Unfortunately for South Vietnam, Khanh had his own ambitions and he proved to be highly opportunistic. In August, he proclaimed a new charter known as the Vung Tau Charter that was intended to replace the constitution of Diem's First Republic. Under it, the chief of state would enjoy broad powers similar to those of France's government under Charles de Gaulle. University students protested, fearing this action would pave the way to military dictatorship. Khanh reversed himself and personally tore up the charter, shouting in unison with the students, "Down with the Vung Tau Charter!" He was a brave airborne officer but he lacked the strength of his convictions.

The Army of the Republic of Vietnam now had 192,000 men in nine divisions, an airborne brigade and four Ranger battalions with a separate Marine brigade. There were also 181,000 men in militia organizations. The South Vietnamese Air Force had 190 aircraft, mostly armed T-28 training planes, while the United States provided an additional 140 planes—fighter bombers—and 248 helicopters. The South Vietnamese Navy had only a few landing craft and some patrol boats and minesweepers.

While a decision awaited in Washington as to the proper course for the United States to pursue, the debate over strategy reached a new high. Walt W. Rostow, chairman of the State Department's Policy Planning Council, stated that he believed North Vietnam was vulnerable to bombing. He said the North Vietnamese no longer were fighting a guerrilla war with nothing to lose. Now, he said, they had an industrial complex to protect. W. Averill Harriman and Roger Hilsman, Harriman's successor as assistant secretary of state for Far Eastern affairs, disagreed and they opposed escalated bombing measures against North Vietnam. They said that the Laotian infiltration routes appeared to be little used. Even a casual appraisal of intelligence reports would have demonstrated how wrong they were.

A policy of gradual response to communist aggression was established in March in a series of Pentagon papers. In a memorandum March 2, 1964, to McNamara from the chairman of the Joint Chiefs, two methods of terminating the conflict in Southeast Asia were offered in the hope that war with the People's Republic of China could be avoided. First it was recommended that small-scale, cross-the-border operations by South Vietnamese forces be used against the Ho Chi Minh Trail. Second, the Joint Chiefs recommended attacks against North Vietnam, especially with strong airpower. The memoranda stated that sudden or heavy air attacks against North Vietnam would demonstrate United States determination to halt their aggression in the South. The memoranda also called for gradual attacks, at first by the South Vietnamese Air Force, on a constantly accelerating severity basis.

Instead, McNamara in mid-March recommended to President Johnson a gradual campaign of covert and naval military pressure against North Vietnam. The president approved the approach March 17, but he insisted upon prior approval by allies of the United States.

Pressure in small doses is always a mistake and, in the end, is more expensive in lives, weapons and national resources because the conflict is protracted. The traditional system of choosing a political goal, adopting a strategy and then granting the armed forces responsibility to attain that goal would have been far preferable than the method selected by the Johnson administration.

While a major decision awaited final approval in Washington, General Khanh on March 6 fired three corps commanders and five of nine division commanders. Next, he ordered the wholesale removal of twenty-three province chiefs. Such indiscriminate action completely disrupted South Vietnam's leadership and shook the confidence of the people in their armed forces. Military desertions soared and Vietcong prestige reached a new high as North Vietnam increased its support to its followers in the South.

Such actions dominated discussions at a conference with the Secretary of Defense at CINCPAC headquarters in Honolulu. The general consensus was that the military situation was discouraging.

Eleven days later a National Security Council memorandum stated that unless an independent non-communist South Vietnam could be maintained that almost all of southeast Asia probably would fall to the communists. Staffers who prepared it admitted that United States programs were limited to prevent such an occurrence.

Uncertainty in Indochina reached a new high when Cambodia's Prince Sihanouk authorized a demonstration during the month against the United States' and Great Britain's embassies in Phnom Penh. Both were severely damaged.

The weaknesses of the South Vietnamese government became more apparent as corps commanders stored up more power against the decentralized military command. Adding to the confusion was the increasing rancor between ground commanders and province chiefs.

President Johnson sent McNamara and Chairman Taylor of the Joint Chiefs to Vietnam for an assessment of the situation. They realized quickly that the military situation had worsened far more than they had realized. Nearly 40 percent of the countryside was under Vietcong control, including the critical provinces around Saigon. They learned that in eight out of forty-three provinces communist insurgents held 75 to 90 percent of the land. Prime Minister Khanh assured McNamara and Taylor that government troops would clear the country, but he said that he doubted his government's forces could hold on to it. He said he preferred covert action against North Vietnam until rear-area security was established.

McNamara replied that men, money and materiel were no object. He said that the United States had to press on with the war. After discussing the possible mining of North Vietnamese ports, McNamara and Khanh directed that mine-laying training begin at once for Vietnamese pilots.

Ambassador Lodge continued to object to any talk of massive air attacks against North Vietnam, particularly until a "carrot and stick approach" was first used. He said the United States could offer advantages to North Vietnam for ceasing aggression, while confronting its government with covert actions such as unacknowledged air strikes. His views were naive, to say the least. Photoreconnaissance flights had revealed Vietcong bases in Cambodia, but hot pursuit across the border was ruled out in light of American negotiations to keep Cambodia neutral and from becoming a part of the North Vietnamese/People's Republic of China association. Lodge insisted that the political damage of attacks against North Vietnam would far outweigh any military gain.

McNamara was also advised that the Vietnamese Air Force had to improve or that additional United States Air Force aircraft would be needed. He was told by the head of the Military Assistance Command that American aircraft had to "fill in the gaps caused by lack of motivation" on the part of the Vietnamese Air Force due to "its inability to produce fast reaction strikes, and its reluctance to fly at night and on weekends."

McNamara and Taylor stopped at Honolulu en route home for additional talks with CINCPAC officials. Back in Washington, they agreed on twelve steps to recommend to President Johnson for changing the course of the war. They stressed actions within South Vietnam and suggested steps to control South Vietnam's border inside Laos and Cambodia on seventy-two hours' notice. Their recommendations called for tit-for-tat bombing strikes and commando raids by Vietnamese forces on such targets in North Vietnam as lines of communication, training camps and infiltration routes. They recommended standby plans for gradually tightening the screws on North Vietnam. Plans should be triggered on thirty days' notice, they said, and should involve air attacks on military and possibly industrial targets.

The Joint Chiefs urged quick action against North Vietnam. The director of the Central Intelligence Agency, John A. McCone, called the proposals "too little, too late." He urged swift operations in the South to match intensive air and naval moves against the North.

Air Force Chief LeMay added his recommendations, saying that military tools and concepts were generally sound and adequate. But he deplored the shackling of sound military activities with artificial political bonds that, he said, events had long made obsolete.

The National Security Council did not concur in McNamara's recommendations and warned, "The United States should commit itself to the clear objective of preventing the fall of South Vietnam to communism." It warned that otherwise the Southesast Asia Treaty Organization would be destroyed.

President Johnson expressed doubts about these recommendations but he approved them, saying he preferred McNamara's approach to the National Security Council's recommendations for attacks against North Vietnam. The president believed that South Vietnam's political and military situation was too fragile to invite expanded enemy hostilities. Furthermore, he said that striking North Vietnam might bring the Chinese and the Russians into the conflict. In approving McNamara's recommendations the president ordered all agencies to support them.

In a major address March 26, 1964, Secretary of Defense McNamara said that the president had four options. The United States could withdraw from South Vietnam, he said, but he rejected that option as completely untenable. South Vietnam could be neutralized, he said, but such an occurrence would risk eventual communist takeover. Military actions could be spread into North Vietnam, he said, and that was a choice that was under continuing study. Finally, he said the United States could focus its assistance to help South Vietnam to win the conflict. That was the option, he said, that President Johnson had approved.

In Southeast Asia, the Military Assistance Command was authorized

March 27 to use strike aircraft against targets up to North Vietnam's borders if such targets involved a river or a road. Elsewhere, aircraft could fly as close as a mile and a quarter to a border when directed to do so by a forward air controller, or three miles when not so directed. Aircraft were forbidden to fire across the frontier, or to violate it, without diplomatic clearance. These rules guided air strikes throughout 1964. North Vietnamese government officials were amused by these restrictions, and they certainly placed no such restraints on their own armed forces.

After a Southeast Asia Treaty Organization's council meeting in Manila April 15, Secretary of State Rusk and General Wheeler went to Saigon to weigh the risks of pressuring North Vietnam with further covert actions by using air strikes and mining, but no decision was reached.

It was believed in the spring of 1964 that the war in Laos had been satisfactorily settled by the 1962 Geneva Accords. Since then, however, President Diem's assassination in South Vietnam and the growing Vietcong insurgency in that country had caused problems for the Laotian government.

President Johnson recognized that the problem of North Vietnamese infiltration of Laos posed an increasing threat to both that country and to South Vietnam. On April 23 he publicly called for other countries to assist the United States in what became known as the "more flags" program to assist so-called beleaguered friends.

In a similar move, the Ministerial Council of the Southeast Asia Treaty Organization that month declared that the defeat of the Vietcong was essential to Indochina's security and that treaty nations should fulfill their obligations.

McGeorge Bundy, head of the National Security Council's staff, in a related memorandum May 25 recommended a high-level strategy conference of SEATO nations to obtain specific force commitments. The conference proposal—and it remained just a proposal—was the last official attempt to place free world assistance under the aegis of the Southeast Asia Treaty Organization. Certain members, France in particular, were expressing a growing resistance to the American policy in Indochina. When the issue of free world support for South Vietnam surfaced again in December it was discussed outside the context of SEATO commitments.

North Vietnam's military successes in the South made them more belligerent. The Vietcong had taken the district capital of Kien Long on the Ca Mau Peninsula on the night of April 12. There were heavy losses on both sides and nine Americans were killed. The capital was left in ruins.

The American involvement escalated after Vietcong underwater demolition experts sank the United States aircraft ferry *Card* May 2 while it was delivering helicopters at a berth in the Saigon River.

With the military situation throughout South Vietnam growing worse each day, Prime Minister Khanh told Ambassador Lodge that he wanted to declare war on North Vietnam. Unrealistically he sought 100,000 Special Forces troops to seal the borders between South Vietnam, Cambodia and Laos that now were wide open to Vietcong intrusions. He also asked Lodge to recommend the bombing of North Vietnam by United States planes.

In Washington, there was a serious split between members of the Joint Chiefs of Staff. Air Force General LeMay and Marine Corps Commandant General Wallace M. Greene, Jr., had repeatedly urged low-level reconnaissance and air strikes against North Vietnam by American aircraft. Other members of the Joint Chiefs still did not believe such pressure was warranted.

North Vietnam's economy was largely agrarian but there were a few industrial targets that, if wiped out, would have had an immediate impact. Heavy attacks against manufacturing facilities and power plants would have severely hurt North Vietnam's economy and its ability to wage war. CINCPAC headquarters in Honolulu, therefore, continued to make plans for bombing North Vietnamese targets and also for air operations in Laos and Cambodia.

During a visit to Saigon May 12 and 13, Secretary of Defense McNamara and Chairman of the Joint Chiefs Taylor had told Khanh that bombing North Vietnam was no substitute for clearing the Vietcong from South Vietnam. In discussions with General Harkins, as head of the Military Assistance Command, he continued to express optimism about the overall situation, but his deputy, General Westmoreland, disagreed. Ambassador Lodge also expressed general satisfaction with American efforts. "Further large-scale contributions are not warranted," he said. Harkins and Lodge were both completely out of touch with reality.

Their optimism received a severe jolt when South Vietnam's defenses south of Saigon in the Plain of Reeds collapsed May 17 and it soon became obvious to almost everyone that some American action was needed to reverse the situation.

The Soviet Union early in 1964 had advocated a new meeting of officials of those nations who had earlier met in Geneva to discuss the war in Indochina. Polish diplomats took the initiative and called for a conference on Laos. There had been numerous charges of border violations by the communists, and the United Nations Security Council suggested that observers be placed along the Cambodian frontier to ease tensions. Officials of the United States and South Vietnam welcomed the suggestion but representatives of the Vietcong and Cambodian officials turned it down.

While acting temporarily as chairman of the Joint Chiefs while Taylor was in the Far East, General LeMay told the service chiefs May 28 that the United States was losing "Southeast Asia fast." He urged them to present a clear record on how to start winning the war when they met for the upcoming Honolulu conference. LeMay argued that the only way to end North Vietnam's support of the insurgency in South Vietnam and Laos was to destroy their means of doing so. He said that air attacks should be made against infiltration points at Dien Bien Phu and Vinh. LeMay still wanted to attack strategic targets but he knew these targets were the only ones with a possible chance of approval at that time. On the 30th the Joint Chiefs accepted his view and passed them along to McNamara. The Secretary of Defense proposed even more limited actions against targets less risky than those at Vinh and Dien Bien Phu. Ambassador Lodge also favored a more limited bombing campaign to bolster the Khanh regime that seemed about to collapse. In the end, the decision was made to see how the situation developed.

At the Secretary of Defense's conference in Honolulu June 1 and 2 the atmosphere was gloomy. There was talk among the participants of obtaining congressional approval for wider actions in Southeast Asia, including the possible commitment of American Army and Marine divisions, and even discussion about the merits of possible mobilization of reserves and the National Guard. The conference ended with little more than talk.

Meanwhile, James B. Seaborn, Canadian member of the International Control Commission, visited Hanoi and advised officials of the Democratic Republic of Vietnam about American thoughts on a negotiated peace. His appeal was based on the premise that both sides would make concessions. His suggestions included an end to the sending of men and arms from North Vietnam to the South, and Seaborn explained that if such terms were met that the United States would respond with economic aid. If the war heated up, Seaborn told them, the Americans had advised that they would unleash their bombers and devastate North Vietnam. The Canadian member of the International Control Commission repeatedly stressed President Johnson's desire to abide by the Geneva agreements of 1954 and 1962. North Vietnamese officials were not impressed by the American president's terms. They demanded instead a United States withdrawal from South Vietnam, and insisted that a neutral regime be established in South Vietnam with the communist's National Liberation Front charting the country's future.

General Harkins had long sought control of all American forces in

South Vietnam and Thailand. Admiral Felt at CINCPAC headquarters, who exercised complete military control of all services, disagreed. A proposal by General LeMay that Harkins assign an air deputy to his Military Assistance Command was rejected by Harkins. Later, after Westmoreland took over Harkins' job he appointed Army Lieutenant General John L. Throckmorton as his deputy. In justification Westemoreland said he was opposed to an air deputy because the war in Vietnam was a ground battle and that he needed a soldier to share command responsibilities.

General Harkins once was asked why the United States should not have command of South Vietnam's armed forces. He replied that such an arrangement was contrary to national policy. This may have been the case with the Johnson administration but it was not true in World War II where coalition armies were the rule rather than the exception. One of the problems faced by the Military Assistance Command was South Vietnam's refusal to agree to such a command relationship since it jealously guarded its sovereign right to accept or reject American advice. They should not have been permitted to get away with weakening the overall command structure.

It had been hoped that General Moore's replacement of General Anthis as head of the 2nd Air Division in late January might increase the Air Force's counsel at the decision-making level in South Vietnam. When the command change took place the division had 140 aircraft and 4,600 people. This number was far in excess of the level required for their operations—almost thirty-three people for each airplane. When the Military Assistance Advisory Group was eliminated May 15 and its functions turned over to an expanded Military Assistance Command headquarters, the Air Force had pressed Harkins for an air deputy but he had replied that he did not need one. Later, after Westmoreland took command June 20 General Moore was named as Westmoreland's deputy commander for air operations—a lesser job than command deputy. Since they had been close friends since boyhood, there was harmony between the two men that transcended the responsibilities inherent in Moore's limited role in commanding air operations.

Of major concern to all officers of the Military Assistance Command was the performance of the Vietnamese Air Force. Use of available Vietnamese aircraft was totally inadequate, and its effectiveness was further reduced by assignment of individual squadrons to each of the four corps commanders. Thus its use was splintered four ways, and the Air Force hardly ever was used effectively to repel a mass attack in a corps area. Nguyen Cao Ky, who had won command of the Vietnamese Air Force for his part in General Minh's coup against President Diem, had increased his prestige by supporting Khanh as prime minister. Ky continued to assure General Moore that he would not relinguish centralized control over airpower, but he did not have the authority.

The rule that restricted United States Air Force advisers from engaging in battle often was strained to the breaking point, but it was never completely broken. There were now eighty-nine Air Force pilots flying in Vietnamese aircraft but no pilot was permitted to lead a flight, be first to fire at the enemy, or to continue a mission if the Vietnamese flight leader aborted it. Despite these restrictions, twenty-eight American airmen had been killed in Vietnam since January, 1962.

At the end of June, 1963, General Taylor, chairman of the Joint Chiefs of Staff, had retired from active duty for the second time at President Johnson's insistence, to become ambassador to Vietnam replacing Henry Cabot Lodge, who had resigned to seek the Republican nomination in the presidential campaign. Army Chief of Staff General Earle G. Wheeler replaced him. Alexis Johnson, a respected career diplomat, was appointed as Taylor's deputy. Taylor's new status recognized his role as one of the major architects of the war. Now he was entrusted by the president with the entire military effort in Southeast Asia.

In the Pacific, Admiral U.S.G. Sharp succeeded Admiral Felt as commander-in-chief and was replaced as commander of the Pacific Fleet by Admiral Thomas H. Moorer.

The new ambassador stopped at Honolulu July 5 and Taylor showed Admiral Sharp a letter from President Johnson. "As you take charge of the American effort in South Vietnam I want you to have this formal expression not only of my confidence, but of my desire that you have and exercise full responsibility for the effort of the United States government in South Vietnam. In general terms this authority is parallel to that set forth in President Kennedy's letter of May 29, 1961, to all American ambassadors; specifically, I wish it clearly understood that this overall responsibility includes the whole military effort in South Vietnam and authorizes the degree of command and control that you consider appropriate.

"I recognize that in the conduct of the day-to-day business of the Military Assistance Command, Vietnam, you will wish to work out arrangements which do not burden you or impede the exercise of your overall direction.

"At your convenience I should be glad to know of the arrangements which you propose for meeting the terms of this instruction so that appropriate supporting action can be taken in the Defense Department and elsewhere as necessary.

"This letter rescinds all conflicting instructions to United States officers in Vietnam.

Sincerely,

Lyndon B. Johnson."

The president's letter seemed to indicate the elimination of CINCPAC in the command chain and Admiral Sharp was disturbed. Taylor assured him that he would not interfere in day-to-day activities, and he was true to his word. Once established in Saigon he also assured General Westmoreland the same thing.

Taylor's appraisal of the Khanh regime was blunt. He called it weak. He wrote later, "We lived dangerously in this period, never sure from night to night when a new coup might overthrow another feeble government, or when we might lose some important town to a surprise attack or a military base to mortar fire."

It was soon apparent to Taylor that heavy deliveries of modern weapons by North Vietnam to the Vietcong, and the infiltration of North Vietnamese Army units to the South, called for greater American effort.

The Joint Chiefs had long advocated a shift from advisory assistance to more direct aid. In May, they had proposed the assignment of United States Special Forces teams to provinces and districts as advisers to Regional and Popular Forces. Westmoreland opposed flooding the country with American servicemen. He believed the key to success was honing the cutting edge of small fighting units. On two occasions, June 25 and July 16, Westmoreland recommended that United States military strength in Vietnam be expanded by about forty-two hundred men but to work only as advisers at the district level.

A reinforced battalion of several hundred Vietcong launched a coordinated attack at 2:30 A.M. July 6 against Nam Dong, an outlying defense position that had been scheduled to close down. It lacked adequate personnel, and its defenses were not in good shape. This was an old French position and it was considered too small to defend. The first shattering mortar barrage hit most installations.

The district chief of Khe Tre, a village at the other end of a valley about a three-hour march from Nam Dong, had insisted before the battle that his Civil Guard companies do all the patroling west of the airstrip and he refused to permit the Nam Dong garrison to send any patrols into the area adjacent to the campsite in the direction from which the attack came. This was a peculiar decision on the chief's part, and his motives later were questioned.

The Vietcong approached across a river and northwest of the airstrip and so achieved tactical surprise. Ten mortar concentrations within fifteen minutes shattered the night and momentarily paralyzed the defenders. Only a brief message was sent to Special Forces headquarters at Da Nang because the radio shack was hit early. The Special Forces radio operator, who slept in the shack, tapped out a message at 2:35 A.M., saying, "Under intense mortar attack." Eighty percent of the casualties were suffered in the first fifteen minutes.

As the barrage lifted, an assault force rolled over the outer perimeter while the strike force was asleep in their barracks. But Nung soldiers were at their posts and they quickly manned their machine guns and resisted the attacks in their trenches.

The Nungs continued to fight well as the Vietcong crept up to the exterior lines of barbed wire through tall grass that should have been removed, and apparently breached the barbed wire before launching their attack. The Vietcong tossed hand grenades into an open mortar emplacement. Detachment Commander Captain Roger H. C. Donlon, wounded himself, repeatedly tried to rescue a team member who had been wounded by grenades. His heroic action later earned him a Medal of Honor.

Two more assaults were directed at the inner perimeter as the Vietcong charged but were stopped at the first line of defenses. These were special shock troops—well-muscled young men with close-cropped hair and clean fingernails and toenails indicating they had not been long in the jungle.

The defenders held their position until dawn the next day despite the fact they were low on ammunition and relief had not arrived. This was the Vietnamese Independence Day weekend and Vietnamese pilots were celebrating in the city of Da Nang. A flareship finally got over the target two hours after the attack and reported that the camp was ablaze.

The Vietnamese district chief at Khe Tre, once he heard the firing, assembled his two Civil Guard companies for a march to Nam Dong but, fearing an ambush, he refused to start until it was light. As his column approached the village in daylight the last Vietcong were withdrawing.

In civil action programs designed to help villages around such defense positions as Nam Dong the people generally were receptive to medical assistance and welfare aid. Tangible aid was something they could appreciate. In programs involving larger community improvement projects they were willing to work if they were paid for their labor and the materials were provided. But the concept of cooperative self-help with an unpaid contribution from each participant was foreign to their nature and culture. This was just one of many aspects of dealing with the Vietnamese that made fighting so exasperating to Americans in Vietnam.

Admiral Ulysses S. G. Sharp, who was appointed Commander-in-

Chief, Pacific, July 1, 1964, replaced Admiral Felt and took over a command where Army officials weren't talking to their counterparts in the Navy and where Air Force officers were at odds with Army officials. Most generals were not even talking to officials at CINCPAC. Admiral Felt's abrasive manner had made them mad: mad at him and mad at each other. It took Sharp two or three months to get everybody to understand that they were all going to be on the same team, that they would pull together or there would be changes

Sharp ordered his component commanders—Pacific commanders of the Army, Air Force, Pacific Fleet and General Westmoreland as head of the Military Assistance Command, Vietnam, to meet with him at his Honolulu headquarters at least once a week—often more frequently—for briefings. After they learned that Sharp intended to be a tough-minded boss, they tried to help one another and work together in a cooperative spirit. Sharp had quicky learned that Westmoreland's command had a tendency to isolate itself from his overall authority and to think they were running the entire war. He quickly squelched such attempts to bypass him. McNamara did his best to separate Westmoreland from the Commander-in-Chief, Pacific, but Sharp would not tolerate abuse of his command relationships. He made it clear that he was the boss and Westmoreland proved cooperative. But there were times when Sharp disagreed with Westmoreland and he was not backward in telling him so.

Sharp's responsibilities in the Pacific covered all areas from the west coast of the United States to the Indian Ocean and specificially included Indochina. As Commander-in-Chief, Pacific (CINCPAC), he exercised overall authority for military operations in South Vietnam, but largely left the strategy and tactics of the ground war to officers on the scene. However, the air war over North Vietnam was under his personal direction and he exercised control through the commanders of the Pacific Fleet, the Pacific Air Forces and the commander of the Military Assistance Command in Saigon.

CHAPTER 10

The Big Lie

PRIME MINISTER KHANH DELIVERED AN EMOTIONAL ADDRESS JULY 18 AT a rally to mark Vietnam's division in 1954 that he called its "day of shame." He said his government was unwilling to remain indifferent in the face of the firm determination of people who wanted to "push northward" as an appropriate means to fulfill "our national history."

A government spokesman clarified his comments the following day. "If Communist China and Communist Vietnam obstinately continue their war of aggression, the government and the entire people of Vietnam will step up the war with determination until total victory liberates the whole of our national territory."

These were bold words but they lacked the motivating force to win what was necessary to achieve such a goal. The Americans had been trying to inspire South Vietnam's leaders for years to take action aganst the invaders of their country.

In a discussion with Ambassador Taylor on July 23 Khanh insisted that the war had entered a new phase, and that it needed a new emphasis. The next day he asked Taylor whether he should resign for the good of his country, but the American ambassador avoided a direct reply.

Taylor sent a cable to the State Department in Washington saying that if the United States opposed a march against the North, the Vietnamese might break with American policy. He said a single "maverick pilot taking off for Hanoi with a load of bombs" could touch off an unwarranted extension of hostilities. Such an act, he said, would cloud the chances for internal pacification of South Vietnam. The chief need, Taylor said, was a stable Vietnamese government and that required time. To gain time, the American ambassador suggested that the Vietnamese armed forces make contingency plans for heightened actions against North Vietnam.

No one should have taken Khanh's threat seriously, least of all Ambassador Taylor. The South Vietnamese armed forces could not even control Vietcong activity in the South, so they were hardly in a position to invade the North.

The United States government announced July 27 that it was sending an additional 5,000 men to South Vietnam—still in a so-called advisory role—to bring the total number of Americans there to 21,000.

The South Vietnamese Navy, using fast patrol boats, was ordered into North Vietnamese waters to blow up beach installations and to intercept and destroy North Vietnamese junks and fishing vessels that were being used to ferry arms and equipment to the Vietcong. Two boats were directed to make landings on the island of Hon Me, seven miles off the North Vietnamese coast at 19 degrees north latitude to destroy a radar station. The other two boats were directed to bombard Hon Ngu, an island three miles from Vinh.

These four South Vietnamese patrol boats, operating under American guidance, left Da Nang July 30 and sailed north. Two boats tried to storm Hon Me but resistance was too strong to make a landing. Instead they shelled the radar station on the island while the other two boats shelled a radio transmitter on Hon Ngu island. Both islands were deeply involved in Vietcong infiltration into South Vietnam.

At the time, the old American destroyer *Maddox* was 120 miles to the south, and it was ordered to remain eight miles off the coast—North Vietnam recognized a five-mile limit as its territorial waters—and not to approach the islands in the gulf. It had been assigned July 27 to investigate coastal activity in North Vietnam's waters.

Before dawn August 2 the *Maddox* encountered hundreds of North Vietnamese junks. Her skipper, Captain John J. Herrick, steered eastward to avoid a clash with them. When his radio operator intercepted a North Vietnamese message indicating possible military operations he recommended to his superiors that his ship's itinerary be changed because of what he termed an unacceptable risk. His request was denied and he was advised to resume his course but to exercise prudence.

Later, three high-speed North Vietnamese patrol boars approached the *Maddox* in international waters twenty-eight miles off the coast of North Vietnam. They were first detected on radar and were tracked at a closing speed of 40 knots. When the boats fired at the *Maddox*, the destroyer took evasive action and fired warning shots. When these shots were ignored Herrick ordered his ship to return the fire. He also sent an emergency appeal to the carrier *Ticonderoga* for air support. The *Ticonderoga* immediately sent aircraft and Task Force 77 went into action for the first time, starting a thirty-seven-month carrot-and-stick effort against North Vietnam to persuade its leaders to stop its aggression against South Vietnam.

At the time it was believed in Washington that direct American involvement would be sufficient to influence North Vietnam's leaders to cease their aggressive acts.

Commander James Stockdale of VF-51 responded to the *Maddox's* appeal at 2:25 P.M. by rushing to the scene from the *Ticonderoga* with four fighters. He spotted the torpedo boats headed north at high speed thirty miles off the coast fleeing in a ragged single file and directed his fighters to charge their guns.

A new pilot, Lieutenant Richard Hastings, called that he had been hit. Stockdale checked his plane but failed to see any evidence of enemy damage. He suspected that Hastings in his excitement had made a jerk on his stick and over-stressed his airplane. He ordered Hastings to remain out of action as he joined Commander Robair Mohrhardt and Lieutenant Commander Everett Southwick who were making attacks on the boats. Their first Zuni missiles failed to make contact but the fighters wheeled back and made strafing passes. Hits were scored and one boat lay dead in the water as its crew threw equipment and themselves overboard. Stockdale reported to the carrier that one boat was sinking and the other two were damaged.

The next day President Johnson warned that "United States ships have traditionally operated freely on the high seas in accordance with the rights guaranteed by international law. . . . They will continue to do so and will take whatever measures are appropriate for their defense." He warned North Vietnam to be under "no misapprehension as to the grave consequences which would inevitably result from any further unprovoked military action against United States forces."

Johnson ordered the Tonkin Gulf patrol reinforced by a second destroyer, the *C. Turner Joy*. The carrier *Constellation* was ordered by Pacific Fleet Commander Admiral Moorer to leave Hong Kong and it headed for the gulf to reinforce Carrier Task Force 77, and he also sent the carrier *Kearsarge* with its anti-submarine warfare task force. A continuous combat air patrol was instituted to provide instant retaliatory power if the North Vietnamese attacked again. Rear Admiral R. B. Moore ordered his ships to retire each afternoon to a night steaming area about one hundred miles offshore to reduce the risk of night torpedo boat attacks.

August 3 the destroyers *Maddox* and *C. Turner Joy* formed a task group under Captain Herrick and again entered the Gulf of Tonkin with orders to fire only in self-defense. They were restricted from pursuing possible attackers. This day ended with no further attacks.

The night of August 4 the two destroyers proceeded easterly at 20 knots and the *Maddox's* radar reported at least five high-speed contacts thirty-six miles away. These radar blips were tentatively evaluated as probable torpedo boats. The American ships were ordered to change course by Admiral Moore and to increase their speed. It appeared from these radar images the torpedo boats were sixty miles off the North Vietnamese coast and only fourteen from the American destroyers. Torpedo noises were reported by the *Maddox*'s sonar and this information was relayed to the skipper of the *C. Turner Joy.* Once it was believed that torpedo boats were within range at 6,000 yards both ships fired their guns and began evasive maneuvers to evade torpedoes. While both ships twisted on the ocean's surface, a torpedo wake was reported passing 300 feet to port of the *C. Turner Joy.*

Commander Stockdale responded to this new alarm at 9:35 P.M. He and other *Ticonderoga* pilots flew back and forth over the ships, noting their gyrations on the surface and the constant firing of their guns, but they could see no torpedo boats nor torpedo wakes. In responding to an appeal to fire at targets supposedly attacking the American destroyers Stockdale fired his guns in the area where the patrol boats supposedly were operating although he continued to see no evidence of enemy attackers.

Less than half an hour after the first attack August 2 Admiral Sharp at CINCPAC headquarters recommmended air strikes by Task Force 77's planes against North Vietnamese torpedo boat bases. At first, McNamara thought this attack was the impulsive act of a local commander. But after the second attack was reported he changed his mind. He now believed these attacks were a deliberate provocation by North Vietnam's leadership.

Two hours after the start of the supposed second attack Sharp was given authority by the Joint Chiefs to take immediate punitive air action against North Vietnam at first light the following day.

Now Moorer and Sharp received a report from Captain Herrick of his doubts that his ships had been attacked, saying they were reinforced by reports from the pilots who had expressed a growing conviction they were shooting at shadows. He advised his superiors that the situation should be re-evaluated, and that daylight aircraft reconnaissance was advisable and a complete evaluation made before any further action was taken.

Sharp maintained telephone contact with General Wheeler, chairman of the Joint Chiefs of Staff, and McNamara as they tried to determine whether a second attack had, in fact, taken place. After a few hours, Moorer and Sharp agreed that there was sufficient information available to indicate that an attack had occurred. Sharp called McNamara and informed him of their evaluation. He said that while reports were not conclusive, the weight of evidence—including radio intercept intelligence—supported their conclusion that a second attack had taken place.

A review of all facts later convinced Navy officials that there had been no torpedo boat attacks that night.

After numerous telephone conversations wth Washington officials, McNamara approved Sharp's original recommendation for air attacks and he was supported by President Johnson. General Westmoreland discussed the contemplated action with Prime Minister Khanh, who concurred. Four torpedo boat bases and oil storage facilities at Phuc Loi and Vinh were approved as targets.

President Johnson announced publicly that the United States was making a measured response to North Vietnam's aggression but that he did not intend to start a war. "Our response for the present will be limited and fitting."

The air strikes were delayed, however, until the carrier *Constellation* could join the task force.

Sixty-four strike aircraft were launched from Task Force 77's carriers the morning of August 5. Ten of the *Constellation's* planes struck torpedo boat bases at the northernmost target at Hon Gai. Farther south twelve other planes from the *Constellation* struck PT bases at Loc Chao. Meanwhile, six fighters from the *Ticonderoga* led by Commander Mohrhardt hit torpedo boat bases at Quang Khe, while twenty-six others blasted the oil storage dumps at Vinh. Eight gunboats and torpedo boats were destroyed, with twenty-one others damaged. Smoke from the ten Vinh storage tanks rose to 14,000 feet and damage was estimated at 90 percent as a result of attacks led by Commander James Stockdale of VF-51. Two aircraft from the *Constellation* were shot down by anti-airacraft fire at Hon Gai. Lieutenant Everett Alvarez went down after his aircraft was hit and he became the first United States pilot to be captured by the North Vietnamese.

These strikes were too limited to be effective in changing the aggressive intentions of the North Vietnamese. Actually, they now brought thirty MIGs from China to Phy Yen airfield. This was the beginning of an effective defense system that later would take a heavy toll of American aircraft and their crews.

North Vietnamese infiltration of the South had steadily increased since 1959. The communists had taken advantage of South Vietnam's 200-mile coastline and its equally long border that traveled through mountains and jungles in all corps areas. The North Vietnamese not only used the demilitarized zone for infiltration but also the supposedly uninvolved countries of Laos and Cambodia, making a mockery of their neutrality. In each nation the communists had almost a free hand in building sanctuaries, supply installations and transit stations. Cambodia's major port, Kompong Song, was used as an entry point for weapons and ammunition for Vietcong forces in South Vietnam.

Since 1961 consideration had been given to establishing an international force in the demilitarized zone. In the spring of 1964 President Johnson had appealed for such a force to be assigned there and in Laos.

Most Vietcong and North Vietnamese war materiel came overland into South Vietnam, but some of it came by sea. United States officials believed that selective but gradually increasing attacks should be made against North Vietnam's military installations and power plants, her refineries, supply storage areas and industrial facilities that supported her war effort. They also recommended that attacks against vehicles, roads and bridges by which war materiel moved south would choke off communist aggression. Emphasis was placed on the avoidance of damage to non-military targets and non-combatants. Therefore aerial bombing was inhibited by major restrictions. At first sanctuaries, base camps and supply depots used by the communists in Cambodia were off limits, and hot pursuit was forbidden. The key port of Haiphong, through which 85 percent of North Vietnam's imports flowed, was only mined years later. Thus war materiel arrived in shipload quantities at a safe harbor, and had to be bombed all along its journey south truck-by-truck, and storage-site-by-storage-site.

After the second reported patrol boat incident against the American destroyers, although it was now known that there had not been such a second attack, President Johnson sent a message to Congress August 5 about the Gulf of Tonkin incidents and asked for a joint resolution of support for his Southeast Asia policy. A resolution was prepared by the administration and introduced by the Chairman of the Senate Foreign Relations Committee under J. William Fulbright and Chairman of the Foreign Affairs Committee of the House of Representatives under Thomas E. Morgan.

The United States Congress passed a joint resolution that termed the attacks on the American destroyers part of a "deliberate and systematic campaign of aggression that the communist regime in North Vietnam had been waging against its neighbors and the nations joined with them." The resolution assured the president of the Congress's determination to "take all necessary measures to repel any armed attack . . . and to prevent any further aggression" until the president determined that peace and security of the area was reasonably assured.

This resolution gave President Johnson authority he should not have had without a declaration of war by the Congress. It is inconceivable that his administration did not know at that time that the so-called second torpedo boat attack never occurred. In effect, the resolution was passed under false pretenses.

United States efforts to involve other free world nations in the war in

South Vietnam improved August 10 when the Royal Australian Air Force sent a detachment with six Caribous. They were placed under American control at Tan Son Nhut and became a valuable addition to fulfill growing airlift needs.

William Bundy (McGeorge's brother) as assistant Secretary of State August 11 outlined his country's next course of action. He proposed intensive military pressures against North Vietnam until they ceased their aggression in the South. He warned that Khanh's fragile regime would crumble without positive American moves.

Bundy's warning about Khanh proved correct. South Vietnam's volatile political situation worsened again August 25, 1964, when Prime Minister Khanh resigned. His restrictive new laws had outraged students and Buddhists. Two days later the Military Revolutionary Council named a triumvirate of provincial leaders as an interim ruling body until a permanent government could be formed. Khanh agreed to remain as acting prime minister in a coalition with General Tran Khiem, who had helped Khanh seize power in January, and General Minh. But South Vietnam again reverted to anarchy.

Military Assistance Command officers frequently criticized Vietnamese ground officers for failing to use tactical air support for ground operations. In Phu Yen Province, when three battalions were attacked August 19 by 500 Vietcong soldiers, their commanders did not even call for air strikes and there were heavy losses. This was a major fault of most such operations.

McNamara asked the Joint Chiefs August 31 to answer three questions. One, after a full-scale assault on the ninety-four targets previously selected by them for air attacks, would there be sufficient ordnance and fuel remaining to defend Southeast Asia from an attack by the People's Republic of China? Two, what effects would each of the suggested four patterns of attack have on North Vietnam's economy, on its capacity to support the Pathet Lao in Cambodia, the Vietcong in South Vietnam and its ability to enlarge North Vietnam's military forces in South Vietnam and Laos? And lastly, if the destruction of the ninety-four targets failed to stifle North Vietnam's will to wage war, what course of action was feasible?

Meanwhile, South Vietnam's fifteen-member leadership committee replaced its ruling triumvirate September 3 but again picked General Khanh as acting prime minister with General Minh as chairman.

Ambassador Taylor, Secretary of State Rusk, Secretary of Defense McNamara and Joint Chief's Chairman Wheeler now weighed courses of action. They sharply revised McGeorge Bundy's outline of graduated response against North Vietnam. They believed that the South Vietnamese government would be weak for several months and that it would be conterproductive to increase American action. It was decided that the United States should reduce the risk of confrontation but keep the military situation under control in South Vietnam. It was agreed that American patrols in the Gulf of Tonkin should be continued but that they should be divorced from actions in South Vietnam. Task Force 77's commander was advised to be on the alert to respond to an attack, but not to deliberately provoke one.

These proposals were forwarded to President Johnson and the Joint Chiefs. General LeMay protested these courses of action because, he said, they did not convey a clear and positive signal of United States resolution to North Vietnam. Marine Commandant Greene agreed with LeMay but McNamara and General Wheeler disagreed. They were concerned that drastic American action might trigger a strong reaction against the South Vietnamese regime that it could not meet.

This cautious approach was accepted by President Johnson September 10, and he agreed to talks with the Laotian government to approve limited air and ground operations in the Laotian panhandle.

Administration officials were agreed that the United States' first order of business was to shore up the South Vietnamese government. They continued to have but slight success.

The IV Corps' commander started a coup September 13, charging that Khanh had capitulated to Buddhist and student demands when he promised them in August that he would liberalize his regime. He led armored elements into Saigon, occupied public buildings and disarmed the national police. The Vietnamese Air Force remained loyal to Khanh and made a show of force. The American State Department also remained loyal and the rebellious forces withdrew.

Khanh now carried out sweeping changes among his military commanders, and he appointed a high national council of seventeen civilians to draft a constitution and to designate a civil chief of state. September 26 the council elected Phan Khac Suu as chief of state and former Saigon mayor Tran Van Huong as prime minister, although the real power still was held by the generals. These actions offered scant improvement. Pacification efforts in the countryside had collapsed because the military staff in Saigon was virtually paralyzed.

During a visit to Peking in the People's Republic of China Cambodia's Norodom Sihanouk met with Pham Van Dong, North Vietnam's prime minister, and asked him to recognize Cambodia's territorial integrity. Dong dodged the issue, telling Sihanouk to refer the matter to the

National Liberation Front that, he said, was the only organization that could represent South Vietnam in this matter. This communist-front organization had no authority whatsoever to make such a political decision without North Vietnam's approval.

Sihanouk, playing both sides against the middle, sent Cambodian officials to New Delhi, India, for a meeting in December with American representatives to discuss their differences. The meeting, arranged through the good offices of the Indian government, was cordial but they failed to resolve the tense relationship between the United States and Cambodia.

Seaborn, Canadian member of the International Control Commission, tried again during another visit to Hanoi in August with no better success to achieve a negotiated peace. He warned communist officials that American patience was wearing thin, but Vietnamese officials were unimpressed.

With the adamant stand taken by the North Vietnamese, McNamara and General Taylor asked the Joint Chiefs and CINCPAC to forge a three-phase air offensive against North Vietnam. Such a step, it was believed, would signal American readiness to attack all major military targets in the North. Planners approved the ninety-four strategic targets for attack that had been previously recommended by the Defense Intelligence Agency. They included twelve railroad routes. By 1967 the list had grown to 244 active and 265 contingency targets.

The distrust that had been building up between the Montagnards and the South Vietnamese flared into an armed uprising in September. The Montagnards struck five camps in II Corps, and restricted the use of United States advisers as they rebelled against their government. Some Vietnamese leaders were killed as the disorders spread in an armed challenge to the government. By the evening of September 20 most insurgents had returned to their camps although Montagnard leaders continued to press their demands for a fair policy in regard to land ownership and relations between them and the government. They sought representation in the National Assembly and at district and province levels. They also requested larger quotas in the officer and non-commissioned officer ranks, a Montagnard flag, and their language taught in primary schools.

The South Vietnamese government was shocked by the insurrection because these camps were an excellent source of intelligence about Vietcong activities. Government officials agreed to some of the demands and promised to study the rest.

Opposition to the war was growing in the United States, and American communists used the racial discrimination issue effectively. Thus the stage was set for a massive confrontation December 2, 1964, at the University of California at Berkeley with crowd agitation, rallies and civil disobedience. The goal was to split the campus wide open. Leaders advised that if such a revolt were conducted with toughness and courage it could spread to other campuses across the country. Radicals engaged in a sit-in at Sproul Hall. The next day there was serious trouble. There were fake charges of police brutality to fire up the students to new demonstrations. Hundreds cheered as a Communist Party member urged students to join the Vietcong. Few, if any, did. They weren't *that* courageous! Leaflets were distributed calling for a "class war." At one gate a sign called on students to attend Marxist classes taught by revolutionaries. It was signed by a campus unit of the new Peking-oriented Communist Progressive Labor Party. Added in red on the sign were the words, "Wanted for Murder—Lyndon B. Johnson." He was charged with wanton slaughter of thousands of innocent victims of his "Wars of Aggression in Vietnam and the Dominican Republic."

Under the cloak of academic freedom—that they clearly denied others—the far left tried to take over campuses and to interfere with the freedom of most of America's hard-working six million college students and faculty members.

Most effective of the communist groups were the W.E.B. Dubois clubs, the new youth front of the United States Communist Party that was named for a black communist hero to give a civil rights image to the anti-war demonstrations. The Federal Bureau of Investigation revealed that this organization had secret training schools that were conducted by the Communist Party for its membership. After graduation from such schools students were sent to college campuses, typically with a $30-a-week party stipend.

The free-speech movement was misnamed. The real issue was the seizure of power by the radicals to determine who would run the universities. Mario Savio, a twenty-two-year-old student associated with the Student Non-Violent Coordinating Committee, led sitters into Sproul Hall December 2 at Berkeley's University of California campus. One eyewitness said, "They acted like sheep herded together. They cheered on cue, they booed on cue. They were caught up in a carefully manufactured myth of 'academic freedom and civil rights.' It was the Nazi big-lie technique and it was frightening because the mob believed it." Savio elected himself as their spokesman. He carried a sign reading "I am a human being. Do not fold, bend, spindle or mutilate." He told reporters, "There's a time when the operation of the machine becomes so odious, makes you so sick at heart, that you can't take part. You can't even tacitly take part. And you've got to put your bodies upon the gears and upon the wheels, upon the levers, upon all the apparatus, and you've got to make it stop."

At 11:00 P.M. December 2 Governor Edmund G. "Pat" Brown directed police to clear Sproul Hall and known communists were arrested. It took 350 policemen twelve hours to carry out 773 demonstrators. Among them were eighty-six non-students, thirty-eight of whom had criminal records, and forty-five with known subversive and radical backgrounds. The vast majority of students were silent witnesses but they needed help in overcoming this attack against their university. Authorities were much too slow in assisting them.

Berkeley's ringleaders moved eastward and their free-speech movement spread to other campuses. Russian leaders were delighted, and a so-called diplomatic representative of the Vietcong in Moscow gave American newsmen clippings of United States press reports about campus unrest. He said, "We do not need to rely on our military prowess. The pressure of United States public opinion will drive your imperialist government out of South Vietnam."

The anti-war, anti-draft movement was led by articulate members of the "new left." This was a loose network of undergraduates, graduate students, dropouts and young marrieds who, united by suspicion of the adult establishment, thought of themselves as the "movement." These young radicals made civil rights, university reform and a decentralized ideal called "participatory democracy" their catchwords. In retrospect it appears that the movement was marked by an unwillingness—especially where collaboration with the communists was concerned—to absorb the lessons of history. These young people enjoyed thinking the worst of their country and its leaders. Unfortunately, their activities only served to prolong the war that they refused to fight, and increased the casualties on both sides.

CHAPTER 11

Open American Combat

IN STRATEGY DISCUSSIONS IN WASHINGTON, STATE DEPARTMENT COUN-
selor Walt Rostow pressed his case that "an insurgency supported by
external power must be dealt with through measures to neutralize the
success of its support." Such measures, he believed, would convince a
nation supporting an insurgency—such as North Vietnam—that it was in
its own best interest to reduce or eliminate its support. Criticism was
levied at his views that called for using graduated military actions as well
as economic and political pressures, but they were given serious consideration by the Johnson administration.

The importance of taking some positive steps was dramatized November 1 when the Vietcong staged a mortar strike against an important air
base at Bien Hoa, twenty miles northeast of Saigon, and five Americans
were killed while seventy-six others were wounded. Five B-57 bombers
were destroyed, and eight others were damaged. Despite this direct attack
against Americans President Johnson decided against retaliatory action.
This was the eve of the 1964 presidential election so he opposed recommendations by Ambassador Taylor and the Joint Chiefs when they sought
air strikes against communist targets in Laos and aerial reconnaissance
south of the 19th parallel in North Vietnam. Such strikes, they said,
would provide cover for American installations in South Vietnam. At the
time North Vietnam's defenses against air strikes were minimal, and
American air attacks could have been made with few if any losses. And,
they might have helped to stabilize the situation in the South.

Taylor's recommendations for reprisal raids had been approved by
Admiral Sharp. In a message to the Joint Chiefs Admiral Sharp called for a
steady, relentless movement toward convincing the North Vietnamese and
the Chinese that they would pay a prohibitive price if they continued
subversion and aggression in South Vietnam. Sharp insisted that

McNamara's concept of a graduated response to provocations by the communists would fail. He claimed that the United States must deal from a posture of strength before sitting down to the bargaining table.

Despite repeated attacks against American military personnel President Johnson continued to refuse retaliatory missions against the North Vietnamese.

General Moore had long recommended more aircraft for the Vietnamese Air Force and in November McNamara approved their fifth and sixth fighter squadrons, plus an increase in Vietnamese liaison squadrons.

As commander of the 2nd Air Division General Moore believed that his friend General Westmoreland was the Tactical Air Force's biggest booster in Vietnam. However, Westmoreland's requests for more air resources in mid-1964 had hewed to Army aviation's tactical doctrine—support for ground troops. There were four squadrons for supply missions, and a second squadron to handle deliveries between corps areas, plus two new Army squadrons with seventy helicopters. Some of these were used by command personnel but others were converted to gunships in addition to the two mobile platoons. Pacific Air Force officials agreed with the use of helicopter gunships for tactical airpower but General LeMay expressed a dislike for armed helicopters and the manner in which tactical airpower was being used. In particular, he objected to helicopter gunships. LeMay contended that strike aircraft provided more firepower.

Adaptation of existing weapons in the American arsenals for use in an unconventional war was realistic and necessary. The United States at all times had air superiority so use of tactical airpower for support of ground operations increased in importance. The United States Air Force had earlier seen the need to saturate enemy ground positions from the air, to interdict enemy reinforcements, and to defend isolated hamlets and outposts under attack. Flying equipment for such multiple tasks had to be flexible and survivable. At first the Air Force had nothing to use in such a role.

The theory of a gunship, first tested in 1926, that could aim side-mounted guns in a tight turn at fixed points on the ground was not new. The first Vietnam-era gunship was the venerable C-47 transport, but it grew into a highly complex weapons system.

After Vietnam tests were authorized by General LeMay, the C-47 proved ideal as a gunship. LeMay later changed his mind about their use in such a role, saying, "You don't have the range, staying capacity, or anything else. They're too vulnerable both on the ground and in the air."

Gunships proved themselves as night protectors of friendly villages, bases and Special Forces camps. They helped to strip away the Vietcong's shield of darkness. The AC-130 was later pre-eminent as a truck-killer. It was used as the primary interdiction vehicle to choke off North Vietnamese support for insurgents infiltrating into South Vietnam.

Despite doubts among top Air Force officers such as General Walter G. Sweeney, Jr., head of the Tactical Air Force, that the C-47 gunship could survive in combat, the concept had its supporters because the plane could loiter around targets, change firing patterns, and deliver great quantities of firepower. It proved ideal at night and its six 7.62 mm. miniguns could hit targets even on steep mountain slopes.

General Sweeney, who had followed the C-47 gunship trials closely during research and development tests, claimed that "this concept will place a highly vulnerable aircraft in a battlefield environment in which I believe results will not compensate for losses of Air Force personnel and aircraft." His concern was largely due to battle losses, because in these early days the Air Force was not allowed to put decent equipment on a gunship. Sweeney was also concerned that a successful gunship would weaken the Air Force's case against the Army and its overuse of helicopters for offensive fire-support missions. Although LeMay still had his own doubts, he rejected Sweeney's position.

Captain Ronald W. Terry arrived in South Vietnam December 2 to test two C-47s equipped with miniguns at Bien Hoa air base near Saigon. They carried a crew of seven with one Vietnamese observer. They flew their first combat missions successfuly December 15. Their first night mission was flown eight days later in the Mekong Delta and the Vietcong broke under the intense fire of 4,500 rounds from its miniguns after seventeen flares lighted up their positions. Terry said later, "Saving forts or hamlets at night was the only thing we ever got to do." This was unfortunate because these gunships had proved themselves. Their success, in large part, was due to the lack of enemy air defenses in the South.

After their initial success General Moore, the 2nd Air Division's commander, sought a squadron. He recommended that each plane use rapid-firing miniguns or 30-caliber guns if miniguns were not available. His request was denied for the present but a sixteen-plane squadron was approved a year later.

The first true gunship—the AC-47—despite the twenty-plus-years of age and obsolescence, proved to be a highly versatile, rugged and reliable craft. Henceforth all C-47 transports that were modified as gunships were given the letter "A" to designated their attack role.

United States and Vietnamese psychological warfare flights proved too limited in number to be effective. This could be said of most air operations. Messages broadcast from the air to people on the ground in remote areas often were distorted by aircraft and helicopter noise and there was little comprehension of the messages that were beamed to the Vietnamese people.

During the last half of 1964 Vietcong night attacks doubled against outposts and hamlets. They were particularly severe in the III and IV Corps areas. By October, the Vietcong also scored military successes in II Corps, an area that had been considered pacified just a few months earlier.

At the end of Johnson's first year in office he admitted that his principal advisers had made no unanimous recommendations for air activity against North Vietnam. This was true, but some of his advisers had done so, and he was listening to the wrong people. The problem lay within his administration because it remained sharply divided about more aggressive actions.

In reply to McNamara's earlier questions about the ninety-four strategic targets recommended for air attacks, the Joint Chiefs and CINCPAC assured him that these targets could be attacked without depleting the fuel and ordnance needed to meet a possible Chinese intervention. Secretary of Defense McNamara was told by Admiral Sharp that his command was set to attack these targets in twenty days after approval was granted. General LeMay and General Greene again added their voices in favor of such attacks. LeMay said there never would be a sound government in Saigon without morale-building offensive operations. He said the Vietnamese military establishment was a solid, stabilizing force. If that collapsed, he said, the United States might well have to fight to get its military advisers and their dependents out of the country.

After the Vietcong attack against Bien Hoa the Joint Chiefs had recommended strong reprisals. Ambassador Taylor, angered by the attack, favored limited retaliation against selected North Vietnamese targets by American and Vietnamese aircraft. Secretary of State Rusk and McNamara counseled patience. The president, concerned about possible Vietcong action against American dependents in Saigon, ruled out instant response but he ordered that lost aircraft should be quickly replaced.

Johnson's hand was strengthened when he crushed Senator Barry Goldwater in the November election by a margin of 16 million votes. This was the highest margin ever scored by a presidential candidate. In addition, the Democrats obtained huge majorities in both houses of the Congress. Now he could use his wide support to take strong action. He refused to do so.

In lieu of such action, he directed the National Security Council's staff, chaired by McGeorge Bundy, to outline political and military options available against North Vietnam.

The Joint Chiefs December 18 again called for a hard-hitting air campaign against North Vietnam to be completed within twenty days. As a fall-back position they proposed tightly controlled but gradually increasing air pressure over a two-month period.

Air Vice Marshal Ky led a reprisal raid by the Vietnamese Air Force when thirty-two attack bombers struck a Vietcong camp near Saigon, and supposedly killed five hundred soldiers. On the ground, Vietnamese troops battled the communists for six hours near Ben Cat as Major General Khanh directed the operation. This limited action did not deter the Vietcong. Severe floods from the November typhoons, along with Vietcong successes in the area, had caused the virtual collapse of government authority in ten central provinces. As the floods receded, the Vietcong took almost complete control of the countryside in populous Quang Ngai and Binh Dinh Provinces.

This situation prompted Ambassador Taylor to inform the president Novemer 21 that the principal problems in South Vietnam were the country's inability to form a solid national government and to stop Vietcong reinforcements.

In Washington, Bundy's group within the National Security Council suggested three possible courses of action. 1. Reprisal attacks, intensified covert operations, resumption of offshore naval patrols and stepped-up Laotian air attacks. 2. Heavy bombing of North Vietnam as favored by the Joint Chiefs. Bundy called such actions almost reckless—an open invitation to Chinese intervention. 3. Modest use of air attacks against infiltration targets in North Vietnam. He said he preferred the last option because it would give the impression of a steady and deliberate pressure against North Vietnam while permitting the United States to halt at any time.

Ambassador Taylor flew to Washington November 26 and advocated that the United States take steps to restore an adequate government in Saigon and to increase covert actions, anti-infiltration attacks in Laos and reprisal bombings to stiffen South Vietnamese morale. In a second phase he called for more air attacks against infiltration targets in North Vietnam. Thirdly, he recommended destruction of all important fixed targets in North Vietnam. Like Bundy, he believed that covert actions, attacks against infiltration routes in Laos and reprisal bombings should start at once.

President Johnson was briefed by his principal advisers December 1, and he accepted the premise that a stable South Vietnamese government was essential to end the insurgency and he approved first-phase military actions. He said subsequent phases would project a progressive air bombardment against the North rather than attacks against functional target systems.

In line with the president's decision, a joint State Department/Defense Department message was sent December 8 instructing the Laotian ambassador in Vientiane to seek approval for American air strikes against hostile North Vietnamese communications targets inside Laos. Approval was granted on the 10th and McNamara authorized two missions a week, each consisting of four aircraft. This restricted bombing campaign was nicknamed Barrel Roll. Armed reconnaissance flights also were initiated.

Vietcong attacks continued to increase in South Vietnam against hamlets and outposts and they soared to a new high despite the Laotian bombing, and the greater use of American and Vietnamese planes and helicopters.

When the issue of free world support for South Vietnam surfaced again in December, it was discussed outside the context of Southeast Asia Treaty Organization commitments.

Such troop commitments were discussed at the White House meeting December 1 and a resolution was reached that aid should be sought from America's key allies. Thailand was asked to support the United States program and to intensify its counter-insurgency efforts. Prime Minister J. Harold Wilson of Great Britain was briefed on the position of the United States and his support was sought. The State Department was charged with the responsibility of seeking additional help from Australia and New Zealand and also consideration of sending small combat units to South Vietnam when and if the United States moved to the second phase of its strategy of increasing the military pressure against North Vietnam. It was agreed that the Philippines should be asked for a commitment of approximately eighteen hundred men. The conferees concluded their session with a decision to press for more outside aid.

At the time sixteen countries, including the United States, already were providing aid—some of advisory assistance to South Vietnam's armed forces—but mostly economic and technical aid. By the end of 1964 the Philippines, Korea and Nationalist China had said through diplomatic channels that they were ready to provide military assistance to South Vietnam.

Ambassador Taylor was advised by President Johnson following this White House meeting to let him know what kind of assistance would be needed after he discussed the matter with South Vietnam's government officials. The president said that the initiative in seeking allied help should not come from the United States but from South Vietnam which should have a voice in determining the nature of the allied assistance.

The previous month Major General Nguyen Khanh, the real power in the government, had said his country had only a general need for additional manpower and police. But December 7, at a meeting with Khanh,

Ambassador Taylor emphasized that free world assistance was important from the United States' domestic point of view, but he stressed that the United States did not want to internationalize the war although participation by other nations was needed. Khanh agreed.

At this point, aside from tentative probes of the attitudes of the governments of Australia and New Zealand, no effort was made to secure foreign combat troops but it was made known that economic assistance and military advisers would be welcomed. State Department messages since May had stressed that no foreign troops were sought.

An incident in downtown Saigon brought the United States to the verge of direct all-out intervention. That was the Christmas Eve bombing of the Brink's Hotel where bachelor officers of the Military Assistance Command were housed. Two Americans were killed, and sixty-four were injured along with forty-three Vietnamese.

Following the bombing President Johnson criticized Ambassador Taylor for not doing all that could be done to protect American installations.

Taylor replied, "We are faced here with a seriously deteriorating situation characterized by continued political turmoil, irresponsibilty and division within the Vietnamese armed forces, lethargy in the pacification program, growing anti-United States feeling, signs of mounting terrorism by the Vietcong directed at United States personnel, and deepening discouragement and loss of morale throughout South Vietnam." He said he had as many American advisers as could be absorbed. The introduction of combat troops, he said, might result in South Vietnam letting the United States carry the ball and, in view of past colonialism, lead to open hostility against Americans. Taylor noted that many factors were beyond America's capability to change. He said something new had to be done to make up for those things beyond American control. He recommended bombing the North, urging that retaliation be made within twenty-four hours of any North Vietnamese attack in the South. "To take no positive action now," he wrote, "is to accept defeat in the fairly near future." Actually, both Westmoreland and Taylor had doubts about using American combat troops.

Admiral Sharp and the Joint Chiefs recommended reprisal raids December 29 but President Johnson again rejected their advice. His overwhelming victory less than two months earlier in the presidential election had given him a mandate to pursue steps that would conclude the war. He just wasn't strong enough to make them. The Vietcong bombing was a direct attack against the United States and an open challenge. However, the defeat of South Vietnamese troops at Binh Gia, forty miles east of Saigon in the final days of 1964, was potentially more disastrous. In a departure from its usual hit-and-run guerrilla tactics, two regiments of the

9th Vietcong Division ambushed and virtually destroyed two South Vietnamese battalions, including the 4th Marine battalion. Heavy casualties were inflicted on elements of the armored corps that attempted to relieve them. Westmoreland said the Binh Gia battle marked the beginning of the final communist offensive. He claimed it meant the start of an intensive military challenge that the Vietnamese government could not meet with its own resources.

Meanwhile, the generals who controlled the South Vietnamese government December 20 had dissolved the civilian High National Council established earlier, although Chief of State Suu and Prime Minister Huong remained in their respective positions.

Ambassador Taylor realized that the South Vietnamese defeat at Binh Gia was directly related to their inadequate use of air support, and he was most anxious to use Bien Hoa's bombers in retaliation. He decided, however, that attacks against North Vietnamese targets should be done by B-52 bombers from Guam and by carrier planes from the Gulf of Tonkin.

Security of American bases, maintained by Vietnamese Army soldiers, came in for even greater attention. General LeMay had frequently recommended that security duties be turned over to American soldiers, but the Army had objected saying that four divisions would be needed. With an in-country team of approximately twenty-one thousand men, such a statement was absurd.

Despite Ambassador Taylor's recommendation for attacks against North Vietnam President Johnson in early 1965 rejected air strikes. In the face of contrary advice from many of his advisers, the president's adamant stand is well-nigh unbelievable. Americans and Vietnamese were being killed in increasing numbers but Johnson seemed insensible to their fate, caring little whether they were being saccrificed in vain. His indecision about military operations was matched by his inability to decide whether to support South Vietnam more vigorously or to disengage from the war.

Great Britain and the United States now agreed to call an international conference to guarantee Cambodia's national boundaries in an apparent attempt to slow Cambodia's slide toward communism. It was already too late because Sihanouk was firmly on the side of the People's Republic of China and North Vietnam. The latter continued to insist that only the National Liberation Front represented South Vietnam. Such a situation could not last. Four months later, May 3, 1965, Sihanouk severed diplomatic relations with the United States.

Sihanouk's decision is understandable. The political and military situation in South Vietnam had so deteriorated that he was convinced of the rightness of his decision.

Cambodia was one of the first countries to identify itself as a non-aligned nation—although this nomenclature is false—as it joined other such designated nations at international conferences. The first such meeting had been held in Belgrade in 1962. Since then independent states of Asia and Africa, those of eastern Europe, and other emergng nations gave an impetus to the movement, especially when officials of the movement permitted admission of nations from communist and socialist blocs.

Sihanouk, once he broke his country's ties with the United States, sought aid from China and the Soviet Union and it was readily granted.

The policy of Sihanouk's double-dealing practices favored the Vietnamese and Khmer communists and eventually had disastrous results not only for Sihanouk but for Cambodia. He understood the situation and he denounced their efforts. But Sihanouk's divorce from the United States and the free world, and his marriage to the communist world, permitted a new level of communist control of Southeast Asia. His action significantly changed the face of the war in South Vietnam and provoked in Cambodia's neighbors a sense of the danger of communist expansion. Communists in Cambodia now openly surfaced and threatened Sihanouk's regime. Their defiance of the government posed the greatest danger to religious and intellectual circles. Sihanouk's practice of abruptly changing loyalties, and his policy of consistent inconsistency, wrought havoc in Cambodia. Before Sihanouk turned totally to the communists, Vietnamese communists had already occupied large portions of Cambodia in the east, southeast and south. Their populations, weary of bearing violent persecutions and exactions, abandoned their homesites and retreated farther into the interior. Through the Cambodian population spread a silent rage as Sihanouk's political trickery became evident even though he repeatedly denounced the communists who had gained stature because of his policies.

President Johnson continued to procrastinate about using more forceful measures as he ordered limited air strikes against North Vietnam in a series of attacks called Rolling Thunder although these air strikes were delayed for two weeks by political and military turmoil in Saigon, and by bad weather that engulfed the area.

The Vietcong seemed to thrive on bad weather—for one thing they were mostly free of air attacks—and Saigon itself was threatened by the Vietcong's 9th Division. General Westmoreland authorized light bombers to attack their base camps but it was too little, too late.

General Westmoreland was convinced the United States was not fully committed to winning the war and he wanted to change the nature of the American involvement. He sought more extensive use of American jet aircraft within South Vietnam, the restoration of United States markings on American-manned aircraft and abolishment of the requirement that Vietnamese observers fly in American planes. His first step was to order light bombers and fighters to attack an elite communist battalion that had surrounded South Vietnamese units in the Central Highlands. This action marked the end of the long United States advisory phase, and the beginning of open American combat against the Vietcong.

The Joint Chiefs agreed with most of Westmoreland's views and March 9, 1965, United States aircraft were officially authorized to perform combat operations, although no strikes were permitted from Thailand's airfields into South Vietnam. They also insisted that American aircraft not be flown on missions that could be flown by Vietnamese. The restriction against American insignia on American aircraft was removed, and they no longer were required to have a Vietnamese airman on board.

Despite its limited effectiveness, the Vietnamese Air Force was a formidable force. Since 1955 it had expanded from a few obsolete aircraft to fourteen squadrons and almost three hundred modern planes at five major air bases. The United States Air Force had increased to two hundred and twenty-two planes in South Vietnam while another eighty-three were based in Thailand.

It was now clear to most American military and political leaders that the United States advisory mission had failed to end North Vietnam's support of the insurgency in South Vietnam and Laos. It was apparent that communist infiltration was growing rather than tapering off, and the government of South Vietnam was still unstable seventeen months after President Diem's assassination. Defeat was obvious unless some new approach was tried. The decision was to discard the purely advisory American function in favor of direct United States air and ground operations.

After the Gulf of Tonkin incident, former President Dwight D. Eisenhower had told President Johnson that he saw merit in General Wheeler's suggestion of putting an American division into Vietnam just south of the demilitarized zone to help protect the South, but Johnson decided against such a forceful step. Eisenhower said he did not favor a large deployment of American troops at the time but later he told Johnson that he could not let Indochina fall. Eisenhower said he hoped it would not be necessary to use the six or eight divisions in Vietnam about which he had heard some speculation. If it should prove necessary, he added, "So be it," and he offered Johnson his full support.

CHAPTER 12

Rolling Thunder

OFFICIALS OF THE DEMOCRATIC REPUBLIC OF VIETNAM REGARDED THE start of 1965 as the beginning of the war's final phase, during which South Vietnam's army would be destroyed by direct military action, and the government and its people would lose their will to fight. They correctly judged that the government of the Republic of Vietnam at Saigon had been weakened by a series of coups following President Diem's assassination in 1963. Since then the South Vietnamese Army had suffered a series of defeats that had led to widespread demoralization. Government control of the rural areas was continually eroding as the Vietcong expanded their control. With the start of the new year North Vietnamese Army units for the first time moved into the Central Highlands in regimental strength. Furthermore, infiltration from the North increased and soon reached a rate of more than 1,000 a month.

At this critical juncture most United States authorities believed that South Vietnam's armed forces no longer were able to contain the rising military threat to the security of their country without extensive American military and economic assistance. Ambassador Taylor and General Westmoreland recommended that this assistance would have to include the commitment of American ground forces. President Johnson agreed with them. This decision had an immediate impact on the command and control structure that had been designed primarily to accommodate only a United States military assistance program. Despite proposed increases in military assistance, Ambassador Taylor retained overall responsibility for all United States activities in Vietnam. To assist him, and to provide a mechanism for high-level coordination and discussion, a Mission Council had been formed the previous July. Now senior officials of the civilian and military elements of the United States mission met weekly with the ambassador as chairman.

The Attack Carrier Striking Force, Seventh Fleet, known as Task Force 77, established an operating area in the northern part of the Gulf of Tonkin known as Yankee Station—a reference to the American Civil War and the northern Yankees. A few months later, a similar position off South Vietnam was named Dixie Station for the same reason. This southern station was dedicated to air operations in South Vietnam and was considered temporary until adequate air fields could be established for United States Air Force aircraft. Yankee Station forces at this time operated against targets in North Vietnam and Laos.

After much discussion about command authority, Westmoreland recommended the establishment of several Army corps headquarters in Vietnam that, under his operational control, would conduct combat operations in their respective tactical zones.

The United States Marines were the first members of the American armed forces to deploy large numbers of ground combat units in Vietnam. About eight hundred Marines had served earlier, mostly in the northern provinces. Sixty Marine advisers had been attached to the South Vietnamese Army while a rifle company was assigned to base security at Da Nang. Other Marines were guards at headquarters installations.

When it was decided to make a sizable deployment of Marines to Vietnam those most combat ready were selected, including elements of the 3rd Marine Division on Okinawa and the 1st Marine Aircraft wing in Japan.

Following the attack against the United States destroyers in the Gulf of Tonkin the Pacific command had activated the 9th Marine Expeditionary Brigade under Brigadier General Raymond G. Davis, a Medal of Honor recipient, with regimental headquarters and three battalion landing teams. The preceding August 6,000 Marines had embarked on board Seventh Fleet amphibious ships. The composite aircraft group was alerted, but not embarked. Further orders to deploy to Vietnam were placed in abeyance and this force bacame an effective one in readiness awaiting further orders.

Brigadier General Frederick J. Karch, who had taken command of the American amphibious forces in the Pacific, at this stage was advised to place his command on alert due to the unstable conditions in South Vietnam.

President Johnson sent another fact-finding team to Vietnam February 4, 1965. Such a step apparently was easier than making the tough decisions a stronger president would have long since made. This team was headed by McGeorge Bundy, and it coincided with a visit to Hanoi by Soviet Premier Aleksei N. Kosygin. Since Kruschchev's removal from power in October, 1964, Kosygin had tried to restore closer Russian relations with North Vietnam. According to Chinese sources, the Americans learned that Kosygin hoped to persuade the North Vietnamese to halt their military aid to the Vietcong as a precondition to negotiations to end the war, but Kosygin evidently sensed an imminent Vietcong victory and he wanted the Soviet Union to share it. American intelligence sources reported correctly that Kosygin now planned to offer more economic and military aid to assist the North Vietnamese in stepping up their warfare in the South.

After the American team arrived in Saigon a small United States advisory detachment in II Corps, four-and-a-half miles north of Pleiku, was hit by the Vietcong, and a nearby aviation battalion was also attacked. Bundy, Westmoreland and Taylor jointly called for reprisal strikes.

For once President Johnson had the courage to accept the advice of his top counselors. United States Air Force and Navy aircraft were ordered to attack North Vietnam.

A carrier strike was scheduled for February 6, 1965. Rear Admiral E. C. Outlaw, who commanded Carrier Task Force 77 off North Vietnam's coast, received the go-ahead for high-priority strikes. He immediately ordered crews briefed and they were in their planes when another wire cancelled the strike. No reason was given.

Within an hour another message arrived, advising him that he could not use the seventy-eight A-4 bombers, and that the force would have to be reduced. Bombing load now had to be changed because the use of napalm was forbidden. New targets were assigned for the following day. Outlaw was furious because these targets were insignificant. They included military barracks at Dong Hoi that Outlaw's intelligence officers claimed housed no troops.

Outlaw and Captain Richard Hanecak, his air operations and plans officer, met in the War Room February 7 with the staff after the strike was launched. In listening to calls from strike leaders, they heard one say, "Report to Admiral that the squadron commander reports 'foul ball.'"

"What the hell is foul ball?" Outlaw demanded as the five-foot, nine-and-half-inch admiral literally leaped off his chair.

"I really don't know," Hanecak said.

"Goddam it, find out!"

Hanecak called VA-50's squadron commander Peter Mongolardi. He got the duty officer instead. "What does foul ball mean?"

"I don't know."

"Is Commander Mongolardi in there?"

"He's in the Ready Room."

"Put Pete on."

When Mongolardi came on the line, Hanecak said, "Pete, this is Dick Hanecak in the War Room. What does foul ball mean?"

"Foul ball. Foul ball," Mongolardi mused. "To me it means let's throw another ball in and get on with the game."

Hanecak, in growing desperation, said, "No Pete. I've got the Admiral here and he wants to know what the hell it means."

"Okay, wait a minute."

The night before the strike the air commander and Hanecak's controller had agreed on the code words they would use once the shoreline was crossed and they were over land. Mongolardi explained that foul ball meant they were over Vietnam.

Due to the change in targets, and the reduction in force, the Dong Hoi barracks attack caused insignificant damage.

In the weeks and months that followed, Outlaw grew more and more incensed about the directions he was receiving from Washington through CINCPAC. He was particularly upset with the orders that he was given about how to run his task force. At first, he had to telex his intentions a week ahead of a contemplated strike. This time period was later stretched to a month. When the war heated up, and quick response was mandatory, he was told to make his intentions once a week or twenty-four hours in advance under emergency conditions. Even then the answer was usually no. His instructions for approved strikes went far beyond the point of common sense. Strike crews were ordered to come in from a certain heading, regardless of ground defenses that normally determined such areas of attack, and where they could engage enemy aircraft. McNamara gave specific orders that all enemy aircraft must be visually identified before they could be fired upon. This almost precluded the use of air-to-air missiles because they were normally fired at distances beyond an identification point. It was true that commercial aircraft flew in and out of the Hanoi-Haiphong area and that these aircraft must be protected. Despite the war, civilian traffic operated just as if the nations were at peace. The Sparrow missile was practically ruled out, despite its effectiveness, because it could not arm itself if it was fired too close to an enemy aircraft.

Outlaw became so upset with McNamara's way of controlling his operations, never permitting him to operate with any degree of independence, that he protested to friends in CINCPAC and among the Joint Chiefs that such regulations were jeopardizing his fliers. He was told to shut up or he would be fired. Restrictions were frustrating because he honestly believed that destruction of high-priority targets in North Vietnam would shorten the war. He had served in World War II so his views should have been given the respect that they deserved.

When Carrier Task Force 77 first started operations it had more aircraft than the whole Seventh Air Force in Indochina. In early 1965 it had three carriers at Yankee Station, and Dixie Station in the south was set up for interdicting targets of evacuating Americans if South Vietnam should fall to the communists.

Air Force F-105s in Thailand had to refuel at least once going to and from North Vietnam so the carrier task force was the best source of adequate fighters and bombers at this time to attack North Vietnam.

The carrier task force operated without fear of reprisal raids. After the Gulf of Tonkin incident, when torpedo boats attacked elements of the Seventh Fleet, no serious attack was ever made again. A station north of Yankee Station—manned by the heavy cruiser *Long Beach*—had a missile capability. It was ninety miles southeast of Hanoi and it was called the Piraz Station (positive identification, radar advisory zone) at a geographic location in the northern gulf.

At Yankee Station, there were two carriers on line at all times while a third was undergoing replenishment by moving back and forth over an eighty-mile area to the southeast. Carriers could operate about three days before they needed replenishment at sea, and they were restricted to a distance of thirty miles from the Chinese-controlled island of Hainan.

After the first mission, every detail was provided by Washington, even the time over target regardless of whether the circumstances might make a particular route or time dangerous to the crews. There could be no deviation in any detail. Airfields were off limits but some of the pilots tried to provoke North Vietnamese fighter pilots to come up and fight, but their challenges were largely ignored.

After the first attacks the Vietcong retaliated February 10 and struck Qui Nhon, killing twenty-three Americans and seven Vietnamese.

In coordination with these attacks the Joint Chiefs ordered four-and-a-half Tactical Air Force squadrons transferred from other Pacific bases to Vietnam, and moved thirty additional B-52 bombers to Guam.

It had been almost too late for an American response because South Vietnam's control in all areas had deteriorated to the disintegration point as Vietcong action quickly expanded in all four corps areas.

President Johnson addressed the nation February 7 and announced that he was ordering the withdrawal of American dependents. He warned that the United States might take further actions. "I have ordered deployment to South Vietnam of a Hawk air defense battalion," he said. "Other reinforcements, in units and individuals, may follow." Hawk was an acronym for "homing all the way killer," and it was used against low-flying aircraft.

McGeorge Bundy was asked by the president to discuss the value of further North Vietnamese air strikes with Westmoreland and Ambassador Taylor during his visit to South Vietnam. After he did so Bundy recommended that the United States develop a sustained reprisal policy using air and naval forces against North Vietnam. He wrote the president that the situation in South Vietnam is "deteriorating and without new United States action defeat appears inevitable—probably not in a matter of weeks or perhaps even months, but within the next year or so. There is still time to turn it around," he said, "but not much."

This was true. The North Vietnamese continued to reinforce their units in South Vietnam and they were able to move almost at will against major population centers. It appeared that the North Vietnamese Army was about to cut the country in two, across its midsection. In General Westmoreland's judgment the defeat of aggression by the North Vietnamese could not be achieved without deployment of United States combat forces. With Ambassador Taylor's concurrence, he recommended such a move.

Two days prior to the February 11 Vietcong attack on an enlisted men's barracks at Qui Nhon that killed twenty-three Americans, Westmoreland gave his official appraisal of the war. He recalled that in the past he had considered a request for American combat troops to provide security for United States bases but that he had rejected the idea because he feared the South Vietnamese might lose interest in the war and relax their vigilance. He said that the February 7 attack on Pleiku marked a new phase and that American troops must be protected. He said he needed at least a division. "These are numbers of a new order of magnitude, but we must face the stark fact that the war has escalated."

Following the attacks on Qui Nhon and Pleiku the Joint Chiefs forwarded to the Secretary of Defense a program of reprisal actions to be taken against communist provocations. They said retaliatory air raids against North Vietnam had been too small to be effective and they recommended sustained pressure on the North Vietnamese, including air strikes against selected targets in North Vietnam, along with naval bombardment, covert operations, intelligence patrols and cross-border operations in Laos and the landing of American troops in South Vietnam.

Two days later President Johnson approved a "limited and measured" air campaign against North Vietnam. Air strikes were delayed, however, until March 2 due to bad weather.

The explosive political situation in South Vietnam erupted again in February, 1965, as another power struggle began. Dissident military leaders revolted against Khanh and troops seized Saigon. The Armed Forces Council February 15 declared that it alone had responsibility for selecting the prime minister and the chief of state. While veteran politician Phan Khac Suu remained as chief of state, the council appointed a Saigon physician, Dr. Phan Huy Quat who in 1964 had served as foreign minister, as prime minister. Six days later a group of senior generals led by Major General Nguyen Van Thieu, commander of IV Corps, and Air Vice Marshal Nguyen Cao Ky who commanded the Air Force, deposed Khanh, the veteran of other coup attempts, as commander-in-chief of South Vietnam's armed forces. To Ambassador Taylor's great relief Khanh went into exile and never returned to South Vietnam.

With the military and political situation assuming disastrous proportions, Westmoreland directed his deputy, Lieutenant General John L. Throckmorton, to determine what American ground forces were needed for base security. Throckmorton recommended deployment of a three-battalion Marine expeditionary brigade to Da Nang because of the importance of the base for any air campaign against the North, and the "questionable capability of the Vietnamese to protect the base."

Although the need appeared urgent, and Westmoreland agreed with Throckmorton's concern, he hoped to keep the number of United States ground troops to a minimum and recommended instead the landing of only two Marine battalions while a third was held offshore in reserve.

Admiral Sharp, Commander-in-Chief, Pacific, agreed and forwarded his recommendations to the Joint Chiefs in Washington. Although Ambassador Taylor had strong reservations about sending ground troops to Vietnam he agreed to place Marine battalions at Da Nang "in view of General Westmoreland's understandable concern for the safety of this important base."

President Johnson agreed at the end of February to commit two battalions of the Marine expeditionary brigade to Da Nang to protect the base.

The State Department cabled Ambassador Taylor February 27 that he should seek approval of the Vietnamese government before the Marines were introduced. Although the Vietnamese agreed they expressed concern about the reaction of the Vietnamese population and requested that the American forces be brought to Da Nang "in the most inconspicuous way feasible."

Pentagon officials had considered bringing the Army's 173rd Airborne Brigade by air from Okinawa instead of the Marines. They believed that light infantry toops would be less conspicuous. General Westmoreland disagreed because the Marines would be more self-sustaining, and Admiral Sharp added his negative thoughts. With such high-level opposition, the Joint Chiefs ordered the 9th Marine Expeditionary Brigade to Da Nang.

The brigade's commander, Brigadier General Karch, waiting ten miles offshore the night of March 7 aboard the *Mount McKinley* for the decision to land his troops, was handed a dispatch. He read it quickly and when Rear Admiral B. W. Wulzen came in Karch read the dispatch to him. "It said, "Close Da Nang, land the landing force."

Karch looked again at the dispatch before he said, "Don, do you think in Washington they know what time it is in Da Nang? This means a night landing if we close Da Nang at this point."

Karch was disturbed because the fleet was encountering the worst weather it had even seen in the South China Sea. Visibility was limited to 150–200 yards, and it was midnight. The move into Da Nang harbor from which the landing would be launched was going to take four to five hours.

Karch instead set the landing for 8:00 A.M. March 8. Visibility was five miles with a light wind. Near the shoreline waves crested from two to four feet, spilling gently onto the beach. But in the transport area swells reached eight to ten feet and slowed the debarkation of the first troops.

Once they were landed, I Corps Commander Major General Nguyen Chang Thi and the mayor of Da Nang welcomed them while a group of Vietnamese university students, led by a vanguard of pretty girls with leis, greeted the Marines. Prior to the landing Vietnamese troops had secured the beachhead and the route to the air base. Karch was bedecked with flowers and, when pictures of him were distributed to the press later he was criticized for his stern demeanor. His response to the criticism was that "when you have a son in Vietnam and he gets killed, you don't want a smiling general with flowers around his neck as the leader." There were banners everywhere to welcome the troops. Later, the 1st Battalion, 3rd Marine Division, was airlifted to the air base. The 3rd Battalion was landed from ships that afternoon.

A new phase of the war had begun. With these landings of 5,000 troops a third of the Marine ground forces and two-thirds of its helicopter squadrons in the Western Pacific were committed to South Vietnam. Despite these two battalions, however, the Marine intervention was still limited. The Joint Chiefs made their position clear in a March 7 dispatch that "the United States Marine Force will not, repeat, will not engage in day-to-day actions against the Vietcong."

General Westmoreland assigned the Marines to protect Da Nang's air base from enemy attack, but instructed Karch that overall responsibility for the defense of the Da Nang area belonged to the armed forces of the Republic of Vietnam.

The Air Force base at Da Nang at first was a fenced off area with a 10,000-foot runway. Personnel slept in tents, and they were vulnerable to attacks by communist sympathizers. The men most feared Vietnamese women and children. The base was run by the Vietnamese and at first civilians had free access. After a kid smuggled in a hand grenade and threw it into a fuel compound and blew it up, destroying the tent compound, even mothers with babies in their arms were almost strip searched. A baby would be practically disrobed while the mother's purse and her body were carefully checked for explosives. The Americans were never sure who was or who was not a Vietcong. Often Vietnamese loyal to their government were forced to do things by the Vietcong to protect their loves ones or themselves.

General LeMay's problems with McNamara and President Johnson had become so acute by June, 1964, that the president offered him an ambassadorship if he would step down as Air Force chief of staff. LeMay had no interest in such a position and with that fall's election coming up the President wanted to avoid a donnybrook such as occurred when Chief of Naval Operations Anderson was fired by McNamara during the Kennedy years. So, he continued LeMay in the job.

After Johnson was overwhelmingly elected, LeMay knew that it was only a question of time before he was asked to leave and this time there would be nothing offered except a demand for his retirement. This came early in 1965.

LeMay, and General John P. McConnell who succeeded him as Air Force chief of staff February 1, 1965, had long pressed for a series of systematic air attacks against North Vietnam. They believed that earlier attacks had been too restrictive because they were confined to lines of communication in Laos and in North Vietnam below the 19th parallel. They wanted attacks against North Vietnam's ports, railroad yards, bridges, power plants and supply centers. There were not a great number of important strategic targets in North Vietnam but those that existed were far more important than interdiction of supply routes in the South because of the primitive network over which most supplies were carried along jungle trails on the backs of soldiers. The generals had argued that it was more efficient to destroy supplies at the source: such targets as the Kep Marshalling Yards, the Paul Doumer bridge in Hanoi and the port of Haiphong.

When he took over from LeMay, General McConnell proposed to the Joint Chiefs a twenty-eight-day campaign against ninety-four strategic targets. They agreed that the South Vietnamese needed air support; otherwise a prolonged war of attrition would result. He said the war should be brought home to the people of North Vietnam and supplies cut off where they were most vulnerable. Phase 3 would last two weeks, he said. During these attacks the ports would be destroyed, the sea approaches mined, and ammunition and supply areas in the Hanoi-Haiphong area would be destroyed. Hopefully, he said, North Vietnam would decide that the war in the South was not worth the price. By the end of Phase 4 the Air Force chief of staff said that all ninety-four targets would be destroyed.

With the situation in Vietnam growing more desperate in late February President Johnson, Secretary of State Rusk and McNamara approved a strategic air offensive to be called Rolling Thunder, but only against targets below the 20th parallel. Also, McNamara insisted that the size and frequency of the air offensive be decided in Washington, and that he personally must approve each target. This was an unfortunate decision because after attacks were authorized later above the 20th the threat to American planes had multiplied and it became a perilous area for fliers. Even by the summer of 1965 North Vietnam's defenses above the 20th parallel had become formidable. President Johnson placed even further restrictions by saying that strikes against surface-to-air (SAM) missile targets could only be made if they were firing at American planes! All other sites were off-limits. McNamara was convinced that the air campaign would make little difference to United States operations in the South and that the risk of Chinese confrontations against American fliers was too great.

Years later, when President Richard M. Nixon authorized massive bombing of the Hanoi-Haiphong area in December, 1972, the Chinese did not intervene. In effect, to use one of their own expressions, the Chinese had become paper tigers. The Americans were out-bluffed, and this decision extended the war and increased the casualties on all sides.

In South Vietnam the war continued to be fought on the ground with inadequate air support. Army Chief of Staff General Harold K. Johnson said he believed it would take approximately five-and-a-half divisions to seal off the demilitarized zone. Marine Corps Commandant General Greene was more realistic, saying it would eventually take 500,000 troops in South Vietnam. Air Force General McConnell and his field commanders believed that only a strategic air campaign could end the conflict, but they were denied a chance to prove it.

The Joint Chiefs continued to seek McNamara's approval to attack some of North Vietnam's more important targets, particularly those with a direct bearing on the fighting in the South. Twelfth on the list of targets long recommended by them was the Paul Doumer railroad and highway bridge on the outskirts of Hanoi. The 14th target was the Thanh Hoa railroad and highway bridge just north of the city of Thanh Hoa, seventy miles south of Hanoi. They were both key links in North Vietnam's transportation system, and were destined to become two of the most famous or infamous targets in North Vietnam depending upon which side you talked to. Destruction of the southern railway system had long had the highest priority to reduce the flow of men and materiel to South Vietnam. South of the 20th parallel there were five other large bridges and a railroad yard at Vinh with 115 miles of usable rail lines. The bridges, however, were the most vulnerable links in North Vietnam's lines of communication. The Joint Chiefs had repeatedly recommended attacks against the southern portion of this rail system to overwhelm its defenses in a single effort. The Dang Phuong railroad and highway bridge and the Thanh Hoa bridge were recommended as first targets in order to trap the maximum quantity of rolling stock south of the 20th parallel where it could be destroyed in other attacks.

The Joint Chiefs submitted a four-phase program to McNamara March 27, 1965, that incorporated some, but not all of McConnell's earlier recommendations. They proposed a twelve-week program to isolate North Vietnam from all external sources of supply, and then further attacks to destroy her internal military and industrial capacity. In the first phase—to last three weeks, all lines of communication south of the 20th parallel would be attacked starting with a strike against the Thanh Hoa bridge. In a second phase to last six weeks all rail and highway links with China, including the destruction of the Paul Doumer bridge, would be bombed. The third phase, scheduled for two weeks, recommended air attacks against all port facilities, the mining of the seaward approaches during the ninth week and the destruction of ammunition and supply dumps during the 10th week. In the final phase, previous targets would be restruck as necessary during a two-week period as well as attacks against industrial targets outside populated areas.

The key point of the railroad system was on the outskirts of Hanoi where four of five major railroad lines came together to cross the Red River over the Paul Doumer bridge. Its destruction would sever Hanoi from communication with southwest and southeast China and North Vietnam's major seaport at Haiphong. With this bridge knocked out, truck traffic would have to be rerouted from National Highway 1 to Routes 2 and 3 northwest of Hanoi over a Red River ferry. The Haiphong-Hanoi road traffic would also have to be ferried across the Red River. The Joint Chiefs emphasized to McNamara and the president that any delay in authorizing the destruction of this key bridge would allow time for building an extensive bypass system of river ferries and the development of an effective air defense system for the bridge's protection.

The second bridge recommended for early destruction was seventy miles south of Hanoi. The Thanh Hoa bridge was known to the Vietnamese as Dragon's Jaw because it funneled men and materials to South Vietnam's battlefields and into southern Laos.

McNamara approved attacks against the southern rail lines in March but he withheld approval of other targets for the time being. The Paul Doumer and Thanh Hoa bridges were not attacked until after they became well defended and perilous to American fliers.

Vietnam's 1,300-mile railroad system was conceived by Governor General of French Indochina Paul Doumer and was built between 1896 and 1902. By 1960 the system was a major factor in North Vietnam's movement of military supplies from China and Haiphong into Hanoi and then south to the battlefields. All supplies coming into Hanoi by railroad passed over the Paul Doumer bridge, while those moving south crossed the Thanh Hoa bridge. The Doumer bridge was 5,532 feet long and 38 feet wide, the longest in Vietnam. The Thanh Hoa spans the Song Ma River. It was a new bridge completed in 1964 after the Vietminh destroyed the original French bridge. It was 548 feet long and 56 feet wide.

The Air Force's tactical aircraft carried the early strike burden against the highly-defended targets in North Vietnam, although the Navy played the major role later in attacks against the bridges. Political reservations about committing strategic bombers made the use of fighter-bombers necessary. The Air Force's F-105 Thunderchief and the Navy's F-4 Phantom, due to their superior speed, maneuverability and bomb-carrying capacities, were ideal for this role. These fighter-bombers and Navy tactical fighters made outstanding contributions, particularly as bridge "busters." The F-105 was the largest single-seat fighter in the world, weighing 50,000 pounds. It was called the Thud—at first sarcastically and later with some affection. It has other derisive nicknames: lead sled, ultra hog and the squash bomber. But it was tough and it could take incredible punishment. The F-4 gained equal fame as a MIG killer and was known for its excellent bombing capability. Initially an all-weather, high-altitude, two-place interceptor for the Navy's fleet defense, it filled many other roles. It was ugly to look at with its drooping horizontal tail and bent-up wing tips. It was first developed for the United States Navy and then converted to Air Force use.

Approval to attack the Thanh Hoa bridge seventy miles south of Hanoi was finally granted by McNamara April 2 and the job was assigned to the Air Force's 67th Tactical Fighter Squadron—the Fighting Cocks—led by Lieutenant Colonel Robinson Risner flying out of Korat, Thailand, in F-105s.

For the first mission, sixteen of the forty-six F-105s were loaded with a pair of Bullpup missiles while others carried general purpose bombs. Half of the planes were scheduled for flak suppression. In the first attack Bullpup missiles merely bounced off the bridge's upper steel structure.

The bridge was hit repeatedly but it refused to go down, and two planes were lost.

Two days later the bridge was attacked again. This time three planes were lost as MIGs attacked for the first time during the war. The bridge remained in place, although it was damaged. It was like bombing a spider web. The 750-pound bombs used in these attacks were not powerful enough to destroy a bridge of this size, a fact learned in World War II but ignored in this new war.

Other targets were hit with greater success including a thermal plant that was virtually destroyed, and a locomotive and twenty-two trucks. These attacks convinced the North Vietnamese that in the future supply trucks should travel at night.

The Thanh Hoa bridge was attacked again May 7 after it was noted that repairs had been made and the bridge was back in service. The new attacks closed the bridge again temporarily to traffic, and made truck and rail traffic more vulnerable.

By mid-May, twenty-seven of North Vietnam's bridges had been attacked and all but one was destroyed. The Dragon's Jaw remained because the missiles and 750-pound bombs were inadequate against the sturdy Thanh Hoa bridge.

During one such flight May 15 to the Hanoi area Lieutenant Colonel Robinson Risner's plane did not come back. Crew Chief Charles Thompson, who only a few months earlier had arrived at Da Nang fresh out of technical school in the States, anxiously scanned the sky awaiting his commander's return. He was one of a large number of enlisted men servicing the F-105s who quickly had to take on responsibilities far beyond their years. At each promotion time, it was experience in the field that counted and Thompson went up in grade as quickly as regulations permitted.

Thompson turned as the chief master sergeant spoke up behind him. "We've got a problem."

"Is it Colonel Risner?" Thompson said anxiously.

"I believe so."

Thompson walked over to a plane that had just parked, wondering why the captain remained in his seat. He noted that the pilot was close to tears. Thompson unstrapped him, and said, "Do you know what happened to Colonel Risner?"

"He went down and we didn't have time to go back and check," the captain said. "Nobody saw a chute. All we saw was his plane going down. We called for recon to come in and they searched the area for an hour but they had to leave because of ground fire."

Thompson was shocked by Risner's loss. They had all admired the young commander. Risner had a steady look that could get action from associates without saying a word. They did not know whether he was killed or captured until two years later when his picture appeared in an American magazine as a prisoner of war.

CHAPTER 13

An Old Play with New Actors

GENERAL WESTMORELAND COMPLETED HIS ESTIMATE OF THE SITUATION in Vietnam March 26, 1965 and forwarded his recommendations to Admiral Sharp and the Joint Chiefs. He said there were three alternatives. First, the United States could give more aid to the buildup of the Vietnamese armed forces, continue and expand air strikes against North Vietnam, and use resources of the Seventh Fleet to interdict infiltration by sea. He did not believe that these actions were sufficient. In his second alternative, he suggested that five divisions could be deployed, including three American divisions, across the Vietnamese and the Laotian panhandle near the 17th parallel. Such action, he added, coordinated with a stepped-up air campaign against the North, could be taken along with the strengthening of South Vietnam's armed forces. Thirdly, Westmoreland said that other American and free world troops could be sent to help deal with the Vietcong insurgency. He did not believe the lines of communication or port facilities in South Vietnam could supply and support divisions strung along the parallel, claiming that by the time this was done the war would be lost. He claimed that the one feasible solution was to continue to build up the Army of the Republic of Vietnam, intensify the air war against North Vietnam, and to deploy the equivalent of two United States divisions with their necessary combat and service support in South Vietnam. These divisions would be used, he said, to protect vital United States installations, to defeat communist efforts to control Kontum and Pleiku Provinces, and to establish enclaves in coastal regions. He said he realized this would involve 33,000 troops by June, but that he believed such American strength would blunt the communist offensive in the two northern corps areas and stiffen the backbone of South Vietnam's forces throughout the country. In addition, he recommended reinforcement of the Marine Expeditionary Brigade by 4,685 men, and to include a third battalion at Da Nang, with a fourth assigned to the airstrip eight miles south of Hué. Westmoreland was disturbed about possible enemy action against other bases, notably the United States Army communications facility at Phu Bai and its small airfield. It was not a good airfield, he said, but it was the best available north of the Hai Van Pass.

Admiral Sharp and the Joint Chiefs had already recommended deployment of troops to Phu Bai but Lieutenant General Victor H. Krulak, commanding general of the Fleet Marine Force, Pacific, and a leading theorist on counter-insurgency warfare, was opposed. He believed this was an example of dollar economics wagging the tail of military deployment. He believed that Phu Bai was tactically indefensible. Westmoreland disagreed, pointing out there was a $5 million investment in the unit and he firmly believed that Phu Bai must be defended. Some of Westmoreland's staff agreed with Krulak saying that better uses for a Marine battalion could be found elsewhere. Krulak continued to maintain that the unit should be moved to another place so that Marine forces could be concentrated. Westmoreland insisted on Phu Bai's defense and Admiral Sharp refused to override him.

Westmoreland's new estimates of the situation in Vietnam were hand-carried to Washington for a special April 1 meeting with the National Security Council. At this meeting President Johnson made several far-reaching decisions. He approved an eighteen to twenty thousand increase in United States forces to include an additional Marine battalion. The 9th Marine Expeditionary Brigade was also permitted to use Marines "in active combat under conditions to be established and approved by the Secretary of Defense in consultation with the Secretary of State."

Westmoreland had predicted in March that within six months the South Vietnamese armed forces would essentially be located in a series of islands of strength clustered around districts and province capitals that would be clogged with large numbers of refugees while the rest of the provinces were communist-controlled. And he expressed his conviction that once this situation developed the South Vietnamese government would be besieged by groups demanding an end to the war. He told Ambassador Taylor that the only alternative was the maximum use of airpower against the North and American support of the Vietnamese in the South and against the enemy's supply lines in Laos. At first Taylor had opposed the use of more American combat troops, although he had agreed to the entry of the Marines at Da Nang. It was not until later that the Marines were given approval to make offensive operations within fifty miles of their bases.

The South Vietnamese armed forces now had 275,058 regular troops, 137,187 Regional Forces, and 185,000 Popular Forces. They greatly exceeded the number of Vietcong and North Vietnamese regulars. If used properly they should have been able to contain the aggression but they were poorly trained, especially in counter-insurgency operations. For American advisers the language barrier was always a problem. But the shortage of South Vietnamese junior officers was still a strong factor behind the marginal combat effectiveness of their army. Once the Vietcong buildup started it soon put too much of a strain on South Vietnam's widely scattered battalions, and desertions escalated. The primary factor was the gross inefficiency of the generals trying to run their country.

South Vietnam's critical political situation created instability and unrest throughout the country. This came at a time when the communist strength rose from 30,000 in November, 1963, to 212,000 by the middle of 1965. North Vietnam's units now were armed with modern weapons such as the AK-47 assault rifle that gave them a firepower advantage over South Vietnam's World War II rifles.

As South Vietnam's desertion rate soared, some paramilitary units simply disbanded and went home. The war was in a new phase that American political and military officials did not yet fully comprehend.

Westmoreland now divided the United States military effort in two parts—a tactical effort to destroy the Vietcong and North Vietnamese Army's main units, and second, to help South Vietnam develop a viable government to exercise effective control throughout the country. These two aims were closely related with emphasis placed on the establishment of security control. To accomplish this second objective advisory teams worked with the South Vietnamese government at the province and district level and their efforts focused on specific programs and goals. Pilot teams, each with an officer and a non-commissioned officer, had started operating a year earlier as a team was deployed to each of the thirteen districts in provinces surrounding Saigon. Within a month there were encouraging signs that districts formerly isolated were becoming close members of the provincial family. Therefore, the program was expanded in 1965.

With the increase in United States combat and advisory forces, a massive buildup and training program was established to train South Vietnam's armed forces. The program was created to establish South Vietnamese armed forces that would be capable of defending their country with minimal outside asistance.

Manpower was a major problem for the South Vietnamese. It was caused by an ineffective conscription program and a continually high desertion rate. South Vietnam's military authorities never made any real effort to enforce conscription laws. By the end of 1965 an estimated two hundred and thirty-two thousand youths had evaded military service.

Westmoreland called for a study of the problem, and he warned that if the current situation continued South Vietnam's primary manpower sources would be exhausted by 1969.

John A. McCone, United State Director of Intelligence, sent a memorandum April 2 to Secretary of State Rusk, Secretary of Defense McNamara, McGeorge Bundy and Ambassador Taylor. "I feel that the latter decision (to change the mission of American ground forces in South Vietnam) is correct only if our air strikes against the North are sufficiently heavy and damaging really to hurt the North Vietnamese." His next words were prophetic. "I think what we are doing is starting on a track which involves ground operation which in all probability will have limited effectiveness against guerrillas, although admittedly will restrain some Vietcong advances. However, we can expect requirements for an ever-increasing commitment of U.S. personnel without materially improving the chances of victory." In conclusion he said that if the United States was to change the mission of the ground forces then the ground rules on strikes against North Vietnam must be changed.

McCone's successor, Vice Admiral William F. Raborn, considerably watered down McCone's views when he was asked to report to Rusk and McNamara May 6, and he supported most of the limitations that the Johnson administration had used to make the air war ineffective.

In a memorandum April 6 the National Security Administration urged the president to deploy two additional Marine battalions and one Marine air squadron and its support units. They recommended more active use of Marine battalions and approved urgent exploration with the Korean, Australian and New Zealand governments of rapid deployment of significant elements from their armed forces in parallel with the deployment of American Marines. The president agreed and also approved a slowly ascending tempo on air raids as Vietcong attacks increased in number and severity. He still refused to approve heavy raids against all of North Vietnam's strategic targets or to agree to a blockade of her ports or their aerial mining.

During April Seventh Fleet's carriers established regular close support missions against the Vietcong in the South. They proved so successful that Westmoreland sought for a permanent assignment of a carrier off the northern half of South Vietnam to support the ground forces. Dixie Station was given that designation May 16, 100 miles southeast of Cam Ranh Bay. Three of the four carriers on duty in Indochina had to spend an unacceptable 80 percent of their time at sea with little time for rest and maintenance. By June 5, however, with five carriers assigned to the western Pacific, seatime was reduced to 75 percent.

In May, President Johnson had ordered a suspension of bombing attacks against the North in hopes of getting the North Vietnamese to talk seriously about ending their aggression. The bombing halt lasted eight weeks but there was no serious move on the part of the North Vietnamese to start peace talks.

Navy pilots began a three-year effort in June to destroy the Thanh Hoa bridge. After each attack the bridge remained upright although its girders were battered and there was a crescendo of bombs and missiles. There would be a lull in between each attack while the North Vietnamese repaired the bridge. It soon became an old play that reopened regularly with new actors. United States Navy pilots hit it twenty-four times with sixty-five aircraft in the next twelve months for a total drop of 128 tons of bombs. Not once was a span dropped due to the intrinsic strength of this incredible bridge. The general area around it looked like the valley of the moon due to the hundreds of bombs that missed the bridge and struck the ground instead. After each attack the North Vietnamese would put up pontoon bridges to continue the traffic while the indomitable bridge was repaired. Attackers increasingly met heavy ground fire and MIG fighters attacked aggressively while the bridge continued to fulfill its function of permitting trucks and box cars to cross its battered spans.

A year earlier air defenses in North Vietnam had been weak and limited. But in the spring of 1965 this situation no longer prevailed. The first SAM (Surface-to-Air Missile) site was spotted April 5 southeast of Hanoi. By mid-July numerous sites were active. When Admiral Sharp recommended that they be knocked out, McNamara refused saying he feared Russian technicians might be killed. Some Washingtonians claimed that the SAM sites were defensive only, and that if our aircraft did not attack Hanoi or Haiphong the enemy would not fire at them. American aircrewmen could have told them differently but the Washington politicians refused to listen. Finally, after one American plane was destroyed by a SAM the United States Air Force was permitted to attack two sites northwest of Hanoi. The order to attack was for just one day, and specifically forbade any attack against air bases from which enemy MIGs might oppose the mission. Fifty-five aircraft bombed the two sites and lost four aircraft. Another strike was authorized in August but photographs showed the sites had been moved.

United States Marines April 10 received more reinforcements for their air and ground units. The Marine Expeditionary Brigade reached a strength of 8,878 by the end of April. With a four-battalion regiment and a four-squadron aircraft group, artillery and engineer groups and a support group General Karch was convinced he could handle any emergency.

With President Johnson's approval, Karch was authorized to engage in counter-insurgency operations. Westmoreland ordered the Marines, in coordination with I Corps' Vietnamese army, to take the offensive and destroy the Vietcong in the Da Nang area.

Major General Thi, who commanded the corps' army, strongly opposed offensive actions outside the airfield's perimeter. He said of the area south of the field and on the bank of the Da Nang River, "This is enemy country. You are not ready to operate there." Despite his too-cautious views the Marines started patrols April 20 beyond their bases at Da Nang and Phu Bai. Vietnamese troops and civilian officials went along to avoid incidents with civilians. There was an almost total lack of intelligence. But nowhere did they encounter the Vietcong in strength such as had been reported by the Vietnamese.

Karch believed their presence accomplished their basic mission—defense of the two bases. During a visit to Da Nang General Wallace M. Greene, Jr., the Marine commandant, had other views. "You don't defend a place by sitting on your ditty box." This was the first common-sense remark that had been uttered since the Marines arrived.

A high-level conference at CINCPAC headquarters April 20, 1965, was attended by Ambassador Taylor, General Westermoreland and Admiral Sharp. They agreed that the relatively light Vietcong activity they were experiencing was the lull before the storm and they recommended deployment of 42,000 United States servicemen, including 5,000 Marines. The Marines would establish another defense enclave at Chu Lai, fifty-seven miles southeast of Da Nang, and be supported by three jet aircraft squadrons. The Chu Lai coastal plain lay astride the boundary dividing the two southern provinces of I Corps—Quang Ngai and Quang Tin. A few miles inland and west of the plain was heavy jungle with the rugged Annamite Mountains. Route 1, the all-weather, macadam road that paralleled the sea, bisected this plain. This national highway connected Saigon with the demilitarized zone and went through Da Nang to the northwest and Quang Ngai City, twenty miles to the south. Chu Lai was selected because of an extended Pentagon debate concerning the building of an expeditionary airfield south of Da Nang, but the proposal originated with General Krulak. He had selected Chu Lai after an inspection tour the previous year and he gave the future base its name. When his accompanying Navy officer remarked that the place looked good but that it was not marked on the map, Krulak replied that its name was Chu Lai. He explained later that he had simply given the officer the Mandarin Chinese characters for his name.

Secretary of Defense McNamara had tentatively approved the base March 30 but a final decision was not given at the Honolulu Conference.

It was proposed first to establish a short airfield for tactical support aircraft but later the runway was extended to 8,000 feet.

Ships of the Navy task force arrived off Chu Lai May 7. After an amphibious landing, seven of the nine infantry battalions of the 3rd Marine Division were ashore supported by most of the 12th Marines, a division artillery regiment, and a large portion of the 1st Marine Air Wing.

The 9th Marine Expeditionary Brigade was now deactivated and replaced by a new organization—the III Amphibious Force. The dropping of the word expeditionary had been recommended by General Westmoreland because of his concern that the name had bad connotations for the Vietnamese because the earlier French forces had been called expeditionary. He now ordered that defense of the three bases be coordinated with General Thi, and that the Marines conduct deep patrolling and offensive operations with their Vietnamese counterparts. Relations with the Vietnamese were sensitive. The Americans were considered guests who could offer advice but not compel action. In other words, the American were told to cooperate but not to give orders to the Vietnamese. Once the Marines were established, Westmoreland ordered the start of American operations in three successive stages: base security, deep patrolling and finally search and destroy missions.

At Da Nang, rudimentary pacification efforts were started at the village complex of Le My. There had been little security for more than a year. Marines took over village security and successfully helped villagers to fend for themselves with self-help projects, and they created an administration supported by the people. The Marines helped them to rebuild bridges, and their success with the villagers appeared to show promise for the future. General Krulak, during a mid-May visit, said, "It is a beginning, but a good beginning. The people are beginning to get the idea that United States security is a long term affair. This is just one opportunity among many. . . . it is the expanding oil spot concept of action."

Meanwhile, the building of the Chu Lai air base went ahead. Colonel John D. Nobel, Air Group 12's commanding officer, brought a four-plane division of Skyhawks into Chu Lai June 1, although the runway was not fully extended to maximum length. Later, more planes flew in and the first combat strikes were flown the same day.

Major General Lewis W. Walt relieved Major General William R. Collins as commander at Chu Lai when the latter was rotated home June 4, and Major General Keith B. McCutcheon replaced Major General Paul J. Fontana as commander of the 1st Marine Aircraft Wing. The change-of-command ceremony was held indoors because American colors were not permitted to be displayed outside. McCutcheon, a short, slim officer with a distinguished combat record, and Walt, a former college lineman whose bulk made him look the part, were welcomed briefly to their new jobs. Both men were junior major generals in the Marine Corps but highly decorated.

Shortly after General Walt assumed command of the Chu Lai forces he did a survey that showed 150,000 civilians were living within mortar range of the airfield. His response was that the "Marines are into the pacification business." Other than pacification efforts at Le My, little was accomplished. There was a need for overall guidance since civic action was too important to leave to the good will and natural enthusiasm of individaul Marines. With positive direction later improvements began to be shown and some villagers moved their homes under Marine protection. It would have been far preferable if the Marines had been permitted to expand the perimeters of their enclaves instead of bringing people into them.

June 15 Westmoreland ordered search and destroy missions and by the end of the month activity was stepped up in all three Marine enclaves although such actions placed a strain on available men and materials. During the month Walt requested that the remaining battalions of the 3rd Marine Division be sent from Okinawa. His request was viewed favorably in Saigon and Washington whose officials were convinced that additional American forces would be needed. Overdue was a reconsideration of the total United States commitment to Vietnam even though there was little combat involvement between its forces and the Vietcong. The communists deliberately avoided contact and concentrated instead on attacks against the South Vietnamese.

A "new life" hamlet program was given priority by the South Vietnamese government with consolidation of secure populated areas through a combination of military and social reforms. This was a variation of Diem's Strategic Hamlet Program but it was more realistic and it held greater promise of acceptance by the villagers. Under the new program security was restored in one area before teams went along to the next. It was a program based on static defense and that was its greatest weakness. At this time South Vietnam's pacification plans were too ambitious. In I Corps the campaign for 1965 called for pacification of the coastal plain inland to the railroad at Quang Nam and Quang Ngai Provinces. By March, however, only the areas surrounding the provincial capital were controlled by the Army of the Republic of Vietnam.

Further compounding the government's pacification efforts was another political crisis. Chief of State Suu and Prime Minister Quat disagreed over the makeup of the cabinet and were unable to resolve their differences.

Both stepped down and handed the reins of power to the military directorate who on June 11 appointed Nguyen Van Thieu as chief of state and Nguyen Cao Ky as prime minister. Saigon's military efforts and related pacification programs sputtered to a halt at the national and local levels. It appeared to the Americans that there was neither the time nor the inclination on the part of South Vietnam's various governments to deal with anything except the most urgent military threats.

During the spring and summer Vietcong offensive that started May 30, Army of the Republic of Vietnam units were caught widely dipersed in support of the pacification program. The Vietcong were able to destroy South Vietnamese battalions piecemeal. I Corps' 1st Vietcong Regiment ambushed the 1st Battalion, 51st Regiment, outside the small hamlet of Ba Gia, twenty miles south of Chu Lai. Of five hundred men in the South Vietnamese battalion only sixty-five and three United States advisers were able to break through the communist lines. General Thi threw in his last reserves—the 39th Vietnamese Ranger Battalion and the 3rd Vietnamese Marine Battalion. Marine F-4Bs from VMFA-531 flew close support for South Vietnamese units. When the battle ended it was a disaster for the South Vietnamese. Two battalions of United States Marines had been alerted but they were not committed to the battle. President Johnson issued a statement June 8. "If help is requested by the appropriate Vietnamese commander, General Westmoreland also has the authority within the assigned mission to employ these troops in support of Vietnamese forces faced with an aggressive attack when other effective reserves are not available and when in his judgment, the general military situation urgently requires it."

Westmoreland had only the III Amphibious Force in I Corps close enough to intervene. The United States Army's 173rd Airborne Brigade was the only other organization that could be committed but it was at Bien Hoa near Saigon.

The situation became so serious that the South Vietnamese Army was losing the equivalent of one infantry battalion a week to enemy action.

Westmoreland was more than ever convinced that the South Vietnamese were incapable of holding back the Vietcong, now reinforced by North Vietnamese regular troops, and he so informed the Joint Chiefs on June 7, 1965. "I believe that the DRV (Democratic Republic of Vietnam) will commit whatever forces it deems necessary to tip the balance and the government of Vietnam cannot stand up successfully to this kind of pressure without reinforcement." Specifically he asked for approval to deploy to Vietnam those forces already being considered in future plans. These included the remaining two battalions of the 3rd Marine Division, as well as two Army brigades and an airmobile division. Also under consideration was a Republic of Korea division and possible deployment of more American troops at a later date.

In January, 1965, the United States government had intensified its efforts to seek combat units from other nations to join its forces in South Vietnam. This was done to ease the conception that the Vietnamese war was an American undertaking supported only by non-Asians. In particular, the United States sought help from non-aligned nations, including those in Latin America, for non-military assistance. Donor countries were asked to meet as much of the cost of their aid as possible.

McGeorge Bundy had written President Johnson February 7 saying that he believed the government of Vietnam would collapse by 1966 without more United States help and action. At the time he had recommended increased military pressure on the North. The Joint Chiefs also had recommended such action and proposed that a brigade be sent to Da Nang.

That same month General Wheeler, chairman of the Joint Chiefs, notified Westmoreland that a major policy decision had been reached at the highest level to "do everything possible to maximize our military efforts to reverse the present unfavorable situation." Thus the foundation was laid for increased United States aid and deployment of free world combat troops.

February 20, 1965, the Joint Chiefs had recommended deployment of a Republic of Korea Army division for counter-insurgency and to assist in base security. Such a division, it was said, would number about twenty-one thousand and would be used in conjunction with additional United States Army, Air Force and Marine Corps combat personnel. Two problems were cited. One involved logistics and the other the relationship of the Korean division to the Military Assistance Command.

Ambassador Taylor originally had expressed strong reservations about sending United States Marines to Da Nang but he had agreed to support Westmoreland's recommendation for a battalion landing team to provide security.

After the Joint Chiefs approved such deployment, the State Department sought Taylor's views on the possible use of an international or multilateral force in Vietnam. He expressed strong opposition. Both he and the Australian envoy to South Vietnam believed that such a force might encourage the South Vietnamese to let the United States assume an even greater share of the war.

Upon his return from Vietnam in March, Army Secretary Johnson recommended the commitment of troops from Australia and New Zealand to take over responsibility for training Vietnamese Regional Forces and thus broaden the international character of the war. Secretary of Defense

McNamara agreed, but he also suggested inclusion of a Korean division. He said it was the policy of the United States government to send anything that would strengthen the position of the South Vietnamese government.

Army Secretary Johnson sought to resurrect the notion of invoking terms of the Southeast Asia Treaty Organization to deploy a four-division force across the demilitarized zone from the South China Sea through Laos to the Mekong River to prevent further infiltration. He was emphatically turned down by the organization's leaders.

While the Marines were given primary responsibility for I Corps, the United States Army was assigned II and III Corp including the Central Highlands, its adjacent coastal regions, and the area around Saigon. South Vietnam's armed forces retained responsibility for the IV Corps delta region.

In April the United States government agreed to send more troops to Vietnam and to the commitment of free world forces. The matter of free world troop contributions was discussed April 1 at the highest level in a policy meeting at which Army Secretary Johnson's 21-point proposal, including troops from Australia and New Zealand, was approved. Two days later, while Ambassador Taylor was in Washington, President Johnson and McNamara said they favored the idea but recognized serious political problems in obtaining troops from the Republic of Korea. The president said the Vietnamese government had expressed reluctance to have them in South Vietnam. Despite these views the president agreed April 6 to request free world combat troops and to explore with the governments of Korea, Australia and New Zealand the possibility of rapid deployment of combat troops from these countries.

In a speech April 7 at Johns Hopkins University, President Johnson stressed the nation's desire for peace and a reluctance to get further involved in the Vietnam war, but he said that United States pressure on North Vietnam was not a change in purpose but a change in what "we believe that purpose requires."

He said further, "Our objective is the independence of South Vietnam and its freedom from attack. . . . We will do everything necessary to reach that objective, and we will do only what is absolutely necessary.

"We will not be defeated.

"We will not get tired.

"We will not withdraw, either openly or under the cloak of a meaningless agreement.

"And we remain ready . . . for unconditional discussion."

These words may have seemed forthright at the time but, in retrospect, they have a hollow ring.

North Vietnam's Prime Minister Pham Van Dong rejected Johnson's proposal the next day.

In Vietnam, the military situation in I and II Corps was rapidly deteriorating as more North Vietnamese troops entered the South. General Westmoreland outlined the command relationship for deployment of free world troops to take this problem into account. He decided that the Korean division would not be attached to the United States Marine Corps but would constitute a major free world component of an international military security task force to block infiltration through the demilitarized zone. He said he wanted it deployed in Quang Ngai to provide security for the port and its base. Admiral Sharp agreed April 10 that free world units would not be attached to United States brigades but would have combined staff representation to give these forces an international flavor, and still allow the United States to retain full authority over its own forces. General Westmoreland proposed a "mechanism at the national level to control international forces involving the joint exercise of authority by the Commander-in-Chief, Vietnamese Armed Forces, and the Commander of the Military Assistance Command." In other words, he sought approval to form a single, small, combined staff headed by a United States general, with a Vietnamese deputy chief and a multinational staff. Their first mission, he said, would involve base security to permit release of Vietnamese troops from such tasks.

The already muddled chain of command would grow even worse under this arrangement. The fault did not lie with Westmoreland or Sharp but with the politicians in Washington who were afraid of creating hard feelings among their allies.

The Korean government, not wishing to have the only free world combat forces besides those of the United States in South Vietnam, expressed fear that its aid might be seen not as independently and freely given but "as the fulfillment of the obligation of a vassal state." Therefore, Korean misgivings caused the United States to weigh more carefully the pros and cons of obtaining Korean combat troops. It was decided, therefore, to ask the government of South Vietnam to seek combat troops directly from the Republic of Korea.

Westmoreland received word from the Pentagon April 5 that more United States troops would be sent because of the deteriorating military situation. Ambassador Taylor was somewhat taken aback. While he had been in Washington he had thought that Johnson would exercise caution on requests for additional deployment of troops. He asked that the decision to send a United States brigade to Bien Hoa or Vung Tau be held in abeyance and that he be given instructions on how to present to the Vietnamese government this new United States policy of seeking free world ground troops. He said he realized that the Joint Chiefs evidently believed that twenty new battalions were needed to keep the war from going on indefinitely.

The points raised by Taylor were resolved at the Honolulu Conference April 20 at which time it was agreed to deploy one Australian battalion to Vung Tau and a Korean regimental combat team of three battalions to Quang Ngai. The problem of command relationship remained unresolved.

Later these decisions were revised at Honolulu and Korea was asked for a full division, instead of a regimental combat team. Its arrival in South Vietnam was set for mid-June 1965. It was also decided later that national forces should retain their command identity and that the United States would not place its forces under the Vietnamese armed forces although, in some cases, the Army of the Republic of Vietnam might put its forces under allied commanders. Allied forces, however, agreed to accept operational control by United States commanders. Combat units would normally be placed under control of United States commanders at the brigade level or higher.

In early June Australia sent the Royal Australian regiment plus the 79th Signal Troop and a support company, and they were attached to the United States 173rd Airborne Brigade at Bien Hoa. With the addition of support elements, the Australian troop strength reached 1,557 by year-end.

In May, New Zealand replaced its engineer detachment with a combat force and a howitzer battery. They arrived June 21 and were attached to the 173rd primarily to support the Australian battalion.

Westmoreland revealed to his staff that his long-range goal for Australia and New Zealand was to deploy a full Australian division and a New Zealand Army Corps brigade during the coming year.

The Republic of Korea had earlier sent an army engineer battalion with support and self-defense troops—the Dove unit—March 16 to a base at Di An in Bien Hoa Province. An understrength Army infantry division and its supporting elements were approved August 21 for deployment by the Korean government. The Republic of Korea Capital Infantry Division and the 2nd Marine Brigade were completely deployed by November and given security duties at Cam Ranh Bay and Qui Nhon.

The Republic of the Philippines, Thailand and the Republic of China on Taiwan each provided assistance but only in the form of non-combatants to act in either advisory or civic action roles.

By the end of the year there was a new drive in Washington to encourage other free world nations to increase the amount of their aid, or to start giving it. Most nations preferred to provide civic action and medical asistance and were opposed to giving military aid. Military assistance from the Republic of China could not be accepted due to fear of Chinese communist intervention in Vietnam.

The Joint Chiefs, in a message to Admiral Sharp and General Westmoreland June 22, cited an eventual 44-battalion-size force for Vietnam exclusive of South Vietnamese forces. These would largely be United States Army soldiers and Marines, although they could be supplemented by units from South Korea, Australia and New Zealand. The Joint Chiefs discussed the immediate approval of sending twenty-three battalions but no mention was made of the 3rd Marine Division's two battalions. They sought the opinions of Admiral Sharp and General Westmoreland whether a forty-four battalion force "would be enough to convince the DRV/VC they could not win."

Westmoreland opposed any withdrawal of United States units and he objected to any suggestion that forty-four United States Army and Marine battalions would meet the upper levels of his needs. "I saw forty-four battalions as no force for victory," he said later, "but as a stopgap measure to save the Army of the Republic of Vietnam from defeat. The premise must be that we are in for the long pull. . . . it is time all concerned face up to the fact that we must be prepared for a long war which will probably involve increasing numbers of United States troops."

At the end of the month the Joint Chiefs informed CINCPAC and Westmoreland that the forces the general sought June 7 and in subsequent requests were approved. Now 8,000 more Marines would be dispatched to Vietnam, and the 101st Airborne Brigade and a brigade from the 1st Infantry Division were also authorized.

Westmoreland had requested authority to employ American forces on offensive operations against the Vietcong. He claimed that the enemy's shift to big-unit war was drawing Army of the Republic of Vietnam troops away from heavily populated regions and that American and Allied troops would have to assume the role of fighting the big units, leaving the South Vietnamese Army to protect its people. He said there should be no more niceties about defensive posture and reaction, and that the United States had to forget about enclaves and take the war to the enemy.

CHAPTER 14

Search and Destroy

THE NORTH VIETNAMESE HAD SEVENTY MIG 15S AND 17S WITH EIGHT Il-28 jet light bombers by mid-June 1965. The United States Navy repeatedly had requested permission to attack their North Vietnam airfields but all requests were denied by McNamara.

A division of Phantom fighters with Commander Lou Page and his radar intercept officer Lieutenant John Smith and Lieutenant J. E. D. Batson and his radar intercept officer Lieutenant Commander Robert Doremus made their first contact with the MIGs June 27 at 10:25 A.M. Page picked up the enemy fighters thirty miles ahead on radar. The Phantoms and MIGs began to close at 1,000 knots—a mile every three-and-a-half seconds. At ten miles both F-4s locked on and were ready to fire their long-range Sparrow missiles. They were forced to withhold their fire, however, because McNamara's rules of engagement did not permit firing until positive identification was made, a restriction not observed by the MIG pilots. When Page positively identified the huge nose intakes, the mid-wings and the prominent bubble canopies of four silver MIG-17s at a mile distance he pickled off his missiles at the second MIG flying with its companions in a ragged, single file. Batson fired at the third and puffs of orange flame and black smoke erupted as the two North Vietnamese fighters were hit.

A third MIG was bagged June 20 by two propellor-driven A-1 Skyraiders flown by Lieutenant Clinton B. Johnson and Lieutenant (jg) Charles W. Hartman from Midway's VA-25. Four Skyraider planes led by Lieutenant Commander E. A. Greathouse were jumped by two MIG-17s. They dove for the deck and scissored just above the tree tops to avoid the enemy jets. It was a wild melee of turns and reverses during a five-minute dogfight but the slower Skyraiders outturned and outmaneuvered the

MIGs. Johnson and Hartman finally got on the tail of the MIGs and one of them was blasted out of the sky by their 20 mm. cannon.

An Atlantic fleet carrier, the *Independence*, arrived at Yankee Station in June with a much-needed squadron of all-weather A-6A Intruders.

After Westmoreland received permission from Washington April 26, 1965, to seek out main force North Vietnamese units, he was given authority to conduct search and destroy missions "in any situation . . . when in ComUSMACV'S (Commander, United States Military Assistance Command, Vietnam) judgment, their use is necessary to strengthen the relative position of GVN forces." This authority for the first time gave him a relatively free hand to employ his ground forces, which he should have had all along.

Infiltration of North Vietnamese regular units into II Corps had caused increasing concern. Therefore, Westmoreland gave the highest priority to the prevention of a linkup of North Vietnamese regulars in the mountains with the Vietcong on the coast. The key route was 19 from the city of Qui Nhon to Pleiku City where it joined Route 14 and continued north to Kontum.

The United States Army's 1st Cavalry Airmobile Division was specifically designed to be moved quickly from one trouble spot to another. It was now requested for dispatch to Vietnam. "If the VC choose to mount a major campaign against Highway 19," Westmoreland said, "this is a better place than most for a showdown." This was true because the area could be supplied either overland or by air.

Admiral Sharp and Ambassador Taylor disagreed. They wanted the 1st Cavalry Division based at Qui Nhon until both Route 19 and the vital coastal area had been secured to assure supplies for the division. Westmoreland compromised and agreed to base the division at An Khe, thirty-five miles west of Qui Nhon, where it could be launched into the Pleiku highlands and into Binh Dinh Province. However, the 1st Cavalry Division could not arrive until September, and the request to move two III Amphibious Force Marine battalions into the Central Highlands was rejected because of concern that the security of the Army's Qui Nhon logistics base was no longer adequate. To resolve this situation a Seventh Fleet special landing force composed of one battalion of the 1st Division's 7th Marine Regiment was sent July 1 to Qui Nhon. Its stay was short. General Westmoreland advised Admiral Sharp the day after its arrival that it would be necessary to release the 173rd Airborne Brigade from its static role protecting the Bien Hoa air base and use it as a mobile reserve due to increasing enemy attacks in II Corps and in the northern part of III Corps. He recommended, therefore, that the 1st Infantry Division's battalion at Qui Nhon be diverted to Bien Hoa and that one of the Marine battalions slated to reinforce the III Marine Amphibious Force relieve the 3rd Battalion at Qui Nhon and again become a floating reserve as part of the special landing force. The incoming battalion then would remain at Qui Nhon until it was relieved by Republic of Korea troops scheduled to arrive later that year. Admiral Sharp approved the changes and forwarded the recommendations to Washington.

Establishment of an enclave at Qui Nhon made General Walt's mission in I Corps difficult. He lost the services of one infantry battalion that could have been used at Phu Bai or Da Nang, but he also had to position a detachment of ten helicopters at Qui Nhon to provide support for the Marines stationed there.

Vulnerability of Da Nang's air base was exposed July 1 when the Vietcong attacked with mortars and infantry troops. Although little damage was caused, and there were few casualties, the spectacular nature of the Vietcong attack caused worldwide publicity. Westmoreland's command became increasingly alarmed by vulnerability of American bases whose defenses were so slim that they almost invited attacks.

To counter one such situation Lieutenant Frank S. Reasoner, commander of Company A, 3rd Reconnaissance Battalion, 3rd Marine Division, led a patrol July 12 into heavily controlled enemy territory. Their deep penetration soon brought them under heavy fire from an estimated one hundred Vietcong insurgents. With an advance party of five, Reasoner deployed his men for an assault on several concealed positions. The slashing fury of the Vietcong's machine gun and automatic weapons fire made it impossible for the main body of the company to move forward. Reasoner repeatedly exposed himself to enemy fire, he killed at least two Vietcong and silenced an automatic weapons position as he tried to evacuate one of his men. His radio operator had been wounded and he moved quickly to his side to attend to his wounds. When the operator was hit a second time while attempting to reach a protected position, Reasoner again ran to his aid while machine gun bullets slashed around him and he was mortally wounded. His courageous act permitted his patrol to complete their mission without further casualties and he was posthumously awarded the Medal of Honor.

General Walt had repeatedly sought permission from Vietnamese General Thi to put some type of defense outside the base on the east and south sides but the head of I Corps replied that such action should be delayed "until the people of Da Nang became more used to the Marines' presence." After the attack on Da Nang, Thi gave tentative approval but he told General Walt, "You are still not ready to try and search for the VC."

After the last units of the 3rd Division arrived Walt increased his airfield security, and tactical control of the area was extended beyond the confines of his enclave. The infusion of American units was often resented by the South Vietnamese although it temporarily solved some of their nation's military problems. The North Vietnamese were quick to exploit the situation, saying that they did not use their friends in combat. As in the past, North Vietnam's officials used the American military presence as a pretext for their invasion of the South to "assist our blood fellow countrymen." Despite misgivings about the growing American presence, the South Vietnamese believed that foreign troops would eventually bring them victory. Without them, they faced almost immediate collapse.

At a Saigon conference in July Westmoreland was asked by Secretary of Defense McNamara what he would need to fulfill his mission. He replied that he would need 175,000 American troops at the start, with another 100,000 later. He based his estimates on the need to fulfill three phases that he considered necessary to reverse the deteriorating military situation. In Phase 1 he wanted to commit American and allied forces to halt the losing trend by the end of the year. In the first half of 1966 he said he wanted to take the offensive in high priority areas in a second phase to destroy enemy forces and reinstitute pacification programs. In the last phase, he said, if the enemy persisted, they could be defeated within a year by forceful allied action.

The Johnson administration made some far-reaching decisions in July, 1965, for the future. McNamara decided to visit Vietnam to discuss various alternatives with field commanders. The Secretary of Defense met with outgoing Ambassador Maxwell D. Taylor, and his successor Henry Cabor Lodge who was starting his second tour as United States ambassador to Vietnam. McNamara and Lodge arrived in Saigon July 16. In the next four days they met with officials of the Military Assistance Command and completely reviewed the military situation. Westmoreland told them that South Vietnamese troops no longer were able to hold the critical rural areas and were unable to cope with the Vietcong threat. He said it was obvious that unless further American and allied forces were deployed, "there was little chance of arresting the trend." McNamara was convinced and he so advised President Johnson.

The president then went to the American people to say that the American troop level in Vietnam would be raised to 125,000 and that Westmoreland would receive whatever reinforcements he needed. In a prepared statement to the White House press corps July 28, Johnson said, "I have asked the commanding general, General Westmoreland, what more he needs to meet this mounting aggression. He has told me. We will meet his needs. I have today ordered to Vietnam the Air Mobile Division and certain other forces which will raise our fighting strength from

75,000 to 125,000 men almost immediately. Additional forces will be needed later, and they will be sent as requested . . . ."

The bombing pause that President Johnson had approved in May had been a total failure, and Johnson knew it. His critics insisted that the pause had been too short—it lasted eight weeks—and that the United States should have held off a little longer. They displayed an abysmal ignorance of communist aims and intentions.

Johnson said later that once the troop deployments he was recommending had been completed he would consider another intensive effort to find a way to negotiate peace.

Lieutenant Colonel Verle E. Ludwig, commander of the 1st Battalion, 9th Regiment, was ordered August 3 to seek out the Vietcong at Cam Ne and destroy them. This complex of villages favored enemy hit-and-run attacks. It was an innocent-looking collection of crude structures that harbored punji sticks (sharpened bamboo stakes coated with excrement to cause disease), spider holes, and interconnecting tunnels between houses and a cooperative civilian population. Marines would search a hut only to have a sniper turn up behind them, fire and then disappear. Marines routinely burned huts from which they received fire. Lieutenant Ray G. Snyder told his superiors that Cam Ne was an extensively entrenched and fortified hamlet. He said burning the houses was the only way to ensure that they would not become active military installations after his troops moved past it. The lieutenant's company uncovered 267 punji-stick traps and pits, six Malayan whips—bent bamboo fences that, when tripped, whipped pointed sticks into the intruder. There were countless booby traps and crude mines. Troops demolished fifty-one huts and thirty-eight trenches and tunnels. With darkness approaching a withdrawal was ordered. The Vietcong opened fire again and the retreating Americans were covered by their own mortars until the firing ceased.

The Vietcong used civilians as shields during the fight and a ten-year-old Vietnam boy was killed and four villagers were wounded when they were caught in crossfires.

A Columbia Broadcasting System camera crew caught the nastiness of village war. American viewers at home later saw a film made by the crew showing a Marine casually setting fire to a house with his cigarette lighter while an old woman pleaded for her home. The film showed little or no resistance and Morley Safer, who narrated the film, said, "If there were VC in the hamlets they were long gone." The Marine Corps took exception to Safer's comment and said that Cam Ne was a fortified Vietcong village and that Marines had received fire from an estimated platoon of the enemy. The film did not misrepresent the facts but it did not tell the whole story. General Walt was upset, believing that Safer had misrepresented the facts. Shown in the United States, the movie had a strong impact on people who were seeing a side of warfare long familiar to combat men but one that most civilians had never seen before.

General Westmoreland issued stern orders that civilians should be protected whenever possible but he stressed that it was the inherent right of all individuals to protect themselves if attacked. In this case, although mistakes were made due to inadequate knowledge about the people of Cam Ne, the Marines had every right to take such action.

In an action near Camp Bon Song in II Corps' Binh Dinh Province, Captain Paris D. Davis and three members of the Special Forces attached to the 883rd Vietnamese Regional Forces Company started a raid shortly after midnight against a Vietcong regimental headquarters. They killed 100 Vietcong and Davis gave the signal to pull in the security men along the river bank. Master Sergeant Billy Waugh was with the second platoon and Staff Sergeant David Morgan with the third platoon while Specialist Fourth Class Brown was assigned to the fourth. The first platoon was hit by automatic fire and Davis ordered it to pull back to the main body. The captain had been hit in the hand by a grenade fragment. When he heard firing ahead, and saw a wounded Vietnamese soldier running towards them, he knew the remainder of the 883rd company was under attack. Retiring to the main body, he found the Vietcong had them pinned down in an open field. Davis ordered his platoon to open fire but only a few did. Davis fired his own weapon, moving up and down the line, encouraging the members of the company to return the Vietcong fire. He noted most of the fire was coming from their right flank, so he moved there and ran into six Vietcong coming over their trench line. He quickly tossed a grenade and killed four of them. Now his M-16 rifle jammed so he shot another Vietcong with his pistol and repeatedly hit another until he killed him.

Sergeant Waugh screamed that he had been shot in the foot. Davis ran to the middle of the open field and tried to get Waugh but the enemy fire was too intense and he was forced to move back to safety. At the edge of the field Sergeant Morgan, who had been knocked out by a mortar blast, revived. Davis spotted another sniper in a camouflaged manhole and killed him. Then the captain crawled over and dropped a grenade in the hole, killing two more.

Davis next made contact with a forward air controller who dispatched a flight of F-105s who dropped bombs on the enemy position. During this period Davis ran out and pulled the wounded Morgan to safety. Although slightly wounded and in shock Davis rallied his men by picking up a machine gun and firing at the Vietcong when they tried to overrun his position. He saw four or five drop before the remaining Vietcong broke under his intense fire and fled the battle. Now Davis set up a 60-mm. mortar and dropped a half a dozen rounds down the tube in rapid succession before he ran out and tried to rescue Waugh. Meanwhile Morgan, partially recovered from his own wounds, opened up on the enemy with a machine gun while Davis tried to pick up Waugh who by now had four wounds in his right foot. Davis struggled to lift the wounded man but he was unable to do so. When he received a slight wound in his back, Davis was forced to run for cover.

The forward air controller now had a flight of F-4s overhead and they started to drop bombs on the enemy position. During these attacks, Davis ran out again and this time was shot in the wrist but he was able to pick up Waugh and carry him to safety despite a hail of automatic weapons fire. Davis called for a Medevac for Waugh after he carried him 200 yards up a hill. When it arrived SFC Reinburg got off the plane and ran to where the company was dug in. Almost immediately he was shot through the chest and Davis had to run to his side to give him first aid and, with Morgan's help, pull him to safety.

The Vietcong tried again to overrun their position. Davis fought back desperately, throwing grenades and firing any weapon at hand. He killed at least six more Vietcong. Now he received orders to take his remaining troops and leave the site. He radioed the colonel in the command aircraft overhead that he had a wounded American, and another that he did not know. He refused to leave until he got all the Americans out. Reinburg was taken out first and the fighting continued until mid-afternoon.

Despite two more attempts by the Vietcong to overrun the site, the company held stubbornly to their position. Finally, reinforcements arrived and they were able to rescue Brown who had lain in the middle of the field for twenty-four hours ever since the battle began. Under great odds, the South Vietnamese had whipped the Vietcong decisively under the leadership of an incredible American captain and his three sergeants.

Master Sergeant Bradley Spencer, assigned to the Intelligence Section of the Second Battalion's 1st Marine Regiment, returned to Vietnam in January, 1965. Three months earlier he had helped flood victims at Chu Lai above Da Nang.

In the summer of 1965 his battalion participated in raids mainly at the request of province chiefs who complained about Vietcong attacks. Each time they were sent to clean out an area the enemy would fade into the jungle without making contact. At times they got behind the Vietcong by going in with a helicopter group while others used amphibious vehicles across the salt marshes. For Spencer these forays were exasperating because the Vietcong always seemed to know where they were headed.

A conference was held at CINCPAC headquarters in Honolulu the first week in August to determine the units to be deployed and their timing. The Marines decided to reinforce the III Amphibious Force with the 7th Marine Regiment and the remaining two battalions at Okinawa. After the regiment arrived at Chu Lai August 14 it was possible to plan for the first major offensive against main-force Vietcong and North Vietnamese. There had been ample evidence since July that the Vietcong were building up their forces in the southern section of I Corps, especially in the area south of Chu Lai. It was believed by American headquarters that they could attack with as many as three regiments in hit-and-run raids against Marine bases.

Westmoreland advised General Walt July 30 that he expected him to undertake larger offensive operations against the enemy in conjunction with South Vietnamese Army troops at greater distances from his base areas. Walt reminded him that the Marines were still bound by the May 6 letter of instruction that restricted the III Marine Amphibious Force to missions in support of South Vietnamese units heavily engaged against the enemy. Westmoreland replied, "These restraints are no longer realistic." He invited Walt to rewrite the instructions, working into them the authority he needed. He promised quick approval.

Walt received permission to take the offensive August 6, 1965. With the arrival of the 7th Marine Regiment a week later he moved against the 1st Vietcong Regiment. This regiment had launched a second attack against the hamlet of Ba Gia twenty miles south of Chu Lai, causing extensive casualties. Now ensconced in the mountains west of the hamlet it was reported by intelligence officers that they were ready to move again. But in a one-battalion operation, the Marines encountered only scattered resistance.

A defector later positioned the Vietcong twelve miles to the south, and a Marine attack was planned before they were expected to move. It was decided that some Marines would move against the Vietcong by sea, and some over land. Again, most Marines met little resistance.

Pockets of resistance were encountered August 18 when combined Marine and South Vietnamese attacks moved across rice paddies ringed by dikes and hedgerows. The Vietcong were holed up in bunkers, trenches and caves scattered throughout the area. The Marines swept the area but did not find a single soldier although sniper fire followed them as they retreated. Marines often had to dig out the enemy or blow up his tunnels otherwise they never made contact.

Corporal Robert E. O'Malley led his 3rd Battalion, 3rd Marine Division squad near An Cu'ong 2 on August 18 in an assault against strongly entrenched Vietcong soldiers. When Company I came under intense small arms fire O'Malley disregarded his own safety and raced across an open rice paddy to a trench line where the Vietcong were located. He jumped in and attacked them with rifle and grenades, killing eight. Next he led his squad to the assistance of an adjacent Marine unit that was suffering heavy casualties. With no thought for his own safety, O'Malley pressed forward. He reloaded his weapon, and charged the enemy emplacement. He personally assisted in the evacuation of several wounded Marines. After regrouping remnants of his squad, he returned to the point of heaviest fighting. When ordered by his lieutenant to evacuate, he gathered his besieged and badly wounded squad and led them under fire to a waiting helicopter. In total disregard to his streaming wounds—he had been hit three times—O'Malley refused evacuation and continued to cover his men from an exposed position until the last of his wounded men were on board the helicopter. Then he consented to board it. His acts of courage were recognized later when he was awarded a Medal of Honor.

That same day Lance Corporal Joe C. Paul, a fire team leader with Company H, 2nd Battalion, Fourth Marine Regiment, was in action near Chu Lai. His platoon was pinned down by heavy mortar and automatic weapons fired from entrenched positions. They quickly sustained five casualties and when the wounded Marines were unable to move from their perilously exposed positions they found themselves the target of phosphorous rifle grenades. Paul dashed across the fire-swept rice paddies and placed himself between his comrades and the enemy troops and immediately opened fire to divert the Vietcong long enough to permit evacuation of his wounded comrades. Although critically wounded, Paul remained in his exposed position and continued to fire at the Vietcong until he collapsed and died. For saving the lives of his fellow Marines Paul received a posthumous Medal of Honor.

For five days two battalions systematically swept the Phuoc Thuan peninsula and there was no organized resistance by the time they finished. But civilians in the combat zone presented complications. The first attempts to evacuate them proved difficult. The people were frightened and they did not trust the Marines. Most were placed at local collecting points where they could be fed and given medical attention. Some villages were completely destroyed when it became obvious that the enemy used them as fortified positions. The Marines liquidated the 60th Vietcong Battalion and badly mauled the 80th. Westmoreland reported to General Walt that some Vietnamese generals had made disparaging remarks about his operations. He said he wanted the Vietnamese included next time. At General Thi's insistence, Vietnamese units had not been advised of the operation. When the successful operation received wide press coverage, there was resentment because similar-type all-Vietnamese operations in the past had been largely ignored. Although both Vietcong battalions suffered heavy losses, General Walt knew they would soon be back to full strength.

In an anti-SAM strike mission called Iron Hand, Task Force 77 received permission to strike missile sites in North Vietnam. Although five planes and two pilots were lost to anti-aircraft fire, only one missile site was located during operations August 13 through 17, 1965, and it was destroyed. If the sites could have been attacked earlier, they would have been easily knocked out. However, permission to strike was not received until the SAM site was completed.

The III Marine Amphibious Force entered a new stage when it began to strike enemy main-force units. General Walt now considered that the time was right to complete the destruction of an enemy regiment that, intelligence sources revealed, had withdrawn to the Barangan Peninsula eight miles south of Van Tuong. He consulted first with General Thi before ordering plans for a coordinated attack.

In contrast to his command's first operation, this one was carefully prepared and by September 2 Lieutenant Colonel James F. Kelly's 1st Battalion, 7th Regiment, and Lieutenant Colonel Joseph E. Muir's 3rd Battalion, 3rd Regiment, prepared to embark on Seventh Fleet ships while Lieutenant Colonel Charles H. Bodley's 3rd Battalion, 7th Regiment, prepared to make a heliborne assault. The plans called for Kelly's battalion to land across the beach north of Batangan Peninsula and push southward while Bodley's airlifted battalion would set up blocking positions two-and-a-half miles inland. Muir's battalion was ordered to remain in reserve. The South Vietnamese 2nd Battalion, 4th Regiment, and the 3rd Marine Battalion would be moved by helicopter into the region south of Bodley's position. There the South Vietnamese would seek out the Vietcong on the An Ky Peninsula separated from Batangan by the Sa Ky River.

The operation began September 7 with air strikes. Only light resistance was encountered by infantry battalions, and during a three-day operation only Kelly's 1st Battalion found significant numbers of Vietcong. As it turned out, the 1st Vietcong Regiment had withdrawn so this large operation was unnecessary.

Chinese Defense Minister Lin Piao revealed in September that the People's Republic of China would not intervene directly in Vietnam as Mao Tse-tung began the Great Proletarian Cultural Revolution and unleashed the Red Guards in a devastating purge of Communist Party ranks.

October 19 three Vietcong regiments of 6,000 men attacked the Civil

Irregular Defense Group's camp with its United States Special Forces at Plei Mai near the entrance to the Ia Drang Valley in what was believed to be the start of a thrust to cut the country in half. With the assistance of massive air strikes, elements of the newly arrived 1st Cavalry Division thwarted the enemy in a series of engagements that lasted nearly a month. This action was the most costly to date but the successful defense of this region improved security in and around the Central Highlands.

In the spring of 1965 the United States and South Vietnamese had stopped using riot-control ammunition such as tear gas because of public uproar. When McNamara visited Saigon in July he reiterated his earlier views that American public opinion would not support use of such weapons. Tear gas continued to be used, however, to rout out Vietcong from caves and trenches. It was ridiculous to stop using an agent long used for crowd control in the United States. Even the New York *Times* editorially denounced the prohibition, saying it would mean certain death or injury to more Americans and South Vietnamese and that non-lethal use of riot control gas was far more humane than any other methods. Most people in the United States concurred and McNamara finally agreed to permit Westmoreland to use tear gas in tunnel clearing.

In the fall, the III Amphibious Force, supporting the Vietnamese in I Corps, increased the number of battalion-size operations against Vietcong main-force elements outside the enclaves but with disappointing results. For two months the Vietcong refused to give battle, except on their own terms.

McNamara wrote a detailed memorandum to President Johnson November 7, 1965, in which he set forth his views on Vietnam. He said he was convinced that the United States would never achieve its desired goals with a force of 160,000 Americans in Vietnam, and the 50,000 who were scheduled to be sent, and that more men would be needed. He called for a halt of the bombing of the North, saying such bombing would not force Ho Chi Minh to sue for peace.

Johnson was skeptical of McNamara's views and so were McGeorge Bundy and Secretary of State Rusk.

That same day Ambassador Lodge in Saigon gave his personal assessment of the war. "An end of the bombing of the North with no other quid pro quo than the opening of negotiations would load the dice in favor of the communists," he said, "and demoralize the government of Vietnam. It would in effect leave the communists free to devastate the South with impunity while we tie our hands in the North."

Westmoreland, Sharp and the Joint Chiefs all raised their voices against a bombing halt.

Soviet Ambassador Anatoly Dobrynin and a Hungarian diplomat told Rusk that a "few weeks" of bombing halt would be enough to bring North Vietnam to the conference table. They offered no guarantees—just hope.

In November, the 1st Vietcong Regiment, now recovered from an earlier beating, attacked South Vietnamese outposts at Hiep Duc, twenty-five miles west of Tam Ky. This district capital, on the headwaters of the Song Thu Bon, was the western gateway to the fertile mountain valleys that later became known to the Marines as the Nui Loc Son basin. It was named for a rugged narrow hill that protruded from its center to the valley floor. It was also known as the Que Son valley, a broad, heavily populated expanse of farmland that constituted one of the most strategic areas between Da Nang and Chu Lai. During the northeast monsoon season heavy rain clouds shrouded the valley and its western approaches, permitting the enemy freedom of movement without being observed from the air.

On the evening of November 17 an enemy regiment overran the small Regional Forces garrison. Air strikes were called in and two South Vietnamese battalions were readied to be air lifted to the area. During a preflyover the area seemed ominously quiet. Not a living soul was in sight although there was evidence of the fight the day before. Observers noted that the typical triangular-shaped French fortifications in the village had been penetrated in several places. Corpses hung on barbed wire around a few of the outposts.

Colonel Thomas J. O'Connor, commander of Air Group 16, chose a site for a landing zone that was small but could accommodate two helicopters at a time. The hill on which the landing zone was situated was at the western end of the ridgeline east of Hiep Duc. Unknown to Colonel O'Connor and his staff, the Vietcong had placed machine gun positions on the hill that dominated the landing zone.

The first helicopters landed without incident November 18 but then the Vietcong opened fire. O'Connor, flying over Hiep Duc, reported that enemy gunners were actually firing down on the landing helicopters. He knew those guns had to be knocked out after two of his helicopters were hit. He stopped further flights and directed them to circle east of the hill while air strikes were called in. There was a risk in stopping the airlift because the Vietcong began to converge on the landing zone occupied by only a company of troops. After a twenty-minute wait for airplanes to knock out the Vietcong guns, O'Connor ordered the helilift to resume. Fortunately there was no further opposition. South Vietnamese troops soon gained control of the situation, particularly with the help of close support from the air, but General Thi decided to withdraw his two battalions despite Bodley's agreement to reinforce the zone with his reserve battalion.

He was overruled and his battalion was committed to an engagement at Thach Tru, sixteen miles to the south of Quang Ngai. It arrived November 22 but his help was not needed. Two Regional Forces companies and the 37th South Vietnamese Ranger Battalion had repulsed an attack by the 18th North Vietnamese Army Regiment.

These two actions at Hiep Duc and Thach Tru typified the enemy's monsoon strategy. They moved during periods of poor weather because it hampered American air operations, attacking isolated outposts and then establishing ambushes to trap relief forces. At Thach Tru the Vietcong had miscalculated but at Hiep Duc, in forcing the South Vietnamese to abandon the zone, the 1st Vietcong Regiment was in an excellent position to enter the strategic Nui Loc Son basin and thus threaten outposts at Que Son and Viet An.

General Walt was ordered by Westmoreland November 16 to hold two battalions on alert to conduct search and destroy operations against more distant Vietcong base areas to destroy or drive them out.

General Krulak, commander of Fleet Marine Force Pacific, in Honolulu, was not in the operational chain of command but he called for the Marines to recapture the initiative. He suggested enticing the Vietcong to attack a supposedly weak position that actually would be loaded for bear.

The III Marine Amphibious Force now activated a temporary task force under Assistant Division Commander Brigadier General Melvin D. Henderson. He was given two battalions and furnished artillery support and ordered to coordinate his activities with his Vietnamese counterpart, Brigadier General Hoang Xuan Lam, commander of the 2nd Division. Henderson was a colorful personality who wore a black beret with silver badges, a tanker's jacket and swagger stick. In the largest combined operation to date the troops entered the Que Son valley along the Thanh Binh-Hiep Duc road December 8. The 1st Vietcong Regiment supposedly was west of this area. An American battalion was inserted behind enemy lines to force them eastward towards the advancing South Vietnamese. Halfway to Que Son the Vietnamese Ranger battalion was ambushed by the 70th Vietcong Battalion, losing a third of its men and its position was overrun. The battalion withdrew and called for American air support. Replacements were sent forward and the next day, despite heavy attacks, the South Vietnamese held firm. Henderson now committed the American Marines by air but few Vietcong were found as they landed five miles west of the South Vietnamese troops. During linkup of the Rangers and the Marines there were some stiff firefights and more Marines were airlifted to the battle zone. One company landed near the village of Cam La, five miles southeast of Que Son, and ran into heavy and intense fire that surprised the Marines. The Marines who landed at the first site reported they were in trouble and they called for reinforcements. Since the rest of the battalion had landed to the west, Henderson ordered a company to move south to aid the hard-hit unit. Company E, 2nd Battalion, 7th Marines, pushed southward but was hit on its right flank by enemy fire. With some difficulty the company reached an area from which it could support the stranded company, and Company F began to withdraw under the relief force's covering fire. Ten hours after the first helicopter landing, various companies joined forces, and Companies E and F from Lieutenant Colonel Leon N. Utter's 2nd Battalion suffered substantial casualties.

That night General Walt removed Henderson and Brigadier General Jonas M. Platt was named task force commander. Once Platt was appraised of the tactical situation he ordered another of Utter's companies to reinforce the 2nd Battalion, 1st Marine Regiment.

Platt took to the air December 11 to review the situation. When his aircraft encountered no anti-aircraft fire he figured that the Vietcong had withdrawn. He ordered Colonel Utter to seize the strategic hill from which heavy fire had come and this was done without opposition. Other searches proved that the Vietcong had fled the scene except for a few snipers.

That afternoon, suspecting the Vietcong regiment had retreated into the Phuoc Ha valley—a smaller valley paralleling the Que Son valley—Platt informed General Thi of his beliefs.

Thi replied, "Be very careful, very careful."

Westmoreland's staff operations officer suggested that Guam-based B-52s strike the valley before the Marines tried to enter. Platt agreed and the first of several heavy bomber raids was completed the following morning, and on the next day.

Immersion foot, an extremely painful foot condition, became a serious problem. Feet swelled and took on a puffy, crinkled look. The condition was caused by wearing wet footgear for extended periods, and became an increasing problem as long as Americans were in Vietnam. It was a minor annoyance but it was nothing like the frustration felt by most Marines who believed they should have hit the beach the first day and headed inland as far as they could go. They were anxious and eager to go after the Vietcong in force and end the war so they could go home.

CHAPTER 15

"Hey, Hey, L.B.J., How Many Kids Did You Kill Today?"

WHILE THE WAR HEATED UP IN THE FAR EAST, DEBATE AGAINST THE war's escalation grew hotter. Senator Wayne Morse of Oregon spoke to the Senate October 19. "What America needs to hear is the tramp, tramp, tramp of marching feet, in community after community, across the length and breadth of this land, in protest against the administration's unconstitutional and illegal war in South Vietnam. Those protests must be within the law. Those protests must not violate the law. But the administration must also act in keeping with the rights of the protesters under the first amendment.

"Those who violate the law must be held accountable to the law. But also I forewarn the administration that it cannot, because of the actions of some of these demonstrators who may be law violators, breach the rights of the legitimate protesters; that it has the obligation to see that the rights of the legitimate protesters are protected, even though the government itself is violating the Constitution of this country.

"I shall continue to protest the war," Morse said. "I shall continue to vote against giving the president any vote of confidence for what I think is his inexcusable course of action involving us in the war in South Vietnam in the absence of a declaration of war."

Most protesters were not as moderate in their words or actions. There was a growing, organized protest about the war. It was met by official rage and counterattack. The cries and accusations from both sides—those supporting the demonstrators and those condemning them—were raising issues that were deeper than the war itself. The values and moral structure of each group was at stake.

Protesters were denounced by church groups, but also applauded by some church members. Newspapers called them the "bearded bums" and members of an "acne alliance." Former President Eisenhower referred to them as "beatniks." He said the women were as bad as the men—their hair stringing down over their faces. He suggested the way to bring the males to their senses would be for the "girls to turn their backs on boys like that." He added, "Sloppy dress indicates sloppy thinking."

Representative L. Mendel Rivers of South Carolina called them "filthy buzzards and vermin" who ought to be arrested. Senate Minority Leader Everett M. Dirksen said, "The spectacle of young men willing to perjure themselves to avoid the draft and willing to let the world know that they do not support other young Americans arrayed in battle in Vietnam in the cause of freedom is enough to make any person loyal to his country weep."

The director of Selective Service, Lieutenant General Lewis B. Hershey, said, "Every generation has its small minority who are perpetual adolescents. Nowadays, many of them are on the college campus, where they are easily misled and misguided by, probably, their counterparts from somewhat older generations. We've become a very permissive people in recent years."

Throughout 1965 more than 100,000 people marched in anti-war parades and took part in rallies. The movement was not entirely communist manipulated. The greatest number of protesters acted out of moral and humanistic reasons.

Demonstrations escalated in 1965 after fourteen University of Michigan faculty members started an all-night teach-in in March to denounce the United States' role in Vietnam. A nationwide campus movement was started through telephone calls that led to a national teach-in May 15 in Washington. Twenty-six sponsors of the televised event were alleged by the FBI to be communist fronts, some dating back decades.

Although President Johnson was not at home, protesters picketed the White House April 17 calling for an end to "United States aggression in Vietnam." Signs proclaimed "I will not fight in Vietnam—except for the Vietcong." Twenty thousand demonstrators later thronged the grounds of the Washington Monument and paraded with Vietcong flags while some solicited for the communist National Liberation Front. A "declaration of conscience against the war" was sent to the White House with 4,000 signatures collectd by pacifists.

At a June convention at Camp Maplehurst, Michigan, Students for a Democratic Society—a new-left group claiming three thousand members in ninety colleges and communities—sought to enlist recruits to fight against American troops in Vietnam. They offered guerrilla training, and some were taught to manufacture explosives and to make Molotov cocktails for use as fire bombs.

In Oakland, California, 200 demonstrators tried to block trainloads of Vietnam-bound troops August 12 and again on the 23rd. "Suckers!" they shouted, brandishing signs that said "Off to the slaughter!"

Students on campuses that fall burned their draft cards and Congress made such action punishable by five years in prison and a $5,000 fine. The law was defied.

By mid-October disorders erupted all over the United States and 10,000 peace marchers thronged New York City's Fifth Avenue. The FBI charged that communists sponsored the New York demonstrations.

Outside the Pentagon November 2 a thirty-two-year-old Quaker, Norman Morrison, father of three children, burned himself to death in protest to the war. A week later, Roger La Porte immolated himself at the United Nations for the same reason.

Senator Gale W. McGee of Wyoming, a former professor, said, "As one who has vigorously defended America's tough line in Vietnam. . . . we must not destroy our fundamental freedoms in the name of preserving them. This we threaten to do if we ban pickets or smear them as communists. I am sure there must be some communists in the ranks. But I deplore labeling every protest movement as communist-inspired . . . . This smears the overwhelming majority of the protesters in a way detrimental to their free right to object, or to oppose."

Selective Service Director Hershey warned again that there was grave danger that other nations might over-emphasize these protests by what he called "a tiny majority of our least promising young people and misjudge the essential clear-sightedness of the American people."

Dissenters in California and New York City issued "guides" for beating the draft. They advised a man how to pretend he was a homosexual, an epileptic, to fake an allergy or pretend to be addicted to drugs.

As 1965 drew to a close there were further evidences of militant youth in action. Students kept saying that their movement was not an ideology but a rallying cry against the war. In a sense that was true because the movement was a coalition of forces and personalities that included groups ranging from religious pacifists to militant supporters of the Vietcong. They ranged from children of left wingers of the 1930s to students who simply hoped to evade the draft in any way. President Johnson bore the brunt of their wrath as hecklers chanted, "Hey, hey, L.B.J., how many kids did you kill today?"

Dr. Benjamin Spock, whose books on baby care had been translated into twenty-nine languages, became a controversial figure as he toured the nation at his own expense. He gave speeches like "Raising Our Children in a Cold War Age." Mothers flocked to his appearances to hear about raising their children but they also heard about his pleas for peace. His theme was the same everywhere: the Vietnam War was militarily hopeless, morally wrong, and politically self-defeating. "It is a very dangerous war for the United States," he said. "If we are not careful, we are going to escalate ourselves right off the face of the earth."

Spock was called foolish, ignorant and even unpatriotic. In his defense, he said, "I am certainly not unpatriotic. I have always believed in standing up to aggression. But in Vietnam we are not standing up to aggression. We provoked it by trying to establish a sphere of influence on the other side of the world."

Most servicemen in Vietnam would have disagreed with him, particularly men like Lieutenant Harvey C. Barnum, Jr., a forward artillery observer attached to Company H, 2nd Battalion, 3rd Marine Division who was at Ky Phu December 18, 1965. Here, during a two-battalion sweep of the Phuoc Ha valley, the Marines encountered heavy resistance despite two days of B-52 bombing. His company was pinned down by extremely accurate enemy fire and was separated from the remainder of the battalion by over 1,300 feet of open and fire-swept ground. With casualties mounting, Barnum made a reconnaissance of the area seeking targets for the artillery. When he found a rifle company commander mortally wounded, and his radio operator dead, Barnum gave aid to the dying commander. He removed the radio from the body of the operator and strapped it on himself. Assuming command of the rifle company he moved into the middle of the heaviest fire and rallied its units. After reorganizing them to replace the loss of key personnel, Barnum led an attack on enemy positions from which deadly fire continued to come. He remained calm and his decisions were quick and sound, serving to stabilize the badly decimated units by his example as he exposed himself repeatedly to point out targets. After his unit was provided with two armed helicopters Barnum moved ahead despite enemy fire to control the air attack against the firmly entrenched Vietcong while he directed a platoon in a successful counterattack on key enemy positions. Once a small area was cleared he directed two transport helicopters to evacuate the dead and wounded while he assisted in mopping up the enemy and finally directing the seizure of the battalion's objective. His country recognized his extraordinary bravery with a Medal of Honor.

With such stiff opposition the Vietcong retreated. By December 19 the Marine battalions had completed their withdrawal from the area after the capture of a large quantity of supplies and materiel. Airpower played a major role in their successful sweep of the Nui Loc Son basin.

This was the last of the big battles fought by the Marines in 1965. During the year they had conducted fifteen operations of battalion strength or larger.

General Krulak, head of the Pacific Fleet Marine Force, was critical of their operations. "We cannot be entrapped in the dangerous premise that destruction of the Vietcong's organized units per se is the whole answer to winning the war, any more than we can accept the erroneous view that pacification and civic action will solve the problem if major enemy forces are free to roam the countryside."

With President Johnson's approval, General Westmoreland had divided the war effort into three phases. The first, to end in 1965, was to commit those American and allied forces that were necesssary to halt the war's losing trend. In 1966 he planned to take the offensive in selected high priority areas. At an undetermined date, total destruction of the enemy's forces and their base areas would be accomplished. He planned to use American combat troops to protect developing bases, although some troops were committed as fire brigades whenever enemy big units posed a threat.

The III Amphibious Force was given responsibility for securing coastal enclaves, and to extend them gradually as manpower and materiel became available. By such means it was hoped to win the loyalty of the people to the government's cause. The most pervasive Vietcong guerrilla strength was in the rich and heavily populated rice lands south of Da Nang. General Walt insisted that his first priority was to clear the region of Vietcong. Westmoreland's perception was different. He believed the growing North Vietnamese Army and Vietcong forces should be the main target of United States forces. General Krulak said that differences between Army and Marine strategy were more of emphasis than substance.

In the summer of 1965, General Walt had informed Westmoreland that he needed two Marine divisions and a reinforced Marine air wing. He said if he were made responsible for the entire area from Quang Ngai Province to the demilitarized zone that he would need three more battalions. In August, McNamara had authorized a 30,000-man increase for a total of 223,000 men. Now Walt sought another 55,000 to allow formation of the 5th Marine Division in California, eighteen infantry battalions for Vietnam and three for Okinawa. By the end of the year his request was approved and funds were provided for the increased number of units.

The 1st Marine Division under Major General Lewis J. Fields had been established August 24 on Okinawa, and was in a position for movement to Vietnam if that became necessary.

By the end of 1965 the III Marine Amphibious Force in Vietnam had eight fixed-wing squadrons and eight helicopter squadrons. It had received 25,000 troop reinforcements since July 1 and now totaled 45,000 Marine and Navy personnel.

As small-unit patrolling expanded into the populated ricelands beyond

Marine enclaves, General Walt realized the futility of such actions unless the Vietcong infrastructure was destroyed. He set up several programs to accomplish this end. Pacification became the name of the game as joint-action companies were formed in a cooperative effort rather than a Marine-officered native constabulary. The Marines for this assignment were hand-picked and highly motivated. They lived in the surrounding hamlets and Marines were assigned to Popular Forces platoons. Normally a Marine was platoon commander while the Vietnamese non-commissioned officer was his assistant. The main obstacles to establish mutual trust between the Marines and the Vietnamese villagers was the sub rosa control the Vietcong maintained in most of these villages.

Joint-action companies were coordinated with civic action programs in what General Walt called the use of the "velvet glove." Marines worked hard to assuage the effects caused by the ravages of war, poverty and sickness. It was more than benevolence. The companies were used as a weapon against the Vietcong and they hoped to remove the populace from their control and to induce loyalty to the Saigon government. By late December, Marines realized that serious problems still existed, although they had started seriously to challenge the Vietcong in the countryside. They knew they had much to learn and that there was still much to accomplish before the villages were free of communist control.

President Johnson met in the Cabinet Room with his chief advisers December 18 to discuss a bombing pause. He opened his remarks by saying "the military says a month's pause could undo all we've done."

"That's baloney," McNamara said.

"I don't think so," the president said. "I disagree. I think it contains serious military risks. It is inaccurate to say suspension of bombing carries no military risks."

McGeorge Bundy and McNamara countered that the bombing could be resumed at any time. Johnson talked extensively with his advisers, and later with representatives of other countries. Finally, he agreed to a bombing halt. He had done so before, and he would do so again—a total of eight times between 1965 and 1968. Five other times the president had ruled out attacks on military targets in or around Hanoi and Haiphong for extended periods. Johnson later conceded in his memoirs that nothing had been gained by these halts because North Vietnam used every pause to strengthen its position.

The Rolling Thunder air campaign had achieved only limited success because the most important targets had remained off-limits. In 1965, an average of 200 tons of bombs were dropped each week. The tonnage increased to 1,600 the following year when more lucrative targets were authorized. The Navy alone lost one hundred and five airplanes and eighty-two pilots and crew members who were sacrificed needlessly on the altar of political expediency. Many of the targets were worthless and the pilots took the same risks as they would against high-value targets. All too many air strikes merely splintered thousands of trees in Laos and South Vietnam.

Despite attacks by North Vietnamese aircraft, and a growing array of missile and anti-aircraft sites around targets below the 20th parallel, the request by the Joint Chiefs to neutralize North Vietnam's airfields that accommodated MIG 21s was turned down even though seven American planes and a drone were shot down August 24 and 25. Every time the Joint Chiefs sought retaliatory strikes McNamara disapproved saying that the Chinese Air Force might take over defense of North Vietnam. This do-nothing strategy remained unchanged for the rest of 1965.

The last strike of the year against North Vietnam—before President Johnson's seven-week bombing pause—was made against the first industrial target authorized by the Joint Chiefs. On December 22 planes from three carriers struck the Uong Bi thermal power plant fifteen miles north of Haiphong. Heavy damage was caused and Haiphong's electrical power was reduced for weeks. All further attacks were suspended to help the peace negotiations. The raid caused the loss of two planes. One pilot was killed and the other was captured.

Crop destruction acreage constituted 42 percent of the total land area covered by herbicides in 1965 while the remainder was sprayed for defoliation. In July, Ambassador Lodge had cabled the State Department requesting authority to expand the crop destruction program to make a greater impact on the Vietcong's food supplies. He also requested authority to change the May, 1963, guidelines to permit crop destruction operations in more populated areas if the insurgents dominated them, and if significant military gains would result. In evaluating past crop destruction programs, Lodge concluded that the Vietcong had suffered considerable hardships, while the adverse reactions of the local people had been manageable. He said he had perceived a similarly favorable evaluation from the Military Assistance Command that had just published a positive opinion of crop destruction.

More liberal guidelines were approved August 7, 1965, and authority was given to continue the practice of requiring the United States ambassador and a senior South Vietnamese official to approve personally each crop destruction operation. These guidelines extended the range of permissable targets to include remote and more highly populated areas where the Vietcong were experiencing significant foot shortages.

In December, the program called Ranch Hand expanded its area to include parts of southern and eastern Laos traversed by the Ho Chi Minh Trail. Ambassador William H. Sullivan in Vientiane opposed defoliation in Laos saying he believed it would aggravate an already tense situation.

Westmoreland said, in the fall of 1965, that he was convinced that there were sufficient targets beneath the jungle canopy in southern Laos to justify major efforts against the Ho Chi Minh Trail. Admiral Sharp proposed several actions in Laos November 7, including the defoliation of selected lines of communication and the destruction of crops. Despite objections, the program to use herbicides in Laos was approved December 1.

Various groups of scientists in the Untied States expressed their growing concern, particularly the use of arsenical herbicides such as Agent Blue, and they urged that the use of this type of herbicide cease until more was known about the ultimate fate of the arsenic in these chemicals once it was released in the land. There were arguments that using 2,4-D and 2,4,5-T on forests was a military device for saving lives that caused a level of harm to the environment that was unprecendently low, presumably compared to alternatives such as high explosives or napalm.

Professor E. W. Pfeiffer of the University of Montana, one of the original scientists, asked the American Association for the Advancement of Science to request a United Nations analysis. He specifically requested field studies in Vietnam. One of the two scientists who had gone to Vietnam told the press in New York that it was "completely unrealistic to expect American commanders in Vietnam to stop defoliation missions because the use of these chemicals unquestionably saved American lives." He said he had seen few living plants on a journey by boat from Saigon to the ocean, but that if the vegetation along the way had not been killed, he would probably not have survived the journey.

Defoliation operations continued despite misgivings, because it was believed that herbicide spraying was fulfilling a military need.

It was widely believed by most American Army officers that Vietnam's monsoon climate, together with its jungle terrain and countless rice paddies, constituted an environment too hostile for use of armored units. French armored units in Vietnam from the end of World War II to 1954 had been largely unsuccessful. Their failure convinced doubters in the American Army.

Although early American aid had envisioned a buildup of an armored force within the South Vietnamese Army, it was not until 1967 that the potential of armored forces was fully described to the United States Army's top leaders. General Arthur L. West, Jr. had sent the results of a study to the Army Chief of Staff and to the Secretary of the Army that pointed out armored cavalry was the most cost-effective force on the Vietnamese battlefield. It was then too late to alter basically the structure of the forces already sent to Vietnam or those earmarked for deployment. By then constraints on the size of American forces imposed by McNamara, and the decisions on deployment that extended well into 1968 had already been made. This was a regrettable error of the highest significance because armored units of the Army of the Republic of Vietnam had been successful in fighting the elusive Vietcong, although they were used only in the limited number available.

From early March 1965 to the end of the American involvement in 1973 armored units participated in virtually every large-scale offensive and worked closely with South Vietnamese forces. They were found to be powerful, flexible and essential battle forces. In large measure they contributed to the success of the Allied forces, not only in close combat, but in pacification and security operations. When redeployment was started back to the United States, armored units had proven so successful that their departure was held off until close to the end.

France's failure to use armor effectively was due to the fact that their World War II tanks and armored vehicles were not suited for cross-country movement, and their age often made them inoperative. When they took to the field they clung to the main roads where the Vietcong could easily avoid or attack them at will.

Westmoreland's lack of faith in armored units in Vietnam was due to the failure of the French at Dien Bien Phu—a situation that haunted his thoughts. But that battle was not lost because of failure of armored units. It was basically an infantry battle after the French had positioned themselves in an untenable position.

Once Americans became directly involved in Vietnam there was a basic lack of knowledge about the country's terrain that, in many places, was ideal for armored operations. When armor officers studied the terrain in 1967 they found that over 46 percent of the country could be traversed all year by armored vehicles. Actually, armored units conducted operations in every geographic area and were most limited in the Mekong Delta and the Central Highlands. Land in the delta often was below sea level and was rarely more than 13 feet above sea level. It was wet, fertile and extensively cultivated. It was poorly drained and on the southern tip of the Ca Mau Peninsula there was an expanse of stagnant marshes and low-lying mangrove forests. The entire delta was criss-crossed with streams, rivers and canals so traffic was forced to follow the dikes, dams and the few roads. In the Central Highlands, the rugged small mountains of the Annamite chain had peaks that rose to 7,000 feet. They were heavily forested with tropical evergreens and bamboo, difficult to traverse by armored vehicles, but the terrain was not impossible for them. The roads were poor and population centers were small and scattered. Armored units were first introduced in the Highlands to clear roads and to escort convoys. As larger enemy forces appeared, combined task forces operated against the mountain and jungle strongholds of the Vietcong.

Other regions along the coastal plain and plateau generally had rolling or hilly terrain that could be used by armored units 88 percent of the time. This area had been used by the French and South Vietnamese forces before the Americans arrived.

South Vietnam's weather was controlled by two seasonal wind flows—the summer or southwest monsoon, and the winter or northeast monsoon. The summer monsoon had the strongest winds from June through September that blew out of the Indian Ocean causing a wet season in the delta and in most of the western Highlands and in the plateau region. The wet season for the rest of the country was from November to February during the winter monsoon when onshore winds from the northeast dropped moisture over the northern one-third of South Vietnam.

In the transition period between the wet and dry seasons, and during dry periods, use of motorized vehicles was feasible in most parts of Vietnam. Even during the wet season they could operate in most areas with relative ease.

Westmoreland and most of his officers during the early 1960s believed the Vietcong was a loosely organized body that could not fight against a modern army. Actually, it was some time before these officers realized that the Vietcong actually were well organized in regular main forces, particularly after 1959 when Vietcong units began to organize into companies and battalions.

South Vietnam's armored units were well organized under their American advisers by 1962 when their new mechanized forces achieved success in the Plain of Reeds. These units, part of the 7th Infantry Division, fought well in September despite difficult terrain and poor tactical decisions. Many senior Vietnamese commanders were still ignoring or did not understand the capabilities of an armored force. Part of the problem was the palace guard syndrome that caused Vietnamese commanders to parcel out armored units among several provincial headquarters as security elements. At this stage, armored units could have been overwhelming if they had been used properly because the Vietcong had none, and they did not have anti-tank weapons. By 1965, however, the Vietcong were using armor-destroying weapons down to the company level and these new weapons became a distinct threat.

Once General Thieu came to power he insured the loyalty of his armor leaders by giving assignments to the Saigon area to his most trustworthy officers where armored forces could be combined on short notice to support or suppress any attempt to overthrow his government. Until the mid-1960s, political appointees as commanders of armored forces were a fact of life and had a disastrous effect on development and use of armor. These officers were not always the best leaders, and they were primarily concernerd with advancement of their careers, and thus reluctant to fight the Vietcong for fear of losing their jobs. Only in 1968 when political stability later became a serious reality were armored units finally able to shed the stigma of not fighting the Vietcong but interested only in protection of the political leadership.

United States Army armored units were sent to Vietnam in 1965. These were a mixture of M-48 and M-60 tanks, M-113 Armored Personnel Carriers and M-109 self-propelled 155 mm. howitzers.

Most senior armor officers, who had spent years in Europe, dismissed the Vietnam conflict as a short, uninteresting interlude that was best fought with infantry troops. Armored units did not demonstrate their full capabilities until these officers were weeded out in the field.

The two United States Marine battalion landing teams that were sent to Da Nang in early 1965 at General Westmoreland's request to provide air base security, brought their tanks with them. The 3rd Marine Tank Battalion was the first armored unit to send men to Vietnam. They took part in the first major battle in mid-August when a large Vietcong force was reportedly preparing to attack Chu Lai's airfield, southeast of Da Nang. Helicopters and armored teams were used to break up the attack. In a short, bitter firefight that lasted two days, the Vietcong were pressed against the sea and over 700 were killed. This was the first introduction of Marine armored units in Vietnam, but it would not be the last.

The decision to send American ground forces to Vietnam was due to the cumulative effect of a rapidly changing strategy but without clearly stated long-term goals with definite troop commitments. In the hectic days and months of the first half of 1965 no one could predict the length of the war, the enemy's intentions or the capabilities and extent of future commitments.

Three principal ground strategies were developed: security, enclave, and search and destroy. The first two did not require the use of large mobile forces because it was believed United States troops would not long remain in Vietnam. Under security guidelines, Marines were sent to defend an airfield and they took their tanks along because this was basic Marine Corps strategy. Prior to their arrival, Military Assistance Command planners had not examined the makeup of a Marine battalion landing team and incredibly did not realize that such a team had tanks! The Marines saw no need to leave their tanks behind because tanks were an integral part of their combat operations. When Ambassador Taylor learned that the Marines had brought their tanks he was surprised and displeased, saying, they were "not appropriate for counter-insurgency operations."

Base security by its very nature is limited in scope to a purely defensive role. The so-called enclave strategy also was primarily defensive. Neither called for use of armored units. Troops authorized for Vietnam to carry out both strategies—the Marines, the Army's 173rd Airborne Brigade and an Australian infantry battalion—therefore were supposed to be infantry elements whose stay in Vietnam was considered temporary. The Airborne Brigade had specifically been assigned to temporary duty. Military Assistance Command planners, therefore, in trying to obtain all the combat troops that were needed, and stay within troop ceilings established by McNamara, selected infantry units that could be easily deployed and that required only minimal support.

When the 1st Infantry Division was approved for deployment, directives were issued to eliminate units designed for nuclear war, the division's two tank battalions, and all mechanized infantry units. The rationale for this decision was offered by Army Chief of Staff General Harold K. Johnson July 3, 1965, to General Westmoreland. He said he had overruled his staff's proposal that one tank battalion be retained with the division. Johnson cited the Korean War experience that demonstrated the ability of orientals to employ relatively primitive but extremely effective box mines that defied detection. He told Westmoreland that he had seen few reports of light tanks among the North Vietnamese and that he did not believe there was any need for them. He said that the distances planned for the 1st Division to operate indicated that rapid movement would be slowed by tanks. His statement is almost unbelievable. But he compounded the error by concluding that the presence of a tank formation would tend to create a psychological atmosphere of conventional combat, as well as recall the image of French tactics in the same area. He did agree that the division's 1st Squadron should keep its medium tanks to test their effectiveness.

Westmoreland demonstrated his own lack of comprehension of the terrain in which his military units would operate by replying, "Except for a few coastal areas, most notably in I Corps, there is no place in Vietnam for either tanks or mechanized infantry units." Unfortunately, this was the prevailing viewpoint in top command circles.

The 1st Division's commander, Major General Jonathan O. Seaman, was concerned by this decision, and rightly so. Even worse, after his brigades were sent to three different locations, and the 1st Squadron was split into a platoon for each brigade, the squadron's effectiveness was even further reduced.

General Westmoreland now flatly stated that he wanted "no tanks in the jungle" and he ordered the M-48s withdrawn from their cavalry troops and held at the squadron's base at Phu Loi. It took Seaman six months to convince Westmoreland that he was wrong.

As North Vietnam's political and military power grew during 1965, Westmoreland and his planning staff became convinced that the United States would have to provide even more troops if the South Vietnamese government was to survive. President Johnson approved his requests for additional men and this time additional armored units were authorized. Late in the year Westmoreland requested the deployment of the 11th Armored Cavalry and the 25th Infantry Division which had armored units. Major General Frederick C. Weyand, commander of the division, insisted that the armored battalion be deployed with his division despite resistance from staff planners in both the Department of the Army and in Saigon.

The battle of Ap Bau Bang November 11 and 12, 1965, was an early example of a combined arms defense of a night position. It demonstrated their effectiveness in jungle warfare. This battle went on for more than six hours before the Vietcong withdrew to the northwest. In it the 1st Squadron's 4th Cavalry made a strong case for armored forces. General Seaman and other officers recommended that armored units of the 25th Infantry Division be sent to Vietnam in early 1966. He said the M-113's heavy fire had broken the enemy assault.

Within three weeks after their arrival, three armored units of the 25th Division participated in Vietnam's first multi-battalion armor operation. It was carried out in jungle and among rubber plantations twelve miles north of Saigon where heavy growth favored the concealment of the Vietcong's base camps. The soft, marshy soil impeded tank movements but generally the vegetation did not restrict the movement of either the tanks or armored personnel carriers. This was the first time large armored forces had invaded a Vietcong jungle stronghold and forced them to move their camps. The myth that armor could not be used in jungle operations was finally destroyed, although some doubters remained within the Military Assistance Command.

The first armored units to arrive in Vietnam literally had to invent tactics and techniques and then convince the Army hierarchy that they worked. Several generals advocated the deployment of more armored units. General Seaman, 1st Division commander, and later head of the II Field Force, constantly recommended deployment of more units, and a growing number of other generals added their appeals. It had been a difficult task to demonstrate the truth to higher headquarters but these officers who laid their careers on the line against strong opposition had the courage of their convictions.

One significant fact emerged after a series of engagements. Contrary to tradition a tank-led armored force had sufficient combat power to withstand a massive ambush until supporting artillery, air and infantry support could be brought up to destroy the attackers. Engagements with armored elements actually forced the Vietcong to fight while infantry battalions provided the necessary reinforcement to encircle the enemy and cause his destruction. Such operations became routine in the next two years, despite Westmoreland's earlier doubts about their effectiveness in Vietnam.

CHAPTER 16

"Without Reinforcements, Kiss Us Goodbye!"

AT THE HONOLULU CONFERENCE IN JANUARY, 1966, ADMIRAL SHARP insisted that United States Air Force and Navy aircraft be employed more aggresively against North Vietnam. If war is to be ended soon, he told conferees, massive air strikes on all communist bases must be approved not only against North Vietnam but against their bases in Laos and Cambodia. He also called for mining of Haiphong's harbor, saying it was evident the North Vietnamese were unwilling to negotiate. The Joint Chiefs promptly endorsed these proposals made by the Commander-in-Chief, Pacific.

At the start of the new year, the 173rd Airborne Brigade launched the first American attack in the Mekong Delta by moving into the notorious Plain of Reeds by land and air from Hau Nghia Province.

The 1st Brigade of the 1st Cavalry Division also set out to destroy the Vietcong in Pleiku and Kontum Provinces, but the enemy fled into Cambodia. The division then shifted to Binh Dinh Province where some of its units had been committed since their arrival in Vietnam the previous summer for a major effort to control the Ia Drang Valley.

While the Marines supported the South Vietnamese in I Corps, Army troops performed the same function in III Corps in the central region and around Saigon.

The 1st Brigade, 101st Airborne Division, the Korean 2nd Marine Brigade and South Vietnam's 47th Regiment set out January 19 to locate and destroy the North Vietnamese 95th Regiment believed to be located in the Tuy Hoa valley. Their primary mission was to protect the rice harvest in the coastal region. They were successful and the enemy suffered serious losses before a temporary ceasefire was proclaimed in honor of the

Lunar New Year, although minor clashes continued throughout the Tet period.

Until this year the American part in the war had been largely one of words. Now the air strategy changed slowly and some of the recommendations long advocated by General LeMay, and his successor General McConnell as Air Force chief of staff since the previous year, were approved by Secretary of Defense McNamara. For one thing, Admiral Sharp and his field commanders were given greater control of air operations, and the Pacific commander was allowed to determine how much effort should be applied, and how often. There were still restraints, and they continued to irritate the admiral because the new rules still fell short of using airpower at its full potential. Most important targets still remained off-limits and attacks were largely restricted to lines of communication and against targets below the 20th parallel. Those above this line were released by the Defense Department on a one-by-one basis.

McNamara set the tone by saying publicly February 3, 1966, that United States "objectives are not to destroy or to overthrow the communist government of China, or the communist government of North Vietnam. They are limited to the destruction of the insurrection and aggression directed by North Vietnam against the political institutions of South Vietnam. This is a very, very limited political objective." It was limited all right—so limited as to be tragically unsound. For those laying their lives on the line almost daily it was no wonder many said privately, "Why are we here?"

McNamara continued to insist that there was only an insurrection in South Vietnam whereas in reality there was full-scale war.

Admiral Sharp and the Joint Chiefs disagreed with McNamara. They continued to seek a total air campaign against the North Vietnamese heartland as the only viable alternative to a full-scale ground war. Sharp repeatedly stressed that the United States could control events and stop reacting only through the proper use of airpower. In the South, he said, the North Vietnamese maintained the initiative by fighting where and when they desired, and then retreated into the jungle to their sanctuaries in Laos and Camabodia. Sharp and the Joint Chiefs were convinced that treating the war as an insurgency was wrong.

In the United States many sincere, well-meaning people were speaking out against the war. Senator Robert F. Kennedy, the former president's brother, said February 19 that the National Liberation Front might be included in a coalition government. Unfortunately such words and actions gave aid and comfort to North Vietnam. The chants of activists at peace demonstrations resounded across the nation, "End the war now!"

In a tally of 1,200 recent Harvard graduates it was learned that only 4.6 percent, or a total of fifty-six had been drafted. Most of these men were in stateside non-combat positions and only two were in Vietnam. Thus the war was being fought largely by non-college, low-income draftees.

North Vietnam's newspaper *Nhan Dan* wrote with great satisfaction February 27, "In America the debates on the Vietnamese problem will become increasingly fiercer [*sic*]. The United States Imperialistic rear will be the scene of great confusion, which in turn will exert great influence upon the morale of the United States serviceman on the front line. That is why the Johnson clique is very perplexed and afraid, faced with the ever stronger anti-war movement which, like a sharp knife, is stabbing them in the back."

The protest movement was valued highly by the communists who praised the American "peace champions" whom they said, "courageously turned the courts trying them into forums to condemn the war."

President Park Chung Hee of Korea announced January 29, 1966, that subject to ratification by the Korean National Assembly he had approved South Vietnam's request for an additional regiment and a division. His request was promptly approved by the Assembly.

In the coming months, Thailand authorized the activation of a military assistance group and an Air Force contingent. The Australian government agreed to provide another battalion, and New Zealand offered to increase its contingent to 500. The Australians later reached a peak of 7,672 men. Korea eventually had 50,000 men in Vietnam, and Thailand 11,568.

Thailand's decision to participate actively in the war with a reinforced battalion was a departure from its earlier non-intervention stand. In Bangkok alone more than 5,000, including twenty Buddhist monks and the prime minister's son, volunteered for Vietnam. A thirty-one-year-old monk said, "The communists are nearing our home. I have to give up my yellow robe to fight them. In that way I serve both my country and my religion." This allied help was welcome, but it did pose logistical problems for the United States because it had to supply these units.

President Ferdinand Marcos of the Philippines, who was elected in the fall of 1965, refused to send combat troops but he did authorize a 2,000-man civic action group to aid pacification efforts.

The Korean Capital Division, first introduced the previous fall to protect Highway 19 up to An Khe from Qui Nhon, was given responsibility in the new year for all of the area north of Qui Nhon to east of Highway 1 and up to Phu Cat Mountain.

After the 9th Korean "Whitehorse" Division arrived, Westmoreland reached agreement with Major General Myung Shin Chae to develop a Korean corps area at Nha Trang close to I Field Force with Chae as commander. With 50,000 troops it was now possible to sweep the area that had been dominated by at least two North Vietnamese battalions and to occupy key points in a matter of days.

President Park Chung Hee had personally selected each senior officer. General Chae was an excellent officer who had the difficult job of pleasing his government and staying on good terms with American commanders. The Korean divisions had remarkable discipline and they fought with proven competence. There was never any formal agreement on the employment of Korean forces although Chae made it clear that he did not consider his corps under American control, although he cooperated with American commanders in an amiable spirit. Chae had specified that he wished his forces deployed in a significant, prestigious area on a densely populated coast where their presence would have the greatest impact at home and abroad. President Park had insisted from the beginning that all those going to Vietnam would be volunteers, and those who did not measure up were quickly sent home.

On a trip to South Vietnam President Park told General Westmoreland that he was proud to have Koreans fight under his command. This was as close as any Korean ever came to such an admission.

I Corps' volatile Vietnamese commander, Lieutenant General Nguyen Chang Thi, had led an abortive coup against President Diem as early as 1960, and he played a large role among the younger military commanders who dominated South Vietnam's policies following Diem's assassination November 1, 1963. In I Corps, Thi controlled both the civilian government and the armed forces. Although not openly defiant of the various military governments in Saigon since Diem's death, he carefully selected the directives that he chose to obey. In early 1966 there were rumors in Saigon that Thi was about to lead a coup against the flamboyant Air Marshal Nguyen Cao Ky and the more reticent General Nguyen Van Thieu who respectively served as commissioner in charge of the executive branch and chairman of the Joint Directorate—the official name for the ruling military junta governing South Vietnam.

General Walt refused to concern himself with the machinations of Vietnamese politicians, but confined his efforts towards the establishment of a working relationship with General Thi. He respected Thi's courage and military competence but he realized that Thi also had political responsibilities. Walt admitted later that in South Vietnam the military purpose sometimes got on a collision course with the political purpose, but he said they always found ways to talk out their problems. Walt knew that Thi was politically ambitious, but he believed that he was interested in making I Corps an example for the rest of his country.

The American buildup of the III Marine Amphibious Force under Walt reached approximately seventy thousand troops, including Major General Fields' 1st Marine Division. Fields was an experienced artillery officer who had served in both World War II and in Korea.

The American buildup had been approved by McNamara the previous year and paralleled South Vietnam's inability to cope with an increase in communist forces within South Vietnam from 138,000 in March the previous year to 226,000. Almost half of these men were guerrillas, but the remainder were North Vietnamese Army regulars. Allied forces had made their first encounter with the latter the previous fall. Walt's interest, however, was in the 30,000 Vietcong and North Vietnamese regulars in his area. But his primary concern was the Vietcong infrastructure that he believed controlled a third of the population and, through terror tactics, influenced another third.

In the previous year the Marines had emphasized small-unit, counter-guerrilla tactics rather than multi-battalion operations against main-force units. General Krulak had persistently opposed such tactics. Known as "Brute" in jesting reference to his small stature, but also in recognition of his forthright and commanding personality, Krulak was one of Sharp's advisers. He repeatedly attempted to convince Sharp there was no value in seeking out North Vietnamese Army units in the mountains and in the jungle. He said as long as they stayed there they were not a threat and American efforts should be addressed to the rich, populous lowlands. "It is our conviction," he said, "that if we can destroy the guerrilla fabric among the people, we will automatically deny the larger units the food and intelligence and the taxes and the other support they need. At the same time, if the big units want to sortie out of the mountains and come down where they can be cut up by our supporting arms, the Marines are glad to take them on, but the real war is among the people and not among these mountains." This was too simplistic an approach to the problem. The Vietcong and the North Vietnamese used these mountains as sanctuaries to attack at will, at points of their selection and thereby maintain the initiative.

Westmoreland disagreed with Krulak's views. He said North Vietnamese Army units in the South created an entirely new situation. He said he believed that the communists wanted to develop multidivision forces in relatively secure base areas, while at the same time continuing extensive guerrilla actions to tie down allied units. With the inteligence data at his disposal Westmoreland was convinced that the communists planned to mount major offensives in 1966 in provinces northwest of Saigon and in the Central Highlands. He expressed his belief that the communists hoped to control the Pleiku-Qui Nhon area and thus isolate I Corps from the rest of Vietnam. Westmoreland insisted that 1966 was the year of transition and he hoped to build up allied strength, protect vulnerable bases and then launch spoiling attacks to keep the enemy's main forces off-balance. He had long had reservations about the Marine Corps' pacification program ever since the preceding November when his operations officer reported that the the Vietcong controlled all but a tiny part of I Corps outside the enclaves. Brigadier General William E. De Puy had recommended that the Marines start a large offensive against Vietcong-controlled areas, but Westmoreland was reluctant to issue such orders, relying instead on specific projects that gradually would get the Marines out of their beachheads. Strong leadership on Westmoreland's part would have resolved the problem, regardless of the sensitivities involved.

In contrast to the Marines, the men of the 1st Cavalry Brigade encountered North Vietnamese regular troops early in 1966. In heavy fighting that lasted from January 28 through February 3 they engaged the 18th North Vietnamese Army Regiment in the coastal region of Binh Dinh Province, eight miles north of Bong Song. They killed six hundred and captured half that many more, for a brigade loss of seventy-five. This was a coordinated offensive against the enemy buildup in I and II Corps. For the first two weeks the Marines encountered only small groups of Vietcong and despite extensive commitment of units there was little heavy fighting. The Vietcong would strike the Marines, pull back, and then repeat the tactic. After being reinforced by the 1st Cavalry Division's 2nd Brigade near Bong Son, Colonel Harold G. Moore's 1st Brigade moved into the rugged interior of An Lac to link up with the Marines where they smashed the 18th North Vietnamese Army Regiment. Following this defeat, the enemy withdrew after suffering 2,000 casualties. Until March 6 the cavalry troopers and the Marines met only sporadic resistance.

This was no great victory for the Americans and General Krulak summed up the situation by saying that the operation failed because it taught people in the area that Marines "would come in, comb the area and disappear, whereupon the VC would resurface and resume control."

At a Honolulu meeting February 8, 1966, with President Johnson, Chief of State Thieu and Prime Minister Nguyen Cao Ky the two governments issued a declaration. President Johnson renewed the American pledge to support South Vietnam in its struggle against the communists, while Ky and Thieu promised renewed dedication to the eradication of social injustices, building a viable economy, establishment of a true democracy and defeat of the Vietcong and its allies. Both governments committed themselves to winning the pacification war. Ambassador Lodge told the gathering, "We have moved ahead here today in the fight to improve the lot of the little man at the grassroots. That is what this is all about."

Prime Minister Ky delivered an address to the conference pledging to carry out a social revolution to guarantee the people of South Vietnam "respect and dignity, and a chance for himself and his children to live in an atmosphere where all is not disappointments, despair and dejection."

Johnson expressed his pleasure with thoughts that he had often used to describe his Great Society program, by telling Ky, "Boy, you speak just like an American."

When Ky asked Johnson, "Isn't it possible for America to help us and yet keep out of the picture? Instead of making us look like the puppets of the giant Uncle Sam, let us fight the actual war. It will make us better soldiers."

Johnson's reply was not enthusiastic because he had little faith in South Vietnam's ability to defend itself. "Yeah, we'll consider it."

Westmoreland's strategy for using large units was not repudiated. McNamara and Rusk gave him a memorandum of understanding approving an increase in South Vietnamese and United States regular forces, directing him to intensify attacks against major enemy forces. This authority almost doubled the battalion months of offensive operations from forty to seventy-five. Westmoreland said that the conduct of the war was not a matter of either pacification or actions to thwart enemy mainforce units, but involved both.

Back in South Vietnam not much changed for the time being. The Marines continued to experiment with pacification techniques to convince the people that it was in their best interests to support their government in Saigon because victory was assured. These were just words at a time when action was needed.

There were growing encounters in southern Quang Tri and Thua Thien provinces and February 28 a 1st Division unit was ambushed seventeen miles north of Hué. Phu Bai was ordered reinforced and the Marines were confident they could control the situation. The campaign during these weeks was in the same area—the Street Without Joy—where the French in 1953 used twenty battalions against a Vietminh regiment, and three of them were severely mauled along Highway 1 between Quang Tri City and Hué.

While the Marines reinforced Phu Bai in response to the communist buildup, a threat developed at the A Shau Special Forces outpost in western Thua Thien Province, thirty-three miles southwest of Phu Bai. It was manned by a South Vietnamese irregular defense group with an American Special Forces detachment. This camp was ideally situated to monitor enemy movements through the A Shau valley, a major communist infiltration route two miles from and parallel to the Laotian border. It was surrounded by steep jungle-covered mountains, and its key road extended for fifteen miles. One branch ran westward and joined the elaborate Ho Chi Minh Trail. Other trails led into the populated area around Hué and Phu Bai. There had been three such bases in the area the previous year but all had been abandoned except the A Shau base in the southern part of the valley.

Acting upon information from a captured Vietcong soldier that A Shau would be attacked, its commander asked for reinforcements. The South Vietnamese said they were too committed elsewhere but the 5th United States Special Forces Group at Nha Trang authorized a mobile strike force company and it arrived March 7, raising the number of defenders to 400.

The following day the base commander placed the camp on alert. Early the next morning heavy North Vietnamese artillery fire struck the camp while 2,000 Vietcong and North Vietnamese soldiers probed its outer defenses. On the 9th an Air Force ground-support plane was shot down, although a rescue helicopter saved three of its crew. Despite ground fog two Marine helicopters, one flown by Lieutenant Richard A. Vasdias and the other by Lieutenant David E. Brust, tried to evacuate the wounded. Vasdias's craft was hit and crashed. Brust quickly touched down, picked up the crew and flew to Da Nang.

Shortly after noon on the 9th the commander radioed, "We suspect we are heavily infiltrated. Don't think camp will last the night without reinforcements."

Until the weather cleared there was no hope of helicopter support but reinforcements were requested. Brigadier General Marion E. Carl, assistant wing commander, flew from Da Nang to Phu Bai where he discussed the A Shau situation with the commander of the helicopter squadron. Then Carl flew over A Shau personally to analyze the situation. With improving weather Carl ordered an airlift to start at 4:20 P.M., but then he had to postpone it when the weather deteriorated and he learned that the Vietcong had surrounded the camp. It was clear to Carl that there was no possibility of reinforcements that day.

The communists began their final assault during the early hours of March 10. Some South Vietnamese irregulars fought well but most surrendered. American Detachment Leader Captain John D. Blair, IV, said later the commander of the irregulars hid in the camp's bunkers and made no effort to lead his men during the entire battle. At 10:00 A.M. Blair radioed for planes to bomb and strafe the camp except for the communications bunker and the north wall.

The Marines and Air Force now rushed in with close air support despite heavy cloud cover and the proximity of steep mountains surrounding the valley. Lieutenant Augusto M. Xavier, leader of a two-plane flight from Chu Lai, arrived over the camp and ordered his wingman to orbit above the cloud cover. Xavier descended through the overcast aided by the glow of parachute flares dropped by an Air Force plane. He maneuvered his attack bomber around the mountains and made a low level pass on emeny positions. Despite heavy ground fire he made a second pass, strafing enemy positions with cannon fire. This time his plane failed to pull up and it crashed into the side of a mountain.

Conditions on the ground continued to deteriorate and the defenders radioed shortly after noon, "Need reinforcements. Without them kiss us goodbye!" Twenty minutes later they radioed again, "Do not have area where you can land reinforcements."

Bad weather hung over the camp and Walt, recently promoted to lieutenant general, chaired an emergency meeting. Carl, who had made another reconnaissance flight over the valley, attended. He warned that the Marines stood a chance of losing one out of every four helicopters in a rescue attempt, but added, "We cannot abandon the troops encircled there."

Walt urged him to try and despite the continuing bad weather Carl called his squadron at Phu Bai and asked them to attempt to rescue members of the beleagured camp. "If the Special Forces have to 'bug out' they will be outside the camp over the north wall," Carl said.

In response to an emergency call for Air Force support, Major Bernard F. Fisher and Captain Francisco (Paco) Vazquez were first to take off from Pleiku. Upon arrival over the A Shau camp they found the valley floor ringed with more than twenty anti-aircraft guns and hundreds of automatic weapons. Fisher thought grimly that it was like flying inside Yankee Stadium with people in the bleachers firing machine guns. He and Vazquez joined four other A-1s orbiting above the valley. Spotting the precise location of the camp proved difficult due to the clouds but Fisher found a hole and led the Skyraiders through it. They broke out at 800 feet with the clouds obscuring the tops of the hills. The valley was like a tube because it was less than a mile wide and six miles long permitting little maneuvering for bombing or strafing. It was obvious to Fisher that they could attack in just one direction—straight down the valley to deliver their ordnance, and then make a tight 180-degree turn and escape back up the valley.

Fisher led four Skyraiders on the first pass and they were met by a deadly curtain of ground fire. He listened carefully as an Army radioman on the ground described the enemy positions along the valley's south wall.

Gunners quickly found their range and the canopy of Captain Hubert King's aircraft was shattered. Unable to see clearly, King desperately swung his Skyraider around and headed back to Pleiku.

Fisher and the others continued down the valley. Major Dafford W. (Jump) Myers felt his A-1 lurch. He had been hit by 50-caliber guns before and he knew this was something bigger—possibly a Chinese 37 mm. cannon. His engine sputtered and cut out. With his cockpit full of smoke, he called on his radio, "This is Surf 41..I've been hit and hit hard."

Fisher, in Hobo 51, replied, "Rog, you're on fire and burning clear back past your tail."

Myers made a quick decision. He was too low to bail out and his only recourse was to land on the A Shau strip. What he did not know was that the airstrip's borders were controlled by the enemy and they had heavy guns. Myers had no choice and he began a gliding turn towards the edge of the strip. His forward vision was blocked by smoke and flames so Fisher talked him into a proper alignment and rate of descent. The crippled Skyraider crossed the landing threshold and Fisher realized it was going too fast to stop on the short strip. He radioed Myers to raise his landing gear and Myers retracted his wheels just before the aircraft landed on its belly. He had tried to release his belly tank while in the air but it would not drop. It blew up and separated from his plane as it touched the runway. A huge billow of flames erupted and they streaked after the careening airplane until it came to a shuddering stop. Up above, Fisher watched with growing horror as the Skyraider was enveloped in flames with Myers still inside. Fisher made a 270-degree turn, taking about forty seconds, while he circled the strip and notified the airborne command post that Myers probably was hurt and trapped inside the blazing aircraft.

On the ground Myers hurriedly removed his parachute and helmet, grabbed his gun and survival kit, and quickly exited through the flames.

Fisher finally spotted Myers as he jumped out of his cockpit and dashed away from the burning plane—seemingly on fire. Actually it was only smoke streaming from Myers' body.

Myers hid in the brush across from enemy positions on the other side. He waved as Fisher flew directly overhead, but Fisher did not see him and did not know whether Myers was badly hurt. He was relieved that he was still alive. Fisher learned now that the airborne command post had requested a rescue helicopter and that one would arrive within twenty minutes.

Fisher was now joined by Captains Jon Lucas and Dennis Hague in their Skyraiders as they repeatedly strafed enemy positions to protect the beleagured fort and their downed comrade.

Ten minutes later Fisher heard over the radio that the rescue helicopter was still twenty minutes away and the airborne commander asked him to rendezvous with the chopper above the overcast and escort it down.

Fisher expressed doubt that Myers could last that long on the ground. If he left, he said, the Vietcong would quickly capture him. They had not been able to spot him because he was so well-concealed by brush. Instead, Fisher called the airborne commander to tell him that he would land and pick up Myers. The commander expressed strong opposition and even Fisher conceded such an act was unwise although he had to do it. Myers was one of his men, and they were like a family. It was unthinkable to desert him without a rescue attempt.

Fisher advised the command plane that he was going in and he proceeded on his approach with "Paco" along with him strafing enemy positions. Fisher carefully monitored his descent, knowing he was coming in too hot, and then he noticed that blowing smoke concealed the runway. On his final approach, he had to fly through the smoke so he kept full power on until he could see through it. Noting he was still too fast, he quickly reduced power so he would not overshoot. He released his gear to slow his descent but he was still too far down the runway. It was debris-littered as he touched down and slammed into several small objects although he dodged the bigger ones. He was still going too fast to stop so he decided to go around and immediately went to full power and took off. He made a quick 180-degree turn in order to land in the opposite direction from his first approach. He wheeled through a hail of enemy fire and touched down, using his brakes to stop on the 2,500-foot runway. For the first time he was scared, doubting he could bring the Skyraider to a stop. He pressed hard on the brakes and dropped his flaps to put more weight on the wheels. The steel planking was slick with dampness and he skidded and his plane went off the end of the runway where 55-gallon drums were hidden in the weeds. Now he had a new fear that he would hit them. Only his tail touched them when he turned around but his wing went right over their tops.

At breakneck speed Fisher taxied down the runway. It was like running an obstacle course among the litter while he searched for Myers. When he taxied by him, Myers frantically waved both arms. Fisher jammed his brakes but his speed carried him 100 feet beyond the downed pilot. When Myers did not come he thought he must be hurt so he set the plane's brakes and climbed over the right seat to get out on the side that Myers was on. In looking through his mirror he saw two red, beady eyes as Myers frantically crawled up the back of the wing. Fisher grabbed him by the seat of his pants and pulled him headfirst onto the cockpit's floor. Myers hit hard on his head but he did not complain. He was too glad to be rescued.

While Fisher jammed the throttle to the firewall and maneuvered his Skyraider around shell craters and debris, the North Vietnamese concentrated their fire on the fleeing plane. The Skyraider lifted off at minimum speed and Fisher held her on the deck until he had sufficient speed to pull into the clouds and head for Pleiku. He learned later his plane had taken nineteen hits. Myers was profuse in his thanks, saying he had run to the plane as fast as his forty-six-year-old legs could carry him.

The three other Skyraiders helped to make the hair-raising rescue possible by bombing and strafing the enemy positions. They were out of ammunition by the time Myers was picked up. Fisher's selfless act earned him a Medal of Honor.

Now another flight of Skyraiders took over as the defenders stubbornly clung to their position at A Shau throughout the 10th and made several unsuccessful counterattacks on the North Vietnamese positions. Each time they were forced by heavy fire to give up the attempt. It was noted that there were 300 dead Vietcong along the wall of the camp. By 3:00 P.M. Captain Blair realized the end was in sight. There was little ammunition left and no food or water had been available for the last thirty-six hours. He ordered most weapons destroyed but at 3:30 he received word that Marine helicopters would arrive within an hour-and-a-half. Blair promptly ordered the camp's evacuation and established a landing zone about 900 feet from the camp. Able-bodied South Vietnamese troops and irregulars were ordered to fight a rear-guard action while the wounded were placed first in the helicopters.

Shortly after 5:30 P.M. Lieutenant Colonel Charles A. House led sixteen UH-34s from his squadron with six UH-1Es and fixed-wing aircraft to support the rescue operation. As they approached the valley House's helicopter came under severe fire. Veering away, House noticed that the camp's survivors were pouring over the parapets on the north side. He turned around and began to descend to the improvised landing zone.

There was chaos on the ground when the helicopters landed. South Vietnamese irregulars panicked and abandoned the wounded. They clambered over one another to get into the helicopters. So many tried to get out first that they hung on the helicopters' cables, almost pulling them into the zone as they descended. South Vietnamese regulars clubbed some of them off the helicopters with their rifle butts. When this failed, the Americans fired into the midst of this hysterical mob. Some had to be killed to maintain order. It was either that or sacrifice everybody.

As House's helicopter began to rise a North Vietnamese recoilless rifle bullet struck the tail rotor and sent his plane spinning to the ground, while his wingman was also shot down and other helicopters were damaged. Now House and his men had to join the South Vietnamese on the ground. With darkness the airlift had to be temporarily suspended, and only one helicopter had gotten out with sixty-nine defenders, including four American advisers.

On the ground House took command and escaped with the survivors into the jungle. On the afternoon of the 11th Marine pilots found House and his men in a small clearing, and helicopters landed to rescue them. It was a repeat performance of the day before as irregulars panicked and South Vietnamese regulars had to shoot thirteen of them before they could be brought under control. One South Vietnamese threw a grenade that killed ten of the irregulars struggling to board the helicopter, but no Americans took part. South Vietnamese officials later denied such actions, saying control had been maintained by rifle butt strokes and firing in front of the feet of the terror-stricken men. Helicopters were able to rescue sixty of the group, including House and six other Americans. All aircraft got away but heavy damage was caused to twenty-one of the twenty-four helicopters, forcing them to be scrapped. One survivor said of the Skyraider support, "It took all the pressure off the east wall of the fort and enabled us to escape."

Reporters interviewed Lieutenant Colonel House and he said that he had told senior commanders that he was highly critical of the A Shau operation. When the press reported unfavorably on the operation, House was given a medal for bravery and a letter of reprimand for his part in the evacuation. In addition to the heavy loss of aircraft, 248 out of 434 men in the garrison were either missing or dead, including five Special Forces soldiers. The fall of the camp proved serious because it opened the area to increased infiltration of men and materiel through the valley into the central part of I Corps.

Before the evacuation, the pros and cons of using ground troops to rescue the men at the camp had been debated, but in the end nothing was done. On March 15 General Chuan, who had just relieved General Thi as corps commander, due to his falling out with Prime Minister Ky, urged the South Vietnamese General Staff to intercede with Westmoreland's command for use of American Marines to make up the major attacking force to retake the A Shau valley. Due to the buildup of enemy forces in the northern provinces, this plan was rejected.

Meanwhile, the Phu Bai forces were increased. General Walt's III Marine Amphibious Force and the Military Assistance Command in Saigon still differed on the extent of the enemy threat in the northern provinces. Walt believed that successful operations earlier in the month, along with the buildup of his northern forces, combined to contain the enemy. He was soon to learn how wrong was his assumption. He said that although A Shau had fallen, there had been no apparent attempt by the

95th North Vietnamese Regiment to move toward the coast. In contrast, Westmoreland's intelligence chief reported that he expected a major enemy offensive in the north. He referred to a new enemy division and other units that, he said, were known to plan an attack on Phu Bai. At a meeting with Walt, March 24 at Chu Lai, Westmoreland expressed concern at the fall of A Shau, saying I Corps' western flank was now exposed to the enemy. He pointed to reports of North Vietnamese Army troops in the demilitarized zone and near Khe Sanh's Special Forces camp in northwest Chang Tri Province as evidence that the enemy was on the move. Walt promised Westmoreland that his Marines would continue to watch developments in the north. A promise of more aggressive action was not only needed, but would have been more than welcomed by Westmoreland.

CHAPTER 17

"General, We Will Die Together!"

THE INCREASING COMMUNIST THREAT FROM THE NORTH DURING THE spring was of major concern but the internal political crisis in I Corps overshadowed the North Vietnamese Army buildup. Beneath an outward show of national unity several groups dissatisfied with the Saigon military regime took action. These disgruntled politicians maneuvered to restore civilian authority. Various Buddhist leaders had criticized the National Leadership Committee, or Directorate, and now demanded a national assembly. Within the government itself military factions jockeyed for power. The resulting schism, mainly bewteen Catholics and Buddhists, threatened the delicate fabric of South Vietnam's political cohesiveness.

Until the end of February, 1966, Prime Minister Ky had managed to keep his political opponents off-balance by granting piecemeal concessions. He promised a constitution approved by a referendum, and the creation of a representative government. He said reform would take a year or more. He scheduled a referendum to consider a constitution for October, and he promised elections for a national assembly sometime in 1967. In effect, Ky was offering his rivals the possibility of a share in authority sometime in the future, while he and his supporters remained in charge for an indefinite period.

Prime Minister Ky considered General Thi his most dangerous rival. Born of peasant stock, and a native to the I Corps region, Thi was popular with troops and the people. He capitalized on this sentiment, as well as the population's traditional distrust of the government in Saigon, and he carved out his own power base centered at Hué where he maintained his residence. Since the start of the new year Thi had continued to consolidate his position in I Corps by appointing officials personally loyal to him, including the mayor of Da Nang, Dr. Nguyen Van Man, a civilian physician with little administrative experience.

After his return from the March conference at Honolulu, Prime Minister Ky viewed the political situation in I Corps with increasing alarm. He personally flew to Hué to investigate allegations that Thi was directing agitation against the government. There was a lively confrontation between Ky and Thi and they exchanged charges and countercharges. After this session Ky returned to Saigon and called for a special meeting of the National Leadership Council to settle the dispute.

In an extraordinary session March 10 Ky asked his military colleagues for a formal vote of confidence. He said he would resign if Thi was not stripped of his command. In a secret ballot, a majority called for General Thi's dismissal on grounds of insubordination. Thi was present and he gracefully accepted his firing. The following day a government spokesman announced that Thi had requested sick leave because of sinus trouble, and that Brigadier General Nguyen Van Chuan, 1st Division commander would be the new I Corps' commanding general. Brigadier General Pham Xuan Nhuan was appointed to replace Chuan as division commander.

Thi's removal caused shock waves through I Corps. Soldiers and civilians alike marched through Da Nang in protest. Buddhist forces later joined those loyal to Thi, and anti-Ky coalitions were formed in the northern cities. A group in Hué called themselves the Popular Forces to Struggle for the Revolution. Their first action was to initiate a strike that quickly paralyzed the city.

Prime Minister Ky tried to placate the opposition March 15 by permitting Thi to return for a brief visit, supposedly to announce that he had accepted his dismissal in the best interests of the country.

Thi was met by enthusiastic crowds and he expressed reservations about the government. He moved into his official residence in Hué for what he called an extended rest, and he remained there two months as the political ferment escalated.

Despite the internal Vietnamese political crisis the United States continued its military buildup and revamped its command structure. In March, the Secretary of the Navy approved establishment of United States Naval Forces, Vietnam, while the Air Force changed the name of the 2nd Air Division to the Seventh Air Force. Westmoreland made additional changes March 15 by establishing field forces in II and III Corps areas. They were responsible to him for all United States ground operations in their respective areas.

Similar changes were made in I Corps among the Marine commands. Through the first three months of 1966, units of the 1st Marine Division continued to arrive from Okinawa under General Fields at Chu Lai. There the 1st Division was made responsible for this tactical area and the 3rd Division retained control of the Phu Bai and Da Nang enclaves.

General Walt restructured his command in March to conform to the transformation of his III Amphibious Force into a two-division ground force supported by a large aircraft wing. March 18 Walt relinquished direct command of the 3rd Marine Division to devote more time to his duties as head of the amphibious force, and Major General Wood B. Kyle assumed command of the 3rd Division. Despite these changes the basic mission of the Marines continued to be support of operations by the Army of the Republic of Vietnam.

While strikes continued to cripple Da Nang following General Thi's dismissal, General Walt kept his men out of the internal dispute. It was almost impossible, however, to continue operations and to keep the antagonists apart. There were many minor incidents that could have become explosive.

When dissidents continued to hold positions of political power in I Corps, Prime Minister Ky decided to re-assert his authority. He told a press conference April 3, "I consider Da Nang to be in the hands of the communists, and the government will organize an operation to retake [the city]." Ky flew to Da Nang the following night with two members of the Directorate and three Vietnamese Marine battalions. Apparently General Chuan persuaded Ky not to move against the dissidents because the Marines remained at the airfield. In a radio broadcast Prime Minister Ky said the city was not under communist control as he had stated. He returned to Saigon that night but the Vietnamese Marine battalions remained at the air base while the rebels continued to hold the city.

General Walt was in an uncomfortable position and he wanted to keep the antagonists apart. In particular, he did not want to even give the appearance of meddling in South Vietnamese politics. He feared this political crisis would not only interrupt his prosecution of the war, but that United States troops might become embroiled if fighting broke out between the two factions.

The climax came April 6 when Colonel Dam Quang Yeu led an armored convoy of anti-government Army forces towards Da Nang along Route 1. Major General Wood B. Kyle directed that the Americans block the highway, and this was done close to Dien Ban. The danger of a serious confrontation at Thanh Quit Bridge, nine miles south of the air base, remained. There American Marines faced a heavily armored South Vietnamese convoy. Colonel John R. Chaisson, head of the 9th Marine Regiment, warned Colonel Yeu that if his troops continued to advance or shell the base, the Americans would consider it an attack upon themselves and act accordingly. On signal, a flight of Marine A-4s armed with bombs and rockets appeared overhead, and General Walt ordered Marine artillery to lay their guns on the rebel positions but to fire only on his personal command. The situation was tense but Chaisson's forthright action convinced Colonel Yeu that aggressive action by his rebel faction was not in anyone's best interest. Yeu ordered his artillery unit to return to Hoi An, but he and his infantry remained.

Prior to this confrontation, the Marines evacuated American civilians, United States military personnel and foreign nationals from Da Nang in accordance with Westmoreland's orders.

The following week there was a lessening of tension. General Ton That Dinh replaced Chuan as I Corps commander April 10, and he defused the situation. Two days later the remaining Vietnamese Marines returned to Saigon.

At the government-sponsored national political Congress April 14, Chief of State General Thieu announced elections would be held within five months. Most dissidents were satisfied by the announcement. Even outspoken Thich Tri Quang, who had led the 1963 Buddhist revolt and was still the key leader in central Vietnam, called for a moratorium on strikes and demonstrations. Da Nang and Hué returned to a semblance of normal.

But this situation did not last and General Thi on April 15 demanded that the government step down immediately. Radical Buddhist leaders announced that sixty monks and nuns were prepared to immolate themselves if Ky did not resign as prime minister.

Ky aggravated the situation May 7 by announcing that the constituent assembly the government had promised to organize within five months would not be transformed into a national assembly. He said the body would simply draft a constitution and be dissolved until the national assembly was elected some time in 1967. Demonstrations erupted again in the north. In retaliation, Ky replaced the director general of the National Police, a Thi supporter, with Colonel Ngoc Loan—an officer loyal to Ky.

Prime Minister Ky acted forcefully to put down the revolt in Da Nang. Charging that the dissidents had committed acts of terror the previous night, he airlifted two Vietnamese Marine battalions and two Airborne battalions to Da Nang. Their arrival caught officials of the III Marine Amphibious Forces by surprise because Ky had not consulted General Walt. I Corps' commander General Dinh, in trying to negotiate with the rebels, also had no knowledge of Ky's action. Both he and Walt were caught in the middle of another unpleasant crisis. Fortunately, there were only a few confrontations with American Marines. General Walt's advice that Ky support his I Corps commander and withdraw his forces was rejected by Ky who refused to compromise. Further inflaming the situation was Ky's action May 16 in replacing General Dinh with Major General Huynh Van Cao. The new commander was a Catholic, who had been IV Corps commander under the late President Diem. His appointment was a red flag to the Buddhist leaders.

Da Nang is essentially an island city. Every exit had to be made over one major bridge. Any force that held this bridge, controlled the city. Therefore, General Walt wanted to keep the Da Nang River Bridge intact. He tried to reach a compromise between government and dissident forces, but by May 18 the Vietnamese Marines had pushed to the western edge of the bridge connecting Da Nang to the Tiensha Peninsula. When the Vietnamese government Marines tried to cross, dissident troops fired at them from entrenched positions on the other side. The leader of these rebel troops sent General Cao a message that he had wired the bridge with demolitions and that he would destroy it if government Marines continued their advance. Cao relayed the message to General Walt, reminding him that this single-span bridge was highly important to his amphibious command because it was needed to transport most of his supplies. Walt did not need to be reminded and he ordered his operations officer, Colonel Chaisson, to work out a compromise. Chaisson met the South Vietnamese Marine commander at the bridge and requested that he pull back his troops to permit American Marines to occupy the bridge. The government commander agreed and Company M of the 3rd Marines, at the time part of an airfield defense battalion, replaced the Vietnamese government Marines on that side of the river.

Before crossing the bridge to talk with the dissidents' leader Chaisson asked for a reinforced squad from the 3rd Battalion to meet him on the eastern side. Then the colonel flew across in a helicopter but he failed to persuade the Vietnamese rebels to abandon their entrenched positions. Chaisson ordered Captain William L. Lee, commander of L Company, 3rd Marines, who had accompanied the reinforced squad, to move his troops towards the dissidents. The Americans advanced directly into the midst of the rebels and simply sat down, making no attempt to dislodge them.

Chaisson boarded a helicopter and reported to General Walt. Both returned to the bridge in Walt's staff car. As General Walt walked across the bridge a Vietnamese dissident warrant officer ordered him to stop, intimating he was going to blow up the bridge . . . and the American general.

Walt argued that the demolitions should be removed. When the rebel officer refused, Walt gave him hell and tried to intimidate him, but the short Vietnamese officer refused to back down.

"I'm going to stay right here and send for a platoon of Marines," Walt said. He ordered a Vietnamese government platoon to come to the bridge just as the rebel warrant officer held his hand up as though he were about to signal for the bridge to be blown up. Walt remained defiantly in place.

In a commanding voice the warrant officer said, "General, we will die together!" He brought his raised arm down smartly to his side. There was no doubt in Walt's mind that the Vietnamese expected the bridge to blow up on his signal. His expression turned to incredulity when nothing happened.

A Vietnamese government platoon now marched from the west side and went over the rails to remove the wired charges as General Walt returned to his staff car and drove away.

Walt's report to Westmoreland was laconic. "After considerable debate, Army of the Republic of Vietnam engineers succeeded in removing the demolitions from the bridge."

Once the bridge incident was over, attention focused on the fighting in the city. Rebel forces had barricaded themselves in several pagodas and refused to surrender. The main point of resistance was the Tinh Hoi Pagoda where 350 heavily armed rebels held out against government troops. General Cao did not want unnecessary casualties so he refused to order a direct assault.

The new National Police chief, Colonel Loan, went to I Corps headquarters, pulled a gun and threatened Cao's life unless he gave the order to attack the pagoda. General Cao beat a hasty retreat to the American headquarters compound where he asked General Walt for asylum and for transport to the United States. Despite his action Prime Minister Ky did not immediately relieve Cao. Next day Ky directed government forces not to attack the pagodas. Instead, he ordered them to encircle each stronghold and to starve out the defenders.

The situation on the Tiensha Peninsula remained tense as dissidents continued to control the east bank of the Da Nang River and exchanged shots with government troops on the west bank. They threatened to blow up a large supply dump if government troops crossed the river. General Walt ordered a battalion of his Marines to occupy the site and to seize the ammunition dump if necessary. When a Vietnamese Skyraider made strafing passes on Marine positions, Walt warned the Vietnamese Air Force that his jets would shoot down any Vietnamese planes that did it again. He ordered four Marine Skyhawks to fly a combat patrol above the Vietnamese Skyraiders. The Vietnamese commander then ordered four more Skyraiders to fly above the American jets. Walt topped them with four more Skyhawks above the second layer of Skyraiders. For over an hour General Walt sat in his command center with two telephones, one connected to the Marine air commander, and the other to the Vietnamese air leader. He told the Vietnamese air commander that if his planes fired one round, one rocket or dropped one bomb that he would order his pilots to shoot down all his planes. On the other phone he told his Marine air commander to immediately carry out his orders if he was instructed to do so. The Vietnamese commander backed down and ordered his planes to land.

This was a ridiculous and dangerous situation, one that should have been resolved at the highest levels in Washington and Saigon. If President Johnson had threatened to withdraw all Americans unless this nonsense did not immediately cease, something might have been salvaged from the war effort. As it was President Johnson never could make up his mind whether to fight the war or to get out.

After this episode, there were no more air strikes although rebel forces fired mortars into the ranks of the 2nd Battalion, and eight Americans were wounded. Retaliation was threatened, and that ended the mortar attacks. The dump was finally turned over to the Marines.

The rebel movement collapsed in Da Nang May 23, 1966, with the surrender of dissidents in the Tinh Hoi Pagoda. One hundred and fifty Vietnamese had been killed on both sides, and twenty-three Americans were wounded in this fratricidal exchange. Apparently General Thi decided against further attempts to return to power when he and Prime Minister Ky met and he agreed to accept a new assignment. Such a reassignment was never forthcoming and he went into exile in the United States.

General Cao proved unacceptable to Prime Minister Ky so the Directorate named loyal 2nd Division Commander, Brigadier General Hoang Xuan Lam, as I Corps' commander.

With General Thi's departure the situation in Hué worsened and mobs rioted. A Buddhist nun sat in front of a pagoda and doused her robes with gasoline, and then set herself on fire. That night another nun did the same, and a monk emulated them in Da Lat the following morning.

Buddhist leader Thich Tri Quang blamed President Johnson for the fiery suicides and several days later he began a publicized hunger strike to protest American support for the Saigon government. His followers burned the United States information office in Hué June 1, and continued their protests against all Americans.

As a result of the increasing violence the Saigon government granted concessions to the Buddhists. At a meeting of the Armed Forces Council June 6 the Directorate was enlarged to include ten civilian members, including two Buddhists. A week later Prime Minister Ky established a predominantly civilian eighty-member People/Army Council to advise the government. His action did not quell the opposition but the Buddhists resorted mainly to non-violent harassment. In northern cities, they placed family altars and statues in the streets. United States personnel were ordered not to touch religious figures since desecrating would precipitate more anti-American actions. Da Nang's cluttered streets now became snarled by traffic so General Walt restricted vehicular use, and movement of supplies from the piers came to a halt.

I Corps' General Lam ordered police to remove all shrines. This was done in Da Nang, but police and 1st Vietnamese Division troops refused to participate in Hué. Buddhists did the same thing on highways and made the passage of vehicles impossible due to the shrines that effectively obstructed traffic.

Prime Minister Ky ordered General Lam to rectify the situation in Hué. This time government forces acted with restraint so there was little opposition. Vietnamese policemen bowed three times and carefully removed each altar and demonstrators were jailed. Although General Thi's earlier removal was a loss to General Walt, he acknowledged that government forces had put down the revolt without civil war. For the time being Ky and members of the Directorate achieved a solidification of their control, but at the expense of instability in I Corps.

This spring political crisis had caused serious disruption of Marine offensive operations. At Da Nang they not only had to fight the communists, but try to prevent their so-called friends from destroying one another. These dissident actions were a boon to the Vietcong and the North Vietnamese as the Marines tried to expand their pacification efforts beyond the Da Nang enclave.

In the rest of South Vietnam, General Westmoreland stressed mobility of operations. Mobile guerrilla forces were formed and sent to enemy-controlled areas. These strike forces doubled in number starting in May and participated in operations where camps needed additional strength at critical times. Twenty-two new irregular camps were opened with Special Forces advisers while nine were closed in relatively pacified areas.

There was a lack of understanding throughout all ranks about the war in Vietnam. Most Army schools failed to incorporate many of the lessons learned during the Korean War that would have been applicable. March and counter-march across the European plain remained the staple instruction at Army schools throughout the 1960s.

Once reports filtered back from Vietnam that the Vietcong and North Vietnamese had become adept at so-called insurgency warfare, military schools in the United States hastily juggled their courses to add new instructive courses to their curriculum. Despite these efforts each new group of Americans had to re-learn the elemental lessons of infiltration, scouting and patrolling. One lesson that was learned the hard way in

South Vietnam was that nighttime and jungle operations belonged to those soldiers who could use them best.

In April, General Westmoreland requested a Women's Army Corps detachment with its own commander and staff to provide fifty clerk-typists for duty at his headquarters in Saigon. This number was soon raised to 120 and they served well under Captain Peggy E. Ready. Unlike the Korean War that was fought by males only, Westmoreland sought women for headquarters jobs along with the traditional nurses.

About 300 Army, Navy and Air Force nurses were now serving in South Vietnam and Thailand in field hospitals and aboard hospital ships. Still other nurses flew with evacuation crews. At first, male nurses had been requested but it was soon apparent there were not a sufficient number. Actually, women nurses were preferred because they gave an enormous lift to morale in combat zones. Before the American involvement ended approximately six thousand nurses and medical specialists saw combat duty, while another fifteen hundred women served in other capacities. Many were wounded, and eight were killed, and a great many were decorated for acts of valor and service.

North Vietnamese Army units north of the demilitarized zone continued to pose a serious threat to the security of Quang Tri and Thua Thien Provinces. From the earliest days they had tried to gain control of these provinces. They were 450 miles from Saigon, bordered on the west by the mountainous Laotian frontier and on the east by the South China Sea.

Except for the narrow coastal plains lying at the base of the mountains, the terrain was dominated by hills and the Annamite Mountains. The Central Highlands was characterized by steep slopes, sharp crests and narrow valleys covered mainly by dense evergreen forests. Most peaks rise from four to seven thousand feet—a few to eight thousand. The narrow coastal plains flanking the Highlands on the east are compartmented by rocky headlands with belts of sand dunes and, in areas where the soil was arable, with rice fields.

From the crests of the mountain peaks streams flow either towards the South China Sea or into Laos or Cambodia. Those that flow east are swift and course through deep narrow valleys over sandy bottoms. Streams going west follow longer routes, sometimes through deep canyons while others traverse poorly drained valleys that, like the coastal plains in the east, are subjected to seasonal flooding.

From the military point of view operations were affected by the monsoon weather, the rugged mountains and the seasonally flooded lowland plains with their dense pattern of farms. In the canopied forests, steep mountains, dense undergrowth and jungle along the demilitarized zone at key strategic points like the Rock Pile, Khe Sanh and A Shau much of the action would be centered in the next few years.

Transportation facilities in the region were poorly developed. One all-weather road, Route 9, connected the coast of Quang Tri Province with the western mountains. In Thua Thien Province, the extremely primitive Route 547 ran south and west from Hué into the A Shau valley. The major north-south road was Route 1 through the Hai Van Pass to Hué. From there the road continued north through the towns of Quang Tri and Dong Ha to the demilitarized zone and thence into North Vietnam.

After removal of United States and Vietnamese Special Forces in the A Shau valley, Westmoreland decided not to re-occupy the remote camp. Another two years would pass before his forces would return. In the meantime, North Vietnam developed the area into a major logistical base and constructed roads into Laos to tie in with the extensive network of routes leading south from North Vietnam. During 1966 more than 58,000 men—the equivalent of five North Vietnamese divisions—infiltrated South Vietnam. By the end of the year North Vietnam had 280,000 men in the South plus 80,000 others in political cadres.

Westmoreland believed that North Vietnam now intended to open a new front in northern I Corps to divert free world forces from the heavily populated Saigon area—the preferred objective. Intelligence sources noted the increasing use of 120 mm. mortars, and both Vietcong and local guerrillas were increasingly equipped with the AK-47. This was a Chinese copy of the Soviet assault rifle and it was a highly effective automatic weapon. Westmoreland believed that North Vietnam hoped to seize the northern areas as a base for its so-called National Liberation Front for use in winning concessions from South Vietnamese officials in future peace talks. North Vietnamese leaders knew that Thua Thien Province was in a state of political unrest and that the South Vietnamese government had been openly challenged there. From March until mid-summer the Saigon government experienced a series of political crises as militant Buddhists and students resorted to riots and civil disobedience throughout the country. The situation was most acute in Hué and Da Nang but it was serious elsewhere. The anti-government movement became so infiltrated by communists that it appeared for a time that they would take over the northern part of the country. Prime Minister Ky had removed Lieutenant General Thi, but this action did not stop mass protests that continued into late summer.

Gunships continued to play an important role in ground operations and the versatility of the AC-47s became clearer as the months went by. Two major types of interdiction increased along the Ho Chi Min Trail: actually not a trail but an intricate network of roads and trails that ran through Laos. Gunships were now based in Thailand as well as South Vietnam. A road-watch, truck-busting mission on the night of February 23, 1966, was typical of those throughout the war. Captain William Pratt and his crew spotted a truck convoy halted where bomb craters gutted the road. The road traversed a valley with sheer cliffs but Pratt moved in and set the first truck on fire. He then orbited above the trapped trucks while the convoy replied with intense small-arms fire. Pratt kept his gunship on target, and destroyed eleven trucks while damaging several more.

In most small operations the North Vietnamese adopted methods and procedures for each situation that typically involved old-fashioned American resourcefulness and know-how. Too many high officials in the United States armed forces thought only in terms of high technology. Since most such technology was unavailable to the communists they fought with what they had. Despite the primitiveness of much of their equipment, and the smaller numbers of people available to them, they refused to accept defeat even though they lost one battle after another.

Their resourcefulness was admired—but hardly ever emulated. They would crouch behind rice paddy embankments, and American soldiers and Marines would hardly ever see them because they'd poke holes in the banks and fire through them. In returning the fire, Americans continued to fire too high. When fire was directed at these holes, communist casualties started to rise. Americans walking across an open area seldom survived. For the Marines it was difficult at first to get them to change their basic firing-range procedure. Mounting losses could not long be sustained and changes had to be made.

Excessive firing by Americans and South Vietnamese was incredible. Areas were sprayed without any selectivity. Marines were taught, however, that fire from a bamboo thicket assuredly meant an enemy and such rapid fire was permitted. Still, most North Vietnamese and Vietcong fired from positions dug in the ground and even when they were sitting up they still could not be seen.

It was often frustrating to determine if any of the enemy had been killed or wounded because casualty victims were almost always removed when they retreated. In an entrenched area, there was frequently a half-mile or more of tunnel systems. Smoke was used but it soon became apparent that smoke could not penetrate deeply enough to drive out the enemy soldiers. Parts of tunnels were routinely blocked off, and frequent air holes with tubes of bamboo made tunnel life survivable for the occupants.

In hamlets it was impossible to check each hootch to see if they concealed entrances to tunnels. At times as many as 500 men occupied these tunnels.

Mines were always in short supply so the Vietcong resorted to heavy use of punji stakes, coated with excrement or anything that would cause illness to those who fell into the traps and were pierced by the coated stakes. Such traps were cleverly hidden along trails, dikes or along the walls of rice paddies. Mines usually were placed along main roads and on bridges. The Americans did not use mines to a great extent, and the ones they used were portable. Often the Vietcong would turn the American mines around to use them against their owners. Trip wires were used to send electrical impulses to discharge them. Such mines were seldom buried deep so they could be easily removed.

Concertina and tangle-foot wire proved most effective. Cans filled with stones, and tied to the wire to make a noise, quickly alerted sentries of the enemy's presence. Communist-made Malay gates that slammed into a body when a wire was tripped were made of wood, string and a piece of wire. When one of these gates, with its pointed stake, struck a man he could be killed, or die of infection. Combat men tried to tell their superiors in Saigon that they were relying too much on sophisticated equipment that often did not work as well as primitive weapons. They were seldom listened to.

In villages, the Vietnamese frequently changed their allegiance. Basic Vietcong cadres in most villages consisted of four or five people. Commissars were always giving lectures about the fundamental goodness of the communist system, while Vietcong collected taxes in rice or other foodstuffs. Communist death squads sought out village chiefs who remained loyal to the Americans. In effect, Vietcong cadres controlled most villages. For villagers, it was often a Catch 22 situation—they had to pay both sides. The Vietcong's most vital food needs were salt and rice and they took what they wanted at harvest time. They also would take young men to be indoctrinated, and assassination was common.

Master Sergeant Bradley Spencer, intelligence chief for the 1st Marine Regiment's 2nd Battalion, was often hard put to answer questions when one operation after another appeared to resolve nothing. The refrain was repeated endlessly, "Hey, Sarge, how come? We've been taken back in there twice, we've lost people every time we've gone back."

Spencer had few answers. He knew as well as his men that once the Marines vacated an area, the Vietcong would soon be back. Often you could see them moving back over the hills as you left. It was frustrating because the Americans controlled the daylight hours, but the Vietcong moved freely at night.

Spencer watched apprehensively as kids came through the base perimeter during the day to sell cokes, knowing this same kid might be back that night with the Vietcong to guide them through their defenses. All too often a Marine would walk by a small kid to get into a jeep only to find that the youngster had stuck a grenade in it. Young kids were the most ardent Vietcong of all. Perhaps his family needed money, or oftentimes a brother or other family member was held captive, so the kid did as he was told. The Vietcong would tell them that for every American they helped to kill the family would get another bag of rice. Americans have always been suckers for children. Vietnam was no exception. They freely gave them candy and gum. Reporters were often duped by seeing soldiers picking up young kids, or throwing tear gas at them. What the reporters often did not know was that these kids five minutes earlier had been throwing grenades.

Spencer was frequently asked by young Marines how they could recognize a Vietcong. At first, they had all been told that you could distinguish them by their black pajamas. But most Vietnamese wore them along with what became known as Ho Chi Minh slippers made of rubber tires, and conical hats. Young Marines quickly developed a morale problem because they had never been adequately indoctrinated before they reached Vietnam. Few understood communism, or its timetable of world revolution and how to achieve it. They could not understand dedicated guerrillas who would fight for twenty years if necessary, and lose half of their population, to achieve victory. The Vietcong peasant had nothing but his faith in the better life promised by the communists. Often rifles were in such short supply that they were loaned to different soldiers on different days. A grenade was saved until it could be used with assurance that a number of Americans would be killed.

In the countryside Vietnamese families were often divided in their loyalties much like American families during the Civil War. American politicians were taken on sanitized tours of villages that were known to be trouble-free places, whereas some nearby villages would have been much too dangerous. Young American soldiers and Marines witnessed these things and they became cynical.

The concern about body count went on endlessly. In war, casualties should number four to one in your favor if victory is to be achieved. Such a count was almost impossible to verify in Vietnam because the communists removed their dead and wounded as they retreated. Still, orders were standardized that after a fight there must be a check for bodies, number of captured weapons, marks on the ground possibly indicating the number of casualties who had been dragged away. Any estimate was just that. Even the Vietcong did not know their real losses. Some of the confusion was due to the fact that duplicate reports reached the headquarters of the Military Assistance Command in Saigon. There is no evidence that these reports were falsified, but errors cropped up due to the inability of getting verified reports and through duplication of paper work.

CHAPTER 18

Bouncing Bettys

ONE OF THE PROBLEMS IN THE FIELD WAS THE M-16 RIFLE. ANY LITTLE substance such as dirt or inadequate cleaning would cause it to jam. Not so the AK-47 that was reliable under all conditions. These weapons were not as smoothly finished as the American guns, and they had rough spots. But their mechanism was superior, and they fired all the time. Field reports consistently harped on the fact that a gun would not fire any better just because it had a smoother outside finish.

Master Sergeant Spencer was in battalion headquarters in Phu Bai in April when an aerial observer radioed, "I just saw some pink elephants."

Everyone laughed, and the operations chief told the headquarters staff, "Hey, we've got pink elephants out here."

After the laughter died down Spencer said, "Where?"

He gave the coordinates, saying they were near one of the rivers that flowed over red clay. They decided that after the clay dried on the elephants it changed their color to pink. Spencer sent in a report to higher headquarters, with an explanation. Back came a report from Da Nang. "Somebody's been drinking. You're all crazy up there."

Spencer decided to see for himself and he flew with an aerial observer. Sure enough, they found the elephants and their hides definitely looked pink. He noted they were hobbled next to the river and evidently were used as beasts of burden. There were six of them, and they probably had come from the back country off the Ho Chi Minh Trail west of Phu Bai.

While at Phu Bai in July Spencer became concerned about the consistent reports of radio jamming. He had reported the problem but higher headquarters said the Vietcong did not have the capability to jam radios. Spencer took a number of scouts and one of the radiomen and went out to find out what was going on. A helicopter dropped them off in a village area where jamming had been reported. They found two bamboo poles fifteen to twenty feet high with wire strung between them and leading into a hootch. On further examination they found that the wire ended in a bucket of water with a piece of metal. There was no radio, just a piece of metal spinning in the bucket and creating noise on the American frequency they wanted to jam. This simple device caused a snap, crackle and pop on their radios so nothing could be heard on that frequency. Spencer noted ink, pen and paper and realized the Vietcong had been copying their codes. Scouts earlier had been looking for more elaborate equipment but this simple mechanical device performed just as well. They tore everything down, knowing that such a simple arrangement could easily be set up again. There were just a few old women there. Spencer marveled at the simple ingenuity of the Vietcong who, with almost nothing to work with, found a way to jam radios that higher authorities claimed was impossible without expensive jamming equipment. This old-fashioned know-how should have been understandable to American officialdom but they were too enamoured with their high-technology gadgets.

An innovative solution to focus the huge energy of certain high explosive weapons against the Thanh Hoa bridge had been underway for months during tests in the United States at Eglin Air Force Base. But the weapon that was developed was eight feet in diameter and two-and-a-half-feet thick. Only a cargo plane could carry it. Shaped liked a large pancake, and weighing 5,000 pounds, it was decided to float the weapon down the Song Ma River where it would pass under the bridge and detonate once its sensors detected the metallic structure. It was a bold plan and specialists in many fields contributed to its development. After tests were completed two C-130 transports and their crews were sent to Eglin to train for releasing the new weapon. Major Richard T. Rembers headed one crew and Major Thomas F. Case the other. It was decided to drop five of the weapons one to two miles up river from the bridge under cover of darkness. Planes would fly in and out at 500 feet to avoid radar detection. A route of forty-three miles was planned precisely for seventeen minutes over enemy territory in these unarmed cargo planes. It was decided to use two fighters to make diversionary attacks with flares and bombs on the highway ten miles south of Thanh Hoa shortly before the C-130s made their drops while another plane jammed radar transmitters in the area.

Rembers and his crew took off from Da Nang for the first drop at 12:25 A.M. May 30. Within an hour they turned towards the North Vietnamese coast flying at 100 feet above the water. Navigators, Captain Norman C. Clanton and Lieutenant William "Rocky" Edmondson, quickly figured the drop point. As they approached the first zone Rembers climbed to 400 feet and slowed to 150 miles an hour. When no enemy fire erupted, he headed for the first drop zone. Flak guns now opened up and their fire grew in intensity as they headed in. It was too late to turn back but they were fortunate in flying through the hail of shrapnel without being hit. Five bombs were dropped in their prescribed zones and Rembers banked his Herky Bird sharply to the right and dove back to 100 feet as he boosted the power of his engines and headed for the Gulf of Tonkin.

It had been a flawless operation but reconnaissance photographs detected no damage to the bridge, or even a trace of bomb damage.

A second mission was set up for May 31, this time with Major Case's crew, but including Edmondson as navigator. When they flew away that was the last ever heard of the plane and its crew. A flight of fighters making a diversionary attack reported a fire and a large ground flash in the vicinity of the bridge two minutes prior to the scheduled drop time. The bridge remained intact and no additional damage could be detected.

Navy carrier attacks continued against the bridge, but they were as unsuccessful as their earlier attempts.

When no progress was made with the North Vietnamese in arranging peace talks, Rolling Thunder attacks had been resumed January 31, 1966, but again they were limited to the southern part of North Vietnam. While American crew losses rose, important strategic targets still remained off-limits.

It was now decided that Task Force 77 at Yankee Station should have a permanent commander after it began to work closely with Air Force units in South Vietnam and Thailand. Rear Admiral James "Sunshine Jim" Reedy was given the assignment aboard the *Kitty Hawk*, with Captain Martin D. "Red" Carmody under him as task group commander.

A modification of the procedure for assigning Rolling Thunder targets was made in February. In the past, the Seventh Air Force and Task Force 77 had shared the air war over North Vietnam on a time basis, alternating each week. But this arrangement did not provide continuity, particularly as far as intelligence information was concerned. Now the six "route packages" were permanently assigned. The Navy was given responsibility for areas 2, 3, 4 and 6B because they were closest to the carriers in the Gulf of Tonkin. The Air Force was assigned areas 1, 5 and 6A with Route Package 1 under Westmoreland's area of control as part of the extended battle zone adjacent to I Corps in South Vietnam.

Route Packages 5, 6A and 6B contained the most lucrative targets in North Vietnam but the sanctuaries imposed by Washington officials placed the major targets in them off limits. There was a five-mile sanctuary surrounding Haiphong and a ten-mile limit around Hanoi. There was also a thirty-mile-wide buffer zone along the North Vietnam-People's Republic of China border that was also restricted.

Permanent areas of responsibility were assigned by Admiral Sharp in

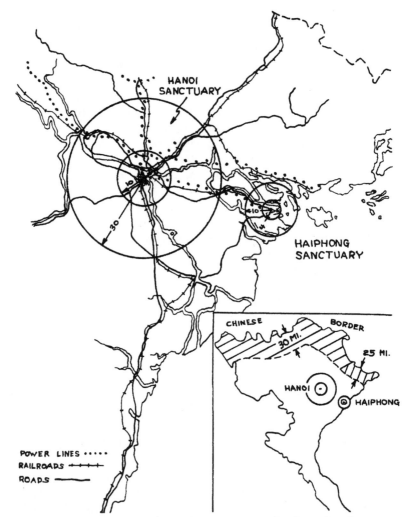

POWER LINES · · · · ·
RAILROADS +·+·+·+
ROADS ————

Sanctuaries—Around Hanoi and Haiphong, and 30 miles from the Chinese border to the northwest, and 25 miles from that border in the northeast, prohibited zones were established and American fliers were not permitted to drop bombs without special permission from the Secretary of Defense. There was also another area within a 10-mile radius of the center of Hanoi, and an area within a radius of four miles form the center of Haiphong designated as prohibited areas. No targets in such areas could be attacked without approval of the Secretary of Defense. Although the most important targets were in these areas, approval was seldom granted. In addition the areas between the 10 and 30 mile radii of Hanoi's center, and the four and 10-mile radii from Haiphong's center, were also designated as restricted areas. The Joint Chiefs of Staff, as directed by the Secretary of Defense, imposed severe limitations within these areas. *(Drawn by Master Sergeant Bradley A. Spencer M.C., Ret.)*

Honolulu. Establishment of operational zones had the immediate effect of reducing aircraft and aircrew losses. Pilots became more familiar with assigned targets since they repeatedly flew against the same targets. In this way they got to know enemy defense systems and could better plan attack procedures and detect meaningful changes on a daily basis.

Task Force 77's Chief of Staff, Captain James D. Ramage, looked up as Carmody barged into the operations center with a message April 19. "I think we've got it," he said excitedly. "The chance to hit Cam Pha." The Seventh Air Force commander had asked CINCPAC if a target in the vicinity of Kep would qualify as an armed reconnaissance target—one located within the prescribed distance from a line of communication. The response was affirmative.

Ramage studied the exchange of dispatches. "Red, you're right. Let's show this to 'Sunshine.'"

Admiral Reedy spotted the similarity immediately. Cam Pha, one of North Vietnam's major coal exporting ports, was adjacent to the railroad as well as a major highway center. Therefore it was close to two lines of communication. They realized this was an opportunity to attack a major target that was off limits. It would take moral courage, but Ramage and Carmody knew that "Sunshine Jim" had plenty of that.

The admiral listened carefully. He nodded. "Launch 'em."

Carmody was commanding officer of the carrier *Kitty Hawk* and also air commander of a carrier task group. He sent an OPREP (the system used to send notice through channels to higher authorities of an intent to make an immediate strike). He launched his armed reconnaissance strike of twenty-four aircraft simultaneously. Reedy knew this was circumventing the routine that required that an OPREP be sent the previous night for approval. In other words, the operation would be executed unless the various echelons up the line all the way to the National Command Center in Washington did not cancel it. Using the emergency OPREP was the only way to get the planes on target before anyone up the line cancelled it.

The men of Task Force 77 had watched helplessly as communist-block ships sailed through the Gulf of Tonkin, loaded with coal at Cam Pha, and steamed to their respective countries with high-grade anthracite to fuel their factories. On occasion it was noted that some of the ships were headed for so-called friendly nations. This coal, therefore, was a valuable source of hard currency for North Vietnam. Now, by using a broad interpretation of the rules of engagement for armed reconnaissance it might be possible to eliminate this lucrative target.

The mission was a complete success. The coal-washing and loading machinery was demolished, the railroad yards were destroyed, and loaded trucks were strewn throughout the target area. As always when the communists were hurt, they squealed. A Polish collier in the harbor had been shaken up. Both North Vietnam and Poland immediately protested the attack. Before the aircraft had landed aboard the *Kitty Hawk* Reedy received a message from Washington ordering the operation to cease. Therefore, a second launch had to be diverted to less lucrative targets.

Ramage received an informal message from fleet headquarters warning that a major flap was brewing. He was pleased to note that Reedy was not overly concerned.

Three days later a formal message arrived from Admiral Sharp at CINCPAC headquarters. He indicated to Reedy that he had exceeded his authority, but he was not overly critical. He ended his message by saying, "This appears to have had a salutary effect upon the enemy."

It was a stupid way to operate, but that was the way much of the war was fought.

A shortage of pilots now developed, along with an adequate supply of ammunition, rockets and bombs. The chief of naval operations announced that no naval aviator would fly more than 150 combat missions during a seven-and-a-half-month deployment, or more than two tours. Many shore jobs were eliminated to release pilots for Vietnam, and training was increased but that did not help the immediate situation. It took eighteen months or more to train new pilots.

In April, losses reached a new high with twenty-one aircraft down for a loss of fifteen crewmen. Much of the bombing effect had been directed at the Vinh-Ben Thuy complex due to the poor weather farther north. The Y Uong-Bi thermal power plant near Haiphong was hit for the second time. It supplied one third of Hanoi's power and nearly all of Haiphong's. The attack surprised the North Vietnamese and was a success.

These attacks were important in association with other attacks against oil targets. North Vietnam's petroleum needs were 20,000 metric tons per month. It took two Soviet tankers each month to supply North Vietnam's petroleum needs, or 170 railroad tank cars from China. Attacks during June eliminated Nam Dinh and Phu Qui as petroleum storage centers in North Vietnam's southern section, and the storage capacity at Vinh was cut by two thirds.

Major petroleum storage areas near Hanoi and Haiphong still remained off-limits and by spring tank farms had either been buried or their tanks were bunkered across the countryside. The majority were located in or near major military and industrial centers and clusters of fifty-five-gallon drums were spotted from the air at widely dispersed points making them costly to attack. The effort wasn't worth the cost of making so many multiple attacks against small clusters of oil drums.

McNamara's opposition to some important targets was reduced somewhat in June when he permitted attacks against seven petroleum facilities and the radar installations at Kep airfield. He directed that ships belonging to Russia, China or communist-bloc countries be avoided as well as attacks that could endanger civilians. Specifically, Navy pilots were ordered not to attack ships in the Haiphong Harbor unless they were fired upon, and "only if the craft is clearly of North Vietnamese registry." How Navy pilots flying at subsonic speed would make such a determination he did not say. He also ordered American planes not to attack piers servicing ships at Haiphong "if a tanker is berthed off the end of the pier."

The strike was delayed for a week due to a news leak in the United States but it was finally launched June 29 despite fears in some government quarters in Washington that the strike might precipitate Chinese or Russian intervention.

Commander Wynne F. Foster of VA-163 was flying an A-4E when he was hit by a shell that almost severed his right arm below the shoulder. He radioed that he was bleeding badly but he managed to steer his crippled Skyhawk with his knees while holding the stump of his shattered arm to restrict the flow of blood. Once he was over water near a destroyer, and growing faint from loss of blood, he succeeded in making a left-hand ejection and was promptly rescued by the ship's whaleboat and evacuated to the *Oriskany* where his arm was amputated. During the change of command ceremony in Subic Bay a few days later Foster conducted it from a stretcher, concluding with the traditional but left-handed salute.

During this series of precision strikes all targets were hit, and the huge fireballs that erupted proved their success. By the end of July no Soviet tankers arrived, a further indication of the extent of damage. Later, tankers were forced to off-load oil drums rather than bulk fuel because of the destroyed storage tanks. Two Soviet tankers that normally used Haiphong were forced instead to off-load in China and the oil was transferred by tank car to North Vietnam.

By the end of the year the campaign had wrecked the largest oil storage facility in Hanoi and Haiphong and incoming fuel was reduced to marginal levels. North Vietnam still had sufficient reserves, however, buried underground in drums and in caves. The oil strikes had started too late, giving North Vietnam a chance to disperse its stocks. Still the loss of precious oil caused the communist leadership to order strict regulations of its use, and their propaganda gave every indication of how seriously these attacks were regarded by the country's leaders.

Admiral Sharp said, "Despite our interdiction, the enemy has accommodated to our lines of communication attacks by ingeniously hiding and dispersing his logistic activity. His recuperative capability along these lines has been remarkable."

During the year 89 Navy airmen were killed, captured or missing and 123 aircraft were lost.

For government financial specialists the escalating Vietnam War was a nightmare. It was like starting to play a game of baseball but, in the third inning, the players found out they were playing basketball. It was believed at first that financial matters would be handled like those during the Korean War with no requirement for stringent accounting controls or budgeting, and that significant amounts of funds would be available. This assumption was responsible for the lack of an adequate organization for financial management during the early days of the buildup. McNamara had told the heads of Pentagon departments and the major field commanders, "Under no circumstances is lack of money to stand in the way of aid to that nation." After his rules were clarified it was found that the Army was expected to establish virtually a peacetime system for financial control and reporting. Such an order came almost too late. Many transactions had already occurred and it was impossible to document them in normal fashion. Some never were specifically identified. The concept developed by the Centralized Financial Management Agency proved almost impossible during wartime.

Never before had the Department of Defense been called upon to budget for war activities. Even during the Korean War, when reasonably accurate records were kept, no attempt was made to limit the funds needed to prosecute the war. As the Vietnam War increased in scope the Congress insisted upon more information about expenditures despite the fact that a year earlier McNamara had signed a memorandum to service secretaries in effect giving them a blank check to spend money for the war.

In the spring of 1966 McNamara's new approach to budgeting called for the extensive use of supplemental budgeting. McNamara had requested $1.7 billion in August, 1965, for the war in a separate account and there was little surprise in Congress when he submitted a supplemental request in early 1966 for that fiscal year. During hearings, it was officially recognized that Vietnam no longer fell within the purview of the Military Assistance Program, and a request to transfer all balances from that program to other appropriations was granted. Now there was a growing congressional concern because of the Defense Department's assumption that enemy activity would continue at the level that existed at the time of the preparation of the budget and that no end to the war was in sight. They could foresee even higher budgets.

Major General Leonard B. Taylor appeared before the Senate Committee on Appropriations and he was questioned by Senator Stuart Symington, a member of the Senate Armed Services Committee. "I saw the Secretary of Defense on a television show last night," he said. "To the best of my recollection he said the Vietnam War was costing a billion dollars a month minimum, and that they could not figure all the overhead. Some of us figure that it is costing a great deal more than a billion a month. As the budget officer for the United States Army, do you have any figure that you have drawn up as to what the total cost is per month for the Vietnamese operations?"

Taylor replied that no attempt had been made to put a price tag on the war's cost, and he cited several reasons. "The rationale is simple. Each estimate would depend entirely on the assumption that you use to determine what price you derive. For example, the very large procurement appropriation that we received in fiscal year 1966 provides for things which won't be delivered for another year or eighteen months. So you really can't charge these to any one particular fiscal year. I am aware that Secretary McNamara used the $1 billion figure and I have no reason to depart from that."

Symington turned to the committee's head. "What worries me, Mr. Chairman, is that one sees headlines about saving $4 billion, $3½ billion, the same time you are heavily increasing the cost of the war. It is hard to correlate that. I personally view with grave apprehension the danger to the future value of the United States dollar incident to these various programs."

Despite such strong reservations the Congress approved the supplemental appropriation.

In contrast to the extended anti-guerrilla, small-unit war waged in Da Nang's tactical area, Marines in the southern part of I Corps fought a series of sharp engagements during late winter and early spring in 1966 against North Vietnamese regulars. Many defense complexes were destroyed by these Marines and they learned that they faced a brave and resourceful enemy but they certainly were not supermen.

One such complex was seven miles southwest of Da Nang, near where two French battalions were wiped out years earlier. Colonel Edwin Simmons, the 9th Regiment's commander, was responsible for clearing the area. After a number of brisk skirmishes Delta Company's effective manpower was reduced to 120 from 175, including the loss of a high percentage of its leaders. Their work was ugly and unrewarding because the Vietcong sniped at them and then ran—leaving mines behind that took a heavy toll.

The 1st Platoon went out on patrol June 8 although it was down thirty-two men. Captain John Hart, Delta Company's red-headed commander who had been with them for several years and with another company in Vietnam before that, was a shrewd, natural leader and understanding of his men. He ordered two amtracs (amphibious landing vehicles) to travel in advance of his men to set off mines before they reached them. Sergeant William Cunningham was in charge of the patrol and hopefully believed that the amtracs would solve their mine problems. They followed closely in the tracks of each 35-ton vehicle as it traversed the flat lowlands, smashing fences and tearing up mine fields. Snipers were more bothersome than dangerous and Marine 60 mm. mortars dealt with them. The men of Delta Company's 1st Platoon knew this area well—and hated it. Rice paddies and fields stretched for miles in a checker-board pattern, separated by thick tree lines and numerous hamlets. Mud clung to their boots like glue, and the tree lines could be penetrated only by using machetes and axes. There were scattered hamlets of one to ten houses, and each house was surrounded by a thorn fence that was harder to break than barbed wire. The level ground prevented the scouts from seeing beyond the next hedgerow, and there were mines everywhere, with no pattern to their placement. The Vietcong had buried them where they anticipated the Marines would walk after long observation of their movements. If one patrol passed a point safely, the Vietcong would scurry out of their hiding places, dig up their mines, and save them for another day. Sergeant Cunningham was well aware of these tactics. He directed that the same routes be used as the day before so the amtracs would explode the mines. The Vietcong's supply, he knew, was not inexhaustible. Most mines were "bouncing Bettys" or anti-personnel mines that exploded in midair and were particularly dreaded because their shrapnel caused dreadful damage to a man's genital area. Cunningham repeatedly reminded the new Marines to remain in the tracks of the amtracs. Veterans needed no such reminder. Each Marine was equipped with a helmet and body armor and each infantryman carried 150 rounds of ammunition with two or more grenades. The men who manned the machine guns were draped with belts of linked cartridges. Two 3.5-inch rocket launcher teams had grenadiers who carried 40 mm. shells. Cunningham had also given his men six portable anti-tank weapons for additional firepower. Captain Hart never permitted his men to patrol without ensuring they had all the firepower they could carry.

They had moved out at 11:00 A.M. when it was 102 degrees and no breeze or shade. They were quickly soaked by sweat as they plodded south, strung out over a quarter of a mile. There was no flank section. The fear of mines was too great and Hart had told them that they would get quick support if it was needed. Directly in front of the lead amtrac was a thorn and bamboo fence at right angles to their line of march. Six hundred feet to the right there was a thick tree line in which the thatch rooftops of four houses could be seen. To the left, a dirt field stretched for a thousand feet.

Sergeant Cunningham was cautious. He had earlier seen his radioman and one of his squad leaders trip a mine attached to a fence and die. The day before they had been fired upon while on patrol. He insisted that no foolish risks be taken today. He yelled at the lead tractor driver, "Rip that thing apart. Really tear it up."

The driver turned left to hit the fence head-on. The amtrac lumbered forward, crushed thirty feet of fence before its left track slipped into a drainage ditch, and it churned to a halt. The second amtrac eased forward, attached a tow rope to the front of the stranded vehicle and pulled it out.

Cunningham gave orders to continue south through the minefields saying that other holes would be torn in the fence on their return trip that afternoon. "Move out," he yelled. "We'll come back to that bear later on. It'll still be here."

One amtrac roared ahead while the second idled by the fence, waiting to turn into position near the center of the column.

The hard dirt around the fence had been churned into jagged clods by treads of the two amtracs. Point Marines, including Cunningham, carefully picked their way across the fence, stepping only in the tracks, and fell in again behind the lead amtrac as the rest of the column followed.

Cunningham had walked 250 feet from the fence when he heard an explosion. Even before he turned his head he knew what he would see. A thick, black cloud hung in the air beside the fence. Three Marines were sprawled on the ground. Before the shower of loose dirt and shrapnel stopped falling the platoon's senior corpsman, Hospitalman 3rd Class Robert E. Perkins, had reached the side of the most seriously wounded Marine.

Corporal Raymond Lewis, leading the point squad, burst out, "Why the hell don't they follow the goddam tracks?" Cunningham ran back, yelling in anger and frustration, "I told you to follow me through here— we came through here," he said, pointing to the ground. His anger quickly subsiding, he said with resignation, "O.K. Who got it?"

Tired, feeling secure because there were so many tracks near the fence and nine Marines had walked safely past, the 10th Marine had wandered off the path of the tread marks. For twenty feet he had followed the trail of old tank treads. The Vietcong had placed a mine on the old trail against the torn fence. The Marine had tripped a bouncing Betty that flew knee-high before it exploded—felling him and two companions behind him.

The column was halted, spread out and without cover. Platoon leaders clustered at the fence, checking the condition of the wounded.

There were scattered sniper shots, but they were ignored. This happened on every patrol and Cunningham refused to divert his attention from the wounded because of the incoming rounds. Ten seconds later there was steady fire aimed at the wounded as the Vietcong found the range and Cunningham heard the whine and snap of close misses.

While Cunningham and platoon guide Sergeant Peter Hastings discussed possible counter-action, a helicopter was ordered to evacuate the wounded. Corpsman Perkins worked swiftly to prevent the most seriously wounded Marine from bleeding to death. He did not even look up from probing the man's legs when bullets started passing close by. He had been with the company for nine days and he had already tended nine wounded Marines.

Most of the fire seemed to come from a hamlet on the west flank, not more than 600 feet to the right of the point squadron. Some fire was coming from the distant tree line to the left. There were flat, low reports of several carbines and the short bursts of a machine gun. The Vietcong had carefully planned their trap. The mine had stopped the column in the open less than 600 feet from their firing position. To confuse and spread the Marines, they had posted snipers on the other flank. They knew from experience that the leaders would cluster around the wounded, and they had sighted their weapons on the fence line. Cunningham quickly analyzed the situation and he knew the Vietcong had better positions than his platoon as well as fire superiority. He never had a chance to contact his three squad leaders as Marines flopped down and began returning the fire without waiting for orders, but their return fire was ragged and lacked direction.

Corporal Raymond Lewis moved out in front of the column to lead an attack. A veteran of dozens of firefights, his squad was not under fire and it was closest to the hamlet. To his left he could hear the crack of sniper rifles from the tree line. He directed his machine gunner to rake it, keeping his fire low and continuous. Squad grenadier, Private First Class Michael Stay, was pumping 40 mm. shells into the hamlet as fast as he could reload. Lewis decided he needed more punch. He directed the fire of his bazooka team toward the hamlet. Corporal John Martin quickly had his rocket launcher ready. They agreed fire should be directed at the houses. Martin had seen men firing from raised flaps on the roofs. He placed the long tube on his shoulder, sighted swiftly, and fired from a kneeling position. One house shuddered and pitched at an angle. He placed another white phosphorus rocket in his launcher and fired. A second house burst into flames, then another as he fired again. The machine gun stopped firing. Meanwhile, rifle fire was directed at the hedgerows bordering the huts.

Sergeant James Gibbs and his 60 mm. mortar crew riding on the second amtrac took up where Martin left off. When the enemy machine gun fired, Gibbs jumped off the tractor and yelled to Cunningham, "Should we try for the gun?"

"Go ahead," Cunningham yelled back, "but watch it when the choppers get here."

The crew set up their tube less than 900 feet from the hamlet. Gibbs aimed it by line of sight while Lance Corporal Joe Dykes estimated the range and Private First Class Peter Vidaurie hauled ammunition from the amtrac. "Can we fire now?" Gibbs yelled.

"Sure, any time you want," Cunningham replied.

The 60 mm. mortar crew walked rounds back and forth across the 600-foot length of tree line. Under cover of this firing, Cunningham directed his 2nd Squad into position to secure a landing zone for the helicopters. He wanted to get his wounded out before the enemy machine gun resumed firing.

By the time the firefight was four minutes old most of the small arms fire had died down. Steadily, however, two grenade launchers kept busy and their rounds crunched in the wood line. Three houses were blazing and their bamboo sides were expanding and popping like the firing of hundreds of .22-caliber rifles.

Cunningham directed the second amtrac toward the tree line. It lumbered forward for several feet and stopped before a three-foot embankment 200 feet from the hamlet. The three-man crew and two demolition engineers lay on top and fired at the burning village. The amtrac's commander, Staff Sergeant Howard G. Plummer, feared the fire in the village. He was carrying explosives and 500 gallons of fuel and he had no intention of risking a "cook-off" in the intense heat.

The lull in the fighting broke. On the left, an enemy light machine gun chattered. On the right, an automatic carbine and several rifles opened up. The guerrillas who had lived in the area for years had used familiar tactics against the Marines—setting mines and sniping from a distance, while employing ambushes at close range only when they had numerical superiority. This time the Vietcong were surprised. They had not expected the Marines to recover so quickly from the mine explosion. Now squad members ran quickly to their nearest amtrac as the Vietcong concentrated their fire to stop them.

The crew of the amtrac preceding Lewis's squad at point was confused by the fighting. Without orders they had fired their rifles at the hamlet.

When the infantry pushed forward to attack, the amtrac started forward, still without orders, with no flankers or supporting fire. Corporal Lewis, once he saw the amtrac move alone to attack, ordered his riflemen to throw out protecting fire on the flanks and his grenadier to fire over the vehicle into the tree line beyond. When the amtrac reached the edge of the trees the driver hesitated, looking for a route through the hedgerows. The fire grew in intensity, and Private First Class Billy Adams, a maintenance mechanic on board, heard bullets strike the hull. To him they sounded as if someone were pounding it with hammers. "Time to button up!" he called. He started to pull down the steel hatch cover when he saw a Vietcong on the roof of a house firing at the infantry seeking shelter behind the other amtrac. The Vietcong soldier and Adams saw one another simultaneously. Adams flipped his weapon to automatic and stitched the roof, igniting it just as the Vietcong ducked into the house.

The turret machine gunner on Plummer's amtrac started to fire, spraying the village while incoming bullets bounced off the amtrac's left side. On the right side of the vehicle Marine riflemen engaged Vietcong who were lying on the roof of a house. They fired long bursts while the Vietcong returned the fire with their automatic carbines. Both sides had abandoned cover so intent were they on what had become a very private duel. Standing in the off-hand position, a Marine finally remembered to sight carefully and squeeze off a few rounds instead of spraying the houses. This time the Vietcong fell limply off the roof.

Corporal Jerry Payne brought his squad up behind Plummer's amtrac. "Move it out! Let's roll!"

Plummer hesitated, looking for a way out that was not blocked by flames.

"Come on," an angry Marine yelled. "The hell with waiting for this thing," gesturing at the amtrac. "Let's go get 'em!"

Payne grabbed him by the shoulder as he started around the tractor's side. "No, you don't. That whole field is mined. They're just trying to sucker you in. Stay behind the trac."

Three hundred feet to the left, Adams' amtrac had already reached the hedgerow and was smashing its way into the embankment until it pitched down into the level field and rumbled toward the village. Payne yelled, "We're going in." The five Marines clustered around him nodded nervously but said nothing. They were too apprehensive. They were ready to follow Payne but they wanted someone to lead the way. Payne scrambled up the embankment into a burst of machine gun fire. His helmet spun off and he pitched forward head first. The squad froze. Payne was their leader, the most experienced man, and the one who knew what to do. They were shocked, believing him dead.

Payne got up slowly, shaken but unhurt. "Come on," he muttered. They dogtrotted across the field after the amtrac.

By now Adams' amtrac had entered the line of trees. Lewis ordered his squad to cease fire. The amtrac passed the house where Adams had fired at the sniper hiding in the roof. Private First Class Larry Blume, a demolition engineer riding in the amtrac, saw two men run from the house on the left, but he could not get a shot at them. Adams watched from the observer's window to the right of the driver's seat. He spotted a Vietcong trying to dodge across the path of the tractor, stumble and fall. The amtrac rolled over him, crushing his body into the soft soil.

Plummer's amtrac reached the thorn fence surrounding the village. He turned his vehicle right to avoid the flames ahead as Marines peeled off to the left and ran along the fence line looking for an opening. They went in at the center of the village. There the point Marine hesitated and turned to the right. Payne knew the machine gun lay to their left but he, too, turned right thinking that since the point man was ignoring the machine gun he must be attacking another target. But the point man did not know about the machine gun. His sudden appearance behind the amtrac at the start of the assault had caught the enemy machine gunner by surprise, and he was the first to be fired upon.

While the assault force rushed to the right the Vietcong slipped out to the left. Adams saw six of them moving towards his amtrac, four dragging two bodies. He could not fire his machine gun for fear of hitting the Marine squad sweeping in the other direction. Nor could he pursue them through the burning village. The tractor, breaking out of the tree line on the far side of the hamlet, pivoted right and raced along a cane field to turn the Vietcong troops. They slipped away toward the left bank.

While this assault was going on the wounded lay where they had fallen. Helicopters had been called but it took time to fly from Da Nang, sixteen miles to the rear. Only eight minutes had elapsed before two helicopters were circling overhead, looking for the green smoke grenade signaling a secure landing zone. Sergeant Hastings threw the grenade and one of the choppers clattered down while the other continued to circle overhead, ready to fire on any enemy position. Fortunately the landing zone was secure because the third squad was pushing the Vietcong from the hamlet. Sergeant Cunningham had settled the fire teams of the second squad in the outskirts of the surrounding trees, ready to stifle any enemy who tried to down one of the helicopters. Still a fight was raging and one of the wounded became concerned that the helicopter might choose not to land. "Give me a rifle," he said. "I'll secure this damn landing zone myself, if it means I'll get out of here afterwards."

The helicopter settled in and Hastings was extremely careful to direct it to land on the tracks of the amtracs so it would not detonate another mine. The wounded were placed on board and the helicopter took off and headed for Charlie Med—slang for Company C of a medical battalion. Thirteen minutes after the mine had exploded, the wounded were being tended by doctors, and all survived. The evacuation helicopters were like city ambulances in the States—only they responded quicker.

Meanwhile, the battle continued and Adams told the assault force it was going the wrong way. They had stopped, gasping for breath, and stumbled out of the back of the village in the trace of the amtrac. A trench line ran from the village to another tree line and hamlet 1,200 feet in the rear of the burned village. Eight Marines trotted beside this trench and most had burns where their hands or arms had accidentally brushed their heated rifle barrels. Their flak jackets and helmets weighed them down, but they did not ease up.

Six hundred feet from the tree line, Payne ordered his machine gun team to drop off and cover their advance. The amtrac stopped at the tree line and readied its machine gun. Marines swept the village in pairs, covering each other's advance, but the village was deserted, and so was the trench line. There were numerous fighting holes, but they were also empty, and there were punji traps and bamboo stakes everywhere. It was a typical armed village.

The Marines were ordered to withdraw and they did so cautiously. They were exhausted as Cunningham joined them near a machine gun emplacement, bringing two squads and the other amtrac with him. Adams and Blume told the sergeant where they had seen the Vietcong and the bodies. The information puzzled Cunningham. He said he had passed that area five minutes after the amtrac and had seen only women, old men and children fleeing to the left flank. He had seen no Vietcong and certainly no bodies. He realized that in a short time the Vietcong or the villagers had policed the battlefield and removed their dead and wounded.

Cunningham ordered their position consolidated and he sent engineers into the village to blow up the bunkers and trench lines. The entire action had lasted less than forty minutes. Within six minutes an assault against their attackers had been launched. Not a single Marine was wounded in this attack. Their sudden and fierce reaction had taken the Vietcong by surprise. The Marines were surprised themselves. In seven months in Vietnam this was the first time that Payne and his men had ever had a chance to charge the Vietcong.

The action had been sharp, brief but inconclusive—like most such actions. The assault forces, assuming that the Vietcong would pull back, had been fooled by their flank escape, probably through tunnels or trenches. Carelessness and inattention had caused the mine casualties as the men on patrol had relaxed their vigilance under the hot sun. Most importantly, the platoon had responded to the sudden Vietcong attack like veterans, which they were, most having more than four months of experience in seeking out an unrelenting enemy.

CHAPTER 19

It Was a New Day—and They Still Held

THE 1ST MARINE DIVISION AT CHU LAI HAD TWO INFANTRY REGIMENTS with its artillery and support battalions by June, 1966, totaling over 17,000 men, and it had increased the size of its enclave by more than a third to 340 square miles. The division continued to use the same combination of battalion strength or independent small-unit actions that had characterized its earlier operations. At the beginning of the month the division turned its attention to the Do Xa region that harbored an enemy base, thirty miles southwest of Chu Lai near I Corps' border. While plans were underway to mount an exploratory operation, disturbing reports reached headquarters that the 620th North Vietnamese Army Division had entered the Que Son Valley straddling the Quang Tin/Quang Nam provincial boundaries northwest of Chu Lai. Control of the Que Son Valley was important to both sides, and it had been the scene of operations the preceding December. Bounded by mountains on the north, south and west the valley extends some twenty-four miles on an east-to-west axis from Route 1 to Hiep Duc. The valley was populated by 60,000 people due to its rich farmland. Former I Corps commander General Thi had said that the Que Son area was one of the keys to control of the area.

When the North Vietnamese incursion was confirmed, the Do Xa operation was cancelled and a reconnaissance of the Que Son Valley was approved and the Marines and the 2nd Army of the Republic of Vietnam Division joined forces to attack the North Vietnamese.

An eighteen-man team led by Staff Sergeant Jimmie L. Howard was first helicoptered June 13 to a 1,500-foot hill that provided excellent observation, and Howard reported events for the next two days. The joint Marine-South Vietnamese operation began officially June 17 and ended five days later, but it never expanded beyond the reconnaissance stage. Actually, relatively few Marines, supported by air and artillery strikes, prevented the North Vietnamese from massing forces and penetrating the Que Son Valley in strength.

Substantial progress was made against the communist forces throughout I Corps' southern section by the end of June, and in further pacification of the Chu Lai sector. In contrast to Da Nang and Phu Bai, the spring political crisis had little impact at Chu Lai because the South Vietnamese under General Lam had remained loyal to their government and the general had temporarily become commander of I Corps.

Extensive Marine operations in Quang Ngai and Quang Tin Provinces and the armed reconnaissance in the Que Son Valley succeeded in keeping North Vietnam's larger units out of coastal populated areas. By now nearly 30,000 of the 160,000 in the Chu Lai sector lived in villages that were more than 80 percent on the Marine Corps' pacification schedule. As a result, there was optimism at mid-year that progress was being made.

Throughout the period of political unrest in the spring, and the expansion of the base areas at Da Nang and Chu Lai, Westmoreland continued to be concerned about defense of the northern part of I Corps and communist intentions in that area. As early as February, 1966, at the monthly Honolulu Conference, he had told President Johnson that if he were the enemy general he would attempt to capture Hué. He said the former imperial capital was a "symbol of a united Vietnam," and that its loss would have a traumatic effect upon the allied war effort. He said such a thrust by the enemy would shorten their lines of communication and that the mountain spur north of Da Nang effectively isolated the two northern provinces of Thua Thien and Quang Tri from the rest of Vietnam, thus making them particularly vulnerable. Westmoreland had told his staff that any allied reinforcement along Route 1 and the railroad—the only north-south arteries—had to wend its way through the narrow confines of the strategic Hai Van Pass and was subject to enemy harassment. The Marines had kept the pass open only through extensive patrolling and armed "rough rider" road convoys. Half of the time through the month of March the communists had effectively closed the railroad between Da Nang and Hué.

Westmoreland's intelligence officers agreed that the enemy was using the area as a staging place for a major offensive. During the first quarter of the year it was estimated that the communists averaged 7,000 men in the area and in Laos along the border. General Walt and his staff disagreed, seeing little buildup for a major offensive.

At the Military Assistance Command conference April 21, 1966, Westmoreland asked Walt if his III Amphibious Force had any reason to doubt the number of major North Vietnamese Army units in I Corps as reported by his staff. Walt replied that extensive reconnaissance had failed to verify the existence of any large body of enemy troops. "If they [the North Vietnamese] were there, they were hiding in the mountains not far from the Laos border." After this session Walt resisted attempts to "get us extended" and away from pacification programs further south.

Despite such reluctance, Westmoreland insisted that the Marines conduct a one-battalion operation near the isolated Special Forces camp at Khe Sanh in the northwest corner of Quang Tri Province. Westmoreland advised Walt that he placed high strategic importance on this base. In January, mortars had been used against it but no ground attack had yet been made.

Although the communists avoided any contact with Marines in Thua Thien Province during April, Westmoreland continued to insist on development of contingency plans to meet any enemy offensive. At the April commanders' conference, Westmoreland had asked all subordinate commands to "work up detailed scenarios of what the enemy might do." He suggested the communists "will try to suck us into a fight on a field of their choosing." He insisted that it was "necessary to the war game in order to avoid barging into battle at a disadvantage." He advised General Walt not to count on Army reserves since the enemy might strick in more than one place.

The Army's Pacific commander presented a plan to CINCPAC to deploy a two-division army corps along the demilitarized zone in the North and west to Laos. It was suggested that such a move would take the war out of the South, and towards the North where "we can fight better and make the enemy mass its forces near the demilitarized zone."

Westmoreland was reluctant to move Army troops into I Corps. At the April commanders' meeting, he had brought up the idea of a corps-size strike force of three divisions that would be capable of moving anywhere in South Vietnam to confront strong enemy thrusts. He cautioned such a plan was still in the conceptual stage.

North Vietnamese Army troops attacked two Republic of Vietnam outposts just south of the demilitarized one May 19, causing heavy losses. That same date a North Vietnamese soldier surrendered and revealed that the North Vietnamese 324B Division had infiltrated through the demilitarized zone into South Vietnam. A reconnaissance in force failed to find sizable communist units.

The political confrontation between dissident South Vietnamese elements against the central government during this period had a great impact on the war effort in the two northern provinces. It was worse with the 1st Army Division of the Republic of Vietnam that was responsible for the northern sector. The men of this division were recruited locally, and were loyal to General Thi who had been ousted as I Corps commander. The division's Buddhist chaplain had led the men in demonstrations against the government while the division's commander, Pham Xuan Nhuan, refused to commit himself to either side and conveniently became ill or disappeared at strategic moments. After the burning of the United States Information Center in Hué June 1, the new I Corps commander, General Lam, considered using the division to put down disorders in the city but had decided against such a move because the division was so politicized that it was no longer a dependable fighting force.

The Joint General Staff replaced General Nhuan with the airborne's commander, Colonel Ngo Quang Truong, after Nhuan refused to move against dissidents in Hué.

With the breakup of the dissidents in Hué, Truong instilled some measure of discipline in his division. With two of his own battalions in Hué, and two South Vietnamese Marine Battalions supported by armored troops and United States Marine aircraft, the 808th North Vietnamese Battalion was defeated. This communist unit, emboldened by the political crisis, had entered Quang Tri's coastal plain from its mountain base on a rice-gathering expedition. The two-day engagement was fought June 21–23 and the North Vietnamese were routed, despite brisk attacks.

If General Walt's III Marine Amphibious Force still had reservations about the North Vietnamese buildup in the north, their doubts were quickly dispelled June 28 when the base at Cam Lo suffered a heavy mortar attack. Patrols now were met by regular troops. Despite the reconnaissance force that Walt had ordered to the north there were now more and more instances of regulars moving across the demilitarized zone.

Twenty miles inland, and west of the Marine base at Chu Lai, the Vietcong and North Vietnamese were using a steep mountain range with its twisting valleys to prepare for attacks against heavily populated seacoast hamlets. They massed only when they were ready to attack. American intelligence reports in June continued to indicate that a mixed force was gathering by the thousands in the mountains, although they were widely dispersed in squads and platoons.

Lieutenant General Walt ordered American infantry battalions to seek out these small bands before they could join together. He ordered a reconnaissance battalion of the 1st Marine Division to scout the mountains in small teams of eight to twenty men. If large enemy concentrations were encountered, Marine infantry would be flown in. If, as expected, only small Vietcong groups were encountered they were to be destroyed by calling in air and artillery strikes.

Lieutenant Colonel Arthur J. Sullivan of the 1st Reconnaissance Battalion had given his men individual instructions because he had learned in Vietnam that the small unit leader—corporal, sergeant and lieutenant— often had to be independent.

Captain Howard "Tim" Geraghty was a tall, rugged officer in his thirties, and well liked by C Company's men. Under him was Staff Sergeant Jimmie Earl Howard, acting commander of the 1st Platoon.

At dusk June 13, Howard and 17 of his platoon settled on a slope of a hill twenty-five miles west of Chu Lai following a helicopter airlift. They quickly climbed to the top that rose 1,500 feet and dominated the terrain for miles. Three narrow strips of level ground ran along the crest for several hundred yards before falling abruptly away. Seen from the air, the top resembled the three blades of an airplane propeller. Howard chose the north point for his command post, and placed observation teams on the other two sides.

Enemy foxholes dotted the ground, each with its small shelter scooped out two feet below the surface. During daylight hours Howard permitted his men to use small, one-man caves to avoid the hot sun and detection by the enemy. There was no other cover. There were no trees, only knee-high grass and small scrub growth.

The Vietcong were in the surrounding valleys and its villages. For two days Howard called in fire missions but not all requests for air and artillery support were honored. Sullivan, the battalion's commander, was concerned that the platoon's position would be spotted by the enemy. Most of the firing at targets located by the platoon was done only when an observation plane circled in the vicinity to deceive the enemy. Sullivan's concern rose after the second day and he decided the risk was too great to leave Howard's platoon stationary any longer. Howard radioed his disagreement, saying that his observation post was ideal and that he had encountered no difficulties. He told Sullivan that he believed he had a secure escape route along the ridge to the east. Reluctantly, Sullivan gave him one more day.

But the communists knew of Howard's platoon and they decided to eliminate it. On June 15 the North Vietanmese moved a well-equipped and highly trained battalion to the base of the hill. In late afternoon hundreds of troops started to climb its three sides, hoping to annihilate the eighteen Marines in a surprise attack.

Army Special Forces under Sergeant 1st Class Donald Reed and Specialist 5th Class Hardey Drande were leading a platoon of Vietnamese irregulars on patrol near the hill that afternoon. When they spotted elements of a North Vietnamese battalion moving towards the hill they radioed the information to their base camp at Hoi An, several miles to the south. Howard's radio, purposely set on the same frequency, alerted the sergeant to the threat against his position. He listened as Reed and Drande tried to convince the South Vietnamese into hitting the enemy from the rear, but they violently disagreed with their American advisers.

Listening on his radio, Howard chuckled over the raw language crackling over the air as the two sergeants tried to convince their Vietnamese troops.

Howard quickly developed a defensive plan before the communists attacked. He gathered team leaders and selected an assembly point, instructing them to stay on full alert and to withdraw to the main position at the first sign of an approaching enemy. Corporals and lance corporals crept back to teams and briefed them in the growing dusk. Then they tensely settled down to wait.

Lance Corporal Ricardo Binns had placed his observation team on the slope 120 feet forward of Howard's position, while the four Marines of Binn's team lay in a shallow depression discussing in whispers their sergeant's warnings. Binns quite casually propped himself up on his elbows and placed his rifle butt against his shoulder. Without saying a word he pointed his rifle at a bush and fired. The bush pitched forward and fell thrashing twelve feet away.

Other Marines jumped up, each throwing a grenade, before grabbing their rifles and scrambling up the hill. Behind them grenades burst and automatic weapons pounded away.

Other outposts withdrew to the main position. Now the Marines commanded a tiny rock-strewn knoll with only the rocks to provide protection. Placing his two radios behind a large boulder, Howard set up a tight circular perimeter, not over sixty feet in diameter, and selected a firing position for each Marine.

The North Vietnamese were also setting up while they continued to climb the steep slopes. Howard admired their professionalism. There was no talking, no clumsy movements. When Binns killed one of their scouts, they were less than 150 feet from the top.

Howard knew that he and his men were surrounded after the communists starting throwing grenades from all sides. Some bounced off the rocks and rolled down the slopes, endangering the throwers. Others failed to explode and some landed right on their position and casualty reports started to come in. Navy Corpsman Billie Don Holmes was soon busily crawling from one place to another to attend to the wounded. One grenade exploded between Holmes and a wounded man and Holmes collapsed, losing consciousness.

Howard realized his platoon was in serious trouble as .50-caliber machine guns from the rear fired in support of the communist assault troops while heavy projectiles arced in from four points of the compass. Red tracer rounds from light machine guns streaked toward the Marine position, identifying the direction for communist reinforcements gathering in the valley. Sixty millimeter mortar rounds exploded, adding rock splinters to the shrapnel whining through the air.

The North Vietnamese followed this barrage with a well-coordinated assault directed by shrill whistles and the clacking of bamboo sticks. They rushed forward from different directions firing automatic weapons, throwing grenades and screaming at the top of their lungs. At first, Howard was not sure how his troops would react. They were young, and the situation looked hopeless, but they stood firm and he was proud of them. They were all shocked by the ferocity of the attack and the screams of their wounded provided added horror. They reacted savagely, cutting down the first lines of enemy skirmishers seconds after they stood up and exposed themselves. As a result the enemy assault failed to gain momentum and the rear communist troops went to earth to seek a weak spot through which they might drive. Small bands were seen by Howard and his men as they tried to crawl close to a Marine, overwhelm him with a burst of fire and several grenades.

American hand grenades had twice the blast and shrapnel effect of the Chinese stick grenades and the Marines used them with deadly effect. Also, the Marines could throw farther and more accurately. A Marine listened for movement, gauged the direction and distance, pulled the pin of his grenade and threw. High-pitched yells and excited jabberings mingled with the blasts. The North Vietnamese finally decided they had had enough and withdrew to regroup.

During the lull, Sergeant Howard contacted Captain Geraghty and Lieutenant Colonel Sullivan at Chu Lai. He explained that his escape route was cut off and that his platoon faced overwhelming odds. "You've gotta get us out of here. There are too many of them for my people."

Sullivan called for flare ships, helicopters and fixed-wing aircraft to support his beleaguered men, but their response was delayed.

Shortly after midnight, enemy forces again rushed forward in strength. The Marines threw the last of their grenades and fired their rifles semi-automatically, relying on accuracy instead of volume to save precious shells. Again the communists fell back. By now every Marine had been wounded. The living took the ammunition from the dead and they lay tensely under a moonless sky. Howard doubted they could repel another massed charge by the determined enemy.

Up the slopes came the enemy's singsong taunts that Marines had heard in many another war. The voices screeched, "Marines, you die tonight!" And, "Marines, you die in an hour!"

After receiving Howard's permission to respond, Marines cursed and used every invective in their vast reportoire. The North Vietnamese screamed back, and Howard told his men to laugh. Rollicking laughter rolled down the slopes and continued until the Marines were exhausted.

Now the communists were strangely silent. The mocking laughter had disconcerted them. At 1:00 A.M. an Air Force flare ship appeared overhead. Howard talked to the pilot and the plane dropped its first flare, lighting up the hillside. Lance Corporal Ralph Glober Victory stared with the others. "Oh my God, look at them." Communist reinforcements filled the valley. Twenty-year-old Private First Class Joseph Kosoglow said later, "There were so many, it was like an ant hill had been ripped apart."

Above the hill, attack jets and armed helicopters swarmed in now that they had light from the flare. Jets concentrated on the valley floor and the approaches to the hill, firing rockets that hissed and blanketed large areas with their blasts. Then helicopters scoured the slopes with gunfire. As low as twenty feet, they skimmed the brush, firing their machine guns in long, sweeping bursts. Then the helicopters pulled off to spot for the jets, and fighter bombers slipped down, releasing bombs and napalm. The helicopters scurried back to pick off the stragglers, to survey the damage, and to direct another run.

Two helicopters remained over Howard's position all night. When one got low on fuel it was replaced by another.

By flare light, jet pilots could see the hill and distinguish terrain features but they could not spot Howard's perimeter. To mark specific targets for the jets, the flare ship was directed to drop flares on the ground as signal lights and then the jets were called down to pulverize the spot. Howard identified his position by flicking a flashlight on and off and, guiding on that mark, helicopter pilots strafed within seventy-five feet of the Marines.

The fight on the perimeter continued. In the shifting light of the flares pilots, fearful of hitting the Marines, left space free of fire in front of the Marines' front lines. The communists quickly realized this and crawled into it.

With no more grenades, Howard passed word to fire only at an identified target, and only one shot at a time. The enemy freely used automatic weapons, and hurled grenades while the Marines were forced to throw rocks back. This was a good tactic. A Marine would hear a noise and toss a rock in that general direction, and crawl to a spot from which he could sight and wait. The communist soldier would think it was a grenade and dive for another position. In a few seconds, the communist would raise his head to see why the grenade had not exploded and the Marine usually got him with one rifle shot from less than 30 feet.

Corpsman Holmes, after regaining consciousness following the grenade burst, saw a North Vietnamese dragging away the dead Marine beside him. Another soldier reached over and grasped him by his cartridge belt and tugged.

Lance Corporal Victory was lying on his stomach behind a rock. He had been hit twice by grenades since the first flares were dropped, and he could scarcely move. He saw an enemy solider bending over a fellow Marine. He fired and the man fell backward. He saw another enemy soldier tugging at a Marine's body. He fired again. The North Vietanmese slumped dead against Holmes' chest. Holmes pushed the body back and crawled to the Marines' lines, although his left arm was lanced with shrapnel, his face was swollen and his head rang from grenade concussions. For the rest of the night Holmes crawled from position to position to take care of the wounded, taking occasional shots at the enemy.

The flares finally flickered out and the planes had to break off to avoid crashing into one another. Artillery, under control of the Special Forces and manned by their South Vietnamese gunners, filled the gap.

"Stiff balls," Howard radioed the Special Forces camp at Hoi An, three miles south of his position. "If you can keep Charlie from sending another company up here, I'll keep these guys out of my position."

"Roger, Carnival Time," Captain Louis Maris of the Army Special Forces replied, using Howard's own peculiar call sign. Both sides kept their part of the bargain and artillery concentrations continued to concentrate on the enemy.

In periods of darkness, each Marine fought alone. At 3:00 A.M. a flight of helicopters whirled in to extract the platoon. The fire was too intense so they were unable to land and Howard was advised they would have to fight until dawn. Shortly thereafter, a ricochet bullet struck Howard in the back while he was talking on his radio. His voice faltered and died out. Special Forces personnel, pilots, high-ranking officers of the 1st Marine Division all thought the end had come. Then Howard's voice came back strong.

Fearing the drowsy effect that morphine can induce, Howard refused to permit Corpsman Holmes to administer the drug to ease his pain. Unable to use his legs, Howard pulled himself from hole-to-hole while he encouraged his men and directed their fire. Wherever he went, he dragged their lifeline—his radios. The redoubtable sergeant had been wounded three times during the Korean War.

Binns, the man whose shot had started the battle, was also a Korean veteran. Now, despite severe wounds, he crawled around the perimeter, urging the men to conserve ammunition while he gathered enemy weapons and grenades for his men and provided assistance whenever it was needed.

The long night ended. At 5:25, Howard shouted, "Okay, you people. Reveille goes in thirty-five minutes." At 6:00 A.M. his voice pealed out, "Reveille, reveille." It was a new day—and they still held.

On all sides the Marines saw enemy bodies and equipment. The communists would have normally raked the battlefield clean but the Marine fire had been so deadly that their dead cluttered the defense perimeter.

Howard noted that the firing had slacked off but he knew the enemy still ringed them and would not leave. While Marine sharpshooters sought a moving target, air and artillery fire proved so deadly on the slopes that the communists withheld another attack until they received reinforcements so they could go in again that night.

Still, bursts of fire from light machine guns chipped rocks above the Marines' heads. Firing uphill from concealed foxholes, the enemy could cut down any Marine who silhouetted himself against the skyline.

A helicopter buzzed low over the hill's crest, while a gunship hovered to one side, ready to pounce if the enemy took the bait. No one fired. Pilot William J. Goodsell decided to mark the position for medical evacuation. His helicopter fluttered slowly down and hovered. Howard thought the maneuver too risky and he said so. But Goodsell had run risks before and he came in anyway, dropping a smoke grenade. Still no fire. He waved to a relieved Howard and skimmed north over the forward slope only 10 feet off the ground.

Machine guns drowned out the sound of the helicopter's engines. Tracers flew toward it from all directions. The helicopter rocked and veered sharply to the right and zigzagged down the mountain. Co-pilot First Lieutenant Stephen Butler grabbed the stick and brought the crippled helicopter under control, crash landing it in a rice paddy several miles to the east. The pilots were quickly picked up by their wingman, but Goodsell died before reaching the hospital.

The medical helicopter did not hesitate. It came in although Howard frantically waved it off. He did not want another plane shot down. The pilot saw the signal and turned off while bullets clanged against the armor plating around the undercarriage.

Jet aircraft and helicopters attacked again, flying lower and lower as they criss-crossed the slopes searching for the communist machine gun emplacements, even offering themselves as targets in daring attempts to get the communists to fire back and reveal their positions.

On the ground communists gunners took the challenge and opened up and another helicopter was hit and spun into the ground. But their .50-caliber machine guns were exposed and they were quickly silenced. Still the communists held their ground despite persistent air attacks. Howard, watching the attacks anxiously from his hill-top position, was convinced that the communist assault company, with its automatic weapons and its brave young troops, had been ordered to wipe out at any cost the few Marines still alive.

Welcome assistance arrived to avert certain tragedy for the Americans when Marine infantrymen were flown in. They had left their bases at dawn and now circled overhead for forty-five minutes despite intense enemy fire as American jets and artillery blasted a secure landing zone.

During this period Lieutenant Richard E. Moser, a helicopter pilot, monitored Howard's frequency and heard the sergeant talking about communist soldiers in holes in front of him. "You've gotta get this guy in the crater because he's hurting my boys," Howard called.

On the northern slope the helicopters dropped down and members of Charlie Company of the 5th Marine Battalion, jumped out and climbed the slope quickly, ignoring sniper fire and wiping out small pockets of resistance. With their first rounds, a Marine 60-mm. mortar team knocked out the enemy mortar that had caused so many casualties. Sergeant Frank Riojas, weapons platoon commander, cut down a sniper at 1,500 feet with a tracer round from his rifle. Marine machine gun sections detached from the main company and set up along the flanks of the hill to support the company's forward movement. Now the communists were the hunted as Marines scrambled up the slopes, attempting to pinch off the enemy before they could flee.

Charlie Company's main column climbed straight up. A quarter of a mile away the point man spotted Howard's platoon on the plateau. The boulder that served as Howard's command post was the most prominent feature on the peak. The men hurried forward but had to step over enemy bodies to reach the perimeter. Howard's men now were down to eight rounds of ammunition for each rifle.

The relieving force found one Marine propped against a rock. In front of him lay a dead enemy soldier. Muzzles of their rifles touched each others' chests. Two Marine entrenching tools were recovered near a group of mangled North Vietnamese. Both shovels were covered with blood. One Marine was crumpled beneath a dead enemy. Beside him lay another Vietnamese. The Marine had a bandage around his chest and head, but his hand still clasped the hilt of a knife buried in the back of the soldier on top of him.

Howard called to the relieving force and his voice was sharp. "Get down! There are snipers right in front of us."

One of his Marines shouted, "Got any cigarettes?" Others repeated the request. Not one word of relief was uttered at being rescued. During the night few of them had expected to see the sun rise. After they survived, they knew the infantry would be coming. However, the fight was not over. Before noon, despite almost continuous artillery and air strikes, four more Marines died.

Lieutenant Ronald Meyer quickly deployed his platoon along the crest. He was new in the field, and he wore no shiny bars. Officers and men alike called him "Stump," because of his short, muscular physique.

With no identifying insignia Howard had assumed he was a corporal or sergeant and he shouted orders to him. Meyer sensibly obeyed, respecting Howard's knowledge of the situation. Howard continued to direct tactical maneuvers of the relieving company, determined to wipe out the small number of enemy troops still dug in 60 feet downslope.

Meyer yelled for grenades and lobbed them toward the snipers' holes. By peering around the base of the boulder, Howard was able to direct his throws but they had little effect. Air strikes were called in. Lance Corporal Terry Redic, one of the company's sharpshooters, thought this procedure was too slow. He raised up, sighted down the slope looking for a target, but he was killed instantly.

Meyer swore. "Let's get that bastard. You coming with me Sotello?"

Lance Corporal David Sotello nodded. He followed as Lieutenant Meyer started forward with a grenade in each hand.

Howard yelled a warning. "Keep your head down, buddy. They can shoot."

Meyer crawled for several yards, threw a grenade at a hole, and blasted an enemy soldier. He turned, looked upslope, and a sniper shot him in the back.

Hospitalman 3rd Class John Markillie crawled to the lieutenant.

"For God's sake," Howard yelled, "Keep your head down!" While Markillie tried to attend to the lieutenant, a sniper shot the corpsman in the chest.

Corpsman Holloday, and squad leader Corporal Melville now crawled forward. Meyer's pulse could not be felt, but Markillie was still breathing. Ignoring the sniper fire, they began to drag and push his body up hill. Melville was hit in the head and he rolled over, his helmet bouncing off. He shook his head and continued to crawl. The round had gone in one side of his helmet and ripped out the other, just nicking the corporal above his left ear. Finally, Melville and Holloday dragged Markillie into the perimeter.

At Chu Lai, the battalion commander called his company commander Lieutenant Marshall "Buck" Darling. "Is the landing zone secure, Buck?"

There was a pause.

"Not spectacularly," came the tense reply.

Two noncoms were listening to the radio communication. "I wonder what he meant by that?" asked a sergeant.

"What do you think it means, stupid?" the other said. "He's getting shot at."

Ignoring his own wounds, Corpsman Billie Holmes was busy supervising the new corpsmen from Charlie Company as they administered to the wounded. While the firefight continued evacuation was impossible so the wounded were taken to the rear on the south slope.

It was a difficult situation for the medical evacuation pilot orbiting overhead. He knew he had to come in perpendicular to the ridge, then cock his bird around before he set her down.

Holmes reported to Howard one Marine could not be accounted for. He was either dead or missing. Howard stubbornly refused to leave the site until he received assurances from the infantry that the body was recovered. To get the body, however, the last of the enemy had to be destroyed.

Lieutenant Philip Freed flopped down beside Corporal Melville. He was a forward air controller attached to Charlie Company. He contacted one of two fighter jets circling overhead. "This is Cottage 14. Bring it down on dry run. This has to be real right. Charley is dug in right on our lines." Lieutenants Richard W. Deilke and Edward H. Menzer listened to Freed's instruction carefully. The forward air controller was lying in a pile of rocks on the crest of the hill's northern finger. He had flown an F-8 Crusader so he was uncertain whether these pilots could help by attacking that close without hitting the Marines on the ground. The pilots were also concerned when they learned they would have to drop 60 feet from their positions. Menzer told his wingman, "As long as we're flying parallel to the people, it's okay because this is a good shooting bird."

The pilots turned their Crusaders toward their objective, knowing that the slightest variance would rake the Marines. They made four passes 10 to 20 feet above the ridge. On the ground, Freed feared they would crash as their wing tips almost touched the hill's crest. Their cannon shells showered the infantrymen with dirt as the pilots made eight attacks against an area 300 feet long and 60 feet wide. Freed noted that the hillside was gouged and torn as if a bulldozer had churned back and forth.

Freed cautiously lifted his head. A round cracked by his head. He ducked. At least one enemy soldier had survived. Someone shouted that the round came from the position of the sniper who had killed Meyer.

The fighter pilots now were out of cannon shells but they offered to make dummy runs over the position if the Marines thought they would be helpful. Freed agreed.

Company Commander Darling watched the jets. As they passed, he noticed that the firing stopped momentarily. He decided that the planes would provide good cover for what he had in mind. "I'm going to get Stump," he yelled. "Coming, Brown?" he asked the nearest Marine, Lance Corporal James Brown.

Brown followed the lieutenant and they tried to pull Meyer's body back while crawling on their stomachs, but they lacked the strength.

"All right," Darling said. "Let's carry him." Brown looked at him incredulously, knowing what had happened on the slope to anyone who raised his head. "We'll time our moves with the jets," Darling said. When the jets passed low, they stumbled and scrambled forward a few yards with their burden. They flattened as the jets pulled up. Sniper shots chipped rocks around them, but they still had thirty feet to climb. It took them more than a dozen rushes before they made it.

Now the infantrymen went after the sniper. Corporal Samuel Roth led an eight-man squad around the slope's left side. On the right, Sergeant Riojas set his machine gun up on the crest to cover them. Automatic fire struck his gun's tripod as the sniper continued to fire at the machine gun. His low position enabled him to aim exactly on the gun. The Marines would duck until he fired, then reach up and let loose another burst downhill, forcing the sniper to duck into his hole. With the firing the sniper could not hear the squad moving through the brush on his right side. Roth brought his men in a line facing the sniper. With fixed bayonets they walked forward. There was no movement in the clumps of grass and torn earth. During a lull in the firing the sniper finally heard the squad, spun around and fired. His bullets whipped by the Marines. Roth's helmet spun off and he fell. His steel helmet saved his life. Not aware that his helmet was off, Roth said, "When I give the word, kneel and fire. Now!" They rose and rounds kicked up dust and clumps of earth in front of them as the sniper fired first. The Marines missed the sniper because he popped back into his hole.

Roth swore as the Marines lay back. "All right. Put in fresh magazines and let's do it again. Now!"

As the Marines rose, the sniper bobbed up like a duck in a shooting gallery. This time a bullet knocked him back against the side of his hole. Roth charged and the other Marines sprinted behind him. Roth drove forward with his bayonet. A grenade with the release pin intact rolled from the sniper's left hand. Roth jerked his blade back and the sniper slumped forward—silenced at last.

By noon, Darling decided that the position was secure. After a search, they found the body of the missing Marine. They quickly searched the bodies of the thirty-nine dead communists for documents, gathered up their Chinese weapons, and boarded a flight of helicopters to fly off the plateau. Of the original eighteen Marines in Howard's reconnaissance platoon, six had been killed and the other twelve were wounded. Charlie Company accounted for two of the dead and two pilots from the Hué squadrons were also lost.

Staff Sergeant Howard's incredible deeds were justly recognized by a Medal of Honor.

It was a small operation, limited in scope, but one that would soon become all too familiar.

CHAPTER 20

"You No Warn VC No More."

A TASK FORCE WAS ESTABLISHED JULY 12, 1966, UNDER BRIGADIER General Lowell E. English supported by the 1st Marine Aircraft Wing to counter the communist buildup in the northern part of I Corps. English set up a command post near Cam Lo, seven miles west of Dong Ha and south of the Cam Lo River; a tributary of the Cua Viet River that empties into the South China Sea.

Two days later, a two battalion helicopter assault was made into the Ngan Valley. There was no initial resistance but some small arms fire took a toll. It was not until the Marines tried to cross the Song Ngan River that the North Vietnamese attacked in strength. With the enemy on high ground south of the river blocking their attempts to cross, English directed two battalions to move out of the valley July 18 along a corridor to the northeast. The first battalion was ordered to clear the enemy and establish blocking positions astride the river a mile south of the demilitarized zone. The other battalion was told to seize a commanding hill July 19 a mile southeast of the other battalion's blocking position.

English planned to insert a third battalion on the 18th into a small valley suspected of being used as a North Vietnamese marshalling area south of Song Ngan. B-52s had bombed the area on the afternoon of July 17. Actually, Guam-based B-52s carried out five strikes during the entire operation but the raid on the 17th was the only one exploited on the ground.

During a surprise North Vietnamese attempt July 18 to obliterate the Marine rear guard, the 3rd Battalion's Company K was struck hard. It had remained behind at the former landing zone to provide security for battalion operations while engineers blew up captured enemy ammunition and destroyed the three American helicopters downed in a collision. The enemy struck first with mortars, followed by their infantry. The Marines had already filled in their fighting holes so there was nothing to do but clear out on the double but the rear guard was not fast enough and was still in the area at the start of the enemy's infantry attack. Company K's 1st Platoon, under Staff Sergeant John J. McGinty III, became separated from the rest of the company and endured the full thrust of the enemy's assault. McGinty rallied his thirty-two-man platoon to beat them off. In one bitter assault, two squads became separated from the remainder of the platoon. With total disregard for his safety, McGinty charged the communists through intense automatic weapons and mortar fire. Many men were wounded and the medical corpsman was killed. McGinty quickly reloaded ammunition magazines and directed their fire upon the enemy. Although painfully wounded himself, his first thought was for his men as he continued to direct fire against their attackers. The North Vietnamese were beaten off, and when they tried to outflank his position he personally killed five at point-blank range with his pistol. When they again seemed on the verge of overrunning his small force, McGinty called for air strikes close to their position. This fire routed the enemy who retreated, leaving an estimated 500 bodies on the battlefield.

Company K's commander, Captain Robert J. Modrzejewski, had led his men in the capture of an enemy position three days earlier that contained a large amount of ammunition and supplies. That evening he had led the successful defense of the captured position even though they were assaulted by overwhelming numbers. Although wounded in the three-day operation, much of it fought at close quarters, he continued to lead his men. Once he crawled 600 feet to provide critically needed ammunition to an exposed squad.

July 18, when Company K was attacked by at least one thousand communists, Modrzejewski reorganized his men and urged them to continue to fight although their position was critical. He called in air and artillery strikes to drop within 150 feet of his troops and such action finally drove off the enemy.

Everyone looked up when a Marine shouted, "Here are some more Marines!"

He was wrong. They were North Vietnamese troops. When the communists heard his cry they ducked into the river. All the Marines could see were bobbing heads and rifles above water. It was like shooting floating pumpkins, and there were few misses.

The 3rd Battalion's commander, Lieutenant Colonel Sumner A. Vale, radioed for help July 18 and shortly before 5:00 P.M. Company L joined K. These reinforcements relieved the pressure and they were able to withdraw but in a state of complete exhaustion.

McGinty and Modrzejewski were later awarded Medals of Honor for their valorous conduct.

After the heavy fighting of July 18, the North Vietnamese avoided battle and fought only when they had no choice. This particular operation was completed with a series of sharp clashes followed by temporary withdrawal of the North Vietnamese. There was bloody fighting July 24 and 25 but this marked the end of large-scale actions.

The head of the 3rd Marine Division, Major General Wood B. Kyles, met with English at Dong Ha to discuss the battle. He ordered his task force commander to withdraw his battalions to the south and southeast because the difficult terrain offered obstacles to infantry maneuver and because there was a paucity of landing zones for helicopter assaults. Kyle suggested the Marines saturate areas in the vicinity of the demilitarized zone that contained enemy military activity with maximum artillery and air strikes.

English withdrew his infantry battalions to the south, but casualties continued. Although reconnaissance patrols were dangerous, their extensive use with artillery backup was one of the major innovations of the war. Hereafter reconnaissance elements hiding among enemy units proved to be deadly to the communists, particularly when artillery strikes were called in on precise targets.

The last significant sighting of a large body of enemy troops was made July 28. It was believed that the 324B Division had either crossed into the demilitarized zone or was hiding in the inacessible jungles to the west. During this period, Marine aircraft maintained a sortie rate of 100 per day.

Following this operation General Walt said that the North Vietnamese attacked in mass formations and died by the hundreds, and that their leaders had misjudged the fighting ability of the United States Marines and South Vietnamese troops fighting together. Then, too, the Americans had a superiority in artillery and total command of the air. Walt concluded, "They had vastly underestimated . . . our mobility."

Farther south, seven miles southwest of Chu Lai, there was consistent activity. Charlie Company of the 7th Marine Regiment continued to fight with South Vietnamese militia units in the village of Binh Yen No. Their goal was to develop Popular Forces to protect it. There were many such operations, and some success was achieved.

Sergeant Joseph Sullivan went out on patrol with company executive officer Lieutenant Thomas J. O'Rourke on the night of July 16. With five other Marines and two members of the Popular Forces they departed their base at 10:00 P.M. with one of the Vietnamese at point. When the point man entered the blackness of a main village street he quickened his pace. O'Rourke, second in the column, held to a slow, cautious tread. Seeing he was all alone, the South Vietnamese scurried back and frantically gestured for the Marines to walk faster. He was ignored. The Vietnamese returned to point and they walked more slowly, trying to set up an ambush.

From inside a house there was the loud sound of forced coughing. The patrol stopped in its tracks. The coughing stopped. When the patrol proceeded, the coughing started again. The Marines had been waiting for such a tip-off. O'Rourke checked with the point man.

"Yes, yes, very bad man, number 10." This was Marine slang for the bad man of a situation—Number 10. "No VC himself, but him warn VC," the point man said.

Members of the Popular Forces refused to apprehend the man. This was their village. They wanted the Marines to take action. The Marines were more than willing. Three of them converged on the house. Lance Corporal Bettie walked to the open door. A Vietnamese man inside looked at him for a moment and then made threatening gestures of hostility and contempt. Bettie struck him and the man fell, spitting blood. Bettie leaned over him. "When Marines pass, you no talk, you no cough." Bettie made a loud and false coughing sound. "You no warn VC no more. I come back sometime. I see."

The man nodded after every word. He understood. Perhaps next time he would not cough. Or perhaps he would use a lantern instead. Maybe he had learned his lesson. If not the Marines had orders to shoot out all blinking lights.

The patrol moved towards the river, and O'Rourke knew the Vietcong had been alerted but he knew their position could be easily defended. The traffic across the river was heavy. He could hear Vietnamese voices and splashes of water but he could not spot any movement.

A sound alerted O'Rourke. Someone was stalking their rear. All he could see were dark shadows because they were facing the river and the rice paddies were at their backs. He watched carefully but the shadows did not move. Slowly the lieutenant pulled his body over the bank, twisted around and raised up on his elbows. Now he was facing the rear with his back to the river. He checked for shadows again. They were closer than before— not over sixty yards away. Later, Lance Corporal Guadalupe Garcia told of glimpsing infiltrators as they crept by his flank position. He did not report them because he was not absolutely sure what he had seen.

O'Rourke nudged Sullivan and Corporal Leland Riley. They peered into the darkness and Riley whispered, "Yes, two of them."

The Marines waited until one Vietcong crept closer but the man lost his nerve. He jumped up and ran diagonally away. A Marine heaved a grenade that traveled over 150 feet before it exploded behind the fleeing soldier.

The others fired their automatic weapons. Riley said, "I think I hit one." A search found no body.

"This ambush is blown," O'Rourke said. "The VC are getting wise to us. We're just going to have to think these things through more. It's going to take more planning. Let's head back in."

In the northern sector of I Corps reports indicated that the North Vietnamese were moving two more divisions into the demilitarized zone. Marine General Krulak told Westmoreland that the North Vietnamese were attempting to avoid direct contact with the Marines. Westmoreland disagreed. "Just the reverse is the case and North Vietnamese forces are not seeking to get away."

The Marines recognized there was a buildup but they took exception to such Military Assistance Command terms as "massive buildup." Unfortunately, all commands used the identical intelligence data but continued to interpret it differently.

In August, 1966, a small task force continued to monitor the potential threat to the north. Major Dwain A. Coldby's Reconnaissance Marines were relied on for information as four- or five-man teams were dropped by helicopter along suspected enemy avenues of approach. They could immediately call for artillery support if they were attacked. This was an active month for both the Marines and the North Vietnamese in a series of operations. Generals Walt and Kyle watched the intensifying action in northern Quang Tri Province with growing concern. Westmoreland was the most concerned. He foresaw the likelihood of large numbers of North Vietnamese troops moving south through the demilitarized zone and he was apprehensive of what might happen if two North Vietnamese divisions moved into the area. He feared the North Vietnamese might skip around the main Marine defense position—a 700-foot mountain called the Rockpile with a commanding view of the surrounding terrain—and Dong Ha and attempt to open a corridor in the northwest corner of Quang Tri Province in the mountains bordering Laos and North Vietnam. Westmoreland suggested to Walt that he reinforce Khe Sanh ten miles southwest of the Rockpile, and thirteen miles south of the demilitarized zone, with a Marine battalion. Walt resisted. Several Marine generals believed Khe Sanh had no basic military value.

In the spring of 1966 the same militant Buddhist group that had precipitated events leading to Diem's downfall began to demand a return to civilian rule. Their protests grew more violent as they were brutally suppressed by government forces. In one three-week period ten Buddhist monks and nuns set themselves on fire in protest. Buddhist leader Tri Quang tried to bring order to the developing chaos but the rebellion was out of control, especially in the major cities. Before her immolation one nun wrote a letter to President Johnson. In it she labeled America's support for the Saigon government as "irresponsible," and Tri Quang blamed the president for her death.

United States officials urged Prime Minister Ky's government to broaden its base to include political parties and religious groups and they called for elections at the rice-roots level. The situation was so fraught with peril that the ruling generals agreed to a Constitutional Assembly—the nation's second—and set a date for an election that September.

A new method for close support to enable ground commanders to call for B-52 bomber strikes was approved July 6. A "combat sky spot" bombing program was initiated using ground radar control to direct bombers to a target and indicate the exact moment of release. This assured precision bombing in almost any kind of weather. B-52s had made their first strike almost a year earlier. Guam-based bombers were personally ordered by Westmoreland against enemy supply routes and suspected bases. They were effective but this was a terrible misuse of airpower that would have been more effective against strategic targets in North Vietnam.

The 2nd Korean Marine Brigade arrived August 18 in the II Corps area and was later assigned to northern Quang Ngai Province on the Batangan Peninsula, seventeen miles southeast of Chu Lai. Their arrival posed a delicate command relationship with the Marines because General Walt did not have operational control of the brigade. In effect, he could not order them to do anything. But he and Brigadier General Le Bong Chool had earlier attended Marine Corps schools together and they now formed a good working relationship. However, the arrival of the Koreans permitted a greater concentration of United States Marine 1st Division troops in the Da Nang area that allowed, in turn, more effective use of the 3rd Marine Division in the two northernmost provinces.

Secretary of Defense McNamara became increasingly interested in a physical barrier across the demilitarized zone and along the Laotian panhandle to stop North Vietnamese infiltration. A report was released August 30 that an air-supported barrier (one not manned by ground troops) could be operational in a year after a go-ahead was given. The report said such a barrier would consist of two parts: one to kill or maim foot soldiers and the other to destroy or damage vehicles. The barrier against soldiers would extend along the southern edge of the demilitarized zone into Laos while the other would be located farther to the west. A series of early warning devices, including a pressure system to indicate any increase in weight against the ground, and acoustic sensors to detect vibrations caused by men walking would be positioned at strategic points within the entire barrier to prevent attempts at penetration. The detectors were similar to burglar alarms and used electronic eyes. It was suggested that Air Force aircraft could monitor the area around-the-clock, analyze sensor signals, and call in air strikes against suspicious movements.

The Joint Chiefs forwarded the plan to Admiral Sharp September 8. After evaluation he reported that the barrier would have to be tended. If it was not, he said, it could be breached with ease. The Joint Chiefs concurred and they told McNamara the plan needed further study. There was much discussion in Saigon and Washington about the plan's merits but its huge cost and doubtful effectiveness were apparent unless strongpoints were manned on the ground.

General Kyle, in a memorandum to Walt, reiterated the views of most Marines that a barrier defense system "should free Marine forces for locations elsewhere and not freeze them in a barrier-watching defensive role." The head of the 3rd Division proposed instead that two divisions be used to halt enemy infiltrations through the demilitarized zone. "A two-division mobile defense force," he said, "could accomplish the same mission as a barrier without tying down more forces to fixed positions, and this course of action would have the additional advantage of requiring a much less extensive engineering effort." Walt agreed but the decision was not his to make.

In January, 1967, Westmoreland made some modifications to the plan—removing the word barrier and substituting anti-infiltration system—but the basic concept remained the same. His command said the eastern portion of the barrier should be completed by November 1, with the remainder completed at a later date. Westmoreland submitted revisions to Sharp and the Joint Chiefs and the plan caused a great deal of controversy throughout the year. McNamara was opposed to the changes. General Walt said the barrier discussion placed undue emphasis on the infiltration problem, and that he believed the primary enemy was the guerrilla and that infiltrators could only support local forces, but not replace them. Time proved him wrong. These defensive barriers demonstrated the thinking of the Washington operations analysts but they served no useful purpose. They warned of infiltration but the Johnson Administration would not free American commanders to seize the areas that supported the infiltration. These base camps were well disguised and generally located in Laos. Construction of the barrier or anti-infiltration system was begun in early April, but the project was shelved when enemy activity slowed down the project and the buildup of United States forces in I Corps preempted the logistical support needed to supply the construction materials.

In the summer of 1966 a North Vietnamese general said, "Our basic intention is to win militarily. We must gain military victories before thinking of diplomatic struggles. And even when we are fighting diplomatically, we must go on with our war effort; we must multiply our military victories if we want to succeed diplomatically." In other words, he saw no reason to negotiate because North Vietnam was not suffering badly due to restrictions imposed upon American airpower.

While the buildup of American troops continued, Westmoreland initiated search and destroy operations to clear main force communist units from population centers and to drive them into areas where they could be destroyed. Basically these operations were designed to create favorable conditions for pacification of the countryside. Air power was used extensively to bomb the Ho Chi Minh Trail. This was an expensive and ineffective use of allied airpower.

In September, 1966, Army forces launched operations against the Vietcong's 9th Division in an area west of the Michelin Plantation that was the heart of the enemy's war effort in the northwestern part of Tay Ninh Province along the Cambodian border. Results were so successful that it was believed that multi-division operations of this type were the key to success in South Vietnam.

In late September, after the North Vietnamese concentrated their forces nine miles from Khe Sanh, it became obvious that Westmoreland's view of that area was correct. Lieutenant Colonel Peter A. Wickwire's 1st Battalion, 3rd Marines, that had been alerted to move from Da Nang to Dong Ha, now had its orders changed to prepare to move to Khe Sanh. General Walt gave the order with reluctance. Westmoreland had long insisted that the base at Khe Sanh was needed to launch intelligence operations into Laos by cross-border patrols and small aircraft. He considered Khe Sanh a northern anchor to the defenses south of the demilitarized zone, and a base from which operations could be launched to cut the Ho Chi Minh Trail in Laos if authorized to do so. Westmoreland wanted the Marines to become familiar with the area and to gain confidence in fighting there if it became necessary.

It was not until September 29 that Wickwire's battalion, reinforced by an artillery battery, was sent to Khe Sanh. There, Wickwire established immediate contact with the United States Army's Special Forces adviser who informed him that the area was in imminent danger of being overrun.

Despite extensive patrolling by the Marines little contact was made with the enemy, but the original thirty-day stay of the battalion was extended into 1967.

At the time of the battalion's move to Khe Sanh, the Military Assistance Command kept getting reports of an unprecedented buildup of enemy forces along the entire length of the demilitarized zone. These reports convinced Westmoreland the North Vietnamese planned a massive advance into Quang Tri Province.

A task force was organized to reinforce the northern border area under General English. Many changes in command were made but despite III Marine Amphibious Force preparations, or perhaps because of them, the expected enemy offensive never materialized. The North Vietnamese chose to remain inactive during the northeast monsoon season, but there was every indication that fighting would start once the rains stopped.

The forward base at Dong Ha now became the center of operations for the northern area. Its airfield, and the one at Khe Sanh, was lengthened to handle four-engine transports. The Marines and the Navy also developed a sizable port at Dong Ha to accommodate craft bringing supplies up the Cua Viet River.

During the last major operation near the demilitarized zone in 1966 the Marines prevented the communists from establishing an operating base in northern Quang Tri Province, and killed over 1,000 enemy troops. By the end of the year Marines were running into poorly equipped young soldiers and frustrated commanders. But the battles for control of this northern region cost the Marines 200 dead.

In the southern part of I Corps, Vietcong guerrillas during the summer continued to probe Popular Force and Regional Force outposts near Marine positions, and one Marine company was ambushed, resulting in several deaths. There were other encounters that killed 24 additional Marines but resulted in the deaths of 380 of the enemy.

General Fields had informed headquarters of the III Marine Amphibious Force that he was prepared to carry out operations against Do Xa—the operation cancelled by the necessity of moving into the Que Son Valley—with his 1st Reconnaissance Battalion. He said that if there was a large enemy force at Do Xa that a two-battalion strike force stood ready to exploit the situation. General Walt agreed and so did Westmoreland. The South Vietnamese were not enthusiastic, requesting that the Marines coordinate their activities with their 2nd Division to avoid mistakes.

On the morning of July 6, 1966, Marine helicopters transported

Lieutenant Colonel Arthur J. Sullivan's 1st Reconnaissance Battalion, together with his command group and Company A, to the district town of Hau Duc in the northern fringes of the Do Xa sector, thirty miles west of Chu Lai. There were few sightings so the operation was ended July 14 without inserting infantry units. Fields was dubious about the importance of the Do Xa region. At a commanders' conference, he said, "We found there is nothing big in there."

His 1st Marine Division was particularly concerned about the 620th North Vietnamese Army Division that had once again penetrated the strategic Que Son Valley. Intelligence experts reported that the 3rd North Vietnamese Regiment had departed its mountain bastion south of An Hoa and had advanced southeast towards the coastal plain after taking on the Marines at Nui Vu. The 21st North Vietnamese Division was also believed to be near the district town of Que Son and Thang Binh—a village twelve miles north of Tam Ky on Route 1.

As early as July 18 Fields had informed Walt that he wanted to follow up this intelligence information with a multi-battalion operation in the Que Son region. He was granted permission and a combined search and destroy operation was launched August 6. There was heavy fighting on the 10th and the North Vietnamese battalions retreated to the north where they engaged South Vietnamese Marines three days later. With air support, the South Vietnamese forced the communists to retreat. This operation succeeded in driving the North Vietnamese 2nd Division out of the Que Son Valley temporarily and was the first in a series of operations that brought the entire Hiep Duc-Que Son area under the blanket of III Marine Amphibious Force security. Increasing commitment of Marine forces near the demilitarized zone after August pre-empted Walt's plans for pacifying the valley at this time. It was not until April in the following year that the Marines were again able to enter the region in force.

In September, 1966, a nationwide election selected delegates for a Constitutional Assembly to draw up a new constitution for South Vietnam. This was a precarious undertaking at a time of heavy fighting and discord. But the electoral turnout in I Corps was approximately 87 percent of the 900,000 eligible voters who lived in relatively secure areas, but where government control all too frequently could be maintained only during daylight. Nationwide, 81 percent of the people voted and their demonstration of courage was outstanding. During this period Marine units kept out of populated areas although harassment by Vietcong and North Vietnamese regular units kept up. General Walt was so concerned by Vietcong threats to dismantle the electoral process that he had nine battalions in the field on search and destroy missions before and after the election. Despite success of the electoral process, there were few successes for the Marines in the pacification program in central and southern I Corps.

The southward flow of men and supplies from North Vietnam was drastically reduced in 1966. Navy jets concentrated heavily on railroad lines and yards. At Phu Can a Hancock flight hit a twenty-five-car ammunition train that exploded like a string of fireworks. Pilots reported, "Large red fireballs completely disintegrated the cars and there was heavy smoke, many fires and numerous rail cuts."

During April, May and June United States planes encountered increasing resistance from SAMs, MIGs and anti-aircraft guns. As a result, improved tactics and newly developed electronic countermeasures had to be quickly put into use. Despite increasing resistance, a kill ratio of three MIGs for each carrier plane shot down was maintained.

In June, after numerous delays caused by Washington officials, carriers and Air Force wings were turned loose against the most significant targets they had yet been assigned—the extensive petroleum storage system of North Vietnam. On June 29, Navy pilots hit the Haiphong petroleum storage areas, causing three huge fireballs and leaving columns of black smoke rising to 20,000 feet at the complex. "It looked like we had wiped out the world's supply of oil," one pilot said. He could still see the smoke from as far as 150 miles away. Twenty storage tanks and a pumping station constituting 80 percent of the installation were destroyed.

Simultaneously the Thailand-based Seventh Air Force's fighters and bombers hit the petroleum storage area near Hanoi. This tank farm, second in size to the Haiphong petroleum storage area, was completely obliterated by precision bombing. This one-two punch was completely successful but, due to the prolonged delay and forewarning in the United States media, the North Vietnamese had already provided an alternate dispersed system.

During succeeding strikes Navy aircraft swept far inland to obliterate petroleum storages at Bac Giang, northeast of Hanoi. As a result no more tankers were pulling into Haiphong by July because there were no storage tanks left.

On the first of July the North Vietnamese reacted with an attack against two United States search-and-rescue destroyers, the *Coontz* and the *Rogers,* steaming fifty-five miles southeast of Haiphong. Navy planes counterattacked and both enemy PT boats were destroyed. Ships picked up nineteen enemy survivors. These men were the first to become Navy prisoners of war.

During the summer of 1966, strike operations increased in intensity. In August, three carriers became permanently available farther north.

When Rear Admiral David C. Richardson became commander of Carrier Task Force 77 in August, he was appalled by the depth of Washington's control of air operations into North Vietnam. Local realities clearly had not penetrated McNamara's thinking about how to conduct the war. None of the civilian leaders in the Pentagon appeared aware of the enormous fallacy of slowly increasing the intensity of operations, then reducing them before the desired result could be achieved. They did not seem to understand that the target selection process that seldom permitted attacks against militarily significant targets gave the communists needed time to complete measures that reduced their dependency on those targets. A large number of targets that were militarily significant remained off-limits to on-the-scene commanders until they were specifically authorized for attack by McNamara. Every four to six weeks a list of targets authorized for attack, usually involving four to eight targets, would be received from McNamara. All too frequently these targets were so insignificant that they bordered on the absurd, leaving operational personnel to question the competence of those who made the selections. For example, one set of authorized targets consisted of buried and dispersed petroleum stocks—each containing between 75 to 100 50-gallon drums spread over a large area. Richardson reckoned that his planes would consume fifty times the fuel they might destroy but at great danger to the pilots from surface-to-air missiles. He knew that the loss of such a small amount of fuel would make little or no difference to communist military operations. Meanwhile, his men were providing a lot of target practice for the North Vietnamese. He was continually upset because of the high risks his men were forced to take in comparison to the gain they could expect to achieve. He protested and received Admiral Sharp's support, but nothing changed.

A year later, after reporting for duty in the Pentagon, Richardson inquired into the processes for selecting targets. He learned that the Joint Chiefs, having been repeatedly rebuffed on their recommendations to McNamara's staff, decided that their chairman, General Wheeler, should carry their nomination of targets to be authorized for attack to the White House when he deemed the circumstances favorable. Richardson was advised that the periodic submission of their recommended targets bore little resemblance to the list authorized by the White House. He was unable to learn who actually selected the targets that were authorized.

Strategic targets often were deleted and each one was approved only after it was personally authorized by the president. Johnson boasted that they could not hit an outhouse without his approval. In general, only three or four important strategic targets were approved each six weeks so the long delays between strikes permitted the North Vietnamese to rebuild their defenses. By the time they were allowed to hit power plants North Vietnam had already brought in mobile generators by the thousands to provide electrical power so they were no longer dependent on their major plants. Destruction of their power plants, therefore, was not as disabling as if they had been hit earlier.

Task Force 77 at Yankee Station concentrated on supply dumps and railroad lines to the south in the fall of 1966. One particularly successful series of missions occurred when a morning armed reconnaissance flight noticed a series of railroad cars passing through the town of Ninh Binh. Captain James D. Ramage, Richardson's chief of staff, advised the operations officer, Captain Samuel Gorsline, to concentrate all airborne aircraft on this target.

A later report indicated that there were possibly three trains of 100 cars in the Ninh Binh area. An alert reconnaissance leader dropped bombs and cut the line to the north of the town and the trains were immobilized. Ramage immediately alerted Richardson and he pointed out that some of the rolling stock was in the town, and requested orders.

Richardson replied, "The target is the trains."

Ramage returned to strike control. "Tell the pilots to take them all."

Strike aircraft from three carriers pounded the targets for three hours. Pictures later showed that workers were trying to offload material from the burning railroad cars to store under adjacent cover, despite secondary explosions from the cars' contents. During the next three days Navy planes poured tons of ordnance on the train and trucks attempting to unload and transfer the cargo. A key target was a prominent road outcropping that had been tunneled to store ammunition. Direct hits, aerial photographs disclosed, caused massive explosions in the rock.

The same type of operation took place during this period a mile from Thanh Hoa. A train, isolated by cut tracks, was halted near an important train ferry, a major railroad bridge and a transshipment point.

Three days after the Ninh Binh strike Ramage was sent to Saigon to brief the "Five O'Clock Follies"—the daily briefing given to the press in a downtown theater. He described how a tactic called "interdiction in depth" had in six days destroyed 229 railroad cars and more than 200 trucks and caused serious disruption of military traffic through two important North Vietnamese cities. He said that one element of planes was assigned to paralyze large supply trains by cutting the tracks in front and behind them and destroy the cars inbetween at leisure. Once this was done, another element concentrated almost all of their fighter-bombers from the attack carriers on the trains and nearby targets. Ramage told the press that he believed interdiction in depth worked best at what he called "choke points" or North Vietnamese cities where vital railroad, barge and highway routes converged and where important military supplies were transshipped and temporarily stored.

Ramage said the Seventh Fleet hit the jackpot earlier that month at the vital cities of Ninh Binh and Thanh Hoa, respectively fifty and seventy miles south of Hanoi. He said the raids pretty much disrupted traffic meant to support North Vietnamese infiltrations into the South. Ramage described how three carriers had almost incessantly bombed a railroad and storage area near Ninh Binh from September 14 through the 17th and destroyed two locomotives, one hundred and four railroad cars and two bridges. He explained that one element of interdiction in depth is to take quick advantage of an unexpected opportunity. This was done at Ninh Binh, he said, when a reconnaissance plane saw a large freight train the day the first strikes were underway and succeeded in isolating and paralyzing the train by cutting the rails at one end and knocking down a bridge at the other.

Ramage's forthright remarks, backed up by pictorial evidence, was appreciated by the news media. After the briefing a newspaperman asked the Army colonel who ran the briefing whether the carriers were continuing strike operations in the North. This was during one of the many standdowns imposed by President Johnson. The colonel avoided the question by saying he was not permitted to discuss it.

Ramage was upset over this nonsensical answer because the North Vietnamese knew we were no longer striking up north. After the briefing he sought out the correspondent and reminded him that he knew very well that the United States was not bombing North Vietnam.

The correspondent agreed. He said, "I just wanted to ask the question to see what kind of a stupid answer I would get from these guys."

Episodes like this one turned off the press and many military men like Ramage knew that some criticism of military actions was deserved.

At first Richardson's command was permitted to hit concentrations of trucks and storage areas, as well as trains, but they were seldom permitted to hit barges. Why, he never learned, but he suspected the reasoning was idiotic, that such attacks might damage the canals. Richardson pressed for attack against barge traffic because it could be seen from photographs that barges were part of the transportation system that moved supplies to North Vietnamese units in the South, and were so critical to the North Vietnamese economy. One day Ramage displayed a picture of such traffic. Both agreed that there were so many barges that an Olympic runner could leap from one to another. Richardson went to Military Assistance Command headquarters in Saigon with the photographs. It took three weeks before he was permitted to attack the barges. By then most of them had been dispersed.

Richardson was disturbed by periodic orders from Washington that limited the number of aircraft to be assigned to a target because the risk for the crews was intensified. In response to his outraged complaints, Department of Defense officials said that if there were too many planes some of them might miss the target and kill civilians.

Following one attack close to Hanoi, Richardson received a message asking, "Did you kill any civilians?"

The admiral was incensed. He had never received a message asking how many pilots had been lost. They were more concerned for North Vietnamese civilians than for his pilots. In this case Richardson checked the strike photographs and replied that all bombs were on the target.

Those on the carriers knew that it was necessary to have a high proportion of attacking aircraft to suppress the numerous missile batteries around a target to reduce the risk. After the query whether North Vietnamese civilians had been killed Richardson told his staff that we sure as hell won't mention this message to the strike group pilots.

He complained to Admiral Roy Johnson, commander of the Pacific Fleet. "Why send a message out like this? Doesn't anyone consider our pilots?"

Johnson replied that this was an urgent message from the White House that was sent out from his headquarters before he had a chance to see it.

Richardson was also dismayed that about half of his staff's time was devoted to the preparation of reports. These reports involved their intentions, modifications and all aspects of each strike operation. Details had to be furnished in five different categories from planning, execution and reporting the results. Each day his command had to send Washington voluminous information relating to their intentions, and this data was fed into computers. There was also a time frame within which each mission could be cancelled. After submitting this data, Richardson's staff hoped that its interpretation in Washington would make sense. However, it went to systems analysts who were unable to comprehend the significance of the information they had requested. This sometimes led to message exchanges that bordered on the hilarious. Occasionally, the consequences were serious.

Despite their attack effectiveness the old propellor A-1 Skyraiders began to encounter anti-aircraft defenses in North Vietnam that were too hot to handle. Richardson withdrew them and informed Pentagon officials. He explained that the risk was too high for them to continue flying attack missions in North Vietnam, and that the benefits of their operations were too low for the risks involved to the pilots and crew members. Richardson forwarded this message to the Seventh Fleet commander, that he was grounding the Skyraiders for attack missions to the North. The fleet commander agreed with him.

Richardson received a message from the Operations Analysis office under McNamara. "We don't understand why you can't continue to fly the A-1 in North Vietnam." The message stated that an A-4C jet aircraft carried three bombs, but that an A-1 carried three times that number, and the loss rate for the A-4 was one for each thousand bombs dropped—the same as the A-1. "Therefore we think the A-1 should continue to be used."

Such reasoning was sound in a static environment. But in combat operations conditions change quickly; often radically. Those statistics covered the period when North Vietnam had very little air defense capability. McNamara's target limitations by now had given the communists time to create a significant anti-aircraft defense system.

Richardson responded that in measuring the equivalent number of bombs on target between the two aircraft the A-1 would lose more pilots even though it got more bombs on targets. What disturbed him most was that this type of problem was mathematically calculated without any recognition of the human factor. Such computations made no sense to men who were risking their lives.

After Richardson had arrived at Yankee Station he was upset when he noted there was a serious shortage of bombs and weapons. As a result he was forced to send less than the number of aircraft that were needed on a strike. To make the need clear, he scheduled strikes as they should have gone but then canceled those for which bombs were not available. He was deliberately feeding the Pentagon computer with data to get some action.

Admiral Johnson, commander-in-chief of the Pacific Fleet, wired back, "Knock it off!"

Secretary of Defense McNamara, who allocated bomb expenditure rates from Washington, had established production rates for ammunition and ordnance according to criteria known only to himself. Therefore, the sizes and quantities of bombs were grossly inadequate, and comments from the war zone were not welcomed.

Richardson recognized this shortage was a typical instance that if a certain amount of money was spent, it would produce a measurable return. McNamara's whiz kids had programmed the production line and they did not want to disturb it. By doing so they would have to admit they were wrong. One of the problems was that 250-pound bombs were too small. Thousand pounders were more useful but 2,000-pound bombs were the most needed. But they were in such short supply that their use had to be curtailed. It took over a year for the production lines to gear up to meet the desperate need in Southeast Asia.

Air Force and Navy bombers had done an excellent job of destroying thirty major bridges—twenty-one in October—in North Vietnam, but their efforts were thwarted when the communists paved the river bottoms so vehicles could cross when the water was low. They also used barges tied together as temporary roadbeds over rivers when bridges were destroyed.

Captain Robert Wood, Richardson's operations officer, repeatedly stressed that if small bridges were destroyed between towns that the traffic would be reduced far more than if larger bridges in the towns themselves were knocked down. The latter, he stressed, could be bypassed. Wood cited the critical areas as the plains to the north and south around Vinh where roadways were constrained by steep hills. The Vinh area had a particularly large number of canals, railroads and roads where attacks would have a great impact on North Vietnam's supply lines. Farther inland, Wood said, the mountainous terrain made it difficult for the communists to open roads. Actually, it took the North Vietnamese years to create a road through the mountainous terrain and thus bypass this area of vulnerability.

Richardson recommended amphibious landings in this coastal area. It was clear that hit-and-run raids would accomplish much more than air activities, especially during the monsoon season when aircraft were unable to see their targets. But such raids remained off-limits.

Bad weather constantly plagued the operations of Carrier Task Force 77. Poor visibility restricted air operations for over 300 days out of the year.

Later, during a period of duty at the Pentagon in the summer of 1967 Richardson wrote a memorandum to the chief of naval operations, Admiral Thomas H. Moorer, saying that he thought the Navy could determine whether the United States was winning or losing the interdiction campaign. He said an analysis of the effort (attacks against enemy supply lines) was the key, and not the strategic air effort against major targets given the restraints and the poor quality of targets permitted by McNamara. "If you agree I would like to take several people from the Intelligence group who are familiar with reconnaissance photographs and let them analyze targeting opportunities in three categories: the situation in early 1966, in December 1966 and in May 1967. We should ask ourselves are the communists developing bypasses or other means that are alleviating their difficulties? Are their anti-aircraft capabilities increasing? What are the consequences or dynamics of these developments during the next couple of years?" He added that despite better aircraft and improved evaluation techniques from photographic evidence the enemy was improving its bypasses and now had more SAM missiles to protect their routes. The study concluded that many bypasses had been completed during the year examined and that many more were being constructed, anti-aircraft defenses were increasing appreciably, and that time was working against them. Richardson said that the United States Navy should re-examine its basic strategy.

He warned that weather conditions were not adequately considered by planners in Washington, or the attendant risks involved to crews. He said those who assigned targets appeared to believe that the United States had such overwhelming forces arrayed against North Vietnam that the communists would see the futility of their efforts. Richardson said such assumption was not true. He ordered a chart kept of day-to-day weather conditions. A good weather day was defined as one in which visibility exceeded five miles on a line-of-sight basis for at least four consecutive hours. There were many days when visibility lasted only two or three hours before clouds closed in and operations had to be cancelled. The records demonstrated that in the summer months—July, August and September—the average number of "good" days was fifteen. During the monsoon season, operations were seldom possible. In the winter, there might be four or five days of marginal weather but the average was about two days a month when pilots could be assured of hitting a target during a four-hour period of good visibility. This meant that crews had one or two good strike days and then had to stand down for a week or more with no activity, thus allowing the North Vietnamese to repair the damages.

Few recommendations to attack strategic targets from Richardson through CINCPAC were approved in a short time. Those that were approved took anywhere from three weeks to two months and a great many targets remained on the prohibited list. Actually, the Joint Chiefs were getting only a third of their strategic targets approved by McNamara.

In September and October Richardson's command destroyed more than 1,000 supply boats and barges, 450 railroad cars, and 350 trucks before bad weather in mid-October cut their missions more than in half. Prior to that they had been averaging 300 bombing aircraft flights a day during good weather. Despite the bad weather, after the middle of October the carriers destroyed 21 bridges and destroyed or damaged 600 supply boats, 130 railroad cars and 100 trucks. This was a good record, but this air effort would have been more usefully employed against North Vietnam's strategic targets.

Admiral David MacDonald, while he was chief of naval operations in 1966, had specifically selected Richardson for his job. Before Richardson reported to his new assignment in the Pacific, MacDonald told him, "I put you in this job out there and I am telling you one thing that I want you to do. Take care of the pilots." It was apparent to Richardson that Mac-Donald believed there were too many nonsensical orders being issued by the Pentagon. His final instruction was, "Don't get out there and be reckless with the pilots. The cake isn't worth the eating."

Admiral MacDonald visited Richardson's flagship while the latter was a carrier task group commander but had not yet relieved Admiral Reedy as commander of Carrier Task Force 77. He was pragmatic about the war. When Richardson expressed strong views about the way things were going, MacDonald replied, "Settle down. Can you guarantee that the Chinese won't come into the war?" He stressed that assessments indicated the Chinese might intervene, and that the United States did not intend to provoke them.

At that time the situation in China was far different from what it was later, because rebellious youths unleashed by Mao Tse-tung as part of the cultural revolution were tearing apart the fabric of the communist state and it appeared to many Americans in authority that the People's Republic of China might intervene in the war. In retrospect, we know that intelligence estimates at the time were completely in error.

Occasionally there was some relief from the monotony of combat operations when entertainers came out to the ships. The crews enjoyed the better ones, and they were most warm in their welcome of a group of talented young Mormon men and women who put on a clean show without off-color remarks. Some entertainers seemed to think sailors preferred dirty jokes and obscene material. Such was not the case. Richardson noted with surprise that when such material was used, many of the sailors drifted away. The higher the quality of entertainment the more attractive it was for most of the men.

Admiral Sharp sent another message to the Joint Chiefs October 26, 1966, claiming that self-imposed controls on the use of airpower against North Vietnam had had an adverse effect upon the effectiveness of airpower in reducing North Vietnam's capability to support the insurgency in the South. He said air attacks had disrupted their operations and prevented them from seizing significant portions of I and II Corps. Sharp added, however, that air operations had not reduced their support to the South to a satisfactory level and that these air attacks had failed to bring them to the negotiating table. He called for an air campaign that would bring the war home to the communists. Reporting on operations for the year, Sharp said of 104 targets in the northeastern part of North Vietnam he had been permitted to hit only 20. He claimed that the Rolling Thunder campaign did not apply steady pressure on the communists solely due to restrictions posed by McNamara and President Johnson.

Navy interdiction operations in North Vietnamese waters had only been authorized in October, and they were limited to 17 degrees, 30 minutes north latitude—an area of thirty miles. Although often fired upon, Navy planes suffered their first casualty December 23 when two men were killed and three were wounded. Sharp had argued forcefully for permission to bomb targets whenever such attacks were desired. He was turned down. The president and McNamara were reluctant to authorize an all-out aerial offensive of North Vietnam.

After forty-eight-hour bombing halts on Christmas and New Year's, strikes concentrated again on stopping the southward flow of war supplies and troops, and all-weather A-6s struck major targets in the North's military industrial complex as some target restrictions were lifted temporarily so Air Force and Navy pilots could bomb closer to Hanoi and Haiphong although the cities themselves remained off-limits.

That same month McNamara returned from a visit to South Vietnam and told President Johnson in a memorandum, "Pacification has if anything gone backward" and the air war has not "either significantly affected infiltration or cracked the morale of Hanoi." He recommended a limit to increased forces and the consideration of a bombing halt. Either that, he said, or shift the bombing of targets from the vicinity of Hanoi and Haiphong to infiltration routes to increase the credibility of peace gestures.

The Joint Chiefs opposed a bombing cutback, and they proposed strikes against locks, dams and rail yards. They were turned down.

In November, however, McNamara had given the Joint Chiefs new authority to raise the ceiling of American troops in Vietnam to 469,000 by the end of June, 1968.

By the end of 1966, two Marine divisions were still fighting two separate wars. The 1st Division assumed responsibility for Da Nang and Chu Lai, and the 3rd Division was fighting a more or less conventional war in the northern section of I Corps. The 1st Division, meanwhile, continued its combination of large unit and counter-guerrilla operations south of the Hai Van Pass. Walt wanted to reduce the size of his forces along the demilitarized zone, but this pattern of warfare continued well into 1967.

The United States started 1967 with 385,300 military personnel in South Vietnam. In a year-end report, Westmoreland said, "During 1966, airmobile operations came of age. All maneuver battalions became skilled in use of the helicopter for tactical transportation to achieve surprise and out-maneuver the enemy."

Close to 60,000 North Vietnamese regulars had entered South Vietnam during 1966. They now had five divisions with a total strength of 282,000 men, plus another 80,000 in political cadres.

Westmoreland's request for a 30 percent increase in troops—leveling off at 500,000 men—with a reserve of three divisions in the United States shocked Washington officials who began to wonder where it would all end.

What Westmoreland did not know, however, was that the North Vietnamese had decided in late 1964 to move in large units to build up their strength and give greater support to the Vietcong.

According to allied plans, the South Vietnamese would take over more of the pacification program in the coming year. In I Corps, South Vietnamese troops were assigned the primary mission of supporting the villages while the Marines operated against enemy main-force units. Unfortunately, the South Vietnamese Army was not ready to take over pacification duties. This was shown dramatically in December 1966, when the III Marine Amphibious Force learned that not one hamlet had been added to the secure category in I Corps that month. General English summed up Marine frustrations, saying that there was too much real estate and the Marines did not have enough troops. Actually, failure to secure and hold outlying areas was to blame. The Vietcong were aware each time a Marine squad and some local militiamen departed a village that their hold on the population would crumble.

Pacification gains during the year were modest at best. The South Vietnamese government had hoped to place teams in over 300 villages. Only one-third of that goal was reached. Westmoreland estimated that the percentage of the South Vietnamese population that lived in relative security had risen from 50 to 60 percent, due largely to the presence of American troops rather than efforts by the Vietnamese. Lack of success was due to a variety of reasons but mainly can be attributed to the fact that the government of South Vietnam had provided little protection for the hamlets. Although emphasizing pacification, Westmoreland said, "Our strategy will be one of a general offensive with maximum practical support to area and population security." He said American forces had come to fight the enemy "by attacking his main forces and invading his base areas."

Under Admiral Richardson his carrier command established excellent relations with Air Force commanders. He was critical, however, of the Air

Force propensity for long, detailed strike orders from Saigon that went into too much detail, leaving strike commanders at their bases no flexibility. In the Navy, air commanders participated in planning strikes, often making recommendations for changes because of weather conditions or upon discovering fleeting targets of opportunity. During one period the Air Force had 2,000 people in various Saigon headquarters. Some of this over-staffing was due to the vast number of reports required by Pentagon authorities. The Military Assistance Command personnel reached a peak of 3,500, a number far in excess of need.

Although Richardson believed that special intelligence operations by the United States were good, he thought greater use should be made of transmitting misleading data to confuse North Vietnamese monitors. He was aware that there were certain things that could not be hidden, but he expressed his concerns to higher authorities about the lack of adequate decoy information (imply that you are going to attack one place but go to another). Such methods were used effectively by air officers in World War II against the Germans. He believed strongly that many people in decision-making positions in Washington did not understand air warfare. He was disturbed that lessons learned in World War II and Korea often had to be relearned again with unacceptable and unnecessary losses. If more decisions could be made in the theater of operations he believed this problem could be alleviated. He resisted constraints on operations but they were made by people at the highest levels of government and could not be changed. In his messages through the chain of command, Richardson reminded those at the top that modern warfare depended in part upon electronic warfare to create confusion among the enemy. Unfortunately, the North Vietnamese and their Russian and Chinese advisers proved more adept at electronic warfare despite their less sophisticated capabilities.

CHAPTER 21

All Targets Must Be Struck

ADMIRAL SHARP MADE A NEW ATTEMPT IN EARLY 1967 TO GET PERMIS-
sion to deny North Vietnam access to the flow of supplies from China and
Russia. In particular, he wanted to curtail the flow of men and supplies
from North Vietnam into Laos and South Vietnam. Through channels, he
said there were six basic target systems in North Vietnam: electric power,
war supporting industries, transportation support facilities, military complexes, petroleum storage depots and the air defense system. He reminded
the Joint Chiefs that attacks against these target systems, rather than
against individually selected targets on a stop-and-go basis, would steadily increase the pressure against North Vietnam heretofore denied his
command due to operational restrictions.

He recommended January 18 that targets in these target systems—all
of which needed approval by higher authority—should be approved as a
package and not doled out a few at a time. At the beginning of the year,
Sharp said, there were 104 important military targets in the northeastern
section of North Vietnam but only 20 had been authorized for strikes.
Actually, he later designated 242 fixed targets in the North and he sought
permission to hit 15 new targets each month.

From the beginning of his tenure as Commander-in-Chief, Pacific,
Sharp had urged the Joint Chiefs to hit all strategic targets in North
Vietnam before the communists were given a chance to build up their
defenses. The Joint Chiefs had agreed but each time McNamara had
turned them down. Sharp continuously pointed out that more than 85
percent of the war materiels that arrived in North Vietnam came by sea
through Haiphong. Cargoes were unloaded on a twenty-four-hour-a-day
basis from Russia and her satellite countries. He had strongly recommended that North Vietnam's harbors be mined but this request was
rejected.

In 1972, when President Nixon authorized mine operations, it cost less than $1 million and not one person on either side was killed. It should have been done in 1965 when mining might well have been decisive in ending the war. Early in his tenure, Sharp also recommended that overland supply routes from China to Hanoi be destroyed. His request was denied because of a disproportionate fear by the Johnson administration as to how the People's Republic of China might react. We know now they would have protested, but would not have intervened.

In his State of the Union address January 10, 1967, President Johnson said, "Our adversary still believes that he can go on fighting longer than we can. I must say to you that our pressures must be sustained . . . until he realizes that the war he started is costing more than ever." These were empty words because he never exercised the full authority to do what was necessary to end the war. The basic strategy was one of attrition: to reduce the flow of infiltrators and increase the cost of fighting until North Vietnam decided it was paying too high a price to gain control of the South. It was not a convincing argument then, and time has not dealt kindly with a policy of fighting a ground war merely to destroy the enemy's manpower. Instead, airpower should have been unleashed on the North to destroy their resources and their will to fight. The North Vietnamese had an abundance of men to sacrifice—probably two million eligible men—and even the huge might of America's military machine was insufficient to gain victory in only land battles against such a determined foe.

President Johnson wrote to President Ho Chi Minh in early February suggesting that their representatives meet in secret to find a peaceful solution to end the conflict. He said he was ready to stop all bombing and freeze the level of America's forces in South Vietnam. His letter was delivered to the North Vietnamese embassy in Moscow on the 8th. That same day Johnson ordered a halt to all bombing of North Vietnam as part of a general truce surrounding the Tet holiday.

North Vietnam used the bombing halt to send a thousand sampans and other vessels south along the coast carrying enough supplies and equipment to support a large-scale military operation for a long period. A Navy pilot reported that the roads in North Vietnam's panhandle were jammed with trucks dashing south. He said the roads looked like the New Jersey Turnpike.

The British appealed to Premier Aleksei Kosygin before he left on a visit to Hanoi. The Russian premier headed back to Moscow February 12 as Hanoi broadcast Ho Chi Minh's uncompromising answer to an earlier appeal for peace by Pope Paul in Rome. The North Vietnamese president insisted that all bombing and other military actions against North Vietnam must be stopped unconditionally, and that all American and other allied troops must withdraw from South Vietnam. Ho Chi Minh said that South Vietnam's future must be settled in accordance with the political program of the communist National Liberation Front. This meant surrender of South Vietnam, and the extended bombing pause was ended February 13 after Kosygin was safely back in Moscow.

President Johnson received a reply to his letter to Ho Chi Minh the same day but it was almost identical to the one sent to the Pope.

Demonstrators against the war now increased their shrill attacks against the administration and Radio Hanoi acknowledged their help by broadcasting, "It is clear that the American people's protest movement has become a real second front against United States imperialists on the very soil of America. It is the largest, most stirring, and most organized mass movement in United States history."

In late January and early February air strikes were authorized against sixteen fixed targets in North Vietnam's northeastern quadrant. Again there was piecemeal approval of targets and the previous restrictions remained in effect.

Search and rescue crews did an outstanding job. They were often life insurance for pilots who knew that every possible effort would be made to rescue them. These crews often prevented the communists from exploiting downed pilots either as a source of intelligence or as political hostages. Each pilot who was rescued meant that a replacement need not be trained. It costs hundreds of thousands of dollars to train each jet pilot.

Aerial mining of selected areas of North Vietnam—but not Haiphong's harbor—was approved February 23 because of the increased use of barges and sampans for the transport of men and supplies. The dropping of mines in selected river areas proved their effectiveness, and it is regrettable that North Vietnam's major harbors were also not mined. A-6 Intruder pilots proved adept at this kind of warfare because of the need to make precise drops at night—often in bad weather—on straight-in, low-level passes.

It was now evident to Westmoreland that another major enemy offensive was building up along the demilitarized zone and he instructed his staff to prepare plans for a task force of four United States Army brigades, later reduced to three, with supporting units for deployment to I Corps.

After several damaging attacks against South Vietnamese Army units in the La Vang area in I Corps' southern section, Westmoreland ordered

Army troops to move in under Major General William B. Rosson's command. April 26 the head of the 1st Marine Division turned over responsibilities for the defense of Chu Lai's air base and supply complex to Rosson. This was the first deployment of large Army units to this area. Now the Marines could concentrate farther north where the enemy buildup was most ominous.

There was activity in other areas. Forward Air Controller Captain Hilliard A. Wilbanks had often flown over the Central Highlands near Bao Lac and Di Linh. These small cities, 100 miles northeast of Saigon, were surrounded by rolling, forested countryside with occasional plantations. The Montagnards, or mountain people, were the area's chief inhabitants.

The 23rd South Vietnamese Ranger Battalion and their American advisers sought the North Vietnamese February 24 as Wilbanks flew above to direct accompanying American gunships. The night before the Vietcong had planned an ambush. Local tea plantation workers had been persuaded to help them dig foxholes and bunkers on the hills west of Di Linh in preparation for the attack. The Vietcong decimated one South Vietnamese platoon and killed its American advisers. They set another trap for dusk.

Rangers advanced slowly through the plantation because the low tea bushes offered no protective cover. Wilbanks spotted the trap from above. The enemy was hidden in camouflaged foxholes on the hillsides and he saw that the Rangers were walking into a trap. He quickly warned Army Captain Gary V. Vote on the ground and the pilots of the two gunships just as the hills erupted with enemy fire.

The Vietcong, aware that their trap had been sprung, attacked the Rangers and fired at the planes overhead. Wilbanks fired a white phosphorus rocket toward the center of the enemy to mark them, and the gunships wheeled to attack. One gunship was soon crippled and Wilbanks ordered the other to escort it home. He requested backup, and fighters were en route. He knew he would need their firepower.

Wilbanks spotted movement on the ground. The Vietcong had abandoned their foxholes and, with bayonets and knives, they charged down the slope toward the badly outnumbered Rangers. There seemed scant hope for their survival now that the gunships were gone.

Wilbanks sent a smoke rocket into the middle of the enemy troops, and the Vietcong directed their fire at him and sent a hail of bullets towards his small observation plane. He turned again and sent another smoke rocket at them despite withering return fire. With his last rocket gone, he could have pulled off until the fighters arrived. Instead, he took up his rifle—normally used only for survival on the ground—and pointed the nose of his plane at the enemy troops. He released his airplane's controls and aimed his rifle at the Vietcong through a side window. The light plane careened above the tree tops so he again grabbed the controls to recover and evade the enemy's fire. The Vietcong were caught off-balance. Wilbanks headed towards them again, after inserting another clip in his rifle. Each attack was so close to the ground that his plane was hit repeatedly. His luck ran out on his third rifle-firing pass and the aerial ballet ended as his plane was seriously damaged.

Captain Vote, the Ranger adviser on the ground, had watched Wilbanks' actions as he flew barely 100 feet off the ground. He watched with increasing concern as the plane performed eratically—first up, then down—before banking to the west over his head. He decided the pilot must be wounded and was looking for a friendly place to land. Vote jumped up and waved his arms. But as the plane banked again, he could see that the pilot was unconscious. The plane crashed 300 feet away in no man's land between the two forces.

Captain Vote pulled Wilbanks from his plane and he was still alive as two new gunships attacked the communists. Four times they tried to set down to rescue Wilbanks but each time enemy guns drove them off.

Two fighters appeared and raked the enemy with cannon fire under the direction of another forward air controller who appeared on the scene. At last a helicopter, despite withering ground fire, picked up Wilbanks, but he died en route to base. His unselfish act earned him a posthumous Medal of Honor.

Admiral Sharp continued to insist that mining North Vietnam's ports was the most effective naval operation his fleet could perform. After several previous attempts he sent another message to the Joint Chiefs in February 1967, that such action would drastically reduce North Vietnam's external support. He pointed out that exports were equally vital to Hanoi's strained economy. Haiphong, he said, received 85 percent of North Vietnam's imports. If the port was closed, he said, everything would have to be re-routed through China or off-loaded by barges. He reminded them that the People's Republic of China had refused to permit the Soviets to use China's rail system. They were allies at the time, but they did not trust the Russians. Sharp reminded the Joint Chiefs that China's rail systems were of marginal importance anyway. He said port facilities in North Vietnam offered his command twenty-five lucrative targets besides the gains of mining the waters. His request was again denied.

In Navy attacks against bridges the Walleye Glide Bombs, or Smart bombs, were used effectively. This was a free-fall glide bomb with a thousand pound warhead and a television camera in its nose to track the target. The pilot positioned crosshairs on the preselected point of impact as he headed towards a target. Pilots liked the bombs because they could release at a distance from a target and the bomb would glide to it and often hit it with pinpoint accuracy. Smaller bridges were easily destroyed, but the larger ones proved too sturdy for that size of bomb.

The F-105 Thunderchief was designed as a nuclear strike fighter-bomber for the United States Air Force but it was limited in air-to-air combat. Despite this shortcoming it was widely used over North Vietnam as strike aircraft and Wild Weasels that attacked SAM sites. In circumventing North Vietnam's ground defenses, it was ideal because it could break the sound barrier at low level and streak at more than twice the speed of sound at high altitudes. It was an all-weather plane that could carry six tons of ordnance—some in an internal bombbay. Once a crew was alerted by a hostile radar signal—a rattlesnake-like tone and a bright blip on their warning radar scope—they immediately attacked by unleashing a radar-homing, air-to-ground missile from a comparatively safe distance, or by diving directly over the site to drop conventional bombs. An experienced North Vietnamese missile crew could decoy Wild Weasels by sending all the electronic indications of a SAM launch without actually firing a missile. With a plane's warning scope cluttered with many threat indications, the Weasels could never be sure where and when the next SAM would be fired. The pilot and his countermeasures operator had constantly to scan the horizon in all directions to determine if deadly "telephone" poles (SAM missiles resembled them in size and length) were rising to meet them so the pilot could pull his aircraft into a violent maneuver to evade the missile. A crew's biggest fear was that a SAM would be fired from directly behind and streak in unnoticed to send a lethal blast through the Weasel bird. Flak and SAM suppression efforts were vital to spare the bombers, but the job was inherently dangerous. Weasels deliberately flew within North Vietnam's defenses to force enemy gunners and missile crews to commit themselves. Meanwhile, MIG interceptors were waiting to sneak in with their air-to-air missiles or cannon. As a result, each Weasel mission involved death-defying risks to protect the main strike force.

Nicknamed the Thud, F-105s were based in Thailand and had to refuel—sometimes as many as three times—in order to strike deep into North Vietnam's heartland in the Red River Valley. Fortunately its superior speed permitted it to outrun the MIGs and, if warned in time, it could turn into an approaching missile and evade it.

Northwest of Hanoi was a range of mountains that soon became famous as "Thud Ridge." It was an easily recognizable checkpoint for navigation, and a natural shield that protected the F-105s from the valley's bristling defenses. F-105s, hit by flak or SAMs, often crashed on the mountain's slopes.

A flight of F-105s took off from Takhli Royal Thai Air Force Base March 10, 1967, with Captain Merlyn Hans Dethlefsen in the number three position of a four-plane formation as part of the strike force. They were headed for the Thai Nguyen steel mill and an industrial complex in a valley forty miles north of Hanoi and seventy miles from the Chinese border. This target had only recently been approved for attack.

After a flight of 500 miles, they were directed to knock out the ground defenses that ringed the target. Normally, these pilots tried to deliver on one pass and then pull off at maximum power with violent evasive maneuvers, and head for home. Those who tried to make a second run rarely lived to tell about it. Dethlefsen and his wingman were nearly a mile behind the first element when he lost sight of his leader in intense flak. The number two plane broke hard to the right and Dethlefsen followed with his wingman Major Kenneth Bell. A moment later he heard a parachute beeper signal on his emergency radio confirming that the lead crew had ejected from their crippled aircraft. The leader's wingman now reported that his plane was badly damaged, and he would try to escape.

Dethlefsen took command of the flight. He was still ahead of the strike force and they were vulnerable. The suppression job remained because the lead aircraft's missile had not scored. He decided to stay in the target area and circle as he studied the flak pattern. He realized he could not avoid all the flak so he sought the less-intense areas. He knew by the flak's intensity that this must be a vital target.

Dethlefsen and his backseater Captain Kevin "Mike" Gilroy had located the SAM site on the first pass. The pilot now spotted two MIG 21s closing from the rear. He quickly fired his radar-seeking missile at the site and veered sharply as the MIGs triggered missiles. He broke to the right, diving through the flak. He figured this maneuver would be his best chance to evade the heat-seeking missiles and the MIGs' guns. He did not believe the MIGs would follow through their own flak, and they did not.

It was standard procedure under MIG attack to jettison your ordnance, engage the afterburner and head for the treetops where the "Thud" could outrace the interceptors. In a dogfight, the Thud was no match for a MIG. With the flak-suppression job still unfinished, he decided to hang on to his ordnance. He positioned his plane for another pass, meanwhile evading two more MIG 21s with a tight break to the left.

Now an anti-aircraft shell hit his plane, jolting the Thud with a direct hit. The flight controls and engines still responded so he carried on. He learned later that chunks of shrapnel had torn through the bottom of his plane's fuselage and damaged his left wing tip without hitting vital systems. He received permission from the mission's leader to stay over the target and turned back towards the SAM site. By now the main strike force was already leaving the target. The steel mill had proved too big to knock out on one strike but Dethlefsen decided to get that troublesome SAM site today before it got him.

Manuevering around a flak pattern, he spotted another site dead ahead so he squeezed off a missile and the site's radar shut down.

Smoke and dust from the bombed targets drifted over the defensive positions on the ground as Dethlefsen strived to locate the original SAM site. When he could not see it, he went down on the deck for a closer look.

Throughout these maneuvers, his wingman Bell stuck to him like glue despite hits by anti-aircraft fire and by the MIGs. With a damaged aileron, Bell could only turn to the right as he went down the chute once more. This time Dethlefsen dropped bombs squarely on the missile site. He followed that up with a pass using his 20 mm. cannons. He noted with satisfaction as he pulled off that the site was burning.

In recognition of his bravery, he was awarded a Medal of Honor.

The first woman Marine to arrive in a combat theater was Sergeant Barbara J. Dulinsky who was assigned to Bien Hoa Air Force Base March 18, 1967. The next morning she journeyed by bus to Saigon with an armed escort through thirty miles of enemy-infested countryside for duty with the Military Assistance Command. Most Army and Marine women were assigned to the command's personnel section but they often had to go out into the field for on-the-spot audits of records. Eventually thirty-six women Marines served in the combat theater.

Other women followed her pioneering assignment but the majority were nurses—Army nurses. The war in Vietnam was fought largely with small arms and traps so multiple wounds were common, often of the most mutilating types, and nurses found their onerous work almost impossible to bear.

Other Army, Navy and Air Force nurses served in evacuation duties and often went along with doctors into villages to help civilians as part of medical teams.

Army units were moved from South Vietnam's central and southern sections to I Corps' border with the demilitarized zone. A further increase in military activity in April prompted Westmoreland to send additional troops to I Corps' southern section to permit Marine units to move farther north adjacent to the demilitarized zone.

President Johnson wrote Ho Chi Minh again April 6, and expressed his disappointment with his earlier request to get peace talks started.

A spring air offensive had been approved by President Johnson in February to include attacks against power plants, the mining of rivers—but not harbors—and some relaxation of restrictions on air raids near Hanoi and Haiphong.

In March, Westmoreland asked for 200,000 more troops for a total of 671,616. The Joint Chiefs forwarded his request to McNamara and the president and called for mobilization of the reserves. They also proposed extending the war into Laos and Cambodia and possibly North Vietnam.

In response to the troop request, Johnson said, "When we add divisions, can't the enemy add divisions? If so, where does it all end?"

In one of the largest raids of the spring, Haiphong was left without lights on the night of April 20 when strike and fighter jets from two carriers attacked a power plant a mile northwest of the city, and another facility two miles east of it. Together the two plants produced nearly 14 percent of the national power capacity. Navy pilots encountered anti-aircraft fire that became extremely heavy on these strikes, the closest made to the port city.

Major Leo K. Thorsness and his backseater Captain Harold E. Johnson led four Thuds toward the North Vietnamese border from Thailand April 19. They headed for Xuan Mai, an Army barracks on the edge of the Red River delta where rice paddies gave way to forested mountains. Approaching the target, Thorsness climbed to a higher altitude to let somebody shoot at them. Once the gun and missile installations were located they would go lower to attack them. He likened the tactic to trolling for sharks in a canoe.

The familiar rattlesnake tone sounded in Thorsness's ears at the same time flickering strobes appeared on Johnson's scope. This eerie rattlesnake sound signaled that the missile crews were homing in on a target. The sound grew louder as they flew deeper into North Vietnam. Although their warning gear could detect a SAM's tracking and guidance radar, this was no guarantee that a missile was being launched. Thorsness respected the lethal SAMs but he knew that by turning into one as it was accelerating it could be avoided—most of the time. SAM IIs were another matter. They had proximity fuses and even if one exploded near your aircraft the blast would toss you upside down just by passing in your vicinity. Most of the time you could see the forty-foot-long, three-foot-wide SAMs. In this case, they could be avoided by pointing the nose of your plane directly at it to see where it was headed. Once the missile committed itself at high speed it was difficult for it to change course. SAMs were always a threat at high altitudes but even if they did not shoot you down a large concentration could force your plane to a lower altitude where conventional anti-aircraft guns were a problem.

Thorsness and his backseater scanned the ground at frequent intervals hoping to spot a SAM rising from its pad in a cloud of dust. Otherwise they hoped to locate the missile while there was still time to avoid it with a desperation maneuver.

Thorsness ordered two of his planes north of Xuan Mai as he and the other pilot headed south. This was done to force the ground gunners to divide their attention. He maneuvered his plane toward a strong signal and fired one of his radar-seeking Shrike missiles. The target was seven miles away and obscured by haze so he did not see it hit. The abrupt disappearance of the enemy signal, on whose beam the missile guided itself, indicated that it might have done its job. He picked a second site visually and rolled into a diving attack through a curtain of anti-aircraft fire. He pickled off his cluster bombs and pulled out of a steep dive.

Thorsness's plane thundered across the tree tops, giving him the best chance to survive, but his wingman was in trouble. Thomas Madison's plane had been hit and Thorsness told him to head for the hills to the west but Madison's beeper later indicated that he and his backseater, Thomas Sterling, had already bailed out. During this tragedy in the sky Thorsness fired another Shrike missile at a third SAM site.

To the north, the other two planes in the flight had encountered MIGs but both had survived. However, one plane's afterburner refused to light and without its added thrust the plane could not sustain the high speed necessary to outrun its attackers. Both planes continued to fight off two more MIG attacks as they turned south towards their base in Thailand. Now Thorsness's plane was the only Thud left in the Xuan Mai area.

He circled Madison's and Sterling's descending parachutes while he relayed information to the rescue aircraft. Spotting a MIG off his left wing, Thorsness feared the MIG pilot might attack the men in their parachutes. He dropped his plane down a thousand feet and headed towards the MIG—ending up on its tail practically driving up its tailpipe at more than 600 miles an hour. At 3,000 feet he opened up with his 20 mm. cannon, but missed. He attacked again and while triggering more cannon blasts Johnson in the rear seat yelled that there were MIGs on their tail. Thorsness continued to fire at the MIG in front until the plane blew up. Low on gas, Thorsness turned his plane south to pick up the tanker. Now he heard that prop-driven A-1 Sandys were on the scene to direct the rescue helicopters picking up the downed Weasel crew.

He was refueled by an aerial tanker and, with full tanks, but only 500 rounds of ammunition, he flew north again. He quickly briefed the Sandy pilots about defenses around Xuan Mai, and then spotted three communist interceptors. One MIG flew right into his gunsight's crosshairs at 2,000 feet and his guns tore the aircraft to pieces.

Johnson warned him that four MIGs were closing from the rear and Thorsness dove for the deck, thus eluding his pursuers, as his Thud raced through mountain passes with his afterburners blazing.

The MIGs turned back to attack the slow Sandys. Thorsness radioed, "Okay, Sandy One. Just keep that machine of yours turning and they can't get you." He was low on fuel again and out of ammunition but Thorsness turned toward the MIGs with only one idea—to get them to attack his plane. He knew the Sandys were sitting ducks for MIGs.

But a flight of F-105s arrived and now the MIGs were on the defensive.

Thorsness finally turned towards his rendezvous with the tanker as flames and smoke rose high above the target. He could see them for forty miles.

After Thorsness refueled again he was still not satisfied. A Sandy had been shot down and the rescue effort for Madison and Sterling had been called off. He learned later that both had been captured. At the time, however, he faced a crucial decision. When he heard a fellow Thud pilot call that he was in trouble, Thorsness did not hestitate. "Leo," the other pilot called. "I'm not with the rest of the flight, and I don't know where I am. I've only got 800 pounds of fuel. What should I do?"

Thorsness knew it was not unusual to get lost in battle and he knew it was up to him to help the pilot. He sent the tanker north toward the lost pilot and the rendezvous was successful. Thorsness again was low on fuel and he continued south toward the nearest recovery base at Udorn, Thailand. He knew if he could get to "The Fence"—the Mekong River— that he could coast across. With seventy miles to travel, he pulled the power back to idle and glided in. His fuel gauges were indicating empty when the runway came up in front of him and he landed long.

His bravery was acknowledged with a Medal of Honor.

President Johnson's approval of attacks above the 20th parallel against targets in North Vietnam were limited because important targets within thirty miles of Hanoi were still off-limits.

Even in late spring, when more targets close to Hanoi were released, and transportation targets were hit heavily, there were still too many strategic targets that could not be attacked. Now would have been the time to release all targets advocated by Seventh Air Force General Momyer and Admiral Sharp. Such attacks should have been made two years earlier but it was still not too late to go all out to end the war by destroying North Vietnam's power complexes, communications network, and the factories that produced war materiel. Her harbors should have been mined but this request was again rejected because McNamara and his staff, and President Johnson, were concerned about getting more deeply involved in the conflict. For those fighting in Vietnam, it was all-out war. So, the war went on, with no end in sight.

Following the attacks on military targets in Haiphong and other cities Hanoi Radio denounced raids on so-called "populated areas" and claimed that over 1,872 planes had been destroyed. The extent of their concern was manifest even with this limited air campaign when they called on the "peace-loving and justice-loving countries in the world to condemn energetically the United States aggressive war in Vietnam and take timely action to stay the United States war criminals' hands."

After a raid March 11, Radio Hanoi reported the capture of a number of American "pirates." One, they said, was captured in Hai Duong Province at noon while rice farmers were weeding, but had their rifles with them. The radio report said militia men and women quickly fanned out in combat formation when airplanes were heard in the distance and they heard the firing of nearby anti-aircraft batteries. Militiawoman Pham Thi Diem supposedly ran in the direction of one plane that streaked towards the ground in flames. When she spotted a white parachute she shouted to the others to follow, despite a swarm of American planes that she feared would try to rescue the American pilot.

As the parachute neared the ground another militiawoman, Nguyen Thi Van, rushed toward the American, shouting, "Hurry up, comrades, this way!"

The communist report said the American pilot dropped into a pond and Diem, according to Radio Hanoi, waded in holding her gun towards the pilot. She signaled him to surrender, saying in Vietnamese, "Give up and you'll be spared. I'll bring you down if you resist." She said the American was trembling as he saw the fierce look of his captress and joined his hands to seek mercy and slowly raised both arms.

Meanwhile, Nguyen Thi Van brought a rope as others arrived and the pilot was tied up and taken prisoner. Only then, the report said, did Diem and Van notice that their captive stood at least a head taller than they were.

The Foreign Ministry of the Democratic Republic of Vietnam said on March 10 and 11 that United States aircraft had launched many attacks against the town and steel complex of Hai Nguyen, the town of Hon Gai, and a number of industrial establishments in Quang Ning and Ha Sac Provinces, and had fired missiles at populous areas in Haiphong City. The statement said many civilians were killed or wounded and many houses were destroyed. In one town, it was said a kindergarten and a parish church were completely destroyed and many children and Catholic believers were either killed or wounded. The attacks were labeled as an extremely brazen escalation step—an utterly inhuman crime perpetrated by the United States imperialists against the Vietnamese people.

This was clever propaganda, but it was not true. Certainly some civilians were killed in these attacks, but North Vietnam's strong condemnation indicated their intense concern that, if continued, such attacks might have a devastating effect on their war effort.

Radio Hanoi frequently read so-called letters from American fliers who were prisoners saying that many pilots were refusing to fly missions and were courtmartialed because they would not use cluster bombs and napalm which they called barbarous weapons, against schools, hospitals and children. They actually used the names of prisoners who supposedly confessed. There was no truth to these allegations, but some prisoners were tortured and "confessed" to crimes under extreme duress.

Westmoreland appealed to South Vietnamese government officials again in May that the nation's manpower be mobilized for war. Although a partial mobilization was authorized in the fall, no legislation was approved to enforce mobilization. There was general dissatisfaction with militia life and tolerance by military and civilian authorities towards desertion made a mockery of mobilization plans.

Early in 1967 Westmoreland had approved withdrawal of all American funds for unproductive and ineffective Vietnamese army units. One of the most unsatisfactory policies of the Vietnamese armed forces was the officer-commissioning system that emphasized formal education, thereby eliminating potential leadership ability in the enlisted ranks. The Military Assistance Command continued to urge that deserving enlisted men be commissioned from the ranks. Steps were finally taken to consider those who had served two years in the grade of corporal first class or better.

Improvements were evident in 1967 in South Vietnam's armed forces and a tenth infantry division was activated and other support units were formed. Desertions remained high, and Westmoreland knew that performance in the field was the only gauge by which their training's effectiveness could be judged.

The first Navy strikes of the war against MIG bases were launched April 24 with a series of attacks on Kep airfield, thirty-seven miles northeast of Hanoi. A-6 Intruders from the *Kitty Hawk* hit the runway, control tower and maintenance and support buildings. The airfield had 20 MIGs out of an estimated 120 in North Vietnam.

In the largest combined strike of the month during the next two days Navy jets from three carriers faced heavy SAM, MIG and anti-aircraft fire to blast a cement plant at Haiphong and nearby ammunition and petroleum storages. The plant was a major manufacturer of construction products used by North Vietnam to build military installations. After the raids one pilot said kiddingly, "If they had cement made, they could have shoveled what was left into a bag."

With good weather in May, and four carriers on station, more than 3,100 missions were launched. This effort was directed mainly against electrical power sources and MIG airfields, with repeated strikes against the thermal power plants. At Kep, on the first of the month, eight MIGs were destroyed on the ground and two shot down in the air.

Ellsworth Bunker replaced Ambassador Lodge May 1 when United States involvement was at its peak. His appointment was expected to be brief but it lasted six years. Throughout his tenure as ambassador to South Vietnam Bunker supported the policies of both President Johnson and President Nixon, thereby earning him the enmity of war critics.

Bunker entered government service after years in private business. A wealthy Ivy Leaguer, he had been introduced to public service by President Truman in 1951, serving first as ambassador to Argentina and then in a number of other important diplomatic posts. His ambassadorship of South Vietnam proved to be the most trying of all.

Long after the war Bunker acknowledged that these policies failed because of self-imposed United States restrictions and the lack of public support. He said publicly, "To try to fight a limited war with limited objectives and, by inference, limited in time because we are an impatient people, against an adversary whose objectives are unlimited and who has the means or is given the means to wage unrestricted warfare—this is not a viable policy."

CHAPTER 22

"What Will I Tell the President?"

MAJOR GENERAL JOSEPH A. MCCHRISTIAN, WESTMORELAND'S CHIEF OF intelligence, forwarded an estimate of communist troop strength in May that totaled 500,000. The figure had been acquired from Army intelligence sources, and the Central Intelligence Agency. It included the Vietcong's self-defense militia because some intelligence personnel believed they had caused 40 percent of American casualties. Although the militia included older men, women and children they had always been counted in the past, dating back to the years of the French occupation.

Colonel Gains B. Hawkins personally briefed Westmoreland about the new figures. Westmoreland was upset because he had estimated that communist troop strength in South Vietnam was around 300,000. He asked, "What will I tell the president? What will I tell the Congress? What will be the reaction of the press to these high figures?" Hawkins testified at General Westmoreland's post-war libel trial against the Columbia Broadcasting System in early 1985, after the network had charged the general with deceiving the Johnson administration, that Westmoreland had said that this higher figure was "politically unacceptable."

At this same trial, McChristian testified that Westmoreland refused to forward the higher enemy troop estimates and that he had imposed a ceiling of 300,000. He said Westmoreland had ordered that the Vietcong militia be dropped from the rolls because they included old men and women and pre-teen boys with no military capability.

The higher figure proved more accurate during the 1968 Tet offensive. Most disturbing of all, intelligence analysts shamefully confessed under oath that they had helped to write what they regarded as a fraudulent estimate of enemy troop strength.

While Air Force General William W. Momyer and Admiral Sharp continued to call for air strikes against all targets in North Vietnam, President Johnson and his secretary of state were advocating a bombing halt as a step toward the initiation of peace negotiations. McNamara continued to be negative on the subject of bombing North Vietnam, citing as proof the so-called failures of bombing in World War II and in Korea, a subject about which he knew little.

In mid-June, 1967, word was sent to Admiral Sharp that McNamara and other Washington officials planned to attend a conference in Saigon in early July. General Wheeler, chairman of the Joint Chiefs of Staff, advised Sharp that this meeting would determine the future of the Rolling Thunder bombing campaign. He said he and the Chiefs still believed in it, but they faced a determined McNamara who wanted to stop bombing above the 20th parallel. Sharp informed his component commanders that he would present his views to McNamara on the importance of the air campaign against North Vietnam and that he expected them to support his views. He reminded them that they needed to emphasize continuance of the campaign. To each commander he forwarded a summary of the views that he would present, saying that the air defense situation in North Vietnam had improved in their favor, and that there were indications of delays in getting materiel through North Vietnam's ports causing military supplies to pile up. His comments stressed that attacks had made inroads in North Vietnam's rolling stock and truck inventories, and that power shortages were progressively interfering with North Vietnam's industrial activity. He asked Vice Admiral John J. Hyland, commander of the 7th Fleet, and General Momyer who headed the Seventh Air Force to be prepared to amplify his analysis, pointing out their successes with armed reconnaissance along the northeastern railroad network since the first of May. He stressed that statistics were essential to prove their case that he termed was crucial to the war effort.

Sharp made a special trip to Saigon June 28 to hold a planning session with Westmoreland, Hyland and Momyer. After reviewing their presentations, he found them inadequate and insisted that they redo them. He told Westmoreland, "And Westy, I don't want any screwed up things from you. I want you to support it, too." He also pointed out to Westmoreland the importance he attached to his participation in all preliminary meetings so he would be knowledgeable about the briefings that Sharp planned to give.

Sharp returned to his headquarters in Honolulu. With the Saigon conference scheduled for July 7 he returned two days early, stressing again to his commanders that the meeting was vital to continuation of Rolling Thunder.

Sharp and his top officials met with McNamara and a delegation from the State and Defense Departments and the Joint Chiefs July 7, 1967, to start the two-day conference. In reviewing the bombing campaign, Sharp said that since January, 1966, he had been recommending an air campaign centered around attacks against vital target systems in the North marked by a sufficient weight of effort to convince North Vietnam's officials that their aggression was not worthwhile compared to the damage they were suffering. He reminded the conferees that his command had been authorized to strike North Vietnam's petroleum stocks since June of 1966, but that the communists had been forewarned and had dispersed their stocks. He said that bombing strikes had not been as effective as they would have been if the attacks had caught them by surprise. He reminded them that in February, 1967, six basic target systems had been approved for attacks including power plants, ports, airfields, transportation systems, military complexes and war-supporting industries. He admitted that bad weather had reduced the potential impact of such raids but that by April the weather over North Vietnam had improved and they had received permission to bomb all six target systems. He said that nine of the ten newly authorized targets had been hit by May 1, five of them more than once. With continuing favorable weather, Sharp said that ten additional targets had been authorized and that by mid-May the bombing campaign was putting greater strain on North Vietnam's government than ever before.

Sharp decried the reaction of Washington's officials who had responded to communist outcries and imposed restrictions on his command May 23 against targets within ten miles of Hanoi after command aircraft had successfully attacked a vital Hanoi thermal power plant three days earlier. He claimed that his command had been forced to remove the pressure against the communists just when they were being hurt.

Sharp concluded his remarks by saying that the sector within ten miles of Hanoi was North Vietnam's most important support area and militarily vital to them. "Our continued failure to strike decisively in that area gives them a virtual sanctuary from which to operate." He highlighted the fact that changes in enemy resistance were due to the thirty enemy fighters destroyed in air combat over the last five weeks. These losses, he said, resulted in their failure now to challenge American planes. Sharp claimed that three airfields had been heavily damaged and that attacks against missile sites and anti-aircraft batteries had reduced their effectiveness and lowered American plane losses. He stressed again that the trend in the air war was in their favor, and that the momentum of air attacks must be maintained. Sharp insisted that imposition of prohibited and restricted zones around cities in North Vietnam—imposed by civilian authorities in the Pentagon—continued to hamper air operations. He emphasized that the majority of important targets—59 percent of the industrial targets— were still off-limits. "To have the greatest impact on the communists," Sharp insisted, "all target systems must be attacked and re-attacked if, like transportation targets, they are repaired." He maintained that it was self-defeating to concentrate on one target system because all must be struck if air strikes were to be effective.

Momyer and Hyland then took over the briefing with summaries of Rolling Thunder in support of Sharp's views. Westmoreland also supported the air campaign but made a strong pitch for more ground troops.

After their presentations, Sharp summarized his remarks by saying that in the past eighteen months his command had flown about 18,000 sorties in the North and another 185,000 in the South, including Laos, and that a large number of vehicles, rolling stock and watercraft had either been destroyed or damaged. He said disruption of the enemy's lines of communication were partially indicated by the number of bridges and ferries destroyed. He admitted that some had been replaced and would need to be hit again. But he said that 86 percent of North Vietnam's power capacity had been destroyed, 30 to 50 percent of war-supporting industries had been disrupted, while 40 percent of major military installations in the North, and all fixed installations in the South, were either destroyed or disrupted. In that period, Sharp said, 81 MIGs had been shot down or destroyed on the ground. He claimed that in North Vietnam's northeastern sector a reliable intelligence source in Hanoi estimated that 30 percent of the war materiel supplied to North Vietnam had been destroyed en route to Hanoi by air strikes. He said that this informant claimed that "the effectiveness of American air action and the seemingly infinite capacity of the Americans to escalate to the degree necessary to overcome any increased support rendered, are the principal causes of the disillusionment among representatives of the Soviet and bloc countries in Hanoi, and their conviction that the North Vietnamese cannot win. They also feel that the problem must be negotiated if the complete destruction of North Vietnam is to be avoided."

Sharp repeated for emphasis that not until late April did Rolling Thunder begin to reach the level of intensity in the northeast quadrant that he considered necessary to do the job. Since late May, he said, maximum effectiveness is not being achieved because of restrictions and the lack of authority to hit the more vital targets. Sharp claimed that restrictions came at a time when two factors were in their favor: first, good weather months and, second, important and perhaps decisive changes in the enemy's capability to defend himself. He charged that a momentum had been established that was now endangered. "To retrench ever further and limit our attacks to the south of the 20th parallel will have adverse and, I believe, disastrous effects. War-supporting industries in the North would be brought back to maximum output. Morale of our own forces would decline while that of the enemy would be greatly enhanced. It would allow North Vietnam to operate out of a virtual sanctuary with complete freedom to move supplies to the South without damage.

"We are at an important point in this conflict and an incisive air campaign, including sustained attacks in the northeast quadrant against all target systems would assure interrelated effects against the enemy's military, political, economic and psychological posture. There is ample evidence that the enemy is hurting. I consider it essential that we continue this effective, successful air campaign."

His recommendations included: closing of Haiphong Harbor to deep-water shipping by bombing and/or mining, destruction of the six basic target systems, deletion of Hanoi's ten-nautical mile prohibited zone, reduction in Hanoi's restricted area to ten nautical miles and mining of inland waterways.

At the conclusion of the conference, McNamara said, "General West-moreland that was a fine presentation." He pointedly ignored Admiral Sharp.

The next morning Sharp told General Wheeler, "Goddamn it. I'm getting sick and tired of that son-of-bitch making a comment like that to Westy when I'm the senior officer present and I have made a presentation and he didn't say a word to me."

"Oley," Wheeler replied, "he was furious at you. He came out here to stop the bombing above 20 degrees and you made it impossible for him to go back and say that everyone agreed."

Sharp understood. He knew from past experience that McNamara frequently wrote his report on the way out, and used these presentations to justify his report. McNamara would have cut off Rolling Thunder if anybody had agreed with him. But now he could not report a consensus to stop the bombing campaign.

Although McNamara refused to permit attacks against all targets on the list of ninety-four approved by the Joint Chiefs, he did not urge President Johnson to stop the bombing. However, he refused to close the ports, and targets within the prohibited areas in Hanoi and Haiphong remained off-limits.

President Johnson approved the additional troop deployments that Westmoreland had sought at the conference.

Despite McNamara's views, Sharp and Wheeler continued to press for attacks against North Vietnam's airfields—especially the one at Phuc Yen—the site of North Vietnam's main operational air base. They stressed that aircraft losses to MIGs and SAMs were on the increase and they urged him to protect Air Force and Navy pilots by destroying North Vietnam's air defenses. Otherwise, they said, they would continue to lose pilots and planes unnecessarily.

In late July, McNamara was informed by Senator John C. Stennis that the Preparedness Subcommittee of the Senate's Armed Services Committee intended to conduct extensive hearings in August into the conduct of the air war against North Vietnam. He was informed that he would be expected to testify, along with the nation's top military leaders. Sharp was one of those asked to testify. The committee was known for its hardline views and its sympathies for the military services. Committee members had long defended airpower advocates in the services against what they called unskilled civilian amateurs in the Defense Department. Stennis, and most committee members, viewed bombing restraints as an irrational shackling of a major instrument that could help to win victory in Southeast Asia. With more than half a million troops in South Vietnam, and a war costing $2 billion a month and no clear end in sight, their patience with the restrained bombing campaign was wearing thin.

Sharp appeared before the committee and went over some of the material that he had presented at the Saigon conference. He said recent air strikes against military and economic targets had resulted in a major increase in the level of damage inflicted on North Vietnam. He claimed air strikes had caused widespread disruption of economic activity, and that over 500,000 people were engaged in repairing damage to North Vietnam's lines of communication. Sharp claimed that port congestion at Haiphong was so heavy that some large cargo ships had taken sixty days to turn around. Railroad traffic, he said, had been seriously disrupted. He estimated that seven thousand enemy anti-aircraft weapons had been installed in North Vietnam to counter their air strikes, and 40 percent were in the Hanoi/Haiphong area. Sharp estimated that there were over sixty MIG 15s and MIG 17s, and fifteen to twenty MIG 21s in North Vietnam. Most, he said, were based in South China and flown in daily since North Vietnam's airfields at Kep and Hoa Lac had been attacked. He reported that the earlier restrictions imposed by McNamara were still in effect.

Sharp concluded his remarks by saying, "The best way to persuade the ruling elements in North Vietnam to stop the aggression is to make the consequence of not stopping readily and ever more painfully apparent."

Under questioning, Sharp admitted that after the committee hearings had been announced he had received permission to strike various targets that he had been requesting for months.

The senators made quite a point of the timing.

McNamara was the final witness August 25. He took issue with the military view of air warfare, and defended the bombing campaign as being carefully tailored to limited objectives in Southeast Asia, primarily the routes of infiltration. "The bombing of North Vietnam has always been considered a supplement to and not a substitute for an effective counter-insurgency land and air campaign in South Vietnam. The bombing campaign has been aimed at selected targets of military significance, primarily the routes of infiltration." In this light, he said, the bombing had been successful.

The subcommittee issued its report August 31, 1967, and castigated the administration for its conduct of the bombing campaign, and for not deferring to the authority of professional military judgments instead of McNamara's civilian analysts. The report advocated an escalated pressure against North Vietnam.

The report caused a furor by exposing a rift within the administration. President Johnson called an unscheduled news conference September 1 to deny differences among his advisers, and generally over-ruled his Secretary of Defense on bombing strategy.

Cam Pha, North Vietnam's third largest port, had been one of the targets that McNamara had specifically counseled against attacking in his testimony. It was struck again September 10.

McNamara's year-end resignation was the only logical course for some-one who found himself so far out of line with administration policy, although he continued to press for his former policies while in office.

In early September the Joint Chiefs asked Sharp for an air plan to attack North Vietnam and they suggested several objectives.

Sharp called Wheeler to tell him that he did not agree with these limited objectives. "What we should do," he said, "is to destroy North Vietnam's economy."

Wheeler was aghast. "Oh God, we can't say that! We just can't say that. We'd be howled at in Washington. We can get the same job. . . . it's not what we say, but what we do that affects the North Vietnamese. And I think we can get it done without raising all this hullaballoo."

Wheeler's words gave Sharp an indication of what to expect. He was disturbed by the chairman's words because this was the first time that the Joint Chiefs had failed to support his views.

Sharp responded with a plan that cited three basic tasks: to deny external existence to North Vietnam, destroy in-depth resources within

North Vietnam that contributed to aggression, and to disrupt the movement of men and materiels in South Vietnam and Laos. He sought the mining of three deep-water ports: Haiphong, Cam Pha and Hon Gai. His plan called for destruction of war-supporting industries within Hanoi's and Haiphong's prohibited zones and air strikes against major lines of communication between these two cities.

John Colvin, consul general of the British Mission in Hanoi during 1966 and most of 1967, said long after the war that by September, 1967, the Americans had won the war, and then renounced victory by ending the bombing. Prior to that time he said Hanoi's streets were lined with war materiel from China, some parked outside the British and Canadian missions, but by September there was none at all.

When Colvin returned to England that month he believed that North Vietnam was no longer capable of maintaining itself as an economic unit nor capable of mounting aggressive war against its neighbors. He said the key to the effectiveness of the bombing in 1967 was its consistency that "for the first time allowed the North Vietnamese no time to repair war-making facilities." He said their will had been eroded to near extinction, and that their capacity to wage a major war had been broken by the continued cutting of railroad lines from China and Haiphong to Hanoi and by putting its ports out of action.

In his opinion, Colvin said prompt use of air power against North Vietnam's industrial northeast would have won the war in 1965 and would have spared both sides the agonizingly higher costs of gradualism advocated by McNamara.

In July, Navy carriers had launched an unprecedented barrage of major attacks against North Vietnam's vital northeast industrial sector, hitting railroad yards, petroleum storage yards as well as bridges and transshipment points.

During August targets were released within the buffer zone sanctuary along the border between Red China and North Vietnam. Strikes were made against the Port Wallut naval base, the Long Son railroad bridges, and the Na Phuoc railroad yard. In that month, the Navy lost sixteen aircraft, the highest monthly total of the war.

Throughout August and succeeding months strikes were made against bridges, rail lines and warehouses near Haiphong to isolate the port, although its facilities were not directly struck. On the 14th, a 1,150-foot highway bridge across the Red River, seven miles north of the center of the city, was blasted by A-6 Intruders and A-4 Skyhawks. Flying from the Constellation, they were successful in dropping two spans into the river.

In Washington, Senator Stuart Symington was one of many of his colleagues who viewed the rising cost of the Vietnam war with alarm. A supplemental budget request for fiscal year 1967 was submitted to the Congress by President Johnson June 24 for $12¼ billion. McNamara stoutly defended the budget when he was questioned about the unusual increase in the use of supplementary budgets. "The main reason is we are fighting a war and they aren't [meaning other departments] and it is absolutely impossible for us to predict the actions of our enemy twenty-one months in advance."

Although the fiscal year 1968 budget was prepared using different guidelines, there was need for another supplemental budget later in 1967. In size, however, it was approximately one-third that of the supplementals for fiscal years 1966 and 1967. Evidently congressmen were too resigned or frustrated to protest very much.

The Army emerged from the conflict with a reasonably good reputation with Congress. Actually the Department of Defense bore the brunt of ridicule. The general impression among congressmen was that the Army was making every effort to maintain a reasonable degree of financial control while insuring that no commander in the field was deprived of anything that was absolutely necessary to pursue the war.

President Johnson met with Premier Kosygin in Glassboro, New Jersey, June 23, 1967. There, Johnson was informed by Kosygin that he had received a message from the North Vietnamese an hour earlier saying that if the bombing of the North ceased, Hanoi's representatives would talk with officials of the United States.

They met again two days later and Johnson assured the Russian premier that the United States was ready to stop bombing of North Vietnam if private talks were agreed to.

This was no time to let up on the pressure against North Vietnam. Air attacks had hurt her economy but, due to restrictions on targets, her ability to wage war in the South had not seriously been impaired.

During April, May and June most attacks were against waterborne supply vessels and 620 were destroyed or damaged while another 826 targets on shore were hit by naval gunfire.

In the air, MIG losses approximated 50 percent and the North Vietnamese ordered their pilots not to challenge Navy and Air Force fliers. Three of their airfields were knocked out. Later, when the North Vietnamese again called upon its pilots to contest their air space they lost thirty more aircraft in five weeks, while more MIGs were destroyed on the ground.

With continued air attacks North Vietnam was faced with importing more food, and its transportation system could not keep up with demands upon it. Of 3,500 trucks that were destroyed during a previous period, only 2,000 were replaced.

Admiral Sharp reiterated again that "the best way to make Hanoi cease its support of aggression and to convince President Ho Chi Minh to stop his aggression against the South is to impress upon him the consequences if he does not desist. All target systems must be struck. It has been estimated that only 55 tons per day, or 18,000 metric tons per year, are required to support operations in South Vietnam. Even if this amount were tripled it is insignificant compared to the nearly 2 million metric tons entering North Vietnam through the ports, rail lines and roads of Route Package 6 [northeastern North Vietnam]."

He claimed that interdiction in the northeast, instead of in the south, cuts directly into North Vietnam's capability not only to support the aggression, but also to support itself. "Interdicting the imports into North Vietnam, combined with strikes against other vital target systems, particularly the rather limited but important industrial base, is the best way to raise the plateau of pain to a sufficient level to affect the North Vietnamese's will to resist. There is evidence that the Haiphong area is used as a sanctuary for the storage of materiel. Precise attacks against warehouses and storage yards would be the most direct means of preventing safe storage. Mining ports remains the most effective way to reduce maritime imports. Rail lines from China provide a similar example."

Battles in the northern provinces continued with emphasis on the Khe Sanh plateau where the mountainous countryside provided a natural infiltration route for the North Vietnamese. Battles had started late in April when a Marine forward observer party engaged a large enemy force. Evidently the Marines prematurely triggered a major enemy attempt to overrun Khe Sanh. In a series of hard-fought battles Marine units were supported by massive air strikes and artillery and pushed the communists out of the surrounding hills. There were heavy losses on both sides but North Vietnam's 325C Division was so battered that it posed no threat to Khe Sanh for some time.

The action shifted to the eastern part of the demilitarized zone near the town of Con Thien, two miles to the south. A small defensive position on top of a hill ten miles northwest of Dong Ha provided a commanding view of the countryside. It became the anchor for the western end of a barrier extending eastward eight miles to Gio Linh.

In May, the North Vietnamese made repeated attempts to capture or destroy the Marine base at Con Thien. Their attacks were countered by a Marine multi-battalion sweep that developed into a number of fierce small-unit engagements.

The North Vietnamese introduced 152 mm. artillery guns in the fighting during July that could be fired from the demilitarized zone, or even North Vietnam. This was the heaviest artillery they had ever employed, and these guns were immediately attacked by Marine artillery, air strikes and naval gun fire.

The Paul Doumer bridge was almost as important symbolically as it was militarily because it was vital to transport supplies into South Vietnam. It had not been listed for attack, despite pleadings by airmen, until the summer of 1967 when United States leaders permitted attacks against some targets within and near Hanoi. Now the bridge was given a high priority. After numerous attacks failed to destroy the Thanh Hoa bridge, it was decided to use F-105s against the Paul Doumer bridge with 3,000-pound bombs. The job was given to the 355th, 388th and 8th Tactical Fighter wings in Thailand, and the 355th was selected to lead the mission.

Strike pilots set out August 11 with Wild Weasels in front carefully scanning and looking for SAMs and radar-directed anti-aircraft guns as they set out for Hanoi in full sunshine.

As the Air Force planes crossed the Red River, ninety-five miles northwest of Hanoi, speed was increased. Four minutes prior to bomb release, the formation turned the corner at the northwest end of Thud Ridge, the limestone outcropping that ran northwest from Hanoi. This mountain range provided a region over which one could fly relatively unhampered by ground defenses.

Turning towards the target, puffs of flak appeared around the lead airplanes of the 355th Wing. Now they varied their altitude to confuse the gunners and evade the flak. Some pilots reported MIGs were taking off from Phuc Yen a few miles away. Soon the MIGs were climbing towards them, but it soon became evident they could not catch them before the target. Down below, the bridge stood out like a black snake spanning the brownish, turbulent waters of the Red River. Time was short and a last turn was made to the south and the formations climbed to 13,000 feet for the bombing run. There were four aircraft in each section. A precise point over the ground had been established to start the 45-degree dive angle for the final run and, when it was reached, each aircraft commenced its roll and started down. All aircraft swept down with their engines on afterburners. Each wingman flew formation just off the wing of his leader. Flak grew thicker, and the SAMs started to rise from their launching pads. The bomb run lasted seven seconds—the longest seven seconds in the world with the flak bursting around them. This was the moment of truth.

The flak suppression flight had destroyed a site with seven guns west of the bridge. The first flight leader released his bombs at 8,000 feet and the others followed suit. Speed brakes were retracted and the planes pulled up, making hard left turns to exit down river to the east. These strike pilots now were overflying the Hanoi "Hilton" and their sonic booms were heard by American prisoners of war who thrilled at the sound, knowing what it signified.

One pilot, glancing back, saw a span of the bridge drop into the river. The codeword "Giraffe" was flashed by radio to indicate success.

Now the other wings prepared to attack, and two highway spans were dropped into the water by their bombs.

Lieutenant Colonel Harry W. Schurr, of the 469th Tactical Fighter Squadron, watched as the bombs hit the bridge, and those 3,000 pounders seemed to pop like big orange balls.

Later, photo reconnaissance showed the bridge was out and a span was down. One railroad span, and two highway spans on the northeast side were also destroyed. The damage prevented an average of twenty-six trains per day, with a capacity of 6,000 short tons, from crossing. It was not until October that the bridge was restored to vehicular and rail traffic. Bad weather during the monsoon season prevented further attacks until October 25 when the bridge was again rendered unserviceable with the destruction of two spans—the eastern pier supporting span and the highway deck. It was again serviceable twenty-five days later. Two attacks in December further damaged the bridge, but it was repaired again, and not attacked later due to the bombing halt in April, 1968.

In the August 11 attack only two planes were damaged although Hanoi "Hannah" exaggerated the American losses.

In October, Navy fliers continued the pressure on Haiphong by destroying all three boat yards in the city.

They spent the last two months of the year maintaining the pressure against MIG bases, thermal power plants and lines of communication throughout North Vietnam.

Multi-divisional ground operations were conducted during 1967's first half, marking a turning point in the war. They caused the North Vietnamese temporarily to re-evaluate their tactics and revert to small-scale guerrilla operations. Hundreds of their best troops were killed and many of their base camps were destroyed. Those who survived fell back into Cambodia where they were free from attack.

Americans learned that the war in Vietnam was the most complex their armies had ever fought. There were no front lines, or rear areas for that matter, and communists could be found almost any place. Despite use of the world's most sophisticated weapons in the hands of the 448,800 Americans in Vietnam by July 1, 1967, a highly disciplined and motivated enemy who employed no airpower in the South, little naval support and, during this period, comparatively few mechanized vehicles still managed to fight on because they absolutely refused to accept defeat.

CHAPTER 23

A Hammer and Anvil Operation

THE LAO DONG, OR WORKER'S PARTY, THROUGH ITS CENTRAL OFFICE IN South Vietnam, controlled military and civilian communist operations. Providing the administrative apparatus was the Vietcong's shadow government—the National Liberation Front—but everything was controlled by the Lao Dong's Central Committee in Hanoi.

The previous year the United States had accelerated its buildup of both American and South Vietnamese units so that by 1967 they were ready to take the offensive against enemy troops controlled by their central office at a headquarters near Saigon and in major areas close to the capital such as the Iron Triangle and Vietcong base installations close to the Cambodian border.

In the spring of 1966 an enemy move on the capital had been thwarted and the United States 1st Infantry Division had uncovered large quantities of supplies near the Cambodian border. During June and July of that year American and South Vietnamese divisions had joined forces and defeated the Vietcong's 9th Division, and carried out other successful operations. The 9th suffered such a mauling that it did not return to South Vietnam from Cambodia until the following spring.

After the 9th's disastrous defeat, Westmoreland instructed Lieutenant General Jonathan O. Seaman, head of the II Field Force, to plan an operation against the enemy in northern Tay Ninh Province in early 1967. It was named Junction City and it was designed as a multi-divisional force with a parachute assault capability. It was scheduled to start January 8.

Seaman built up his II Field Force for an invasion of the Iron Triangle, an area bounded on the southwest by the Saigon River, on the east by the Thi Tinh River, and on the north by a line running west from Ben Cat to

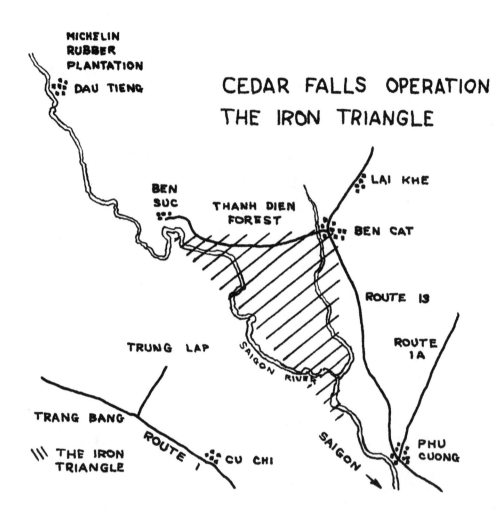

Cedar Falls Operation: the Iron Triangle. *(Drawn by Master Sergeant Bradley A. Spencer, M.C., Ret.)*

the town of Ben Suc. The Iron Triangle had long been a dagger pointed at Saigon only twelve miles away, and it provided the communists with their closest haven to the capital. It was heavily fortified and contained the Vietcong's Region IV headquarters that directed military, political and terrorist activities in the Saigon-Gia Dinh region. Their control permitted the Vietcong to dominate key transportation routes in the surrounding area. Westmoreland had long known it would have to be attacked in force to neutralize it.

During planning meetings in the fall of 1966, Seaman discussed the operation with Westmoreland who suggested a co-ordinated operation with forces on both sides of the Saigon River. Westmoreland envisioned troops moving into position on one side to form an anvil with a rapid movement from the other side to hammer the enemy into submission against the anvil. They discussed the necessity of stripping the entire area to deprive the enemy of concealment.

General Seaman received a call in early December, 1966, from Brigadier General Joseph A. McChristian, assistant chief of staff for the Military Assistance Command's intelligence section, saying he would like to brief him on new data concerning III Corps' tactical zone. Seaman agreed and McChristian came out with several of his officers who had been pouring over voluminous reports, saying they had a good idea where the communist headquarters was located, and its supporting elements. Seaman was impressed, believing they had given him sound information. He told his staff to prepare plans for an operation to seal off the southwest side of the Saigon River and the Iron Triangle to see what could be learned about the enemy's defenses.

He invited Westmoreland to a briefing and he proposed that the Junction City operation be postponed for two reasons. First, he said that he believed his new intelligence information was so good that he had to capitalize on it. Second, he advised Westmoreland that if Junction City was postponed for a month, or a little more, he would have another division available for other important operations when the 9th arrived from the States in early January.

Westmoreland agreed and a new operation, Cedar Falls, was scheduled to start January 8, 1967. II Field Force was ordered to attack the Iron Triangle and the Thanh Dien Forestry Reserve to destroy enemy forces and their installations. The civilian population would first be evacuated, and the Iron Triangle would become a strike zone to preclude its use as a support base for Vietcong operations. The plan called for an attack on the Iron Triangle with all available forces. It would be a hammer and anvil operation using deceptive deployments on seemingly routine operations to pre-position forces. The anvil would be positioned first and then the hammer swung through the Iron Triangle with the area tightly sealed to prevent enemy troops from escaping.

The Thanh Dien forest and the Iron Triangle were known to contain strongly fortified positions with their approach routes mined and booby trapped. There were dense forests and wet rice lands. Vehicle movement, therefore, would be restricted to existing roads and some trails.

Deception tactics included use of the 11th Armored Cavalry Regiment from Xuan Loc, sixty-two miles to the east, and the 173rd Airborne Brigade operating between Ben Cat and Phuoc Vinh. Elements of the 1st Infantry Division would be air transported to complete the seal and invade the area. Numerous small-scale movements were planned under the guise of local operations to position other forces. Strict security was enforced and only a minimum number of people were informed of the operation, and only preliminary air operations were scheduled.

The operation was set for two phases. Units would be positioned on the flanks of the Iron Triangle-Thanh Dien Forestry Reserve January 5–8. D-Day was set for January 8 with air assaults on Ben Suc on the triangle's western terminus. This area would be searched, and, after civilians were evacuated with their possessions, all installations would be destroyed. Phase II would start January 9 with an armored force attacking west from the vicinity of Ben Cat to penetrate the eastern side of the triangle. Simultaneously, air assaults would be ordered for an arc around the Thanh Dien forest from Ben Cat to Ben Suc to complete the encirclement of the northern portion of the triangle. These forces would attack south through the triangle at the confluence of the Saigon and Thi Tinh rivers after all civilians had been evacuated, and then it would be cleared and its tunnels and installations destroyed. This phase was scheduled to last two to three weeks.

The II Field Force had three divisions: the 25th Infantry Division under Major General Frederick C. Weyand, the 1st Infantry Division under Major General William E. De Puy, and the South Vietnamese 5th Infantry Division under Brigadier General Quoc Thuan with supporting air force and navy units.

The 25th Division, with its attached brigade, was positioned along the Saigon River on the southwest leg of the Iron Triangle to conduct search and destroy operations and prevent the North Vietnamese from escaping. Under its control was the South Vietnamese 7th Regiment, 5th Infantry Division. The 1st Infantry Division, and its attached brigade, had a three-fold mission. Prior to D-Day they would position their elements along the Thi Tinh River, conduct search and destroy operations, and assume a blocking position to keep the North Vietnamese from escaping to the east. On D-Day, January 8, one brigade would seal, search and destroy the village of Ben Suc. The third swing-hammer element of this anvil operation was assigned to attack west and south with one brigade through the triangle while another brigade advanced through the Thanh Dien forest. Deception moves began on schedule January 5.

The first contingent of troops was airlifted to their forward base within 500 yards of the Saigon River near its junction with the Thi Tinh River and more than a mile east of Phu Hoa Dong. Some enemy resistance was met on the second day but allied losses were light due to effective air and artillery strikes. The communists withdrew after dark, and this was the only instance where they resisted the intrusion. Two companies of the 2nd Brigade now were anchored on the southeast flank of the 25th Division. To the northwest of this position, the brigade's other two battalions attacked to the northeast from Cu Chi and by nightfall were in position at the edge of the Filhold Plantation 400 yards south of the Saigon River.

To the northwest of the 2nd Brigade's position, the 196th Brigade continued its search of the Ho Bo Woods, uncovering a small quantity of enemy supplies. The anvil now was in position.

Brigadier General John R. Deane, Jr.'s 173rd Airborne Brigade moved into its blocking position along the eastern leg of the Iron Triangle. All that remained now was to position the hammer forces—the 173rd Brigade and the 3rd Brigade of the Big Red One. Deane's men had been airlifted by helicopters from Bien Hoa to Phu Loi and then to the staging area six miles east of the triangle. On D-Day, the 11th Armored Cavalry Regiment under Colonel William W. Cobb came under the operational control of the 1st Division and subsequently under Task Force Deane. Colonel Sidney M. Marks moved his 3rd Brigade to staging areas at Lai Khe and Dau Tieng without incident. The hammer was now raised awaiting D plus one.

To the northwest of the Ho Bo Woods the 1st Division's 2nd Brigade under Colonel James A. Grimsley launched its 1st Battalion, 26th Infantry Regiment, under Lieutenant Colonel Alexander M. Haig by air into the village of Ben Suc. This village had given the Vietcong dominance of the area because it was located in a loop of the Saigon River at the triangle's far northwestern corner. Ben Suc was a fortified supply and political center, and the hub of an area estimated to contain approximately six thousand people. The American commanders were aware that Ben Suc's perimeters were heavily mined and booby trapped so the attack had to be swift and decisive. It had been under enemy control at least since 1964 when a South Vietnamese battalion was driven out, and the Vietcong's central organization was located in Ben Suc at a secret base. Just as the Iron Triangle was the key to Vietcong influence in the Saigon-Gia Dinh area, Ben Suc was the key to Vietcong control of the Iron Triangle. It was essential, therefore, that the village be captured. The civilians and their possessions—including their livestock—were scheduled to be moved out to the government relocation camp at Phu Cuong.

Sixty helicopters zoomed towards Ben Suc in formation with an infantry battalion and another attached company during the early hours of January 8. The villagers were caught by surprise and there was complete confusion as the choppers swooped in and soldiers occupied the village.

At 8:30 A.M. a blocking force landed south of the village to seal its exits. In the first two-and-a-half hours, forty communist troops were killed with only light battalion losses.

After the village was sealed and the troops consolidated their positions, a South Vietnamese battalion was brought in by air to search the village and interrogate its inhabitants. This was the same battalion that had been driven out in 1964. Their search uncovered a number of tunnel and bunker complexes that were destroyed. Under some houses, there were three levels of storage rooms where rice and medical supplies were found in great quantities.

The South Vietnamese were give responsibilities for evacuating the residents, and resentments mounted. The people were told that they could take their water buffalo and almost 6,000 people were evacuated. Some Americans were disturbed as natives and their possessions including chickens, hogs and buffalo waited to be taken to Phu Cuong. To them it was a pitiful sight although they understood the evacuation's necessity. A few South Vietnamese soldiers tried unsuccessfully to get a huge and dangerous water buffalo on a boat. They were chagrined when an eleven-year-old boy talked his animal on board. It soon became obvious that the resettlement phase had not been as well planned as the military operation. As a result, Vietnamese families suffered unnecessary hardships.

Once the villagers were evacuated a systematic demolition of everything was started. Twenty acres of scrub jungle land was found infested with tunnels where Vietcong popped up by the dozens and were quickly captured. Tunnels and homes were systematically destroyed throughout Ben Suc. Finally, a large cavity was scooped out near the center of the area and filled with 10,000 pounds of explosives no longer suitable for normal operations. They were set off in the hope that any undiscovered tunnels in the village would be crushed.

At dawn January 9 units forming the operation's anvil were maneuvered into final position following the successful occupation of Ben Suc. Meanwhile, the hammer forces of the 1st Infantry Division, including its own 3rd Brigade and Task Force Deane, initiated their assault at 8:00 A.M. with simultaneous attacks across the Iron Triangle and into the forestry reserve. The hammer's impact against the communist forces was poised to strike.

The 1st Infantry Division's 3rd Brigade was assigned airmobile assaults with five battalions into the forest to evacuate its inhabitants and to destroy enemy installations.

Extensive air and artillery strikes were made in preparing the first landing zone at the northernmost point of a ring of men and weapons soon to be formed around the forest. The 3rd Brigade, and the 1st Battalion under Lieutenant Colonel William C. Simpson, were flown out first aboard sixty helicopters and all landed safely within five minutes against mild enemy reaction. As darkness fell that night, defensive positions were established by the five combat battalions within the forest.

At 8:00 A.M. that same morning the 11th Armored Cavalry Regiment attacked west from their staging area near Ben Cat. After securing the bridge across the Thi Tinh River, the regiment headed for its objectives four miles to the west. Two hours later, the Blackhorse Regiment had penetrated the entire width of the Iron Triangle from east to west and had severed it from the Thanh Dien Forestry Reserve on the north, meeting only light resistance.

By the next day, the 25th Division's anvil forces were in their final blocking position and were searching the Saigon River's west bank and destroying enemy installations.

The entire operation was characterized by small-unit actions as allied forces proceeded into the Iron Triangle and the Thanh Dien forest as the hammer continued to swing toward the anvil.

General Seaman sent messages to the commanding generals of the 1st and 25th Divisions. After congratulating them on achieving surprise and the results revealed so far, he said, I want a thorough search of the entire area. "I particularly desire that the Iron Triangle be completely covered." This was done sixteen days later and large supply caches were uncovered, and everything was stripped from the countryside that might be of value to the enemy. Seaman was surprised that there had been no organized defense or counter-attacks.

New jungle-clearing techniques, using dozer-infantry teams, combined with the use of acetylene torches and tunnel demolitions with high explosives, was credited for much of their success. M-48 medium tanks were equipped with bulldozer blades and they proved very effective. Their heavy armor protected crews from most mines, booby traps and snipers. Another innovation was the "Rome Plow"—a large tractor for heavy duty land clearing that had a curved blade with a protruding, sharply honed lower edge that was curved to one side to form a spike for splitting trees too large to cut with the blade alone, although the blade could slice through a tree three feet in diameter. Bars on top of the blade forced trees away from the tractor and a "headache" bar over the operator's position protected him from falling debris. Some Rome Plows were modified with light armor for further operator protection. They were used in conjunction with infantry troops to cut through enemy-infested jungle. Often a formation of two tankdozers was used at the "point" followed by two others abreast, with two more as a cleanup team to remove cut vegetation. They were most effective on search and destroy operations. During contact with the enemy the men in the vehicles provided their own fire support until infantry troops could move forward to silence the enemy. Their use helped infantry troops who, without tankdozers, would have been forced to clear trails by hand—a lengthy operation that the dozers performed in minutes.

General Seaman realized, despite the operation's success, that the three to four weeks planned for completion was inadequate and that only strategic roads and landing zones could be cleared in addition to the wide swaths made by his mechanized forces. Actually, only 7 to 8 percent of the triangle's sixty-three square miles was cleared.

Extensive tunnel systems were found throughout the Iron Triangle-Thanh Dien Forestry Preserve. Troops were forced to flush out the Vietcong with tunnel rats or riot control agents. Smoke was often used to locate air holes and tunnel entrances. If the Vietcong could not be driven out of their tunnels, they were sealed and destroyed inside. A tunnel rat team had six to ten men led by an officer or a non-com. Sketches were drawn of the underground complexes from information relayed by team members within the tunnels. The lead element of a tunnel rat team usually was armed with a pistol equipped with a silencer (to fire in a tunnel without a silencer was to risk broken eardrums). Poor communications, and lack of fresh air, were always a problem so air compressors with blower attachments were used to force fresh air into the tunnels. Tunnel rats had a difficult job. It was hot and dirty work and they were soon gasping for air with their bodies squeezed through shallow openings while crawling on all fours, never knowing whether the tunnel might collapse or what might be found around the next turn. Tunnel rats were a special breed—modern combat spelunkers who gained valuable intelligence information.

Flame throwers, normally used to destroy windrows of trees and brush, proved effective in tunnels and against bunkers. They not only reduced the amount of oxygen in tunnels, but their hot flames had a psychological impact on the communists and terrified them.

The Vietcong lost at least 750 men—those confirmed by actual count—and they had heavy losses of ammunition and weapons. Westmoreland called the operation disruptive, and the first in which the number of enemy captured equalled the number of those killed.

In nineteen days the Iron Triangle was temporarily converted from a haven for the Vietcong to a sealed battlefield and finally to a military no-man's land. The communists had spent years tunneling beneath its surface and their hoard of scarce military supplies was largely nullified. Now that civilians had been evacuated, Westmoreland hoped the area could be controlled by air strikes.

Westmoreland and Seaman were not about to permit the North Vietnamese to recoup. Junction City, the operation that had been delayed, was activated to carry the war deeper into enemy sanctuaries to the west for an extended period.

Seaman's II Field Force was ordered to eradicate all Vietcong and North Vietnamese installations and to build various Special Forces camps and airfields. Two United States divisions were committed with as many as twenty-two battalions of infantry troops, fourteen artillery battalions, and four South Vietnamese battalions.

Like the Iron Triangle north and west of it, this fifty by thirty mile area was a major enemy stronghold and sanctuary for insurgents who had been active for twenty years between the Iron Triangle and the Cambodian border. Westmoreland's intelligence officers believed the area housed the headquarters for the communists' Central Office for South Vietnam. The operation into this area a year earlier had unearthed valuable intelligence information.

The 25th Division was assigned the extreme western portion of the area in the vicinity of Lo Go. A second preliminary operation would be conducted by the 1st Infantry Division in Binh Long Province fifty miles to the east in an area defined by the Minh Tranh and Michelin rubber plantations including the village of Bau Long on Highway 13.

Seaman's intelligence officers advised him that the enemy's recent setbacks in the Iron Triangle, and the political rejection of the Vietcong by the population in the previous fall's national elections, would force the communists to increase guerrilla warfare and terrorism in an attempt to wear down his II Field Force. They said that the communists would use main forces only when there was a significant chance of gaining psychological victories at minimum risk to their own forces. This diagnosis later proved remarkably accurate.

Twenty days prior to the start of Junction City, preliminary operations were begun by the 25th Infantry Division and twelve days later on

February 14 by the 1st Division. A combination of airmobile assaults and attacks by mechanized battalions encountered limited opposition as the communists chose not to stand and fight but to use guerrilla tactics.

The 1st Infantry Division penetrated a triangular-shaped area in the southwest corner of Binh Long Province. It was believed this was an enemy sanctuary with numerous camps and storage sites, but only sporadic contact was made.

Seaman ended search and destroy operations after only four days when only a fraction of the rice that was believed to be stored in the area was recovered. It was necessary, however, for the 1st Division to spend three days from February 18th through the 21st to position its troops and prepare for the major operation.

Phase I of Junction City began February 22 with the 1st and 25th Divisions, and some South Vietnamese units, deployed in the shape of a giant horseshoe. The 1st Division was in position east and north of the inverted "U" while the 25th was placed northwest and to the west to drive through the "U's" open end. Major General John H. Hay, Jr. used two of the Big Red One's three brigades, augmented by the 173rd Airborne Brigade and two South Vietnamese units. Later, the 1st Brigade, 9th United States Infantry Division, joined the 1st Division to keep Route 13 open from Lai Khe to Quan Loi. The division was assigned responsibility for air and ground assaults to block the enemy's escape routes in the northern and eastern portions of the area and to destroy installations.

In Phase 1, the 25th "Tropic Lightning" Division under General Weyand was to be used first as the blocking force before participating in search and destroy operations.

D-Day was set for February 22, 1967. Nine infantry battalions conducted air assaults to cordon off the northern portion of the area. At the same time, the 25th Division adjusted its brigade in the blocking position on the west while additional units were positioned for an attack into the horseshoe-shaped area as the 1st Division's 3rd Brigade pushed north on Provincial Route 4 to complete the horseshoe.

On D-Day, 845 paratroopers boarded transports at Bien Hoa and at 9:00 A.M. the 173rd Airborne Brigade began its jump. As aircraft approached the drop zone two miles north of Katum the jumpmaster's voice rose above the roar of the plane's engines. "Stand in the door." General Deane moved to the right door, while Lieutenant Colonel Robert H. Sigholtz took his position at the left door. Deane jumped as the green light flashed on.

By 12:30 the battalion had established itself, and there were only eleven minor injuries.

Almost simultaneously the 196th Brigade of the 25th Division began its air assault in the vicinity of Route 246 on the northwestern side of the horseshoe. They landed unopposed and their battalions were in position by 1:50 P.M.

Meanwhile, the other two battalions of the 173rd Brigade completed the northeastern portion of the inverted "U".

Ground elements had started rolling that morning at 6:10 A.M. as the 1st Division's 3rd Brigade attacked to the north. Throughout the day enemy contact was light and so were casualties, due in part to extensive air strikes.

Now the combined elements of the 11th Armored Cavalry Regiment and the 2nd Brigade of the 25th Division thrust northward through the open end of the horseshoe to trap whatever Vietcong were inside and to destroy the communist headquarters and all other installations. Significant caches of arms and supplies were uncovered en route.

In all areas contact with the enemy remained light and the second day General Seaman called for a thorough search.

Another air assault was made February 24 into a landing zone secured by the 196th Brigade at the northern end of its area near the Cambodian border. Meanwhile, South Vietnamese Marines attacked to the south and prepared to continue operations even further south. Seaman now ordered the 1st Division's 3rd Brigade infantry battalion to move from Suoi Da to positions five miles south of Prek Lok along Route 4.

While the hammer forces of the 25th Division continued to attack to the north, the other two units along the horseshoe strengthened their defensive blocking positions while they continued their search missions.

Six enemy base camps were discovered near the Cambodian border and were destroyed along with their extensive supplies and weapons.

During the rest of Phase I, terminated March 17, units of both divisions continued their searches. Since the hammer forces had completed their operations, they started leaving early and some were airlifted out March 2. Small-unit actions marked most of the operations and the communist dead amounted to 835, but large quantities of supplies and equipment were confiscated by the various sweeps.

The fighting was not all easy. At 8:00 A.M. February 29, Company B of the 16th Infantry Regiment's 1st Battalion went out along Route 4 and proceeded east to assist the 1st Division's search and destroy mission. Up ahead there was a stream called Prek Lok, but the company never reached it. Captain Donald S. Ulm's men found the going extremely slow because of thick and tangled jungle. When he heard heavy small arms fires, Ulm decided that the enemy force facing him was larger than his company. He called the forward air controller and requested air strikes. He believed the Vietcong were not dug in so he recommended cluster bombs. When delivered from the air they exploded at treetop level and burst in a radius of 10 feet. They were lethal weapons against troops in the open, and ground commanders preferred them for such operations.

Ulm was requested to mark the position of his troops with colored smoke, and to give the disposition of his men. Twenty minutes later the communists attacked, but Ulm's men were well protected and they suffered few casualties. He realized, however, that the enemy fire was coming from the trees by well-concealed snipers. He suspected they would attempt to encircle his company. Therefore, the 1st Platoon's fire team was moved to the northwest and a squad from the 2nd Platoon was moved into position. The first air strike was effective as the forward air controller advised the pilots, "Drop within 30 yards of the smoke." Artillery fire was called in even closer, and contact with the enemy was broken at 3:00 P.M.

The brigade's commander, Colonel Sidney M. Marks, brought another company of the 1st Battalion into the landing zone to the northeast of the embattled company. A second company from another battalion was also airlifted into the landing zone after the first was dispatched to help Ulm's company. By 4:45 a third company, also from the 1st Battalion, landed to assist in securing the landing zone and in evacuating the dead and wounded.

It was not until 9:30 that night that Captain Ulm and his company, assisted by the relieving company, reached the landing zone but they had twenty-five dead and twenty-eight wounded with them. A later sweep of the forward positions revealed 167 Vietcong bodies.

The next day an officer walking among the company's survivors asked a soldier, "What did you think of the artillery and air strikes? Were they coming in a little close?"

The soldier smiled, "Sir, I was getting sprayed all over. But God it felt good!"

Platoon Sergeant Mathew Leonard took over as leader of his platoon when its leader was wounded. While dragging a wounded soldier to safety a sniper's bullet shattered his hand, but he refused medical attention and continued to fight. Under cover of the main attack from the northeast, the Vietcong moved a machine gun into a location where it could sweep the position of Leonard's platoon. He rose to his feet, charged the gun, and destroyed its crew despite being hit several times. When last seen alive he was propped against a tree continuing to engage the enemy. His valor earned him a posthumous Medal of Honor.

Junction City's second major battle began March 10 at 10:00 P.M. The Vietcong first mounted a heavy mortar attack against a fire support base at

Prek Lok and Lieutenant Colonel Edward J. Collins of the 2nd Infantry Regiment's 2nd Battalion ordered a counter attack.

In addition to the main attack from the east, the Vietcong launched limited attacks from the northeast and southeast. Air strikes were called in and, after an hour of fierce fighting, the brunt of the attack was repelled.

Two battalions of the 272nd Regiment of the Vietcong's 9th Division made a determined attack, although two of the division's regiments were badly defeated. Their remaining regiments were held back until later.

Junction City's Phase II was scheduled to start a minute past midnight March 18. Some elements of the 1st Infantry Division attacked as they repositioned themselves and strove to complete their preparations before the attack into the eastern side of the war zone.

II Field Force's mission for Phase II was identical to the first phase but this time it was commanded by Lieutenant General Bruce Palmer, Jr. who succeeded Seaman. The Big Red One was made responsible for bridge security along Routes 246 and 244 and for construction of camps and airfields to be occupied by Special Forces and South Vietnamese irregulars. Two brigades were positioned astride these enemy routes in the eastern zone. It was also essential to keep Route 13 open from Lai Khe to Quan Loi over which vital supplies were reaching the field force.

During the twenty-nine days of Phase II's intensive search and destroy operations only three major battles were fought. But there were mortar attacks against fire bases and against battalion positions. Fire Support Patrol Base Cat Sroc Con Trang, one of the largest established during this operation, sustained eleven mortar attacks. And enemy mining and ambush attacks were conducted along Routes 246 and 244. Although there were many contacts and some heated firefights, none of these forces, except in the three battles, was significant.

By the end of Phase II, the enemy was increasingly difficult to locate, although quantities of supplies and equipment were found.

After the battle of Ap Bau Bang II, blood trails were mute evidence of the bodies hauled away by the Vietcong. Most deaths were caused by artillery and air strikes and American losses were only three killed and sixty-three wounded. This was the site of the first major Vietnam action in which the 1st Infantry Division participated November 12, 1965. At that time the 272nd and 273rd Regiments of the Vietcong's 9th Division had attacked the 2nd Infantry's defense perimeter and were repelled at high cost.

1st Division commander, Major General John H. Hay, Jr., sent a derisive letter in Vietnamese to the commanding general of the 9th Vietcong Division after the battle. "This is to advise you that during the battle of Ap Bau Bang on 20 March the regimental commander of Q763 (273rd Regiment) and his battalion commanders disgraced themselves by performing in an unsoldierly manner.

"During this battle with elements of this Division and attached units your officers failed to accomplish their mission and left the battlefield covered with dead and wounded from their units.

"We have buried your dead and taken care of your wounded from this battle."

An egg-shaped clearing close to Suoi Tre, near the war zone's center and fifty-five miles northwest of Saigon, now became the target for United States forces. Four months earlier the 28th Infantry Regiment's 1st Battalion had defeated elements of the 272nd Vietcong and the 101st North Vietnamese regiments at the battle of Ap Cha Do. Now the 272nd had returned.

The area near Suoi Tre was surrounded by sparse woodland that had been blighted by defoliants. After helicopters airlanded the 22nd Infantry Regiment's 3rd Battalion and the 77th Artillery Regiment's 2nd Battalion led by Lieutenant Colonels John A. Bender and John W. Vessey, Jr., a fire support base was established. Heavy action had not been anticipated, but within minutes of the landing the entire perimeter was under heavy fire as waves of Vietcong emerged from the jungle. Three helicopters were destroyed and six more damaged. Air strikes were called in as ground forces fought off human waves. Despite the enemy pressure the lines held, although positions on the east side were drawn back.

Mechanized infantry and armor battalions now moved from the southwest and the 12th Infantry Regiment's 2nd Battalion moved northwest across the countryside to avoid trails and roads that might be mined or booby-trapped. They linked up with the battered Company B and reinforced the battalions under heavy fire as the Vietcong pressed their attacks. Some Vietcong, so badly wounded that they could not walk, were carried piggyback against the Americans by their comrades. With the American reinforcements the Vietcong commander withdrew his troops, leaving 647 dead who had fought with the 9th Vietcong Division's 272nd Regiment. This was one of the enemy's best organized and equipped units and one of the few that dared to make daylight attacks. They scattered now and soon were so completely disorganized that they fled to the northeast under American artillery fire and air strikes.

The 26th Infantry Regiment's 1st Battalion—the Blue Spaders commanded by Lieutenant Colonel Alexander M. Haig—was alerted March 26 to prepare for an assault deep into the war zone near the Cambodian border. They were attached to the 1st Division's 2nd Brigade at Fire Support Patrol Base Cat Sroc Con Trang. The assault was planned for late morning March 30 into a landing zone eight miles to the west. The battalion was told to secure the zone for a follow-up landing by the 2nd Infantry Regiment's 1st Battalion, and Haig was warned to expect enemy opposition. Poor weather at first delayed air strikes so the assault was postponed for two hours. When the battalion moved in there was no enemy contact. That evening Haig's battalion dug in with full overhead cover, interlocking defenses and listening posts were established while patrols were sent out to prevent ambushes.

The next morning the 2nd Infantry Regiment's 1st Battalion under Lieutenant Colonel William C. Simpson was airlanded in the zone without incident, and they were assigned search and destroy operations in the woods northwest of the perimeter. They all quickly learned that the Vietcong had expected the Americans because troops found small signs in English warning them that they would not return if they went beyond the signs.

At 1:00 P.M. a reconnaissance platoon moved farther to the north into a wooded area and made its first enemy contact when the point man was hit. Lieutenant Richard A. Hill went forward to check the situation and he was mortally wounded. Now only Hill's radio operator remained in contact with the battalion's command post. Before he was hit Hill had advised Haig that his platoon was heavily engaged and the colonel immediately called for artillery support and air strikes.

After a sweep of the battalion's defensive position, B Company was advised of the reconnaissance platoon's desperate position, and that its leader had been hit. On his own initiative, the company commander swung his men to the north and proceeded to assist the embattled platoon.

Haig boarded his helicopter but it was not until he was airborne that he learned of B Company's move north. While the move to extract the platoon was necessary, the lack of control over artillery and air support complicated the problem. Therefore, B Company entered the engagement without sufficient preparation and quickly found itself heavily engaged along with the reconnaissance platoon. They faced a battalion and they were quickly pinned down. Haig knew he had to reinforce them and get them out. He alerted Company A and they moved forward to pass through and relieve B Company.

Haig landed near the point of contact and ordered his battalion operations officer to take to the air to control the direction of the firing. Haig found Lieutenant Hill's body, and saw that the commander of Company B was wounded and in mild shock. He decided to remain and he was joined by A Company's commander who had moved his unit through B Company and gained fire superiority over the enemy. Intense and accurate artillery and air strikes now permitted all units, except the two platoons of A Company who were still in contact with the enemy, to be extracted. The Vietcong continued their attacks by leaving their bunkers but they were forced back by air and artillery bombardment.

The 1st Division's commander, General Hay, when apprised of the situation, ordered reinforcements into the area. Soon, the beleaguered men heard the unwelcome sound of heavy enemy mortar fire that sounded like loud, heavy machine guns. American artillery responded and the mortar attack ceased April 1 at 5:15 A.M. Seven minutes later, however, the Vietcong launched a ground attack against the northeast edge of the defense perimeter. As American soldiers, who had been manning listening posts, withdrew to the perimeter the Vietcong followed them in. This movement, coordinated with mortar fire, permitted the Vietcong to make their surprise attack through the tall grass, and three bunkers were captured and a penetration was made in Company C's sector. Hand-to-hand fighting began as the Vietcong sought to overwhelm the American defenders. Haig said later that he had known from the day he selected this night defensive position that it was the most vulnerable along the perimeter. He said the enemy commander had quickly understood this weakness and had exploited it.

Captain George A. Jones, the battalion's operations officer, watched as the Vietcong walked right through their mortar and artillery fire. When they kept coming he realized they had a large force out there. With C Company fighting hand-to-hand in bunkers along with members of B Company, Jones ordered his men to pull back, reorganize and hold their fall-back position.

Despite intense fire, C Company's commander, Captain Brian H. Cundiff, moved among his men to encourage them to make an effective defense. He personally killed six Vietcong in hand-to-hand fighting. Although he was wounded three times, Cundiff refused medical aid as he rallied his men.

The Vietcong changed their tactics by launching diversionary attacks from the east and west while Air Force planes bombed and strafed them every fifteen minutes. Under this heavy volume of fire the Vietcong attack began to falter as light and heavy helicopter planes fired rockets and miniguns, and artillery massed their fire along his eastern flank. When cluster bombs were used, and dropped close to the American positions, the Vietcong ran—many throwing down their weapons in panic.

Captain Cundiff led elements of C Company, now reinforced by the 1st Platoon of B Company, in a massive counterattack that pushed the remaining Vietcong back where they ran into deadly artillery barrages and air strikes. By 8:00 A.M. the perimeter was restored. The cluster bombs, not available at the start of the battle, proved most effective against troops in the open since pilots could release the small bombs from their cannisters at low level—often dropped within 100 feet of American troops. They exploded on contact, leaving United States troops unharmed since their lethal radius was slightly less than that distance. Air strikes, including two B-52 strikes, followed the Vietcong as they withdrew. In the two-day battle, 609 Vietcong were killed for an American loss of seventeen.

Air strikes may have helped but the determined fighting of all men, and the proper use of artillery and automatic weapons, made the difference.

Phase II ended April 15, but the first two phases had proved so successful that a third phase was initiated. This time the 25th Division was solely responsible to commit a brigade, with the same goals as the first two phases. Junction City was brought to a close May 14.

In these operations, all regiments of the 9th Vietcong Division were severely trounced, losing 2,728 dead and large stockpiles of food and military supplies. The communist headquarters was withdrawn to Cambodia and, for a time, this affected its control over the Vietcong. Westmoreland believed that all objectives had been reached but the communist main forces had not been destroyed.

General Giap called the operation a big victory that had resulted in crippling American losses; but captured enemy documents proved later that the communists privately acknowledged they had suffered a decisive defeat. They realized that basing main units in close proximity to a key population area was foolhardy, at least for the time being. They now increased their use of Cambodian sanctuaries.

Elements of the 1st and 25th Infantry Divisions, the 11th Armored Cavalry Regiment and South Vietnamese units swung back towards Saigon to clear the enemy from Long Nguyen, just north of the triangle.

South Vietnam's armed forces now demonstrated their capabilities as their Special Forces took over several camps and manned them for the first time without United States advisers and proved their worth in major operations on their own.

Westmoreland believed he had insufficient forces to continue to operate in the Iron Triangle and prevent the Vietcong from returning. This was a mistake because Vietcong troops returned within two days following the departure of the American forces.

Unfortunately for the allies, the 1968 Tet offensive was made possible because of heavy reinfestation of the Iron Triangle, so most of Junction City was fought in vain.

CHAPTER 24

"God, I've Got It."

THE GHOST RIDERS—VA-164—FLEW THEIR FIRST MISSION FROM THE *Oriskany* July 15, 1967, in A-4 Skyhawks. Their first two missions were scheduled over South Vietnam to give them combat experience in an area less dangerous than North Vietnam.

When they started to fly missions up north in late July they were part of daily maximum efforts with strikes scheduled at 8:00 A.M., noon and 4:00 P.M. although individual pilots flew only two of them. On the following day only one strike was set up at noon and this schedule was repeated for twenty days prior to a standdown for rest and recuperation.

Lieutenant Commander Robert Arnold, the squadron's operations officer, was briefed the night before their first mission into North Vietnam against a truck-storage target sixteen miles outside Hanoi. Eight airplanes from his squadron and eight from their sister squadron VA-163 were assigned to the mission with eight fighter escorts. Two of his Skyhawks were made responsible for missile suppression. In the States, they had received limited training for this type of warfare and the suppressors received on-the-job experience over heavily defended areas of North Vietnam. These "Iron Hand" pilots performed similarly to the Air Force's "Wild Weasels" in seeking out SAM sites so their Shrike missiles could come in on their acquisition radar beams.

Early the next morning the *Oriskany* was already a hot-box of heat and humidity because water rationing had been initiated due to the ship's inability to make sufficient fresh water, and there was little or no air-conditioning. There were no showers to relieve the heat that rose to 90 degrees and even higher.

None of them felt inclined to talk as they went to breakfast and got in their flying suits prior to their 5:00 A.M. briefing. Arnold soon learned that the worst part of getting up was the knowledge that you were going on a mission. The tension and apprehension drained him as they waited in Strike Operations for the first briefing with their knee boards ready, to make notes.

The strike leader rose to brief the two squadrons, describing the target and its location. He referred to it as a strategic target because it contained rolling stock. He said Iron Hand pilots would drop "daisy cutters" (bombs with 36-inch extended fuses that scattered fragments above ground) and the strike force would use 500-pound bombs.

VA-163 pilots were briefed to concentrate on installations north of the road that divided the target area, while Arnold's squadron was assigned to the south. Pointing to a map, the strike leader indicated a bend in the river. "This is your roll-in point. You'll cross the beach at 12,500 feet in a slight descent. Roll in, pull off to the left, and head out. Keep it moving after pull out and keep jinking all the way to the beach. Call out any missiles or flak over the air. If you see a SAM, call out immediately." Arnold nodded his understanding, thinking that they would be going in like an old-fashioned cavalry charge but coming out anyway they could.

The electronic counter-measures briefing was next and they were informed that an A-3 would be jamming radars up and down the coast. Some Air Force planes were also assigned this job but to date they had not been effective.

A weather briefing followed and finally an intelligence briefing where they were shown flak installations marked with pins on a chart. This part of their briefings was a standard joke among the crews. When the air intelligence officer told them to expect fire from guns of various millimeter-size shells they all recited in union, "37, 57, 85, 100" because the charts were covered with red pins. The intelligence officer, in pointing out these installations, said, "There's a gun here, a gun there," and so on and on. Someone from the rear yelled, "For Christ sake, there are guns all over the place!"

These briefings did not furnish meaningful information because the briefing officer only spoke of the most active sites. Most sites were mobile, so their location was not specific.

Pilots now left for either division briefings—those involving four planes—or the Iron Hand pilots went to a special briefing.

Despite the sweltering heat, it was time for hot coffee and to put on the rest of their gear, including a "G" suit that was snug when zipped up. When a pilot pulled "Gs" the suit would fill with air to keep him from blacking out as the inflated suit pressed against arteries so blood did not drain away from his head. A pilot earlier had been shot in the legs and the flight surgeon had radioed that he should inflate his "G" suit to shut off the flow of blood through his wounds. It worked, and the pilot got back aboard his carrier in good shape.

Arnold checked his survival equipment: knife, gun, water, food and maps, and prepared for launch. The worst part was sitting and waiting. It always gave him a queasy feeling in his stomach. He kept wanting to go to the head for a last nervous pee, but this was impossible just prior to launch.

The heat of the flight deck was even more oppressive than below decks. The planes were air-conditioned, but the system could not be turned on until they were in the air. Arnold watched the activity on deck around the parked planes. Some ordnance was still being loaded, and there were bomb carts under several airplanes with 520-pound shaped bombs—half of iron and the other half of explosive material—being fitted with their fuses. Airplanes often were pre-flighted while the bombs were loaded. Squadron ordnance officers now began to check the setting of each fuse.

Over the loudspeakers came the voice of the air boss. "Stand clear of all intakes and exhausts." He was like a tower operator at an air base. A senior officer, he supervised the launch and all deck hands were responsible to him.

Arnold watched intently as a yellow cart came up to each plane to act as an engine starter. Planes were still tied down and everyone was off the flight deck except those necessary for the launch.

Arnold received the signal from the plane director that the power was on, and he cranked up his engine as the director went on to the next plane. He turned on his radio to check with his strike leader, Commander Douglas Mow. He called, "Magic Stone 1—Magic Stone 3 up and ready."

Arnold was sweating as the sun beat down. He could not wait now until he was airborne so he could turn on his air-conditioning. Sweat trickled down his back, and he developed an itch, but the confines of the cockpit were too tight for the necessary movement to scratch it. With his engine running, after hours of preparation, he wanted to be on his way. Then, he knew, much of his apprehension would fade away.

The *Oriskany* turned into the wind as the planes were moved forward. Fighters were taking off first and the signal was given for the removal of the planes' tie downs, although chocks remained under each wheel. Then the signal came for removal of the chocks. Arnold pressed his brakes and signaled he was ready to go. The plane director passed each plane up the deck and onto the catapult. Meanwhile, checkers made a visual inspection of the airplane as it moved forward to detect leaks, or malfunctioning systems, including a final inspection of any rockets or missiles to determine if all connections had been completed.

The taxi director brought Arnold's plane slowly on to the catapult. An hour-glass fitting in the rear of his plane was hooked to the catapult's cable as a hold back, while catapult hooks were attached to his plane with tension cables. Now his plane was in the hands of the catapult officer. It was stretched by cable two ways—one holding it back while the others were prepared to hurl it forward. Arnold went to full power, checked all gauges, and signaled he was ready to go. The catapult officer gave him a pronounced signal with his arms so no one could mistake the gesture. The catapult was fired and Arnold's plane was flung off the ship. To Arnold it always felt like a kick in the ass as his plane accelerated from zero to 160 knots within 150 feet with his head jammed back against the headrest. For seconds he was on a fast ride in a plane over which he momentarily had no control. He smiled, recalling the old joke at such times, "God, I've got it," once he was in the air. The feeling of control was a relief because one never knew what was going to happen—especially at night—when there was a black void ahead. Each time he hoped there would be no electrical failure. This time everything went smoothly and he brought up his gear. Once he was comfortably airborne, he brought his flaps up from their full-down position.

Arnold climbed his plane to their rendezvous and it seemed to take forever, actually only fifteen minutes as he circled the ship. He checked in with his skipper as he watched the rest of the planes launch from the *Oriskany's* deck. "Magic Stone 3, aboard."

Commander Mow tersely replied, "Roger." He checked off each pilot, noting that the ship had called that one of his planes had a mechanical problem and did not get launched.

After they left the ship's vicinity they switched on their radios to the strike frequency as they went through the slot—the Red River Valley—the most direct and heavily defended corridor to Hanoi. There was only one way to go. Besides it did not matter because the communists always knew they were coming.

Arnold flipped on the switches to his five bomb stations. He left number three off because it contained the center fuel tank. He checked his gunsight and its two filaments—one for use as an alternate—and he established the millimeter setting for the dive at the target. Ballistics were pre-calculated in the sight and all he had to do was keep the "pipper" centered on the target. He flipped on the master armament switch. They had been told to wait until they crossed the beach (North Vietnam's shoreline) but they had learned from experience that often it was too late to do it then. He was now ready to drop his bombs. On release, an exploding cartridge would eject the bombs away from his airplane.

Arnold picked up radar signals from missiles on the ground. With tension mounting, knowing anti-aircraft guns and missiles around Hanoi were the worst ever faced by American fliers, he was keyed up with mounting tension. Formations in this area reported the firing of thirty SAMs in two minutes—one every four seconds. Navy and Air Force pilots often said this was a great testing ground for the Russians who supplied the equipment but let the North Vietnamese do the fighting. What embittered Arnold and his fellow fliers was that the North Vietnamese were quite aware through American news media reports of the restrictions placed upon American fliers and what targets could or could not be attacked.

Arnold listened anxiously to the radar signals coming from the ground. He likened their sound to a symphony of death, with musicians warming up their instruments. First was the enemy's search radar so he knew they were picking them up. Next, was the height-finding radar with a different pitch. Their "chut chut, chut chut" sounded like crickets chirping. Next was the gun control radar for the heavier guns. He spotted three large bursts of flak off to one side, and they immediately varied their flight path, but they still felt the concussion bumps as the shells exploded. Anti-aircraft guns were not all that effective, but this early in his tour Arnold did not know that. Now the search radar was going "zip, zip" along with the "blip, blip" of the height-finding radar while the gun-control radar kept repeating "brr, brr." They crossed the "beach" at the most unpopulated point that could be found flying at 400 knots and 12,000 feet. Overhead was a loose formation of tactical bombers with their covering fighters, and the Iron Hand suppressors on either side.

The frequency of the radar sounds grew louder as Arnold's pulse raced. The "zip, zip, blip, blip and brr, brr" sounds grew in intensity and his heart seemed to be in his throat. Now there was the new sound of the acquisition radar—a sing-song undulating tone that was particularly unnerving. With this sound he knew that the missile's radar was actively tracking them—a sound someone called "singer low."

The guidance radar, or "singer high" emitted its peculiar sound and Arnold knew that a SAM had either been shot or was ready to be fired. It was locked on to somebody. Their planes carried chaff to upset the ground radar, but it was not foolproof insurance against a missile.

Arnold watched his skipper and hugged closer to his plane as they tried to find the bend in the river.

Someone screeched, "There's a missile in the air! A missile in the air!"

Another shouted, "Somebody's on fire. He's going down."

Arnold feared at first that his plane was on fire until reality reached his consciousness.

He looked down quickly as they neared the target and he saw more guns than he had ever seen before. He was overwhelmed as literally hundreds of gun flashes winked on and off. He followed his leader, never once seeing the target. When Mow dropped his bombs Arnold and the others also dropped.

This was his first mission over North Vietnam and he felt totally inadequate, and there were times when he thought he would not get out alive. This feeling disappeared later, but it was strong at first.

Arnold's nerves were on edge as hysterical voices sounded through his earphones. "Break right! Break right!" one pilot called. "Going down. Going down," screamed another in high-pitched urgency.

With his bombs gone Arnold felt a freedom and an exhilaration, and now all he wanted was to get out of the target area. It had taken only twenty seconds to roll down to release altitude at a speed of 500 knots and they were away from the target in thirty seconds, but it had seemed like an eternity as the bombs slowly rippled off one at a time.

Once at the "beach," after jinking to throw off ground radar, each pilot flew independently to the ship, after checking in with the strike leader so he could determine possible losses. Only one fighter was lost and its pilot was picked up the next day.

Arnold's squadron lost four planes during its first week of operations.

Later that month, Arnold was sent out on a rescue mission to aid the pickup of two pilots who had been shot down. One pilot was picked up right away but the other was still on the ground.

Arnold took off at 4:00 A.M. as a flak suppressor with two rocket pods and cluster bombs. The downed pilot was on a karst ridge with a big valley to the south of him. A-1 Skyraiders were overhead, talking to the pilot on the ground. They were subjected to small arms fire while they waited for a helicopter to pick up the pilot. Six or seven trucks came roaring down a road, pulling up at the base of the ridge. When they started firing heavy anti-aircraft guns at the A-1s, Arnold called control, saying, "We've got some trucks that are shooting at the Spads and I'm in a position to roll in." He wondered why he had to request permission but it was quickly granted. The trucks saw him coming and turned their guns on his plane rocketing down the valley. He fired one rocket pod with nineteen rockets and the noise was deafening. They roared ahead like a freight train. He turned and came back, noting that three or four trucks were burning while the others were hastily departing the scene.

The Skyraiders kept in touch with the man on the ground through his survival radio. Supposedly there was a North Vietnamese army barracks a few miles to the south. Now a helicopter arrived and started to make its approach. Somebody shouted a warning to the pilot, "Stay out of the valley. Stay over the ridge. Be sure you don't go over the valley."

The helicopter pilot ignored the warning and flew over the valley.

He was warned again, "Don't go over the valley! Stay over the ridge."

Now the helicopter pilot learned the reason for the warning as several hundred troops started shooting at him.

"This is Clementine. I am hit. Hit!"

Arnold watched with horror as the helicopter caught fire while the ground troops increased their shooting, and it crashed killing all on board. Arnold had cluster bombs but their use was so sensitive that special permission had to be given. Each bomb opened up like a clamshell and balls with all-way fuses tumbled out and exploded on contact. He called Lieutenant Commander Leon A. Edney and permission was granted. Arnold started to head in but he was called off by Edney who knew that he could not get the man out and there was no sense in making the enemy ground troops any madder. He knew they might take out their anger on the pilot on the ground, Lieutenant Commander Richard Hartman, if they captured him.

Hartman called as Arnold pulled away. "Hey, fellows. Don't leave me here."

Arnold was distraught as he turned away. He learned later that Hartman was killed by the communists the next day.

His wingman, Lieutenant Barry Wood, desperately needed to refuel but the tanker was still on the carrier. He ran out of fuel and had to eject.

Arnold was also running out of fuel as he reached the shoreline. He knew he had to get home quickly. He still had two cluster bombs so he salvoed them into the ocean to lighten his plane. He was at 25,000 feet but the *Oriskany* was 175 miles away and he knew it was impossible to reach the carrier with such a short fuel supply. He tuned to the carrier *Constellation* and called, "Warchief, this is Magic Stone 403. Do you have a ready deck?"

"Magic Stone, what's your problem?"

"I am 75 miles out and I've got 400 pounds of fuel." Gauges were accurate only to 200 pounds so his situation was critical. His Skyhawk normally burned 1,200 pounds of fuel an hour so he figured he had only ten minutes before his fuel ran out. He pulled back the throttle and knew that, at most, he would have but one shot at the carrier's deck. In coming aboard he would have one hand on the throttle and the other on his ejection curtain.

"What's your position?" The *Constellation* radioed.

"Seventy five miles out."

"We're launching the tanker." There was a pause. "Magic Stone, what's your position?" the pilot of the tanker called.

"Seventy miles out." He gave the tanker his bearing from the ship. He had no hope that the tanker would arrive on time.

The tanker pilot called again. "We're heading on your radial and we're at 15 miles."

"I'm at 60."

"We're at 25."

"I'm at 40."

"We're at 30."

"I'm at 38."

As they closed on one another the tanker reported at a distance thirty-three miles that they were starting their turn to head back towards the ship to meet him streaming his fuel drogue so they would not miss one another.

An overwhelming sense of relief filled Arnold as he spotted the tanker and inserted his probe just as his fuel gauge registered 200 pounds.

"How much do you want?" the tanker plot called.

"I'll take a couple of thousand, if I can."

He was given 2,000 pounds and when he unplugged that was the amount registered on his fuel gauge. It had been close.

"Thanks," Arnold radioed. "I owe you a bottle of whiskey."

Arnold flew back to his own ship, the *Oriskany*, whose crew had thought him lost because he had been off their frequency so long.

In the Gulf of Tonkin, where up to sixty American ships of Task Force 77 cruised with as many as six carriers, ships of other nations headed through the fleet en route to Haiphong. Missile containers were clearly visible on the decks of the ships from Russia and Iron Curtain countries. American fliers were frustrated, knowing these missiles would be shooting at them within a few days and they could no nothing about it. Russian ships in particular scouted the fringes of the American fleet to report on its movements, and the plane takeoffs and their direction.

Despite its importance, the port city of Haiphong remained off-limits. The sports arena was specifically prohibited because it was listed as a cultural center. Actually, the communists used it for gun emplacements, knowing it was off-limits. Pilots flying in the area at night frequently said it looked like Los Angeles with someone shutting the lights on and off as the guns and missiles were fired. Pilots watched in deep frustration as SAMs lifted off from the center of Haiphong, and headed for them as they bypassed the city. Many missiles crashed into the city and North Vietnamese officials quickly denounced the Americans for using terror bombs against civilian when, in fact, the damage was caused by their own exploding missiles.

There was a growing number of prisoners held by the communists in North Vietnam. The majority were Air Force and Navy pilots and navigators who had ben shot down over the North.

Major George E. Day was flying as a forward air controller August 26 when his fighter was hit by ground fire and he was forced to eject. In the process his right arm was broken in three places and his left knee was badly injured. Day was captured immediately and taken to a camp where he was tied up, interrogated and tortured while his captors refused to treat his injuries. Two days later a doctor crudely set his broken arm. Despite continued torture Day refused to give the communists any information.

Feigning a back injury, Day slipped out of his bonds and escaped into the jungle. He trekked south towards the demilitarized zone to evade enemy patrols, surviving on a diet of berries and uncooked frogs. On his second night, a bomb or rocket detonated near him and he was hit in his right leg, and he started to bleed from his nose and ears due to the shock effect of the explosion. He hid in the jungle for two more days to recover from his new wounds.

When he started out again a barrage of American artillery almost killed him near the Ben Hai River separating North Vietnam from the South. With the aid of a bamboo log that he used as a float he swam across the river and entered the demilitarized zone. Now he became delirious and disoriented from his injuries as he wandered aimlessly for days trying to signal American aircraft. Once two forward air controllers flew directly overhead but they failed to spot him. Even more frustrating, Day limped toward two Marine helicopters but they pulled away before he could reach them.

Twelve days after his escape, weakened from exposure, hunger and multiple wounds, Day was captured by the Vietcong. He suffered additional gunshot wounds to his left hand and thigh while trying to elude them. He was returned to prison and brutally punished for his escape.

Day was placed on a starvation diet and his 170 pounds shrank to 110. He repeatedly was refused medical treatment for his broken bones, wounds and infections. Although he was constantly tortured he refused to give them the information they sought, even when he was bound under his armpits and suspended from the ceiling of his cell for two hours. Now the interrogating officer ordered a guard to twist his mangled right arm, breaking his wrist.

When Day appeared to cooperate with his captors they believed he had at last broken but he deliberately gave them false answers and revealed nothing of significance, knowing that he faced death if they found out he was lying.

Two months after he was shot down Day was transferred to a prison near Hanoi. By now he was totally incapacitated, with infections in his arms and legs, and with little feeling in his twisted hands. He could no longer perform the simplest tasks for himself but he was still tortured. Incredibly, Day's refusal to give his captors military intelligence never wavered as he sought to protect airmen still flying missions against North Vietnam.

Five-and-a-half years later he was released, still defiant, and the nation he served so well honored him with a Medal of Honor.

In late April, 1967, the Marines set up an operation to destroy North Vietnamese forces in the Thang Bien, Que Son, Hiep Duc Valley where they planned to establish control of the valley and to retake the Hiep Duc Special Forces Camp. Colonel Kenneth J. Houghton's 5th Marine Regiment was assigned to make the attack April 25.

First contact was made at La Nga when a Marine rifle company encountered heavy enemy fire and Houghton ordered his regiment to exploit the contact. The 21st Regiment of North Vietnam's 2nd Division made its stand at the hamlet of Phouc Duc. For four days, commencing May 12, the 5th Marines attacked fortified enemy positions despite heavy mortar barrages and counterattacks, but the Marines finally overran the entrenched communist forces.

The second phase of this operation (code-named Union and Union 2) by the 5th Regiment, now expanded to six battalions, was launched May 26 with a helicopter assault that was met by a tremendous volume of rocket and mortar fire. This led to the belief that elements of the 2nd North Vietnamese Division were in the area with perhaps a general officer in command. The Marines maintained the pressure throughout a day of fierce hand-to-hand fighting.

F Company, under Captain James A. Graham from the 2nd Battalion defending An Hoa on the other side of the valley, was attached to the 1st Battalion's A and D companies and Graham's F Company, "Cassandra Foxtrot" came under mortar and small arms fire that inflicted a large number of casualties. Hardest hit was F Company's 2nd Platoon. It was pinned down in the open by intense fire from two concealed machine guns. At this point, Major Richard Alger, the regiment's executive and operations officer, and Colonel Houghton decided on a night attack to relieve the pressure on the 1st Battalion—F Company in particular.

Houghton and Alger followed the action by radio, marveling at the audacity of the North Vietnamese who at mid-day June 2 were taking on the Marines despite their preponderance of air and artillery support.

Up front, Graham grew increasingly concerned about his 2nd Platoon. By the book, he should not have personally tried to relieve them, but he would not have been a Marine if he had not tried to extricate his men. He formed an assault unit from members of his small company headquarters and led an attack that forced the North Vietnamese to abandon their first machine gun position, thereby relieving some of the pressure on the platoon. The wounded then were quickly evacuated to a more secure area.

Now the second machine gun had to be silenced because its devastating fire was taking a heavy toll. Graham's small force stood steadfast in its hard-won position and during the afternoon Captain Graham suffered two minor wounds while personally accounting for an estimated fifteen enemy killed. But they were now almost surrounded, and in deep trouble.

Battalion Commander, Lieutenant Colonel Peter Hilgartner, whose call sign was "Cottage," called Graham. "Cassandra Foxtrot, this is Cottage 6. I want you to pull back and assume control of your company."

Graham replied, "Cottage 6, this is Cassandra Foxtrot. I've got eight wounded up here and I don't want to leave them." He added that it would take "Dislodge 6 Actual" (Houghton's call sign) before he would pull back.

Hilgartner appealed to Houghton but the colonel refused to intervene, hoping that the impending night attack would relieve the pressure on Graham's company.

Minutes later, Graham called, "Cottage 6, this is Cassandra Foxtrot. They are all around us. I want you to pull the fire in right on top of my position. There are men here with me still alive, but pull it in. It's been my pleasure soldiering with you. My apologies for disobeying your order. They are in the assault now. This is my last transmission. Cassandra Foxtrot, out."

Tears cascaded down Houghton's, Alger's and Hilgartner's cheeks now that they realized there was no hope the brave captain would survive.

The night attack was launched by the remaining companies of the 2nd Battalion under Lieutenant Colonel Mallard Jackson. His operations officer, Captain Richard Esau, led the attacking companies. This night attack ruptured the enemy's defenses and drove the tattered vestiges of a North Vietnamese division from the field.

After Hilgartner's troops moved forward they found eighty-seven dead communist soldiers around Graham's position. Among the wounded Americans whom Graham had refused to leave was Gunnery Sergeant John S. Green, but Graham was dead.

Prior to the company's relief Sergeant Green had led a frontal assault across a fire-swept rice paddy and overran a Vietcong machine-gun position. He personally killed ten communist soldiers. Without concern for his own safety, he carried wounded men to positions of relative safety while he consolidated his position.

Houghton recommended Sergeant Green for the Navy Cross and it was approved by higher headquarters. When President Johnson visited Vietnam in December 1967, Green went to Cam Ranh Bay for the awards presentation. The sergeant stood at the head of the line because his medal was the highest award to be presented that day. Behind him were admirals and generals waiting to receive their Distinguished Service Medals—good conduct medals for general officers.

Two weeks later, Westmoreland's deputy, General Abrams, visited III Marine Amphibious Forces headquarters. There was a grin on his face as he got out a cigar, clipped off the end, and said, "Houghton, you pulled a good one. You Marines sent that gunnery sergeant down there and upstaged the entire United States Army. Westy damn near dropped his teeth."

Houghton later attended a ceremony at the Marine Barracks in Washington, D.C., when Graham's widow, with her two small children in attendance, was presented with her husband's posthumous Medal of Honor for his outstanding courage throughout a day of heroic achievements.

In both operations the North Vietnamese lost a total of 1,200 men killed, while another 1,800 were wounded. The North Vietnamese 2nd Division was eliminated from further operations for several months following this battle.

A year later Houghton was directed to come to the White House to accept a Presidential Unit Citation for this battle on behalf of his 5th Marine Regiment. When he was asked whom he wanted to attend the ceremony he suggested inviting the enlisted men who had earned the honor for their regiment. He was advised that there had to be fewer than 400 participants because that was the number who could be accommodated inside the White House if inclement weather prevented use of the Rose Garden. When these men gathered for the affair with their left breasts covered with individual medals, including a large number of Purple Hearts they had received for combat wounds, it was a heartwarming sight for Houghton. President Johnson personally made the presentation, but there was no warmth to the occasion because the president seemed preoccupied. Houghton was glad to see that Johnson did seem to enjoy talking to some of his men.

The president stopped in front of one sergeant, noting that he had four Purple Hearts. There were standing orders from the Pentagon that once a man receive three Purple Hearts he was to be immediately shipped home. The president said, "Where did you get those four Purple Hearts? You must have gotten some of them in Korea."

"Oh, no sir, Mr. President. I got them all with Colonel Houghton."

Houghton winced, not realizing beforehand that the sergeant had four Purple Hearts. Later he was ordered by the White House to explain the situation and he discovered that the sergeant was being evacuated after his third wounding but that his helicopter had been hit at the village of La Nga and shot down. He was wounded again, and qualified for his fourth medal.

Three battalions of the United States Army's 1st Cavalry Division moved into I Corps' Quang Ngai Province in August and penetrated into the Song Be Valley that had long been a Vietcong stronghold. This picturesque terrain consisted of numerous hillocks along the valley's floor with fertile fields of rice and well-fed livestock. The 2nd Battalion of the 8th Cavalry Regiment under Lieutenant Colonel John E. Stannard selected a landing site for an air assault along a ridgeline to the southwest of an abandoned airstrip. Unfortunately, the landing zone was in the middle of a well-prepared enemy position. Army troops fought back with heavy firepower, losing eleven compared to seventy-three enemy dead. This was a dress rehearsal for what was to come.

Soon to be introduced was the Huey Cobra or AH-1G. This was a major step in armed helicopters because it was agile and heavily armed. It could place fire within a few yards of its own troops to support them. It carried a 40-mm. grenade launcher, a minigun and 2.75-inch rockets. The Cobra was a vast improvement over earlier jury-rigged gunships that had proved inadequate.

In September the North Vietnamese concentrated their attacks against Con Thien with heavy shelling and rockets, but they slackened when they ran into strong resistance.

North Vietnamese activity flared again in the western demilitarized zone near Khe Sanh. Their first heavy probes made it obvious that heavy fighting was in the offing.

Once it was evident that Khe Sanh was seriously threatened, some of the sensors ordered for McNamara's electronic fence—an idea that was now definitely abandoned—were made available to the South Vietnamese and also to Khe Sanh's defenders. These devices could be dropped from the air, hung on trees, placed along river banks or buried underground. Some commanders appreciated their usefulness because they forewarned of a possible attack. These sensors were most useful in locating enemy troops, and keeping track of their movements.

Republic of Korea Marines, Australian advisers, and United States Special Forces were all taking an active part in I Corps' defenses. The Special Forces often reported enemy activities in sparsely populated regions. Not so well known were their long-range patrol teams that roamed areas normally thought to be under enemy control. They gained valuable information and frequently harassed the communists with ambushes or raids, even in places where the North Vietnamese felt secure.

The Koreans had entered I Corps in August, 1966, when their 2nd Marine "Dragon" Brigade moved south of Chu Lai in northern Quang Ngai Province. They were adept at dealing with the local population because most of the men were farmers. They conducted a number of imaginative and skillful war operations. The Koreans quickly proved themselves masters in the patient collection of intelligence information and its effective use.

During 1967 the role of the 1st Vietnamese Army Division in I Corps expanded. The division had been given priority for new equipment and this firepower increase made the division more effective.

During Vietnam's war with France the French developed a remarkable riverine force, particularly in the north where most of the fighting occurred. They used flotillas of boats for transport and attack purposes because 90 percent of all traffic moved by inland waterways.

In late 1966 and early 1967 the North Vietnamese had a political and military organization in the Mekong Delta where the Vietcong numbered about 82,500 men of whom 25 percent were combat troops, but they also had over 50,000 part-time guerrillas. The Army of the Republic of Vietnam had only 40,000 men. South Vietnam's naval force included six river assault groups, and eleven coastal groups known as the Junk Fleet. The assault troops were under the control of IV Corps' commander and supported the army's riverine operations. Each group could lift an infantry battalion to a threatened area, but in 1966 these assault groups were used only 10 percent of the time in such a role. Army commanders preferred airmobile operations instead of riverine. Despite their greater capability as assault forces, riverine forces were primarily used to support small-unit operations by Regional or Popular Forces under the control of province chiefs. All too often they were used as escorts for commercial craft.

In 1966, despite Ambassador Lodge's remark that he would not be surprised "to see the Mekong Delta totally clear of communist forces by the end of 1965," Vietcong control had been extended to 25 percent of IV Corps' population.

In recognition of this situation, an American riverine force was created in late 1965. It was agreed that two land bases should be developed—one for an infantry division headquarters with a brigade, and another for a brigade in the delta's northern sector—probably in Long An Province. A third brigade would be based on the water. With a mobile floating base, the mingling of United States troops with the population would be reduced—a prime consideration in view of the reluctance of the Vietnamese to accept American ground forces within the delta. Westmoreland approved, calling the concept of a floating base most imaginative.

Initial operations of the Mobile Riverine Force started in June, 1966, in the vicinity of Dong Tam to make that land base more secure and to test operational procedures.

Basically, offensive maneuvers were planned to drive the enemy against a blocking force, with open flanks covered by Army helicopter gunships, or to encircle him. These maneuvers were based on the theory that enemy troops would choose to fight only when they thought that they could inflict heavy casualties or when they were forced to fight.

The Mobile Riverine Force left Dong Tam June 11 and sailed down the Mekong River to Vung Tau where it received additional assault craft. With them, the flotilla numbered fifty-two armored troop carriers, ten monitors and support ships. They sailed to an anchorage sixty miles southeast of Saigon at Nha Be. From there they conducted operations June 13 through 17 as part of the operations of the United States 9th Division that brought greater security to the Long Tau shipping channel although no enemy contact was made. Later operations were equally successful.

During operations in southern III Corps and northern IV Corps the Mobile Riverine Force added to the capabilities of corps commanders by providing water mobility to complement air and ground movements.

In areas where the Vietcong relied heavily on waterways and where they had operated largely unopposed by South Vietnamese armed forces, the Mobile Riverine Force throughout 1967 posed a threat to remote enemy outposts outside the range of artillery positions and almost inaccessible to tracked vehicles. Mobility of barge-mounted artillery enabled this force to cover troops and support them. All operations were planned so the force could move freely among provinces north of the My Tho River, and eventually into the southern delta. By inflicting major losses on Vietcong units, the Riverine Force took away the security provided to local guerrillas and their secret political organization.

In 1967, Admiral Sharp continued to stress the importance of Haiphong's port as the major entry for military supplies, plus the ports of Cam Pha and Hon Gai. He pointed out that Russian aid to North Vietnam in 1965 totaled $300 million, and that two thirds of it was destined for her armed forces. He said their aid rose to $720 million—$520 million in military aid—in 1967. He argued that Hiaphong should be blockaded, but each request was rejected because McNamara and

Johnson believed the risk of damage to Third World ships was too great. Sharp persisted. He said that if North Vietnam's ports were not blockaded the United States should isolate North Vietnam by destroying her major bridges, and mine trans-shipment points near Haiphong and cut all railroad lines from there to Hanoi. This was a much more difficult task for his command, but he was willing to undertake it.

North Vietnam needed to keep Haiphong's harbor free of heavy silt deposited by the Red River, and her dredging operations had to cease during persistent American air attacks. This forced deep-draft ships to anchor in the outer channel and off-load cargoes into lighters that were prime targets. Planes from the carrier *Bon Homme Richard* sank the first dredge July 6, 1967, and the camouflaged vessel rolled over on its side, caught fire and sank. To save its largest suction dredge the North Vietnamese towed it to China. Now increased shipments to South Vietnam were secretly sent to Sihanoukville in Cambodia and transferred by trucks, barges and sampans. War supplies were surreptitiously moved into sanctuaries along the border which were not attacked until the spring of 1970.

Meanwhile, the Russians increased their deliveries of military supplies and more water craft were used to transport them over North Vietnam's inland waterways.

The almost continuous American attacks against targets around Haiphong began to have an effect. By August 25 an evacuation order of the city was given, and the communists indicated they would welcome negotiations.

Air attacks reached their peak in 1967 from June through October with targets in the Iron Triangle northwest of Saigon receiving maximum attention. In August, as a direct result of the pace of air attacks, sixteen Task Force 77 aircraft were shot down, six by SAMs. This was the highest loss to missiles in a single month.

By the end of 1967 Haiphong was the most heavily defended city in the history of air warfare. There were fifteen SAM sites—each with multiple launchers—and five hundred and sixty known anti-aircraft guns of various calibers plus thirty-three MIG-17s or 21s at nearby airfields. During this period, one American aircraft was lost for the expenditure of fifty-five SAMs.

McNamara was not impressed by the air campaign. He said October 10, "I do not think [the bombing] has in any significant way affected their war-making capability. The North Vietnamese still retain the capability to support activities in South Vietnam and Laos at present or increased combat levels and force structure.

"All of the evidence is so far that we have not been able to destroy a sufficient quantity [of war materiel in North Vietnam] to limit the activity in the South below the present level, and I do not know if we can in the future."

For the pilots, risking their lives daily under the restrictive rules imposed by McNamara, who were not allowed to destroy the supplies where they could be seen almost daily, it was a disheartening judgment.

President Johnson did release North Vietnam's major air base at Phuc Yen for attack October 24, but limitations on the number of strike aircraft and the timing of the attacks persisted.

Despite bad weather, missiles, MIG fighters and anti-aircraft guns plus the restrictions imposed on Sharp's command, Task Force 77's accomplishments were impressive: 30 SAM sites and 187 anti-aircraft gun batteries destroyed, 955 bridges knocked out and 1,586 damaged, 734 motor vehicles demolished and 410 locomotives and railroad cars destroyed in addition to the destruction of 3,185 watercraft.

Eleven carriers were used during 1967 and 40,000 sorties were flown over North Vietnam while fourteen MIGs were destroyed in the air and another thirty-two on the ground. The Task Force paid a heavy price: 133 aircraft lost—33 to SAMs, but approximately one-third of the crews of downed aircraft were recovered. North Vietnam's leadership responded to these attacks by ordering 500,000 civilians to participate in air defense and repair work to counter the air campaign. Air Force and Navy strike missions were never prevented by North Vietnam's fighters. Air battles over North Vietnam were usually won by American fliers because air superiority was maintained throughout the war.

CHAPTER 25

Enemy Buildup

A CONDITION AROSE THAT SERIOUSLY HAMPERED CARRIER OPERATIONS. On board the *Oriskany* a year earlier ordnance from a strike aircraft was being removed from airplanes October 26, 1966, and carried back to magazines. Among the bombs were a number of parachute magnesium flares. A seaman, tossing flares from an ammunition cart on the hangar deck to another seaman at the storage locker, mishandled a flare and it fell to the deck. It was about to ignite when the seaman put it into the locker where it set off the others. The resulting fire killed forty-four men, including twenty-five pilots, most of them by asphyxiation, and injured thirty-eight. Bombs had to be jettisoned from the hangar and flight decks to save the ship.

A similar tragedy occurred July 29, 1967, aboard the carrier *Forrestal* when a Zuni rocket inadvertently was fired from a parked fighter on the aft starboard quarter of its flight deck. The rocket went through a belly tank on a nearby attack plane and struck a 1,000-pound bomb on its far wing. There the rocket motor broke up into many small, blazing fragments that spread across the flight deck and ignited the spilled fuel from the belly tank. Within seconds the aft flight deck was enveloped in flames. The fire was brought under control within an hour, but fires below deck were not extinguished for twelve-and-a-half hours. One-hundred-and-thirty-four lives were lost, twenty-one aircraft were destroyed and another forty-one damaged. The *Forrestal* had to be sent to a shipyard for repairs.

Admiral James S. Russell, former vice chief of naval operations, was recalled to active duty in October to review carrier operations and enhance their safety.

The veteran carrier pilot soon realized that both fires should have been prevented. He noted the mishandling of the Mark 24 flare on the *Oriskany* was caused by an inexperienced seaman who, when he dropped the flare and activated the ignition cord, should have taken it to the adjacent hangar deck and thrown it into the sea instead of putting it in the locker with the other Mark 24 flares and dogging down the door. When the flares exploded under pressure the flames went through the ventilation system and killed a number of pilots asleep in their bunks. In regard to the premature firing of a 5-inch rocket on the *Forrestal* in July, Russell determined that the pace of operations had been so heavy that ordnance was stored on the outside of the carrier's islands where there was no sprinkler system to keep the bombs and rockets cool, or flood them if there was danger that they might explode.

Admiral Thomas H. Moorer, chief of naval operations, was disturbed by Russell's report because it was apparent that carelessness had caused numerous deaths and injuries. He had specifically recalled Russell to active duty because he was an old-time pilot who had long been involved with Essex-class carriers.

Russell and his committee made ninety-six recommendations to enhance safety on the Navy's carriers. Most were simple things such as not putting red warnings on bomb and rocket casings and then trying to read them with a red flashlight that washed out the letters and made them indistinguishable. He also recommended methods to dispose of a burning airplane while bombs were going off on a flight deck. Through his efforts, the Navy adopted a sprinkler system for flight decks and the control switches were placed at the air officer's station in Primary Fly Control and, as a backup, on the navigating bridge. When a fire started, either station could immediately turn on the sprinkler system for any section of the flight deck that needed it. Also, a film-forming fire suppressant mixed with seawater was later installed as part of Russell's recommendations on all carriers.

These were vital and worthwhile recommendations but Russell knew the main problem was the inexperience of most ordnancemen and that this condition would not be rectified until changes were made about the war's prosecution by the Johnson administration. Since the United States was not officially at war, regardless of need, well-trained ordnancemen could not be held on active duty when their enlistments ran out. As a result, inexperienced ordnancemen continued to serve on ships.

Russell was appalled by the feelings of disgust expressed by pilots and others on the carriers about the manner the war was being run. He talked to one young dive bomber pilot in October who was walking out to his plane on the flight deck to prepare for a takeoff for a mission against North Vietnam. Seeing the copious notes on the pilot's knee pad, Russell said, "What's going on, son?"

The pilot replied, "Admiral, these are the targets I can't hit on this strike." He said there was a ten-mile circle around Hanoi with a flying field in it that he could not bomb because it took White House permission. (Special clearance was required to bomb any target within thirty miles of the city.) His knee pad notes, he said, provided warnings against bombing merchant ships of Soviet nationality even though he could see them discharging war cargoes in Haiphong's harbor with a dozen lighters around each ship. He explained that he could not hit the lighters until they were ten miles from the Soviet ship although they were bringing ammunition and war supplies to the enemy.

Russell shared the pilot's exasperation, particularly during a period when scores of American pilots were being shot down while they were denied permission to attack worthwhile targets. Anti-aircraft guns on rice paddy dikes, for example, could not be attacked because activist Jane Fonda had accused the United States of trying to starve the enemy by breaking the dikes.

Thieu had agreed earlier, while he was a figurehead chief of state, to issue a mobilization decree in October, but the month passed and he did nothing to implement it. He remained adamantly opposed to such a step until much later when events forced his hand.

The Second Republic of Vietnam officially came into existence November 1, 1967, four years after the end of the first following President Diem's assassination. Its Constitution, approved a year earlier by delegates to a constitutional assembly, called for a two-house legislature and a powerful president. Nguyen Van Thieu was elected with only 34 percent of the vote, and Nguyen Cao Ky became vice president.

Despite the ineffectiveness of the new heads of government there were other outstanding Vietnamese leaders including General Ngo Quang Truong, the airborne division's commander; General Nguyen Viet Thanh, commander of the 7th Division, and General Do Cao Tri, former commander of II Corps and later III Corps. The last two were killed in separate helicopter accidents but they showed by their zeal what properly led South Vietnamese troops could accomplish.

Many Americans were misled by communist propaganda into believing that North Vietnam's General Giap was the greatest general in Southeast Asia. He made many mistakes, and his armies suffered enormous casualties that would have forced the removal of an American commander under similar circumstances.

One of the few developments of a positive nature was the swift evacuation of wounded Americans to field hospitals. Only 2.6 percent of the wounded died, compared to 4.5 percent in World War II. Air evacuation was so swift that countless lives were saved. Actually, two-thirds of all hospital admissions were for tropical diseases and not for war wounds.

Senator Stuart Symington of Missouri grew disenchanted with the war, noting the extreme restrictions imposed on air crews that forced them to follow circuitous and often perilous routes that exposed them to enemy fire longer than was necessary. Now he refused to support the war effort any longer.

There were indications in the fall of 1967 of another enemy buildup, particularly in areas close to Laos and Cambodia. In late October the Vietcong struck the Special Forces Camp at Loc Ninh. Vietnamese reinforcements saved the camp but at the same time approximately twelve thousand communist troops moved against the Special Forces camp at Dak To in northern Kontum Province where the borders of Laos, Cambodia and South Vietnam meet. In response to this potential threat the United States and South Vietnam committed sixteen battalions to counter the threat to Kontum and Loc Ninh.

On the afternoon of November 9 a North Vietnamese battalion ambushed a small United States/South Vietnamese reconnaissance team near Khe Sanh, and then shot down two helicopters attempting to rescue the survivors. By evening, the communists were certain that another rescue attempt would be made that night, or early the next morning. Using the survivors as bait, they hoped to lure the rescuers into a flak trap.

Captain Gerald O. Young received a call from the Rescue Center at midnight to return to Da Nang in their HH-3E Jolly Green Giant and not attempt the rescue. His co-pilot, Captain Ralph Brower, said with disgust, "Hell, we're airborne and hot to trot." All four crew members agreed that Young should request permission to continue the mission. This was done, and they were assigned as backup to the primary recovery helicopter—another Jolly Green Giant. A C-130 flareship, and three Army helicopter gunships, completed the team.

Shortly after midnight the approaching aircraft brought hope to the survivors, and anticipation to the North Vietnamese gunners. Flares from the C-130 cut through the darkness and illuminated the hillsides, but low clouds and poor visibility forced the choppers to operate within range of the guns on the ground. The enemy took full advantage. The small helicopters evaded the withering fire and answered with a stream of rockets and machine gun bullets. The primary Jolly Green Giant hovered nearby, waiting for a chance to make the pickup. Suddenly, the ground fire ceased.

Like motorcycles preceding a VIP limousine, gunships escorted the first Jolly Green Giant, strafing the silent enemy positions, to protect the defenseless rescue bird. The "Jolly" settled slowly into place on a steep slope just as the hillside erupted again with close-range fire from a nearby ridge. The helicopter was an easy target in the ghostly flarelight. Only three survivors climbed aboard and the "Jolly" broke out of hover and wheeled away from the murderous fire. Leaking fuel, oil and hydraulic fluid the bullet-riddled helicopter struggled to gain altitude. The pilot was forced to withdraw before two wounded Americans and the remaining survivors could be picked up.

Captain Young's co-pilot warned the crippled "Jolly" to head for a landing strip at Khe Sanh, knowing it could not reach Da Nang. The other pilot agreed. He warned Young to suspend the rescue attempt because of the intense ground fire and low fuel level of the gunships.

Young and his crew refused to leave. The pilot maneuvered his helicopter into position while his co-pilot directed the gunships' supporting fire. As soon as the "Jolly" touched down, Sergeant Larry W. Maysey was ready to alight and lift the wounded survivors to Staff Sergeant Eugene L. Clay. Young's steady hands hovered the helicopter over a flat pad. This would have posed no problem in daylight, but it was a difficult maneuver under enemy fire at night. With skill and discipline Young approached the hillside under a hail of bullets, while Brower called out enemy positions. Young set the chopper down but was forced to land with one main wheel on the slope to prevent his rotor from contacting the side of the hill. Maysey leaped to the jungle floor while Clay covered him with the "Jolly's" machine gun. While the chopper hung in suspended animation awaiting the survivors, it was hit repeatedly.

Once the last soldier was aboard, Young applied full power for takeoff just as communist riflemen appeared in plain sight. They raked the "Jolly" with small arms fire and rifle-launched grenades. The right engine exploded, flipping the helicopter on its back and sending it cascading down the hillside in flames. Young hung upside down in the cockpit, his clothing afire. He desperately kicked out a side window and released his seat belt, falling free and tumbling 100 yards to the bottom of a ravine. He beat out the flames but not before suffering second- and third-degree burns over a fourth of his body.

He spotted a man lying unconscious who had been thrown free with his foot afire. Young crawled to his side and smothered the flames with his bare hands. In trying to move up the hill to help those who had been trapped in the mangled helicopter, he was driven downslope by searing heat and whining bullets form the communists. He dragged the unconscious man into the bushes and treated him for shock before he concealed himself in a ravine.

Two A-1 Sandys arrived at 3:30 A.M. They could not make contact with the survivors because rescue beeper signals blocked the emergency channel, making voice transmission impossible. The Sandys circled the triangle of burning helicopters and planned a "first light" rescue attempt when they could fly low and slow over the crash site to attract enemy fire and divert it from those on the ground. Fighter bombers and helicopter gunships then could pound the hostile positions while the Sandys escorted another Jolly Green Giant for the pickup. They knew that nothing could be done before daylight, and the communists knew it, too.

As the eastern sky lightened, the Sandys began to troll slowly over the helicopter graveyard. Their pilots were elated to see Captain Young emerge from hiding and shoot signal flares. He tried to warn the A-1 pilots that the North Vietnamese would probably use him as bait for a flak trap, but the beepers continued to prevent radio contact. Sensing a trap, the lead Sandy made forty low passes but the enemy still did not respond. The pilots wondered if they had pulled out at dawn, but they were not sure. At 7:00 A.M. the Sandys were replaced by another pair of Skyraiders.

Two hours passed with no opposition and the Sandy pilots located the survivors near one of the wrecked helicopters. They escorted several Army and Vietnamese Air Force helicopters for a pickup now that there appeared to be no trap. The Sandy pilots identified Captain Young and an unconscious survivor. They also spotted North Vietnamese troops moving back into the area from the south. Fearing a repetition of the night's scenario, they did not dare risk the "Jolly" in a rescue attempt.

As one A-1 dueled with ground gunners and inflicted heavy losses, the other Sandy laid a smokescreen between the enemy and the survivors and led the rescue chopper from the north. Despite the smoke screen the North Vietnamese opened fire and hit the lead Sandy with so many armor piercing bullets that it was forced to leave. His wingman laid down another smoke screen to shield Captain Young and protect the rescue helicopter.

In the jungle, Young hid the wounded man and stole into the underbrush, deciding to help by leading the enemy away from the crash site to protect the rescue helicopters. His maneuver worked and the communists pursued him throughout the day. Dazed, and in shock, Young hid frequently to treat his wounds. When North Vietnamese soldiers approached he crawled into an open field but soon learned that he was going in circles among the tall elephant grass. He was certain the enemy wanted him to contact the rescue force, but he stuck by his decision not to expose friendly aircraft to another ambush.

Because of his action the helicopters were able to land a rescue party at the crash site and pick up one survivor and the bodies of the crew members killed in the crash.

Seventeen hours later, and six miles away, Young escaped his pursuers and only then did he signal a friendly helicopter for a pickup.

Young's selfless act was recognized with a Medal of Honor.

Captain Lance P. Sijan's fighter was shot down over North Vietnam in late December. He parachuted near Vinh and, despite serious injuries to his left leg and right hand, a brain concussion and severe lacerations, he evaded capture for six weeks. By then the shock of his wounds and lack of food had reduced him to such an emaciated condition that every bone showed through his body.

He was captured around Christmas and taken to a prison camp where he was placed in solitary confinement and subjected to long interrogations while being tortured. But he still refused to tell his captors anything beyond his name, rank and serial number.

With other prisoners he was moved January 6, 1968, to another camp and Lieutenant Colonel Robert Craner was detailed to care for Sijan. By now he could neither stand nor sit erect without help.

The two men were sent by truck the next day on a punishing trip to Hanoi. It was a jolting ride and Craner often believed that Sijan had died, but each time he regained consciousness and insisted that he was all right. He never complained, talking only of escaping.

Sijan was taken to Hao Lo Prison and kept in a section airmen called Vegas. His wounds were not treated and he was only able to take a few spoonfuls of food each day. He grew steadily weaker but requested aid only to put his body into a sitting position so he could exercise his slack muscles in preparation for an escape attempt. During evasion after his bail-out his broken left leg would not support him so he had dragged himself on his hips during his flight through the jungle. Now both hip bones jutted through the skin and exercise became excruciatingly painful.

His condition was aggravated by inadequate diet and clothing and he contracted pneumonia January 18. Fluid built up in his lungs and would have strangled him if he had tried to lie down. On the night of the 21st he was removed from his cell and the next day prison officials announced that he had died. Until the end, this indomitable airman had resisted the communists, never once complaining about his condition, while he awaited a chance to escape. Years later, when his ordeal was revealed, President Ford honored his memory with a posthumous Medal of Honor.

During the early months of 1967 General Nguyen Chi Thanh, commander of all communist forces in the South, had admitted to his superiors that the United States had three major advantages since its forces entered the war with combat troops. He cited its great numerical strength, its powerful air forces and its artillery and armored units. Despite these advantages he had advocated a large-scale offensive with main-force units, and advised that he would need a bigger commitment of North Vietnamese troops. He said he believed the United States was out to disperse communist main force units and force them to revert to guerrilla warfare. He said American commanders would try to spread his forces thin over South Vietnam and destroy them piecemeal with superior firepower. (This was the theory behind Westmoreland's search and destroy operations.) Thanh said that if the Americans were successful North Vietnam would be forced to fight the war on United States terms. He said it apparently was United States policy to expand South Vietnam's rural areas through consolidation and pacification to protect their strategic lines of communication. Such a plan, the communist general said, would isolate North Vietnam from the South and cut off North Vietnamese assistance. Thanh concluded that his most effective strategy was to conduct the offensive on all battlefronts continuously and with determination. He reiterated that this was the only way to gain the initiative.

Thanh's strategy of confrontation had ended in failure, especially after his defeat in the Iron Triangle and the Cambodian border areas so North Vietnam's military leaders voiced doubts and criticized Thanh's conduct of the war.

General Vo Nguyen Giap advocated instead a temporary retrogression to defensive warfare. He believed in the spring of 1967 that the North Vietnamese Army was not ready to confront American superiority. He had recommended that operations be focused on small-scale, harassment attacks to consolidate their defense positions in the South, and buy time for training additional North Vietnamese Army units.

Thanh rejected Giap's plan, saying he was one of those he considered "conservative and a captive of old methods and past experience." He charged, "Because these people could not see beyond their past, they thought only of mechanically repeating the past and were incapable of analyzing the concrete local situation which required an entirely new kind of response."

The Thanh/Giap disagreement was not resolved until North Vietnamese leaders aligned themselves behind Giap to extol guerrilla activities that had been successful in South Vietnam. Thanh stuck to his views until his death of cancer July 6, 1967, in Hanoi. Politburo members pointed to disruption of South Vietnam's pacification efforts throughout the year, and obstruction of United States logistic buildup activities, interdiction of vehicle traffic by ambushes on major routes, and terrorist activities in major cities as irrefutable proof of guerrilla warfare's effectiveness. The results, they emphasized, were producing a favorable psychological impact that greatly enhanced communist prestige throughout the world. They cited the shelling of Independence Palace October 31, 1967. This attack, during a formal reception marking the inauguration of South Vietnam's Second Republic with American Vice President Hubert H. Humphrey in attendance, they claimed was of particular importance.

Giap's viewpoint was discussed in an article published in the *People's Army Magazine* in the middle of September and broadcast by Hanoi Radio under the title "Big Victory, Gigantic Task." This was his fourth article of the year and it was important because it expanded on his views of the military strategy that should be pursued in the years ahead. General Tran Van Tra, who had succeeded Thanh, adhered to Giap's viewpoints.

In his new article, Giap analyzed the United States' numerical strength and strong firepower, saying they were not helping because the American armed forces were unable to maintain the initiative. He said the people's war had kept them dispersed over vast areas, such as the demilitarized zone, where the United States Marines were spread thinly over a defense perimeter more than 300 miles long and where Army units in the Central Highlands had to defend an area of more than 120 square miles. Giap said he recognized that United States firepower was strong but that B-52 attacks were not effective because they were scattered almost everywhere.

Giap said he was convinced that the United States would not maintain large military forces in South Vietnam for a long period because it would be worn down by war and sooner or later it would have to negotiate on North Vietnam's terms.

Giap's plan called for American and free world troops to become the primary targets for the infliction of heavy casualties, in addition to attacks against their supply network. He also promoted the concept of main forces concentrated against a strategic zone instead of dispersed all over South Vietnam.

Giap said the effectiveness of attacks was dependent upon the judicious use of three kinds of forces: main, local and guerrilla. He said they could be combined or operated independently. For the future, Giap stressed that communist forces should place more emphasis on coordinated use of all three forces and greatly expand and improve its guerrilla units. These units, he said, later would become the strike forces of the future.

Giap predicted that the United States would expand the war into Cambodia, Laos and possibly North Vietnam where, he thought, a major landing of American forces would take place. He said he was sufficiently concerned to warn that in such an event, China would probably intervene. He said North Vietnam would be prepared to counter such an invasion.

Giap had always emphasized that the war in South Vietnam would be protracted and might last five, ten or twenty years—or even longer. Ho Chi Minh had said much the same thing at the war's outset.

Giap's article seemed to confirm the opinion of most of South Vietnam's leaders that the communist Politburo still believed the war would be protracted. They placed undue emphasis on this phase of Giap's article and so were misled into believing that North Vietnam was not prepared to undertake a general offensive. As a result, South Vietnam's leaders badly misinterpreted Giap's words because the North Vietnamese had already decided on a general offensive during the coming dry season.

In his article Giap expressed his major concern that the United States would expand the conflict beyond the South's battlefronts and that South Vietnam's pacification and development programs might succeed. He believed that expansion of the war must be prevented at all costs because North Vietnam would be forced to extend its forces over a larger geographical area to include not only the North and the South but also Laos and Cambodia. He said he considered that all operations were strategically independent, like links in a chain, and that a breakdown in any one link would disrupt the entire war effort.

Giap wrote that an American landing in the North might have unfathomable consequences for the North Vietnamese regime. The introduction of Chinese forces was not desirable, he said, because the suppressed popular antipathy to the war would surface, resulting in possible insurrection. He was aware that some high-ranking members of the government were not in favor of the war. For example, in September, 1967, 200 party members were arrested and accused of being dissenters. At the same time, North Vietnam enacted a special law imposing harsh punishment on reactionary crimes such as sabotage, spying and opposition to the war.

Despite the advocacy of protracted warfare conceived as an antidote to the United States' strategy of a quick victory. North Vietnam began to feel its debilitating effect. While its leaders argued that the ratio of human losses—one American for every ten North Vietnamese—was more of a concern to the United States, North Vietnam's leaders now began to have second thoughts. The accumulated damage and casualties of the limited air war were having an adverse effect on the North Vietnamese population. Giap was concerned that further suffering might generate an undercurrent of frustration that could end in bitterness and jeopardize the long-term war effort. North Vietnam's economy, that had earlier shown improvement, now plunged downhill as the result of stepped-up bombing of strategic targets. Increasingly dependent upon Soviet Russia and the People's Republic of China for military and economic aid, North Vietnam was experiencing difficulty in steering a middle course between these two nations without alienating either, while both appeared to be headed toward a period of aggravating animosity.

Giap claimed in his article that United States policy was based on maintaining the political, economic and social life of the American people at a high level with few adverse effects caused by the war. He predicted that policy would change as a result of the growing political unrest in the United States and in South Vietnam. The popular manifestations that had rocked South Vietnam's big cities, he said, indicated that the people there were not only anti-government but anti-war. He said signs of popular sympathy for the communist insurgency were evident. In that respect, later events proved him wrong.

The fall election in 1967 in which Thieu and Ky received only 34 percent of the popular vote was seen by the communists as particularly significant. They pointed to Truong Dinh Dzu's 17 percent share of the total vote as indicative of this reasoning. An obscure lawyer with an unsavory reputation, Dzu had campaigned on a platform of "restoring peace and ending the war." This also was the National Liberation Front's political line.

Giap said he believed these things would have the inevitable effect of a catalyst that would start a popular insurrection. He viewed the basic objective of a people's war as that formulated by Mao Tse-tung that victory should have political significance and toward that end be made to look like a popular rather than a military success such as the proposed general offensive.

In early January, 1968, South Vietnamese forces captured Nam Dong, a political commissar assigned to one of the Vietcong's principal headquarters. He disclosed that North Vietnam was switching its strategy from a protracted war to a general offensive-general uprising. This was a radical departure from the first Indochina war against the French and it was due to the growing strength of American forces. There was now no hope in Hanoi of another victory like the one at Dien Bien Phu, but there was a growing belief among communists leaders that a protracted war would cause them unacceptable losses and might end in their regime's collapse. It was now believed that a general military offensive, coupled with a popular uprising, could succeed. They believed that the United States presidential election in November, 1968, could be used to their strategic advantage and that a communist victory before the election would make it impossible for the Johnson administration to authorize more American troops for South Vietnam. Such a victory, it was believed, might force Johnson's hand and get him to seek negotiations on terms advantageous to North Vietnam. The communist leaders were aware of the increasing American and foreign opposition to the war in Indochina and that a big victory would make the opposition's case that much stronger. They believed such a victory might even force the United States to terminate its involvement. The tactical advantage they foresaw of such an attack was the element of surprise, the captured commissar said. He said his leaders had decided to launch the offensive during the Tet holidays and he reiterated Giap's belief in success although he told his captors that even without total success the communists would be more entrenched in rural and mountainous areas. He said any failure in the cities would simply mean a return to old Vietcong redoubts. Dong said the communist leadership knew it would suffer heavy losses in the cities but believed their replacement capability was three times those of South Vietnam. He said the communist leadership was convinced that South Vietnam's leadership was no longer effective and that most people hated the Americans and the Thieu government. He said the antipathy of the people to their government was demonstrated frequently by violent acts and that many civilians were joining such popular organizations as National Salvation and the Buddhist movement. The communist leadership, he reiterated, was convinced that the time was ripe for insurrection and that most people were ready to join the communists.

Nam Dong's revelations later proved reliable, corroborating several unconfirmed reports. General Giap had stated in his article that the American election was merely a device for the party in power to reshuffle its ranks and that the policy of aggression would remain unchanged regardless of who won the election. Actually, the North Vietnamese leaders were aware that in an election year United States presidents were seldom inclined to make bold policy decisions.

North Vietnam was granted a sizable increase in military supplies in September, 1967, by the Soviet Union. The next month, China and the bloc countries also agreed to increase their military and economic aid. The AK-47 assault rifle and the B-40 rocket launcher now became standard issues in the South with marked advantage over the South Vietnamese in terms of firepower.

Preparations for the general offensive had begun in March and April of 1967 when the North Vietnamese confirmed their switch in strategy through Resolution No. 13. Their strategic objective was to insist upon a coalition government. Once success was achieved politically, such a government would order its armed forces to cease combat in areas where fighting was still not conclusive. Coalition leaders then would initiate negotiations with the United States to solve pending political and military matters in the event of victory. The communist leadership saw this as a possibility even though the armed forces of the United States and South

Vietnam were not defeated. Attacks would be primarily targeted against South Vietnam and thereby isolate United States bases. The ploy was to convince the South Vietnamese people that the United States had privately agreed to a coalition government as a solution to South Vietnam's political future. This was clever propaganda. Rumors abounded in September that the United States had agreed to a deal. Doubts were further aroused in the inquisitive minds of Saigon's people. During September, leaders of the National Liberation Front repeatedly broadcast its political program, guaranteeing among other things such freedoms as religion and thought.

North Vietnam's minister of foreign affairs declared December 31, 1967, that if the United States unconditionally ceased its bombing, North Vietnam was prepared to talk. This was a smoke screen to hide her true intentions of developing a theme that the United States was ready to make a deal with North Vietnam. Of course, with cessation of the bombing attacks North Vietnam could speed up infiltration movements into the South during the dry season without great losses.

Other communist announcements of an extended truce during Christmas, New Year's and the Tet holiday were all intended to achieve the same purpose: diversion, and a free hand for infiltration. The communists took advantage of the Christmas and New Year's truce to move supplies into place and to reconnoiter future battle sites.

On the military fronts, as diversionary actions, communist forces launched several large-scale attacks against Khe Sanh and Dak To in the Central Highlands and Phuoc Long and Loc Ninh further south near Cambodia. These attacks were aimed at forcing United States and South Vietnamese military leaders to reinforce these areas and transfer troops that were needed to defend populous and urban areas. Thus, favorable conditions would be created for communist sapper operations in the cities.

It was learned later that the attack on Loc Ninh gave the communists an opportunity to experiment with street-fighting tactics and to test South Vietnamese reactions, while ascertaining the amount of firepower that would be necessary to take over population centers. Infiltrated sapper units were primary forces employed to attack important targets such as the headquarters in each city with the support of local communist forces. Once these objectives were taken, the attackers were told to hold at all costs for a period of two to five days to afford main force units time to move in. Prisoner-of-war camps were to be seized and their occupants liberated while rebellious elements of the local populace were enlisted.

In the countryside, where the Vietcong had been free to collect taxes, assassinate officials and provide communications and support, the communists expected strong support. They believed that the United States and

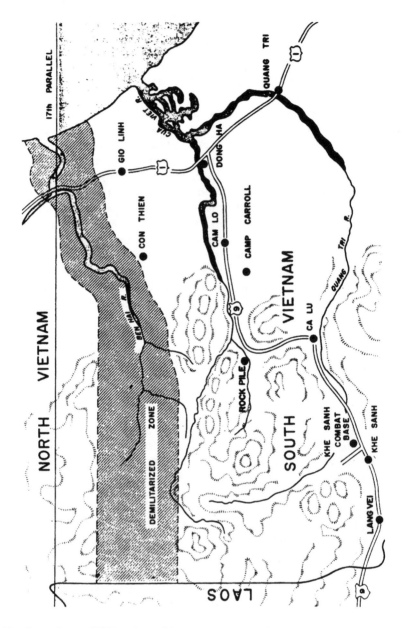

Northern Quang Tri Province. *(Courtesy Historical Branch of the United Marine Corps.)*

South Vietnamese efforts against the Vietcong's infrastructure—the political arm of the communist insurgency—had not been too effective. This, too, was a basic miscalculation. By the end of 1967, 67 percent of the population were living in security under government control, and all but 20 of the 242 districts were secure. Although South Vietnam's economy had improved, the social impact of 485,000 American troops and 60,000 troops of the Third World had caused some disquiet that the communists hoped to capitalize on.

By now there was a total of 1.2 million allied troops arrayed against the North Vietnamese and Westmoreland was optimistic of the outcome. He had told members of the American Congress in November that the United States should be able to initiate limited troop deployments back home by late 1968. He conceded that the border areas were still critical.

North Vietnam's strength in the South was 323,000 in nine infantry divisions plus guerrilla units. North Vietnam had lost 87,500 men killed while over 27,000 had rallied to the other side during 1967. Total United States losses since 1961 were 16,106. South Vietnamese military losses had been relatively light although Vietcong terrorists had caused the deaths of more than 4,000 village officials while 8,000 were wounded and another 5,400 had been abducted.

Thieu and his government officials believed that the presence of almost a half a million American troops, plus those from the free world, would assure their government of survival. The president was convinced that if the communists started anything they would be defeated with heavy losses.

With the approach of the Tet holiday in late January, 1968, there was the usual pre-Tet shopping spree and preparations for the holiday. The government even removed the previous ban on the traditional firecrackers. There were presents for the troops and the under-privileged. Each parcel, in addition to toilet articles, contained a horoscope predicting among other things a bright future for South Vietnam in the Year of the Monkey, and disaster for the communists.

After discussions between President Thieu and Ambassador Bunker, Westmoreland issued a joint declaration of a thirty-six-hour ceasefire effective from the evening of January 29 through the morning of the 31st for the Tet holiday. Westmoreland, concerned by the ominous situation in the North, made an exception in the case of I Corps where increased enemy activity seriously imperiled United States positions. Meanwhile, the Vietcong announced a seven-day Tet truce to last from January 27 to the early hours of February 3. Under cover of this truce, the North Vietnamese used this premeditated subterfuge to prepare attacks of unprecedented scope throughout South Vietnam.

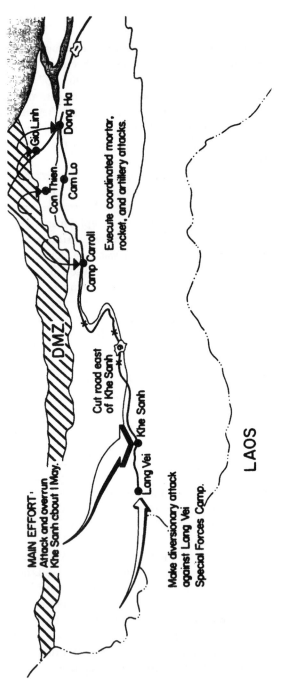

Enemy offensive against Khe Sanh in early 1968. *(Historical Branch of the United States Marine Corps.)*

The Vietcong now hid in cemeteries, drainage ditches and garbage dumps. War cargoes were surreptitiously delivered to the cities in four trips: late November, Christmas and the last two days before Tet. They stole weapons from South Vietnamese units, including artillery guns and vehicles. Once the signal was given they hoped to capture South Vietnamese unit commanders and force them to give orders to their troops to cease combat and cooperate with the communists. Radio and television stations were vital and propaganda programs were prerecorded including Ho Chi Minh's Tet greetings to the South Vietnamese people.

Khe Sanh became a focal point of enemy activity in January, 1968. This was worrisome to Westmoreland's staff because the road over which the base received its supplies had been cut since the preceding August. Now it was no longer possible to fly in supplies with immunity because the North Vietnamese had positioned anti-aircraft guns around the outpost. Therefore, the bulk of daily supplies for the Marines and South Vietnamese stationed there had to be parachuted to them.

The North Vietnamese 325C Division had earlier been identified in the area but a new division—the 304th—now crossed the Laotian border and positioned itself southwest of the base. The 304th was an elite homeguard division from Hanoi that had participated in the battle for Dien Bien Phu against the French.

In the northern provinces the Khe Sanh plateau in western Quang Tri Province had long been viewed by the North Vietnamese as an excellent alternate route to invade I Corps, particularly after two years of attacks across the demilitarized zone had ended in failure. The whole of Vietnam—North and South—could be likened to two rice baskets on opposite ends of a carrying pole. Khe Sanh then would be at the pole's fulcrum in the heart of the rugged Annamite Mountain range. It was a natural infiltration route because most mountain trails were hidden by tree canopies sixty feet in height with dense elephant grass and bamboo thickets. Air observation was difficult because of the depth of the area's cover, and ground sightings were limited to sixteen feet.

Dong Tri Mountain was the highest in the region at 3,000 feet and, along with Hill 861 and Hills 881 North and South, dominated the two main avenues of approach. One, the western access, ran along Route 9 from the Laotian border through the village of Lang Vei to Khe Sanh. The other route was through a small valley to the northwest formed by the Raio Quan River that runs between Dong Tri Mountain and Hill 861. Another key feature was Hill 558 squarely in the center of the northwest approach. In the early days of 1967 the only stumbling block for the North Vietnamese was a small number of United States Marines, their Army Special Services advisers, and South Vietnamese irregulars. The

Green Berets had been the first American troops into the area in August, 1962, when they established a Civilian Irregular Defense Group camp at the site later known as the Khe Sanh Combat Base. In 1966, Marines were in and out of the base.

The Khe Sanh Combat Base was situated on top of a plateau in the shadow of Dong Tri Mountain overlooking a tributary of the Quang Tri River. It had a small, dirt airstrip for helicopters and fixed-wing transports. It had its own artillery and was within range of the 175 mm. guns of Camp J. J. Carroll and the Rockpile.

The largest installation in the entire area, and its brain and nervous system, was located at Dong Ha, eight miles to the southwest of Camp Carroll's artillery base. Several Army batteries of 175 mm. guns could fire into North Vietnam or protect the approaches to Khe Sanh. Ten miles west of Camp Carroll another artillery base was located at the Rockpile whose 175 mm. guns had a range almost to Laos. For additional protection, the Marines had built a series of strong points paralleling and just south of the demilitarized zone. Gio Linh and Con Thien were the two largest sites.

These installations had consistently denied the North Vietnamese Army several forays into eastern Quang Tri Province. The garrison at Khe Sanh and adjacent outposts commanded the approach from the west that led to Dong Ha and Quang Tri City. Without a strategic plateau in American hands—such as Khe Sanh—North Vietnam would have had an unobstructed invasion route into the northern provinces and could have outflanked the allied forces holding the line south of the demilitarized zone. At the time, it was not considered possible for mobile defense of the area with helicopters and fixed-wing aircraft so these bases were used as static defenses with emphasis on patrolling, artillery and air interdiction and occasional reconnaissance in force to stop enemy infiltration.

The North Vietnamese were overwhelmingly defeated in April, 1967, when they first tried to take Khe Sanh. Colonel John P. Lanigan and his 3rd Marine Regiment stopped the main thrust of a regimental-size attack by members of the 325C Division that had hoped to sweep in from the west and seize the airfield, while their heavily reinforced bunkers and gun positions provided direct fire against Khe Sanh in support of their assault troops.

North Vietnamese were blown from their positions in the hills by aircraft of the 1st Marine Aircraft Wing. The ground fighting that followed was bitter for days as the North Vietnamese Regiment held in reserve to attack the airfield had to be thrown into the hill battles in a vain attempt to stop the Marines. It was not until May 5 that all hills were retaken. The hilltops looked like the moon's surface, the once-vivid green reduced to an ugly brown. All vegetation had been blasted away and only churned dirt and blasted trees remained. The North Vietnamese made one more effort to retake the hills but were forced again to pull back.

III Marine Amphibious Force headquarters scaled down the defense contingent at Khe Sanh when the North Vietnamese retreated and the 26th Regiment's 1st Battalion was moved there May 13 to relieve the 3rd Marines who were airlifted to Dong Ha.

After the battle, Colonel Lanigan said it was a conventional infantry battle but the maze of bunkers was a grim reminder of the determination of the Marines to stay and fight. The North Vietnamese had openly challenged the Marines and tried to push them off their hills, but they were the ones who were forced to leave. It was a decisive defeat for the North Vietnamese Army, but it would not be the last at Khe Sanh.

During the second half of 1967 the enemy offensive south of the demilitarized zone was a bloody repetition of the previous year's effort. With more courage than good sense the North Vietnamese streamed across throughout the summer of 1967 only to be chewed up in one engagement after another. They tried to shift emphasis from direct infantry assaults to attacks by long-range rockets and artillery in caves and treelines against Marine fire support and supply areas. Con Thien, ten miles northwest of Dong Ha where the Marines had a commanding view of all activities in the area, was the scene of heavy fighting. There was bitter fighting elsewhere but it was only light and sporadic around Khe Sanh.

Lieutenant General Robert E. Cushman, Jr., head of the III Marine Amphibious Force since June, 1967, made a number of changes. He deployed the 3rd Marine Division from north of Da Nang to the demilitarized zone and east to the South China Sea and west to the Laotian border.

During the fall of 1967 the Marines at Khe Sanh improved their base defenses and installed aluminum matting over the dirt of their 3,900-foot airstrip so four-engined transports could use it. This proved a godsend later.

Westmoreland scrutinized the flow of intelligence reports and January 5, 1968, directed his operations and intelligence officers to plan for a massive aerial bombardment to counter the threat. Two days later he ordered B-52 strikes on an around-the-clock basis plus strikes by other Air Force and Navy planes. The next day he informed the commander of the III Amphibious Force of his plans, saying he was concerned about the demilitarized zone's west end, but that he was also disturbed about reports of an intensification of enemy activity in other areas.

At that time the forces defending Khe Sanh included three battalions of the 26th Marine Regiment under Colonel David H. Lownds and were supported by artillery and tanks. Outside the main base, the colonel had established several important defenses in hill outposts. He was well aware of what had happened to French forces at Dien Bien Phu in early 1954 so he resolved to hold the surrounding hills at all costs. There was one flaw in his defenses because one of the hills blocked the line-of-sight between two other hills, and this stretch of high ground prevented the two units from supporting one another, thereby leaving a corridor through which the North Vietnamese could move to outflank either Marine outpost. This was known and Lownds positioned a company on the ridgeline northeast of one of these hills. Thus the valley's floor was under surveillance by the Marines from all key hills.

On January 21 the communists attacked again with mortars and artillery, causing extensive damage to the Khe Sanh Base, including the loss of a main ammunition dump that was destroyed. Enemy troops once breached the outer defenses until artillery and air strikes broke the enemy attack. After a second attack Colonel Lownds called back some of his isolated units. He knew that the village of Khe Sanh was not in an ideal defensive position so he evacuated it before it was surrounded.

There was widespread criticism in the United States when events on the 21st were revealed. So-called experts expressed doubts that the 26th Marines could hold, saying that the North Vietnamese could skirt the base and ignore it. These critics called for a pull-out, expressing fears that the Marines faced another Dien Bien Phu disaster.

In Vietnam, both Westmoreland and Cushman agreed that the situation was not as bad as depicted by the news media. They knew that the base and adjacent outposts commanded the Khe Sanh plateau and the main avenue of approach into eastern Quang Tri Province. The base was a solid block to an enemy invasion or a motorized supply route from the west. Had the allies greater strength in the northern provinces, they might have achieved the same ends with frequent airmobile assaults—a concept long advocated by General Cushman. In January, 1968, however, there were neither the helicopter resources, troops or supply bases for such operations. Weather was a problem because low visibility prevented airmobile operations during the winter monsoon. Until April the sealing off of Route 9 would have to be left to the 26th Marines.

Westmoreland considered the holding of Khe Sanh a rare opportunity to engage and destroy an otherwise elusive foe. All his previous attempts to box in the North Vietnamese had been frustrated. Now he believed the North Vietnamese had decided to stand and fight. He told his staff that he was anxious to oblige them. He said he was convinced that despite the superior number of the enemy they could be defeated. He said that Lieutenant General Cushman agreed with his decision to reinforce Khe

Sanh and hold the base while destroying the North Vietnamese with massive firepower. Then, he said, his airmobile forces would take the offensive in April when the weather cleared.

Cushman sent in the 1st Battalion, 9th Marines, under Lieutenant Colonel John F. Mitchell January 22 as further reinforcement for the 26th Regiment.

Since three high-ranking North Vietnamese Army officers were killed outside the base, Colonel Lownds had been concerned by the high interest in his western perimeter. He learned the reason when a North Vietnamese lieutenant was captured. He said the eastern avenue of approach was the key that the communists believed would unlock Khe Sanh's defenses. He said that the North Vietnamese first intended to attack and seize Hills 861 and 881S, both of which served as fire bases. From these commanding positions, the enemy would push into the valley and apply pressure along the northern and western portion of the Marines' perimeter. These efforts, he said, would simply be a diversion to conceal the main thrust—a regimental ground attack from the opposite quarter. He revealed that an assault regiment from the 304th Division would skirt the base to the south, hook around to the east, and attack parallel to the runway through the 1st Battalion's lines. Once this compound was penetrated, the North Vietnamese lieutenant revealed that communist forces expected the entire defense system would collapse.

To prepare for the attack, Vietnamese General Lam authorized the 37th Ranger Battalion to be sent to Khe Sanh January 27. This was the fifth and final battalion for Colonel Lownds' command as he prepared for a showdown.

Although it was not known at the time, two other North Vietnamese divisions were being held in reserve, but they were never committed because the defenders of Khe Sanh refused to yield ground to the first two divisions.

In reaching his decision to defend Khe Sanh, Westmoreland had to consider whether he could afford to reinforce Khe Sanh's five battalions, keep them supplied by air, and defeat an enemy that was far superior in numbers until the weather cleared for full air operations. It was a difficult decision and he ordered an overland relief expedition to be ready if one should be needed. He was convinced, however, that Khe Sanh could be held, and the enemy destroyed.

The North Vietnamese directed heavy mortar fire against Khe Sanh and the surrounding hill defenses January 22. Tactical airplanes and artillery responded but two re-supply helicopters and Air Force fighter-bomber were lost to ground fire.

Across the Laotian border three North Vietnamese battalions overran friendly Laotian troops and local inhabitants were forced to evacuate their villages and withdraw to the east. Eventually these refugees reached the Special Forces camp at Lang Vei where the Laotian commander had previously been a reliable source of intelligence about North Vietnamese movements. His report that tanks were a part of the communist attacking force was not accepted.

When the North Vietnamese opened their attack January 21 Westmoreland initiated air strikes against enemy positions by the Seventh Air Force. He also ordered the strengthening of other I Corps positions. The 1st Cavalry Division (Airmobile) was moved forward to the vicinity of Phu Bai, six miles south of Hué on Route 1. That same day the Seventh Air Force began its strikes. These timely reinforcements provided the III Amphibious Force with the necessary units to thwart the enemy's major objective—the capture of Hué and Quang Tri.

On the eve of Tet, Hanoi Radio broadcast a short poem by Ho Chi Minh:

"This Spring [Tet] is entirely different from previous ones
Because every household is enjoying news of victory,
North and South are now forever reunited.
Forward! Total victory will be ours."

This poem was intended to stimulate communist troops in the South and exhort the South Vietnamese people into joining them in the general uprising. The poem's last line also had the code words for attack. His poem was conceived weeks before in the expectation of success. Now all details were completed and the hour to strike was awaited.

Units scheduled to attack first received their orders only forty-eight to seventy-two hours in advance. No unit commander from the middle level down ever knew the attack was part of a countrywide general offensive. Most indications could not be kept secret from officials of the Republic of Vietnam's government and United States officials, so little action was taken to prevent disclosure in the final hours.

There had been several indications of a general uprising earlier. In early October a copy of Resolution 13 by North Vietnam's Politburo was obtained by South Vietnamese intelligence officers; it called for victory in a short time and prescribed the strategy for a large-scale offensive to achieve it. As Tet neared, more and more captured enemy documents confirmed that an offensive was about to be unleashed.

Marine Captain Vera M. Jones walked to the window of her quarters the night of January 30, 1968, as helicopters made machine gun and rocket strikes near the golf course three blocks away. Never before had women

Marines been permitted to serve in a combat theater. That night, as the North Vietnamese violated the Tet truce, she lay sleepless as mortar rounds exploded in Saigon.

Another officer, Lieutenant Colonel June H. Hilton, was asleep in her quarters at Tan Son Nhut. She had led the first contingent of five Women's Army Corps personnel to Saigon the previous June to serve in Westmoreland's headquarters. By mid-1967, the total number of women officers and enlisted personnel had risen to 160 in Saigon and Long Binh—the only locations where enlisted women were permitted to serve. When the first mortars and rockets exploded outside her quarters she was jolted awake. She rushed to a window and was shocked to see buildings on fire.

The raid caught her by surprise, but she was not alone. In some city quarters early commuters the next day noticed strange faces of men in odd uniforms wearing the distinctive Binh Tri Thien rubber sandals. Despite the warnings, the surprise was almost total. Westmoreland and his staff were appalled when it was learned that these attacks were widespread throughout South Vietnam. Although they had known the North Vietnamese were building up to an offensive, and leaves for South Vietnamese and American Marines had been cancelled in the northern provinces and they were on full alert, the size and ferocity of the attacks caught them by surprise.

PART III

A REDISCOVERED FAITH

CHAPTER 26

Tet Offensive

THE NORTH VIETNAMESE EXPECTED THAT HO CHI MINH'S THREE-POINT battle cry, "Defend the North, Free the South, and Unite the Country," would have a patriotic and emotional appeal throughout South Vietnam because the United States was labeled as an imperialist power that had replaced France. They were quickly disillusioned.

South Vietnamese soldiers on guard duty at the main gate of III Corps' headquarters at Bien Hoa January 30 were shocked to be confronted by a Vietcong reconnaissance team. They quickly opened fire and killed a communist soldier.

Can Tho, the seat of IV Corps' headquarters, was also invaded by communist sappers disguised as tourists who earlier had rented rooms in one of the city's hotels for the night. They were discovered and promptly arrested.

South Vietnamese irregulars captured enemy soldiers on Saigon's defense perimeter and one prisoner revealed that communist troops were preparing to attack Saigon, Tan Son Nhut, the Joint General Staff's compound and Saigon's principal radio stations at 3:00 A.M. January 31. This was only a few hours away, and the attack began promptly on Tet's second day.

The Vietcong achieved total surprise everywhere. Even President Thieu took no significant action when he first learned the news because he did not believe his own intelligence reports. At the time he was holding a reunion with his wife's family in My Tho.

Saigon's early risers could not believe their eyes when Vietcong troops in palm-leafed hats and black rubber sandals established themselves in some of the city's blocks. Few had believed the communists would launch an offensive against the cities and towns during the Tet holiday. Urbanites were particularly shocked because they had not seen much of the war.

The Tet offensive quickly revealed serious weaknesses in the plan to defend Saigon. The commanding general of South Vietnam's III Corps had responsibility for the capital but he had no control over the National Police. And the intelligence coordination between the Joint General Staff and the Military Assistance Command was poor. In effect there was no central intelligence control in South Vietnam so the communists were able to achieve surprise almost everywhere.

Some concern had been expressed by South Vietnam's Joint General Staff when two airborne battalions—the last reserves—had been ordered to deploy to I Corps because Westmoreland believed that the situation in the demilitarized zone required additional South Vietnamese troops. They had not departed, however, because of non-availability of air transportation.

President Thieu had reduced the truce time to thirty-six hours a few hours before the Tet holiday because Westmoreland and the United States embassy had told him the situation bore several indications of an imminent enemy offensive. Even then, however, it was not expected that Saigon and other major cities would become objectives. It was believed that the greatest threat would be posed in the northern provinces.

Thieu's last action before he left Saigon was to cancel the truce in I Corps' two northernmost provinces. He also ordered all other South Vietnamese units to confine 50 percent of their troops in barracks. Special Tet leaves were limited to 5 percent of each unit but they were not cancelled. In some areas division commanders and province chiefs took defensive measures based on their own estimate of the situation. At Ban Me Thuot the commander of the 23rd South Vietnamese Division cancelled all leaves after he reviewed captured enemy documents. Other division commanders did likewise.

On the afternoon of January 29 two pre-recorded tapes were seized at Qui Nhon and transmitted to II Corps headquarters where they were forwarded to General Cao Van Vien, chairman of the Joint General Staff. Their contents were so revealing that he warned all corps commanders of imminent enemy attacks, and instructed them to take appropriate defensive measures. Some commanders later complained that the warning gave no true sense of urgency. Few troops took the warning seriously and some slipped off to join their families.

At midnight January 30 every household began celebrating Tet. Three hours later the first attacks began at Nha Trang and during the night all five provincial capitals in II Corps came under enemy attack.

In Saigon most people were in a festive mood at first and they were not concerned about the warnings. But at 9:45 A.M. January 31 radio stations interrupted their regular programs to cancel the Tet truce in view of the enemy's violations. By afternoon all major accesses to the city were subjected to tight control, and the airborne battalion took up duties as a reserve force.

Downtown, police took up defense positions at vital street intersections, but their presence was hardly noticed by the few people on the streets. The uninterrupted noise of firecrackers echoed throughout the city and the first enemy rounds fired into the city at 2:00 A.M. blended with this noisy background. Now groups of armed men could be seen moving silently through the darker streets. Those who watched them believed another coup was unfolding against their government.

The communist attacks were not fully coordinated, probably to deceive the South Vietnamese, as twenty-eight out of forty-eight cities and provincial capitals were targeted. They had six major objectives in Saigon for January 31: the headquarters of the Joint General Staff, Independence Palace, the United States embassy, Tan Son Nhut, the Vietnamese Navy headquarters, and the National Broadcasting Station. Except for Tan Son Nhut the primary enemy force was the C-10 Sapper Battalion with 250 men. They had lived under cover within the city and were familiar with city life and its streets. The battalion had been ordered to gain control of its six objectives and to hold them for forty-eight hours until other local forces could maneuver into the city to relieve them. The attack against Gate 5 at the Joint General Staff compound ended in failure because of the arrival of a United States Military patrol jeep that the sappers fired on, alerting those in the compound. Enemy units also failed to arrive on time at Gate 4. Then they compounded their error by occupying the wrong building. Two airborne companies arrived and promptly drove them off. President Thieu was flown to the compound at noon by a United States helicopter, and convened a staff meeting to adopt plans to counter the threat. During the meeting they received word that the attack against Independence Palace had been thwarted.

Suicide attackers attempted to take over the United States embassy and a few got in the front yard, but not into the locked building. All were quickly killed.

At the National Broadcasting Station, guards were overwhelmed and Vietcong soldiers took over the studios. The transmitter was located several miles away and its operators switched off the lines from the downtown studio as soon as it was occupied and used a standby studio to continue broadcasting with tapes and records. So smooth was the transfer of programming to the transmitter that listeners did not note any change. At 5:00 A.M. an airborne company took over the main studios and Vice President Ky appealed to the population to remain calm.

Attacks against the Vietnamese Navy's headquarters and the Philippine embassy also failed, as did the attempt to kidnap Prime Minister Nguyen Van Loc at his home.

At Tan Son Nhut, three enemy battalions—two of local Vietcong soldiers and the other from the 9th Vietcong Division—attacked Gates 10, 51 and 2 at 3:00 A.M. They broke through 51 but met fierce resistance by airport security guards and their almost immediate reinforcement by two companies of the 8th Airborne Battalion still awaiting transport to the North under previous orders. At the same time the 3rd Armored Squadron of the United States 25th Infantry Division at Cu Chi began to move toward Tan Son Nhut under emergency orders to assist United States forces at the airport. By daybreak the squadron entered Tan Son Nhut and inflicted serious losses to the enemy troops and forced them to retreat.

Despite rapid restoration of control at these major objectives, by dawn January 31 enemy local forces had penetrated several areas in western and southern Saigon. The enemy tried to sever land communications between Saigon and Bien Hoa, seat of III Corps' headquarters, and to close the access road to Vung Tau in the south. The enemy effort in the northern suburb of Saigon was strong and persistent. This area was heavily populated, easy to infiltrate, and provided the enemy with a perfect position from which it could initiate attacks against nearby key military installations.

Vietcong troops in Saigon served as guides for attacking units. A few actually held jobs in United States and South Vietnamese agencies. When the attack began most Vietcong who participated in subversive activities believed that success was assured. They acted as guides and informants for the attackers and helped to arrest South Vietnamese civilian and military officials. They also acted as propagandists, inciting people to support the liberation forces. Fifteen enemy battalions had been introduced into Saigon, Cholon and part of Gia Dinh Province. They occupied a northern Saigon suburb, the 7th and 8th precincts in Cholon, the Hy Tho race track and part of a few city blocks in downtown Saigon. They broke up into small units, taking shelter in people's homes while they organized defenses in buildings and awaited reinforcements.

South Vietnam's armed forces in III Corps consisted of three infantry divisions, a Ranger group and three armor squadrons. In addition to United States II Field Force headquarters, the 199th Infantry Brigade was at Long Binh while three infantry divisions, the 25th, 9th and 1st, were based in the surrounding area.

South Vietnam's General Staff called reserve units to rush to the relief of Saigon. Within hours an additional seven infantry battalions had reinforced the eight battalions in the city.

By the end of the third day South Vietnam's armed forces in Saigon had been increased to sixteen battalions. With these forces the Joint General Staff launched a major relief operation to clear the enemy from Saigon. General Vien took personal command and the city and its suburbs were organized into areas of operation.

A major battle was fought in Saigon February 11. With the support of one United States unit, the South Vietnamese Rangers wiped out a high-level command post in the Phu Lam communal temple. After this battle, that cost the lives of six high-ranking communist officials, fighting in the city declined.

Fighting resumed February 17, however, as a new series of attacks erupted. Rockets caused heavy destruction at Tan Son Nhut and the nearby Military Assistance Command headquarters. This fighting lasted until early March and was highlighted by bitter fighting inside Saigon and Cholon.

In Washington, the Joint Chiefs urged President Johnson to authorize air strikes against Hanoi and Haiphong. They also pressured him to call up the reserves, but McNamara approved only a 10,500-man increase for Vietnam and refused to call up the reserves. In early March, Westmoreland was still seeking 206,736 more men, but he got only 22,000.

After March 7 there was relative calm in Saigon that lasted until May 5 when fighting broke out again. Countrywide the situation was greatly improved except for Hué where the fighting still raged. There the loss of civilians was high, including the massacre of approximately four thousand people who became victims of communist atrocities committed during the twenty-five days the city remained under their control.

Hué, a city of 140,000 people, was the cradle of militant Buddhism. It had consistently defied all central governments, first with its confrontation with President Diem in 1963, and again in 1966 when dissident South Vietnamese soldiers openly defied Saigon's central authority. These demonstrations tinted Hué with a certain hue of political radicalism that the communists identified with their interests. Thus they considered Hué the South's second most important city, and the perfect place for inauguration of a coalition government of their making.

At the time of the first attack, the South Vietnamese Army had only a headquarters for its 1st Infantry Division at Mang Ca, a small and isolated camp in the northern corner of the Old Citadel. The Citadel was a square-shaped area whose outer perimeter was made of earth and stone, twenty-five to thirty feet high and surrounded by a moat. Both rampart and wall were built in 1802 during the reign of Emperor Gia Long, forefather of the Nguyen dynasty. Within the Citadel were the Imperial Palace with its stately Midday Gate topped by a majestic flagpole and constructed in the

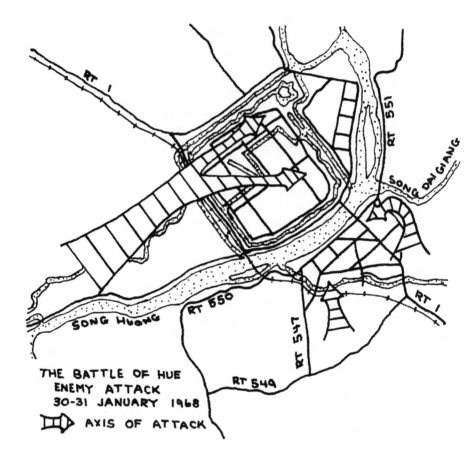

The Battle of Hue. *(Drawn by Master Sergeant Bradley A. Spencer, M.C., Ret.)*

ancient architectural style and, in stark contrast, the modern Tay Loc airfield. South of the Citadel ran the River of Perfume over which two bridges provided access to the more contemporary southern part of the city—Trang Tien and Bach Ho. On this southern bank governmental and military installations were located, including the Thua Thien sector headquarters and the Military Assistance Command compound. There were no American combat troops. The nearest base was at Phu Bai, five miles to the southeast, where the 3rd Marine Division was headquartered.

With only the headquarters staff of the South Vietnamese 1st Infantry Division inside the Citadel, it was almost defenseless. The nearest combat units were the Seventh Armored Cavalry Squadron a mile and a quarter to the southeast at An Cuu, and the 2nd Airborne Battalion ten-and-a-half miles to the northwest of Hué.

Prior to Tet, Hué had been tense due to the constant reports of large-scale troop concentrations near Khe Sanh and north of Quang Tri. The United States 1st Air Cavalry Division had moved from II Corps to its new base ten miles to the northwest of Hué. They were ready for any eventually, but no sign of attacks against Hué were reported at the start of the Tet holiday.

The Lunar New Year's day passed without incident amid traditional celebrations. But the North Vietnamese struck at 3:40 A.M. the following morning with fierce preparatory fire of rockets and mortars. By the morning of the next day, despite desperate resistance, Hué had practically fallen under enemy control with the exception of the key military and governmental headquarters. By 8:00 A.M. the flag of the National Liberation Front flew on the Midday Gate's flagpole.

The commander of the Vietnamese 1st Division ordered his troops to retake the city, and his forces were joined by available United States forces. In addition, Brigadier General Ngo Quang Truong ordered the 9th Airborne Battalion back fron Quang Tri. With a United States airlift they landed at Mang Ca while others were brought in. Tay Loc airfield inside the Citadel was retaken after two days of heavy fighting as United States Marines were placed on full alert.

The communists had overrun the principal prison and had freed 2,000 prisoners, some of whom were used as laborers while the others were given arms to replace combat losses. The Vietcong quickly consolidated their control of the city. They divided it for defense purposes, placing each section under control of a Revolutionary Committee. Civilians were required to register with the committee and turn in weapons, ammunition and radios. Many civilians were asked to report again and evidently were murdered, including those on the Vietcong's black list. Families were told they had to attend a re-education course. Those detailed for work were given picks and shovels and ordered to dig shelters. These holes became their graves. On the campuses of Gia Long and Gia Hoi High Schools, and in the vicinity of Tag Quang Tu Pagoda, the bodies of thousands were found later, while others were located in forests outside the city. This was the worst atrocity of the war, and one largely ignored by the world's press.

Hué was considered by the various Saigon regimes as the most anti-government city in the South. It had always been the breeding ground for the communist-inspired National Alliance for Democracy and Peace. Hué had attracted some left-wing professors and students at its university. It is possible that the pre-planned mass murder was aimed at eliminating the government of Vietnam's organization and its personnel against whom the Vietcong had long harbored a blood feud. General Truong later said he believed the murders were committed to protect Vietcong members whose identity was known after they surfaced, and it was announced that Hué would be retaken at all costs.

Once the weather moderated for air operations, United States and South Vietnamese aircraft attacked two battalions in the southwest corner of the Citadel, and United States Marines and South Vietnamese troops forced their way into the city.

A message was intercepted February 16, 1968, from the enemy head-quarters inside the Citadel that their commanding officer had been killed, and that their losses had been heavy. They recommended withdrawal of the rest of their troops. Their request was denied and they were ordered to fight to the end. Three days later they counter-attacked seeking to retake Tay Loc airfield. It was learned later that this counter-attack covered the escape of high-ranking communists who had been stranded in the Citadel.

The stubborn resistance of the communists inside the Citadel lasted until February 21 when their situation became desperate. Three United States Air Cavalry battalions made a concerted drive against the La Chu area northwest of Hué and occupied it, thus severing all communications and re-supply activities between the Citadel and the outside.

Two South Vietnamese Ranger battalions increased the strength of the attackers and the Imperial Court was retaken February 24 and the National Liberation Front's flag was brought down, ripped into tatters and the Republic of Vietnam's flag run up in its place. For the first time in twenty-five days the yellow and triple-red-striped flag fluttered tri-umphantly in the breeze. This battle ended the communist's occupation of Hué. It had been the most fierce, bloody and destructive of all battles during the offensive. The communists had committed sixteen battalions, or almost the equivalent of two infantry divisions. They lost more than 2,000 killed in Hué alone. Communist leaders later said they lacked accurate intelligence and blamed poor coordination among their units for their failure to retain control of Hué.

In large part the allied victory at Hué was due to the men of South Vietnam's 1st Division who held on to their headquarters in the Mang Ca compound and from there continued to direct operations from the outside. The compound proved a vital base to receive reinforcements and an excellent staging area for counterattacks. The South Vietnamese troops, although few in number, had demonstrated high morale and fought superbly despite repeated calls from the communists to surrender. The gallant fight put up by the 81st Ordnance Company, with only eighty men, fought off repeated attacks for fifteen days as the enemy sought to obtain their stock of 1,400 M-16 rifles. They even moved their stock before their compound was overrun. Militia troops also fought well until they ran out of ammunition and were forced to withdraw.

United States Marines contributed to the clearing of the Citadel. The fighting was so heavy that 80 percent of all houses within the Citadel were destroyed.

Hué's people lived in agony during the communist control of their city, enduring horrors and hardships they had never before experienced. There were shortages of food, water and electricity and the populace lived among decaying corpses that could not be buried and whose smell drove many civilians into hysteria.

During the intense struggle to retake Hué, watercraft were subjected to heavy punishment by rockets, automatic weapons and mines as they tried to deliver supplies on the Huong River. North Vietnam had launched a large-scale assault against supply routes on the Huong and Cua Viet Rivers. When the fighting reached its peak intensity February 20 General Abrams, Westmoreland's deputy, requested that a naval task force be organized to coordinate the protection of watercraft using these rivers to supply Hué and Dong Ha.

Rear Admiral Kenneth L. Veth, commander of Naval Forces, Vietnam, organized a task force under Captain Gerald W. Smith to provide river patrol boats and ground and air units to protect shipping. Once security conditions improved, convoys were discontinued although sweeps by river patrol boats continued along with mine-clearing operations.

By early March the task force took the offensive and began using river patrol boats and armored troop carriers to insert troops behind enemy lines and provide them with gun support. The North Vietnamese retaliated by using more mines, and night patrols became necessary.

Westmoreland belatedly recognized that tactical airpower needed a single manager, and March 8 designated his deputy for air operations,

General Momyer, for this job. Momyer's control included all United States
Marine fixed-wing strike and reconnaissance aircraft. Westmoreland's action was taken as a result of the buildup of Army forces in I Corps to
maintain maximum flexibility in allocating aircraft where they were most
needed. Such control was contrary to Marine doctrine and tradition, and
was not welcomed by officials of the III Amphibious Force.

The northeast monsoon had seriously curtailed air operations
throughout South Vietnam during the early months of 1968. In the Iron
Triangle aircraft averaged only three days per month for visual strikes. In
February, only three percent of the days were flyable.

With such severe weather restrictions, the Navy's A-6 Intruders bore
the brunt of the missions, usually at night.

A vital port facility, newly authorized for attack on the southeast corner
of Hanoi along the Red River and south of Gia Lam airfield, was set up for
attack by the *Kitty Hawk's* VA-75 under Commander Jerrold Zacharais.
When the *Enterprise* arrived at Yankee Station with VA-35, Zacharais
transferred to the nuclear carrier and led raids until the *Enterprise's* squadron could be trained for combat.

On the night of February 21, 1968, Zacharais led his squadron as they
approached Hanoi from the mountains in the northwest. There was no
moon and they used their terrain-avoidance radar to fly at 500 feet above
the peaks. Once they were clear of the mountains they descended to 200
feet so SAM radars could not pick them up. Zacharais could just discern
the ground at this altitude. After leaving the mountains behind he saw a
SAM launched dead ahead as the light from the SAM's booster reflected off
the bottom of the overcast, and from every rice paddy between his aircraft
and the missile. The missile was ten miles away and fired directly at them.
He descended to 100 feet but overshot this altitude and was down to forty
feet above the ground. This was too low so he went back to 100 feet. Now
he spotted a second SAM headed their way, off to the right, so he made a
15-degree course change to the right to place the missile on their left side
where he could see it at all times. Five seconds later the missile made a
course change to compensate for his heading alteration. Zacharais waited
until the proper time and then broke sharply up and to the right. He
passed 500 feet in a 70-degree bank as the first missile exploded underneath, right where he had been. The explosion rocked the Intruder and
Zacharais descended back to 400 feet. On their bombing run no more
missiles were fired at them, possibly due to North Vietnamese concern
that their missiles would land back in Hanoi. Six miles from the target
every gun on the ground seemed to open up as the radar officer picked up
the target. Close in Zacharais rose to 780 feet and their twenty-four bombs
were dropped. He noted that Hanoi was blacked out but there was enough

light from the flashes on the ground for him to see river banks and determine they were on target. Zacharais broke left and went lower as he crossed Hanoi at 530 knots to wake up the city's heavy sleepers. He altered course on his return to the *Kitty Hawk*, frequently going back to avoid flak sites that were hosing the sky with bullets. He knew that at 400 feet you could see it all coming up and could pick the holes that looked lightest to go between.

Hué's occupation by the communists caused most of its civilians to change their minds about their government. Afterwards, they learned to accommodate themselves with their national government and, above all, to reject with determination every political inclination that smacked of sympathy for the communists.

Pham Hung, South Vietnam's communist leader, circulated a memorandum among leaders of the communist hierarchy shortly after the start of the offensive that, despite substantial gains, communist forces still fell short of their objectives. He said they had not been successful in inciting a popular uprising. "The primordial thing we have to understand is that our General Offensive-General Uprising has been conceived to defeat a stubborn and reactionary enemy who has more than 1.2 million troops, all modernly equipped. Ours is a strategic offensive of long duration, which consists of several military campaigns and popular uprisings intended to shatter every enemy counter-attacking effort. As such, it has to be an extremely hazardous fight.

"We must continuously attack the enemy and deny him the chance of rest and to reorganize. We must attack the enemy repeatedly, 3 or 4 times if need be, in those areas under contest, and we must not withdraw just because we fail in our first effort."

From statements such as this it was obvious that the communists did not consider this offensive a one-time effort but part of a multiphased program with each phase including several surges of activity.

The initial phase of the offensive abated during the first week of March, and it was apparent to allied leaders that in view of severe losses the enemy needed a respite to reorganize and refit his battered units.

During January, 1968, Senate confirmation hearings for Clark M. Clifford, Johnson's recommendation to replace McNamara as secretary of defense, Clifford expressed the fervent hope that the bombing of North Vietnam could be stopped if some kind of reciprocal word came from the communist leadership that they were ready to bargain for peace in good faith. "The deepest desire that I have is to bring hostilities in Vietnam to a conclusion under those circumstances that permit us to have a dignified and honorable result that in turn will obtain for the South Vietnamese that goal which we have made such sacrifices to attain."

Senator Strom Thurmond asked, "When you spoke of negotiations, in which case would you be willing to have a cessation of bombing? I presume you would contemplate that they would stop their military activities, too, in return for a cessation of the bombing."

"No, that is not what I said," Clifford replied. "I do not expect them to stop their military activities." He explained that he agreed with the president that the bombing would be stopped if the North Vietnamese would agree to start negotiations promptly, and not take advantage of a bombing pause.

"What do you mean by taking advantage if they continue their military activities?" Thurmond said.

"Their military activity will continue in South Vietnam, I assume, until there is a ceasefire agreed upon. I assume that they will continue to transport the normal amount of goods, munitions and men to South Vietnam. I assume that we will continue to maintain our forces and support our forces during that period. So what I am suggesting, in the language of the president, is that he would insist that they not take advantage of the pause in the bombing."

Once again a top official of the administration was falling into the same trap that officials of the Truman administration encountered in negotiations with the communists during the Korean War. It was learned then that in negotiations with communists that you never weaken your pressure when they seek a cessation of activities. When this was done during the Korean War the communists increased their buildup of offensive weapons and the United Nation's command fought two more years. The Johnson administration was about to make the same mistake.

The State Department shortly afterwards confirmed that Clifford's views represented the policies of the government. There is no question that this viewpoint weakened the American position in Vietnam. Admiral Sharp protested to the Joint Chiefs, saying in effect that if the bombing of North Vietnam were stopped whenever the communists said they would enter into talks, "We would have tossed away our most effective means of applying pressure on the enemy. Although it is agreed that in such a situation we should maintain our momentum in South Vietnam, we would be doing so with our right hand tied behind our back: that is, engaging in a land war on a land mass of Asia without fully utilizing our air and naval offensive power. Such a defensive strategy would be disastrous for the achievement of our objectives in Southeast Asia."

In a speech at San Antonio, President Johnson said that the United

States was ready to talk peace at any time, any place, any where while stopping the bombing and expecting no counter action by the North Vietnamese. In effect the president was telling the communists that all they had to do was be patient and more concessions would be forthcoming.

North Vietnam's failure to win over the populace in the South and its losses on every battlefront called for a re-evaluation. Communist leaders focused on the American homefront and tried to impress upon the American people that the United States was losing the war and that it should withdraw. Communist propaganda won battles for them that their military forces were unable to achieve. President Johnson now was convinced that the majority of the American people were not behind him and he sought to bring North Vietnam to the peace table. He considered offering a cut in the bombing of the North as an inducement, hoping North Vietnam would also halt its attacks on villages and cities throughout South Vietnam.

Johnson sought the views of the Joint Chiefs about stopping the bombing above the 20th parallel. They said it could be stopped briefly to determine North Vietnam's intentions. But they agreed that North Vietnam probably would continue to fight until enough force was applied to threaten their existence as a power base. Since the first of the year bombing had been seriously curtailed anyway due to the northeast monsoon.

While a bombing halt was discussed, the weather changed from the northeast to the southwest monsoon so conditions over North Vietnam would be poor for another month and all but a few strikes would be cancelled anyway. Air Force Chief of Staff McConnell agreed to stop bombing during the month of April. All agreeed that if North Vietnam did not stop shelling South Vietnam's cities, cease its assassination of village chiefs, and withdraw their regular divisions across the demilitarized zone that bombing should be resumed without reservations. They urged President Johnson to set a time for peaceful actions by North Vietnam otherwise, they told him, the bombing halt could be used as propaganda just as the North Koreans had done.

Much of the 1968 Tet offensive in the southern provinces was broken by the middle of February through the combined efforts of the Mobile Riverine Force and units of South Vietnam's armed forces. The integration of Army and Navy units was uniquely tailored to operations in the eight provinces of the Mekong Delta as the Mobile Riverine Force complemented its efforts with other American and Vietnamese units. Its presence in 1967 and 1968 often tipped the balance of power in the northern delta region in favor of the allies.

President Johnson spoke to the Congress and the nation March 31,

1968. "I am taking the first step to de-escalate the conflict," he said. "Tonight I have ordered our aircraft and naval vessels to make no attacks on North Vietnam except in the area north of the demilitarized zone where the continuing enemy buildup directly threatens allied forward positions and where the movements of their troops and supplies are clearly related to that threat. Our purpose in this action is to bring about a reduction in the level of violence that exists."

What he did not say was that his order would spare 80 percent of all targets in North Vietnam.

Johnson also announced that he would not be a candidate for re-election. "With America's sons in the fields far away, with America's future under challenge right here at home, with our hopes and the world's hopes for peace in the balance every day, I do not believe that I should devote an hour or a day of my time to any personal partisan causes, or to any duties other than the awesome duties of this office—the presidency of your country. Accordingly, I shall not seek, and I will not accept, the nomination of my party for another term as your president."

His decision recognized a political truth that he probably would not receive the nomination of his party and that, even if he did, he could not be elected in the fall. A Gallup poll released on this date showed only 29 percent of the American people approved of his handling of the war, and that 63 percent disapproved.

The communists had lost every battle in Vietnam but they had won a resounding psychological victory in the United States. On April 3, 1968, they agreed to discuss an armistice and immediately took advantage of the peace talks to improve their military position while they pushed their political warfare through propaganda. Thus the United States missed a golden opportunity to deal a death blow to an enemy in agony. More troops were not needed now, and it was time to turn most of the fighting over to the South Vietnamese. The missed opportunity proved tragic in loss of lives and prestige for the United States.

North Vietnam's overwhelming defeat in South Vietnam was not recognized by most people in the United States, but it should have been. The combined armed forces of the allies was so overwhelming that it exceeded the communists' manpower by almost three to one and made their defeat a foregone conclusion. Airpower played a key role due in large part to allied air superiority. The United States Seventh Air Force had 650 fighter-bombers while the Vietnamese Air Force had a large force of attack planes and helicopters. United States Army aviation had an impressive fleet of gunships and airlift transports while Marine aviation had been used almost exclusively for support of their two divisions in the northern provinces. In addition, carrier planes of Task Force 77 had played a prominent role. B-52 bombers had flown 1,200 sorties a month against assigned targets. All told, the allies had 1,090 aircraft available for the Tet offensive with more than sixteen airfields plus at least three carriers offshore. In contrast, the North Vietnamese had no aircraft in the South. Fortunately, on the eve of Tet, control of airpower had been centralized and this action proved decisive in holding Khe Sanh and other key points.

Westmoreland made a serious error in not warning the American people of the possibility of such an offensive. He was aware of the buildup before the holiday, although the widespread attacks throughout South Vietnam had caught him by surprise. His briefing officers at the Five O'Clock Follies often gave newsmen the idiot treatment and that did not enhance his prestige with the media.

Basically, the Vietnamese armed forces did most of the fighting and most units fought well. Not one army unit broke under intensive pressure, or defected to the North Vietnamese. In the first phase of the attacks the communists lost 32,000 killed and 5,800 captured. By the end of the second phase in May another 5,000 died. The communists failed to hold any city except Hué and that was only for twenty-five days. The general uprising which they had confidently counted upon to achieve success did not occur. It was a military defeat for North Vietnam and even the Vietcong headquarters admitted that they had failed to seize a number of primary objectives and had not been able to destroy any South Vietnamese units. Most galling of all was the fact the people of South Vietnam had refused to join the uprising. The fighting did disrupt pacification in the countryside, however, generating 600,000 new refugees.

Dragon's Jaw Bridge, crucial to North Vietnam because it was a major part of its transportation system from the North to the South, now was a charred and twisted mass of steel girders after repeated bombing attacks. The central railroad was a patchwork of flimsy boards upon which rested twisted tracks, while its concrete roadbeds were unusable. Both approaches to the bridge were so cratered that movement of vehicles across the bridge was impossible.

With Johnson's bombing halt, substantial repairs were started and it soon became usable, and it was protected from further attacks for the next four years.

During those years, while most of North Vietnam remained off limits to bombers, 25,000 more Americans died as the communists continued to support the war from privileged sanctuaries.

Prior to President Johnson's address to the nation, in which he took himself out of the presidential race, he announced that Westmoreland would be replaced as Military Assistance Commander by his deputy,

General Creighton W. Abrams, in June. Westmoreland was named chief of staff of the United States Army in Washington.

After the Tet offensive it was suggested at the highest levels that American women in uniform should be removed from Vietnam. Such a move was strongly opposed by the women, most of whom were volunteers, and who resented the implication that they could not take combat conditions. Actually women often held up better than some of the men under stressful conditions.

Three years earlier four Navy nurses had been injured during the Vietcong terror bombings in 1965, becoming the first women to receive Purple Hearts in Vietnam. By the end of the war eight Army nurses had died, most in air crashes, although Lieutenant Sharon A. Lane was the first Army nurse to die of shrapnel wounds during a rocket attack June 8, 1969, against the 312th Evacuation Hospital where she served at Chu Lai.

Through the defection of Colonel Tran Van Dac, a deputy political commissar in IV Corps, it was learned that North Vietnam considered it mandatory to follow up with a second offensive. Westmoreland and his staff prepared a coordinated plan to crush this new attempt. It was apparent that the North Vietnamese would use the peace talks to refit their battered units and again take up the fight to conquer South Vietnam.

CHAPTER 27

Khe Sanh

WHEN THE COMMUNISTS LAUNCHED THEIR 1968 TET OFFENSIVE THEY struck in force everywhere in South Vietnam except at Khe Sanh. Most attacks were made by the Vietcong while North Vietnamese Army regulars remained out of the fighting. Two of the four divisions around Khe Sanh were regular North Vietnamese organizations, and they were prepared to seize a portion of Quang Tri Province to give North Vietnam a stronger bargaining position at any future conference.

At first American and South Vietnamese commanders expected a pitched battle similar to the one in 1967 but the communists continued to bide their time, settling instead for artillery exchanges while Khe Sanh's defenses were strengthened.

Defense of Khe Sanh was a part of allied plans to control the area near the demilitarized zone. The North Vietnamese had massed large troop concentrations within this zone, in Laos and in the southern panhandle of North Vietnam. In opening this new front, Nguyen Van Mai, the top communist official in Cambodia's capital Phnom Penh, predicted, "We will entice the Americans closer to the North Vietnamese border. . . . and bleed them without mercy."

There was speculation in the American press that the isolated base at Khe Sanh might fall and end American participation in the war. The media constantly harped on the specter of Dien Bien Phu, but there was no parallel to the two situations. At Khe Sanh possession of the surrounding hills made the base more tenable. Companies on each hill not only denied the enemy an unobstructed firing platform from which they could strike defense installations, but they also served as eyes for the rest of the regiment in the valley that was relatively blind to enemy movements.

Elements of Battalion 3 on Hill 881S were a constant thorn in the enemy's side because men on that most isolated of Marine outposts could observe all three of the main North Vietnamese firing positions.

The Marines had devised a crude but effective early warning system of impending attacks. Motor transport personnel mounted a horn from a truck on top of a tree with lead wires attached to two beer can lids. When a message was received from 881S the Marine who monitored the radio pressed the two lids together and activated a blaring horn that warned of incoming artillery rounds. The radio operator relayed the message over the regimental network and dived into a hole. Men in the open usually had from five to eighteen seconds to find cover or just hit the deck before all hell broke loose.

Company I on 881S bore the brunt of North Vietnamese artillery and their existence became a nightmare. When the sheer weight of the constant enemy bombardment is considered, enemy shells caused a relatively small number of casualties. Men wore flak jackets and were led by topnotch officers who knew how to protect their men.

The North Vietnamese launched three of their heaviest attacks during the first week in February and there was some bitter fighting. A counter-attack deteriorated into a melee that resembled a bloody, waterfront brawl. Darkness and ground fog so reduced visibility that hand-to-hand fighting was necessary. On Hill 861A, a Marine almost decapitated his adversary with a roundhouse right in the face, then leaped on the flattened soldier and dispatched him with a knife. Another enemy soldier jumped a Marine from behind and was about to slit his throat when his buddy jabbed the muzzle of his M-16 between them and, with the selector on full automatic, fired off a full magazine. The bursts tore huge chunks from the Marine's flak jacket but cut the North Vietnamese soldier in half.

"Attention to Colors." Captain William H. Dabney snapped to attention and faced the improvised flagpole and saluted along with the members of his Company I, 3rd Battalion, 26th Marine Regiment.

On battle-scarred hilltop 881S to the west of Khe Sanh his men remained half hidden in trenches and foxholes. Most men had scraggly beards, torn trousers and rotted helmet-liner straps. Second Lieutenant Owen S. Mathews, the only man left in the company who could play the bugle, lifted the battered instrument to his lips and raggedly played "To the Colors" while two enlisted men raced to the radio antenna that served as a flagpole and attached the Stars and Stripes. The American flag was as battered as the men over whom it waved as it snapped open in the light breeze. To the southwest of their position 120 mm. mortar rounds emitted their familiar thunk as they left their tubes and the men knew that in twenty-one seconds those rounds would be bursting around them, but no one moved until the flag was run up high on the hill. With the last note of the bugle the men dove headlong into their foxholes or scrambled into bunkers. Seconds later explosions walked across the hilltop and black smoke, dirt and debris erupted into the air. Rocks, splinters and spent shell fragments whined viciously overhead but the men were hunkered down with familiar expertise and the mortars did no damage. Captain Dabney lifted his head cautiously while smoke drifted away from their position, noting with a tired grin that a much smaller banner now arose above their position. On a nearby pole a pair of red, silk panties waved defiantly in the breeze. A few men stood up and jeered as Maggie's Drawers taunted the North Vietnamese, while other men saluted with an appropriately obscene gesture. The daily flag raising on Hill 881 South was over. There was no particular political significance to the action, merely a show of defiance, but it boosted the morale of the embattled Marines.

When the communists were driven off with heavy losses Hill 881S was not attacked again and so could provide support to their comrades on 861 who were heavily engaged. Now Company I's mortar tubes became so hot that Marines used precious drinking water to keep them cool enough to fire. When water ran out they used fruit juice, and ended up urinating on the hot tubes. Their spirited defense helped to blunt the enemy attack on 861.

The fighting on 861A was especially bitter as Marines used grenades. With their flak jackets to protect them from fragments, Marines threw grenades, turned away and hunched up.

In the early hours of February 7 the North Vietnamese attacked the Special Forces Camp at Lang Vei, five-and-a-half miles from Khe Sanh astride Route 9, with twelve Russian amphibious tanks followed by infantry assault troops. They soon were in the heart of the compound and almost half of the 500 defenders were either dead or missing, but the survivors had destroyed seven tanks and caused as many casualties as they had suffered. Colonel Lownds knew that any attempt to relieve them by land would be suicidal and he ruled out large-scale helicopter efforts when the North Vietnamese withdrew their tanks in fear of just such an attack.

Plans for hit-and-run raids were drawn up by General Cushman's headquarters and Westmoreland approved them. It was agreed that helicopters not needed for the defense of Khe Sanh would be used. The survivors of Lang Vei managed to break out and worked their way to an older camp while helicopters evacuated the South Vietnamese irregulars and their American advisers.

The North Vietnamese troops made their first daylight attack the morning of February 8 against the 26th Marine Regiment. It ended in savage hand-to-hand fighting but they were driven off and quiet reigned for several weeks, although there was continued artillery pressure.

The weather remained miserable but the air effort continued. Pilots learned that the key to their survival was to fly a steep approach through the eastern corridor, make a short roll-out, and a speedy turn-around after landing. A small ramp paralleled the western end of the strip that transport crews used as their unloading point. After roll-out, pilots turned off the runway onto the easternmost taxiway, then wheeled on to the ramp while loadmasters shoved supply pallets out the back. All outgoing passengers were quickly loaded because planes rarely stopped rolling or they would be hit. Each pilot completed the loop by turning back onto the runway via the western taxiway and took off in the opposite direction from which he landed. It was not uncommon for an entire circuit to be completed within three minutes, often while planes were exposed to mortar rounds.

C-130 transport landings were suspended after one was lost and they now had to air drop their cargoes five feet off the ground without landing. With cancellation of C-130 landings, C-123 Providers and helicopters were used but under extremely hazardous conditions. Colonel Lownds was more than satisfied as the transports met his daily requirement of 185 tons of supplies for his five battalions. Through the efforts of Marine and Air Force transport pilots, helicopter crews and ground personnel, the giant umbilical cord that meant life for the combat men was kept open. They could not have survived without it.

While supporting arms whittled away at the enemy's strength, the defensive posture of the 26th Marines grew more formidable each passing day. By the end of February the Americans and the South Vietnamese had erected 510 bunkers, dug miles of trenchlines and laid hundreds of minefields and trip flares. Each sector was guarded by a maze of barbed wire, and there was sophisticated anti-infiltration equipment for night detection.

Unknown at the time to the men at Khe Sanh the North Vietnamese never tried to tunnel under their base. This was probably due to the fact that they were on top of a plateau whose slopes were wrinkled with deep ravines. Colonel Lownds surmised that the communists had decided they would have had to dig too deep to avoid breaking the surface of the ground and that such excavations were impractical.

The North Vietnamese launched their heaviest attack February 29 but they were beaten off by massed artillery and suffered heavy casualties. Never again were they able to muster a force large enough to overwhelm the defenders. This was the turning point in the battle although the communists continued to pound Khe Sanh's defenses with artillery. Clearing skies in March permitted heavy air strikes and they also took their toll.

Radio Hanoi's English-speaking announcer, Hanoi Hannah, changed her line that the Americans would soon be crushed. Instead, she said, "Ho Chi Minh would be unhappy if we wasted our time on only 6,000 Marines." She said the 20,000 men of the North Vietnamese Army had "tied down" the 26th Marines. She was being inconsistent because by mid-March an exodus of major units had started to leave the Khe Sanh perimeter.

In a major operation to relieve Khe Sanh, United States Army, Marine and Vietnamese Army units participated in a deception operation in the early hours of March 30 northeast of Dong Ha, and attacked toward the demilitarized zone along the coastal plains while the 1st Cavalry Division attacked west from Ca Lu to seize high ground along Route 9 in a series of air assaults. Concurrently, the Marines moved forward to secure and repair Route 9.

Once the 1st Cavalry Division moved forward April 1 the deception operation was cancelled. Air support was furnished the attackers, including massive B-52 strikes, as major units reinforced the 1st Cavalry Division. They included the 1st Marine Regiment with three battalions, and an airborne tank force of three battalions.

The relief force, with two Marine battalions in the lead, pushed west from Ca Lu. It was delayed by weather so it was not until 1:00 P.M. April 1, that the initial waves of the 1st Cavalry Division's helicopters were landed five miles from Khe Sanh. There was only moderate enemy contact and Khe Sanh was relieved April 8, and the 3rd Brigade was airlifted into the base to secure the position and become its new landlord. Route 9 now was clear because the North Vietnamese chose to flee rather than face the highly mobile Americans, leaving behind large amounts of equipment in their haste.

In a further operation allied forces returned to the A Shau valley after being driven out two years earlier. The entire operation marked the loss by North Vietnam of a long-held fortress, and demonstrated that the United States and South Vietnamese forces had reestablished control of most areas in the South in the wake of the Tet offensive.

There are several reasons why the siege at Khe Sanh did not turn into a Dien Bien Phu disaster. The Americans first of all possessed overwhelming supporting arms that were not available to the French. Their air and artillery support proved decisive and more than made up for the numerical superiority of the communists. The ability to keep Khe Sanh supplied represented outstanding leadership at all levels of command. The North

Vietnamese and the 26th Marine Regiment stood toe-to-toe in a slugging contest and, despite their numerical superiority, the North Vietnamese destroyed themselves.

The United States Army's Special Forces camp at Kham Duc was attacked by the North Vietnamese a month after the siege of Khe Sanh was lifted. It was named for the small village a half mile from the defense compound south of Khe Sanh in the northern section of Quang Tri Province ten miles from the Laotian border. The camp's 6,000-foot runway was dominated by steeply rising terrain in all directions, and for pilots it was like flying into a green bowl with the field at the bottom. Amidst densely forested hills, the camp was vulnerable to attacks from the high ground surrounding it. It was situated on Route 14 that paralleled the Laotian border and served as an avenue for insurgents to move from Laos north and east to the coastal plain around Da Nang. The camp's Army personnel were assigned to train the Civilian Irregular Defense Group's South Vietnamese soldiers. With the fall of Lang Vei between Kham Duc and Khe Sanh in February, Kham Duc became the only border surveillance camp in I Corps. It was now singled out for a major attack because of its upgrading and apparent vulnerability.

In early April, 1968 there were intelligence reports that Kham Duc might be attacked, so a battalion task force of troops from the American Division was sent May 10 to the camp with 600 troops and artillery units. A few more troops and supplies followed the next day and an airlift was authorized with the highest priority. Now there were 1,760 troops and 272 Vietnamese dependents: a microcosm of the Vietnam war. The others were from American Army, Marine and Air Force units plus American and Australian advisers for the Vietnamese irregulars. The Second Battalion was commanded by Lieutenant Colonel Robert B. Nelson. When he was assigned he knew he would have a battle on his hands so he refused to take any men with less than sixty days remaining in their combat tours.

The camp's forward position at Ngoc Tavark, three miles south of Kham Duc, was overrun by two North Vietnamese regiments May 5, and after four days of bombardment the Vietnamese irregulars, against the advice of their advisers, elected to move back to Kham Duc.

The communists attacked with heavy mortar and artillery shelling on May 10. Some unidentified Vietnamese soldiers approached the Marine section of the compound shouting, "Don't shoot, don't shoot. Friendly, friendly." When the Americans withheld their fire the Vietnamese communists opened up at close range and scored heavy casualties. Some of the fire came from American carbines so the Marines assumed that a few of the attackers were South Vietnamese irregulars who had turned on them. The

Marines were understandably upset and requested a gunship and tactical fighters.

That same day a small contingent of reinforcements arrived at the forward base aboard Marine helicopters but two were shot down. When the camp's defenders were ordered to withdraw to Kham Duc, a small medical helicopter was sent to remove the seriously wounded, but some South Vietnamese irregulars rushed the helicopter, preventing some of the seriously wounded from being evacuated. As the overloaded helicopter took off several irregulars held onto its skids, only to fall off or be shot off high above the jungle.

The camp's equipment was destroyed, with the help of fighter strikes, and those remaining were transported by helicopters to Kham Duc on a number of shuttle flights.

Throughout May 10 and 11 the main camp was subjected to intensified mortar and rifle fire while B-52s dropped hundreds of tons of bombs on suspected enemy positions, but it brought little relief to the defenders.

III Amphibious Force commander, General Cushman, recommended to Westmoreland May 11 that Kham Duc be evacuated. His request was approved because it could not be defended as easily as Khe Sanh. The timing was left to Major General Samuel Koster, the Americal Division's commander. Leaders of the Army Special Forces received word at 1:00 A.M. that the camp would be evacuated May 12 but some units were not informed until hours later.

The pressure on the camp rose during the remaining hours of darkness and outposts were captured one at a time. Ground fog formed at dawn obscuring movements of the North Vietnamese on the high ground. B-52 strikes were made but did little to alleviate the situation. North Vietnamese regiments now made massive attacks against the compound's southeast side. Air attacks were called in but the enemy was too close for effective bombing or strafing. One lieutenant with the South Vietnamese irregulars had to threaten to shoot anyone who left his defense perimeter.

The first helicopter arrived at 7:30 A.M. to start the evacuation but it was hit and destroyed—blocking the runway. Army engineers sent a bulldozer to push the burning hulk off the runway but the communists disabled the bulldozer and killed its driver. Then an attack plane was shot down.

It took an hour to clear the runway before four-engine transports could land. Ground fire punctured the tires of one plane's landing gear and it ruptured its main wing tanks. When the cargo doors opened Vietnamese women and children, and some irregular troops, rushed inside. Some women and children were trampled by the South Vietnamese irregulars. When the aircraft commander, Lieutenant Colonel Daryl D. Cole, decided to evacuate civilians, he found his aircraft was too overloaded, and he was unable to take off on the partly blocked runway littered with debris. He taxied off the runway and the civilians fled the vulnerable airplane. Further evacuation attempts failed and all transport flights were cancelled.

Tactical aircraft were sent to protect the camp after seven aircraft were lost in the previous nine hours. Transports made airdrops and Westmoreland called for additional B-52 strikes. With the camp about to be overrun, it was decided to evacuate.

All air services responded to the evacuation call as another pilot, who had been dropping napalm and cluster bombs on the ridgeline above the camp, had to bail out. An Army helicopter pilot set out to rescue the pilot while a pair of gunships provided fire support. Both gunships were hit but went into orbit around the pilot floating helplessly to earth in his parachute as enemy fire concentrated on him. Once the pilot was down the rescue helicopter prepared to land but the enemy fire was too intense. Gunship pilots made contact with the grounded pilot, surprised that he had survived the intense fire. He was told to remain where he had landed.

The rescue pilot told the gunship pilots, "I'll go down and get him. You follow me." The gunships provided fire while the rescue helicopter settled to earth. There were two companies of North Vietnamese in the area around the downed pilot. They seemed to the rescue pilot as numerous as ants. They stood behind trees and shot at his helicopter. The gunships kept after them but they could not kill them all. The rescue plane settled to earth and the pilot hurried over to the grounded pilot, cut his parachute shroud lines with a knife, and dragged him to his helicopter where he threw him bodily inside and took off. One of the gunship's pilots said the area looked like a World War II movie with burning airplanes all over the place.

The May 12th evacuation was just in time and 1,500 people were taken out although all heavy equipment had to be abandoned. The firepower of the tactical fighters permitted Army and Marine helicopters and large transports to save them. The biggest problem was control of such a large number of aircraft in such a confined space. Unfortunately, some confusion was caused because the order to evacuate was not as widely disseminated as it should have been. Two members of a combat control team had been ordered out of Kham Duc by their commander when he understood that there would be no further air evacuations, therefore their mission was over. Technical Sergeant Morton Freedman and Staff Sergeant James Lundie objected, believing their job was not finished, but they were overruled and flew out.

They were ordered back later by Marine Brigadier General John N.

McLaughlin who believed in the early afternoon that their job was not completed. Major Jay Cleeff and his crew brought them back at 4:20 P.M. While in the landing pattern they saw what was to be the last transport taking off, but no one was sure at the time. After disembarking the control team Cleeff waited five minutes for their return. Mortar shells marched closer and closer to his plane and machine guns started to make his position unhealthy. He decided to leave, not realizing that General McLaughlin was overhead and not knowing what responsibilities he had for the control team. Cleeff took off, leaving the team behind.

In the air Cleeff heard someone say over the radio that the camp was fully evacuated and could now be destroyed at will. He hurriedly called, "Negative, negative." He announced to all who could hear him that he had just inserted a combat control team into Kham Duc. He punctuated his remarks with profanity to emphasize his frustration.

A stunned silence fell on the radio. The men in the airborne control plane were shocked by the news.

On the ground Freedman and Lundie ran to the Special Forces compound but found no one alive and the compound in flames. They crossed the runway and ran to the Americal Division's battalion headquarters but it was empty. Confused, sickened, they realized they were alone on the base with the enemy closing in. They hid in a ditch and Freedman tried to talk to the aircraft overhead with their emergency radio, but it was disabled. Lundie and Freedman almost gave up hope. The North Vietnamese were setting up machine gun positions on both sides of the runway. The Americans vowed not to be taken alive. Freedman told Lundie to take his wallet because it had a lot of money and he did not want the North Vietnamese to get it. He told him to be sure his wife got it, but Lundie's position was just as perilous. They shot two communists in a machine gun nest but they believed their situation was hopeless. They did not believe anyone in his right mind would land on Kham Duc's airfield with the enemy on both sides. Ammunition dumps now started to blow up. Above, no one was sure the men were still alive. A plane was ordered to make low passes over the field to see if they would come out. Lieutenant Colonel Alfred J. Jeonotte, Jr. even touched down but they did not see the men on the ground. As the plane rolled by the men rose up and waved, and tried to chase the accelerating transport but it kept going. Disheartened, they moved back to their hiding place. After Jeonotte's plane took off his crew spotted the men and reported their position. He had insufficient fuel for another attempt and he had to leave. The next plane to make the attempt was piloted by Lieutenant Colonel Joe H. Jackson, the C-123 detachment commander at Da Nang for the 315th Air Commando Wing.

A World War II pilot, and a fighter pilot in Korea, Jackson did not hesitate. He pulled the throttles back to idle, and told his co-pilot Jesse W. Campbell, "Drop the flaps full down."

He replied to a question from the control plane, "Roger, going in."

On his way down he talked to Jeonnotte about the exact location of the team saying that he intended to taxi right up to them. He briefed his crew about what he wanted done on landing and takeoff. To Technical Sergeant Edward M. Trejo he told him to insure that the plane was ready for immediate takeoff and that the jet engines, needed for takeoff, should not be shut down. He advised Trejo that, after landing, to help the load-master, Staff Sergeant Manson Grubbs, to pull the team into the airplane. Jackson side-slipped his airplane to drop rapidly and present the smallest possible target. To watchers in the command plane the C-123 seemed to fall out of the sky and pull out at fifty feet a quarter of a mile from the end of the runway. Jackson was momentarily concerned about blowing the plane's tires because of the runway's debris and the bullets whizzing by them. The transport screeched to a halt and Freedman and Lundie ran to it while firing their rifles back at the enemy.

As Grubbs and Trejo pulled the men inside the airplane Jackson heard Campbell call, "Look out!" Down the runway, straight at them, came a 122 mm. rocket fired from the north ridge. It struck short of the airplane, bounced, spun around several times and skidded to a stop a few feet in front of the plane's nosewheel while they held their breaths, but it failed to explode.

Jackson, using nosewheel steering to taxi gingerly around the rocket now bent like a horseshoe, pushed the throttles to the firewall as he ran up the jet engines and got off the ground in 1,100 feet. They had been on the ground less than a minute. No one talked on the radios. Back at Da Nang Jackson surveyed the airplane with disbelief. There was not a single bullet hole in it. He was the only airlift crew member to win a Medal of Honor for his incredible rescue of the combat control team.

President Thieu proposed April 7, 1968, that all enemy forces with-draw from South Vietnam, and that the communists stop using bases in Laos and Cambodia. He called for national reconciliation, peaceful uni-fication of North and South under international controls to prevent further attacks, and amnesty for communist prisoners if they would renounce violence and abide by laws. His proposal was part of the peace-seeking process, but North Vietnam's leaders had other plans.

As United States strength in Vietnam continued to increase, peace talks opened in Paris May 10 with a delegation headed by Averell Harriman for the United States, and Xuan Thuy, a low-ranking official from the North Vietnamese government. It was soon evident that an agreement was impossible. The United States insisted on withdrawal of North Vietnamese forces inside South Vietnam, a proposal quickly rejected by the communists. The North Vietnamese further muddied the waters by insisting that President Thieu's regime must include Vietcong representatives.

The true intent of the North Vietnamese was revealed before the conference opened when III Corps headquarters received reliable information that the communists would launch a second phase of their offensive on the night of May 4.

The day before, enemy sappers detonated a taxi parked outside Saigon's television and radio compound. Only slight damage resulted but a captured document disclosed that sabotage efforts were intended to impress the Saigon population as to communist capabilities, and as a signal for the start of further attacks. They began as predicted the next day but the communists were soundly defeated in the Saigon area losing 3,000 of their men. All enemy infantry attacks ceased May 12 but a fierce rocket attack was unleashed seven days later commemorating President Ho Chi Minh's birthday.

Calm prevailed throughout South Vietnam until May 25 when there was another surge of attacks. No United States installations were struck in order to convey the impression that the United States was conciliatory towards North Vietnam's peace overtures.

The North Vietnamese had said that rocket attacks against Saigon would last 100 days with 100 rockets fired each day, but this was propaganda. These attacks were not selective, hitting mostly civilian areas, and allied counterattacks curtailed them after twelve consecutive attacks in June.

In both phases of the offensive the communists suffered 170,000 casualties, and lost almost 40,000 weapons of all kinds. A substantial number of communist leaders were killed and the morale of the Vietcong was at a low ebb. More and more North Vietnamese rallied to the South Vietnamese cause and reached such alarming proportions that the communist headquarters in South Vietnam was deeply concerned. To muster more main force units the North Vietnamese deployed their 1st Division from the Central Highlands to the III Corps area and local forces were reinforced.

With the bombing halt against the North, carrier aircraft concentrated on river barges, that often were flak traps, and provided ground support for the Marines.

On one occasion, Morris A. Peelle, commander of the *Oriskany's* VA-23, was on his way to attack targets in Laos with four planes, but was diverted to an emergency target to aid Marines trapped on a hill north of Da Nang close to the demilitarized zone.

Peelle led his formation to the area and checked in with the officer in charge of the Marines on the hill. The ground commander said, "Hey, Navy, we're right down here. We're getting the shit kicked out of us by Vietcong in a clump of trees at the foot of the hill."

Peelle looked down at the thick forest, and was disturbed by the officer's request. "That's awfully close to you," he said, fearful an attack would harm the Marines.

"I know it," the ground officer said. "You come on and drop a couple of 500-pound bombs close to me and I'll let you know how they are in relation to me. As a matter of fact, the guy next to me was just killed."

Peelle was still reluctant, repeating, "That's awful close."

"Come on," the ground officer said. "You can do it."

Peelle decided to make the attack alone and rolled down while the other planes orbited overhead. During his run Peelle's plane encountered small arms fire as he dropped two bombs on the edge of the forest close to the Marines.

"That was perfect," the ground officer called.

Peelle and his squadron mates spent twenty minutes hitting different parts of the grove of trees surrounding the hill—an area of approximately 100 acres.

Once the Marine officer called, "You got us with a little shrapnel that time, but don't worry about it."

After they released their bombs and rockets they swept back and forth, strafing the area.

The small forward air controller cruising fearlessly back and forth in his small plane reported, "You wiped them out."

Upon leaving Peelle called to the Marine officer on the ground. "Sure hope we helped you, Marine."

The officer replied, "Thank God, and thank you Navy."

Although the Tet offensive was put down with heavy losses to the communists those who opposed the war at home insisted on a unilateral withdrawal, saying they had never been given a sound reason for the American presence in Vietnam.

Former President Dwight D. Eisenhower wrote about the criticism in scathing terms. "If they believe this," he said, "it must be because they refuse to read or listen to anything they don't like. There are reasons why it is critically important to fight the communists in Vietnam, and they have been stated often.

"The first and most immediate reason—so obvious that it shouldn't have to be explained—is that we are trying to save a brave little country, to which we have given our solemn promise of protection, from being swallowed up by the communist tyranny. We want the people of South Vietnam to have their chance to live in freedom and prosperity, and even in the midst of a bitter war we are already doing much to help them build up their country."

After the South Vietnamese government weathered the Tet offensive, officials had an increased confidence, and their prestige was enhanced now that their armed forces had been given increased responsibility. Immediately after the offensive, reservists with less than five years of active service were made subject to recall and eighteen-year-old youths were drafted starting May 1. Now personnel in South Vietnam's armed forces would serve an indefinite period as long as a state of war existed. All males eighteen to fifty were mobilized, and those between eighteen and thirty-eight were scheduled to serve in the armed forces, including the Regional and Popular Forces. This general mobilization produced a large number of needed recruits. During 1968, 80,443 men were conscripted and many others volunteered for service. This made it possible by year's end to bring 76.3 percent of the population within government security—a proportion never before equalled. Now only 12.3 percent of the population remained fully under Vietcong control. Although the South Vietnamese armed forces reached a new level of almost 780,000 men, the desertion level remained high—around 10 percent. Part of the problem was the low base pay and allowances because a soldier's pay was below the average cost of living. The Military Assistance Command recommended a 28 percent increase across the board, but this was not enough. Such an increase averaged only $2.80 per man per month.

A major problem with retaining good men was the poor treatment meted out to veterans. Traditionally the Vietnamese armed forces carried physically impaired servicemen on the active duty rolls because of inadequate facilities for their physical and vocational rehabilitation. But this practice misrepresented the number of troops available for duty.

Efforts by the South Vietnamese government under President Thieu were not all in vain. The commendable performance on the part of the South Vietnamese Army and its territorial forces was ample evidence that the United States training effort since 1965 had not failed. In 1968 the Vietnamese Army consistently repelled vicious onslaughts by the communists and their success instilled a new sense of pride and national unity.

There were problems, however, that never were resolved. Qualified leaders were not fully developed, particularly in the higher ranks. Too often American advisers did not take firm stands with their counterparts on key issues, nor recommend relief of unsatisfactory commanders for fear such recommendations would reflect badly on their own initiative. American officers frequently were removed from combat commands because of their unsuitability and given training assignments. If American advisers had insisted upon removal of ineffective South Vietnamese commanders, positions would have opened up affording incentive and opportunity for more junior officers to exercise their leadership abilities. The emphasis should have been on getting the job done, and not on getting along with the individuals being advised.

Before Westmoreland turned over his command to General Abrams on June 11, 1968, he approved the razing of the base at Khe Sanh that American and South Vietnamese troops had fought to defend with so much valor. Allied forces were withdrawn to Ca Lu. This action supposedly was taken because Khe Sanh had outlived its usefulness, and General Cushman believed he could control this enemy invasion route with his mobile units. Westmoreland's action is incomprehensible, and one of the worst command decisions of the war. North Vietnam was handed a strategic base of incalculable value; one that her best divisions had been unable to take in battle.

Admiral Sharp, after reaching the mandatory retirement age of sixty-two, was replaced July 1, 1968, as Commander-in-Chief, Pacific, by Admiral John S. McCain.

Prior to Sharp's retirement there had been concern within the Navy Department that an Army general might be given the top job, one traditionally held by a Navy admiral. At the time, the United States Army had 625,000 men and women assigned to the Pacific theater, far in excess of those in the Pacific Fleet.

CHAPTER 28

A Disastrous Defeat for the Communists

THE NORTH VIETNAMESE BEGAN THE THIRD PHASE OF THEIR 1968 offensive August 17, two days earlier than planned, with a concerted effort in the first three corps areas. This time they made no attempt to propagandize the South Vietnamese people. Their past efforts had failed so they conceded defeat. No main-force units were used against Saigon and local Vietcong troops suffered heavy losses.

In a captured enemy diary one communist soldier wrote, "Everybody is tired and confused. Many don't want the unit to break down into small elements because it would be easily destroyed by enemy attacks. Many others are afraid they will get lost in the city, still others will surely run into difficulties because they can't swim. On the other hand, the enemy is more active, more numerous, and enjoys the initiative."

Another soldier wrote that one-third of the men in his unit were in poor health.

On the propaganda front, North Vietnam's leaders still claimed the general offensive as a great victory. They said the United States and South Vietnam had been edged into a deteriorating defense posture in which they had to redeploy combat units for defense of their cities. They pointed to the evacuation of Khe Sanh and Kham Duc by United States troops as evidence of this deteriorating situation. McNamara's resignation earlier that year and Westmoreland's replacement were also cited as proof that the United States was meeting increasing difficulties in Vietnam.

The third phase was initiated to keep the offensive alive, if only to take advantage of political events that North Vietnam's leaders were convinced were working in their favor.

After announcing another offensive in the fall the political commissar of the 9th Vietcong Division wrote, "I want to remind all of you, comrades, that you should try to live up to your own fame. Let us endeavor to accomplish the mission with which you have been entrusted." The pathetic tone of his appeal was due to his knowledge of the true state of the division's troops which had suffered severe losses.

Actually the Vietcong situation, after Phase Three ended disastrously for the communists, was one of longing for replacements, and reduced activities such as shellings, sabotage and terrorist activities.

South Vietnam's leaders now pushed the pacification program to restore control over the rural areas that had been lost as a result of the general offensive. Both sides knew that the offensive had not yet run its course.

Although the communists failed to achieve any of their objectives, the dictates of politics and the need for a strong bargaining position for peace negotiations continued to keep North Vietnam's leaders under pressure. The communist headquarters in the South issued Resolution 8 in September, 1968, for guidance for a 1969 winter-spring offensive. It was much the same as earlier resolutions and called for complete military victory. This time the approach was different, calling for a step-by-step policy that did not anticipate immediate victory. Communist leaders conceded among themselves that no victory in Vietnam was possible with the presence of American combat forces. It was decided, therefore, to attack major United States units in the hope that the Americans would concede the futility of the war and cease all bombing of the North, instead of targets above the 20th parallel. They had judged Johnson correctly, and he later did cancel all bombing of North Vietnam November 1.

Although the 1968 Tet offensive had been a sound victory for the allies, additional problems were created with three million refugees and an increase in South Vietnam's national budget deficit.

Most South Vietnamese now achieved a better standard of living, although progress would have been more substantial if South Vietnam's leadership had known how to exploit the advantages gained by their military victory. There was now an opportunity for South Vietnam to forge ahead and establish a viable government because most people were behind their leaders. The battle for hearts and minds had never been won in the past but now, due to victory on the battlefields, it was won without much effort. After the communist offensive was crushed most people finally made up their minds as to which side they wanted to live under. There was an almost universal rejection of communism. In the face of disaster, a faith was rediscovered that most South Vietnamese thought had been lost for ever.

This would have been the time for Johnson to start disengagement. By not doing so, President Thieu leaned too heavily on his American ally and proved that he was incapable of leading his country. If he had been forced to do so by an American troop withdrawal things might have worked out differently.

The communists had badly misjudged the mood of the South Vietnamese people. They had completely misread their feelings. Urban unrest had often crippled South Vietnam's government. In the past, political turmoil, coupled with anti-government, anti-United States protests and demonstrations were primarily manifestations of a frustrated urban populace to their ineffective leaders. Their actions were not meant as an expression of communist sympathy. Communist leaders failed to understand this basic truth. Now allied victories instilled confidence in the South Vietnamese people as they gained self-assurance that their armed forces could fight well.

Prior to his departure from Vietnam, Westmoreland had requested an additional 200,000 United States troops. Although he wanted to exploit the gains made by allied troops, his request made no sense. It only fueled anti-war resentment at home. If a gradual reduction of that amount had been requested, it would have been far more logical. Since the enemy had been soundly defeated, fewer United States troops were needed—not more.

South Vietnam now had an opportunity to strengthen its defenses by modernizing its armed forces. Her armies were able to regain the initiative and they drove the North Vietnamese away from urban centers and into the jungles. Two years later its army was able to launch an offensive operation into Cambodia.

In the aftermath of the Tet offensive, South Vietnam's leaders enjoyed the support of their people, the solidarity of their own ranks, and the ascendancy of their cause to free the South of all communist troops. Unfortunately they failed to take appropriate action. They refused to initiate counterattacks and even kept the public in the dark about their intentions. Often the South Vietnamese people learned of actions by its leaders when they were made public by the United States embassy. Now politics again reverted to intrigues and power struggles as if oblivious to every present threat of conquest. Meanwhile, United States politics had irreversibly changed from commitment to disengagement.

President Thieu should have exploited the military victory gained at such cost. If he had done so his country would have been unbeatable. He and his political leaders lost South Vietnam in 1968 because his failure to act aggressively led directly to North Vietnam's final victory seven years later.

For armored forces, the failure of the communist general offensive proved the faith of its proponents. The ability of armored units to move with overwhelming firepower had been of utmost importance throughout the year, and helped to assure defeat of the communists.

Now armored units in combined task forces were spending most of the time in the jungle pursuing weakened Vietcong and North Vietnamese units. The 1st Brigade, 5th Infantry Division, arrived at mid-year. This American mechanized brigade was sent to I Corps in 1968 where the North Vietnamese Army was unused to fighting armored units.

The importance of armor was now so well understood—despite General Westmoreland's earlier lack of appreciation—that long-range plans called for such units to be among the last to leave Vietnam. They proved they could provide mobility and firepower at far less cost in manpower than any other type of unit. It had taken much too long to convince army generals in higher headquarters of their value. Now there was little doubt about the utility of armored forces in Vietnam's jungle warfare. They had been invaluable during the battles of 1968 when the North Vietnamese waged their offensive against the combined free world forces. In seven months the Vietcong and the North Vietnamese had lost 60,000 soldiers without any tangible gains in the South.

In the aftermath of the 1968 Tet offensive both sides changed their strategy. Due to their heavy losses, the North Vietnamese were forced to retire to their sanctuaries.

General Creighton W. Abrams, who succeeded Westmoreland in June, 1968, had an excellent background as a commander of small armored units in World War II. He subsequently commanded an armored division and a corps and served as vice chief of staff of the Army. For the previous year he had been Westmoreland's deputy. He had developed an excellent rapport with South Vietnam's leaders and his confidence in its army was a boost to their morale. Now he gave them broader participation in the war as all forces engaged in small-unit actions to defeat the enemy's remaining forces. American and South Vietnamese armored forces played an important role in this fight to seal South Vietnam's borders. These forces, due to their mobility and heavy firepower, were able to operate in small groups with less chance that any single unit would be overwhelmed. Their mobility permitted them to disperse over wide areas, but still mass quickly when the enemy struck.

After President Johnson had prohibited all air attacks above the 20th parallel March 31, 1968, the North Vietnamese promptly started to repair their rail network. The marshalling yards at Thai Nguyen and Kep, and smaller ones along the northeastern rail system, were soon repaired. Although bombing attacks were outlawed, Johnson still permitted reconnaissance flights and they noted that traffic between China and North Vietnam soon was back to normal. It was also noted that truck travel from the North to the South showed a dramatic increase.

In July, 1968, Secretary of Defense Clark W. Clifford, formerly a strong supporter of the war, became convinced that the war could not be won militarily. He decided to propose to President Johnson that all bombing of North Vietnam should be stopped—not just those targets north of the 20th parallel—and that the United States should begin withdrawal of its ground forces and turn over responsibility for the war to the South Vietnamese.

In Chicago, 10,000 anti-war protestors converged on the city in late August to disrupt the Democratic Convention. Mayor Richard Daley mobilized an equal number of police and National Guardsmen to maintain order. When violence reached a peak August 28 hundreds of protesters were arrested. Their actions alienated many Americans because it was plain that these left-wing dissidents and hippies were bent solely on anarchy. Vice President Hubert Humphrey, the Democratic candidate for president, and his staff drafted a compromise platform that called for cessation of American air strikes against all of North Vietnam, and more responsibility for South Vietnam's armed forces in fighting the war.

Lieutenant Colonel William A. Jones, III, led three other A-1 Sandys on a search and rescue mission from Nakhon Phanom Air Force Base, Thailand, on September 1. When they arrived at their destination northwest of Dong Hoi in North Vietnam, Jones sent two of his planes into high orbit to conserve fuel and remain out of range of enemy guns. Jones and his wingman, Captain Paul A. Meeks, searched for a downed fighter pilot while destroying enemy guns and escorting helicopters for the pickup. Radio contact had been made earlier with the pilot on the ground, but his exact location was not known.

Jones had been warned that he would be in range of ground fire along Route 137, a heavily defended supply road running through North Vietnam into Laos. When the weather got worse, and they had still not pinpointed the pilot's position, Jones led his wingman lower across the rugged hills arising abruptly from the valley floor. A broken cloud layer actually obscured the tops of the highest hills. Without warning his plane was rocked by a violent explosion. His cockpit filled with smoke as Jones regained control and jinked from side-to-side to spoil the gunners' aim. When the smoke cleared Jones scanned his instruments and surveyed his aircraft. It did not appear badly damaged as he realized that he had been the victim of a flak trap with the fighter pilot on the ground as bait.

Jones knew time was important before the communists brought in more defenses, so he and his wingman trolled over the valley and hillsides as fighters pointed out enemy gun positions. When Jones's Sandy passed one point the downed pilot radioed that his plane was directly over his position. At last he had found the man.

An anti-aircraft gun opened up with a barrage of accurate fire from the top of a nearby hill. It was too late for Jones to return the fire and he did not dare call in the fighters because the gun's position was too close to the downed pilot. He racked his Sandy into a tight turn and reversed his course, diving back towards the gun site. He triggered rockets and cannon fire at the hillside, pulled off and rolled in again. During the next pass his plane was riddled by automatic fire. He knew he was in serious trouble. The rocket motor for his ejection mechanism, right behind his head, had been ignited by an exploding shell. Jones looked over his shoulder and saw fire coming out of the rear of his airplane. His instrument panel was clouded with smoke, and fire seemed to burst out everywhere. He knew he had to get out so he attempted to gain altitude and headed for a clear area. He reached down and grabbed the extraction handle with his right hand and pulled. The canopy blew off and he waited for ejection, but nothing happened. With fire all around him, he thought, "This just can't be happening to me. This is not the way it's supposed to be. I've got to get back and see my family." He reached down and grabbed the secondary escape handle to release the extraction gear so he could climb over the side.

When his canopy jettisoned the fresh air increased the intensity of the cockpit fire and the strap that fastened his oxygen mask was burned through, exposing his face to searing flames. His hands were scorched and all he could think was that they looked like mozzarella cheese. Most of his instruments were unreadable and the cockpit was a smouldering shambles. Despite his pain, he tried desperately to broadcast the exact position of the downed pilot and the hostile guns. His radio calls were blocked as other pilots screamed at him over their radios to bail out of the flaming aircraft. Then his radio transmitter failed and his receiver operated on only one frequency.

Incredibly the flames began to die down in the blackened cockpit. He thought desperately that he must make it back to Thailand to report the exact position of the downed pilot and not complicate the rescue effort by becoming a survivor himself. He refused to bail out.

Paul Meeks joined on his wing as the two Sandys headed west. They communicated with hand signals and his wingman took the lead.

Jones, with severe burns on most of his upper body, flew by instinct.

Two-thirds of his windscreen had been shattered by the explosion and the wind blast on his face caused excruciating pain. Even worse his eyes started to swell shut as he trimmed the aircraft to get some protection behind the remaining portion of his left windscreen. The crippled Sandy now was trimmed for uncoordinated flight and skidded through the sky as they passed slowly over the Laotian countryside. Approaching Nakhon Phanom, they learned the weather had worsened so they had to make a ground-controlled approach through a heavy overcast. Despite his mangled hands and blurred vision Jones eased his plane into close formation as Meeks led him down through the clouds. Jones lowered his landing gear with the emergency system and guided his plane to a perfect touchdown and a no-flap landing.

Colonel Leonard Volet reached the gutted aircraft first. He could not believe what he saw. Everything was burned to a crisp, including Jones' helmet, oxygen mask, survival vest, neck and arms. Yet he kept flailing about in his cockpit looking for his maps as he was lifted out. He refused medical attention until he was satisfied that they knew the exact position of the fighter pilot's position on the ground in North Vietnam, and where the enemy guns were located. He continued to debrief intelligence officers as he lay on the operating table. As a result of his detailed information the downed pilot was rescued. Unfortunately Jones died. He was given a posthumous Medal of Honor.

Lieutenant Colonel Richard L. Critz, as operations officer of Marine Aircraft Group 12 at Chu Lai, ordered one of the "nuggets" (a pilot on his first tour) to go out on his first bombing mission where no friendly troops were close to avoid a possibility of error. After he completed his mission, the pilot was instructed to fly to Thailand and fill up the baggage tank beneath his A-4 Skyhawk with soft drinks. The base had been without them for two weeks, increasing a serious morale problem. Critz gave him enough money to get all the cases he could load in the tank.

The young lieutenant fulfilled his mission and returned over the field just after sunset. The center-line lights had been turned on and, as usual, only one out of four was working due to the frequent rocket attacks against the base. In landing the pilot lined up on the runway's right-hand lights instead of those on the centerline. His plane touched down 1,500 feet short of the runway and his right wing snagged the arresting gear in its 500-ton housing. The plane's fuselage was ripped from its mountings and lay over the left wing as the plane skidded in the sand.

Critz got a call from operations. "Hey, we've got a crash!"

He dashed down to the site in a jeep, relieved that the pilot had only sprained his shoulder and noting that the airplane was a total loss along with the soft drinks. There were cans all over the place because the baggage pod had broken open and tossed them helter skelter.

The lance corporal in charge of the crash crew came up. "Colonel, I know what happened. The gooks put those soda pop cans out there and he blew his tire when he landed."

Critz knew better, but he said nothing.

Acting on the advice of Secretary of Defense Clifford, President Johnson ordered all bombing of North Vietnam to cease November 1, 1968. He did authorize continuation of reconnaissance flights and interdiction of supplies through Laos. North Vietnam quickly took advantage of the bombing halt and increased the flow of traffic along its major coastal routes to the demilitarized zone. After that the small harbors in the North were crowded with boats shuttling supplies to the South.

The Joint Chiefs had opposed the halt, saying they were convinced North Vietnam was accumulating large stocks to make another major offensive. Their pleas fell on deaf ears.

American negotiators at the Paris peace talks had yet to begin discussions because the conferences were deadlocked over the shape of the negotiating table, and how the parties should sit around it. This was of significance to South Vietnam's leaders who considered themselves the legitimate government, and they refused to accord equal status to North Vietnam's National Liberation Front.

Meanwhile, the war dragged on. Before noon November 26 a transport helicopter flown by Lieutenant James. F. Fleming and his co-pilot Major Paul E. McClellan inserted a Special Forces team into hostile territory in the western Highlands.

Four hours later the team made contact with the Vietcong and its leader Lieutenant Randolph C. Harrison sent out a radio call for gunship support when he knew they were hopelessly outnumbered. He also requested immediate evacuation.

Overhead an Air Force forward air controller, Major Charles E. Anonsen, responded. He reported that the team was pinned down along a river bank under intensive fire from heavy machine guns and automatic weapons. Anonsen spotted six Green Berets near a clearing 100 yards away with another twenty-five team members in a smaller clearing. It appeared that the Americans were trapped and neither group could provide assistance to the other.

A flight of three transport helicopters and two helicopter gunships heard Anonsen's call. They were en route to a refueling stop but they changed course and headed for the river bank with Lieutenant Fleming in the second transport.

Anonsen briefed the helicopter pilots when they arrived and asked the leader of the ground team to pop a smoke grenade. Red smoke filtered through the foliage and pinpointed their positions. The jungle on three sides of the ground troops came alive as the two gunships sent a stream of fire slanting earthward as the communists fired back. Airborne gunners strained to spot the hostile machine guns as Major Leonard Gonzales and Captain David Miller wheeled their helicopters above the river. Gunship crews finally identified the guns 200 yards south of the men on the ground and ripped the positions with high explosive rockets, destroying two of the heavy guns. The North Vietnamese also found the range and laced Miller's aircraft with machine gun fire.

Despite rapid loss of oil pressure Miller's crippled craft made two more firing passes before it was riddled with an accurate burst. Miller had to pull away and head for base. But, as his helicopter lost power he had to make an emergency landing across the river.

The first transport helicopter, with Major Dale L. Eppinger at the controls, swung in. He touched down beside the crippled helicopter and Miller and his crew climbed aboard. Eppinger's craft was low on fuel as he swung away towards Duc Co.

Within minutes of Eppinger's departure, Miller's helicopter was ripped by enemy fire and destroyed.

Now the second helicopter was forced to leave because of low fuel and only the forward air controller's plane, a gunship and Fleming's transport remained.

The forward air controller radioed the men on the ground to move to a small clearing while Lieutenant Fleming descended toward the river. Meanwhile, Major Gonzales and his gunship forced enemy gunners to keep their heads down as he made multiple passes with guns blazing to cover Fleming's approach.

At treetop level Fleming realized the clearing was too small and overgrown for his helicopter to make a landing. Instead he headed for the nearby riverbank, hoping to hover just above the shoreline with his landing skids bumping the bank and his tail boom extended out over the water. He managed this difficult operation with unbelievable skill as his crew searched frantically for the reconnaissance team. They were nowhere in sight, and the team's radioman could barely be heard above the chatter of hostile guns. Finally, a message came through that they could not make the pickup point.

Fleming's helicopter was an inviting target as he backed out over the river through a hail of bullets. His gunners, Staff Sergeant Fred J. Cook and Sergeant Paul R. Johnson, answered back, raking the concealed emplacements. Gonzales's craft was nearly out of ammunition and both he and Fleming were critically low on fuel. They knew that if they withdrew the soldiers on the ground were doomed. They now had their backs to the river as they hastily ringed their positions with Claymore mines and hoped for a miracle.

Fleming decided to try one more time. For the first time he knew fear as he let down, dropping below the bank to partially shield his helicopter from the deadly enemy fire. The North Vietnamese knew precisely where he was headed so they concentrated their fire on the pickup point and strafed the chopper from all sides.

The six Special Forces men had been under siege for an hour and the communists moved in for the kill. When the North Vietnamese reached the ring of mines, one soldier was blown into the air. The Green Berets killed three of the attackers who had advanced within ten yards of the landing zone, then turned their backs and raced for the helicopter.

In hover, Cook fired at the enemy troops while Johnson tried to clear his jammed gun. As the team reached the rope ladder, Cook continued to fire with one hand, while pulling soldiers aboard with the other. Cook, only five feet, seven inches in height and weighing 120 pounds, helped to lift those 200-pound Green Berets with one hand while Fleming fought to keep his helicopter steady while it rocked as the Green Berets climbed aboard. When the last man was dragged aboard with an assist from Johnson, Fleming sped down river with the ladder dragging in the water.

While Gonzales's craft flew above, supporting Fleming, his helicopter crew ran out of ammunition at the very moment the last of the Green Berets climbed to safety. They had strafed the enemy troops within five yards of the Americans to screen them. They all missed death by inches as the many holes in the windshield proved. For Fleming, his bravery earned him a Medal of Honor.

Throughout the fall of 1968 the South Vietnamese government, with major United States support (United States losses were averaging 200 dead a week), launched an accelerated pacification program. In these intensified operations an area was secured and Vietnamese government units, Regional Forces, Popular Forces, police and civil authorities screened the inhabitants to identify members of the Vietcong. This procedure was successful permitting the expansion of government influence into areas previously dominated by the communists. As a result, two years later at least some measure of government control was evident in all but a few remote regions.

During this period, Richard M. Nixon and his running mate Governor Spiro T. Agnew of Maryland defeated the Democratic ticket headed by Vice President Hubert H. Humphrey and Senator Edmund Muskie of Maine by half a million votes—less than one percent of the total cast during the election. Humphrey's procrastination as to whether he should cater to the wishes of the more liberal wing of his party and defy President Johnson cost him the election. Even Johnson's cancellation of all bombing of North Vietnam November 1 could not overcome the American people's frustration with the way the war was being prosecuted.

Nixon, who had campaigned on the promise of a new look at the war, was expected to bring about a change in the tempo of the fighting in Vietnam as both sides marked time in preparation for what was believed would be an about face in American strategy.

After the election President Johnson ordered fighter escorts for reconnaissance flights over North Vietnam, but the escorting fighters were authorized to attack only if they came under attack. Admiral John S. McCain, who succeeded Sharp as Commander-in-Chief, Pacific, now urged the Joint Chiefs for authority to hit airfields below the 20th parallel because MIGs were threatening the reconnaissance flights. Admiral Moorer, who had replaced Wheeler as chairman of the Joint Chiefs, pushed not only for authority to hit airfields but supply centers above the Mu Gia Pass, and those near Bat Lake thirty to forty miles above the demilitarized zone.

Although the North Vietnamese were constructing airfields south of the 20th parallel and moving SAM defenses even further south until all major passes were covered, posing a threat as far south as Dong Ha in South Vietnam, Moorer's request was denied.

In December, and early January, 1969, President-elect Nixon initiated exchanges with the North Vietnamese, stressing his willingness to engage in serious negotiations, but he was rebuffed. North Vietnam's leaders had achieved a unilateral bombing halt, so they were not about to be cooperative. Instead, they again demanded that the United States overthrow the government of South Vietnam.

By mid-January, the Soviet Union offered a compromise on behalf of North Vietnam to the problem of the shape of the conference table that had deadlocked negotiations since the bombing halt. They suggested a circular table without nameplates, flags or markings. North Vietnam took this action out of fear that President Nixon would again start bombing

North Vietnam. Secretary of State Dean Rusk appealed to President Thieu on behalf of President-elect Nixon to accept this compromise before the inauguration. Thieu agreed and formal truce negotiations got underway January 25, 1969.

The war continued as if there were no peace negotiations.

In early January, the North Vietnamese Army reopened Route 922 from Laos into the A Shau valley, and anti-aircraft guns were installed both in Laos and in the valley. As traffic expanded to 1,000 trucks a day, allied aircraft ran into withering fire from communist guns that took a heavy toll.

Agents reported to 3rd Division officers that communist forces probably would be moved into the Da Krong River area, and possibly into the mountains west of Hué and southwest of Quang Tri. Once in position, the communists would be in a position to make surprise attacks against populated areas as far south as Da Nang.

An operation called Dewey Canyon was organized to deny the communists access into these populous coastal lowlands by destroying his forces and interdicting his access routes from Laos. Colonel R. H. Barrow's 9th United States Marine Regiment was assigned responsibility for the operation.

Attention was focused on Route 922 because it entered South Vietnam from Laos and became Route 548 into the A Shau valley in South Vietnam. It was one of the communist's main supply routes in I Corps.

During the initial phase starting January 19, the 9th Regiment established fire bases to support later maneuver operations. The second phase involved patrolling around the fire bases to eliminate enemy pockets of resistance. The third phase, starting February 11, involved a three-battalion, regimental offensive with supporting aircraft that lasted for seven weeks and covered more than thirty miles of enemy territory.

By the end of February, the three battalions had nearly run out of real estate. They had swept south to the Laotian border, eliminating all enemy resistance, and had captured hundreds of tons of supplies and equipment. Dewey Canyon was officially terminated March 18.

Lieutenant General Richard G. Stilwell, commanding general of XXIV Corps, said later, "Dewey Canyon deserves some space in American military history by sole reason of audacity, guts and magnificent interservice team plays. A Marine regiment of extraordinary cohesion, skill in mountain warfare, and plain heart made Dewey Canyon a resounding success."

In the An Hoa valley southeast of Da Nang Lieutenant Colonel Critz, operations office for Marine Aircraft Group 12 at Chu Lai, responded to a call for close support from Marines who encircled a Vietcong bunker. For the first time since he came to Vietnam Critz saw his target after the strike leader blew the camouflage from an earth and log bunker with Snakeye retarded bombs. After arming his gun pods he came around to make his attack and, after lining up his plane, he squeezed the trigger. The bunker seemed to rise ten feet in the air as his 20-mm. cannon blasted it in five-second bursts. These gunpods could fire 4,000 shells a minute, and they were devastating.

He was about to make another run when he heard the forward air controller say, "Cease fire. No shooting. Cease fire."

He was relieved to learn that the bunker was destroyed although his spent shells had fallen on the Marines who encircled the bunker, although they caused no harm.

In early 1969 the United States Army introduced a new combat vehicle to fill a long-expressed need for an amphibious tracked vehicle with more firepower and mobility than those in use in Vietnam. The M-55 General Sheridan was a partial answer, as the Army replaced its M-49 tanks.

The changing strategy on both sides brought about an increased use of all armored units, especially armored cavalry. Now the ability to move men and vehicles rapidly into battle, especially for small, widely separated engagements, had become acute.

For four years fifty-three Spookies—AC-47s—had filled a critical need for defense of hamlets and outposts. They had earned a reputation as a nighttime defender and they never lost it. Now their long tenure with the United States Air Force was drawing to a close in the rural skies, and by the end of 1969 their operations were turned over to the Vietnamese Air Force.

What began as a search for an aircraft to replace the AC-47 had evolved into a family of gunships, and several allied nations adopted them. The AC-47s were kept in service long after the original intent to use them as an interim attack aircraft. This was due to the fact that the C-130 modifications took longer than expected. By the end of 1968 only four AC-130 gunships were flying combat out of Thailand bases. But the all-weather AC-130 with its sensors, fire-control system and better armament proved far more effective. AC-47s, therefore, filled a critical need, particularly when interdiction missions were authorized against the Ho Chi Minh Trail. Missions were assigned in early 1969 to attack this extensive road and trail network that carried vital supplies to the communists in the South by truck, bicycle or on the backs of porters. The trail's steep mountainous terrain was often covered by a jungle canopy and the communists stored supplies in limestone caves and protected their route system with concealed anti-aircraft guns. Most movement of supplies was made at night. In April, 1968, there were reports that 14,000 trucks were moving through Laos with supplies for South Vietnam's communist troops. This intelligence information imparted a sense of urgency because the traffic was unprecedented and necessary as the communists continued their general offensive.

General George S. Brown, who succeeded General Momyer in August, 1968, as Seventh Air Force commander, had special praise June 9, 1969, for the efforts of the Tactical Fighter Wing. He noted that truck kills in April and May reached new highs, forcing the enemy to replenish his entire truck inventory at frequent intervals.

Some of the problems of getting the AC-130 into service were caused by Air Force Secretary Harold Brown who questioned its worth, and the need to add another costly gunship to the AC-47 and the AC-119. The latter was his choice to replace the AC-47. Pacific Air Force commanders had found the C-119 a disappointment, but Brown insisted on their use because there were large numbers in reserve units. General Momyer, while commander of the Seventh Air Force, argued against the C-119. He wrote June 30, 1967, the "maintenance and logistics problems alone weigh heavily against the C-119." He called its use a regression rather than an advance over the AC-47. Brown later agreed to authorize the modification of C-130s, but valuable time had been lost. When the need for gunships became acute following the Tet offensive, Brown authorized 125 gunships, but the Seventh Air Force believed there was a need for only 72. Brown still held to his conviction that the C-119 would most quickly fill the Vietnam requirement for additional gunships. If he had ever had to fly one in combat—or on any mission—he might have changed his mind. It was never a good airplane for any purpose.

The AC-130 that finally replaced the C-119 proved its superiority by becoming the number one truck killer in Vietnam and an excellent self-contained night attack aircraft.

Major Kenneth Carpenter and his AC-47 had been flying for four-and-a-half hours February 24, 1969, before he received word of enemy activity in the vicinity of Bien Hoa. He turned Spooky 71 toward gun flashes on the eastern and southern perimeters of Long Binh Army base. In their first attack, three thousand rounds were fired. Following their second orbit, he was ordered to give ground troops more flare illuminations and to remain in the area. In the cargo compartment, Loadmaster Airman First Class John C. Levitow set the ejection and ignition controls of the two-million candlepower magnesium flares. Then he carefully handed the flares to one of the plane's gunners, Sergeant Ellis C. Owen, who hooked them into lanyards. He was momentarily diverted by the sound of mortar fire above the noise of the engines. By the way the aircraft was turning he knew that Carpenter was fixing on a new target. Suddenly, a blast shook the aircraft, accompanied by a white flash and showers of flying metal. The crew felt the aircraft start to drop as it veered to the right and then headed down. They were thrown violently about and some were injured. They did not know it at the time but their Spooky had been hit in its right wing by a North Vietnamese mortar shell.

Sergeant Owen had his finger through the safety pin of a flare when they were hit. It was knocked from his hand and now it was armed as it rolled on the floor. They all knew such flares would ignite within twenty seconds and create heat of 4,000 degrees Fahrenheit along with toxic smoke. Levitow, despite shrapnel wounds in his right side, was dragging himself to the open cargo door to pull away one of his injured comrades when he saw the flare for the first time. It was rolling on the floor between two miniguns and a pile of ammunition in storage cans. He took one horrified look at the smoking flare and careened toward it as the AC-47 pitched violently from side to side. Despite his pain he reached the flare and pushed it out the door where it instantly ignited. Carpenter finally got control of the pitching aircraft and flew his injured crew back to Bien Hoa. Levitow's prompt and brave action earned him a Medal of Honor.

The North Vietnamese launched the fourth phase of the general offensive they had started during the Tet holiday a year earlier on February 22, 1969, with a hundred attacks throughout the country: against Saigon and provincial capitals, military installations and outposts. This time there was no surprise and significant attacks lasted only during the first five days. Rockets struck Saigon, Hué and Da Nang as well as key routes in the Central Highlands. The significant feature of this fourth phase was that local forces did not take part. All attacks were confined to North Vietnam main-force units.

There were no enemy ground activities in I Corps due to the success of United States operations in this area, particularly a combined operation that had spanned several months and had just been terminated. The United States 101st Airborne Division, and its South Vietnamese counterpart, plus the 1st Infantry Division had inflicted over 3,000 casualties on the North Vietnamese.

This time the communists were unable to launch an infantry attack against Saigon like it did in Phase 2. In the last two phases their efforts made only inconsequential ripples on the military situation. This time an unprecedented number of communists chose not to fight and defected to the allied cause. Twenty thousand changed sides in the first half of 1969.

This was a threefold increase over the previous year. This defection was due to declining morale and was the first indication that there would be no more all-out offensives for some time. This intelligence estimate proved true and for the rest of the year there were only small-scale attacks by the communists to keep their cause alive for the war's dissenters in the United States and other nations of the world.

In April, the communist headquarters in South Vietnam issued Directive Number 55 in which they admitted the need to preserve their forces for future campaigns. This was a radical departure from previous policies. The North Vietnamese leadership agreed and the rest of 1969 reflected that policy. The war was fought largely with sappers and saboteurs.

The communists' unsuccessful attacks during four phases of their general offensive that began with the 1968 Tet holiday had brought them to the peace table. Talk-and-fight tactics dictated their actions in the years ahead. This was not new, and should have been foreseen by American negotiators. Captured enemy documents in early 1969 clearly stated, "The Paris peace talks cannot bring about any results until we achieve a big victory."

In 1965 Westmoreland had requested authority for B-52s to strike communist supply bases in Cambodia. Prince Norodom Sihanouk had agreed in 1967 provided that no public announcement was made of the attacks. They were not authorized until March, 1969, when the Nixon administration believed that the communists in Cambodia posed a threat to III Corps. B-52s made their first strike March 18 within three miles of the border, and another in April. In May, B-52s were ordered to make a series of attacks against other Cambodian base areas, some within five miles of the border with South Vietnam and all against targets in unpopulated areas. Each strike was approved by the president, and B-52 bombings continued in secret until May of the following year when strikes were made openly in support of allied ground force operations against North Vietnamese bases in Cambodia.

One of the problems associated with all B-52 strikes was that warnings of their attacks were given twenty-four hours in advance to allied commanders, including the South Vietnamese. Throughout the war the South Vietnamese Army was riddled with spies so word of these strikes was almost always leaked to the North Vietnamese so they could evacuate the areas targeted for bombing.

Prior to the Cambodian bombings, Ambassador Bunker had requested private talks with officials of that country and his request was accepted March 22, 1969. Sihanouk never made a public protest against the bombings in his balancing act between the United States and the communists. Oddly the communist delegation to the peace talks never protested these bombings publicly.

However, two months after the bombings started Sihanouk gave a press conference May 13 that almost confirmed the bombings but he denied there had been any loss of civilian lives. He practically invited the United States to continue them, saying, "I have not protested the bombings of Vietcong camps because in certain areas of Cambodia there are no Cambodians."

North Vietnam's General Giap revealed that 500,000 of his men had been killed fighting the United States and South Vietnam. He vowed that his country would "fight on as long as necessary—10, 15, 20, 50 years."

The National Liberation Front was upgraded June 10 to the Provisional Revolutionary Government of South Vietnam in an attempt to give it a political entity of international stature. This was a calculated move to give the National Liberation Front a chance to participate formally in the peace talks on a par with the Republic of Vietnam. The North Vietnamese had finally conceded to the reality of their losses on South Vietnam's battle-fields.

Basis for the new approach was embodied in Resolution Number 9 and the subsequent Resolution 14 on guerrilla warfare. They spelled out the situation at high levels of the party's hierarchy. It was apparent that the communist headquarters was concerned that allied forces might strike into Cambodia where their lifeline lay at the mercy of the allied forces. To the communists, the South Vietnamese seemed more anti-communist than ever—and this was true. They believed that the withdrawal of United States troops and the cessation of bombings in the North would give them the ultimate chance of a final conquest. For the present they were forced to play for time.

CHAPTER 29

Vietnamization

GENERAL EARLE WHEELER, CHAIRMAN OF THE JOINT CHIEFS OF STAFF, told a National Security Council meeting January 25, 1969, that he thought President Thieu would agree to a small reduction of United States forces because such an action would help President Nixon domestically and convey the image of a self-confident South Vietnam. Nixon's new Secretary of State William Rogers said that withdrawal of 50,000 American troops could buy an indefinite amount of time at home.

President Thieu agreed February 6 that a sizable number of American troops could be withdrawn in 1969. General Abrams' deputy, General Goodpaster, reported to another National Security Council meeting March 28 that improvements in South Vietnam's security warranted some withdrawals. "We are close to de-Americanizing the war," he said, "but not yet at the decision point."

Melvin Laird, the new defense secretary, said, "I agree, but not with your term de-Americanizing. What we need is a term like Vietnamizing."

Nixon broke in, "That's a good point, Mel." And the description remained.

Laird remained skeptical about negotiations and the possibility of military victory. He wanted the United States to get out of Vietnam, but without that country's collapse to the communists. Therefore he wholeheartedly supported Vietnamization. Although Laird was a hardliner in negotiations, he believed in rapid troop withdrawals.

Leaders of the Soviet Union reported March 2 that there had been a clash between their troops and 300 members of the Army of the People's Republic of China. The clash, they said, had taken place on an island in northeast Asia. Both countries made much of what should have been an isolated clash on an uninhabited island. In the Western world, there was much raising of political eyebrows at this unexpected announcement, and politicians wondered what it all meant in the global scheme of things. The rumors increased when the Soviet embassy in China was mobbed March 3, and a second border clash occurred March 15 with more troops involved and higher casualties. The Chinese claimed they were only responding to a long series of Soviet intrusions.

At the first private meeting of the new Paris negotiators March 22, Xuan Thuy said that the United States should not expect to gain from divisions between the Soviet Union and China. He insisted that North Vietnam would rely on its own resources, saying that Russian and Chinese leaders had sided with North Vietnam for years in spite of disputes dating back nearly a decade, and that no doubt such disagreements would continue.

With further conflicts along their long border it soon became obvious to the Western world's leaders that there were growing differences between the two countries and that there was always a danger of war between them.

President Nixon decided to explore the possibility of a rapprochement with China, and by fall of 1969 it was apparent through secret diplomatic efforts that the Chinese leaders were interested.

May 8 of that year North Vietnam's leaders proposed a 10-point peace plan to gain control by negotiation what they couldn't achieve on the battlefields. Actually, it was an ultimatum to the United States and it demanded unconditional, unilateral withdrawal, the abolition of the South Vietnamese government and American reparations to North Vietnam. The plan proposed that the South Vietnamese government be replaced by a coalition government to include all "social strata and political tendencies in South Vietnam that stand for peace, independence and neutrality." Of course the communists reserved the right to determine who would stand for peace, independence and neutrality. It was now evident to the communists that the fourth phase of their general offensive was a total failure. In the United States there was great pressure by administration critics not to pass up this "opportunity."

Xuan Thuy said, "If the Nixon administration has a great peace program, as it makes believe, why doesn't it make that program public?"

President Nixon did so May 14 when he told the American people that he would consider abandoning the previous formula that North Vietnam's forces must withdraw six months before the United States, or simultaneously. He agreed to National Liberation Front participation in the political life of South Vietnam and committed that nation to free elections under international supervision, saying they would accept the outcome.

Nixon offered a precise table for a ceasefire and withdrawal of American troops under international supervision. The president refused to consider unconditional withdrawal or any collusion to install a communist-controlled government. It was a fair proposal.

The North Vietnamese disagreed although Xuan Thuy conceded there were points of agreement but that conditions would be attached to such negotiations. In formal negotiations, however, he refused to discuss them and the stalemate continued.

Nixon's new National Security adviser, Dr. Henry Kissinger, issued a directive April 10 requesting that all departments and agencies of the government work to achieve Vietnamization.

Nixon met with President Thieu at Midway Island June 8, 1969, to win his support. A Thieu visit to the United States had been rejected because of concern that his presence might provoke riots.

Thieu promised Nixon he would speed up the process of political and economic reforms, particularly a sweeping change in the land tenure system. Unfortunately this became public knowledge and American advocacy hurt Thieu at home because it appeared he was being forced to make drastic changes. Thieu kept his word and July 11 he offered free elections in which the communists could participate. He also urged the start of a withdrawal of American troops.

At the conference they issued a joint communique emphasizing that both presidents agreed to the principle of "self-determination without interference."

Nixon announced publicly that the first increment of 25,000 American troops would soon be withdrawn from Vietnam and that the United States was determined to emphasize the expansion, improvement and modernization of South Vietnam's armed forces.

The Department of Defense agreed to raise South Vietnam's total armed forces to 953,673 men for fiscal year 1970, and approximately another 40,000 for the following year. This increase was aimed at developing in South Vietnam a modern and balanced military force, capable of supporting itself in combat after United States withdrawals. It was revealed that Regional and Popular Forces would be expanded and modernized with the same basic weapons as the regular forces.

By the end of 1969 population control rose to 90 percent compared to 67.2 percent for the period prior to the Tet offensive. During the year 47,000 enemy troops had rallied to the government of Vietnam—twice the previous year's figure. And the South Vietnamese government resettled or returned to their home villages in excess of 1.5 million people. Now the People's Self-Defense Corps received wide acceptance with approximately two-and-a-half million people volunteering to join it.

Key areas vacated by United States forces were now taken over by South Vietnamese units. In this same time period total communist military strength in South Vietnam was reduced to 243,000. There were an additional 84,000 members in political cadres of the Vietcong infrastructure.

After the Midway conference President Nixon met with his advisers at Honolulu to start the process of troop withdrawals. Some military leaders expressed opposition, believing such action was a reversal of all they had fought for and that with American combat troops out of Vietnam an honorable outcome would be impossible. By now, 36,000 Americans had died. Despite reservations, General Abrams agreed to start the withdrawal of American troops. Actually, it was an awkward situation because President Thieu had personally proposed the withdrawal. Nixon believed that this decision was a political triumph that would buy time to develop a new United States strategy. The decision was well taken, and one that should have been made earlier, but it did cause demoralization problems for the American men and women who remained in Vietnam, and for their families back home. Now the pressure at home increased to speed up the withdrawal.

President Nixon revealed the key points of his so-called Nixon Doctrine on Guam July 25. He called for partnership, strength and willingness to negotiate as basic guidelines of his future policy. In saying that the United States would participate in the defense and development of friends and allies, the president said, "America cannot and will not. . . . conceive all plans. . . . design all programs, execute all the decisions, and undertake all the defense of the free nations of the world. We will help where it makes a real difference and is considered in our interest."

President Nixon made a surprise visit to Saigon July 30, 1969, as part of an around-the-world trip. It was taken against the advice of the Secret Service, but the president believed such a visit was necessary. He told Thieu that continued withdrawals were necessary to maintain American support. He said it was important that such reductions take place on a systematic timetable and on the initiative of the American government.

Prince Sihanouk invited Nixon July 31 to visit Cambodia to formalize the improvement in United States-Cambodia relations. This was four-and-a-half months after the start of the secret bombing of North Vietnamese bases in Cambodia and relations had improved between the two countries. For security reasons Nixon declined the offer.

Although a report in the United States revealed the Cambodian bombings, the reaction was mild. Actually these bombings were of little value. If anything they were detrimental because they drove the communists out of their sanctuaries and into South Vietnam. Their secrecy was merely a means of pressuring the communists without complicating Sihanouk's delicate position.

In Paris the North Vietnamese continued to demonstrate that the so-called peace talks were not a way to seek honorable solution to the conflict but an instrument of political warfare. The Americans quickly learned how skillful they were at it. Although they were the aggressors, Xuan Thuy acted like a stern tutor berating a wayward pupil. He leaked vague clues to the press about goals that had little to do with true negotiations. Many critics of the Americans believed everything they were told by North Vietnam's leaders and, in turn, these critics were privately ridiculed by the communists. The debate over withdrawal of North Vietnam's forces was ridiculous. They never had any such intention.

Kissinger met secretly with Xuan Thuy in Paris August 4. The North Vietnamese negotiator was not a policy maker but only a functionary representing the communist party's foreign ministry. He was sent to Paris with no authority to negotiate. Le Duc Tho, the special adviser to the talks, had the authority. This meeting of Kissinger and Xuan Thuy, although it offered the most comprehensive peace plan the United States had ever placed on the table, got nowhere as Thuy repeated the previous North Vietnamese stand of American withdrawal and total capitulation of Thieu's regime.

When new North Vietnamese attacks were launched, President Nixon on August 23 deferred consideration of the next American troop withdrawal. There were outraged expressions by the Congress and the news media.

President Ho Chi Minh replied to Nixon's conciliatory letter of July 15, 1969, and it was received three days before the North Vietnamese president died. In it he demanded that the United States cease its war of aggression and withdraw all of its troops. Nixon realized that the North Vietnamese were still insisting upon total victory, and he refused to agree to their terms.

September 12 President Nixon authorized an additional troop withdrawal of 40,500 by December 15. He decided that, despite provocations, withdrawals would continue on an inexorable schedule. His decision was reached even though this was a unilateral withdrawal without gaining any concessions from North Vietnam's leaders.

As North Vietnam continued to avoid serious negotiations, the Joint Chiefs devised a plan for mining its ports and harbors, and the destruction of twenty-nine targets of military and economic significance during four days of intensive air attacks. The proposed date for the start of such attacks was November 1, 1969—the first anniversary of the bombing halt of all of North Vietnam. President Nixon refused to implement the plan.

Throughout 1969's summer months public protests escalated. Members of the Women Strike for Peace flew to the University of Toronto July 6 to meet three women representing the Vietcong. In the United States, demonstrators launched a mock invasion of Fort Lewis July 15, and there were weekly demonstrations at the Pentagon, including the pouring of blood on the steps. Twelve young soldiers from a Honolulu base sought refuge August 14 in the Church of the Crossroads as an act of "deep involvement against all the injustice inherent in the American military system." A group calling itself Business Executives for Vietnam Peace called on the White House August 28 to inform the administration that "the honeymoon is over." Nixon's western White House was repeatedly the scene of demonstrations throughout August. September 3 a group of more than 225 psychologists demonstrated outside the White House, protesting that the Vietnam war was "the insanity of our times." Protesters read lists of war dead at public rallies and had them inserted in the Congressional Record. This was done by former members of Congress of the Kennedy and Johnson administrations. By their actions they were condemning their own participation in starting the war in the first place. They demonstrated their indifference to the deaths that they were responsible for while they were in office. In August, leaders of the protest movement announced a series of monthly demonstrations starting October 15 to bring pressure on the government in what became known as the Moratorium. By and large these demonstrations were covered by the press in an approving manner. Few if any of these protesters ever appealed to North Vietnam for even a little flexibility, or admitted that their government had some right on its side.

President Nixon and Defense Secretary Laird, who had earlier asked the Congress for a draft lottery, announced at a White House briefing that the withdrawal of 60,000 men from Vietnam had enabled the administration to cancel draft calls for November and December and that calls for October would be stretched out over the final quarter of 1969. The Department of Defense now limited the induction of nineteen-year-old men, and November 26 the president signed into law a bill permitting a draft lottery.

A campaign on behalf of the American prisoners of war had been launched in August. It demanded North Vietnam's compliance with the Geneva Convention and Red Cross inspection. Forceful statements were made to the North Vietnamese at the Paris peace talks, and at the International Conference of the Red Cross in September. In the previous month 200 members of the American House of Representatives and 40 members of the Senate had signed statements condemning North Vietnamese brutality against prisoners of war. The Johnson administration, fearing reprisals, had earlier been reluctant to take such a step. One of the problems was the undeclared nature of the war that gave the North Vietnamese an excuse for dealing with war prisoners as criminals.

Russian Foreign Minister Andrei Gromyko sought a meeting with Nixon through Kissinger September 27. The president refused, saying that the critical issue in their relationship was Vietnam and that "the train had left the station and was heading down the track." Kissinger told Gromyko that the next move was up to the North Vietnamese.

President Nixon met October 20 with his secretary of state and advised William Rogers that any new diplomatic initiatives were prohibited until North Vietnam responded in some positive manner.

With the 1969 fall semesters, protests quickened at the nation's colleges and universities. Ho Chi Minh's death September 3 was alleged to represent a new opportunity for ending the stalemate at the Paris peace talks. The truth was far different. The United States honored a ceasefire on the day of Ho Chi Minh's death, but it was not honored by the North Vietnamese.

Demands for a ceasefire mounted among congressional politicians. Senator Edward Kennedy attacked Nixon's Vietnamese policy and branded the Saigon regime "as the primary obstacle to a settlement." His brother, the late John F. Kennedy, would never have made such a statement. In fact he would have been appalled by his younger brother's comment.

In response to a letter from a student at Georgetown University respectfully suggesting that the president reconsider his prejudgment about the Vietnam Moratorium, Nixon replied, "If a president—any president—allowed his course to be set by those who demonstrate, he would betray the trust of all the rest. Whatever the issue, to allow government policy to be made in the streets would destroy the democratic process. It would give the decision, not to the majority, and not to those with the strongest arguments, but to those with the loudest voice. . . . It would allow every group to test its strength not at the ballot box but through confrontation in the streets."

There were Moratorium demonstrations throughout the country. Twenty thousand people packed a noontime rally in New York's financial district to hear Bill Moyers, Johnson's former assistant and press secretary, urge President Nixon to respond to the anti-war sentiment.

Fifty thousand people gathered at the Washington Monument October 15, 1969, within sight of the White House. Their appearance was preceded by a walk around the city by several thousand people carrying candles. At George Washington University Dr. Benjamin Spock informed a large gathering that Nixon was incapable of ending the war because of "limitations on his personality." The cry "peace now, peace now" was chanted in major cities. Demonstrators said the American government was an obstacle to peace. Even some of the press took up the cry that Nixon must do more to end the war.

By October the Nixon administration had announced the withdrawal of more than 60,000 troops, a reduction of 20 percent in B-52 bomber strikes and a 25 percent reduction in combat actions by the Tactical Air Command. In Vietnam, General Abrams changed his field orders to practically end American offensive operations.

Despite demonstrations by political activists, 58 percent of the American people supported Nixon's conduct of the war while only 12 percent opposed. The New York *Times* was a critic of the war and editorially it kept insisting that Nixon seize any opportunity for peace.

President Nixon had done far more than his predecessors to deescalate the war and to withdraw American troops. Still, he was castigated for not moving fast enough. Actually the president too often procrastinated in making the harsh, necessary decisions that might have ended the war.

Patrick Moynihan, one of the President Nixon's counselors, sent him a memorandum that said, in part, "Most of them [anti-war activists] are casualties of our affluence. They had had the leisure for self-pity and the education enabling them to focus it in a fashionable critique of the 'system.' Many of the Moratorium marchers were offspring of fathers who attended college under the GI Bill in the late '40s and who went on to vote for Democratic Party candidates. Undoubtedly they were the first generation to reach college from predominantly Democratic urban strata." He concluded by saying he believed the overwhelming majority of these young people remain remarkably open in terms of their future political affiliation. (His views proved accurate in the 1980 and 1984 elections.) "Many are bright and thoughtful," he said. "They are committed to right wrongs and find themselves. They are eager to participate, impatient for tangible results. They are wary of every answer—ready to suspect that arguments for gradual progress mask some sinister conspiracy against the goal." Unfortunately, Nixon did not understand such people and he was frustrated and angered by them. Moynihan concluded, "They have become formidable by adding to their own votes an enormous outburst of political activism bound to have an influence on others as well as on their parents. We have ample proof of this in the McCarthy phenomenom.

"Vietnam is only symptomatic. When that issue is gone, another will take its place. For they are fighting the establishment position as much as a given problem."

President Nixon had a private meeting with the Soviet Union's ambassador to the United States, Anatoly F. Dobrynin, October 20 and they exchanged frank assessments of the Vietnam situation. Nixon pointed out that the bombing halt was a year old. If no progress occurred soon, he said, the United States would have to pursue its own methods for bringing the war to an end. He said if the Soviets would cooperate in ending the war honorably that "he would do something dramatic to improve United States-Soviet relations." Nixon concluded the discussion by saying, "The whole world wants us to get together. I, too, want nothing as much as to have my administration remembered as a watershed in American and Soviet relations. But let me repeat that we will not hold still for being diddled to death in Vietnam."

Like previous talks these were unproductive but Nixon had laid it on the line in words that probably never had been so blunt to an ambassador. All that came out of this meeting was an agreement to start strategic arms talks, but nothing was resolved about North Vietnam. Nixon reluctantly agreed to arms talks October 25 because any escalation in Vietnam would appear as endangering the prospects of a major relaxation of tensions.

Nixon told Kissinger to tell Dobrynin privately that the president was "out of control" on Vietnam. Kissinger procrastinated and waited to see if Nixon would bring up the subject again. When he did not Kissinger ignored the presidential request.

During the summer and fall of 1969 combat operations were increasingly turned over to the South Vietnamese armed forces, as American troops began their withdrawal.

American strength had peaked at 541,500 in April but this number dropped to 505,500 by mid-October. Although enemy attacks were more scattered than earlier, they were concentrated against South Vietnamese positions. American combat deaths were down in early fall as the United States command ordered a switch to small-unit actions. This trend did not remain constant. The death toll, well below 100 a week in the fall, rose above 100 later in the year. This increase was related to communist-initiated attacks signaling the start of the first phase of their winter campaign. These attacks were highlighted by intensified harassment incidents, and attacks throughout the South. In the last two months of 1969 these attacks were heaviest in III and IV Corps, primarily directed against Vietnamese military installations around Saigon to disrupt the pacification program. The most significant enemy activity occurred in November with heavy attacks upon By Prang and Duc Lap in central Vietnam's II Corps.

North Vietnam's leaders viewed the internal United States dispute with growing confidence, knowing that if they held firm they would win everything they sought, not because the anti-war activists were so influential, but that their impact seemed to have almost paralyzed the Nixon administration in carrying out needed actions so that a negotiated settlement could be achieved satisfactory to most parties in the dispute.

In a broadcast to their troops in South Vietnam October 21, North Vietnam's leaders said, "All deceitful tricks and threats of the Nixon clique cannot check the American people's will. In their valiant and persevering struggle, the American progressives will certainly win glorious victories. The Nixon clique will certainly be completely defeated in Vietnam."

In a later broadcast November 15 the communists claimed that the "fall offensive" is sweeping the United States of America. "We express our militant solidarity with and gratitude to the true sons and daughters of the United States. With all of our hearts we wish to thank our American friends."

The president responded to these attacks against his administration November 3 with his so-called Nixon Doctrine that emphasized the United States would keep all of its treaty commitments. He claimed United States military strength was a shield if a nuclear power threatened the freedom of a nation allied with the United States, or of a nation whose survival was considered vital to the United States security and the security of the region as a whole. He said that in cases involving other types of aggression that "we shall furnish military and economic assistance when requested and as appropriate. But we shall look to the nation directly threatened to assume the primary responsibility of providing the manpower for the defense." At last Nixon had stated his position in a clear and decisive manner. It was long overdue.

Nixon, in taking his case to the American people, took a firm stand. He did so against the recommendations of all members of his cabinet except Kissinger. In drawing the line with no concessions to the protesters he took a position of "peace with honor." His appeal was to the great silent majority of Americans to end the war on honorable terms by saying that Vietnamization offered the prospect of honorable disengagement that was not hostage to the other side's cooperation. He said he strongly believed that the American people would not accept sacrifices for a war that had no valid purposes.

Nixon's speech made a major change in his position as expressed May 14 when he had proposed withdrawal of major portions of American forces within one year, with residual forces left for policing the agreement. Now he accepted a total American pullout within a year if there was a mutual withdrawal. This was a public admission of a private position that had been taken with the North Vietnamese in Paris. Nixon also disclosed the secret correspondence with North Vietnam that had taken place prior to his inauguration, the discussions with the Soviet Union, and the secret letters with President Ho Chi Minh, the texts of which were released by the White House. Kissinger's secret meeting with Xuan Thuy was not revealed. Nixon admitted that no progress had been made in the negotiations except the agreement about the shape of the bargaining table.

"In San Francisco a few weeks ago," Nixon told his television audience, "I saw demonstrators carrying signs reading: 'Lose in Vietnam, bring the boys home.'

"Well, one of the strengths of our free society is that any American has a right to reach that conclusion and to advocate that point of view. But as President of the United States, I would be untrue to my oath of office if I allowed the policy of this nation to be dictated by the minority who hold that point of view and who try to impose it on the nation by mounting demonstrations in the street.

"For almost 200 years, the policy of this nation has been made under our Constitution by those leaders in the Congress and in the White House elected by all of the people. If a vocal minority, however fervent its cause, prevails over reason and the will of the majority, this nation has no future as a free society."

Specifically, Nixon said the United States would keep its commitment to Vietnam and would continue fighting there until the communists agreed to negotiate a fair and honorable peace, or until South Vietnam was able to defend itself on its own—whichever came first. The president said he would continue the disengagement policy of American troops at a pace linked to progress in Vietnamization, the level of enemy activity and developments on the negotiating front.

"I have chosen a plan for peace," he said. "I believe it will succeed. If it does succeed, what the critics say now won't matter. If it does not succeed, anything I say then won't matter.

"And so tonight—to you, the great silent majority of my fellow Americans—I ask for your support."

The next Gallup poll showed that 77 percent of the American people approved, and a majority of members of Congress signed letters expressing similar sentiments.

Nixon's speech touched a responsive nerve and there was an outpouring of approval and offers of support. Even the pressures by the protesters slacked off—but only for a short period.

Vice President Spiro T. Agnew delivered a speech in Des Moines, Iowa, November 13 denouncing the "small group of men, numbering perhaps no more than a dozen anchormen, commentators, and executive producers who," he said, "settle upon the film and commentary that is to reach the public. They decide what 40–50 million Americans will learn of the day's events in the nation and in the world." In referring to Nixon's November 3 speech, he said the president's words had been unfairly subjected to "instant analysis and querulous criticism."

In San Francisco November 15, while some 125,000 yelled "Peace!" Black Panther leader David Hilliard said, "We will kill Richard Nixon. We will kill any [one] that stands in the way of our freedom."

In Washington, a quarter of a million demonstrators flocked to the capitol. Dick Gregory was roundly applauded when he said, "The president says nothing you kids do will have any effect on him. I suggest he make one long call to the LBJ Ranch." This time there was scattered violence around the city.

At breakfast with Lyndon Johnson December 11, Nixon was told by the former president that his major mistake as president was in "trusting the Russians" too much. He said all the bombing pauses were a mistake and he had accomplished nothing. He said each halt had been made because of some assurance that he had received, either through Russian or other sources, that there would be a positive reaction from the other side.

With peace talks bogged down in rhetoric, President Nixon sent Kissinger to Paris February 21, 1970, to meet secretly for the first time with Le Duc Tho, the real power behind the scenes in the negotiating process.

The North Vietnamese launched an offensive February 12 on the Plain of Jars in Laos. The next day Prime Minister Souvanna Phouma made a formal request for United States B-52 strikes. The Laotian communists— the Pathet Lao—were dominated by North Vietnam and had long sought Phouma's overthrow. In three American administrations, the United States role in Laos had been kept secret because each president wanted to keep it limited. But starting in the mid-60s the United States found itself extending increasing support to Prince Phouma, Laos's neutralist leader whom the United States had originally opposed, but who had been recognized as the leader by all sides in earlier accords. Financial assistance was granted to Laos because the United States wanted to retain this neutralist government and secure the prime minister's acquiescence to interdict the Ho Chi Minh Trail.

In response to Phouma's request for B-52 strikes, one mission was flown, triggering a domestic outcry, and there were warnings against further escalation of the war.

President Nixon issued a candid report March 6, 1970, about American involvement in Laos dating back to the Kennedy administration. He denied that any men had been killed in Laos. This was not true because a few civilians were killed, including members of the Laotian military who were not in uniform. Nixon had not lied intentionally and he was unhappy when the truth came out.

Laotian government forces, aided by Thailand volunteers, turned back the communist offensive March 31 so the crisis in Laos subsided for the rest of the year.

CHAPTER 30

Fear and Uncertainty at Home

PRESIDENT NIXON GAVE HIS FIRST FOREIGN POLICY REPORT TO CONgress February 18, 1970. It was candid. "Claims of progress in Vietnam have been frequent during the course of our involvement there—and have often proved too optimistic. However careful our planning, and however hopeful we are for the progress of these plans, we are conscious of two basic facts: We cannot try to fool the enemy, who knows what is actually happening. Nor must we fool ourselves. The American people must have the full truth. We cannot afford a loss of confidence in our judgment and in our leadership."

The president described the nation's overall relationship with the Soviet Union as far from satisfactory. Nixon claimed that the Soviets had failed to exert a helpful influence on the North Vietnamese by continuing to supply them with arms. In referring to North Vietnam, he said that country was a "detriment to the cause of peace."

North Vietnam's leaders were determined that the outcome would be total victory. In late 1969 a prisoner of war had carried a major communist policy document that was succinct. Resolution Number 9 of the Central Office for South Vietnam, the southern headquarters of the communist party, was issued to guide its cadres, and stated that American concessions were not efforts at compromise but were evidence of failure. "Their 'limited war' strategy has met with bankruptcy. They are caught in a most serious crisis over strategy and have been forced to de-escalate the war step-by-step and adopt the policy of de-Americanizing the war, beginning with the withdrawal of 25,000 United States troops, hoping to extricate themselves from their war of aggression in our country."

The directive called for the killing of American troops to increase domestic strains in the United States, the weakening of the South Vietnamese Army and its pacification efforts, and to force the United States to accept a coalition government working towards the goal of re-unifying Vietnam.

Vietnam now became a part of a wider problem against communism in the Far East. A United States Navy EC-121, on routine reconnaissance over the Sea of Japan, was shot down by North Korean jets. At no time was it closer than forty-eight nautical miles from Korea. There were no survivors of the unarmed plane. President Nixon refused to make a retaliatory attack against North Korea because he knew the United States could not face another ground war in the Far East.

Cambodia's Prince Sihanouk announced January 6, 1970, that he would leave for France to take cures dictated by his physical condition, and would then travel to the Soviet Union and the People's Republic of China to discuss economic and military aid. By so doing he hoped to solve his nation's growing political problems with North Vietnam and the Khmer communists.

Following his departure there were widespread demonstrations against his government and opposing parties often met in violent confrontations.

The National Assembly and the Council of the Kingdom assembled March 18 and withdrew their confidence in Sihanouk and he was removed as chief of state and replaced by Cheng Heng whom Sihanouk had left in his place as interim instead of acting head of state. Sihanouk was accused of having authorized North Vietnamese and Vietcong troops to illegally occupy Khmer territory and establish bases or sanctuaries during the latter half of the 1960s. This occupation, it was charged, was in flagrant violation of Khmer neutrality as provided by the Geneva Accords. Sihanouk was tried by the High Court of Justice and condemned to death in absentia for high treason.

Representatives of the Cambodian government met with embassy representatives of North Vietnam and the Provisional Revolutionary Government of South Vietnam March 16 to discuss an agreement whereby communists would evacuate their forces from Cambodia, but no agreement was reached. South Vietnam's communists then broke diplomatic relations with Cambodia May 5.

Chinese communist emissaries were sent from Peking to Phnom Penh to meet with General Lon Nol, Cambodia's new government head. They told him that the "matter between Sihanouk and the Khmer government was nothing more than an internal problem" and that the Chinese would overlook personalities involved if the Cambodian's accepted three conditions: permit China to use Khmer territory to re-supply the North

Vietnamese and the Vietcong with weapons, authorize the North Vietnamese and Vietcong to establish their bases in Cambodia as before, and continue to support North Vietnam and the Vietcong with propaganda. Such demands were promptly rejected by the Cambodians.

While in Moscow Prince Sihanouk learned from Premier Kosygin that he had been deposed.

Later, in Peking, Sihanouk hugged Premier Chou En-lai as if nothing had happened, and later turned violently against the United States. He blamed that nation's Central Intelligence Agency for his overthrow, charging that it had been in collusion with the "traitorous" group in Phnom Penh. He defended North Vietnam on grounds they were "resisting imperialism."

North Vietnam's leaders called Cambodia's new leaders a "pro-American ultra-rightist group." In early April, North Vietnamese troops left their base areas and moved deeper into Cambodia to overthrow the government. This was weeks before the United States took any military action. When Lon Nol sought aid from the United States and other countries Nixon approved limited aid of $10 million.

Yakov Malik, the Soviet Union's permanent representative to the United Nations, suggested at a news conference April 16, 1970, that "only a new Geneva Conference could bring a new solution and relax the tension on the Indochina peninsula." This suggestion surprised American leaders and, while weighing its meaning, Malik two days later retracted his proposal.

By February, 1970, North Vietnam's winter campaign had shifted to I and II Corps and attacks increased steadily, reaching a peak in April. Hostile forces staged their heaviest attacks in the Central Highlands near camps of the Civilian Irregular Defense Group. The communists also conducted numerous small-scale attacks against United States support bases. This level of enemy activity continued throughout May.

From November 1, 1969, until May 1 of the following year United States and allied forces concentrated on operations to destroy enemy main and local forces, the penetration of their base camps and installations, and the seizure of enemy supplies. These operations sought to deny the initiative to the North Vietnamese and to inflict heavy losses. While these actions were underway, there was further improvement in Vietnamization and the armed forces of the Republic of Vietnam demonstrated through their actions that they were improving. As a result, three brigades of the 1st United States Infantry Division and several major Marine Corps units were withdrawn from Vietnam.

The communists made several efforts to take the offensive at Dak

Seang, that was attacked April 1 and that remained under siege throughout the month, and at Quang Duc in the By Prang-Duc Lap area where 12,000 South Vietnamese fought the communists on their own throughout 1970.

South Vietnamese units took the offensive April 14 in a bold three-day operation in the Angel's Wing area of Cambodia. Without United States support, the Vietnamese Army inflicted heavy casualties on the North Vietnamese and suffered only light casualties. This was further evidence of their growing proficiency.

Leaders of the Khmer Republic of Cambodia, in a note March 25, for the second time invited North Vietnam's government officials to discuss the problem of evacuation of their forces. But they were informed by the embassy of the Republic of Poland that the North Vietnamese and Vietcong embassies had departed March 27.

After renewed attacks by communist forces against Cambodia, Prince Sihanouk made appeals to the United Nations Security Council for an end to this aggression. In reply, United Nations officials said that in view of the fact that Cambodia was governed by the 1954 Geneva Accords, the Khmer Republic should apply to the co-chairmen of the 1954 Geneva Conference—the Soviet Union and Great Britain. He did so but without receiving any satisfaction.

The United Nations Secretariat April 6 announced that Secretary General U Thant had decided "to deal with the authorities who effectively controlled the situation in Cambodia." Thus Sihanouk's appeal to the United Nations as the legal holder of Cambodian authority was rejected and the United Nations decided to deal with the new Lon Nol government while Sihanouk took refuge in China. Meanwhile, the communists increased their countrywide attacks and Lon Nol appealed to all world blocs to aid him in his fight against the Vietnamese communists.

These forces penetrated Cambodia along two separate axes: first, across the Vietnamese borders with Laos and South Vietnam with the complicity of the Khmer communists, and second by way of the port of Sihanoukville or Kompong Son.

As early as 1962 communist forces had infiltrated the northern and eastern provinces of Cambodia and by 1969 there were 50,000 men in so-called sanctuaries. At the time, Sihanouk ignored them to cover up his complicity with North Vietnam and the Vietcong on the one hand, and to reject the pretext of enemy pursuit by United States and South Vietnamese forces on the other.

Pol Pot, who became secretary of the Khmer Communist Party in 1963 after its secretary was assassinated, had belonged to the anti-French underground for a year starting in 1953. Now he worked closely with the North Vietnamese.

The sudden attacks launched by the North Vietnamese March 29 shocked the Lon Nol government and United States assistance was sought. By early May, Cambodia's provinces along South Vietnam's border were virtually in the hands of the communists. Lon Nol called on the entire population to organize for resistance under direction of his military command to fight a new war for independence.

While announcing another incremental withdrawal of United States troops, President Nixon said April 20, 1970, "The enemy would be taking grave risks if they attempted to use American withdrawal to jeopardize remaining United States forces in Vietnam by increasing military actions in Vietnam, in Cambodia, or in Laos; if they were to do so I shall not hesitate to take strong and effective measures to deal with the situation."

During the first four months of 1970 Kissinger's talks with Le Duc Tho had been unproductive. Nixon stressed April 22 that a "bold move" was needed in Cambodia because it appeared that country was falling to the communists. He wanted to do something symbolic to help the Lon Nol government to survive.

Eight days later Nixon delivered a speech saying, "The actions of the enemy in the last ten days clearly endanger the lives of Americans who are in Vietnam now and would constitute an unacceptable risk to those who will be there after withdrawal of another 150,000." Using a map, he explained how the communists were threatening Phnom Penh and that they had expended their previously separated base areas into a "vast enemy staging area and a springboard for attacks on South Vietnam along 600 miles of frontier." The president spoke of three options: do nothing, massive military assistance to Cambodia, or to clean out the sanctuaries. He said he favored the latter course and called for a combined assault on the headquarters of the entire communist military operation in South Vietnam. He said that the United States would not be humiliated and succumb to anarchy and that his government would not act like a "pitiful, helpless giant." In recommending this step he said he rejected all political considerations "whether my party gains in November is nothing compared to the lives of 400,000 brave Americans fighting for our country and for the cause of peace and freedom in Vietnam." Nixon said he would rather be a one-term president than for America to become a second-rate power and to see the nation accept the first defeat in its proud 190-year history.

Critics promptly claimed that his speech was divisive, and that he had expanded the war and exceeded his presidential authority. When Nixon mentioned that the United States had not heretofore moved against sanctuaries, he was not telling the truth. He conveniently overlooked the secret bombing raids.

After Lon Nol took over as head of the Cambodian government South Vietnam's Vice President Ky twice met secretly with him in Phnom Penh in April, and later made an official visit in May, to establish diplomatic relations and agree on mutual assistance.

President Thieu May 8 revealed Lon Nol's consent and authorization for an incursion into Cambodia three days before the start of cross-border operations. To further cement the bonds of friendship between their two countries President Thieu flew to Neak Luong where he paid a courtesy call on Lon Nol but this visit took place only after their respective armed forces had cleared the Mekong River and Kompong Cham. By May, the capital of Phnom Penh was surrounded on three sides and the only corridor still open was along Route 5 to Battambang and then on to Thailand. Survival of the new regime had depended on clearing the Mekong River, and Lon Nol had admitted that it could not have been done without South Vietnam's military forces.

In late April, President Thieu had sent a secret directive to the Joint General Staff authorizing it to conduct operations in Cambodia. A copy of his order was also sent to the Military Assistance Command. Operations were authorized along the Cambodian border to a depth varying from twenty-five to thirty-seven miles inside the neighboring country. Thieu authorized offensive operations against North Vietnamese bases in possible cooperation with American forces, and also those of Cambodia. He said that weapons and ammunition captured from the North Vietnamese would be given to Lon Nol's forces.

The United States April 17 had discreetly dispatched 6,000 AK-47 rifles captured from the communists, and transported about 4,000 civilian irregular troops of Khmer origin by air into Cambodia to help Lon Nol's forces.

Thieu's plan was to drive communist units from their bases and destroy their storage areas. United States forces assigned to the operation would withdraw no later than June 30. Allied leaders agreed it would take two to four weeks to complete the joint operation. There were two important communist supply areas: one in the so-called Fishhook, and the other west of Saigon in what was called Angel's Wing and Parrot's Beak. The Fishhook area was fifty miles from Saigon and had numerous enemy bases as well as the communist headquarters that directed war efforts in South Vietnam's lower half. The other area, just west of Saigon, not only provided the communists with bases, but with the shortest possible route for attacking Saigon. From this base area the 9th Vietcong Division had penetrated into the western suburbs of Saigon during the 1968 Tet offensive.

South Vietnamese forces crossed the Cambodian border April 29 and encountered stiff resistance. Four days later, III Corps forces linked up with IV Corps units from the south, and each force searched for enemy installations. While South Vietnamese forces attacked enemy base areas to the west in Svay Rieng Province, the United States 1st Air Cavalry Division and the 11th Armored Cavalry Regiment, in cooperation with the South Vietnamese Airborne Division, on May 1 launched another offensive into the Fishhook region north of Binh Long Province. Fighting now spread over almost the entire Cambodian border area as refugees spilled over the border and into South Vietnam in large numbers.

After regular South Vietnamese forces vacated the Parrot's Beak to prepare for the next phase, Civilian Irregular Defense Group and Regional Force units of Tay Ninh Province deployed from Angel's Wing to Parrot's Beak to continue their search for enemy stores. On the same day the United States 6th and 31st Infantry Regiments and the 3rd Brigade of the 9th Division also moved into the area to prevent the enemy from returning.

Phase 2 began May 2 as a large South Vietnamese IV Corp task force took part. It was organized into four armor-infantry elements and moved north from Kien Tuong Province in Cambodia on three axes to link up with III Corps units in the Parrot's Beak. The largest operation was conducted by IV Corps forces when an armored-infantry task force advanced rapidly with its strong firepower and mobility and cut up the area into small pockets to facilitate search and destroy operations. During two days of heavy fighting this IV Corps task force seized several enemy supply centers. At the conclusion of this operation in cooperation with III Corps, the IV Corps task force had killed more than a thousand of the enemy, captured 204 others with a loss of 66 killed.

After destroying enemy installations south of Route 1, III Corps units switched their offensive to the north. During this operation United States and Vietnamese Navy units were active along the Kompong Spean River.

Captain Alan D. Milacek and his nine-man AC-119 gunship crew were reconnoitering a heavily defended road section near Ban Ban, Laos, when they spotted two trucks and quickly destroyed them. Captain James A. Russel and Captain Ronald C. Jones, the sensor operators, located three more trucks. As Captain Milacek banked his plane into an attack orbit six enemy positions on the ground opened up with a barrage of anti-aircraft fire. Co-pilot Captain Brent C. O'Brien cleared their fighter escort for attack and the gunship circled as the fighters worked to suppress the ground fire. Meanwhile, Milacek's gunship destroyed another truck.

About 1:00 P.M. their cargo compartment lit up as enemy rounds tore into their right wing. The plane went into a sickening dive to the right and Milacek yelled, "Mayday, Mayday, we're going in." He shouted to Staff Sergeant Adolfo Lopez, Jr., the illuminator operator, to jettison the flare launcher.

Milacek directed the crew to prepare for instant bailout. The gunship had dropped about a thousand feet in the last few seconds as he and O'Brien pooled their strength to pull the aircraft out of its dive. By using full-left rudder, full-left aileron and maximum power on the two right engines, they regained level flight. Navigator Captain Roger E. Clancy gave the pilot the heading to reach their base but warned they were too low to clear a range of mountains between them and friendly territory. What's more Milacek learned that his fuel consumption had been so high that their tanks would be dry before they got out of enemy territory. He ordered the crew to toss out everything possible to lighten their load and the aircraft slowly climbed to 10,000 feet. The flight engineer, Technical Sergeant Albert A. Nash, reported that their fuel level had fallen precipitately so Milacek elected to land his damaged plane. Near the base he checked his controls, noting he had almost full left rudder and aileron control but that there was uncertain flap damage. He chose a no-flap landing approach at 150 knots and they landed hot—but safe.

Upon leaving the plane the crew noted that one third of their right wing—a 14-foot section and its aileron—had been torn off.

The gunship's role had changed through the years from strikes by a single aircraft to a complex team effort of many aircraft, particularly with fighter escort. They were now filled with heavier armament like the 40 mm. gun and the 105 mm. howitzer and had become an escorted aerial artillery platform somewhat analogous to a Navy battleship and its protective screen of destroyers. The relatively small gunship program had surprising impact in many areas.

President Thieu made an inspection visit of South Vietnamese units May 11 with Vice President Ky. He was briefed by Lieutenant General Do Can Tri on results of the operation. He was informed that the general situation throughout Cambodia was becoming more serious every day. He was told that Vietnamese residents in Phnom Penh were being mistreated by the Khmer authorities and that they needed to be repatriated as soon as possible. Thieu ordered his III Corps forces to clear Route 1 and be prepared to relieve Kompong Trach. All three task forces were ordered to link up with IV Corps forces at Kampong Trabek who were clearing the Mekong River delta.

While directing operations to clear Route 1 from Svay Rieng to Kompong Trabek, General Tri sought to coordinate an attack by IV Corps forces along the Mekong River toward Kompong Cham. Lieutenant General Ngu Kzu, commander of the IV Corps forces, disagreed. He believed this was too remote an objective for his corps.

Route 1 was cleared May 22 but the Vietcong 9th Division occupied the area north of Kompong Cham, Cambodia's third largest city, now defended by only a thousand Khmer infantrymen. The Vietcong started to shell the city and quickly isolated it. South Vietnamese forces set out to relieve the siege May 23. With United States air support, two task forces moved forward but were unable to free the city from its encirclement by communist forces. Three task forces attacked June 21 and they succeeded in clearing the area southeast of Kompong Cham. This operation was one of the most successful ever conducted by South Vietnam's armed forces without American advisers, and it upset the communist plan to overthrow Lon Nol's government.

Heretofore the area of Ba Thu and Angel's Wing had been considered invincible. Now 90 percent of the enemy's supplies in this area had either been destroyed or seized by South Vietnam's armed forces. Most important, enemy troop strength had been reduced by 25 percent.

Earlier, Major General Elvy B. Roberts, head of the 1st Cavalry Division, had received orders to prepare for an operation to destroy the communist headquarters in the Fishhook area. For three days in late April the American division commander and Lieutenant General Du Quoc Dong, South Vietnam's Airborne Division commander, developed plans. Both had worked together in the northern most province of III Corps since the first of the year. Their plan called for advance support by B-52s, and tactical air and artillery strikes followed by the heliborne insertion of the 1st Air Cavalry Division's 3rd Brigade into three landing zones north of their objective to block the enemy's escape routes. Next, the airborne element would advance south to link up with a task force that would attack northward from positions in the south, with the 3rd Brigade to the west, and the 11th Armored Cavalry Regiment to the east and southeast.

In conjunction with this pincer movement in Cambodia the 9th Regiment, 5th South Vietnamese Division and the 1st South Vietnamese Armored Cavalry Squadron were to conduct reconnaissance patrols along the western part of Binh Long Province, opposite the area of operation. After objectives were occupied, all units would continue to search for enemy installations.

Six B-52 bombers pounded the Fishhook area during the early hours of May 1, then allied artillery opened up. The first of a new series of 15,000-

pound bombs was dropped to clear a landing zone. Possibly due to the lethal characteristics of this bomb the allied assault force met little resistance.

In an area called "The City" substantial quantities of supplies were discovered during the next two weeks. This proved to be the most important enemy supply base in Cambodia and its underground shelters were full of war materiel.

Meanwhile, on May 6 III Corps' forces and Field Force II launched three simultaneous attacks against communist base areas in Binh Long, Phuoc Long and Tay Ninh Provinces, and all were destroyed.

The quantities of weapons, ammunition and rice surprised the allied leaders. Most captured crates bore the markings of communist bloc countries, and weapons were still wrapped in their original packages.

IV Corps' commander was given responsibility for clearing the Mekong River as far as Phnom Penh, and to repatriate Vietnamese in refugee camps in the Cambodian capital.

The North Vietnamese evaded these thrusts and shifted their army operations to the west. The communists struck at targets along the roads and waterways connecting Phnom Penh with provincial cities to the south and west of the capital.

In Phnom Penh fuel and food became scarce and Khmer government officials asked the South Vietnamese to clear the enemy from the Mekong River and to reopen communication routes to the south.

After the Mekong River and Route 1 were cleared the Khmer government authorized South Vietnam's armed forces to maintain a permanent force at Neak Luong.

A day after Sihanouk had been deposed President Thieu had boasted, "If Cambodia and South Vietnam and her allies cooperate along the border, then I believe the communists would find it impossible to stay."

Despite the continued modernization of South Vietnam's armed forces they still had to prove their combat capabilities in large-scale military operations, particularly in a country whose terrain was unfamiliar. There was considerable American concern about what would happen in South Vietnam with unreliable irregular troops taking the place of regulars. South Vietnam was still limited in artillery, helicopters and tactical aircraft. Her tactical air squadrons numbered only five and they were equipped with old fighter-bombers with low speed and limited capacity. Even within South Vietnam tactical air support for outposts under attack or units engaged in combat operations had to depend upon the United States Air Force.

During April, South Vietnam's armed forces were still able to initiate operations in Cambodia without concern for security at home because American units were still there in large numbers. These Cambodian border crossings were the largest they had ever conducted with 50,000 troops fighting alongside American units. This also was the first time major South Vietnamese units had fought together in such numbers—the equivalent of six divisions. They included the Airborne Division; the 9th 21st, 22nd and 23rd Infantry Divisions; five Ranger groups; a Marine brigade and nine armored cavalry squadrons. Previously these organizations had performed only pacification support activities while United States forces played the major role in fighting the North Vietnamese. Although forced to fight on unfamiliar terrain, South Vietnam's armed forces proved combat effective despite initial shortcomings in the coordination of their armor and infantry actions. They held the initiative throughout and all planning and supervision were performed by Vietnamese staffs. They fought with pride, knowing they were on their own, and they fought well.

North Vietnamese Army units withdrew beyond the point where Americans were not permitted to operate and avoided contact to conserve their forces. With more flexibility, United States forces might have been able to inflict serious losses on the North Vietnamese but the rules of engagement prevented such action.

The Cambodian invasion caused serious losses to North Vietnam in men and war materiels. Most base areas and storage points along the border were practically paralyzed. A total of 22,892 rifles, or the equivalent number to arm 54 enemy main force battalions of 450 men each, were captured, plus thousands of other weapons. The ammunition and guns destroyed or captured would have sustained communist forces against South Vietnam's III and IV Corps areas for possibly twelve months and the 7,000 tons of captured rice would have been sufficient for six months. While the invasion's primary objective was the destruction of enemy bases and supplies, 11,349 communist troops were killed and 2,328 were captured. This number equalled the men in a division. Others were killed in air strikes and they could not be counted. Allied losses were one-eleventh of those sustained by the communists. Of greatest importance, enemy main-force units were driven away from South Vietnam and its borders and enemy activity inside the country was reduced.

During the rest of the year, and throughout 1971, South Vietnam's armed forces held the initiative on all battlegrounds within their country. The men and their leaders had gained confidence, and their success on the battlefields demonstrated it. The Cambodian incursion also resulted in Cambodia under Lon Nol becoming a partner instead of an enemy. With this new confidence, security increased in the South Vietnamese countryside and a "Land-to-the-Tiller Program" was launched to improve radically the lot of the country's farmers.

Despite its propaganda North Vietnam was forced to come into the open in Cambodia and commit flagrant acts against the Khmer regime. No longer could its leaders claim innocence about the presence of North Vietnamese troops in the country.

With failure of the North Vietnamese to overthrow Lon Nol's government, the regime was given time to equip and re-train its army. Unfortunately allied assistance in Cambodia gave Lon Nol's government only a temporary respite as North Vietnam plotted to dominate all three countries in the region. In spite of losses, the North Vietnamese succeeded in taking control of Cambodia's northeastern provinces, and one-fourth of the country came under communist domination. But the bulk of Cambodia's armed forces—about forty thousand—was still intact in the other three quarters, and as long as North Vietnam controlled vital areas the Phnom Penh government was in mortal danger.

South Vietnam had its own problems and had to concentrate on its security, so no plan could be developed to keep the communists from returning to their former bases in Cambodia. So, despite the success of the incursion, the long-range effects were catastrophic.

The United States had re-established diplomatic relations with Cambodia in August, 1969, and a Defense Attaché Office was established in Phnom Penh after an absence of four years. It was small, and kept a low profile, and was run by only five officers. But the office was greatly expanded after Lon Nol's government survived the North Vietnamese invasion.

President Nixon declared June 30, 1970, that the only remaining American activity in Cambodia after July 1 would be air missions to protect the security of American forces in South Vietnam.

In the United States, throughout the spring of 1970, there was violent campus unrest involving disciplinary regulations, administration and minority admissions. A crowd of students began throwing rocks and chunks of concrete at National Guardsmen at Kent State University in Ohio forcing them up a small hill. At the top, the soldiers turned and someone started to shoot. Two bystanders and two protesters were killed. Their deaths triggered a nationwide wave of campus protests.

A National Day of Protest was hastily called to take place in Washington May 9. At a press conference the day before, President Nixon faced questioners about his authorization of American troops into Cambodia. "I made the decision, however, for the very reasons that they are protesting. I am concerned because I know how deeply they feel. But I know that what I have done will accomplish the goals that they want. It will shorten the war. It will reduce American casualties. It will allow us to go forward with our withdrawal program. The 150,000 Americans that I announced for withdrawal in the next year will come home on schedule. It will, in my opinion, serve the cause of a just peace in Vietnam."

That night, when Nixon saw small groups of young people gathering on the Ellipse between the White House and the Washington monument he went out to talk to some of them. Some said he was not concerned about why they were there and spoke of a tired and dull Nixon who rambled aimlessly from subject to subject. Actually, Nixon tried to explain his goals, telling them he realized they would not agree with his position, and that he hoped their hatred of war—that he said he understood—would not turn into a bitter hatred of the American system and what it stood for. He soon realized that his appeal was a wasted effort.

By now the evolutionary cycle of violent dissent had spawned an ugly offshoot: an urban underground of political terrorists who urged murder and bombing. Most prominent were the Black Panthers and the Weathermen. J. Edgar Hoover informed the president that his FBI agents had begun to pick up rumors of a calculated nationwide terrorist offensive by radical student groups using arson, bombing and kidnaping of university and government officials. They had brought fear and uncertainty to a majority of the American people.

Despite growing criticism of Nixon's actions the Gallup Poll showed that 48 percent of the American people favored sending arms and materiel to Cambodia while 35 percent disagreed and 11 percent had no opinion. Nixon's personal approval rating stood at 50 percent. Before the year was out Cambodia would receive $200 million in American aid.

The United States Senate approved the Cooper-Church Amendment June 30 that, in effect, gave the communists a free hand in Cambodia even though in the judgment of the executive branch this doomed South Vietnam. When the bill was sent to a House-Senate conference committee House members refused to agree on the Senate-passed amendment.

The McGovern-Hatfield amendment to the Defense Procurement Bill was aimed at ending the war by cutting off all funds by the end of 1970. It was defeated by the Senate September 1 by a vote of 55 to 39.

North Vietnam's interest in the Paris peace talks was primarily to keep the United States from resuming the bombing in the North. Its leaders kept insisting that no serious talks were taking place. Kissinger believed that a senior appointment to the American team of negotiators would deprive the North Vietnamese of a propaganda issue. He suggested that David K. E. Bruce be appointed a special ambassador and this distinguished public servant was enthusiastically endorsed by President Nixon. Although Bruce was 72 years old and in poor health he agreed to take on the assignment despite the knowledge that the North Vietnamese would use his fragile health to try to wear him down.

When Kissinger and Dobrynin had met for a general review of the world situation the previous December, the Russian ambassador said that his government expected they would have to deal with Nixon for seven more years, and he suggested that the leaders of his government had no real interest in Southeast Asia. He said the Soviet Union had become involved because of a misunderstanding. He said China was the sole beneficiary of the war's continuation. It was now evident to Kissinger and Nixon that Russian relations with China were not as secure as they had believed.

CHAPTER 31

Agent Orange

THE KINGDOM OF CAMBODIA WAS TRANSFORMED OCTOBER 9, 1970, into the Khmer Republic. The strategy of the Lon Nol government now was to keep supply routes open with priority to maintain control of highly populated regions near and south of the capital of Phnom Penh. The economic situation had deteriorated to the point where there were no longer sufficient rice-growing areas under government control. General Lon Nol, commander-in-chief of the country's general staff, now ordered the armed forces to regain control of some of these regions.

Admiral John S. McCain, Jr., Commander-in-Chief, Pacific, had earlier proposed to General Abrams in 1969 that herbicide operations for defoliation and crop destruction be reduced by 25 percent by July 1, 1970. He said that the Military Assistance Command's projected high use was unrealistic. Abrams agreed and cut the spraying even more, by 30 percent.

President Nixon had announced November 25, 1969, his intention to resubmit the Geneva Protocol outlawing chemical and biological warfare to the Senate for ratification. This protocol reaffirmed the United States policy of renouncing first use of deadly chemicals, and extended the rules to include incapacitating agents. He proposed the prohibition of all uses of lethal biological weapons and "all other methods of biological warfare." This was a strong position, but it did not apply to herbicides.

Dr. Lee A. DuBridge, Nixon's science adviser, referred to the president a report by the National Institute of Health that offered evidence that 2,4,5-T—a component of Agent Orange—could cause malformed babies and stillbirths in mice when administered in relatively high doses.

Deputy Secretary of Defense David Packard directed the Joint Chiefs to insure that Agent Orange—so-called because it was packed in orange-striped barrels—would be sprayed only in areas remote from populations pending a decision about its use in the domestic market.

DuBridge sent the National Intitute of Health report to the Weed Society of America for evaluation. The society's president, Glenn C. Klingman, and other scientists, criticized the use in these tests of DMSO (dimethylsulfoxide) as a solvent for the herbicide. They said that because DMSO was rapidly absorbed and transported to all parts of the body it was likely the 2,4,5-T would reach internal organs that it would not otherwise do. They also criticized the use of subcutaneous injections as an artificial method compared to the natural exposure of 2,4,5-T. They said oral doses in tests were massive compared to normal exposures. They concluded the data failed to support the conclusions, particularly in regard to birth defects.

In a growing number of scientific investigations, opposing views were presented that the 2,4-D and 2,4,5-T used in Vietnam might be causing birth defects and an end to their use was demanded.

Admiral McCain said an investigation in Vietnam was impractical and he suggested the possibility of genetic defects from herbicides be investigated in the United States where they had been used for more than twenty years and where medical records were much better.

The Department of Defense learned in April, 1970, that several Nixon cabinet members planned to call for immediate suspension of 2,4,5-T except for carefully controlled applications. The director of Defense Research and Engineering, Dr. John S. Foster, Jr., advised Secretary of Defense Laird that 2,4,5-T was a major component of Agent Orange being used in Vietnam at the rate of 200,000 gallons a month. He said Agent White could be substituted for Agent Orange but only about 100,000 gallons of Agent White were in Vietnam—an amount equal to fifteen days of defoliation spraying at the current level of operations. He said the Dow Chemical Company could produce over 200,000 gallons of Agent White if given thirty days to do so. Foster pointed out that Agent White was more expensive than Agent Orange and was also more persistent in the soil, increasing the likelihood of long term ecological damage if Agent White replaced Agent Orange in large quantities. Foster said the Defense Department had three choices concerning the future of Agent Orange. First, it could continue the present policy of using the chemical in areas remote from populations, or that Laird could endorse the position of three executive departments and direct that Agent Orange be applied only to sparsely populated, non-agricultural areas and avoid ponds, lakes and rivers. Finally, he said that Laird could temporarily suspend the use of Agent Orange pending further study and the establishment of specific guidelines for future use. Foster argued against the first two options because they would cause adverse public reaction. He said the second option would be confusing without specific criteria for answering queries. He said the Joint Chiefs' chairman favored the second option because restrictions tighter than those governing civilian use of 2,4,5-T should not apply to military use, and because a temporary restriction might be difficult to remove. Foster said he favored the last option because he believed it would be difficult to apply criteria applicable to civilian uses of 2,4,5-T in the United States to military operations in Southeast Asia. His view was accepted by Laird.

General Abrams asked that the ban be lifted to allow Agent Orange to be sprayed on enemy-controlled areas with very low population densities (less than eight inhabitants per square kilometer). As an alternative, he requested 128,000 gallons of Agent White per month, or a suitable substitute.

Admiral McCain reaffirmed the requirement for herbicides April 24 and endorsed Abrams' request. He said he objected to limitations on Agent Orange that were greater in Vietnam than those on 2,4,5-T in the United States.

Admiral Thomas H. Moorer, acting·chairman of the Joint Chiefs, petitioned Laird May 14 to lift the temporary ban on Agent Orange. He said this request was the best of three options, with the other two being to terminate defoliation operations or to buy enough Agent White to replace Agent Orange. Moorer said that ending all defoliation would take away from General Abrams an important capability to reduce jungle concealment and expose enemy camps, storage locations and lines of communication. Moorer said defoliation enabled fewer military personnel to provide security around fixed installations and had helped to save lives. He said he did not favor Agent White as a substitute since defoliation took four months with it, compared to three or four weeks with Agent Orange.

General Earle G. Wheeler, chairman of the Joint Chiefs, wrote Laird June 2 asking for early decisions on the continued use of Agent Orange. Deputy Defense Secretary David Packard wrote June 22 that the suspension of Agent Orange would be continued.

Between the original ban on Agent Orange, and this decision by Packard, there had been the American ground operation in Cambodia and the campus protests in the United States. It was obvious to Nixon that public protests against the war were mounting, and the president was reluctant to generate any unnecessary controversy such as lifting the ban on Agent Orange.

In Vietnam, the Seventh Air Force units involved in spraying operations turned to Agent White until it was used up and they flew their last defoliation mission May 9, 1970, although crop destruction missions continued.

Without herbicide missions the 12th Special Operations Squadron began leaflet operations, and two of their six planes were used to spray malathion for the control of mosquitos. The 12th soon after was dissolved as a unit.

The American Association for the Advancement of Science sent an investigative group to South Vietnam but the four-man team quickly became involved in serious conflict with military authorities over access to herbicide data.

In its preliminary report at their December 30 meeting, the scientists revealed that their inspection of sprayed mangrove areas revealed little regrowth of the forest after three or more years. In sprayed hardwood forests, they said they found areas of dead trees where bamboo had spread over the forest floor. They admitted records were inadequate in South Vietnam to determine whether or not herbicides had caused birth defects. In conclusion, they said South Vietnam's civilian population—and not enemy troops—would have consumed nearly all the food that was destroyed by the crop destruction program.

Dr. Ivan L. Bennett, Jr., a White House scientific adviser, wrote to Dr. Du Bridge June 16 urging that crop destruction in Vietnam be completely halted. He said the Geneva Protocol, soon to be formally submitted to the Senate, would likely become embroiled in controversy over the continued use of tear gas and herbicides in Vietnam. He said that he had not been able to produce convincing arguments against the military effectiveness of tear gas and the herbicides used for defoliation, but he thought the benefits of crop destruction were questionable while the political costs were high.

Du Bridge endorsed Bennett's views a week later in a letter to Dr. Kissinger, Nixon's assistant for National Security Affairs.

President Nixon, July 6, 1970, asked Laird to assess the program and CINCPAC provided a detailed justification for crop destruction five days later. McCain repeated the claim that crop destruction had been an integral part of the resources denial program in South Vietnam since 1962. He said the crop destruction program was a most efficient and effective method of keeping food from reaching the enemy. He cited the situation in Laos where he attributed a significant role to herbicides in General Vang Pao's capture of the Plain of Jars in August, 1969. McCain said both he and Abrams considered crop destruction an essential part of the Vietnamization program.

Secretary of Defense Laird replied to Nixon's request for an evaluation with a memorandum July 18 to Kissinger. In it he repeated CINCPAC's arguments. He said he believed crop destruction had proven itself "an effective adjunct to our total military effort in Southeast Asia."

While the public uproar against the war continued in the United States, Nixon procrastinated. There was one unauthorized use of Agent Orange over remote areas of Quang Tin and Quang Ngai Provinces to defoliate base perimeters and to destroy crops. This use was explained by the fact that Agent White was not available. After that mission all stocks of Agent Orange were kept in central storage points to prevent their unauthorized use.

Dr. Edward E. David, Jr., Nixon's science adviser, and Du Bridge's successor, wrote Kissinger November 20 recommending reconsideration of herbicide policies. He said he had reason to believe the American Association for the Advancement of Science's Herbicide Assessment Commission would report to the Senate Foreign Relations Committee and the public that Agent Orange used in Vietnam contained a level of dioxin—an impurity in Agent Orange—higher than that permitted in the United States. At the time, dioxin was known to cause birth defects in experimental animals, and researchers suspected this chemical could cause damage to human fetuses if ingested by their mothers in sufficient quantities. He told Kissinger that all substitutes for Agent Orange had drawbacks. He said 2,4-D was a suspected carcinogen and that picloram (sold commercially as Tordon) was persistent as a soil sterilant. He urged Kissinger to propose to President Nixon that in Vietnam the United States should only spray those chemicals approved for use in the United States and governed by the same restrictions.

Defense Secretary Laird informed the chairman of the Joint Chiefs December 7, 1970, that he had decided to continue to supply American forces in South Vietnam with both riot control agents and herbicides at a level based on appropriate military and economic considerations.

Three days later Kissinger asked Laird to re-assess the impact of adopting the policy proposed by Dr. David. Laird asked the Joint Chiefs for their opinion and they reiterated the value of herbicides they had expressed in the past. They claimed there were no direct parallels between the way herbicides were used in Southeast Asia and in normal domestic use. They said compliance with the current Department of Agriculture standards of no more than one-half to one part per million of dioxin in 2,4,5-T was not feasible because some of the Agent Orange in South Vietnam contained higher levels of contamination. The Joint Chiefs argued that the scientific evidence concerning the alleged danger from 2,4,5-T and dioxin was weak and did not justify a continuation of the suspension placed on the use of Agent Orange. They cited a test in Florida where more than 500 pounds of Agent Orange had been sprayed on a range over the past eight years. In contrast, they said, only twenty-five pounds of herbicide were deposited per acre during a single spraying in Vietnam. They claimed that investigators had found no detectable dioxin in the soil of this test area, and there were no abnormalities in the animals living there. The Joint Chiefs, therefore, expressed their opinion that there was no factual basis for restricting Agent Orange in areas remote from population centers, and they argued for continuance of the herbicide program.

Laird presented these arguments to Kissinger but he said he did not agree with the Joint Chiefs. He said the overall military impact of implementing Dr. David's policy recommendation would be minimal considering that 95 percent of the South Vietnamese lived in relatively secure areas and that the rapid progress of the pacification program had made herbicides less important. Laird recommended that the Defense Department retain the option of resuming the program. He said he had ordered disposal of all Agent Orange supplies that did not meet United States agricultural standards. He said the adverse political and psychological costs of using the 1.63 million gallons of the chemical then in South Vietnam would outweigh the dollar value of its original price ($12 million purchase cost versus $6 million to dispose of it).

The Joint Chiefs protested Laird's views and Admiral Moorer spoke for them saying that the risk of human injury from this herbicide was even less than originally suspected.

In early December, 1970, Ambassador Bunker and General Abrams decided after consultation with their staffs to phase out the use of herbicides to destroy crops. They agreed there would be no public announcement but the stocks on hand would be used with no new procurement. Their decision was based on continued strong opposition in the United States Senate and President Thieu's finding that herbicides had destroyed 20 percent of South Vietnam's forests. Thieu's advisers now urged him to ask the Americans to cease such operations.

Laird informed President Nixon December 22 that, in future, the use of herbicides in Vietnam must be in strict conformance with policies at home. He explained that Ambassador Bunker and General Abrams had decided on an orderly yet rapid phase-out of other herbicides. The defense secretary said that during the phase-out herbicides would be restricted to remote unpopulated areas and in the vicinity of fire bases and United States installations. This policy change was made public in the last week of December and it was mentioned there was a possibility of reassessment.

The last Ranch Hand mission—code name for the herbicide sprayings—was flown January 7, 1971. Nine days later, Deputy Secretary of

Defense Packard ordered the immediate termination of all crop destruction operations by United States forces.

In June of that year Admiral McCain proposed that herbicides be used to spray opium poppies—the source of heroin—but political barriers were too strong. There was another proposal that the South Vietnamese be permitted to use herbicides, but Ambassador Bunker's strong opposition was sufficient to kill that request.

One-and-a-third million gallons of Agent Orange were removed from South Vietnam by April, 1972, while an additional 850,000 gallons remained in the States. Tests showed that the average concentration of dioxin was about two parts per million, or a total of forty-four pounds of this toxic contaminant. Department of Agriculture standards were one-half to one part per million but the dioxin in Agent Orange had two to four times the amount allowable for domestic purposes. Various methods were considered to get rid of Agent Orange so as not to harm the environment. It was finally burned in special furnaces aboard a ship in the North Pacific specifically equipped to destroy toxic substances. The last of the herbicide, once destined for the jungles of Southeast Asia, was destroyed September 3, 1977. It cost $8 million to destroy it.

President Nixon signed a bill October 7, 1970, that was mandated by the United States Congress for an extensive study of herbicides in South Vietnam. Some scientists had long demanded such a study but during wartime ground investigation in many areas was impossible. The National Academy of Sciences was assigned the task but they failed to find any clear evidence of direct damage to human health from herbicides. They did discover a consistent pattern of largely second-hand reports from the Montagnards who claimed that occasionally herbicides had caused acute or fatal respiratory problems in children. The scientists, however, were unable to visit these people so they could not confirm the reports. On the question of herbicide-related birth defects, the scientists could not find evidence to substantiate such a link. The president of the academy concluded that, on balance, the untoward effects of the herbicide program on the health of the South Vietnamese people appeared to have been smaller than one might have feared.

The effects on land and vegetation were also less than some scientists had expected. The main impact on vegetation was the immediate killing effect resulting from direct spray contact. Since herbicides disappear quickly in the soil, there was no significant effect on plants the next growing season. Herbicide spraying devastated mangrove forests in South Vietnam and, without reseeding, areas were not expected to return to their prior state for a century. Almost all mangrove trees died after one spraying, and herbicides destroyed about 36 percent of all mangrove forests.

These scientific studies showed that herbicides had not had any lasting harmful effects on the amounts of nutrients in the soil with the possible exception of potassium. Scientists noted that bombing and shelling may have had a worse effect on inland forests. Besides the trees killed, bomb and shell fragments in trees made future attempts to saw them costly and hazardous.

After the war, as veterans complained of the effects of herbicides, the Surgeon General in 1978 directed the United States Air Force's Occupational and Environmental Health Laboratory to update previous assessments of human health effects from exposure to herbicides—Agent Orange in particular. The report was published in October. It disclosed that 2,4,5-T's toxicity was minimal considering the degree of use. The report said that none of the herbicides used in Southeast Asia were new or experimental and that all had been used for several years in commercial agriculture in the United States and other countries. They said the use of 2,4-D and 2,4,5-T worldwide since the middle 1940s with minimal adverse effects was an indication that these chemicals were safe if used properly. They found that large doses of 2,4-D had been given to humans in controlled circumstances without adverse effects. If such a dose were significantly high, they said, a number of organs might be affected including the skin, liver and central and peripheral nervous system. They concluded that adverse effects of 2,4-D and 2,4,5-T should manifest themselves soon after exposure. Air Force researchers concluded that symptoms arising for the first time months to years after the last exposure were probably due to a cause other than herbicides. Although no research could confirm cancer, fatal deformities or mutations caused by exposure to phenoxy herbicides or dioxin were not ruled out although the report reached no conclusions.

The United States Air Force June 4, 1979, announced a twenty-year study of the health of twelve hundred Ranch Hand veterans to compare their health with a control group of similar men to determine whether there were any detrimental health effects from exposure to Agent Orange. They are the most likely group to have had a significant exposure to herbicides.

The Air Force's third mortality analysis was released in 1989. It states there is no significance difference in the deaths between the Ranch Hand group and the comparison group. Officers had a slightly lower death rate while ground personnel had a slightly higher rate but neither statistic is considered significant.

President Ford signed an executive order April 8, 1975, that prohibits first use of riot control agents except in a defensive mode to save lives. Of herbicides, he said, "The United States renounces, as a matter of national policy, first use of herbicides in war except under regulations applicable to their domestic use for control of vegetation within the United States, its bases and installations or around their immediate defense perimeters."

Without assuming liability, seven United States chemical companies that manufactured Agent Orange agreed in 1984 to a $180 million settlement for veterans who claimed they suffered deadly or disabling diseases due to exposure to herbicides in South Vietnam. The United States government still maintains there is insufficient evidence to associate herbicide exposure to birth defects among veterans and their families although officials concede there may be some health problems related to herbicide operations.

The aftermath of the use of herbicides in Southeast Asia, where 19 million gallons were spread over 5.9 million acres, cannot be foreseen. Its wide use did not prevent the allies from losing the war so its use as a military weapon may have caused more problems than it was worth.

The North Vietnamese deliberately escalated the war in Cambodia and Laos during 1970 while they engaged in secret peace talks with American officials. They had violated the frontiers of both countries since 1965 without a shred of legality.

In Kissinger's four private talks with Le Duc Tho in Paris from February to April the communist official had rejected neutrality for Laos and Cambodia. He emphasized that it was his people's destiny to take over these countries as well as South Vietnam.

Despite these communist views the Nixon administration continued to bear the brunt of criticism when, in fact, North Vietnam was making a mockery of democratic institutions. Kissinger had been meeting with communist officials in a series of secret meetings since August 4, 1969. Nixon remained skeptical, telling his cabinet, "I don't know what these clowns want to talk about, but the line we take is either they talk or we are going to sit it out. I don't feel this is any time for concessions."

Le Duc Tho, the man with whom Kissinger carried on secret negotiations in 1970, was a gray-haired man with intense eyes and a dignified manner. He usually wore a black or brown Mao Tse-tung suit. As a boy of sixteen he had joined the anti-French communist guerrillas. A passionate communist, he dealt with Americans with great skill. He frequently accused the United States of the entire responsibility for the war, calling North Vietnam an oppressed people. Kissinger told him that the United States wanted a practical end to the war and that it was prepared to withdraw all its forces and retain no bases in South Vietnam. Unfortunately for South Vietnam, Kissinger did not insist upon mutual withdrawal by placing North Vietnamese troops on the same legal basis as the American forces.

Technically, Le Duc Tho was only special adviser to North Vietnam's Paris delegation with Xuan Thuy as its formal head. Actually, he was the official who made the decisions. He continued to insist to Kissinger that before any negotiations the United States must set a deadline for unilateral withdrawal. He said that the fighting would continue against South Vietnam until its government was overthrown. There was no mention of the return of prisoners of war. At the regular meetings, Xuan Thuy dismissed the announced departure of over 100,000 troops as "withdrawal by driblets." He said he was not impressed by reduced air operations. Le Duc Tho claimed the American strategy was only to withdraw enough forces to make the war bearable for the American people while simultaneously strengthening South Vietnam's armed forces. He claimed that the United States could not win.

In a speech October 7, 1970, President Nixon presented a comprehensive program that could serve as the basis for negotiations. It called for a standstill ceasefire, and a halt to bombing throughout Indochina. He suggested that a peace conference be held to bring an end to war in all countries in Southeast Asia, and he said he was ready to negotiate a time table for total withdrawal of American forces.

The speech was greeted with almost unanimous praise in the United States. A number of senators sponsored a resolution calling the president's new peace initiative "fair and equitable." Senator Fulbright expressed his hope that the president's initiative might lead to a breakthrough. Senator Mike Mansfield said the speech was excellent and he would do his best to support it. The New York *Times* editorially called Nixon's approach "a major new peace initiative."

The following day Xuan Thuy rejected Nixon's proposal and refused even to discuss it. The North Vietnamese were not about to share power with anyone.

Negotiations collapsed because the same old story was endlessly repeated. Le Duc Tho could see no reason to modify his demands for unconditional withdrawal and the overthrow of the South Vietnamese government. He remained steadfast in his convictions for two-and-a-half years until a changing military environment left him no choice.

Cambodia's General Lon Nol suffered a stroke February 8, 1971, that left him paralyzed and incapacitated. He was evacuated by a United States aircraft to Honolulu for treatment and then returned to his country April 12. In recognition of his services, he was promoted to marshal April 21 by

Cheng Heng, chief of state for the Khmer Republic since Sihanouk's removal.

Upon his return to Cambodia, Marshal Lon Nol's ambition was to see Cambodia's armed forces transformed into a powerful organization in the image of South Vietnam's armed forces, or even the United States military establishment. He was unrealistic because such a step forward in military capability would have to bypass fundamental principles of operation that animated the armed forces of these two countries. Through the Commander-in-Chief, Pacific, Lon Nol presented a plan to the United States for development of his armed forces to an eventual strength of 600,000. He also said his country needed an additional 53,000 so-called paramilitary forces. His decision makers were operating in a dream world and their plans were based on unreality. Those decision makers included himself, his younger brother Lon Non, and a small inner circle of military personnel and civilian advisers. His plan was not taken seriously by United States officials who complained that it was totally unrealistic and made no sense in the real world of military preparedness.

A year later, in March, 1972, Chief of State Cheng Heng resigned and transferred his authority to Marshal Lon Nol who was elected the Khmer Republic's first President June 4 after a constitution was adopted by a popular referendum in April.

Marshal Lon Nol's personal integrity was above reproach. Unfortunately, during the war period many Cambodians exploited the situation and pursued their own interests without concern for the ill effects of their acts on their country. They were all to pay a bitter price later on.

South Vietnamese troops crossed the Laotian border February 8, 1971, to cut the Ho Chi Minh Trail in an operation called Lam Son 719 (named for a battle where the Vietnamese won an ancient victory against the Chinese). In the first phase the 1st Brigade, United States 5th Infantry Division, occupied the Khe Sanh area with its mechanized units and cleared Route 9 to the Laotian border. In the meantime, the United States 101st Airborne Division moved into the A Shau Valley as a diversion. In the second phase, American forces provided artillery support, helilift and air support for the South Vietnamese units. But the South Vietnamese moved too cautiously and it soon became evident after three weeks that there was a stalemate and Lieutenant General Hoang Xuan Lam decided to withdraw his units. American military leaders learned later that President Thieu had ordered his commander to cease fighting once his command suffered 3,000 casualties. Although the operation was not a success, it may have forestalled a communist offensive that spring.

The hurried retreat of the South Vietnamese caused a violent escalation of anti-war sentiment in the United States by those who believed the South Vietnamese were not worth fighting for. In May, 1971, 200,000 demonstrators converged on Washington and, led by hard-core agitators, openly encouraged by North Vietnam, mounted a violent but unsuccessful attempt to close down the government for a day.

Lieutenant William Calley, Jr. was found guilty March 29, 1971, by an Army courtmartial for the premeditated murder of twenty-two South Vietnamese civilians at My Lai three years earlier. Calley had led his platoon into My Lai, a small hamlet 100 miles northeast of Saigon, in March, 1968. The village was a Vietcong stronghold and it had cost many American casualties. Calley and his men had rounded up the villagers and ordered 347 of them shot. Calley personally used a machine gun when some of his men refused to fire at these helpless civilians. It was an inexcusable act, justly condemned by the American people. The war's critics roundly assailed the massacre, but in the past they had ignored similar and often worse incidents of atrocities perpetuated by the North Vietnamese and the Vietcong.

There were appeals for clemency so two days after the court martial's verdict President Nixon advised the chairman of the Joint Chiefs of Staff, Admiral Moorer, that Calley should be released from the stockade and confined to his quarters pending his appeal of the verdict.

Three years later Calley's sentence was reduced to ten years with eligibility for parole as early as the end of 1974. Nixon personally reviewed Calley's case and decided not to intervene.

The Secretary of the Army paroled Calley three months after Nixon's resignation as president in August of 1974.

The Calley case was a classic example of a breakdown in the officer selection process.

Kissinger resumed negotiations with the North Vietnamese in May, 1971, and made two major concessions. He said United States forces would withdraw six months after an agreement was reached and that President Thieu would step down one month before general elections took place. These proposals were turned down May 3.

In the next three months Kissinger and Le Duc Tho met five times and all United States proposals were rejected. Their last session in 1971 was in September. Now it was clear to American negotiators that the communists wanted South Vietnam to be turned over to their control even before United States troops were withdrawn.

The United States Senate June 22 passed the Mansfield amendment by a vote of 57 to 42 that called upon the president to withdraw all American forces from Vietnam within nine months if North Vietnam agreed to release all prisoners. Now, most of Kissinger's bargaining points lost their credibility. To achieve its ends Noth Vietnam's leaders knew that all they had to do was procrastinate.

This was the month when the so-called Pentagon Papers were published. The documents were leaked to the press by those trying to discredit the United States involvement in Southeast Asia. They were formally titled "The History of the United States Decision-Making Process in Vietnam" and had been commissioned by former Secretary of Defense McNamara. They contained verbatim documents from the Departments of Defense and State, the Central Intelligence Agency, the White House and the Joint Chiefs of Staff. They were classified either secret or top secret and were primarily a critique of the manner in which the Kennedy and Johnson administrations had led the nation into the war. The revelation of John F. Kennedy's decision to support the coup that ousted President Diem in 1963, and that resulted in his murder, caused General Maxwell Taylor to comment that one of our worst mistakes was our connivance in the Diem overthrow. He stated that "nothing but chaos came as a result."

News reports said that the documents proved that President Johnson had told the American people that he was not going to escalate the war while privately planning an escalation from 17,000 to 185,000 Americans. James Reston of the New York *Times* described the actions revealed by the documents as a "deceptive and stealthy American involvement in the war under Presidents Kennedy and Johnson."

The Justice Department tried to stop publication by the New York *Times* June 15 until the government could review the documents and verify that they caused no national security problems. But other papers now had obtained copies, and the Supreme Court June 30 ruled 6 to 3 against the government. One of the majority opinions said that disclosures might have a serious impact on national interest but there was no basis for sanctioning restraint on the press.

Two days earlier, a Los Angeles Grand Jury had indicted Dr. Daniel Ellsberg on one count of theft of government property and one count of unauthorized possession of documents and writings related to national defense. He told admirers outside the Court House, "I think I've done a good job as a citizen." He had worked in the Defense Department and later with the Rand Corporation before he gave the classified papers to the New York *Times*. A federal judge later dismissed the case after it was disclosed that White House agents committed burglary in seeking evidence.

On the Labor Day weekend a group organized by John Ehrlichman, a top member of President Nixon's White House staff, had broken into the office of Daniel Ellsberg's psychiatrist hoping to get information from his files on Ellsberg's motives for revealing the Pentagon Papers, his further intentions and the names of any possible co-conspirators. They found nothing. The raid was led by Egil "Bud" Krogh, a young lawyer on the Domestic Council's staff. Both he and Erlichman subsequently went to jail for the unauthorized break-in.

In Paris, Kissinger believed that North Vietnam's counter proposal to the American peace plan was unacceptable but still negotiable. They had offered nine points versus the seven in the American proposal. The greatest stumbling block was North Vietnam's insistence that the United States not support any particular government in South Vietnam. In rebuttal, Kissinger said his government would absolutely refuse to make a secret agreement to replace the leader of a country that was still an ally. When the July 26 session ended, peace was as far away as ever. Ambassador David Bruce, the official negotiator, candidly admitted that for the past two years there had not been any serious talks and that the peace conference was simply being used by the communists as a forum for propaganda.

Kissinger met with Xuan Thuy August 16. Le Duc Tho was in Hanoi so nothing could be accomplished. This meeting ended as usual with Kissinger saying, "The only thing that remains for me to say is to express the hope that some day Hanoi will approach us with an attitude that will make peace. If there is that attitude I know the minister and I can find formulas to make peace. Until then, until we can find that attitude, we will stay as we are."

They met again September 13. North Vietnam's leaders were disturbed by President Nixon's new approval rating that was well above 50 percent and the announcement of Kissinger's meeting with Chinese officials to consider a summit conference between the United States and the People's Republic of China. But nothing was achieved and this remained the situation for another fourteen months when they met again to consider terms that were essentially the same as those discussed in mid-1971.

CHAPTER 32

A Tidal Wave of Refugees

THROUGHOUT 1971 REDEPLOYMENT OF UNITED STATES TROOPS CONtinued along with Vietnamization. The communists maintained their rocket attacks against major cities and even tried to breach the demilitarized zone. These violations led to a resumption of limited American bombing of military targets in North Vietnam.

South Vietnam assumed full control to defend the area immediately below the demilitarized zone July 11, a process begun by Secretary of Defense Laird in 1969. A month later the United States relinquished all ground combat responsibilities to the Republic of Vietnam. There was some American participation by ground units in Thua Thien Province in October but this was the last major combat operation by American ground forces.

With reduction in United States troop strength, battle deaths were reduced to sixty-six in July, the lowest monthly figure since May, 1967. By early November troop totals dropped to 191,000, and President Nixon announced that American trops had reverted to a defensive role in Vietnam.

Along with morale problems associated with American troops still in Vietnam there was serious corruption in the handling of military and base exchange supplies. The growing drug problem among American servicemen was behind much of this corruption. Most opium, from which heroin is made, was grown in Burma with the rest in neighboring Laos. The major refining center was located in Vientiane where it was flown to Saigon, often in soft-drink cans. Some were dropped from Laotian or Vietnamese military aircraft, but most drugs were landed routinely at Saigon's airport. Opium was openly sold on the capital's streets and around American bases. Almost pure, with very little adulteration, it was cheap compared to prices in the United States. In the early 1970s the Military Assistance Command estimated that 10 percent of its troops were taking heroin and that five percent were addicts.

Throughout 1971 air strikes expanded below the 20th parallel. Now special strikes were directed against many of the supply points that had been targeted before the bombing halt. Nixon approved these strikes because he believed they were necessary for the security of the American men and women still in South Vietnam. Air strikes in the North above the 20th parallel remained strictly limited.

In an election October 3, 1971, Thieu ran unopposed after Vice President Ky was disqualified in his campaign for the presidency, and General Duong Van Minh withdrew knowing that he would lose. Thieu's loyal army and police backers helped to assure his re-election as president.

Now a full commander and skipper of VA-97, Robert Arnold and his wingman were over the demilitarized zone that fall when he called the forward air controller that he still had some 20 mm. ammunition. "We've got some twenty mike mike left. Is there anything you want us to hit?"

He was told there was nothing below worth hitting. They still had forty-five minutes before they were scheduled to return to the *Enterprise*. His wingman was upset because this was his last mission and Arnold was seeking another target.

Arnold tried to contact the airborne control plane Hillsborough. He got no response at first but its pilot finally came on the radio. "What's your ordnance?"

"I'm out of bombs but we still have our twenty mike mike."

"We've got someone who can use you. Go south of Da Nang and contact the Birdseed forward air controller."

Arnold turned south and called Birdseed.

"Where are you?" the controller shouted. "War Ace, where are you?"

"We are on our way. I think we are sixty miles from you."

"We really need you, War Ace."

"Okay. All I've got left are twenty mike mike."

"Hurry up! We need you down here."

Over the radio Arnold heard, "Charlie, how are you doing down there?"

"When in hell am I getting out of here?" Arnold quickly realized that the controller was talking to a man on the ground in an observation post on a ridgeline and that the Vietcong were preparing to charge up the hill and capture him.

"We've got the choppers on the way, Charlie. Hang in there," he said, his voice torn with emotion. This was unusual because most forward air controllers maintained a calm, unemotional voice.

"War Ace, what's your position now?"

Arnold replied, "I'm thirty-five miles from your position." He glanced down but the countryside was just a green expanse. "I think I've got you spotted," Arnold said. "Rock your wings."

The controller did so.

"Okay, I've got you spotted."

"I'm putting smoke in," the controller yelled.

Arnold spotted the smoke as they came in from the north.

The controller called, "I want you to make your runs from the south to the north in a left-hand pattern. Hit my smoke, and hit west of my smoke. Don't hit east of my smoke. We've got friendlies on the east side."

Arnold acknowledged and signaled to his wingman to follow him. He heard the controller call, "How you doing, Charlie?"

"When in hell am I getting out of here?" The man's voice shook and he kept repeating the words.

"We've got the Navy coming in, Charlie. Hang in there." Then to Arnold, he said, "Hurry up, War Ace. We need you down here now."

"I've got your smoke and I'm ready to roll in," Arnold replied.

He and his wingman made six runs shooting at the spot marked by the smoke, and flying just above the tree tops. He couln't see they were doing any damage but then the controller yelled, "You got 'em. You got 'em. They're going the other way." He called Charlie again. "How you doing?"

"When in hell am I getting out of here?"

"The choppers are on the way."

Arnold and his wingman by now had shot practically all their ammunition and they were late in returning to their ship. The last word he heard from the forward air controller as they turned away was, "Hey, Navy, you saved our lives down here today."

It was a great feeling, more than compensating for the 336 combat missions Arnold had flown in Southeast Asia.

Vice Admiral Fred Bardshar, commander of Carrier Task Force 77, flew aboard Rear Admiral "Jig Dog" Ramage's flagship *Oriskany* at noon November 20, 1970. Ramage was in tactical command of the task force at that time. Bardshar advised Ramage that the task force had a high priority job that night. He said the Joint Chiefs had ordered his carriers to support an attempt by American commandoes to rescue sixty American prisoners at Son Tay. Bardshar said planes should be launched at 11:00 P.M. in distruptive operations in the eastern part of North Vietnam to divert attention from the Son Tay rescue force that would be coming in from the west to the prison twenty miles from Hanoi. As Ramage reviewed the plan he admired President Nixon's guts because such an operation could end in utter failure and disaster for the rescue force.

Bardshar told Ramage that the operation was "eyes only" top secret and that he could not tell the crews why they were going out.

Ramage protested. "That certainly doesn't make much sense. I've got to give my guys some reason. It's not pleasant to churn around up there at night."

Bardshar understood. "Okay, go ahead and tell them."

When the pilots were briefed that night they were told that they were to support an attempt to break prisoners out of Son Tay Prison. They were delighted by the news.

In thinking back to the President Johnson years Ramage believed they would get everybody ready for launch and then it would be cancelled. But planes on the *Oriskany, Hancock* and *Ranger* were loaded with anti-radiation missles and cluster bombs along with thousand-pound general purpose bombs. This time there was no cancellation and the 100 planes took off to disrupt North Vietnam's defenses as a diversionary move. Watching them as they launched, Ramage realized there were probably more jet aircraft in the air that night than on any previous occasion. Tankers had been ordered to participate from various Pacific commands and there was an enormous amount of fuel flying around to take care of any contingency.

In a serious intelligence failure, it was not realized that the prison had been closed three months earlier due to fear of just such a rescue attempt. The raid, however, had been meticulously planned and was superbly executed. Once news of the raid filtered down to the prisoners in North Vietnam it had a salautary effect on their morale. According to Americans prisoners of war, it was later revealed that there was a great improvement in their treatment.

During the last week of December United States Air Force and Navy planes carried out 1,000 strikes against North Vietnam below the 20th parallel, the heaviest air attacks since November, 1968. Allied commanders insisted they were necessary because of a huge buildup of military supplies in North Vietnam for possible offensive operations against South Vietnam and Cambodia. Stepped-up North Vietnamese anti-aircraft and missile attacks against American aircraft that bombed the Ho Chi Minh Trail in Laos also contributed to the decision.

The United States continued to reduce its ground presence in South

Vietnam during late 1971 and early 1972, but American air attacks increased while both sides exchanged peace proposals.

In early January President Nixon confirmed that troop withdrawals would continue but he promised that a force of 25,000 to 30,00 would remain in Vietnam until all American prisoners of war were released. Secretary of Defense Laird reported that Vietnamization was progressing well and that United States troops would not be re-introduced into Vietnam even in a military emergency. By the end of March 1972, American troop strength had dropped to 95,500.

Along with troop withdrawals in January, 1972, American planes maintained an intermittent bombardment of missile sites in North Vietnam and on the Laotian border and against North Vietnamese troop concentrations in South Vietnam's Central Highlands.

President Nixon January 25, 1972, announced an eight-part program to end the war that included agreement to remove all American and foreign troops from Vietnam no later than six months after a peace agreement was reached. North Vietnamese and Vietcong delegates rejected the proposal, insisting upon complete withdrawal of all foreign troops from Indochina and cessation of all forms of American aid to South Vietnam.

Nixon decided to lay the American negotiating record before the American people, releasing the record of the twelve secret meetings with North Vietnam's officials. For the first time he publicly released details of his May 31, 1971, offer to set a withdrawal deadline that had been rejected, and the proposal October 11 that spelled out terms of a political settlement of an internationally supervised free election with communist involvement, and President Thieu's willingness to step down a month before the election. The president pointed out that the withdrawal deadline had been reduced from seven months to six. He stated that the "only thing this plan does not do is to join our enemy to overthrow our ally, which the United States will never do. If the enemy wants peace it will have to recognize the important differences between settlement and surrender."

Most Americans were surprised by the long record and the sweep of the American proposals. Various presidential contenders in this election year responded with cautious support. But within a week after the North Vietnamese rejected the proposal, critics were claiming that it was all Nixon's fault. Although the war was unpopular, most thoughtful Americans were not ready to join an enemy in defeating an ally.

The revelations threw the North Vietnamese offstride. For a time they had been outmaneuvered, and they grew increasingly concerned after it was announced that Kissinger had made another trip to Peking to arrange for a presidential visit. They published their nine-point peace plan January 31, 1972, that Le Duc Tho had presented to Kissinger the previous June 26. Their spokesman said there were fundamental differences between them "like night and day." This was true, but it was obvious that North Vietnam was on the defensive.

President Thieu expressed his opposition to the American peace plan because Nixon had dropped the mutual withdrawal aspect as part of his new plan to end the war.

By now 410,000 Americans had been withdrawn from South Vietnam and the military position there had improved. Nixon believed that if he could weather the criticism of the home front he could go to Peking and Moscow with hope of constructing a new international order.

The president stood by his helicopter on the White House lawn February 11 to make a brief farewell speech to congressional leaders before he left for China. He told them that he hoped that the future would record of his trip what was written on the plaque the Apollo 11 astronauts had left on the moon, "We came in peace for all mankind."

Before he left for the People's Republic of China Nixon approved a new set of recommendations for easing trade relations with that country. He ordered that all commodities available for sale to the Soviet Union and eastern Europe be also available to China.

In China, during his meeting with Foreign Minister Chou En-lai, Nixon said he would not impose a political solution on Vietnam, as North Vietnam wanted. If we did, he said, no country would ever trust us again. The implication was unmistakable. American reliability was also relevant to China's security concerns. He warned that he would react violently if North Vietnam launched another major offensive in 1972.

Chou En-lai indicated sympathy for North Vietnam but he said there was no community of interest. He said China's obligation to support North Vietnam was not from ideological solidarity—much less from national interests—but from an historical debt owed to Vietnam from China's imperial past. He said he believed differences between China and the United States could be settled peacefully. Nixon and Kissinger interpreted this comment to mean that China would not intervene militarily in Vietnam, and that China viewed Vietnam in the long-term context of Soviet aspirations in Southeast Asia. In a meeting with Mao Tse-tung, both he and Chou En-lai argued that the war should be ended because it bogged down the United States and deflected its energies from more important parts of the globe.

Nixon's trip to China proved to be a remarkable diplomatic breakthrough between the two countries and reversed United States policy toward the People's Republic of China. The meeting augured well for better relations between these once bitter foes.

The North Vietnamese had initiated their Tet offensive during the 1968 election year and now, four years later, in another presidential election year North Vietnam decided to throw its entire military might behind an invasion to conquer South Vietnam. This time most American ground troops had gone home, but the armed forces of the Republic of Vietnam now totaled 1,048,000, more than half of whom were regulars. Now Vietnamization would be put to the crucial test as more than ten North Vietnamese divisions prepared for what they believed would be the final battle.

It began on Easter March 30, 1972, with heavy artillery attacks as three North Vietnamese Army divisions spearheaded by tanks crossed the demilitarized zone. In attacking from the north and west they overran thinly defended forward outposts held by the 3rd Infantry Division. Three days later, three more communist divisions closed in on An Loc, sixty miles north of Saigon, after taking a district town near the Cambodian border. April 14 two North Vietnamese divisions attacked troops of the 22nd Infantry Division who manned the defenses northwest of Kontum in II Corps while directly to the east, in the lowlands of Binh Dinh Province, another North Vietnamese division attacked the province's three northern towns. Their apparent strategy was to sever the two northern provinces from South Vietnam by pushing a salient towards Pleiku to open the way for a future assault against Saigon.

Although the South Vietnamese Air Force had grown to 44 squadrons and 42,000 personnel, it was structured for a low-scale war. When it was formed a decision was made by United States officials to provide it with relatively low-performing A-37s and F-5s without sophisticated fire controls. Some Americans at the time feared that if the Vietnamese Air Force was given high performance aircraft they would be tempted to mount a large-scale campaign to take over all of Vietnam. This decision was based on the theory that if the South Vietnamese did not have aircraft capable of operations over North Vietnam the potential for keeping the fighting at a relatively low level would be enhanced, increasing the outlook for a political settlement. It was an odd train of thought that made no sense then or later. In the two provinces now invaded by the North Vietnamese the communists set up a massive air defense system and South Vietnam's airplanes suffered heavy losses. South Vietnamese planes were also inhibited by bad weather and a lack of centralized control so its deployment was fragmented. It was seldom used where it should have been, and where it was most needed.

The United States Seventh Air Force had been reduced to half its former strength of 1,000 planes, and President Nixon realized quickly that the communist offensive would not be stopped by further threats of retaliation but only by heavy committment of American airpower. He reduced the restrictions on bombing North Vietnam and ordered the Navy to increase its carriers from two to five.

Nixon made appeals to the Russians, the Chinese and the North Vietnamese to stop this new aggression. There was concern in Peking and Moscow but it was apparent that officials of the Soviet Union and the People's Republic of China had little control over North Vietnam's leaders. Finally, Nixon became so upset over North Vietnam's refusal to set up a meeting with Kissinger and Le Duc Tho that he suspended the Paris deliberations. He had said earlier that North Vietnam was using the Paris forum for propaganda and that on this basis, "There was no hope whatsoever."

General Abrams had performed his difficult task of dismantling his army in Vietnam with dignity for four years in one of the most thankless jobs ever assigned to an American general. Now the more than half million men and women he had taken over were largely gone. Therefore, he had only airpower to use against the North Vietnamese.

At President Nixon's insistence, the Soviet Union was publicly made accountable for the North Vietnamese offensive.

Meanwhile, there was a continued buildup of sea and air forces and April 9 twenty-eight more B-52s were sent to Guam and the following day a fifth carrier was ordered to Vietnamese waters.

North Vietnam again turned down a proposed private meeting with Kissinger and Le Duc Tho for April 24 until the United States agreed to resume public sessions.

While a visit by Kissinger to Moscow was under consideration, B-52s engaged in a two-day attack April 15 and 16 on fuel storage depots at Haiphong's harbor while Navy ships bombarded the depots from offshore. These attacks had been opposed by General Abrams but had been approved by Secretary of Defense Laird.

With intensification of the war in Vietnam, political activists raised their protests to higher levels. There were rallies on the east and west coasts and demonstrations at several universities and military installations. In Washington, 200 law school students protested at the Supreme Court building April 21 against the court's refusal to review the constitutionality of the war. In New York the next day a crowd estimated at over 30,000 marched in the rain. San Francisco had a rally of equal number while a smaller group protested in Los Angeles the same day.

The United States now received an official protest from the Soviet Union that four of its ships had been hit during attacks on Haiphong's harbor with loss of life.

The People's Republic of China April 12 expressed its solidarity with North Vietnam and warned in a private channel that the United States was getting bogged down again in Indochina.

Kissinger left for Moscow on a secret trip April 20. Upon his return to Washington he described his meetings with top Soviet leaders in a memorandum to Nixon. He reported, in part, "In sum, I would have to conclude that Brezhnev personally, and the Soviets collectively, are in one of their toughest political corners in years. They must want the Vietnamese situation to subside and I would judge that there is just a chance that of all the distasteful courses open to them they will pick that of pressure on Hanoi—not to help us but themselves. The dispatch of Brezhnev's confidant, Katushev [Konstantin Katushev was head of the Soviet Central Committee section dealing with foreign communist parties], to Hanoi tends to bear that out.

"The stick of your determination and the carrot of the productive summit with which I went to Moscow, which I used there and which we must now maintain, give us our best leverage in Kremlin politics as well as the best position in our own."

Nixon approved of Kissinger's actions although earlier he had been highly critical of his talks because they included issues other than Vietnam, including a possible agreement to limit nuclear weapons.

April 25—the day it was announced that Kissinger had been in Moscow—the United States gave North Vietnam twenty-four hours to reply to the possibility of a new private session. This time the North Vietnamese quickly agreed to a meeting May 2 whereas in the past they had procrastinated for months.

Within two weeks after North Vietnam opened its offensive large conventional battles were being fought on three major fronts, pitting a total of fourteen North Vietnamese divisions against an equivalent number of South Vietnamese divisions. For the first time almost the entire North Vietnamese armored force was thrown into battle with a significant increase in heavy artillery support. This was the largest offensive ever launched by the communists against South Vietnam. Due to the size of the forces, and the tactics employed, this was a radical departure from their previous methods of warfare.

During preparations for this 1972 offensive North Vietnam had requested huge quantities of modern weapons from Russia and China. It was given MIG-21s, T-54 medium tanks, heavy guns and mortars, SAM anti-aircraft missiles and, for the first time, heat-seeking, shoulder-fired SA-7 missiles. War supplies were sent in amounts never before provided for North Vietnam.

While North Vietnam was receiving these huge supplies, the United States continued to withdraw its troops at an accelerated pace while combat supplies for South Vietnam's armed forces were reduced, despite the fact that it was known that North Vietnam was preparing for a general offensive although the date was not known.

North Vietnam had selected the code name Nguyen Hue for its Easter invasion. This was the birth name of Emperor Quang Trung, a Vietnam hero who in the year of the Rooster 1789 had maneuvered his troops hundreds of miles through jungles and mountains from Central to North Vietnam, surprised and attacked the invading Chinese in the early days of spring and dealt them a resounding defeat on the outskirts of Hanoi. They hoped to repeat this victory in the opposite direction. Unlike Nguyen Hue's army, the North Vietnamese failed to achieve surprise.

The American Joint Chiefs of Staff had sent warnings to all military commanders in Vietnam to be prepared for a major attack early in the year. They thought it would come before Tet or in late January but nothing happened. Remaining American troops were ordered to stay in their barracks.

Some Vietnamese commanders believed that North Vietnam was not ready for an attack in 1972, even though American troop strength—down to 70,000 by the end of April—was not considered significant. The North Vietnamese decided otherwise. They wanted their invasion neither too far ahead of the American presidential election, nor too late in the dry season when torrential rains in late May might impede their efforts along the border.

North Vietnam committed its entire combat force of fourteen divisions, twenty-six separate regiments and supporting armor and artillery units except the 136th Division that was operating in Laos. The fierceness of this classic frontal assault turned parts of South Vietnam into a blazing furnace.

At the time of the offensive all United States combat units had gone home except for the 196th Infantry Brigade, that was waiting its return to the United States while conducting defensive operations around Da Nang and Phu Bai. All other ground forces were South Vietnamese although they still had American advisers and tactical air support aircraft plus ships at sea. North of Hai Van Pass, where 80,000 Americans had been stationed, there were only two South Vietnamese infantry divisions supported by newly activated armor and artillery units with a total strength of 25,000.

I Corps' backbone was provided by three South Vietnamese infantry divisions—the 1st, 2nd and 3rd—plus smaller units and territorial forces. They were under Lieutenant General Hoang Xuan Lam, an armor officer and a native of Hué. On the eve of the invasion the 3rd Infantry Division was assigned the northernmost frontier. It had been activated six months earlier and had never fought as a division although its battalions were seasoned combat veterans. Most soldiers were native to the region and familiar with the terrain and hardened by its harsh dampness. Their dependents lived in nearby hamlets. The division and its reserve Marine brigades were responsible for Quang Tri Province and its headquarters was under the leadership of Brigadier General Vu Van Giai, former deputy commander of the 1st Division.

South of the Quang Tri-Thua Thien provincial boundary, and north of the Hai Van Pass, was the 1st Infantry Division's tactical area of responsibility under Major General Pham Van Phu. Phu's forces were assigned to defend the western approaches to Hué.

The three provinces composing the southern part of I Corps south of the Hai Van Pass were the responsibility of the 2nd Infantry Division under Brigadier General Phan Hoa Hiep. Each of the division's three regiments were assigned to a separate province.

While the 1st and 2nd Infantry Divisions were combat proven, the recently activated 3rd was not, although the men of its two Marine brigades in general reserve had long since proven their worth. But they gave their loyalty first to their commander and not to the 3rd Division's commander. Unfortunately, most South Vietnamese infantry divisions had little experience in multi-battalion operations so their staffs had limited training with combined operations. Some of this fault could be laid to Westmoreland's decision in 1965 to use Americans primarily for main-force operations.

In February, General Lam had been advised by his intelligence officers that the North Vietnamese 324B Division was moving into the A Shau Valley. This was a familiar move to launch an attack against Hué. The 1st Infantry Division clashed with them early in March and Lam did not rule out a full-scale attack across the demilitarized zone although he doubted it. This no man's land was mostly flat, exposed terrain that was unfavorable to maneuver large infantry formations, even with armor support, since they would be under constant observation and exposed to artillery and air attacks. Lam expected the communists to come as usual from the west. Their efforts to open new roads and bring in more weapons seemed to prove this theory.

General Giai of the 3rd Division agreed with Lam, and rotated his troops in and out of this area to familiarize them with the terrain.

The month preceding the invasion, the 1st Infantry Division in the South cleared the approaches to Hué on the west and southwest now that there was an obvious enemy buildup.

At noon March 30 the North Vietnamese surprised General Lam by attacking with four spearheads from the demilitarized zone and west through Khe Sanh. Their long-range 130 mm. field guns north of the demilitarized zone proved deadly as they pounded all strong points and coordinated their fire with infantry attacks. This unexpected assault across the demilitarized zone caught the 3rd Division in movement and only partially settled into defensive positions as the 304th and 308th North Vietnamese Divisions surged forward. The South Vietnamese were out-numbered three to one locally, and outgunned because their defenses were designed to counter infiltration and local attacks—not North Vietnamese divisions. By the evening of April 1 all strongpoints along the northern perimeter had to be evacuated, mostly in orderly fashion.

At 6:00 P.M. Giai ordered the immediate reorganization of his defensive positions. This was done to take advantage of such natural obstacles as the Cua Viet and Hien Giang rivers and establish a line of defense south of them.

The next day the communists launched simultaneous attacks against Dong Ha and its major support base to the west. Bad weather precluded air attacks as enemy tanks and infantry forces repeatedly tried to approach Dong Ha from the north but were repulsed by ground forces and United States naval gunfire when they tried to cross the Dong Ha bridge. A chaotic stream of refugees fleeing the combat zone along Route 1 since early morning affected the morale of the 57th Regiment's troops who broke ranks around noon and fled south with them. A plan for such an occurrence might have prevented the panic that followed. Giai flew to the area and restored some order and the soldiers returned to their units. The destruction of the Dong Ha bridge was ordered to stall the enemy's armor-infantry drive.

Camp Carroll, a major support base to the west, had been surrounded since early morning. Troops of the 56th Regiment endured heavy artillery and resisted repeated assaults but received little artillery or air support. Their commander, Colonel Pham Van Dinh, had often proven his cour-age—he was the officer who restored the national colors at the Hué Citadel during the 1968 offensive—but now he was despondent. He thought everyone had forgotten him. He called his staff together, wanting to save as many men as possible, and ordered his intelligence officer to hang a white sheet at the compound's main gate. This was done and radio contact was made with the communists and terms of their surrender were ar-ranged. Fifteen hundred South Vietnamese troops were surrendered with-out further resistance, along with twenty-two pieces of artillery.

Camp Carroll's loss made the defense of Mai Loc precarious so that base was evacuated, and members of the 147th Marine Brigade fell back to Quang Tri late in the afternoon. The 3rd Division's area of operations continued to shrink as units withdrew with heavy losses.

After four days of arduous fighting and setbacks, the situation at Quang Tri became critical, although for a week enemy attempts failed to break through defense lines. Lam now ran into a serious problem with the South Vietnamese Marines who were assigned to him but were not under his direct command. The 3rd Division commander became frustrated when his orders to the Marines were ignored until their commander checked with his own headquarters. Lam remained optimistic, however, believing he had enough men to stop the North Vietnamese at their present line of defense while he organized a counteroffensive.

Lam trusted Giai but he seldom visited his subordinates in the field, so he was out of touch with the reality of their problems. Therefore, when he ordered a counterattack to the west April 14 his weary troops, who had been fighting for weeks, made little progress. North Vietnam's artillery proved devastating and South Vietnamese tanks bore the brunt of their firing. With Giai's inability to exercise total command over all his units, and morale plummeting with little forward movement, the fighting developed into a costly battle of attrition, and casualties mounted.

General Lam's failure to establish effective control of his units created an increasingly serious problem. Marine Division and Ranger headquarters that had been sent to I Corps to provide control of their units, continued to be left out of combat activities and received no specific assignments. Almost every order from Giai or Lam to their units was questioned by these headquarters. The problem was compounded because Lam frequently issued directives by telephone or radio without going through the chain of command. Giai often learned of them after they had been implemented. The result was total command disruption and control in the frontlines.

After two weeks of rain and heavy cloud cover that inhibited tactical airpower, the weather began to clear and United States aircraft of all types filled the skies over Quang Tri. Their appearance restored the morale of the South Vietnamese troops.

April 18 the communists made their third major attempt to take Quang Tri. Lam thought the situation was under control. He was wrong. He should have reorganized his positions and rotated weary combat units. He also should have had a coordinated defense plan if Quang Tri was to be held. It was never made.

The following week the defense line at Dong Ha and along the Cua Viet River caved in because of a tactical blunder. Reports were received that enemy infiltrations from the west were threatening to cut the supply route between Dong Ha and Quang Tri Combat Base. On his own initiative the 1st Armored Brigade commander directed the 20th Tank Squadron on the Cua Viet line to pull back south along Route 1 to clear enemy elements. As soon as troops saw the tanks moving south they were gripped by panic. They broke ranks and streamed along. Before Giai realized what was happening, many of his troops had arrived at Quang Tri's Combat Base. The Cua Viet defense line, one of the strongest lines of defense from which troops had repeatedly repelled every enemy attack for nearly a month, was handed to the communists without a fight because the tactical commander had initiated a major move without reporting to his superior and without foreseeing the consequences of his action.

Through sheer physical intercession, General Giai succeeded in establishing order, but not for long. There was no way they could send their units back to Cua Viet to restore the lost positions. They were compelled instead to regroup west of Quang Tri City and develop a new defense line north of the Thach Han River. This new line surrounded and protected the Quang Tri Combat Base whose importance as a logistic's support center had greatly diminished in view of the dwindling supplies still there.

The 147th Marine Brigade returned to Quang Tri Base April 23 to take over defense positions after refitting in Hué. Morale quickly deteriorated because they were exposed to daily pounding by artillery and enemy tanks. The long nights were tense and sleepless as they faced the threat of enemy infantry assaults that could surge forward from the dark at any moment. There was such total inertia that the communists could rest or fight at their leisure because South Vietnamese troops were sapped by fear and uncertainty while defending a base of dubious tactical value. Giai decided to evacuate Quang Tri Combat Base and withdraw south of the Thach Han River. He worked on the withdrawal himself, consulting only his division's senior adviser. Giai feared that if other members of his staff learned of his plan they would wreck it by hasty actions. He also withheld his plan from General Lam and this action increased the growing distrust between them and added to the dimension of events that soon would lead to the fall of Quang Tri City.

By the last week of April the strain and shock from four weeks of warfare on South Vietnam's ill-prepared troops took its toll on discipline and effectiveness. They had no self-assurance left, and units fought without conviction and they were practically left to fend for themselves. Meanwhile, the 3rd Division's sector shrank daily.

North Vietnamese attacks from the west near the boundary of Thua Thien Province cut off Route 1 to the south and interdicted friendly vehicular traffic over a five-mile stretch. Therefore, I Corps' forces in

Quang Tri Province were isolated because their lifeline had been severed. General Lam ordered supply convoys to push through enemy road blocks and General Giai was ordered to clear Route 1 from the north. These orders compelled Giai to divert an armored cavalry squadron from its vital frontline role near Quang Tri for operations to the south. Finally, General Lam sent a Marine battalion that had been committed to Hué's defense to clear Route 1 from the south. These movements exhausted fuel and ammunition critically needed in Quang Tri, and failed to reopen the division's lifeline.

Weather was particularly bad April 27 and the North Vietnamese took advantage of the situation. They began a strong push to capture the remaining territory held by South Vietnamese troops in Quang Tri Province. Along the 3rd Division's new defense line, now shrunk to the vicinity of Quang Tri City to the east, north and west, units either reported contact with enemy troops or received enemy artillery fire. Steadily but surely they were forced to retreat as men continued to flee south. The only effective unit still defending the Quang Tri Combat Base was the 147th Marine Brigade and it was under heavy artillery fire.

General Giai, faced with disaster for his 3rd Division, April 30 presented his plan for withdrawal south of the Thach Han River. He said he would hold Quang Tri City with a Marine brigade, and establish a defense line on the south bank of the river and try to reopen Route 1 to the south with tank and armored cavalry units. When informed of Giai's withdrawal plan General Lam concurred although he never gave formal approval or issued a directive.

Lam changed his mind May 1 and called Giai that he did not approve and ordered troops to hold their positions "at all costs." He made it clear there would be no withdrawal without his permission. His orders were merely a reiteration of what President Thieu had told him. Presumably this action was taken because the Paris peace talks were about to resume after being boycotted by the North Vietnamese delegation since the start of the invasion.

Conflicting orders in the field resulted in a nightmare of confusion and chaos. Giai did not even have time to counteract his own orders and send out new ones. Some commanders said their units had already been moved, while others bluntly refused to change their courses of action. Giai insisted that each commander must comply with his orders. Within four hours South Vietnam's defense line crumbled. Units to the north which were manning positions around the Quang Tri Combat Base streamed across the Thach Han River and fled south in panic. Mechanized units at Quang Tri bridge were unable to cross because it had been destroyed. They left their vehicles behind and forded the river, joining the mass rush to the south. On the southern bank of the river infantry units did not remain long in their new positions. When they saw tanks withdrawing to the south they deserted their positions and joined them. They did not get far. Tanks and armored vehicles ran out of fuel and were left behind by their crews along Route 1. The only unit to retain full control was the 147th Marine Brigade defending Quang Tri City. Finally the brigade's commander decided the situation was hopeless and he ordered his unit to move out at 2:30 P.M. leaving behind the 3rd Division's commander, General Giai, and his small staff in the undefended city's old citadel.

When Giai learned what was going on he and staff officers boarded three armored vehicles to catch up with the withdrawing troops although United States helicopters came in to rescue the division's advisory personnel and their Vietnamese employees.

General Giai failed to join the retreating column. Route 1 was clogged by refugees and dispirited troops, military vehicles, and civilians frantically trying to reach Hué under a heavy barrage of enemy fire. The general was forced to return to the old citadel and later he and his staff were evacuated by American helicopters. They were fired upon as they left because the North Vietnamese were already at the citadel. Quang Tri was taken without a fight, the first provincial capital to fall since the war started.

A tidal wave of refugees intermingled with troops along Route 1 as they moved south. The roadway was a spectacle of incredible destruction. There were burning vehicles of all types: trucks, armored vehicles, civilian buses and cars. They jammed the highway and forced all traffic off the road while a frightened mass of humanity was subjected to enemy artillery concentrations. By late afternoon the following day the carnage was over. But thousands of civilians met a tragic death on the long stretch of Route 1 that later was called "Terror Boulevard." The shock and trauma of this tragedy, like the 1968 massacre in Hué, would haunt the population of the northern region for a long time.

The entire Quang Tri Province was in communist hands by May 2, 1972, and North Vietnam's armed forces were in a good position to move against Hué. Lieutenant Colonel Ray E. Stratton, one of the American forward air controllers, was shocked by the magnitude of the tragedy unfolding beneath his small plane. It was an appalling sight. There was a complete litter of United States-built armored personnel carriers, tanks and trucks. In the rice fields to the east of the highway, tank and armored personnel carriers were abandoned in twos and threes. They had simply run out of fuel.

CHAPTER 33

To the Last Man

IN ONE OF THE MOST INTENSIVE AIR CAMPAIGNS OF THE WAR THE
Seventh Air Force and Navy carrier planes tried to choke off the enemy's
resupply effort. Controllers and gunships waged search and destroy operations against communist heavy artillery positions. First, fighter-bombers
brought down all bridges between the demilitarized zone and My Chanh.
After three days, forty-five bridges were unusable although destruction of
the bridges did not stop Soviet-made tanks that could float across rivers.
The dropping of bridge spans did make things tougher for all other
vehicles, particularly self-propelled and towed artillery guns. The communist's 130 mm. guns posed special problems for their handlers. They were
lethal and frightening to the South Vietnamese foot soldiers because they
were so accurate, and capable of firing seven rounds per minute with a
range of seventeen miles. An intensive campaign was started against these
guns May 7. Towed by a tracked vehicle, and capable of traversing almost
any terrain including the jungle and mountainous trails, they were camouflaged and difficult to spot. Forward air controllers and four-engined
gunships flew constantly over areas when such guns were suspected in
hope of sighting their muzzle flashes. They lived dangerously because of
the SA-7 anti-aircraft missiles.

One of the most successful applications of airpower against tanks was
demonstrated north of Hué where the terrain offered little concealment.
From April 1 to August 15 American and Vietnamese aircraft destroyed
285 North Vietnamese tanks in I Corps. Throughout South Vietnam more
than 70 percent of the tanks were destroyed or damaged by tactical aircraft
and gunships. Most effective were laser-guided or Smart bombs carried by
fighter-bombers of the Tactical Fighter Wing at Ubon, Thailand.

Forward Air Controller Stratton flying north of the My Chanh River at
twilight during one operation spotted two tanks. One was trying to pull

another out of a dry stream bed a mile wast of Route 1. He called for strike aircraft, and two fighter-bombers from Ubon showed up. One carried the laser gun used to direct energy onto the target while the other carried the laser-guided bombs. Stratton briefed them hurriedly because they were running out of fuel, and then dropped a smoke bomb to mark the target. One of the pilots asked which tank should be first. Stratton replied that the one that was not stuck should be given first consideration. Within thirty seconds the pilot called, "I've started the music," meaning the laser beam was on target. Their bombs hit on top of the PT-76, blowing the turret off, and flipping the tank over. The blast covered the other tank with mud, so Stratton put down another smoke rocket, and the operation was repeated. In three minutes both tanks were destroyed.

A forward air controller operating northeast of Kontum, north of Fire Base Charlie, reported April 24 that three busloads of refugees were coming down the road. He noted with horror that the North Vietnamese were opening up on them with automatic weapons, blowing the busses apart, and people were flying all over the area. That same night the communists marched 200 civilians into the fire base. The South Vietnamese soldiers left by the back door, unwilling to fire on their own people. The next morning, while an air controller flew overhead, the North Vietnamese prepared to haul away the captured 105 mm. guns, hooking them to trucks. The controller ordered a flight of fighter-bombers from Ubon armed with laser-guided bombs. Three perfectly placed 2,000 pounders took out the three guns and the five trucks.

With the all-out North Vietnamese invasion, the Thanh Hoa or Dragon's Jaw bridge and the Paul Doumer bridge had to be destroyed again. Attacks this time used the "Smart" bombs that had been introduced since the first attacks in 1968. The Dragon's Jaw bridge spanned the Song Ma River northeast of the town of Thanh Hoa, an important railroad junction linking Hanoi and Haiphong and Highway 1 to the south. It was 280 feet in length with open steelwork anchored at each end on massive hewn boulders. The bridge was not only narrow but it would not burn. Near misses had no effect on it.

Twelve F-4 Phantoms from the 8th Tactical Fighter Wing took off April 27 from Ubon in Thailand to bomb the two bridges. Eight planes had one-ton bombs while the other four carried chaff to interfere with enemy radar scopes. Strategic Air Command tankers were assigned to orbit a specific area to refuel the fighter-bombers. The "Smart" bombs could not be used because cloud cover precluded the use of the laser-guidance system. Both bridges suffered heavy damage but the Dragon's Jaw again proved stubborn and needed another attack.

While other heavy strikes were flown against the Hanoi-Haiphong area whose targets had previously been off-limits, the bridge busters went out again May 13 against the Dragon's Jaw. With the target in sight the lead aircraft rolled in, releasing its heavy bombs. Plane after plane followed, each pilot hoping that flashes on the ground did not signify a missile was heading for his aircraft. Below, belches of smoke and flames erupted as bombs exploded on the bridge. Finally it could stand no more punishment and some of its spans collapsed into the river. All planes exited the target area safely despite intense anti-aircraft fire and missile launches. This time post-strike photographs confirmed that the Dragon's Jaw was down.

During May, the interdiction campaign against North Vietnam's armed forces grew in intensity and enemy lines of communication showed signs of crumbling under the continuous American air assaults. By the end of the month thirteen important railroad bridges were down along the two major lines running northeast and northwest from Hanoi. Another four railroad bridges were down between Hanoi and Haiphong, and several more were dropped on lines running south from Hanoi.

The Thanh Hoa bridge across the Song Ma River was quickly repaired so Navy and Air Force pilots made periodic strikes until President Nixon stopped all bombing of North Vietnam in October. With this halt the saga of the Dragon's Jaw came to a close. By December, 1972, it was still in a state of disrepair.

During this period the 8th Tactical Fighter Wing made continuous attacks against the Paul Doumer bridge while other wings provided Wild Weasel and SAM suppression aircraft.

Captain Michael Messet, who had been on the original strike in August 1967 as a back-seater, led a two-ship Wild Weasel element May 10 in support of an attack against the Paul Doumer bridge while other planes attacked the Yen Vien railroad yards. Flak was heavy and 150 SAMs were fired at the strike force and their supporting aircraft at both places. The bridge was left battered and unusable.

F-4 fighters supported the strike aircraft. These fighters had the initial advantage against MIGs because they could fire radar missiles in head-on attacks and the MIGs could not. As a result, most American aircraft shot down by MIGs resulted from surprise attacks. In the earliest days of air-to-air combat, flying at jet-age speeds with a rate of closure of 1,000 knots, pilots used World War II and earlier techniques. They quickly learned that teamwork and air discipline were more important. North Vietnam, with Russian cooperation, had a highly sophisticated ground-controlled radar system. The MIG 21 had one advantage. It trailed little smoke while the American fighter left two large smoke trails that made it easier to spot. And, the MIG 21 turned tighter. This was important in counteracting the higher speed and acceleration of the American fighter. Then too, the MIG was specifically designed for air superiority operations while the F-4 was not. It had to perform multiple missions.

An F-4 flight was flying at 2,000 feet May 10 when radar revealed four MIGs flying high above in pairs about a mile in trail. Major Robert Lodge ordered his Oyster Flight to go after the North Vietnamese fighters. He and Captain Roger C. Locher, his weapons system officer, were highly experienced and had been together for more than eight months. They had agreed they would fire one missile at a time. Two days earlier they had fired two missiles at a MIG and both hit.

After lighting their afterburners, Lodge led his flight up after centering the "aim-dot" and obtaining a good radar firing solution. They covered the eight miles between them quickly, closing at a thousand knots, and Lodge fired his first missile. It started to guide toward the lead MIG but exploded instead in front of Lodge's plane after it armed itself. He quickly fired the second missile. The range was down to six miles and this missile began to guide towards the enemy plane. In five seconds there was a huge red-orange explosion. They had made their third kill.

Lieutenant John Markle and Captain Steven Eaves got an early radar lockon on another enemy plane. As his figher snapped up, the lead missile fired and he immediately checked with Eaves to be sure they still had a good lockon. He was assured that it was still good as they approached the heart of the firing envelope. Markle fired two more missiles and they impacted behind the canopy of a MIG 21, cutting the aircraft in half. The air was filled with enemy missiles that were fired unguided and head on from the remaining MIGs. This was a diversionary tatic by the trailing MIGs because heat-seeking missiles were not head-on weapons.

A third MIG seemed to come out of nowhere and almost hit Lodge's plane. Lodge was in close pursuit of another MIG and directly behind it at a range of 200 feet. This was too close for a missile to be effective because it would not arm in that distance. If Lodge had had a gun he might have shot the MIG down. He realized he had to get some separation to allow his missile to arm. He followed the MIG as it climbed in a gentle two to three "G" turn to the right. Lodge followed him, planning to remain behind on the outside of the turn in order to gain separation as they reached the top of their maneuver.

At the time Markle and Eaves had destroyed their MIG, Captain Steven Ritchie and Captain Charles Debellevue in the number three position had moved to the left and were in good position to converge on the trailing MIG element. The sky was rapidly filling with activity. There were missiles in the air all over the place, fireballs, smoke trails and swirling fighters.

Lieutenant Tom Feezel was on Lodge's wing in good position to protect him but he served only as a pair of eyes because his radar had failed so his radar-guided misiles were useless.

Ritchie and Debellevue spotted the remaining MIGs. Ritchie decided on the one on the left 10,000 feet from the other MIG that was trying to join up.

Oyster Flight was only thirty seconds into its combat sequence. They had made two kills and were now behind the last two MIGs and well in control of the situation. Ritchie placed his sight on the MIG in front of him and switched his fire controls to automatic acquisition after he was sure of a good lockon. He waited a few more seconds to assure that release conditions were good and ripple-fired two missiles. He knew he was in a good position six thousand feet behind and a thousand feet below the MIG fighter and inside of his turn at 18,000 feet. As Ritchie squeezed the trigger the MIG began to tighten his turn. The first missile came off and guided to the target but went under the MIG and did not detonate. The second missile hit the MIG squarely in the center of the fuselage, causing it to explode in a spectacular fireball as the pilot ejected. Ritchie looked to the right at 4 o'clock and noted that Lodge and Locher were trying to drop back into range against another MIG. Markle was with him in good formation position. Suddenly, out of nowhere it seemed, four MIG 19s attacked Lodge and Locher.

"Oyster lead, you have MIGs at your 10 o'clock," Markle warned. He had seen the MIGs as they overshot their MIG 21 and pulled back into formation at the 6 o'clock position.

Lodge now reported MIGs at 10 o'clock and 9 o'clock. He may have thought he could still get another MIG 21, or had not heard the radio calls because he continued to attack the MIG 21 in front.

The MIG 19s opened the first round with their cannon against Lodge's plane. Almost simultaneously Lodge fired a missile at a MIG 21 but he was too close for it to arm.

Markle made a last desperate call. "Hey, hey, break right, break right. They are firing at you." The MIG 19s were so close that they seemed to be firing at Lodge's plane in formation. They continued to fire until Lodge's plane was hit. Locher, the weapons system officer, ejected just before the fighter exploded and carried Lodge to his death.

Markle and Eaves disengaged and went full afterburner away from the scene, picking up a heading of 310 degrees on the deck. The other two planes hit the deck at 650 knots as Feezel and Ritchie spread wide for better mutual support. As they crossed the ridge line west of the Red River at fifty feet Feezel saw a MIG 21 500 feet above him and 100 feet to his rear. It was obvious that the North Vietnamese pilot had not seen them. Feezel used idle power and speed brakes to flush the MIG pilot out in front of him. Unfortunately, his radar was still inoperative and, with no gun, he could not fire at the MIG. He radioed Ritchie who looked to his right and there was a silver MIG sitting on top of him, five thousand feet out. Ritchie decided that ground radar was trying to vector the MIG 21 after them but the pilot still could not see them. Ahead, a huge rain forest tree seemed to rush at him. He put the stick in his lap and climbed out as the tree seemed to fill his windscreen. He just missed it. The MIG pilot now turned to the left, rolled over and looked down, but he still did not see the American fighters. Then, evidently low on fuel, the North Vietnamese pilot turned back to his base. The American planes had a similar problem so they headed for the tanker where they were joined by Markle's plane. They flew the last few miles home as a three-plane formation.

Locher, after he bailed out of Lodge's plane, evaded capture. He was in the jungle for twenty-three days before a combat rescue team reached him.

In addition to the loss of Lodge's plane, one of the strike aircraft was also downed.

Three MIG 21s had been shot down and, in conjunction with their support aircraft, the Yen Vien railroad yards were destroyed including both entrances to the marshalling yards. Other strike planes dropped four spans of the Paul Doumer bridge, knocked out an abutment and severed an adjacent railroad line.

Ritchie became an ace with five kills and his back-seater Debellevue was the first-ever Air Force navigator to become an ace with six kills.

On this same date, Navy Lieutenant Randall H. Cunningham and Lieutenant (jg) Willie Driscoll bagged three MIG 17s near Haiphong to become another ace team.

Captain Messet, who had flown on this mission as a "Wild Weasel" went out again on the afternoon of the following day. Due to an error, chaff was dropped too soon due to a mixup in target times. The MIGs left early, believing that the strikes had been called off, so they encountered no harassment. There were only four aircraft with heavy bombs and they went in with little opposition. It seemed eerie to Messet because they encountered no defenses of any kind. The flight of four did more damage than the entire strike had done the day before. This time another span was dropped in the river and three more were damaged. No additional strikes were needed until September when two more spans were dropped and it was clear that the North Vietnamese had not been able to use the Paul Doumer bridge since May due to the previous damage.

During April, 1972, while the 3rd Division and its attached units were battling the North Vietnamese Army's 304th and 308th Divisions in Quang Tri Province, the 1st South Vietnamese Infantry Division was fighting back attempts by the 324B Division to gain control of the western and southwestern approaches to Hué in Thua Thien Province. Battles seesawed back and forth and continued through May without any solid gains by either side. The North Vietnamese general staff was using this area as a secondary front to contain the 1st Infantry Division and thereby help to support their main effort in Quang Tri Province.

With the fall of Quang Tri City and the province May 1, the communist pressure shifted to Hué. With a full communist attack developing, South Vietnamese Marines fell back to positions south of the My Chanh river with a new defense line to guard Hué's northern approaches. This proved to be the last withdrawal by South Vietnamese troops although during the earlier days of May South Vietnam's position was the bleakest of the war. An Loc, the provincial capital north of Saigon, was under attack and Kontum City was in a precarious position.

From the beginning, enemy pressure in Thua Thien Province had been light. But the fall of Quang Tri was a serious blow because the exodus of panicky city refugees flowing toward Da Nang brought disorder and chaos to Hué where throngs of dispirited troops roamed. They were haggard, unruly and craving for food. They were driven by their basest instincts into mischief and their presence added to the atmosphere of terror and chaos that reigned throughout Hué.

In the midst of confusion and despondency, on May 1, President Thieu replaced General Lam with IV Corps commander, Lieutenant General Ngo Quang Truong, as head of I Corps. Truong had served under Lam, and the disaster in the north was no surprise. He did not consider either Lam or his staff competent to maneuver and support large forces in combat. Once this fact became apparent to Thieu, and Truong's IV Corps area remained static, Thieu made the command change. Truong had expected the promotion and had already mentally selected the staff he would take with him. He flew to Hué and his arrival was greeted with enthusiasm by his countrymen. Earlier he had served as the 1st Infantry's commanding general. Truong was gratified to discover they still trusted him. Truong had long held Thieu's confidence so his selection was a good one. He needed all the reassurance he could get in this bleak hour.

By May 4 Truong had restructured his command, staffing it with senior officers with solid military backgrounds both in field work and in staff work. His staff was a rare assemblage of talents from all three services, and confidence was quickly restored.

A comprehensive plan for Hué's defense was completed the following day. The Marine division was the only capable force north of Hai Van Pass.

It had three brigades, but they had been badly mauled. Truong placed the division under a new commander, Colonel Bui The Lan, and made him responsible for the area north and northwest of Thua Thien Province. He ordered him to block all enemy attacks from penetrating Hué. The 1st Infantry Division under Major General Phu was made responsible for the area south and southwest of Hué, defending its approaches from the A Shau valley. Both commanders were given free reign to initiate limited attacks to destroy enemy concentrations. Truong sought a defense in depth and he created a realistic chain of command with strong reserves for each unit, plus the integration of regular and territorial forces that so far had operated with little coordination.

Truong also initiated a program called Thunder Hurricane to sustain an offensive conducted on a large scale. All kinds of firepower would be focused on each attack wave with sufficient intensity to destroy targets. In particular, the plan called for destruction of enemy mobile targets now streaming towards Hué. He hoped such steps would give his command time to complete the rebuilding of shattered units that had disintegratd during April.

His plans for a defense in depth were in place May 7. With discipline and order restored, the battlefield had been stabilized, although the North Vietnamese Army was building up to an all-out drive with probing tank attacks.

Truong requested the Joint General Staff to give him the airborne forces from II and III Corps. Meanwhile, the Marine Division assumed control of the 1st Ranger Group as it was refitted at Da Nang. Most of the rest of May was used for holding the North Vietnamese away from Hué and refitting, although the 1st Division and the Marine Division caught the communists by surprise, and two fire support bases were recaptured. Under Truong's strong command the morale of the populace and the troops soared to a new peak. His efforts proved worthwhile when on May 21 the communists broke through his northeastern line of defense but were promptly beaten back.

The Marine Division was now ready to make a major assault. In coordination with the 9th United States Marine Amphibious Brigade, naval gunfire, B-52 strikes and South Vietnamese artillery the 147th Marine Brigade conducted an amphibious landing at My Thuy, six miles north of the defense line and made a simultaneous heliborne assault into Co Luy, two miles west of the coastline. Both elements swept through the enemy-held area and returned to the My Chanh Line after several days of successful operations. This was an historic first for the South Vietnamese Marine Division as it planned and executed an assault from the sea.

By the end of May, reinforcements had been brought in and all of Truong's units were refitted and stronger than ever.

General Giai, the 3rd Division's commander, had been placed under arrest May 5 and personally held responsible for the defeat of his division. Thieu even wanted the 3rd removed from the nation's designated divisions, but Truong refused. It was a wise decision because under its new commander, Brigadier General Nguyen Duy Hinh, the division recovered quickly and by year's end was rated by the Joint General Staff as the best of the republic's divisions. Its commander was the only officer promoted to major general during 1972.

South Vietnamese troops needed strong motivation and Truong supplied it, and by the end of June I Corps had regained its former combat strength and was fully prepared to take on the communists. Truong's major problem was to regain the initiative. This was not easy with the heavy losses his organization had earlier sustained and their poor morale before he had taken over. The communists had their own problems. The rapid success they had won in taking over Quang Tri Province had advanced their forces too far ahead of their supply capabilities. They now needed time to resupply them in the forward areas and air strikes against his supply points were hurting.

Captain Steve Bennett and his backseat observer Captain Michael Brown took off from Da Nang June 29 and headed northwest along the coast. The two Marines arrived at Quang Tri and began to circle beneath the low clouds in their OV-10 Bronco. For two hours they adjusted naval artillery fire from ships in the Gulf of Tonkin. Brown's radioed instructions to the heavy cruiser *Newport News* and the destroyer *R. B. Anderson* permitted the ships to pinpoint their fire against enemy positions near Quang Tri. When it was time for them to withdraw, their relief had not arrived so they went back to work. With the approach of darkness, Bennett controlled two flights of A-6 Intruders who were supporting South Vietnamese ground troops. With their maneuvering space limited by the low ceiling, the A-6 pilots would deliver the ordnance where it was needed. Once their mission was accomplished the A-6s departed and Bennett decided to survey the area to see what they had accomplished. A mile to the south he spotted a South Vietnamese platoon with its men pinned at the fork of a creek. Several hundred North Vietnamese troops were advancing along the bank toward them. They were supported by heavy artillery and protected by an anti-aircraft battery and heat-seeking SA-7 missiles. Bennett knew the platoon's situation was critical. With no fighters for protection, Bennett responded. He did not dare call in naval gunfire because of the danger to the South Vietnamese. He had only the Bronco's four machine guns to attack the North Vietnamese. This meant going in at low altitude where enemy anti-aricraft guns would be most effective. He quickly sought permission by radio to attack and it was granted. He made his first attack against heavy fire, but kept going back time after time, leaving many dead and wounded on the ground. His plane was hit several times but he continued his attacks. As he pulled up after his fifth pass a missile struck his plane from behind. The aircraft shuddered as it hit the left engine and exploded. Bennett fought to control his plane as the cockpit was slashed by rocket fragments. He was not hit but Brown suffered minor wounds. His aircraft was crippled, with much of his left engine gone, and its left landing gear hanging limply in the airstream.

When fire broke out he knew he had to jettison his remaining smoke rockets and the external fuel tank before the fire reached them. To do so, he knew, he would endanger the South Vietnamese Marines below. He headed for open water before releasing them.

Brown transmitted a distress signal on the emergency radio channel. "May Day! May Day! This is Wolfman four-five with Covey eight-seven. We are in the vicinity of Triple Nickel [Highway 555] and 602, heading out—feet wet."

Bennett fought to keep the Bronco in the air as the remaining engine tried to force the plane into a bank. He was unable to gain altitude and passed above the beach and the American ships at 600 feet. Over the water he jettisoned the fuel tank and the rockets as they both prepared to eject.

Looking over his shoulder Brown discovered his parachute was gone. Where it had been stowed was a hole about a foot square from the rocket blast, and bits of his parachute were shredded up and down the cargo bay. He yelled to Bennett, "I can't jump."

Miraculously the flames died down and Bennett hoped they might land safely. He turned the plane to the southeast along the coast. The landing strips at Phu Bai and Hué were closest but he knew the battered Bronco would need a foamed runway and the crash equipment at Da Nang. As they passed over Hué, the fire flared again and a pilot in a chase plane confirmed that the OV-10 was close to the explosion point.

Bennett decided to ditch in the water. No OV-10 pilot had ever survived such a ditching because the plane was likely to break up in the cockpit area as it struck the water. Through his mind quickly flashed the admonition, "Punch out or get it on dry land, or whatever you can do, but don't ditch it."

Bennett eased the aircraft into a slow descent toward the water as they completed the pre-ditching checks. They touched down in the water a mile from a sandy beach and the Bronco dug in hard. The landing gear caught in the sea just before the Bronco cartwheeled and flipped over on its back.

In the submerged rear cockpit Brown labored frantically to free himself. He unstrapped and tried to exit through the top of the canopy. When he found his way blocked, he pulled himself through an opening in the side and yanked the toggles to inflate his life preserver. On the surface Brown found only the aircraft's tail section still afloat. He swam around the tail but could not find Bennett. He dove underneath the fuselage, trying to reach the front cockpit. He got only as far as the wing and when he surfaced the second time the plane had gone under. A few minutes later Brown was picked up by a Navy rescue helicopter.

The next day Bennett's body was recovered from his smashed cockpit in the submerged aircraft. He had had no chance to escape. He was awarded a posthumous Medal of Honor.

In the United States, President Nixon's trip to China and Kissinger's trip to Moscow had eased domestic pressures on the administration. But with the new offensive Nixon grew more concerned about the military situation. He had authorized bombing up to the 20th parallel but had denied attacks against Hanoi and Haiphong. He told Kissinger April 30 that he had decided to cancel the summit meeting with the Russians unless they could get a settlement on the war in Southeast Asia.

Kissinger met with Le Duc Tho May 2 and the session was brutal. Quang Tri had fallen the day before, Pleiku was in peril and An Loc was surrounded. It was apparent that Le Duc Tho believed that the Saigon government would soon fall and he stressed that there was no point to the meeting. Again, Le Duc Tho was not interested in negotiations but in laying down terms.

The Chairman of the Joint Chiefs, Admiral Moorer, presented a mining plan and a campaign to bomb strategic targets in North Vietnam at the May 8, 1972, National Security Council meeting. After much argument, Nixon summed up his beliefs. "The real question is whether the Americans give a damn any more. If you follow *Time,* the Washington *Post*, the New York *Times* and the three networks, you could say that the United States had done enough. Let's get out; let's make a deal with the Russians and pull in our horns. The United States would cease to be a military and diplomatic power. If that happened, then the United States would look inward towards itself and would remove itself from the world. Every non-communist nation in the world would live in terror. If the United States is strong enough and willing to use its strength, then the world will remain half-communist rather than becoming entirely communist."

Later that day, despite White House Chief of Staff H. R. Haldeman's concern about the impact on public opinion, and the president's low standing in the polls in this election year, Nixon signed an executive order to mine North Vietnam's harbors and bomb some of its strategic targets. Moorer, Sharp, LeMay and many others had been recommending such a step for years. The Joint Chief's chairman promised President Nixon that the effort would not fail.

These actions had a restraining effect on the offensive, but most importantly they showed that the United States would not permit the capture of South Vietnam. At last a major air offensive was unleashed as most of the original ninety-four-target list was approved. The strategy was to isolate North Vietnam from external support by mining its harbors and destroying its marshalling yards and key choke points along the northeastern and northwestern railroad systems, and to strike major supply areas around Haiphong and Hanoi. But restricted zones were established around and within these two cities as in the 1965–1968 campaign. This time, however, the Joint Chiefs were given greater freedom to attack targets including the frequency and weight of the attacks. Known as Linebacker 1 it was aimed at targets above the 20th parallel to force North Vietnam to realize the futility of trying to conquer South Vietnam by force. It was believed these attacks would restrict the resupply of North Vietnam from external sources, destroy internal stockpiles of military supplies and equipment, and restrict the flow of men and supplies to the southern battlefield. It was hoped that mining and air strikes would break the enemy's will and ability to continue fighting.

Advocates of mine warfare describe it as a less inhumane form of warfare than bombing. This was true in the war against Japan during World War II. Japanese civilian authorities had warned military commanders in the summer of 1945 that if the war continued another year seven million Japanese might be expected to die of starvation because of the mining of the waters around the home islands, and that their agreement to surrender was based, in part, on this fact.

While mine warfare can be correctly labeled a "damn dirty business" as one official of the Naval Air Systems Command has called it, it was effective in World War II. More than a million tons of Japanese shipping was sunk or damaged by mines, while the number of flights necessary to lay the mines around Japan amounted to only six percent of the entire Twentieth Air Force's effort.

During the Korean War, the United States Navy had discovered the effectiveness of defensive mining at Wonson. In addition to losing two minesweepers and more than ninety men, the amphibious landings were delayed a week when intelligence sources learned the waters had been mined. Had it not been for a simultaneous land offensive against Wonson, and minimal resistance by the enemy, there might have been no amphibious landing as a result of the minefield.

Admiral Sharp and others earlier responsible for the prosecution of the war in Southeast Asia had long sought permission to mine Haiphong Harbor and its approaches. With Nixon's approval about forty mines were laid and only one aircraft was lost but the crew was saved. Not one person died as a result of mining operations on either side. After the mines were laid ship movement in and out of the harbor effectively ceased.

Actually, you don't really have to lay mines. If you just say you did, the initial effect can be the same. Fear will accomplish your mission for quite a number of weeks.

Kissinger personally appealed again to the Soviet Union to use its influence to end the war. In a letter to Ambassador Dobrynin from President Nixon the tone was firm but conciliatory. It pointed out that North Vietnam has refused to halt its offensive and renew negotiations. It spelled out Nixon's willingness to proceed with the summit conference, saying it would be Brezhnev's responsibility if he chose to cancel it.

Nixon now demanded of the Defense Department prompt air action against the North Vietnamese. When he received Admiral Moorer's first proposals for bombing attacks against North Vietnam during the first week of May, he was furious because he considered them a timid replay of President Johnson's bombing campaign from 1965 through 1968.

He wrote Kissinger at the State Department, "I cannot emphasize too strongly that I have determined that we should go for broke." He said the United States again was in danger of doing too little too late, and that it was better to err on the side of doing too much while the administration had maximum public support. "This was certainly the weakness of the Johnson administration. To an extent it may have been our weakness where we have warned the enemy time and time again and then have acted in a rather mild way when the enemy has tested us. He has now gone over the brink and so have we. We have the power to destroy his war-making capacity. The only question is whether we have the will to use that power."

Nixon told Moorer that he wanted strong actions, and he made it clear that he was prepared to risk the consequences. The president removed most of the bombing restrictions except for some sensitive targets in Hanoi and Haiphong although specific targets in these areas were approved. In effect, the president removed himself from personal control over selection of the most vital targets to be attacked. Despite his direct orders, Moorer and some members of the Pentagon were more concerned about the political fall-out of such attacks than in dealing the North

Vietnamese a crushing aerial attack. President Nixon was wholly responsible, and willing to accept the consequences, so the civilian repercussions had nothing to do with the military establishment. Moorer's sole concern should have been the success of the aerial attacks. This was yet another instance of Pentagon officialdom talking tough, but performing in an unprofessional and desultory fashion.

President Nixon spoke to the nation the night of May 8, 1972, after signing the executive order to start a strategic air offensive against North Vietnam, and to mine its harbors. He stressed that he would not accept North Vietnam's terms but that a negotiated outcome was still his preference. He said the North Vietnamese had arrogantly refused his latest offer. He repeated the terms acceptable to him: a standstill ceasefire, release of prisoners and total withdrawal within four months.

In a letter to Chou En-lai, Nixon expressed hope that this new crisis would not interfere with the progress made in United States-Chinese relations.

Resumption of bombing of the North, and the mining of Haiphong harbor, caused an uproar in the nation's press and television. The New York *Times* denounced what it called "Nixon's desperate gamble." Some newspapers even praised the Russians for their restraint.

Responses by the Russians and the Chinese were low key, and for the Russians it was business as usual.

In South Vietnam the communist offensive stalled and an attack against Hué never materialized. Kontum withstood communist assaults, and so did besieged An Loc. Now the South Vietnamese developed a counter-offensive to relive An Loc, but it developed slowly.

Nixon fully expected the summit conference would be cancelled, but it was not, and he left for Moscow May 20. Although no agreement was reached about the war in Southeast Asia, an agreement was reached to freeze the deployment of the anti-ballistic missle and to freeze Soviet deployment of offensive weapons in which they had an advantage. The Russians agreed to give up 240 older weapons of large "throw" weight and to stop modernization of its G-class of submarines. The United States had no programs that could be deployed during the period of this offensive freeze so the agreement basically did not effect the United States at all. This SALT agreement was needed to permit the United States to catch up on offensive weapons.

Five men broke into the Democratic National Committee's headquarters to wiretap it June 17, 1972, at the fashionable hotel, office and apartment complex known as Watergate. At the time, the arrest of the men received little attention, but once it was determined that the authorization for the break-in led to the inner circle at the White House, it assumed enormous proportions. Those arrested included a former employee of the Central Intelligence Agency, James McChord, and four Cubans from Miami. Although Nixon denied any White House involvement, McChord was an employee of the Committee to Re-elect the President. In the possession of one of the men caught in the raid was an address book with the name Howard Hunt. Hunt was a consultant to Charles Colson, a member of Nixon's inner circle of aides and advisers. The Democratic National Committee promptly filed a million dollar suit for this invasion of their privacy and violation of their civil rights.

General Truong's plan to retake Quang Tri Province did not call for a blitzkrieg, but for a coordinated campaign to consolidate the defenses of Hué with successive offensive operations from forward positions. First, enemy forces had to be destroyed, Quang Tri-City re-occupied and the provincial government restored.

Truong submitted his plan simultaneously to President Thieu and to the Military Assistance Command. The latter suggested that he continue limited spoiling attacks and consider a counteroffensive later. He was disturbed because his troops were ready to go. He decided to present his plan to President Thieu personally. He flew to Saigon and met with the president, his security adviser General Quang and General Vien. Thieu listened carefully. With a purple grease pencil Thieu drew an arrow on his map, suggesting a spoiling attack in that direction. The others agreed. Truong was so discouraged that he folded up his map and returned to Hué.

Truong worried all night about rejection of his plan to take the offensive. Early the next morning he called General Quang and told him he would present no more plans in Saigon. He said if they wanted him to do anything they should give him whatever plan they wanted to execute and he would comply.

President Thieu called at 9:00 A.M. and said he would like him to return to Saigon and show the plan to him again. The next day, after he presented his plan, the president approved it.

Truong's forces attacked June 28. Airborne and Marine spearheads made good progress but slower than he had expected. Enemy resistance was moderate the first few days except for regimental size clashes when forces crossed the enemy's first line of defense north of the My Chanh River. As the communists fell back, and South Vietnamese forces advanced to the Thach Han River, resistance intensified.

The first airborne elements reached the outskirts of Quang Tri City July 7 and clashed violently with its communist defenders. To relieve the pressure on the paratroopers, and to cut enemy lines of communication with the city, the Marine Division was orderd to helilift a battalion a mile northeast of the city. However, they were unable to make progress and were stopped by the enemy's infantry and armor.

It was evident to Truong that the communists would hold to the last man. Reports to his headquarters indicated ferocious resistance. This was not a primary objective but it became a symbol and a major challenge for the South Vietnamese troops. Meanwhile, the North Vietnamese continued to reinforce their troops, and were determined to go all out for the defense of Quang Tri City. The South Vietnamese drive was stalled, and in a difficult position, but Truong refused to withdraw from Quang Tri because this would be an admittance of total defeat. He switched zones to continue the pressure and assigned the primary effort to the Marine Division. This was a modification of his plan and the Marines were assigned to destroy the communists in the city. They would establish a firm defense line and launch limited attacks against enemy forces up to the Cua Viet River. Meanwhile, the Airborne Division would secure the Thach Han Line and support the Marines. In this manner Truong hoped to destroy the North Vietnamese 304th Division, re-occupy two important fire support bases, and cut enemy supply lines from the west and thus protect Route 1—I Corps' main supply line.

The North Vietnamese fought desperately to hold their gains. In Quang Tri and Thua Thien Provinces the North Vietnamese had six infantry divisions. The 312th had been moved from Laos and introduced into Quang Tri with troop reinforcements from other divisions. Truong knew that a showdown was near.

CHAPTER 34

The Siege of An Loc

DESPITE HEAVY ARTILLERY ATTACKS TRUONG KEPT UP THE OFFENSIVE IN I Corps. He rotated his frontline units, giving them a chance to rest. Constantly on his mind was whether the need justified reinforcement of his region, possibly with an infantry division from IV Corps. He rejected this consideration as neither feasible nor necessary, knowing that the military situation throughout South Vietnam was critical. He knew that redeployment of a major unit from another region would seriously weaken that region.

Truong was convinced that time was on his side. He had firmly established a command and control system; he had a dedicated staff and adequate support. He believed that a drawn-out contest might even be advantageous to South Vietnam if they were successful in retaking Quang Tri. Those six divisions in front of his forces might prevent them from moving against Hué. Truong knew that any diversion of these communist divisions to the western approaches to Hué had to be avoided because his defenses in that rough terrain were more vulnerable. With the communists concentrated at Quang Tri, enemy divisions presented lucrative targets for his combined ground and air forces.

When the offensive campaign entered its tenth week in early September, 1972 without a decisive outcome in sight, Truong decided that enemy troop strength had been sufficiently reduced that a major effort stood a good chance of success. He knew that victory here would not only reinforce South Vietnam's military posture—the North Vietnamese had been defeated by now at An Loc and Kontum—it could also bring about excellent returns in a political sense.

Truong launched three separate operations September 8 to retake Quang Tri City. The Airborne Division reoccupied three key military installations formerly under South Vietnamese control at La Vang, south of Quang Tri City's Old Citadel. Paratroopers now had excellent protection for their Marine Division's flank. The next day the Marines initiated an attack against the citadel. Meanwhile, United States and South Vietnamese forces conducted an incompleted amphibious assault north of the Cua Viet River as a diversion. At first, North Vietnamese resistance slowed the Marine Division's progress, but elements of the 6th Marine Battalion penetrated one side of the citadel's walls September 14. The following day more Marines were thrown into the breach and other Marine spearheads repeatedly assaulted the eastern and southern sides of the citadel. It fell the next night and the following morning the South Vietnamese flag was raised amidst cheers of the troops. This was a day of exaltation for the South Vietnamese people. By late afternoon of the next day the Marines eliminated the last North Vietnamese remnants within the citadel and expanded their control over the entire city that was now reduced to rubble. In the previous ten days, 2,767 North Vietnamese troops had been killed and 63 captured. South Vietnam's Marine division lost about fifteen hundred.

Communist activity in I Corps dropped off markedly and this situation continued until September 30 when the Airborne Division launched attacks to reoccupy fire support bases where fierce resistance was encountered by enemy artillery despite drenching monsoon rains. As October ended the Airborne Division finally reoccupied fire support base Barbara and then shifted its main effort toward the north.

In Thua Thien Province the 1st Infantry Division had earlier sustained the initiative while activity increased against Quang Tri. In addition to its defense of Hué, the division conducted offensive operations to extend its control to the west and southwest. By the end of June enemy attacks turned heavy.

In July, one fire support base was taken and retaken several times in Thua Thien Province. After five months of fighting, the 1st Infantry Division began to show signs of weariness, although it still held its defense line. Truong sent the 51st Regiment to reinforce it and to give some of the battle weary troops a respite from combat. With the aid of B-52 bombers and United States and South Vietnamese tactical aircraft the division retook two important fire support bases. Enemy troops gradually lost the initiative and the 1st Division launched attacks to enlarge its control toward the west. Once the important fire support bases were retaken the North Vietnamese 342B Division lost its aggressive spirit and avoided action. In October, uninterrupted monsoon rains forced the 1st Division to revert to the defense and activities declined to the lowest level in months.

From the time Truong's I Corps troops took the offensive in Quang Tri

Province to the end of July the three provinces south of the Hai Van Pass were able to maintain reasonable control despite their low strength. Although sparsely used, B-52 strikes continued. As South Vietnamese troops in the northern region approached Quang Tri City the communists suddenly chose to initiate several heavy attacks, especially in the area of the Que Son valley, against the 2nd Infantry Division. These attacks by the communists were intended to alleviate the pressure on Quang Tri. The Da Nang air base was heavily rocketed and some outlying bases were overrun by the communists.

The 2nd Infantry Division, under Brigadier General Tran Van Nhut, was directed to concentrate its efforts on the southernmost province, Quang Ngai, where the threat posed by the North Vietnamese was increasing. The 3rd Infantry Division was assigned to relieve the pressure caused by the North Vietnamese 711th Division in the Que Son valley. Both divisions performed well and toward the end of October the situation in I Corps was completely stabilized. As the prospect of a negotiated ceasefire increased the people of Quang Tri, Thua Thien and the city of Hué in particular rejoiced at the prospect of peace. They had already paid a heavy price for freedom. Through the heroic exploits and the sacrifices of the Marine Division, the Airborne Division and the 1st Division they had stemmed the communist tide when at first all seemed lost.

Adjoining the southern boundary of I Corps was the vast territory of II Corps, an area of sprawling high plateaus, rolling hills and dense jungles commonly called the Central Highlands that sloped toward a long, narrow and curving strip of coastal land to the east. II Corps contained almost half of South Vietnam's total land area but was the least populated with approximately three million people, one-fifth of whom were Montagnards.

Along the narrow coast land, where most people lived, ran Route 1 that connected the coastal cities. From the coast, two major highways extended toward the Highlands in the west: Routes 19 and 21. Route 19 connected the port city of Qui Nhon with Pleiku and Kontum on the Kontum Plateau. Farther south, Route 21 connected Nha Trang with Ban Me Thuot, the only city on the Darlac Plateau. Both highways were important supply arteries for this region. Running the entire length of the Highlands from north to south was Route 14 that originated near Hoi An in I Corps and connected Kontum with Pleiku and Ban Me Thuot. The communists frequently cut these routes and road communications between Pleiku and Ban Me Thuot was not always possible. South of the Darlac Plateau lay the Di Linh Plateau with its famous resort city of Da Lat that was connected with Bien Hoa and Saigon in III Corps by Route 20. This was a heavily populated Montagnard area and South Vietnamese lowlanders normally avoided it.

II Corps' weather was under the influence of opposing monsoon cycles, affecting operations by both sides.

In early 1972, all United States troops had left the Central Highlands although support troops remained at Qui Nhon and Cam Ranh on the coast. Two South Korean Divisions were still in II Corps—one in the An Khe-Qui Nhon area and the other in the Tuy Hoa-Ninh Hoa region, but they were preparing to return to their homeland. Republic of Vietnam troops were in charge, but they still had their American advisers. There were two South Vietnamese infantry divisions and a mobile Ranger group to defend II Corps. Along the Corps' western flank, there were eleven border Ranger battalions. All organizations were under Lieutenant General Ngo Dzu at Pleiku.

Intelligence officers had warned in the fall of 1971 that there was a possibility of a major communist offensive in the Central Highlands during the approaching dry season of 1972. They said it would be aimed at Pleiku and Kontum to cut South Vietnam in half roughly along Route 19. Dzu became increasingly concerned by reports of the buildup and the presence of tanks and artillery. He consulted with his senior adviser John Paul Vann and they agreed his forces should counter the invasion but not attack them. At the time, the North Vietnamese were striking Quang Tri, Hué and An Loc. Vann was a legendary individual who had spent nearly ten years in South Vietnam starting in 1962 as an Army lieutenant colonel. He had been critical of the tactics used, so he had resigned his commission and returned to Vietnam as a civilian adviser.

By the second week of April, 1972, the Tan Canh-Dakto area was virtually surrounded. Massive communist assaults soon led to the fall of some fire support bases. And the 22nd Division's defense in Tan Canh became precarious once its northern and eastern flanks were exposed.

A strong enemy force, with elements of the North Vietnamese 2nd Division and other units struck April 23 towards Tan Canh. Here the North Vietnamese made their first extensive use of the wire-guided AT-3 Sagger missile that disabled a number of South Vietnamese tanks and destroyed bunkers with deadly accuracy. The division's tactical operations center took a direct hit and it had to be partially evacuated. Enemy tanks pressed forward and troops of the 42nd Regiment were deeply shocked by their appearance at the gate of their compound. They fought in utter disorder and then broke and fled their defense perimeter. The division's American advisory team fought its way through enemy fire and were extracted by helicopters with Mr. Vann aboard. Colonel Le Duc Dat offered to resign when General Dzu refused to reinforce him with his 22nd Division's two remaining regiments, believing he was being given inadequate support. By then the Tan Canh compound's was without defending troops but Division Commander Dat, his staff and his deputy Colonel Ton That Hung remained behind to destroy the radio sets and the signal information. Dat and his staff slipped out of Tanh Can later in the rain but, with the exception of his deputy, they were never seen again.

As North Vietnamese attacks increased, South Vietnamese troops just faded away and the Tan Canh-Dakto area fell to the enemy. As the battered South Vietnamese troops moved south, they were joined by the local population while United States tactical aircraft tried to destroy the positions and equipment the South Vietnamese had left behind in the haste of their departure.

While the North Vietnamese gained ground in the Central Highlands and prepared to push toward Kontum, the North Vietnamese 3rd Division cut Route 1 at Bong Son Pass and attacked three isolated northern districts. This forced the 40th and 41st Regiments of the South Vietnamese 22nd Division to abandon their two major bases and other strong points. The North Vietnamese now spread northward along Route 1 and southwestward along the Kim Son River and engulfed district towns. With the communist's momentum unchecked, all defenses in the area rapidly crumbled.

With the loss of Binh Dinh Province's three northern districts, South Vietnam's coastal lowland was practically cut in two. If North Vietnam's army succeeded in taking Kontum City, South Vietnam's defense posture would be worsened. All attention now was focused on the Central Highlands where Kontum City braced itself for a big enemy drive.

Many officials, including General Dzu, thought Kontum could not hold despite strong United States tactical air support and raids by B-52s. Dzu's command was demoralized by the loss of the Tan Chanh-Dakto area, and he was remorseful about his refusal to reinforce Colonel Dat. Dzu feared that his own headquarters at Pleiku would also fall to North Vietnamese artillery attacks and feared for himself after what had happened to Colonel Dat. He kept calling President Thieu night and day begging for instructions on the most trivial matters. Thieu and his Joint General Staff quickly realized that Dzu was no longer functioning as a field commander. He was replaced May 10 by Major General Nguyen Van Toan, the armor commander, who also served as assistant commander for operations at I Corps' headquarters.

Days after the 22nd Division's debacle at Tan Canh the communists gradually moved their forces to the southeast toward Kontum City, and it was quickly surrounded. This loss was expected and due to the constant demands in other areas this region was difficult to reinforce. The 23rd Division's headquarters was moved April 28 from Kontum City to Ban Me Thuot—a distance of ninety-nine miles—to command all South Vietnamese troops in the area and to provide some badly needed reorganization. Now Colonel Ly Tong Ba, the commander of the 23rd Division, became Kontum's defender. Although the table of organization called for a major general in such a position, the practice of assigning colonels, brigadier generals and lieutenant generals was widespread, causing serious command problems. Promising colonels should have been given the chance to prove themselves, especially if they had political support. Ba's predicament was not unlike Giai's in I Corps who was in charge of the 3rd Division. Failure to promote to the rank authorized caused a commander to lose full control of his division because some subordinates outranked him or had an established reputation that commanded respect and submission.

The 2nd Airborne Brigade, holding Vo Dinh since the loss of the Tan Canh-Dakto area, was ordered back to Saigon leaving the 6th Ranger Group alone in the combat zone with battalions deployed on a high escarpment straddling Route 14 just south of Vo Dinh. Ranger battalions at Vo Dinh May 1 came under attack and were ordered to withdraw by the group's commander. This moved the defense line back to Ngo Trang, eight miles northwest of Kontum City. This setback exposed the weakness of the command structure. If Kontum held, Colonel Ba's control had to be strengthened. John Paul Vann, the American adviser, suggested to General Toan that he bring in the remaining units of the 23rd Division—the 44th and 45th Regiments—to replace the 2nd and 6th Ranger Groups. This move not only enhanced Ba's command but improved the city's overall defenses. Remnant forces of the 22nd Division were sent back to rear bases in Binh Dinh Province for regrouping.

North Vietnamese attacks increased but the forward troops held their lines, with good support from American tactical airpower. North Vietnam paid a high price in loss of troops by B-52 raids in trying to capture the border camp of Polei Kleng as its defenders fought for three days before retreating May 9 in the face of massive tank-infantry assaults.

The 45th Regiment was assigned to delay the North Vietnamese on Route 14 north of Kontum but due to mounting pressure they had gradually to withdraw toward the city. Intelligence reports now confirmed that the North Vietnamese 320th Division was moving into an area north of the city in preparation for an all-out attack. Here they were so vulnerable to United States air strikes that they would soon either have to attack or withdraw.

Defense arrangements for Kontum were completed by the end of the second week in May after the 23rd Division deployed its units in and around the city. Infantry and armored units blocked the approaches from the north while territorial troops secured the southeast and southern approaches facing the Dak Bla River.

The North Vietnamese attacked on the morning of May 14. They moved down Route 14 toward Kontum with no artillery to support their infantry units. United States helicopter gunships, some armed with the new TOW missile, guided to its target by signals transmitted through a wire, played havoc against the lead communist tanks and the five enemy regiments that followed them. That night a gap between two of the South Vietnamese regiments was exploited and disaster appeared imminent. Colonel Ba called for B-52 strikes and artillery support and ordered his men to pull back slightly for safety. Bombs fell like thunderbolts on the massed communist troops and explosions rocked the small city while the heavy blasts seemed to cave in the rib cages of the city's defenders. There was an awesome silence after the heavy bombers departed. At dawn, hundreds of North Vietnamese troops and their weapons lay scattered over the ground as the remaining communist soldiers retreated in great haste. Kontum was saved. The troops regained their confidence but they knew that without the B-52 strike they would have been in jeopardy.

Colonel Ba realized his units were spread too thin so he tightened the city's defense perimeter.

General Toan and Mr. Vann visited Kontum May 16 and approved of the disposition of his troops. There was no doubt in their minds that the communists would try again as their patrols continued to probe their defense lines. There was an added problem. Air supply was perilous and flights were always difficult and frequently interrupted.

Sapper squads continued to probe Kontum's defenses, seeking to find a weak spot. Some communist reconnaissance elements posed as civilians or South Vietnamese troops. Colonel Ba warned his staff that the communists next time would attempt to take over the city from inside and out. By the end of the week following the first attacks all communist efforts had proved fruitless. Colonel Ba was especially skillful in maneuvering his tanks, which was his specialty. As a result all communist probes were beaten back and the airfield returned to normal operations.

Ba launched a limited offensive against the communists with the assistance of airpower to the north and northwest of the city but always within range of his own artillery. His troops everywhere encountered the evidence of the terrible destruction caused by the B-52s against massed enemy units.

From Pleiku, General Toan launched a major effort May 21 to clear Route 14 north of Kontum, but failed despite B-52 strikes and the use of cluster bombs. It was obvious, however, that the enemy's timetable to take

Kontum had been upset. For the time being II Corps' defenders had maintained the initiative and the morale of its frontline troops remained high.

The North Vietnamese struck again May 25. Communist commanders knew they had to achieve a quick victory or withdraw altogether because the monsoon season was starting with its drenching rains. The attack began with artillery and some infiltration by enemy infantry and tanks. Their artillery fire was devastating and an emergency was called to divert all tactical aircraft and gunships to the area for that day. Despite a vigorous defense, however, it proved impossible to drive the North Vietnamese out of infiltrated areas the next day. Supplies again became critical as transports shuttled in and out.

At nightfall, the North Vietnamese 64th Regiment penetrated between the 53rd and 45th Regiments but B-52s, diverted from other scheduled missions, blunted the major attack against the 45th Regiment with their bombs.

Fierce fighting continued May 27. By late morning the communist advance was halted although North Vietnamese Army infantry units still held the northernmost compound while they harassed the airfield.

To prevent further penetrations, and to consolidate his defenses, Colonel Ba, with the approval of II Corps' headquarters, decided to tighten the defense perimeter again. The move permitted better use of B-52 strikes in close support.

The situation reached the critical stage on the night of the 28th. North Vietnamese forces were still entrenched in the hospital's northern compound and territorial forces engaged in house-to-house fighting in the southern part of the city where the communists still held the schoolhouse and a few homes near the airfield. Now the communists had their own resupply problems. Hourly B-52 strikes had forced them to store supplies at great distance and their lines of communication were disrupted by continuous air strikes.

These air strikes and attacks by helicopter gunships finally permitted the South Vietnamese to counterattack and regain the initiative. They fought from bunker to bunker, using hand grenades. Before noon May 30, the South Vietnamese regained control of the entire hospital complex. Although there were still scattered pockets of resistance in the northeast area, the city was out of danger.

Despite sporadic rocket and mortar fire President Thieu flew to the city. He praised their endurance and fighting spirit and pinned the single star of a brigadier general on Kontum's defender—Ly Tong Ba—"for special frontline merits."

On this day all communist positions were retaken. At midday May 11 the battle for the city was almost over as the communist's main forces withdrew. Thousands of bodies lay scattered over the battlefield with dozens of T-54 tanks, some intact, but most reduced to charred hulks awkwardly perched among the ruins. This was utter defeat for the North Vietnamese Army.

The last vestige of the enemy's resistance was gone June 10. The man who contributed so much to South Vietnam's defense, Mr. John Vann, did not survive to savor the fruits of his labor. A strikingly strong, although controversial personality, Vann was the personification of courage, self-lessness and dedication. At Tan Canh he had personally directed, at extreme risk to his own life, the extraction of the 22nd Division's advisory team. Although his helicopter had crashed at Dakto he had continued his rescue mission. During the battles for Kontum he saved the beleagured city at least twice by making bold decisions on the use of B-52s. He had often goaded South Vietnamese commanders into action. He shuttled, almost daily day and night, in and out of the area with complete disregard for his own safety. One night he was killed in a helicopter crash. He was replaced by Brigadier General Michael D. Healey.

The North Vietnamese 320th Division withdrew towards Tan Canh-Dakto while the 2nd Division returned to its former jungle redoubt in Quang Ngai Province as combat operations in the Kontum area dropped to a low level.

General Toan ordered Ba's command to reclaim territory north and northwest of the city. In particular, efforts were made to clear Route 14 between Pleiku and Kontum. By the end of June, the Chu Pao Pass was cleared and the highway opened to commercial traffic early the next month. Route 14 remained insecure, however, due to frequent communist attacks.

In the coastal lowlands of Binh Dinh Province the 22nd South Viet-namese Division regained its combat effectiveness and in late July with territorial forces the division under Brigadier General Phan Dinh Niem retook two district towns and reestablished communications on Route 1 to the southern boundary of Quang Ngai Province. Little notice was taken of this action at the time but in terms of psychological, political and military impact it equalled other successes such as the reoccupation of Quang Tri and the defense of Kontum.

When the North Vietnamese had crossed the demilitarized zone and invaded Quang Tri Province March 30 the Joint General Staff had ex-pressed serious doubts about the enemy's true objective. It appeared that Hué was the immediate target. It had always been a prime objective because of its historic stature. But the buildup around Kontum had presaged something even more serious. There had been a long-held theory that the communists might attempt an attack across the Central High-lands to the sea to split South Vietnam. Such a possibility remained in the minds of many Vietnamese and American strategists. If so, the Kontum Plateau could become another target of great strategic significance.

During attacks in these areas little attention was devoted to III Corps although there was always the possibility of a communist offensive against Tay Ninh Province and Saigon. North Vietnam's disposition of its troops and its easy access to and from sanctuaries in Laos and Cambodia made the problem of diagnosing North Vietnam's main effort all the more difficult. They had the advantage because the initial success of any thrust could quickly be reinforced and turned into the main effort. If not, it would serve a tactical purpose by supporting other attacks. The communists had the flexibility April 2 to strike where and when they wanted, and the southern arm of their army struck Loc Ninh. Was the ultimate objective Saigon by way of Route 13? South Vietnam's army generals and their American advisers were not sure. Saigon was densely populated with sprawling suburbs with several avenues of approach. Any route could support a main attack, but the northwestern and southwestern approaches were the most important. From the northwest, an attack could originate in the Iron Triangle from its bases there. The approach could follow the Saigon River south where it could be joined by another drive either along Route 1 from Ninh, or along Route 13 from Binh Long. From the southwest, an attack could originate in the Parrot's Beak or the Mo Vat and Ba Thu areas in Cambodia, then cross into Hau Nghia Province to enter Cholon. This was the shortest route of the two possible attack corridors.

Eleven provinces surrounded Saigon, including Bien Hoa. This was the most important because it was an industrial area and the site of III Corps' headquarters. It also contained a large Air Force base and the headquarters of the United States Army. They were both located in the Long Binh Base complex. The second most important province was Tay Ninh—the holy land of the influential Bao Dai sect—whose northwestern corner was a well-known enemy base—and the haven for communist military and political leaders.

III Corps had three infantry divisions, and three Ranger groups in the field, to protect it.

During late 1971, and prior to the 1972 Easter offensive, the Corps' military situation was good. North Vietnam's main divisions had been driven into Cambodia. And South Vietnamese commanders had authority to conduct operations deep into Cambodia as long as they could be coordinated with their counterparts in the Cambodian army.

During 1972's first quarter, three communist divisions were refitting, but in late March captured documents revealed that the 9th Vietcong Division was planning to return to South Vietnam. Its men had been trained in suburban warfare. Their target was Binh Long and not Tay Ninh as predicted by South Vietnamese army intelligence officers. The documents made it clear that the 9th would coordinate its operations with the 7th Division.

Despite this information III Corps' headquarters did not focus adequate attention on Binh Long, partly because the communists had not shown much interest there, although there had been major battles in 1966 and 1967. However, III Corps did take action to reinforce its defenses in this area.

The communists attacked a fire support base April 2, 1972, near the Cambodian border and twenty-eight miles northwest of Tay Ninh City. This base was defended by a battalion of the 25th Division. North Vietnamese tanks contributed to the rapid collapse of the base's defense that was overrun by midday. III Corps' headquarters ordered the evacuation of all advance outposts along the border on the theory that it was better to consolidate defenses further inland. Therefore, a defense belt was built around Tay Ninh City. Heavy losses were sustained during the pullback and the defenders of a fire support base were ambushed and suffered a heavy loss in vehicles and weapons. When reinforcements from the 25th Division arrived the following day they were surprised to find all abandoned vehicles and artillery pieces still there, untouched by the communists. The attacking force had moved away instead of pressing toward Tay Ninh City. The riddle was solved later when a prisoner revealed that the attack on the base had only been a diversion to distract III Corps officials from the main North Vietnamese Army attempt against Loc Ninh as the first objective in Binh Long Province. Although it was not understood at the time, North Vietnam committed three divisions and two separate regiments, all with armor reinforcements, to the Binh Long campaign.

At the request of a battalion commander, who believed his unit would become easy prey to an enemy ambush if it withdrew from Tong Le Chan Base along the border, III Corps' headquarters consented to his remaining. The base was repeatedly besieged, but remained under control until April, 1975, before it was finally evacuated. This was another eloquent testimony to South Vietnamese heroism, and a reminder of what might have been accomplished if all bases had held instead of being evacuated.

The first phase of the communist attack was a diversion in Tay Ninh employing the 24th and 271st North Vietnamese regiments. The second phase was the attack on Loc Ninh by the 5th North Vietnamese Division. The 9th Division was now ordered to attack and seize An Loc, which would be turned into the capital for the Provisional Revolutionary Government in South Vietnam. The 7th Division would block south of An Loc and prevent South Vietnamese reinforcements from reaching the city. After seizing Loc Ninh, the 5th Division would march to Tay Ninh, isolate the city, and destroy the forces of the South Vietnamese 25th Division defending it.

The Loc Ninh attack began April 4, 1972, with an ambush on Route 13, three miles north of the town. South Vietnamese soldiers were ordered to fall back from the border to reinforce the defenses of the town after the armored cavalry squadron attached to the 9th Regiment of the 5th Division was ambushed by an infantry regiment of the North Vietnamese 5th Division. There were few survivors.

Communist armored units were on the move early next morning. A few hours later the communists began to shell heavily before they attacked Loc Ninh. Defenders resisted fiercely with effective American tactical air support. North Vietnam's attempt to capture the airstrip was defeated by cluster bombs. It was overrun the next day, however, by communist tanks. Survivors made it to An Loc as Loc Ninh was overrun despite attempts to reinforce the town's defenses.

Only after the North Vietnamese attack against Loc Ninh was initiated was III Corps' commander, Lieutenant General Nguyen Van Minh, convinced that An Loc City was the primary objective. He knew that if An Loc was overrun that Saigon would be endangered because only two major obstacles would remain on Route 13 north of Chon Thanh and Lai Khe. He ordered the immediate reinforcement of An Loc and specified that it be held at all costs. Two battalions were airlifted to An Loc but now there were no more reserves in South Vietnam.

At a Saigon meeting April 6 at Independence Palace to review the military situation throughout South Vietnam, General Minh pleaded for more troops for An Loc. He was overruled because of heavy attacks in I Corps and the enemy's buildup in II Corps. Most reserves were committed to these regions. The only possibility was to take the remaining airborne brigade and an infantry division from IV Corps.

At a meeting with all corps commanders, Lieutenant General Dang Van Quang, Thieu's assistant for security, and General Vien, President Thieu discussed the requirements for each corps. When it was suggested that the 21st Division be deployed to reinforce I Corps, Quang argued that the situation at An Loc was potentially even more serious than the problems in the north. He said that if the North Vietnamese succeeded in establishing a Provisional Revolutionary Government capital at An Loc the psychological and political damage would be intolerable. Thieu agreed and suggested that the 21st Division, once commanded by General

Minh—III Corps' commander—be used at An Loc where it was hoped that its former commander would get the most out of the division's men. All agreed.

The 1st Airborne Brigade was ordered April 7 to move by road from Lai Khe to Con Thanh. From there it was ordered to conduct operations northward to clear Route 13 to An Loc and to keep this vital supply line open. Upon reaching a point only three-and-a-half miles north of Con Thanh—still nine miles short of An Loc—the brigade's advance was stopped by a regiment of the 7th North Vietnamese Division entrenched in the Tau O area. The North Vietnamese command was determined to dominate the road and to stop every attempt to reinforce or supply An Loc.

After taking Loc Ninh the North Vietnamese 5th Division moved south towards An Loc. The airstrip was first to be occupied April 7. Now An Loc was isolated because air and ground communications with the city were cut off, and the high ground around the city was occupied by North Vietnamese artillery. No attack materialized for several days because the communists were not ready logistically to start their all-out attack. They needed a week to destroy all border outposts. Although An Loc was encircled, it was still supplied by air, and the 21st Division's 8th Regiment was moved in by air to strengthen its defenses. Inside the city An Loc's 4,000 defenders, including Regional and Popular Forces, waited for the attack. The city was tense as refugees poured in from the surrounding countryside.

The North Vietnamese Army started shelling it April 3 and moved up its tanks. The first major attack came from the west, although the main effort appeared to be developing from the north spearheaded by armored units. The M-72 LAW rocket was used effectively and a Regional Force soldier was the first to destroy a tank. The word spread quickly. Their long-established fear of tanks was dispelled in minutes. Despite their newfound optimism communist tanks breached the city's defenses but incredibly there was no accompanying communist infantry. This was disastrous for the communist tanks, and they were quickly destroyed.

Two regiments of the communist 9th Division attacked in force but met strong resistance and allied airpower, including B-52 strikes, that caused 400 casualties. Despite their losses the communists continued to press forward with their tanks but South Vietnamese troop morale remained high. They had developed a hold-or-die attitude.

After the 1st Airborne Brigade was withdrawn from the Tau O area it had been refitted and helilifted April 13 and 14 to join An Loc's defenders. Now there was word that the 21st Infantry Division from the Mekong Delta had reached Tao O on its way north to relieve An Loc. Bolstered by this news the South Vietnamese fought back and nine of eleven tanks were destroyed.

The battle for An Loc abated April 16. After three days of combat the North Vietnamese had lost twenty-three tanks but the northern half of the city was in communist hands and opposing troops were facing one another separated only by the main downtown boulevard. The ring tightened around An Loc although the first enemy effort to overwhelm the defenders had failed. Communist headquarters decided to support their next major attack with a secondary attack against the 1st Airborne Brigade southeast of the city, while the main attack was made by the 9th Division. To protect the communist troops from air attacks, anti-aircraft guns ringed the city.

South Vietnamese officers learned details of the upcoming attack from a handwritten report taken from a dead enemy soldier that had been written by the 9th Division's political commissar. It said their first defeat was due to the intervention of allied tactical aircraft and B-52 bombers that had proved devastating and most effective. Second, the commissar said coordination was ineffective between their armored units and the infantry. The missive included details of the next attack scheduled for April 19. The communists believed that An Loc could be seized in a matter of hours. They were so confident April 18 that Hanoi Radio broadcast that An Loc had been liberated and the Provisional Revolutionary Government would be inaugurated in the city two days later.

The attack began on schedule and initially it was successful as the South Vietnamese brigade headquarters was overrun and had to fall back on the city. But the North Vietnamese 9th Division failed again to make any headway as it attempted to move to Route 13 and attack An Loc from the south. The communists were blocked by two battalions of the 1st Airborne Brigade who were firmly entrenched. Their drive came to a halt April 23.

The northern half of An Loc still remained in communist hands. The city's hospital was destroyed and medical evacuation was impossible. The streets were littered with bodies, most unattended for several days. People were hungry and some were starving. Hospital patients with missing limbs crawled through the streets in search of food. To avoid an epidemic, bodies were buried in common graves. Supplies were rapidly running out including food, medicine and ammunition. Only occasionally could a transport fly in until the United States Air Force took over April 20, using the city's stadium as a drop zone. Due to heavy anti-aircraft fire C-130 four-engine transports had to drop their bundles above 6,000 feet and most fell outside the stadium and into communist hands. Some of the problem was due to improper packing of the bundles. Although it was highly dangerous, the crews elected to try low-altitude drops. After one aircraft took a direct hit and exploded, further such efforts were cancelled. Delivery at night was tried, but it was difficult despite the use of marker lights. After a third transport crashed all resupply drops were discontinued May 4. But with improvements made, and fewer parachute malfunctions, aerial deliveries at higher altitudes were resumed and kept An Loc supplied.

In the parachute drops were special gift packages donated by a grateful Saigon populace for the people and soldiers of An Loc. They included fresh vegetables and barbecued pork along with letters from schoolgirls who wrote of their appreciation. Each time drops were made enemy artillery zeroed in on the drop zone so each pickup was dangerous. Food and medicine were shared with the civilians. Officers never before had seen such cooperation between civilians and soldiers. Most admired by the civilians were the men of the 81st Airborne Rangers and the 1st Airborne Brigade. Both fought so well that they won the hearts and minds of the people.

There was little change in the military situation between April 23 and May 10. By then the defenders had been reinforced by the 81st Airborne Ranger Group, an elite unit with an established reputation dating back to 1968. Food was the biggest problem for the 4,000 troops and the 6,000 civilians.

Plans for a second enemy attack were detected as early as May 1. It was obvious it would be an all-out effort—seven communist regiments against 4,000 defenders—a quarter of whom were wounded.

CHAPTER 35

A Time for Action

THE DEFENDERS OF AN LOC LEARNED FROM AN ENEMY LIEUTENANT who surrendered that the commander of the 9th Division had been censored by communist headquarters in South Vietnam for his failure to capture An Loc. Now, he said, the 5th Division would head the attack and its commander had promised to be in An Loc within two days, the time his division had taken to capture Loc Ninh. The captured lieutenant also revealed that the 5th Division would attack from the southeast in coordination with the 7th Division from the southwest and that the 9th Division would support the attack from the northeast. He was unable to reveal the attack's timing.

Strategic bombers were ordered to break up the enemy's effort. General Abrams and his staff called for maximum tactical air support with priority for B-52 attacks. Precise timing was important but as yet the allied leaders did not know the timing of the communist attack.

It appeared imminent May 9 as heavy artillery opened up against An Loc. Two days later, after several hours of intensified artillery fire, the communists began their ground assault on all sides. They made extensive use of SA-7 missiles against gunships and tactical aircraft. South Vietnamese troops held firm and systematically sought to destroy enemy tanks with their proven M-72s. The main enemy thrust came from the north and northeast as communist leaders pushed their tanks and infantry toward the center of the city where they hoped to link up and split the South Vietnamese forces into enclaves. If that happened, the defenders would risk defeat. At first the situation looked bleak but the South Vietnamese commanders acted promptly when their forces to the west and northeast were threatened with being overrun. They sent an airborne battalion from the south of the city to endangered areas to block the attack. With this prompt reinforcement the North Vietnamese were unable to make further progress.

Vietnamese and American Air Force tactical aircraft kept busy attacking enemy positions. They were so effective that they inflicted heavy casualties on the entrenched communist troops and forced some to flee. The tide turned when B-52s struck at 9:00 A.M. when the intensity of the enemy tank and infantry attack was at its peak. Thirty strikes were made within twenty-four hours and their devastating impact stunned the communists. By noon the attack was broken and the communists fled in panic. They were caught in the open by tactical aircraft and several North Vietnamese tank crews abandoned their machines. Those remaining were either destroyed or abandoned with their engines running. In one area a regiment that had attacked the 81st Airborne Ranger Group was eliminated.

May 12 the communists attacked again but this time their effort was weak and soon blunted by attacking aircraft that kept them off balance. At last a stalemate developed.

Two days later communist tanks and infantry attacked from the west and southwest but again their attack was broken by B-52 strikes. Now the defenders went on the offensive and regained most of the occupied portion of the city. Most communist troops had already withdrawn and it was now apparent that the communists no longer were capable of capturing An Loc. They had paid a heavy price, losing almost their entire armor force. Forty tanks littered the battlefield. Now the communists withdrew completely from the city and there were indications they were shifting their effort toward the 21st Division that was moving north by road toward An Loc.

Despite overwhelming odds An Loc had held. Much of the credit was due to the sheer physical endurance of its defenders and the combat audacity of the elite forces such as the 81st Airborne Ranger Group and the paratroopers. The territorial forces fought commendably under the able leadership of province chief Colonel Tran Van Nhut. But the enemy's back was broken and An Loc was saved by the timely B-52 strikes.

April 12, 1972, the day An Loc was first attacked, the 21st South Vietnamese Division had closed on Lai Khe and established its command post next to III Corps' forward headquarters. To secure Route 13 from Lai Khe to Chon Tanh, the district town eighteen miles south of An Loc, they moved forward against stiff resistance. Communist positions were overrun May 13 and the division gained control of Route 13 to a point five miles north of Chon Tanh.

Pushing northward, the division deployed its 32nd Regiment to the Tau O area three miles farther north. Here the hardest and longest battle was fought, and communist blocking tactics were most effective despite extensive use of heavy bombers and tactical aircraft.

Despite its failure to uproot the communists from the Tau O area, the 21st Division succeeded in holding down at least two enemy regiments, making them unavailable for the An Loc attack. In the meantime, communist pressure on the besieged city made relief from the outside mandatory. The most urgent need was artillery support for An Loc and for the 21st Division's attack at Tau O. A new fire support base was needed and one was established at Tan Khai. The 7th North Vietnamese Division attacked this base May 20 but all attacks were driven off throughout the month of June. The presence of this base alleviated to some extent the enemy pressure against An Loc.

With improvement in the military situation, III Corps' headquarters declared the siege of An Loc terminated, and released the 1st Airborne Brigade to its parent unit. It was a disastrous defeat for the North Vietnamese whose 5th, 7th and 9th Divisions suffered casualties estimated at ten thousand. Not only were they denied a capital for the Provisional Revolutionary Government, but the threat to Saigon was eliminated.

President Thieu flew to An Loc July 7. His helicopter made a high level approach and suddenly dived towards the soccer field where he landed unannounced. He was accompanied by Lieutanant General Nguyen Van Minh, commander of III Corps, who visited the city for the first time since the siege. They were greeted by an emaciated Brigadier General Le Van Hung, An Loc's heroic commander, whose eyes blinked incessantly under the glaring sun. The president later said jokingly to an aide, "Hung looked deceitful to me. Why do you think he kept constantly squinting and blinking his eyes?"

With great seriousness the aide replied, "Why, Mr. President, General Hung had not seen sunlight for a long, long time."

Thieu toured the ruined city and promised its troops that each would be promoted to their next higher rank. He awarded Hung the National Order, 3rd Class.

III Corps spent the rest of 1972 pushing the communists back from An Loc and rotating troops to and from the city. July 11 the entire 18th Division closed in on An Loc to replace the 5th Division. The 25th Division also relieved the 21st Division in its incomplete mission of reducing enemy blocking forces around Tau O. Finally, the 25th Division encircled the remaining communist strongpoints and neutralized them on the 20th.

During August, the 18th Division began operations to retake the Quan Loi airfield but its efforts extended into September without success. In late November, the 18th Division was replaced at An Loc by three Ranger groups that continued to secure the approaches to the city until a ceasefire was arranged the following January.

The grateful people of An Loc erected a monument dedicated to their heroic defenders. This monument was placed in a cemetery especially built for the deceased troops of the 81st Airborne Ranger Group. The epitaph was contributed by a respected elder.

> "Here, on the famous battleground of An Loc Town
> The Airborne Rangers have sacrificed their lives
> for the nation."

During other battles, the Mekong Delta remained quiet but this was deceptive because at least six communist regiments in IV Corps had the capability to reinforce the 1st North Vietnamese Division across the border in Cambodia. They tried to wreck pacification efforts in the area and to strangle the economic lifeline of this rich agricultural region with the nation's capital.

To maintain control of the region the South Vietnamese had three infantry divisions, two mobile and six border Ranger groups, along with 200,000 territorial troops—the most numerous of any region. Despite United States support, the primary responsibility to defend IV Corps had always been vested in the Vietnamese.

At the start of 1972 the situation in this corps area seemed bright because 95 percent of the people lived in secure villages and hamlets. Rice production was up and farmers were aided by several government programs.

The 1st North Vietnamese Division had moved south in Cambodia in mid-March, indicating major actions might be underway in the delta during the dry season.

Kompong Trach, a small Cambodian town nine miles north of the border, saw action first on March 22. In fierce fighting, both sides suffered heavy losses and the allied base there had to be evacuated. This was a major defeat for the communist 1st Division because of their heavy losses, and it was no longer combat worthy.

Although communist troops entered the delta and fought a series of battles, they were driven back each time with losses. Allied air strikes often proved the crucial difference, despite bitter battles. The situation was stabilized by mid-August and after An Loc's siege was lifted the 21st Division returned to IV Corps to help out.

The communists tried to extend their presence in the delta in October in preparation for the standstill ceasefire then under negotiation but their activities declined by the end of the month when no agreement was achieved.

In spite of multiple efforts and heavy casualties during the 1972 spring offensive North Vietnam accomplished little in the Mekong Delta. Route 4, a major objective, remained open throughout the period except for brief periods of traffic interruption. The communists failed to strangle South Vietnam's lifeline and disrupt pacification. Not even the most remote town fell into communist hands and they failed to achieve any additional gains in population control.

South Vietnamese troops in IV Corps fought remarkably well. They prevented the North Vietnamese from achieving big gains and soundly defeated them despite their initial failure to prevent further infiltration. IV Corps' commanders not only won their battles, but they did it by sharing nearly half of their forces with I and III Corps.

Since their major defeats in 1968 and 1969 North Vietnam's leaders urgently needed to accomplish two things. They had to improve their deteriorating strategic posture in South Vietnam, and they had to defeat Vietnamization if they were ultimately to win.

North Vietnam's negotiators in Paris later disclosed that the offensive had been launched because they needed leverage to strengthen their demands for a coalition government in South Vietnam. They considered it mandatory to control as much of the South as possible to accomplish this goal. So, they risked an all-out offensive but it failed. Throughout 1972 North Vietnam hoped to achieve a standstill ceasefire as soon as it achieved territorial gains. Then they hoped their negotiators could end the war on terms most favorable to them. Their campaign failed throughout South Vietnam and North Vietnam virtually exhausted its manpower and material resources. They suffered more than 100,000 casualties, with the loss of at least half of their large caliber guns and tanks. By the end of the year they were no longer capable of mounting another general offensive. And, not one of South Vietnam's provincial capitals—Quang Tri the only exception and only for a brief period—ever fell into communist hands. Out of the 260 district towns, fewer than ten were occupied by the communists and almost all were in remote areas.

North Vietnam's leaders had underestimated South Vietnam's armed forces, their ability to sustain combat and their capacity for endurance. This was especially true of their estimate of the territorials. In the past, the North Vietnamese had held them in low repute. They made a strategic error of great significance when they underestimated the effectiveness and the extent of American airpower. They made other strategic and tactical miscalculations that caused them to lose in every battle they fought. Their strategic error was in dispersing main force units and making major efforts on three widely separated fronts instead of concentrating them in a major thrust against a single objective. Although they were successful in gaining territory in each region, only in northern Quang Tri Province did their gains amount to political and military significance. If they had concentrated their offensive in this area they would have gained Hué and continued south, possibly ending the war in 1972.

Instead of losing one South Vietnamese unit after another as might have happened if the invasion of Quang Tri had been exploited with additional North Vietnamese divisions, South Vietnam was able to deploy its divisions on three fronts, thereby overcoming North Vietnam's initial advantage.

North Vietnam's leaders further compounded their strategic errors. All tactical commanders lacked experience in using armor and they failed to use such units properly. Instead of making deep thrusts into South Vietnam's lines, creating shock and confusion and disrupting rear areas, armored units were employed with hesitancy, primarily in attacks against targets whose armor defenses had been carefully prepared. South Vietnamese troops soon learned to put them out of action with artillery shells.

North Vietnamese commanders squandered their infantrymen in mass suicidal assaults. Several battalions were so badly mauled that they were reduced to less than 50 personnel. Morale reached such a low level that desertion became a problem. Entire units broke contact with the South Vietnamese and retreated, leaving most of their equipment behind. Such actions rarely occurred prior to 1972.

During the offensive's initial stage, the communists had the upper hand, advancing from victory to victory on all three fronts. Success was derived not from their superior strength in firepower, but from the weakness of South Vietnam's defenses. Not only was South Vietnam's geographical position of major vulnerability, but the disposition of her defense forces was not adequate for early containment of an invasion of such proportions. At first, the North Vietnamese seemed invincible. In retrospect, General Truong believes that South Vietnam could have done little to prevent the initial setbacks because South Vietnam's configuration did not lend itself to defense against invasion. From the demilitarized zone to Cape Ca Mau, South Vietnam's narrow strip of land averaged 100 miles in width—only fifty miles at one place. This narrowness would have been no problem if South Vietnam had been a peninsula like Korea but South Vietnam's western border with Laos and Cambodia ranged from the demilitarized zone to Ha Tien City—600 miles. Two-thirds of this area was jungle and mountainous terrain, while the southern 200 miles were swamps and rich ricelands. This was an open border without a natural defense and the communists enjoyed total freedom of movement along the entire frontier. Due to the exposure of South Vietnam's western flank, the North Vietnamese could infiltrate and build up forces with little interruption, attacking when and where they chose. A determined attack could be driven a considerable distance inside South Vietnam before adequate forces could be deployed to contain it. In the face of this vulnerable boundary, South Vietnam was compelled to deploy its forces to protect the entire western border. Its armed forces, therefore, were stationed thinly at fire bases and border camps. Not only could North Vietnam overrun any of these border outposts with a determined attack, but its disposition in Cambodia immobilized a sizable South Vietnamese force. When enemy attacks materialized in several places at the same time it was impossible to commit forces or reserves until it was determined where the enemy would make his main effort. South Vietnam was in the difficult posture of having little tactical flexibility while North Vietnam always enjoyed a definite advantage wherever it chose to attack. South Vietnam's position became more difficult when the United States and its other allies withdrew their forces. Her divisions became over-extended almost to the breaking point to fill areas occupied by departing allies. Meanwhile, North Vietnam sent increasing numbers of troops into the South. They had 149,000 by the end of 1969 when the United States began to withdraw its troops. This number almost doubled to 285,000 by the end of 1972. Vietcong units had been so depleted that their ranks had to be filled by North Vietnamese soldiers.

With the 1972 spring invasion of Quang Tri Province, President Thieu had vowed, "We will not yield even a pebble in Quang Tri or a handful of mud in Ca Mau to the enemy." For a time that proud boast had seemed just that. The decimation of the 3rd Division, and the failure of I Corps' commander and his staff to provide adequate guidance and support for this front-line division had almost led to disaster. Deployments and reinforcements throughout South Vietnam at first were made on a piecemeal basis that was indecisive because command and control procedures were inadequate. The full effect of massed artillery fire was seldom achieved at first by South Vietnamese divisions because they were too dispersed. Once they learned this lesson, they brought the North Vietnamese to a halt and forced them to retreat.

Although South Vietnam's armed forces fought extremely well, in most instances their success was due to support by the United States Navy and Air Force. Without their assistance Quang Tri City could not have been retaken, nor could South Vietnamese forces have held at Kontum and An Loc without Air Force support. South Vietnamese forces became too dependent on B-52 support, often delaying attacks until targets could be bombed. This became a major handicap later. Also, the over-use of ammunition set a bad precedent. The American advisory effort on the ground proved helpful although many Americans at the battalion level had been withdrawn.

No previous communist offensive equalled this one. It was timed to have maximum influence on American politics. Although American ground forces had largely been withdrawn, Navy and Air Force units were still fighting and supply and combat support was still provided by Americans.

With strong American air support, and a clear mission to defend their country, South Vietnam's armed forces proved their worth. Defenders at An Loc had absolutely refused to surrender. At Kontum, when a fresh division was brought in it drove back every communist attack. In northern I Corps, three South Vietnamese divisions not only held Hué against the heavy onslaughts of six communist divisions, but they also crossed the My Chanh line to counter-attack and ultimately recapture Quang Tri City.

With light-weight, antitank weapons South Vietnamese soldiers realized they could disable T-54 tanks. Despite siege conditions, and under heavy artillery fire, most of the time they maintained their morale. This was not only true of the regulars, but also of the territorial troops. The decision by President Thieu to replace ineffective, politically appointed generals with professionals who had earned their rank in combat came almost too late.

In Hanoi, North Vietnam's leaders remained stubborn, and refused to cease their belligerent actions despite losses in the South. They were particularly concerned about political discussions between the United States and Russia and the People's Republic of China. They realized that these two nations, who supplied North Vietnam with nearly all her war supplies, might be persuaded to reduce their support in the near future.

North Vietnam's leaders had hoped in the spring of 1972 that a military victory during this American presidential year might inhibit President Nixon's chances of being re-elected. They had not forgotten the previous presidential election year of 1968 and the reaction caused by their Tet offensive on the United States' internal and international politics. At first, they had thought a communist victory during 1972 might promote the selection of a new president who would repudiate Nixon's commitment to support South Vietnam. Quite possibly this was North Vietnam's major objective in initiating the 1972 offensive.

Although the bloodiest battles raged for three months in the northernmost corner of South Vietnam, North Vietnam no longer had the forces to win a decisive victory. Her army in the South was so exhausted that

North Vietnam's leaders were forced to switch to a course of land and population grab to prepare for a ceasefire standstill.

Much to North Vietnam's chagrin the Republic of South Vietnam emerged from the offensive stronger than ever. Communist leaders were also stunned by the United States' resolve to stand behind its ally. And they were shocked by the staunchness of the South Vietnamese units. They reluctantly gave credit to the individual South Vietnamese soldier. Most had come of age during the war and the communists had to admit they had fought in the noblest traditions of the Vietnamese people.

Nixon replied to a request June 23, 1972, by the North Vietnamese to resume meetings, proposing July 19 for a private meeting. This time Kissinger learned that the North Vietnamese no longer took for granted either a military victory or Nixon's defeat in the coming fall election. Publicly, North Vietnamese officials called the United States' agreement to return to discussions a great victory. In fact, their own military ineptitude gave them no other choice.

The State Department July 14 rebuked actress Jane Fonda over reports that she had made anti-war broadcasts in Hanoi. A spokesman said that it was always distressing to find American citizens lending their voice in any way to a government such as North Vietnam.

North Vietnam's press agency had said in a broadcast the previous day that she had appealed to American pilots, "I implore you. I beg of you to consider what you are doing." It was said that she had visited the Namsach District July 13 and supposedly said, "In the area where I went it was easy to see that there are no military targets, there is no important highway, there is no communication network." She claimed that she saw damaged dikes.

Former Attorney General Ramsay Clark went to North Vietnam July 29 through August 12 to inspect the results of American bombing and visited imprisoned United States servicemen. With other members of the Stockholm-based International Commission of Inquiry they said they wanted to investigate alleged United States war crimes in Indochina in bombing non-military targets. They reportedly visited the sites of damaged dikes. A Hanoi broadcast quoted Clark as saying of the ten American prisoners he saw that they were in good health, getting good medical care and that their living conditions "could not be better." Clark claimed that he had declined a request to broadcast over Radio Hanoi but that he was unaware of what use was made of his tape-recorded comments to journalists. To them he said that he had seen extensive damage to dikes, sluices and canals at six places. He deplored the American air campaign, saying, "There is absolutely no excuse for bombing North Vietnam and there never had been."

In the United States, peace demonstrators failed to delay acceptance speeches by President Nixon and Vice President Agnew at the Republican Convention in Miami Beach. They did stage a massive sitdown August 23 outside the convention's headquarters. More than 1,100 were arrested as splinter groups roamed the streets during the day and tried to block traffic. Some slashed tires and overturned garbage cans.

At the August 1, 1972, Paris meeting, Kissinger told Le Duc Tho that their meetings could no longer be kept secret. The communist leader made some concessions but Kissinger said they were not sufficiently worthwhile to continue the talks.

After Kissinger and President Thieu later reached a consensus as to what could be offered to North Vietnam, a tentative agreement with Le Duc Tho was reached October 12. They settled on all the principle issues except the right of the United States to replace military equipment for South Vietnam and the question of civilians detained by the South Vietnamese. However, a more precise commitment to a ceasefire in Laos and Cambodia was needed. The issue of a coalition government was believed to have been laid to rest. Kissinger and Le Duc Tho agreed to make the announcement October 22 and sign the agreement nine days later.

President Thieu had not seen the latest articles negotiated by Kissinger so Ambassador Bunker October 14 conveyed an outline of the proposed settlement to him. He did not immediately respond.

In other diplomatic moves, officials of China and the Soviet Union were asked for restraint in sending arms to North Vietnam but they, too, failed to reply.

In a meeting October 17 Kissinger and Xuan Thuy argued about the principle of equality on the replacement of military equipment. Kissinger sought one-for-one replacement of worn-out equipment. Xuan Thuy accepted this position if the United States would agree to release communist civilians detained in South Vietnam. This position was rejected.

Kissinger and Ambassador Bunker met with President Thieu October 19. To the draft of the typed text Nixon wrote in long hand, "Dr. Kissinger, General Haig and I have discussed this proposal at great length. I am personally convinced it is the best we will be able to get and that it meets my *absolute* condition that the government of Vietnam must survive as a free country. Dr. Kissinger's comments have my total backing."

President Thieu read the statement without comment.

After many sessions, Kissinger still hoped that by October 21 he would have an understanding with Thieu. He was not concerned about the political battle back home between President Nixon and his Democratic opponent Senator George McGovern. He had been assured by Nixon in writing before he left, and by cable since he arrived in Saigon, that the American election would have no bearing on his negotiations. But on the evening of October 21, although the North Vietnamese had accepted all American demands, including those on Laos and Cambodia, Kissinger still did not have Thieu's concurrence. In regard to prisoners of war, the North Vietnamese advised that there were no prisoners in Cambodia, and prisoners in Laos would be released with those from North and South Vietnam.

Earlier, French journalist Arnaud de Borchgrave, who was also a senior editor for *Newsweek*, was granted a visa to Hanoi that he had not sought and an interview with Prime Minister Pham Van Dong that he also had not requested. This was bad faith on Dong's part but he also gave an interpretation of the draft agreement that was at variance not only with the American interpretation but with the text of what had been negotiated. In the article Thieu was described as overtaken by events, and Dong discussed a three-sided coalition government that would be set up during a transition period. The article stated that all detainees of both sides, including civilians, would be released, but this point had not been agreed to. And lastly, the article said that the United States had agreed to pay reparations.

Thieu's reservations about the agreement had already been high and now they turned to grave suspicions. He was opposed to any ceasefire that left 135,000 North Vietnamese troops in his country. He considered this issue basic to South Vietnam's future and he argued for pressure to be applied to the communist negotiators for withdrawal of all North Vietnamese troops.

Nixon wired Kissinger to apply equal pressure on Thieu without causing a blowup at their October 22 meeting, and to do the same with North Vietnam's leaders. He said that he thought the best solution would be to defer the final agreement until after the election, and to keep the two parties quiet until then.

In a letter to President Thieu, Nixon repeated that he considered the agreement fully acceptable as it stood. He added a warning, "Were you to find the agreement to be unacceptable at this point and the other side were to reveal the extraordinary limits to which it has gone in meeting the demands put upon them, it is my judgment that your decision would have the most serious effects upon my ability to continue to provide support for you and for the government of South Vietnam."

The next day—October 22—Thieu harped on the fact that the agreement permitted continued presence of North Vietnamese troops and argued about the composition of the National Council—which had no function—and in which he was to have a veto. Actually, the council never came into being. Kissinger gave Thieu Nixon's letter. He read it and responded with dignity that for the United States the problem was how to end participation in the war. "For me," he said, "it is a matter of life and death for my country." He said he would consult with his advisers and the National Assembly.

Kissinger cabled Nixon, "I think we finally made a breakthrough." He and Bunker were encouraged by their meeting with Thieu.

Laos and Cambodia were to be dealt with in two sets of documents. Now these two countries posed the most difficult problem. The United States Congress had limited aid to Cambodia to $300 million. In a meeting with Kissinger, President Lon Nol endorsed the agreement, declared a unilateral ceasefire and called for negotiations. Under Article 20 of the Vietnam Agreement North Vietnam had pledged to withdraw its forces from Cambodia and Laos and to refrain from using the territories of Cambodia and Laos for military operations against any signatories of the agreement. In effect, this was a reference to South Vietnam. The Americans hoped that with North Vietnam's forces withdrawn that Lon Nol could handle the Khmer Rouge.

When Kissinger returned to Saigon from Phnom Penh he met with Thieu who was enraged about American meetings with Thailand, Cambodian and Laotian officials. He said the United States had obviously "connived with the Soviets and China to sell out South Vietnam" and that he would not be a party to it. He revealed that his sense of betrayal went back at least a year to the proposal asking him to agree to resign a month before a presidential election. At the time he had accepted the provision without protest.

Kissinger responded angrily, saying, in part, "Your conviction that we have undermined you will be understood by no Americans, least of all President Nixon.

"As to specifics, we have not recognized the right of North Vietnam to be in the South. We have used the language of the Geneva Accords since we thought this the best way to work out a practical solution. Had we wanted to sell you out, there have been many easier ways by which we could have accomplished this.

"We have fought for four years, have mortgaged our whole foreign policy to the defense of one country. What you have said has been a very bitter thing to hear."

Kissinger knew there was no point in staying so he told Thieu he would return to Washington.

He wired his deputy, General Alexander M. Haig, Jr., that there were two options available. He could proceed to Hanoi as originally scheduled, present Saigon's changes, and go back and forth until some concurrence was achieved, or return to Washington. Haig was advised to tell Ambassador Dobrynin that he had encountered major obstacles in Saigon and that we were bound to present them to North Vietnam. He said he still hoped to gain the Soviet Union's support in containing North Vietnamese actions.

A message was sent to Le Duc Tho in Paris that Kissinger had been asked to return to Washington for further discussion of problems encountered with the South Vietnamese government.

Before his departure for Washington, Kissinger met with President Thieu and told him he had requested another meeting with Le Duc Tho to consider South Vietnam's proposals. Thieu was calmer than at their previous meeting but he renewed his objections to the agreement. He asked that the provisions regarding the demilitarized zone be strengthened to prevent infiltration. He agreed with Kissinger that the question of North Vietnamese troops in the South could be settled by unannounced withdrawals but that there was no provision in the agreement for such a contingency.

General Vien, chairman of the Joint General Staff, said control of the ceasefire would be difficult and that a standstill ceasefire in a "leopard skin" pattern carried with it many dangers. With no lines of demarcation he said enemy forces would be allowed to stay where they were, but that he doubted they would do so. He said he expected they would try to take control of villages. One of his officers said, "Before, we went into the jungle to hunt down the wild beasts. Now we have to take them into our arms and sleep with them."

The South Vietnamese agreed that the communists would not abide by the ceasefire and the standstill, pointing to their actions in 1954 and 1972 for justification. Actually, enemy documents found in a district commissar's underground shelter in Quang Tin Province showed that he had been studying the main facts of the text before the South Vietnamese leaders had seen them and the commissar had already received instructions for an appropriate line of action. These documents were given to Kissinger and he was told that this was the first time they had seen the text but that some of the enemy in the frontlines already knew the details.

Thieu expressed his concern about the proposed National Council of Reconciliation and Concord, particularly the kind of structure that was envisioned. Kissinger agreed this point needed clarification. He also agreed to make a copy of the text available in Vietnamese within twenty-four hours. When the copy was given to President Thieu and his advisers it was quickly evident that this text was the original drafted by North Vietnam and definitely not a translated version of the English text. Even the term for United States forces was one that in Vietnamese was derogatory. The term Quan My, instead of the more decent term Quan Doi Hue Ky, was insolent although literally correct. The reference to National Council of Reconciliation and Concord in English referred to an administrative structure but in Vietnamese meant government structure. Thus the North Vietnamese were considering this council an agency with full governmental powers, in effect, a coalition government. The agreement, Thieu pointed out, listed three Vietnamese nations, instead of just South and North Vietnam. He asked rhetorically whether the South Vietnamese government would share its authority with another government.

The South Vietnamese insisted on twenty-six changes to the agreement to make it acceptable. Thieu gave Kissinger a letter for Nixon stating his country could not agree to the agreement because of its shortcomings.

Kissinger returned to Washington October 23 the same day he sent a message to North Vietnam's officials that they rejected as not "really serious." They warned that the war would continue and that the United States must bear full responsibility.

This was also the day the French journalist Arnaud de Borchgrave's earlier interview with Pham Van Dong was released, declaring that peace negotiations in Paris were producing good results and that there would be a three-sided coalition government of transition.

Kissinger sent a cable to Le Duc Tho that the United States was prepared to sign October 31, but it might be difficult to stick to the timetable. He informed North Vietnam's prime minister that all bombing above the 20th parallel would cease as of October 25.

President Thieu went on television to tell his people that South Vietnam would refuse to take part in a coalition government.

The North Vietnamese now released their version of the agreement. They revealed the United States messages of October 20 and 22 in which President Nixon had called the text of the agreement "complete" and had expressed satisfaction with North Vietnam's concessions. In their statement, the North Vietnamese strongly denounced the Nixon Administration's "lack of good will and seriousness." They demanded that the agreement be signed by October 31.

With the president's consent, Kissinger spoke to the press October 26, giving the American side of the negotiations and using the words "peace is at hand." He defended the right of the people of South Vietnam "who have suffered so much. . . . who will be remaining in that country after we have departed" to participate in the making of the peace. He said the United States would not be stampeded into an agreement until its provisions were right.

A North Vietnamese spokesman said that Le Duc Tho and Xuan Thuy would receive Kissinger again only if the United States was prepared to sign the October agreement. He used the words, "peace is at the end of a pen." Kissinger responded that the proposal was ready for final negotiation, and he promised a full bombing halt forty-eight hours after a settlement.

The People's Republic of China now demanded that the United States "put a firm stop to Saigon's behavior." The Chinese implied that these negotiations would be linked to efforts to relax tensions between China and the United States.

Nixon's overwhelming victory over Senator McGovern November 7 prodded North Vietnam to agree to a new meeting November 20.

As negotiations dragged on, Kissinger regretted his "peace is at hand" statement to the press. It had built up unwarranted hopes among the American people and the press. When several meetings with the North Vietnamese proved unproductive, ending with the November 25 agreement to recess until December 4, there was a growing sense of disillusionment about Nixon's hardline stand. The first round of talks had brought about twelve improvements in the agreement, some of which were marginal, but they balanced out three or four demands by North Vietnam for major changes in its favor.

Kissinger asked Ambassador Bunker November 26 to tell Thieu that minimum conditions were unchanged.

The next day Kissinger wired Hanoi that the United Sates would make a maximum effort December 4 and to show good faith was reducing its air operations over North Vietnam.

When the delegations met, Le Duc Tho seized the floor for a violent denunciation of United States tactics. He rejected all proposals from the morning sessions and withdrew nine of the twelve changes he had accepted during the previous sessions in November. He maintained that all of his demands for changes in the October agreement must be met.

Kissinger reported to President Nixon, "The only alternative he offered was to go back to the October agreement literally with no changes by either side."

President Nixon gave renewed consideration to President Thieu's objections to the ceasefire agreement. The major issues were that the demilitarized zone should be recognized as the border separating the two countries as determined by the Geneva Accords in 1954, and a token withdrawal of

North Vietnamese troops—25,000—to be reciprocated by a similar reduction in South Vietnam. There was also the question of whether a ceasefire should involve all of Indochina. South Vietnam wanted an international control force strong enough and ready to take up positions when the ceasefire went into effect. Thieu also insisted that the translated text should be revised to make the English and the Vietnamese texts identical and ensure that there be no misinterpretation about the makeup of the National Council of Reconciliation and Concord.

Kissinger's deputy, General Haig, arrived in Saigon to deliver a personal letter from President Nixon to stress the significance of the American aid program. Haig indicated that if South Vietnam kept refusing to accept the agreement that the United States might go ahead and sign separately with North Vietnam.

Some progress had been achieved four days earlier when the United States State Department revealed that Canada, Hungary, Indonesia and Poland had agreed in principle to participate in a control commission.

Kissinger and Le Duc Tho met again in Paris November 20. The communist prime minister, arriving first, told the press that North Vietnam was suspicious of the United States' sincerity. Although he did not say so, this was obviously a reference to the United States' failure to sign on schedule. At first, while new demands were made by Kissinger to honor South Vietnam's terms, all went smoothly. But three days later Le Duc Tho got tough and rejected all American proposals and again demanded the removal of South Vietnam's government. Obviously, he had received new instructions from Hanoi. Kissinger demanded to know why he had reversed himself. He was told that new demands had brought a change in North Vietnam's attitude. The talks were terminated November 25 and they agreed to meet again in early December.

Nguyen Phu Duc, a special envoy of the South Vietnamese government, was sent to Washington to deliver a letter from President Thieu to President Nixon to clarify his position.

Kissinger met again with Le Duc Tho December 4, but no progress was achieved. Even worse, issues that Kissinger thought had been solved were brought up again. Kissinger left Paris December 12 while underlings on both sides continued to discuss issues.

After Kissinger talked to the president a cable was sent to Hanoi warning that unless serious talks were renewed within seventy-eight hours the United States would resume the bombing of North Vietnam above the 20th parallel that had been halted since late October.

Captured documents during late 1972 indicated that the prospect of an end to the war in October had excited North Vietnamese soldiers. Many of them listened to the British Broadcasting Corporation and South Vietnamese radio stations, and openly discussed their hopes of soon returning to North Vietnam. When the early ceasefire failed many soldiers did not conceal their despair.

Kissinger concluded a meeting in Paris December 13 with a warning to Le Duc Tho of growing impatience in Washington. "We came here twice, each time determined to settle it very quickly, each time prepared to give you a schedule which we would then have kept absolutely. We kept the vice president standing by for ten days in order to start the schedule which we have given you. And we believed that in the last week there has been just enough progress each day to prevent a breakup but never enough to bring about a settlement. I admire the special adviser's skill in keeping the negotiations going."

Kissinger spoke to the White House press corps December 16 to explain the reason for the stalled negotiations. He and Nixon had agreed to tell the press that he would stay in contact with the North Vietnamese.

Kissinger sent a note to North Vietnam's leaders accusing them of "deliberately and frivolously delaying the talks." He proposed a solution to the negotiating impasse and a date for resuming talks. He suggested that they return to the language of the text as it stood at the end of the first round of negotiations November 23 before Le Duc Tho withdrew his concessions.

When there was no satisfactory response from Hanoi President Nixon issued an order December 14 for the reseeding of mines in Haiphong Harbor, resumption of aerial reconnaissance over the North, and for B-52 strikes against all military targets in the Hanoi-Haiphong area.

Nixon was appalled when he learned that bombers had to be borrowed from different commands, involving complicated logistics problems and including a large amount of red tape.

The time for action, and not further talk, had arrived. President Nixon did not hesitate in making the decision that should have been made seven years earlier.

CHAPTER 36

Linebacker II

IN WASHINGTON, PRESIDENT NIXON CALLED ADMIRAL MOORER TO SAY "I don't want any more of this crap about the fact that we couldn't hit this target or that one. This is your chance to use military power effectively to win this war, and if you don't, I'll consider you responsible."

Nixon had said earlier that there was no point in bombing unless North Vietnam was hit hard.

Although it was known that North Vietnam's most important strategic targets were heavily defended by modern surface-to-air missiles and high performance jet fighters—all supplied by the Soviet Union with technicians to train North Vietnamese crews—the Joint Chiefs had long sought such an offensive. If they had judged wrong, and the B-52s failed to survive over such a hostile environment, then the United States would have lost a significant number of its strategic bombers along with incalculable credibility and loss of military stature in the eyes of the world. The Strategic Air Command had long trained for just such a confrontation, and its officials were confident its men and places would meet the test.

The first warning order for a series of raids came December 15 from the Chairman of the Joint Chiefs of Staff, Admiral Moorer, to General John C. Meyer, commander-in-chief of the Strategic Air Command, who relayed it to his Eighth Air Force commander on Guam. The operation was called Linebacker II. In the previous spring, President Nixon had authorized the first Linebacker operation that, for the first time, authorized limited B-52 strikes against targets on the northern coast of North Vietnam. Nixon is an avid football fan. The name for these operations was a natural outgrowth of his passion for the game. That first Linebacker came to an end October 22. It had been an integrated effort by all types of United States airborne forces to interdict the enemy's supply networks throughout Southeast Asia, but mainly in the North. Heavy bombers had concentrated their operations in North Vietnam's panhandle and the demilitarized zone. It is ironic that this great air offensive was executed under a nickname made famous by a defensive position in football.

Since early 1972 B-52s of the 307th Strategic Wing at U-Tapao had been flying support missions for ground operations in the South. Crews from all continental United States B-52 wings had been assigned temporary duty on a rotational basis. At the same time, B-52s assigned to Guam maintained these B-52D aircraft while crews of the 60th Bombardment Squadron were on nuclear alert. The host unit, the 43rd Strategic Wing, also was required to support conventional missions.

The island of Guam—home base for the Pacific area's B-52s—is the top of a 35,000-foot mountain whose roots lie in the deepest part of the Pacific Ocean—the Mariana Trench. It is thirty-two miles long and a scant eleven miles wide. In World War II it was the headquarters for the Twentieth Air Force whose B-29s bombed Japan into submission.

U-Tapao Royal Navy Airfield in Thailand was Guam's sister base.

The crew compartment of a B-52 is filled with equipment. B-52Ds had a tail gunner but in the "G" models all six are in the forward compartment. The pilot and the co-pilot are on the flight deck, the navigator and radar navigator are in a downstairs position called "The Black Hole of Calcutta" while the electronic warfare officer and the gunner sit side-by-side behind them.

B-52s flew in a standard three-plane cell. A wave was a flexible combination of cells committed to a single objective. As in all combat operations, the success of operations hinged on the tireless performance of the men of the 303rd Consolidated Aircraft Maintenance Wing or Bicycle Works. This was the largest maintenance organization in the Strategic Air Command with more than 5,000 personnel. They were responsible for 155 B-52s.

Planning for Linebacker II had started in early August when queries from the Joint Chiefs sought the Strategic Air Command's capability to wage this type of all-out offensive. A lengthy list of potential targets was forwarded August 12.

By fall the number of damaged B-52s flying support missions began to rise, although the extensive use of chaff had reduced losses. It now took the firing of 150 SAMs to destroy one aircraft. Most planes that were lost were due to SAM attacks. When one of these missiles exploded, thousands of hot warhead fragments were dispensed for a considerable distance. Any piece of shrapnel could be lethal if it penetrated a vital spot in a B-52's complex systems. Captain N. J. Ostrozny and his crew bailed out of a B-52 November 22 after an attack against Vinh. A SAM had been set off by its proximity fuse and the bomber suffered heavy damage. This was the first Stratofortress to be lost to enemy fire after more than seven years of combat operations.

Only a handful of officers knew of the first warning order when it was received December 15 by Lieutenant General Gerald W. Johnson, the Eighth Air Force's commander. It provided preliminary instructions for a three-day maximum effort against targets in North Vietnam. But the Eighth Air Force was advised to take no action until they received further instructions.

The next morning, briefings were held to instruct the division and wing commanders and the Eighth Air Force staff. Colonel Thomas F. Rew, commander of the 72nd Strategic Wing, was assigned to lead the first wave. The following day the crews were briefed. At last they would attack strategic targets for which they had been trained. They were told the attacks would be at night at high altitude and by radar. There would be a raid each night, starting with the 18th, they were told. Each night there would be three waves of varying strength, each hitting targets at four- to five-hour intervals. They were advised that they would be attacking the most heavily defended targets in the world, and that these strikes would be a test of their previously untested capability. Admiral Moorer wired from Washington and expressed his and President Nixon's personal concern for the success of the campaign.

The initial concept for the operation as directed by the Joint Chiefs was for around-the-clock bombing of the Hanoi-Haiphong area. Tactical bombers and fighters from the Seventh Air Force and comparable aircraft from the Seventh Fleet would strike during the day and B-52s at night. For the first night there would be eighty-seven bombers from Guam plus forty-two from U-Tapao. The latter crews were assigned targets at Hoa Lac, Kep and Phuc Yen airfields where MIG 21 Fishbed fighters were stationed, while the rest of the force attacked Hanoi area targets, coming in from the northwest. Attack routes were selected to insure ready identification of radar aiming points and to give minimum exposure time to SAM missiles. After their bombs were dropped they were told to exit the target area on west to northwest headings. The second and third days, they were told, would be a repeat of operations on the first, except that there would be ninety-three bombers on the second day and ninety-nine on the third. This three-day effort would tax air and ground units to the limit. Many crew members had been scheduled home for rotation at Christmas.

Crews jammed the briefing room at Guam on the 18th. Colonel James R. McCarthy, who had earlier been assigned temporary duty with the 307th Strategic Wing at U-Tapao and had flown a number of missions, was chosen to brief the crews. He had been assigned the task of reviewing the current MIG and SAM defense tactics and he had recommended changes to improve them. He was an ideal choice.

As the route was displayed on the briefing screen, McCarthy said, "Gentlemen, your target for tonight is Hanoi." That last word captured their attention. After this general briefing crews attended specialized sessions.

The first aircraft started its roll at 2:51 A.M. Guam time. Major William Stocker's black-bellied plane slowly lumbered onto the runway. As the nose of his bomber lined up with the white center stripe, he advanced the eight throttles to takeoff power. Black smoke bellied out of the tailpipes as water augmentation increased takeoff thrust. The plane slowly started to accelerate. The engines not only had to overcome the inertia of the 450,000-pound airplane, but also the 150-foot dip and rise from the middle to the end of Andersen's sway-backed runway. The airspeed increased slowly but soon passed the decision point where momentum prevents the aircraft from being safely stopped on the runway ahead of the plane. Now there was little the crew could do but sweat it out. A blown tire, the loss of power from the outboard engines, or any major failure could spell disaster for crew and aircraft. With all systems "in the green" indicating normal, Stocker eased back on the control column and Rose 1 took off. Seconds later it was over the ocean. Twenty-six airplanes followed in close succession and the Rock's contribution to Wave 1 was airborne.

As Stratofortresses started down the runway at Andersen, the rest of Wave 1 at U-Tapao in Thailand was undergoing its last-minute preparations for launching. Supporting forces at other bases in Thailand and on the aircraft carriers in the South China Sea were launching their aircraft as part of the operation. Navy fighter-bombers would attack coastal gun emplacements plus known or suspected SAM batteries. Specially configured fighters would lay down chaff, the metallic or fiberglass strips of reflective tape that degraded enemy radar scopes. Before the campaign concluded, they dispensed 125 tons of chaff. Along with chaff dispension would be electronic countermeasure aircraft to create additional clutter on enemy radar screens to further hide the bombers.

Other fighters and fighter-bombers would be attacking airfields and SAM sites along the bomber routes in and out. Wild Weasel aircraft would be searching for enemy radar signals against which they would launch Shrike radar-homing missiles. Other fighters would join with bombers to provide a combat air patrol against enemy fighters. EC-121s would provide a special monitoring capability to warn the strike force of close-in threats. Rescue aircraft and helicopters were standing by, ready to provide immediate recovery if it were needed.

The briefing for Wave 2 was conducted in the midst of a flurry of excitement surrounding the first launches, but it was smoother than the first briefing. Now the shock of knowing what lay ahead was past, and briefers had polished their presentations.

The first crisis developed as the pre-strike refueling report was received from Wave 1. Major Stocker reported 196,000 pounds as his total fuel after receiving fuel from his tanker. He should have reported 216,000 pounds. By the book, his mission should have been aborted. Without additional fuel, and flying as briefed, his force would arrive home with dry tanks. A diversion to Thailand would give the bomber time to make it back to Guam for the second and third days' missions.

There was little time for decision making. Commanders discussed alternatives in hastily called meetings at Guam. The only way to complete the mission, and to have the aircraft available for the next day's mission, was to get more fuel. KC-135s in Thailand were already committed to pre- and post-strike refueling of aircraft. The only possibility to obtain tankers was from Kadena Air Base, Okinawa. These tankers were also committed to the refueling of follow-on B-52 waves over the South China Sea. To use these tankers, and keep them for later refueling assignments, meant post-strike refuelings would be stretched to eighteen hours for some crews. The problem was complicated by marginal weather at the refueling altitude near Kadena.

Generals Johnson and Anderson questioned whether the crews were experienced enough to make this type of major inflight modification to their routes and after hitting their targets refuel in marginal night weather. Several questions were in their minds. What condition would the planes be in? Would they be damaged? Colonel McCarthy expressed confidence in his crews and the generals decided to continue the mission. Word was flashed to these planes to refuel over Kadena if they were low on fuel.

All 129 bombers were airborne by midnight and those from Guam had to fly 2,650 miles before they reached their targets. This was the longest sustained strategic bombing flight ever attempted. Actually, the combat routing was much longer because the bombers had to fly internationally approved routes to Southeast Asia to avoid commercial air traffic. And the routes in the forward area were planned to avoid as many enemy defenses as possible and to achieve precision timing. Therefore, the one-way distance exceeded 3,000 miles.

Lieutenant Colonel Hendsley R. Conner's plane took off on schedule at

7:00 P.M. with Wave 2. The commander of the 486th Bombardment Squadron had been assigned as deputy airborne mission commander so he was the seventh man, sitting in the instructor pilot's seat. He had had very little rest the night before so he took a nap on the long flight out, awakening when the plane started to refuel. He tuned his radio to hear how the lead wave was doing. He knew they should be in the target area. He heard Colonel Thomas F. Rew report to Guam by radio after leaving the target area. He said one airplane was known to have been shot down by a missile, two others were unaccounted for, while another had suffered heavy damage. He estimated the North Vietnamese had fired over 200 SAMs, but that there had been no fighter attacks. He said the anti-aircraft fire had been heavy, but well below their flight level. Conner had no illusions. The first wave had achieved surprise, but they would not, and their reception would probably be worse.

The crew was quiet and tense as their bomber entered the target area. Conner saw missiles as they made white streaks of light climbing into the sky. As they left the ground they seemed to move slowly, then pick up speed as they climbed. Each ended its flight in a cascade of sparkles. At first the sight reminded him of fireworks on the 4th of July, but he had no illusions about their deadliness. Conner had flown over 200 light bomber missions but he had never seen so many SAMs. He felt less secure in the B-52 because the smaller aircraft in which he had flown previously could maneuver better.

Just before start of the bombing run Conner checked the emergency gear to assure everything was all right if they were hit. They would be most vulnerable on the run to the target because they would be within the lethal range of the SAMs while flying straight and level. They had been briefed to make no evasive maneuvers so the radar navigator could be positive of aiming at the right target. If he was not sure, each radar navigator was instructed not to drop his bombs but to release them over the ocean on the way back.

Halfway down the bombing run, the electronic warfare officer, Captain James Tramel, called out the number of missiles fired at them. There were four in all but they remained straight and level.

"How far out from the target are we, radar?" Aircraft Commander Major Clifford Ashley asked.

Radar Navigator Major Archie Myers replied, "We're 10 seconds out, Five, 4, 3, 2, 1. Bombs away! Start your turn, pilot."

Ashley turned the bomber to the right. There was a huge explosion, and they all felt like they were in the center of a clap of thunder. Conner felt a slight jerk to his right shoulder. The noise was deafening. Their surroundings glowed brightly for an instant, then it was dark again. Now they could smell the ozone from the burned explosive.

Conner checked the flight instruments. Over the interphone he called, "Pilot, we're still flying. Are you okay?"

"I'm fine," Ashley replied, "but the airplane is in bad shape. Let's check it over and see if we can keep it airborne. Everybody check in and let me know how they are."

"Navigator and radar are okay," Lieutenant Forest Stegelin said. "We don't have any equipment operating, but I'll give you a heading for Thailand any time you want it."

"EW is okay," Tramel said, "but the gunner has been hit. We have about two more minutes in the lethal SAM range, so continue to take evasive maneuvers if you can."

"Gunner is okay," Master Sergeant Kenneth Connor said. "I have some shrapnel in my right arm, but nothing bad. The left side of the plane is full of holes."

Colonel Conner called the lead aircraft to let it know they had been hit. The leader said he could tell because the left wing of their plane was on fire and they were slowing down. He advised him to call for escort fighters.

Incredibly the airplane continued to fly as Ashley resumed evasive maneuvers. Once they were out of missile range he took stock of the situation. The missile had exploded off their left wing and the fuel tank on that wing was missing, along with part of the wing's tip. They had lost two engines, and fire was streaming out of the wreckage where the engines had been ripped off. Fuel was also pouring out of holes throughout the left wing. Ashley noted that most of his flight instruments were not working and that they had lost cabin pressure at 30,000 feet. Their oxygen supply was vital but it must have been hit because the quantity gauge was going down. Ashley took two walkaround bottles for himself and his co-pilot Captain Gary Vickers. If the plane's supply ran out, they at least would have emergency oxygen to get the plane down to breathable altitude.

Ashley turned on the heading for U-Tapao and called again for fighter escort.

"We're here, buddy," came the reply.

Two fighters had joined them and they promised to remain as long as they were needed. One remained high while the other stayed on their wing as they descended to lower altitude. Ashley called to alert the rescue service in case they had to abandon the plane. His first concern was to get out of North Vietnam and Laos. He didn't want his crew to end up as prisoners in North Vietnam, and he knew they did not take many prisoners in Laos. Thailand was a safe haven—if they could reach it.

Ashley noted with concern that the fire in the left pod was still burning, although it appeared to be no worse. Now one of the fighters left them and the other said he would take a close look at their plane before he had to leave, too. This pilot flew alongside their left wing. "I'd better stay with you, friend. The fire is getting worse and I don't think you'll make it."

Conner unfastened his seat belt and leaned between the pilot and co-pilot to take another look at the fire. It had now spread to the fuel leaking out of the wing, and the whole left wing was burning. There was a wall of red flames starting just outside the cockpit and as high as he could see.

Ashley and Conner looked at one another quickly, and they knew it was time to bail out.

"I think I'll head downstairs," Conner said.

"Good idea," Ashley said.

Ejection seats could be fired to abandon the aircraft for the six crew members. Anyone else on board had to go down to the lower compartment and manually bail out of the hold after the navigator or radar navigator ejected. Conner quickly climbed down the ladder and started to plug in his interphone cord to learn their true situation. As he did so the red light to abandon the plane flashed on.

Stegelin fired his ejection seat and he was gone with a bang as the charge blew him and his seat from the plane.

Myers pointed to the hole left by the navigator's seat and motioned Conner to jump. He nodded, climbed over some debris, and stood on the edge of the hole, staring at the ground far below. The airplane shuddered and there were explosions as other crew members ejected. He heard another loud blast, and realized that the wing was exploding. He rolled through the opening and as soon as he was free of the plane he pulled his ripchord. He felt a sharp jerk and then his parachute opened above him. It hurt more than he had expected. Drifting earthward it was quiet and eerie. There was a full moon, the weather was clear, and he could see all around him. He searched for other parachutes and spotted three. Then he saw the bomber coming down in a descending turn to the left with its fuselage enveloped in flames as parts of the left wing descended separately. The plane exploded with a huge flash as it hit the ground.

Conner prepared to land and saw he was going to hit in a small village. He raised his legs to keep from going into a hootch. He hit hard, although he was not injured. Now he noticed blood on his right shoulder and realized that he must have been hit by a piece of shrapnel when the missile burst near them. About twenty-five Thai villagers came out of their homes and stood watching him. They were quiet and friendly and they brought water for him to drink. None spoke English so he tried to communicate in sign language that a helicopter would soon rescue him. A Marine helicopter arrived within twenty minutes and he was picked up. He had bailed out near their base at Nam Phong. All six crew members were rescued without serious injuries. They were flown first to U-Tapao and then to Guam.

Two percent of the total force of bombers was shot down but none due to enemy fighters. Some aircraft, contrary to instructions, had broken formation to dodge missiles. There were problems of communication, primarily over-saturation of radio transmissions in the target areas.

After analyzing the debriefing comments from the first day, Colonel McCarthy was convinced that mutual electronic countermeasures would reduce losses.

As the last cells of the first day's strikes were landing, the first bombers for the second day were starting their engines. Before they departed McCarthy warned crew members of the 43rd Strategic Wing that he would have to consider the court-martialing of any aircraft commander who knowingly disrupted cell integrity to evade the missiles. Such an order was distinctly unpopular. Some crews believed that they could evade the missiles.

The bombing attacks created an uproar in the nation's press and the Washington *Post*'s reaction was typical. They said in an editorial that the raids had caused millions of Americans "to cringe in shame and to wonder at their president's very sanity."

There was joy in Hanoi's Hoa Lo Prison. American prisoners jumped up and down, putting their arms around one another with tears running down their faces. Many tried to look out of their cell windows during the attacks but most were so high that it was necessary to grasp the bars and lift themselves to see out. Guards tried to smash prisoners' fingers with their rifle butts. When the guards heard the long strings of bombs going off nearby they cowered in corners. One guard, trembling like a leaf, dropped his rifle and wet his pants to the great glee of those whom he had tormented. When the bombs continued to fall that night there was no doubt that these were B-52s and the communists had been caught by surprise. There had been fighter-bomber attacks around their prison but those attacks had never generated the kind of abject fear that their guards were now experiencing. For most of the prisoners there was pride that President Nixon was keeping his word and that he would take almost any step to get them released.

Navy Captain Howard Rutledge had been a prisoner for seven years. A guard whom he called the Parrot had been convinced by his country's propaganda that all Hanoi, including the Hoa Lo Prison, would be wiped out. Rutledge and some of the other prisoners tried to reassure him that the prison was the safest place because of the skill of American fliers. The Parrot was not convinced and he went outside in search of a safer haven. When he saw the devastation in the target areas around the prison he hurried back and said he would never leave again. The prisoners comforted him by saying, "Don't worry. Stay with us. We'll protect you."

Colonel John F. Flynn, hearing bombs go off the night of December 18, sent word to all prisoners, "Pack your bags. I don't know when we're going to go home, but we're going home."

Colonel Robinson Risner, a prisoner for seven-and-a-half years, was also convinced that Nixon's decision to step up the bombing in the North, with introduction of B-52 raids against Hanoi and Haiphong, would bring about their release.

Targets for the second day included the Kinh No Railroad and Storage area on the outskirts of Hanoi. It was attacked by twenty-one planes.

Colonel McCarthy, in Major Thomas Lebar's lead aircraft, listened as the electronics officer broke in to say that two SAMs were heading for them. They were northwest of Hanoi, heading for the city. The electronics officer confirmed both missiles were tracking them. The co-pilot reported four missiles coming from the right side. Added to these pyrotechnic displays were Shrike anti-radiation missile firings that gave the bomber crews momentary concern until they were identified. They rejoiced to see something bright heading for the ground instead of at them. The pilot reported two missiles on his side. As they approached Hanoi and the radar navigator prepared to release their bombs the radio became saturated with calls of new missile firings. Once a missile was fired on the ground an area about the size of a city block was lit up by the flash. It looked each time as if a whole city block had caught fire because the flash was magnified by the clouds. As each missile broke through the clouds the large lighted area was replaced by a ring of silver fire that appeared to be the size of a basketball. This was the exhaust of the rocket's motor that grew brighter as the missile approached an aircraft. From the front quarter, a missile's exhaust took on the appearance of a silver doughnut. But they were deadly doughnuts. Those that maintained their shape and their relative position on the cockpit's window caused the most concern because that meant it was tracking your plane. Three SAMs exploded at the precise altitude of Colonel Murphy's plane but they were too far away to do any damage. Two other missiles passed close to the bomber, but exploded above them.

Two minutes prior to bombs away the SAMs were replaced by anti-aircraft fire. Large, ugly, black explosions worried them most because they were from 100 mm. guns. Smaller, multi-colored flak was lower and not as dangerous. Usually they created a silver colored explosion, followed by orange explosions clustered around the first silver burst. The tension was at its peak as SAMs exploded nearby, and sixty seconds remained before bombs away.

A report from a bomber behind them said MIGs were present so a call went out for fighters. Now there were strong SAM lock-on signals. The bomb-bay doors were open, exposing the mass of bombs inside that reflected radar energy to the missile sites and made their plane an even brighter target at which to shoot.

Ten seconds to bombs away and the electronics officer reported the strongest SAM signals of all. Crew members observed Shrike missiles streaking toward the SAM sites. Five seconds later several missile signals dropped off the air and the electronics officer reported they were no longer a threat.

Their B-52 shuddered as twenty-two tons of bombs were released and Lebar had to control the bomber with all his strength as the plane wanted to rise quickly. The B-52 was brought under control with firm hands on the stick and throttles to keep it straight and level. Lebar put his aircraft into a steep right turn away from the target. A second later a SAM exploded where their right wing had been. The turn had saved them but there were reports of more missiles on the way. It seemed to Lebar that the turn would last forever as missiles came closer. Now it was a race to see if their plane could complete the turn before a SAM reached their altitude. Finally the turn was completed and the pilot was free to make small maneuvers as other aircraft in his cell were still in their turn.

McCarthy could not help but wonder "what in hell am I doing here?" He felt sick. After all the missions had been flown he learned that he had double pneumonia.

Their B-52 maneuvered away from the target as SAMs reached their altitude but did not explode. A missile on the left and another on the right formed an arch over their aircraft as they exploded at the apex.

Below, another Shrike missile was launched by a Wild Weasel aircraft and another threat signal disappeared. McCarthy made a note to remind him to write Wing Commander Mele Vojvodich and congratulate his crews of the 388th Tactical Fighter Wing for their magnificent support.

After Lebar's plane departed the target area the SAM signals dropped off. McCarthy got his wave back together and asked for a damage assessment report. Part of his responsibility was to pass such information through encoded radio to those who had sustained damage as to where to land. This time all planes had made it through the defenses unscathed.

The second wave received minor damage but all returned. The third wave struck the Thai Nguyen Thermal Power Plant and the Ven Vien complex. Attacks against these waves were sporadic and the second night's attack was made without loss.

Strategic Air Command headquarters decided to continue the same attack plan December 20th. This night the North Vietnamese put up their heaviest defenses and several cells reported fighter engagements, while others indicated that MIGs flew parallel courses to the attackers and relayed their altitude and speed to the ground. Anti-aircraft fire was heavy but generally it fell short of the high altitude planes. During the night the North Vietnamese fired 220 SAMs at the three waves of bombers making attacks against the Yen Vien Railroad Yards and the adjacent Ai Mo Warehouse area.

All hell broke loose over the Yen Vien target. Captain Rolland A. Scott was in the first wave. He was flying with another crew as substitute pilot. Trouble was encountered early as they lost an engine on takeoff but proceeded on seven engines. In the "G" model this was not a serious problem.

Over North Vietnam Scott listened to the radio as a great deal of fighter activity was revealed. There were numerous sightings of fighters with their lights on, presumably friendly fighters. There was no SAM activity. They approached the initial point on the southeast leg and a MIG 21 appeared on their right wing. They stared with disbelief. Sure enough it *was* a MIG 21 with its lights off flying a tight formation with them. They could actually see the pilot but the enemy plane's approach had not been detected by the B-52's warning systems. The enemy fighter remained for two or three minutes and then departed. Another MIG did the same thing on their left and then he, too, departed.

Now they could see missiles approaching from the front on either side. But the electronics operator reported no uplink or downlink signals. The missiles seemed to adjust their tracks as Scott made slight corrections. He waited for each missile to get as close as he dared and then he made a hard, although small maneuver in hopes of evading them. The missiles approached in pairs and, a few seconds apart, they exploded. Some were close enough to shake their bomber. One came so near that it caused such a loud noise and violent shock wave that Scott told the crew they had been hit. After checking he was grateful to learn they had not been hit. Now they realized why those MIGs had flown formation with them: to give the missile crews on the ground the B-52's heading, altitude and airspeed. It was an old trick that the Germans had used in World War II over Europe.

On the bombing run there were no more SAMs to track although a large ball of fire erupted a few miles ahead and slowly turned to the right and descended. Scott knew a B-52 had sustained a direct hit. He learned later that the crew had ejected safely.

Scott's plane completed its bombing run and made a right turn just as missiles were directed at his plane again. He lowered the plane's nose and steepened its bank. SAMs passed him to the left and exploded above them. They had lost some altitude by this maneuver and, in attempting to climb and accelerate on seven engines, they lagged behind the others in their formation and got out of position. Fortunately there were no more SAMs but a number of enemy fighters were in the air although none was close to them. He heard another crew apparently abandoning its B-52 but over friendly territory. Then his throat constricted as he saw an explosion and fireball on the ground as another B-52 crashed. Three planes were down—the worst loss to date.

There was deep concern at Strategic Air Command Headquarters in Omaha, Nebraska, and pressure mounted from many sources to end the raids. The nation's press reported opposition, with some people saying, "Stop the carnage—we can't lose any more B-52s—it has been a blood bath." Some people termed the B-52 a BUFF—Big Ugly Fat Fellow.

General Meyer, the Strategic Air Command's head, came under heavy pressure. Many politicians in Washington were worried that the Air Force might fail, and that the United States could not bring North Vietnam to its knees through bombing. Some senior Air Force officers were concerned that if the bombing continued too many bombers would be lost and the airpower doctrine proved false. What they did not seem to understand was that if the bombing was stopped it would be construed as a failure of the concept of strategic bombing. Admiral Moorer as chairman of the Joint Chiefs of Staff was upset but he left the ultimate decision to General Meyer.

Midway in this third day's bombing, Meyer assembled his staff. He made it clear that he, and he alone, would make the decision but he polled everyone in the room. He wanted to know, "Can the crews take it?"

He was assured that they could.

"Press on!" he said.

Meanwhile, two cells of B-52Gs already en route to Hanoi were recalled from Wave 2. The losses in the first indicated that there was a pattern to these losses and near-misses. "G" models, modified with more extensive electronic countermeasures packages, had a better record of avoiding missiles. Unmodified "Gs" were neither protecting themselves nor their formations adequately and thus were bearing the brunt of losses to SAMs. These two calls totaled only six aircraft so their removal would not significantly affect the bombing results.

Wave 3, with three of its four targets in and around Hanoi, posed the second half of the nightmare for the Strategic Air Command's leaders. They had both modified and unmodified "Gs" but they were all needed to destroy their assigned targets. Twelve "Gs" had been assigned the Kinh No Complex, an area so extensive that it contained four distinct targets. To withdraw the unmodified airplanes meant that over one-half of the combined effort of Waves 2 and 3 against Hanoi would be deleted. Meyer let them proceed. He understood the risks, but the possibility of failing to complete the mission assigned to them by President Nixon was far worse.

CHAPTER 37

A Blunt, Emphatic Message

MINUTES AHEAD OF THE "G" MODELS HEADED FOR THE KINH NO COM-
plex, nine-B52Ds struck the Hanoi Railroad repair shops at Gia Lam. One
bomber was hit but its crew was able to fly to northern Laos where it
ejected and was promptly picked up by an air-sea rescue helicopter. Eight
minutes later the unmodified "Gs" attacked Kinh No and one airplane was
hit shortly after release of its bombs and it went down. Later it was learned
only two men survived as prisoners of war. Then another bomber went
down as a SAM scored a hit. This time only one man survived. Still a third
"G" went down in a blazing fireball. Captain Chris Quill's bomber, north
of Thud Ridge, saw the flash. "Good lord, what was that?" he said to his
co-pilot.

"Must have been a direct hit," Joe Grinder replied.

Quill's radar navigator Major Richard Parrish was only concerned with
getting their bombs on the target. After release, Quill turned towards the
west, and he considered putting the airplane back on automatic pilot—it
was so quiet. That would give him time to concentrate on what was
happening around the target. First, he took one more look. Looking as far
back to his left as possible he spotted two white streaks coming at them.
He put the bomber into a steep, descending right turn. Almost instantly
Master Sergeant Leo Languirand saw two traces appear on his gunnery
scope. While the bomber maneuvered, the traces continued to climb and
they were closing. For breathless seconds nothing happened and then the
two blips disappeared. The missiles had gone off just behind them.

As they headed for Laos it was quieter but near the border the pilots saw
a large explosion on the ground ahead of their plane. They decided it must
be a bomber going in.

The last bombers attacked the Hanoi petroleum storage area while a
large number of SAMs were fired at them. At last, the third mission was

over but four B-52Gs and two "Ds" had been knocked down while a third bomber was damaged. The "Gs" that were lost were all unmodified aircraft. It was obvious to commanders that a new battle plan was necessary if the Stratoforts were to continue their strikes in the Hanoi area.

Completion of these three strikes marked the end of the first phase for the Guam-based bombers. The weight of the effort for the fourth day had already been assigned to the "D" fleet at U-Tapao. This gave commanders on Guam and in the States a chance to apply their expertise to the problems the "Gs" were encountering while also zeroing in on an analysis of the tactics of the entire force.

This respite for the Guam crews was repeated on days five and seven as a continuing part of the overall plan for the second phase. U-Tapao would provide thirty bombers per day for these missions which was within their capability to handle alone. No air refueling would be needed due to the short distance and the bigger bomb loads.

On the fourth day the target was Bac Mai, a storage area at Hanoi. One crew experienced failure of its radar prior to the initial point. In attempting to change the lead this bomber became separated from the other two aircraft and a missile knocked it down.

Lieutenant Colonel William Conlee, the electronics warfare officer on Lieutenant Colonel Yuill's plane December 21, had flown the first mission. Now, as they arrived at the initial point for the Bac Mai target, he heard co-pilot Captain David Drummond say, "It looks like we'll walk on SAMs tonight." He could spot several firings ahead.

Heading to the target from the IP, ten SAMs were fired. At bombs away, they were bracketed by two missiles, one exploding to their left below them and the other to their right and above them. Shrapnel cracked Yuill's outer window glass, and started fires in their left wing and wounded him. Shrapnel had slashed through the plane also wounding Lieutenant Colonel Bernasconi, the radar navigator, Lieutenant Mayall, the navigator, and Conlee. Cabin pressure was lost by the blast along with loss of electrical power. Yuill rang the emergency bailout signal and all ejected. During Yuill's free fall, SAMs passed him. He tried to locate his aircraft but he failed to see it, and he saw no other parachutes. He was bleeding profusely from wounds in his face and arms. Two hundred feet above the ground he was fired at by small arms and immediately pounced upon when he hit the ground. They were a mixed assortment of civilian and military men and they took his gun, watch and boots. Then, stripped to his underwear he was forced to run a mile at gun point through a gauntlet of people with farm implements, clubs and bamboo poles. They broke his ribs and damaged his right knee before he was halted in front of a Russian truck and taken to Hanoi. He was kept face down but he managed to staunch the flow of blood from his wounds. Finally, he sat up and noticed an old French building. He was pushed off the truck's flatbed, falling six feet to the ground where he suffered a shoulder separation. Unable to move, he was dragged by two soldiers into the yard of the Hoa Lo Prison. He was placed in a small, solitary room in a section known as Heartbreak Hotel. With a spinal compression and other injuries he was unable to move for three days while incarcerated in solitary confinement. Christmas Day he was able to sit in an upright position, and with great effort he was able to stand for a minute or two before getting woozy. During this period he was subjected to several minor beatings and kicking sessions by his captors in an attempt to force him to his feet and get him to talk. They finally left him alone. Although he was unable to eat his Christmas meal, he drank a pot of tea.

At this point, General Johnson, Eighth Air Force commander on Guam, told his staff that the raids would continue indefinitely and that work schedules of all units would be structured to insure support for an extended commitment.

During a review of tactics it was decided to vary the routes so defenders could not establish patterns and predict their routes or altitudes.

Strategic Air Command intelligence officers had been searching for centralized storage areas for the SAM missile sites. After a thorough examination of photographs they found them and recommended that these sites be added to the target list. All eventually were added but it was not until December 26 that the bombers were assigned to them.

In the United States the nation's media started to quote losses that were two or three times the actual number. There were false charges of carpet bombing of urban areas causing the slaughter of countless civilians. This was not true and some elements of the news media played directly into the hands of the communists by reporting such falsehoods. The bombing had been the most precise in the history of strategic bombing. Some crews were lost because of straight runs ordered to protect North Vietnam's civilian population. Actually, the North Vietnamese had never shown an equal concern about civilian deaths in the South. Deaths due to these bombings, it was learned after the war, were remarkably low. Inevitably some bombs fell outside target areas, often due to B-52s that were hit by missiles over the targets. The harsh criticism in the press was particularly hard on the crews and their families. By now, eleven B-52s had been shot down, eight in the vicinity of Hanoi, but three others were able to fly to friendly territory before they bailed out.

On the fifth day, December 22, routes in and out from U-Tapao were scheduled over water because the target was in the Haiphong area. They were routed from the south off the gulf but cells then fanned out on three separate tracks. Sixty miles south of the targets the force was split along six different tracks that were staggered in time and distance to provide spacing for the bombers over their targets. None of these attacks was aimed directly at Haiphong. Three were feints along the coast as though to pass well to the south of the city. It was hoped that the communists would think this attack was headed for Hanoi. Then, thirty miles from their intended release point, every cell abruptly zeroed in on the Haiphong area.

Chaff had been laid by Air Force fighters while Navy planes struck the SAM sites. This concentration of support aircraft gave the enemy the first clue as to what was coming. But the sudden focus by the entire bomber force initially over-saturated the North Vietnamese defense system.

Bomber pilots observed only forty-three SAMs. This low number spoke well for the Navy pilot's suppression of the missile sites. As the bombers pressed their attacks, missiles increased in number and later cells experienced the heaviest pressure as the accuracy of the missiles shocked the crews. Despite these defenses, the petroleum products storage area was hit hard and the bombers left the target without loss. For the second day no B-52s were shot down and this was the first day without even any battle damage. It was an important turning point and it was good news for the U-Tapao crews.

Meanwhile, twenty-eight Guam-based bombers attacked targets in South Vietnam.

December 23 six Guam aircraft joined up on the tail end of the Thailand force to attack the Lang Dang railroad yards, forty-five miles north of Haiphong. Six other Guam aircraft struck a series of SAM sites thirty miles north of the city. Again there were no losses or damage to the bombers.

Crews were told on Guam that there would be no missions December 24 or 25 but that they should be prepared for a maximum effort on the 26th. They took advantage of the layoff to rest up and get into the spirit of the season. The base was alive with excitement as vast numbers of people turned out on Christmas Eve.

While fighting a war thousands of miles away Guam was an island living in the "lap of tropical luxury." Tourists were there in droves—mostly from Japan. Guam had become the "in" place and was particularly favored by newlyweds. Consequently, seeing other people having a good time in a completely carefree mood was disconcerting to say the least to the crews caught up in a war. A song the crews adopted as their theme song was guaranteed to bring down the house any time it was played. It was called "Yellow River." There was nothing special about the tune, but it was the last song the band played on the first night of the raids. The next night, December 19, there had been no losses. Some crew members suggested the song was a good luck charm and that it should be played as the last song every night. When a band played it crew members sang along or clapped in time to the music. As the raids continued, the singing got louder and it was played often each night. By the end of the raids, the 43rd Strategic Wing had adopted it as their theme song.

Christmas Eve at U-Tapao—north of Bangkok—holiday fever was at a peak. The crews could visualize the bright lights and excitement of Bangkok, one of the most cosmopolitan cities in the Orient, but they could not go there until the raids were completed. And there was no standdown for them over Christmas. The pressure had been alleviated somewhat as the Guam bombers shared some of the strikes on the 23rd, and supplemental crews were shipped from Guam.

For the third straight day targets in the immediate Hanoi area were avoided and the strikes diversified to keep North Vietnam's defenses uncertain as to where they would hit next. After two days of penetration from the gulf, the bomber stream from U-Tapao next was sent to the north across Laos to a point northwest of North Vietnam's heaviest defenses. The force then split into two waves for runs on a southerly heading against the Thai Nguyen and Kep railroad yards, forty miles northeast of Hanoi. Additional tactics were used on the bombing run to deceive the SAM-2 crews. In a final deception, waves were split in half during post-target maneuvers as each group exited by varied headings and turn points. Then all planes were funneled back into the common departure route over the Gulf of Tonkin. New tactics now outpaced defenses and Airman First Class Albert Moore got another MIG with his tail guns. Crews landed at U-Tapao in the early hours of Christmas morning and it was a somber day for everyone. While the fliers rested, ground crews worked throughout the day to get the planes ready for another strike.

The basic plan for the December 26 raid was unlike earlier maximum efforts. Attacks were spread over the entire night to permit ten separate bomber waves on nine separate targets. Each wave was assigned the same initial time on target and all subsequent attacks were completed in fifteen minutes for maximum impact on the enemy's defenses. It was hoped that North Vietnam's command and control system would become saturated. Spacing between cells, as well as altitudes of various cells, would be modified in each wave. Electronic countermeasures were also significantly changed. Unmodified "Gs", with their weaker electronic countermeasures capability, had proved to be too vulnerable in the immediate Hanoi area. For the remainder of the attacks it was decided that they would concentrate attacks in other areas and avoid Hanoi.

Major Stocker, who had led the first B-52D wave the first night, was selected to lead the first wave. His bomber would be exposed inside the SAM defenses at Hanoi for the longest time of any strike force during the entire campaign. With him would be Colonel McCarthy as airborne commander. To lead another B-52D wave was Major Tom Lebar. Waves 2 and 6 would be flown by "G" models led by Major Louis Falck and Woody O'Donnell. Wave 7, also "G" aircraft, would be led by Major Glenn Robertson. There would be seventy-seven aircraft from Guam plus forty-two bombers of Waves 4 and 5 from the "D" fleet at U-Tapao.

"D" models from both bases were assigned to strike Hanoi simultaneously in four waves from different directions. Primarily the targets involved key railroad yards and power complexes. Flight separation between the northern and southern streams was only seven miles as seventy-two bombers converged on a relatively small area around Hanoi. With targets only three miles apart, the fifth wave coming from the northwest with a 100-knot tailwind would be making a ground speed of over nine miles a minute. Therefore, a twenty-second overfly of the target would put one of these aircraft on a near collision course with an aircraft coming in from the northeast. Concentration of the bombing effort was crucial to success to the mission and the first cells in each wave had to release their bombs at exactly the same time. Navigation had to be precise to avoid conflict with other bomber waves and to make good each timing point.

Colonel McCarthy, riding with Major William Stocker's lead crew, looked at the aircraft's serial number on the side just before he scrambled up the crew's entry hatch. It was 680. He realized this bomber had been manufactured in 1955. It had flown a lot of missions and it was showing its age. Those seventeen years of hard flying had left their indelible mark.

Thousands gathered as Stocker's bomber taxied out to the end of the runway. Many had worked twenty-four hours straight to prepare the bombers for this mission. They should have been in bed but they wanted to see the results of their labors.

Normally a B-52 makes a rolling takeoff, turning the corner from the taxiway and starting its run. Since his aircraft was a leader, and all other air base traffic had been banned, he requested permission to taxi into position and hold until he got the signal to depart. His request was approved. The minute before takeoff Stocker looked out at the B-52s lined up nose-to-tail as far as his eyes could see. It was an awesome sight, undoubtedly the greatest number of B-52s ever assembled for takeoff at one time.

He heard a Pan American jetliner call Agana Approach Control. This was Guam's commercial airfield and the only other concrete runway available so it was being held open in case of a B-52 emergency.

"Agana approach, this is . . ." The Pan Am pilot described his flight number and designation. "Request landing instructions, over."

"Pan Am, this is Agana. You can expect up to a three-hour delay. No emergency. Tactical considerations."

The Pan American pilot's reaction was spontaneous and included his full reportoire of epithets.

Two hours and twenty-nine minutes after the first bomber started its takeoff roll, the last was airborne. A Russian trawler that maintained a position off the end of the runway also observed the launch of the strike force. Its radio message would reach Hanoi long before the bombers. There was no secret now that the B-52s were coming, or their destination.

North Vietnam had had two days to recover from the last strike and main targets around Hanoi had not been hit for five days. Ground defenders had used the Christmas respite to their advantage. Spare missiles had been brought out of storage and many were installed at new sites.

Fourteen hundred miles from Guam, as aerial tankers prepared to support the strike force, a C-141 inbound to Kadena, Okinawa, had to make an emergency landing. This delayed the departure of the tankers assigned to refuel the "D" models by twenty minutes. Wave 1 was in the middle of refueling when word was flashed that the tankers would be fifteen minutes late for the following wave. By the book, the mission should have been scrubbed. But the success of the mission hinged on having all aircraft on time over the target. In flying the scheduled refueling track, there was no way that Wave 3 could catch up.

As airborne commander, McCarthy called Major Tom Lebar to discuss alternatives. If the refueling point was moved closer to the incoming tankers, some of the time could be made up. If Lebar then took his force on a modified routing and increased its airspeed, while Waves 1 and 2 headed southwest past the Philippines, Lebar's force might possibly catch up with the rest of the strike force as it turned north. For such a change in plans to be successful Lebar's navigation team of Major Vernon Amundson and Captain James Strait had to replan the course within fifteen minutes, and determine rendezvous points with the tankers and the following cells. This would have been a complex and lengthy job to plan on the ground. In the air, it seemed almost impossible. Lebar also faced the problem of compressing his wave, now spread out from refueling. He believed the change was possible if the winds and the weather remained as predicted, all aircraft got their fuel without any problems, and if their over-water navigation was perfect.

Wave 3 was instructed to make the attempt. If they could not get into position by the time Wave 1 crossed the 17th parallel heading north the mission would be scrubbed. The pressure on Lebar's crew was enormous. Fighter and other support aircraft would be taking off from their bases in Thailand, along with the supporting tankers, while Navy and Marine planes would be in the air prior to that time. The massive air armada would have to turn back if the bombing waves could not get together. Much depended on Wave 3's crews. To complete the mission they all had to have fuel. The stream of bombers from the east, scheduled to meet a similar stream of tankers from the north, had to rendezvous at a predetermined time over a specific point in the ocean. This had been acknowledged before the mission as a difficult task but now there was a fifteen-minute discrepancy in arrival times.

In a well-coordinated move, each cell within each wave began a series of airspeed and course adjustments to compensate for the problem, systematically relaying each plane's action backwards and forwards in the stream and passing it to the tanker force. Theoretically, aircraft could meet at adjusted points and times, but the problem was not that simple. Aircraft speeds and the relationship of planes and formations was no longer according to plan. Each crew had to improve his navigation.

Despite the changes, all rendezvous points were achieved and fuel was transferred from the tankers to the bombers.

Now a major problem developed. The original plan had called for the strike force to be over all targets within fifteen minutes. But they were running fifteen minutes behind schedule. Every attention was focused on getting each plane to the target on time. If not, pre-and post-target maneuvers would become as much of a hazard as enemy defenses.

To those on the ground it looked like a highway at night as each wave crossed into South Vietnam and headed north over the gulf. There was a stream of rotating beacons on top of each aircraft as far as eyes could see. In the bombers, the crews observed radio silence. The quiet was eerie, but each aircraft's flashing light was a comforting sight reminding other crews that they were not alone. Soon they would meet more planes using the land route from Thailand.

As Wave 1 headed north over the Gulf of Tonkin, Colonel McCarthy heard Lebar instruct his wave to reach the join-up point on time.

Once across the 17th parallel they were committed. This was the last point at which McCarthy or higher headquarters could recall the bombers. From here on absolute radio silence would be maintained. Radio calls were permitted only if one of the bombers were jumped by a MIG and needed fighter assistance.

McCarthy noted Haiphong off their left wing, and he could see Navy planes working over the SAM and anti-aircraft sites. This place was lit up like a Christmas tree. They flew northeast of Haiphong and headed for the IP where they turned southwest towards Hanoi. There, at their first landfall, they encountered heavy flak. Ugly explosions came closer as 100 mm. guns tried to reach them. They were at a lower altitude than on any other mission and therefore more vulnerable. The closer they came to their IP the more intense and closer came the explosions.

Stocker turned his bomber towards the target and they received their first SAM signal. Captain Donald Redmon, the electronics warfare officer, reported three strong signals tracking their aircraft. Stocker ordered his cell to start a SAM-threat maneuver. Meanwhile, their navigator Major William Francis confirmed the predicted 100-knot headwinds. SAMs lifted off below them and headed up. All six of the first missiles appeared to maintain their relative position versus their bomber. Airman First Class Kenneth Schell reported three more SAMs from his tail gunner's position heading their way.

With the whole force on the bombing run, McCarthy had nothing to do but count the number of SAMs launched. Co-pilot Lieutenant Ronald Thomas reported four more coming up on the right side and two at his position. Stocker reported three more on the left as the first six started to explode. Some were much too close.

McCarthy listened to the navigation team downstairs as they made an unhurried check list. It sounded like a practice run back home as Captain Joseph Gangwish, the radar navigator, calmly discussed the identification of their aiming point with Major Francis.

One hundred seconds before bombs away the cockpit lit up like daylight from the rocket exhaust of a SAM that had come up under their nose. The electronics officer had reported an extremely strong signal and he was correct but it was hard to judge a miss distance at night. This one appeared to be less than fifty feet. The missile's proximity fuse should have detonated the warhead, but it did not. McCarthy breathed shakily knowing, as he said later, that somebody upstairs was looking out for them.

McCarthy quit counting SAMs after he reached twenty-six. They were coming too fast. Evidently the communist gunners were firing a barrage of missiles to make the lead element, or wave, turn back from its intended course. Now, the formation stopped maneuvering for the final seconds because it had to remain straight and level for release of their bombs.

At bombs away, McCarthy likened their situation to being in the middle of a fireworks factory in the process of blowing up as their radio was saturated by SAM calls and MIG warnings. As the bomb-bay doors closed, several missiles exploded nearby. Others could be seen arcing over and starting their descent before detonating. If their proximity fuses did not find a target the missiles were set to self-destruct by the end of a pre-determined time interval. McCarthy noted with satisfaction that the bombs had been dropped at the exact second of their orders.

Minutes after departing the immediate Hanoi area there was a brilliant explosion off to their left rear as a B-52D blew up in midair. All radios went silent to listen for emergency beepers that were automatically actuated when a parachute opened. They heard two, possibly three. Actually, they learned later that four men escaped the plane's explosion and were picked up. Now there was an emergency call from another aircraft that was heading for the gulf. Fighters were vectored to escort the crippled bomber to safety as its pilot reported his plane was losing altitude and he was having difficulty controlling it.

On their withdrawal there was an additional barrage of SAMs. It seemed an eternity before their gunner reported that a missile had gone over the top of their aircraft and exploded out of range. This was their first encounter with missiles.

A cell in one wave reported MIGs closing in and requested fighter support. McCarthy ordered all upper rotating beacons and tail lights turned off. As the Air Force fighters came in the MIG took off. It had probably been pacing the B-52s for the gunners on the ground. Whenever an enemy fighter thought he could get away with it he would sneak in and try to make a kill.

The plane that had reported it was in trouble now was over water and heading south towards friendly ships. Captain James Turner radioed that his B-52 was flyable and that he would try to make it to U-Tapao. But his crew didn't make it. His plane crashed just beyond the runway. This was a tragic loss after such an heroic effort. Only the gunner and the co-pilot survived. Captain Brent Diefenbach, who had landed a few minutes earlier, pulled Lieutenant Robert Hymel from the wreckage. Technical Sergeant Spencer Grippin escaped the burning wreck when the tail section broke free on impact.

After Colonel McCarthy returned to Guam he was sick and weary. His pneumonia had settled into both lungs. After examining him a doctor went away shaking his head, muttering about idiot pilots who fly with pneumonia. McCarthy had reduced the pain by taking 100 percent oxygen during the flight but it took him six months before he was fully recovered.

This proved to be the most successful mission of the series and only one bomber was lost.

On the evening of December 26 the walls of the Hao Lo Prison in Hanoi shook with the bombing. This was a great encouragment to the prisoners. SAMs were fired from the roof, using the prison as a sanctuary from attack.

The next morning ashen-faced Vietnamese guards came into Lieutenant Colonel William Conlee's room and asked him how close the bombs were and what planes were dropping them.

Conlee, who had been shot down on the first raid, replied, "Very close, and you know already." He smiled. This was a mistake because he was badly beaten, the worst he ever experienced. It was obvious that the North Vietnamese were terrified of the B-52s and struck out in fear and frustration at any available target. Conlee was moved to another room where he found his crew had all survived, despite their wounds. Their meals were skimpy and primarily of turnip soup. To the daily lies spread by their guards of the vast number of bombers shot down, they responded with laughs. Even some of the Vietnamese guards were hard pressed to keep straight faces.

It was evident that a two-ship cell—in cases where other aircraft aborted—was not adequate for protection. In the future, if an airplane dropped out of a formation en route to a target, it was decided that the remaining two should join the cell ahead or behind them. Deployment of chaff proved effective. There were numerous reports of SAM-2 detonations when the missiles penetrated chaff clouds. Other changes in tactics were made as a result of suggestions by the combat crews.

The mission on the 27th was a replay of the one the night before, except on a smaller scale, and without attacks against Haiphong. As it turned out the port city had been bombed for the last time. Actually, planners were running out of suitable strategic targets. The bombing had been more accurate than predicted, and North Vietnam was unable to repair damage as quickly as expected.

Morale was high after the December 27 raid because damage assessment photographs for the first time showed the enormous destructiveness of their attacks. And, even more helpful to lift their spirits were news photos showing that friends were still alive although incarcerated in Hanoi's prisoner-of-war camps.

At Strategic Air Command headquarters General Meyer wanted to insure that the SAM sites were destroyed as quickly as possible, even if it meant using B-52s to do the job. There was pressure from Washington and the public because of the losses suffered by his command. One missile site had been a target on the 27th but it had survived the attack, and two B-52s had been lost in this raid.

Although many tactics looked simple on paper, actually they were complex. Pilots had to manhandle the 400,000-pound B-52D because, unlike later models, it did not have power-boosted controls. It took old-fashioned muscle to fly precise formations or make maneuvers with a "D" airplane. It was like driving an eighteen-wheel truck without power steering, air brakes or automatic transmission in downtown Washington during the rush hour.

There was criticism that the Strategic Air Command had used stereotyped thinking and had been slow to change tactics. This was not entirely true. In the past eleven days they had revolutionized modern bomber tactics. Many aircraft commanders had less than 1,500 total flying hours, and some had less than 100 hours as aircraft commanders. For a bomber pilot who routinely flew 25-hour missions, or even longer, this amounted to very little time in the air as an aircraft commander. Their success over North Vietnam is a tribute to their skill and their attitude. They proved that relatively inexperienced combat crews could execute new or revised tactics flawlessly for the first time without ever having practiced them.

On the tenth day, six waves went out from U-Tapao against five targets. Most were in the Hanoi area while others bombed the Lang Dang railroad yards. This last target was a key choke point in the supply routes from China and received more attention in the last days than any other target as every target was successfully attacked and without loss. No MIGs were encountered but an American fighter was shot down. Twenty-eight aircraft attacked targets in southern North Vietnam, Laos, Cambodia and South Vietnam.

North Vietnam did not experience anywhere near the full punishment it might have received because attacks were limited to strategic targets and they soon became scarce.

As fliers returned from their missions on the tenth day to Guam the last aircraft was being loaded for the eleventh strike.

December 29th the command was still geared to an indefinite campaign but later in the day General Johnson notified all crews that bombing operations north of the 20th parallel would be terminated following that day's mission. He said appropriate damage levels had been achieved and the communists were unwilling or unable to repair past damage. Actually, there were no more worthwhile targets left in the immediate Hanoi or Haiphong areas. But there were two lucrative SAM storage targets as well as the Lang Dang railroad yards. This last mission proved to be a carbon copy of the strike the day before. No aircraft were lost or damaged for the second night in a row. One MIG pilot made a half-hearted attempt to engage a bomber but he was unsuccessful.

Bob Hope and his troop of entertainers came to Guam December 31 on the homeward leg of their overseas circuit. His weary troupe played to an equally weary audience but they were called back four times beyond the normal show time.

In eleven days, thirty-four targets had been bombed above the 20th parallel and 15,000 tons of bombs had been dropped. Sixteen hundred military structures were either destroyed or damaged and 372 rolling stock met the same fate. Three million gallons of fuel were destroyed—a fourth of North Vietnam's reserves—and 80 percent of her electrical power production was destroyed. North Vietnam's imports were reduced from 160,000 tons per month to 30,000. There were probably 1,242 missiles fired, or a conservative estimate of 885, and only 24 made hits on the bombers for a 2.7 percent success rate of launches versus hits. Of the twenty-four missiles that hit aircraft, only fifteen B-52s were actually lost. This was a kill rate of 1.7 percent for the number of SAMs launched.

The quality of the airmen who flew the B-52s made the difference. This bomber had been designed in 1949, and was first flown three years later. Despite their valor, there were still some Americans so concerned about the people of North Vietnam that they urged President Nixon to accept any terms to end the war.

Although fifteen B-52s were lost, 94 percent of the Stratofortresses released their bombs on assigned targets. These losses actually were far lower than expected, and considerably less than comparable World War II strikes deep into enemy territory.

The Thailand crews flew 45 percent of the missions, although they made up less than a third of the available aircraft at Guam and U-Tapao.

Of greatest importance, for eleven tense days and nights the United States tactical and strategic air forces had delivered a blunt, emphatic message to the North Vietnamese. They proved by their immediate response that they accepted it with the utmost seriousness.

CHAPTER 38

Ceasefire

THE STRAGETIC BOMBING OF NORTH VIETNAM WAS ALMOST UNIVER-
sally condemned by the world's press. In the United States Congress
criticism mounted, and President Nixon had few defenders. Generally the
bombing was termed indiscriminate carpet bombing of heavily populated
areas. This was not true. Even the North Vietnamese claimed at most that
only 1,600 people died. Such losses, compared to the bombing of German
and Japanese cities in World War II, hardly rated the term terror bombing. It is obvious now that the media over-reacted and that their reports
were based on inadequate and false information.

Two days after the start of the bombing a spokesman for the North
Vietnamese made only a mild protest December 20 when he rejected the
American charge of frivolity and adjourned the technical meeting three
days later.

The magnitude of the bombing effort shocked the communist leadership. For the first time the full weight of America's aerial might had
been unleashed and, with their factories destroyed and their harbors
mined, they quickly became more amenable to reason.

The American government had insisted December 27 that it would not
stop the bombing until technical meetings were resumed January 2, and
that a meeting between Kissinger and Le Duc Tho must be set for January
8 with a time limit on negotiations.

The North Vietnamese responded quickly—in less than twenty-four
hours—and the next day it announced its approval of the American
proposals and asserted its "constantly serious negotiating attitude."

The communists were advised December 29 that as of 7:00 P.M. that
night the bombing would be stopped. They were sternly warned that the
United States would make only one final effort to settle their dispute
within the framework of the October agreement. An American spokesman

573

said that its negotiators could only spend four days and that any repetition of the procedures at other meetings would lead to the collapse of the talks. This statement was announced December 30.

The Democratic caucus in the House of Representatives voted January 2, 1973, 154 to 75 to cut off all funds for Indochinese military operations contingent upon the safe withdrawal of American forces and the release of all prisoners. They made no provision for a ceasefire. The Senate Democratic caucus passed a similar resolution 36 to 12. Neither resolution was helpful and members who voted for the resolutions acted disgracefully.

In a response to a letter from President Nixon, reiterating the conditions for which the United States would settle, President Thieu January 7 urged Nixon to instruct Kissinger to put forward his concerns but he stopped short of endorsing the program, and he did not say he would refuse to sign such an agreement.

The breakthrough in negotiations came on the second day of renewed talks in Paris. January 9 it quickly became apparent to the American delegation that Le Duc Tho had come to settle. Kissinger reported to Nixon, "We celebrated the president's birthday today by making a major breakthrough in the negotiations. In sum, we settled all the outstanding questions in the text of the agreement, made major progress on the method of signing the agreement, and made a constructive beginning on the associated understandings."

Nixon's firmness had paid off. He responded to this news by saying that this was the "best birthday present I have had in sixty years."

Events now proceeded more smoothly and January 13 a draft agreement was completed, together with all understandings and protocols. There was a provision for continued military support to Saigon and the demilitarized zone was reaffirmed in precise terms according to the provisions established in the Geneva Accords in 1954. One provision was added that the parties to the agreement would undertake to refrain from using Cambodia and Laos "to encroach on the sovereignty and security of one another and of other countries." This was aimed to prevent using these countries as sanctuaries by the North Vietnamese. The agreement called for an immediate ceasefire in place throughout Vietnam, withdrawal of all remaining American troops—by now down to 27,000—and release of all prisoners of war throughout Indochina. Infiltration by the North Vietnamese was prohibited and there would be international supervision. The 17th parallel was again made the demarcation line. The matter of a political settlement between North and South was left to them for future negotiation.

Le Duc Tho agreed to arrange a ceasefire in Laos after consultation with communist forces in that country. In fact, the Pathet Lao were totally subordinate to North Vietnam.

The North Vietnamese communist leader refused to be specific about Cambodia. He claimed that North Vietnam had less influence over the Cambodian communists—the Khmer Rouge. It is now known that he was telling the truth. The United States intervened by calling upon Cambodian President Lon Nol for the fifth time in three years to arrange a ceasefire and to cease all combat operations.

Although the Americans and the North Vietnamese had agreed to terms of the ceasefire, President Thieu still had not done so. Nixon was determined to force him to agree. He told Kissinger, "Brutality is nothing. You have never seen it if this son-of-a-bitch doesn't go along, believe me."

Kissinger's deputy, General Haig, delivered a letter from Nixon to Thieu January 16. In it the president summed up the advantages of the agreement and he listed the improvements that had been achieved. He threatened that the United States would sign the agreement with North Vietnam on its own if Thieu did not go along. He told South Vietnam's president that he would explain publicly that the Vietnamese government was obstructing peace. He said the result would be inevitable and there would be an immediate termination of United States economic and military assistance that could not be forestalled by a change of personnel in his government. "We hope," he said, "that after all our two countries have shared and suffered together in the conflict, we will stay together to preserve the peace and reap its benefits."

Haig was instructed to tell Thieu that his answer was required by the evening of January 17. Thieu still complained that the draft lacked balance. He admitted his armed forces could handle the North Vietnamese in the South, but he said their continued presence was a psychological challenge that he was duty bound to resist.

Thieu handed Haig a letter from Nixon January 17 asking one more effort to bring about changes, this time in the protocols.

In reply, Nixon repeated his threats in the previous message and demanded a reply by the morning of January 20. If Thieu did not comply, Nixon said, his action or lack of action would be considered as a refusal. He said the responsibility rested with the government of Vietnam.

Thieu replied on the deadline—Nixon's inaguaration day for a second term—that he was sending Foreign Minister Lam to Paris to take personal charge of the final round of negotiations. This was a face-saving formula indicating that he would sign the agreement although he still demanded a few textual changes.

Nixon replied that he would need Thieu's answer by noon the next day or else he would brief his legislative leaders that Thieu had refused to go along.

President Nixon did promise Thieu January 21 that if he signed the agreement he would intercede more vigorously with the United States Congress for continuing aid to South Vietnam and he pledged that the United States would react vigorously to any serious violation of the ceasefire by North Vietnam.

After consultations with officials of his government Thieu agreed that day but requested some unilateral statements by the United States that it recognized his government as South Vietnam's legal government and that North Vietnam had no right to maintain troops there. These requests were consistent with the agreement and Nixon gave him such assurance. Thieu then wrote a letter of acceptance to Nixon and recommended a summit conference right after the agreement was signed.

Kissinger returned to Paris January 22, and learned that President Johnson had just died. The following day Le Duc Tho kept insisting upon ironclad assurances of American economic aid and generally made himself obnoxious right to the end. This was a matter that Kissinger refused to discuss until the agreement was signed, reminding the communist leader that economic aid had to be approved by Congress. The agreement was formalized by initialing various texts with their improvised closing statements. It was officially signed January 27 by the four parties and a ceasefire went into effect at 8:00 A.M. Saigon time, January 28, 1973.

Prior to the ceasefire the United States had approved financial and military support for 1,090,000 members of South Vietnam's armed forces for 1972, authorizing an additional 10,000 for the following year. The United States had also rushed shipments to South Vietnam before the agreement was signed, but so did the communists in North Vietnam to their cadres in the South. To make up for their staggering losses in the 1972 spring offensive North Vietnam had sent 148,000 replacements to the South. Although it is impossible to arrive at an exact figure, it is believed that the North Vietnamese Army lost 190,000 men during 1972, and 132,000 were killed in action.

To cope with the deteriorating military situation in 1972 the Saigon government had proclaimed martial law, drastically limited draftee deferments, and placed a ban on overseas travel for male citizens from age thirteen to forty-three. President Thieu had been given full legislative power by the National Assembly for the six-month period from July to December, 1972, in matters of defense and national economy. Press censorship was imposed and local elections had been cancelled. Instead of elections, province chiefs received instructions to reorganize their local administrations and to complete the appointment of village chiefs within two months.

By the fall of 1972 the North Vietnamese had controlled the demilitarized zone, a great part of the unpopulated mountain regions of South Vietnam and twenty-one base areas. Control of these areas was part of basic communist strategy to maintain positions intermixed with the South Vietnamese Army in an intricate pattern that ultimately would permit them to gain control of all of South Vietnam.

On the eve of negotiations to reach a ceasefire agreement, South Vietnamese Marines had launched an attack against the Cua Viet Naval Base to deny the communists an opportunity to attack their forces along the northern front lines, and to acquire a position from which the South's armed forces could observe river traffic to the occupied city of Dong Ha and to provide a river route to Quang Tri City. Despite intense United States air and naval support, South Vietnamese Marines were held back by strong enemy resistance. The base was secured, however, a few hours before the ceasefire. Units of the North Vietnamese Army counter-attacked and the South Vietnamese Marines were forced out of their newly won positions although they inflicted a thousand casualties on the communists.

The seaport of Sa Huynh, an important supply entry point from the South China Sea, was linked by a mountain corrider to western high country. This corridor marked the boundary between I Corps and II Corps. January 26, 1973, the North Vietnamese 2nd Division massed an attack against the seaport and overwhelmed it two days later. The following day the communists extended their attacks to the north to the Duc Tho district. The South Vietnamese 2nd Division under Brigadier General Tran Van Nhut was sent into action in a brutal and decisive counter-attack. Sa Huynh was recaptured February 16, and casualties on both sides were heavy.

The communist representative on the four-party joint military commission in Saigon demanded an invesigation, claiming that the takeover occurred after the ceasefire, while neglecting to mention that their capture of Sa Huynh had taken place before the ceasefire was signed. In the last unanimous opinion expressed by the International Commission on Control and Supervision, members sided with South Vietnam. As a result, the head of the Polish delegation was summarily dismissed for not following the party line.

During a press conference, Kissinger was queried as to whether the bombing of North Vietnam and the mining of its harbors had ended the war. "I was asked in October whether the bombing or mining of May 9 brought about a breakthrough in October, and I said then I did not want to speculate on North Vietnam's motives. I have too much trouble analyzing our own. I will give the same answer to your question, but I will say that there was a deadlock which was described in the middle of December, and there was a rapid movement when negotiations resumed on a technical level on January 3 and on the substantive level of January 8. These facts have to be analyzed by each person by himself."

Why he chose this roundabout way of expressing himself only Kissinger knows, but his words are pure gobbledegook. Throughout the bombing it was significant that the North Vietnamese never broke off their communications with the United States government, even when the bombing was at its peak and causing the most destruction. In the final analysis it was North Vietnam and not the United States that sought resumption of negotiations on a serious basis.

Shortly after the ceasefire the United States established the Defense Attaché Office in Saigon with Major General John E. Murray in charge. He was given responsibility to manage American military affairs and his office replaced the Military Assistance Command for Vietnam at Tan Son Nhut that was inactivated March 29, 1973. Instead of American military men and women, the office hired civilian contractors to perform many functions with South Vietnam's armed forces. More than half of these civilians were employed to train South Vietnamese military units. Defense attaché officers scrupulously avoided advice on military operations to abide by terms of the ceasefire.

The United States now officially ended its combat role, although a total of 209 military personnel remained—50 officers from all services at the Defense Attaché Office, and 159 Marine guards assigned to the American embassy in Saigon, plus the four Consul General offices at Da Nang, Nha Trang, Binh Hoa and Can Tho.

Remnants of American airpower remained in Southeast Asia. B-52 bombers and their tankers were still at U-Tapao while fighters, attack bombers and transports were based elsewhere in Thailand. Although a decision had been made to remove them during the fiscal years 1976, the South Vietnamese were not informed. This was done deliberately because the presence of American planes in Thailand gave the South Vietnamese hope they might be used if they were ever needed. Most South Vietnamese refused to believe the Americans would not return if they got into trouble.

When the ceasefire went into effect the North Vietnamese had 293,120 combat troops in South Vietnam. More were available above the demilitarized zone in North Vietnam.

The communist's so-called Central Office for South Vietnam jubilantly claimed that the treaty was an historic milestone and a great communist victory. Its leaders claimed the way was now cleared for a violent overthrow of South Vietnam's government.

In the North, young communist recruits continued to be drafted and an estimated two hundred thousand were readied to reinforce North Viet-nam's army units in the South.

Navy Captain Jeremiah P. Denton was the first man off the plane at Clark Air Force Base in the Philippines February 12, 1973, as the airlift of American prisoners began. He said, "We are honored to have had the opportunity to serve our country under difficult circumstances. We are profoundly grateful to our commander in chief, and to our nation for this day. God bless America."

Most men refrained from immediate comment about their ordeal, but their pride in their country and their belief in the war effort were recurring themes. It soon became clear, however, that they had suffered inhumanely at the hands of the North Vietnamese and had been tortured by their captors.

Navy Lieutenant Commander Everett Alvarez, captured in August, 1964, during the American retaliatory air strikes after the Gulf of Tonkin incident, was the first American pilot shot down in the war. Upon landing at Travis Air Force Base in California, he said, "God bless the President and God bless you, Mr. and Mrs. America, you did not forget us."

The reluctance of the men to discuss details of their ordeal stemmed from fears that they might jeopardize the release of those men still in custody.

Navy Captain Harry T. Jenkins, Jr., spoke out against the anti-war protesters in San Diego February 23. Of those who visited Hanoi during the war, he said, "I think they shamed our nation in the eyes of the enemy."

Air Force Colonel Robinson Risner, a prisoner for seven-and-a-half years, said three days later that he believed that war dissenters "kept us in prison an extra year or two, not just the people demonstrating but the people who were bad-mouthing our government and our policies."

Some freely admitted they had made anti-war statements in North Vietnam, but most called them not voluntary. Few of them repudiated their comments. A very small number of Americans not only disgraced their country but themselves by their anti-American statements.

Commander James B. Stockdale had been a prisoner for over seven years. Upon his release he said that in December, 1972, he could sense that the B-52 raids had at last broken the enemy's will. He reported that there was shock on the faces of the guards as each night's raids went on and fewer SAM missiles were available to retaliate. Right then, he said emphatically, we had defeated the Vietnamese in the North and then we threw it away at the peace table.

The Nixon administration faced a growing problem as Vice President

Spiro T. Agnew was investigated on allegations of conspiracy, extortion, bribery and tax fraud by the United States Attorney in Baltimore, Maryland. Agnew denied all allegations, saying, "I have nothing to hide."

In South Vietnam, the National Liberation Front had a legitimate national status with a government, an army and a national territory. In all respects, except reality, the National Liberation Front was given a political entity equal to the authority of the government of South Vietnam. Never since 1954 had the communists enjoyed such a strong political and military posture. In effect, the United States had forced a coalition government on South Vietnam—something its leaders had said it would never accept.

The government of South Vietnam worsened the problem when President Thieu proved unable to hold his country together to forestall a major political and military showdown with the communists. Long suspected of dictatorial tendencies, he failed to foster and strengthen his nation's solidarity with its disparate groups. The year before he had used his authority to close twenty-four newspapers, and street demonstrations had been outlawed. Even worse, his major criterion for military leadership was loyalty to himself—and not ability.

North Vietnam quickly demonstrated the path she would follow by ignoring the restrictive provisions of the ceasefire agreement that did not suit her purposes. Her leaders refused to deploy teams to oversee the ceasefire and would not pay the prescribed share of the commission's expenses, including the political negotiations in Paris and the two-party Joint Military Commission talks in Saigon. Her leaders now made demands for the overthrow of Thieu's government as a pre-condition for any renewed talks. And, North Vietnam started infiltration of more troops, and expanded her army's weapons and armor in the South. Communist units overran several areas that were clearly held by South Vietnam at the time of the ceasefire. Despite these setbacks for South Vietnam, Vietnamization continued.

In the North, due to the bombing of strategic targets and the mining of its harbors, a severe food shortage developed in the early months of 1973.

During a Kissinger visit to Hanoi in mid-February, he met first with Le Duc Tho and then with Prime Minister Pham Van Dong. It was apparent to Kissinger that North Vietnam had no intention of making the Paris Accords one that it would observe. Violations of the ceasefire agreement materialized in the South, and Kissinger realized that the North Vietnamese withdrawal from Laos and Cambodia, spelled out in Article 20 calling for it to be unconditional, would have to await not only a ceasefire but also a political settlement in both countries. Article 20 specifically stipulated that "foreign countries" should end all military activities in Laos and Cambodia. And Le Duc Tho had agreed that "foreign" meant American and North Vietnamese troops. Cambodia's freedom was doomed by this North Vietnamese attitude, and so was Laos.

Kissinger reported to Nixon that North Vietnam had two basic choices. It would use the agreement as an offensive weapon or it could seek their objectives through gradual evolution. The communists never had any intention of seeking the second alternative.

Kissinger traveled to Peking where he met Chairman Mao and Premier Chou En-lai. Their meeting was cordial and resulted in the establishment of "liaison offices." This was one step below formal diplomatic recognition. It was apparent to Kissinger during his China visit that the Chinese were splitting with North Vietnam's leaders. In regard to Cambodia, China was giving its support to former Cambodian leader Prince Sihanouk. The Chinese were concerned that a complete communization of Indochina would give North Vietnam and its Russian ally control of the region.

The seeds of democratization that had been thrown to the wind with such goodwill by Cambodia's Lon Nol government had returned a poor harvest. Divisions among the nation's leadership had worsened the situation since 1972. As a result, the personal conflict between its leaders had become irreconcilable at a time when the North Vietnamese had succeeded in uniting its forces in a solid front. The gates to Phnom Penh not only were wide open, but they were swung even wider by the enemies of the government in power. There was military dissatisfaction due to a stoppage or slowing of the payment of salaries. There was insufficient rice to feed the soldiers, and decorations and promotions were passed out to military personnel in combat in a totally unfair manner.

During the past year the strategy practiced by the North Vietnamese Army in Cambodia had been marked by a movement toward communization of the country by the Khmer Rouge that had operated since 1970. Now there was open civil war and it compounded South Vietnam's problems. Even worse was the infiltration of 30,000 North Vietnamese troops into South Vietnam from Laos in May.

President Thieu visited the United States from April 2–5. His reception by American officials was reserved but he remained dignified throughout what must have been an ordeal. At San Clemente, Nixon made a polite speech that referred to South Vietnam's capacity to defend itself—dubious under the circumstances of a full-scale North Vietnamese attack with their new Russian weapons. In a final communiqué after their private talks, Thieu received a pledge against "the possibility of renewed aggression" now that all American combat troops had been withdrawn. It stated, "Action which would threaten the basis of the Agreement would call for appropriately vigorous reactions." This was an ambiguous statement but Thieu believed that the United States had been committed by its president to come to South Vietnam's aid in a crisis. By the time the crisis came President Nixon had been forced to resign in disgrace.

The ceasefire agreement also had a provision calling for an end to hostilities in Laos within days of its signing. The Pathet Lao, Hanoi's Laotian clients, continued what Laos's prime minister, Prince Souvanna Phouma, called a general offensive in late February. He sought B-52 strikes from Nixon but the president was reluctant because the North Vietnamese might use such an action as a pretext to delay the release of American prisoners. He did finally authorize them and within forty-eight hours a ceasefire was established in Laos.

February 26 the North Vietnamese failed to produce a list of prisoners due to be released the next day. President Nixon promptly suspended American troop withdrawals and mine-clearing operations. With this positive action the North Vietnamese released the names of the prisoners on schedule.

Kissinger warned Soviet Ambassador Dobrynin March 8 that continued delivery of substantial Russian military supplies would be considered an unfriendly act. He cautioned that a new offensive by North Vietnam would have "the profoundest consequence for United States-Soviet relations."

Dobrynin termed Kissinger's information inaccurate and outdated. He said war materiel was probably brought in by the Chinese. He was lying and he knew it, as did Kissinger.

President Nixon had become indecisive. The Watergate scandal had reached a new high after a Senate investigation disclosed that the break-in was only a small part of a pattern of crimes by the Nixon administration to ensure its reelection. Despite the revelation Nixon denied any personal involvement. He spent long periods with his White House counsel, John Dean, devising strategy to counteract the investigation by the newly constituted Senate Select Committee chaired by Senator Sam Ervin.

After North Vietnam's leaders became insolent between the dates for release of the 3rd and 4th group of prisoners, Kissinger recommended that air attacks be scheduled for March 24–26. He told Nixon the North Vietnamese were exposed both in the Ho Chi Minh Trail area of the Laotian Panhandle and in the northern reaches of I Corps. He said that in both areas they were operating in daylight and the traffic was so heavy that it was congested. He reminded Nixon that the North Vietnamese were clearly taking advantage of the fact that all air action against them had ceased. In his opinion, he said, a series of heavy air strikes over a two- or three-day period in either of these areas would be costly to them in both personnel and materiel.

Nixon advised Kissinger March 21 that he would prefer to hold up troop withdrawals rather than authorize air strikes. He said he would order an air attack "only if it is felt that it will do some real good."

This was the day that John Dean told President Nixon that in addition to other members of the administration the president had a problem. He said, "There is a cancer growing on the presidency."

While Nixon procrastinated about air strikes, North Vietnam continued to rush men and materiel south along the Ho Chi Minh Trail knowing it would soon be shut down by the monsoon season. Instead of action Nixon sent a series of sharp messages to North Vietnam. Now even the discussions in Paris between Le Duc Tho and Kissinger proved futile and they had become a charade.

North Vietnam finally released the last of 590 American war prisoners April 1, but 2,500 were still listed as missing in action.

Chinese leaders became more and more concerned about North Vietnam's domination of Indochina but they, too, were helpless to do anything about the situation.

Cambodia's President Lon Nol earlier had offered the Khmer Rouge a unilateral ceasefire as a first step toward a negotiated peace. His offer was considered a sign of weakness, and further demoralized his armed forces, particularly when there was no response from the communists. Later, further peace initiatives also ended in failure.

Graham Martin, physically frail following an automobile accident and emotionally upset following the death of his wife's son in Vietnam, took over as ambassador in South Vietnam June 24 replacing Ellsworth Bunker. A strong anti-communist who had loyally served both Democratic and Republican presidents, Martin was given a thankless job and he served his country well in South Vietnam's final years.

The United States Congress June 26, 1973, passed a supplemental appropriation bill that prohibited any United States military operations in or over Cambodia or Laos. Nixon vetoed the bill but he was overridden.

Three days later President Nixon authorized House Minority Leader Gerald R. Ford to inform the House of Representatives that a bill cutting off all military action by United States forces in or over Laos, Cambodia, North and South Vietnam after August 15 would be acceptable. After that date the president would have to return to Congress if he wanted to use armed forces in Southeast Asia. With the mood and temper of the American people such an action was unlikely. A bill was passed that, in effect, legislated American disengagement from the war.

President Nixon's staff members told him in August that Justice Department officials were convinced that he would be indicted, convicted and sentenced to a jail term for his part in the Watergate scandal.

September 25 Vice President Agnew went to House Speaker Carl Albert and requested that the House of Representatives undertake a full impeachment inquiry of his activities. He denied that he had ever received any money while he was vice president.

But October 9 Agnew told Nixon that he would resign although he still denied having done anything unethical. The next day he appeared in the federal courtroom in Baltimore and announced he was pleading nolo contendere. Thus, without admitting guilt, he was subject to conviction. It also gave him the option of denying the truth of the charges in a collateral proceeding. He pleaded nolo contendere to one count of having knowingly failed to report income for tax purposes. He also revealed that he was resigning as vice president. The judge sentenced him to three years' probation and a $10,000 fine.

To succeed Agnew, Nixon selected Gerald R. Ford.

The United States Congress further established its control over the war-making policies of a president by passing the War Powers Resolution October 12, 1973, that limited his employment of the nation's armed forces. Nixon vetoed the resolution but again he was overridden. Now future presidents must consult the Congress before introducing armed forces into hostilities or into situations where hostilities may be imminent. The bill states that the president shall submit a report in writing to both houses of Congress within forty-eight hours citing the circumstances calling for introduction of the nation's armed forces and he must specifically relate the authority for so doing and the estimated time of the involvement. The president must also report to them periodically on the status of such hostilities or situation as well as their scope. In no event must a president report to the Congress less often than once every six months.

If the Congress had wanted to curb a president's powers to make war they should not have approved the Gulf of Tonkin Resolution that gave President Johnson almost unlimited authority without a declaration of war.

President Nixon's on-going problems escalated when Archibald Cox, the special prosecutor hired to investigate the Watergate scandal, was fired by Nixon October 30. He had refused to drop a court suit against the president calling for the release of White House tapes and documents believed to contain revelatory information about the president's involvement in the coverup.

The American State Department revealed in January, 1974, that North Vietnam had infiltrated over 170,000 troops into South Vietnam bringing their possible total to 300,000. The communists had tripled their armor strength and, with 400 new tanks and armored personnel carriers, it was obvious they were building up to a new major offensive.

The South Vietnamese Constitution had been amended in October, 1973, to permit President Thieu to run for a third term. This act led to charges of corruption and demands for his resignation. Members of Thieu's oppostion were mostly anti-communists who cared for the future of their country and wanted a change in its leadership. They were joined by a small number of communist agents whose sole purpose was to create disorder. Despite various attempts, Thieu found it impossible to stabilize the situation and by the end of the year he had reshuffled his cabinet four times and replaced a large number of province chiefs and division and corps commanders to strengthen his control of the administration. But opposition increased as those who sought a peaceful change in government pointed to what they termed as Thieu's corrupt and incompetent henchmen who still were part of his government.

In the United States, President Nixon's troubles increased as key members of his administration were indicted on charges of conspiracy and all but one was charged with obstruction of justice. Now there were repeated calls for Nixon's impeachment.

By the middle of 1974 in Cambodia the communists succeeded in isolating the capital of Phnom Penh from contact with various provincial capitals. This fragmentation of the mass of Cambodia's armed forces into small groups, cut off from each other, resulted in their inability to provide mutual support and left them to defend their own zones.

In Washington, the House Judiciary Committee in July, 1974, voted to recommend President Nixon's impeachment on three counts: obstruction of justice in covering up the Watergate scandal, violation of his oath of office, and for defying the committee's subpoenas for evidence.

The Supreme Court in a unanimous decision now ordered the president to turn over evidence subpoenaed by Leon Jaworski who had been appointed the new special prosecutor.

Some of the evidence that the Supreme Court ordered the president to make public was released August 5. It showed that he had obstructed the Federal Bureau of Investigation inquiry of the Watergate break-in to protect his associates. Nixon was advised by Republican leaders in the

Congress that they were helpless to prevent his impeachment and possible conviction.

President Nixon resigned effective August 9, 1974, and was succeeded by Gerald Ford.

A month later, the new president granted Nixon a "full, free and absolute pardon for all offenses" committed during his tenure as president. Now Nixon could not be indicted and placed on trial.

Later, three cabinet members of the Nixon administration, including two of his top aides, plus other administration officials were convicted on charges resulting from the Watergate scandal.

In assuming the presidency, Ford called upon the nation to "bind up the internal wounds of Watergate." He promised an administration marked by candor and openness, but his pardoning of Nixon and his conditional amnesty for Vietnam War draft evaders and military deserters was resented by many Americans.

In February, 1975, Thieu sent the president of South Vietnam's Senate and some of his colleagues to Washington to try and convince the administration and the Congress that his country needed more help. The Honorable Tran Van Lam met with President Ford who wished him success, but his mission was a failure. Senate Majority Leader Mike Mansfield and Minority leader Senator Hugh Scott both refused to see him. President Ford pleaded with Congress for $300 million but his request was turned down.

The war in Cambodia had been going on for five years during which Cambodia the monarchy and its theme "an oasis of peace" had become a republic and was now an "oasis of war." At the beginning it had been a war against aggression carried out against foreign forces. Now it was a civil war pitting Khmer against Khmer. Morale of the armed forces reached bottom in the spring of 1975. Each year the communist's encirclement of the nation's population centers had grown tighter. This was particularly true around the capital. Internal political differences could no longer be tolerated. Divisions between the Social-Republican Party of President Lon Nol and the other parties had deepened to the point where reconciliation had become impossible. Lon Nol had totally isolated himself from his campanions who had helped to found the republic.

Lieutenant General Sak Sutsakhan, who had been a roving ambassador, was asked to accept the post of Chief of the General Staff and Commander-in-Chief of the Khmer Republic. He reluctantly accepted March 12. He viewed his country as a sick man who could survive only by outside means. In its terminal condition, he believed the administration of medication, however efficient it might be, was probably of no further value.

In traveling from one command to another to assess the military situation, Sutsakhan was shocked. There were defeats everywhere for a variety of reasons: lack of resupply, inefficiency, misunderstandings and discontent provoked by the conduct of certain senior officers.

The fight for Phnom Penh was concentrated within a nine-mile radius of the capital. In the northwest, military units were in an increasingly difficult situation. Most other fronts were undergoing various pressures. The Navy and the Air Force were all but impotent. The rapidly worsening situation in March, 1975, was capped in April by the fall of Neak Luong despite strong resistance and days of siege. Its fall opened the gates of the capital in the south. Two days later all friendly positions on Route 1 above Neak Luong held by the Khmer 1st Division fell one after another in heavy combat. All intervention, whether by road or by the Mekong River, was impossible. Frantic civilians converged on the capital from these areas. For all intents and purposes the end came April 5 when the last ring of defenses around the capital were overrun by communist assaults.

President Lon Nol had left the capital April 1 and those remaining knew they had to sue for peace. Many felt his presence had been an obstacle to peace.

In late March, following Sutsakhan's assumption of military command, Lon Nol had been shocked when a delegation urged him to leave the country on a temporary basis. He met separately with each member to test the unity of his detractors. All were adamant so he agreed to leave. He asked those who remained to work for an honorable peace—not simply capitulation—and, failing that, to continue the struggle. It was too late for conditions. He and his family departed by air and they flew to Thailand and later to Hawaii to continue medical treatment for the effects of his 1971 stroke.

The American embassy evacuated its staff April 2, 1975, along with Acting President Saukham Khoy. The United States offered to evacuate other Khmer officials, particularly those whose lives might be endangered, but most declined to leave. To the Americans' surprise the entire cabinet of military and civilian leaders decided to remain with their people.

Phnom Penh and almost all provincial capitals—except those in the east occupied by North Vietnam—were packed with millions of refugees who had voted against communism with their feet. There were roughly six million under government control, with another million under the communists. A considerable quantity of food, ammunition and medical supplies were parachuted each day by American planes, even after Lon Nol had been evacuated.

Sutsakhan checked the military situation April 12. He reported to the Committee of Seven who elected him president and the General Assembly approved their action. The general realized that too much blood had been shed, and too many lives already had been sacrificed. In the first hours of his assumption of office he knew that an honorable peace must be attained, and he made a peace offer to Prince Sihanouk.

Meanwhile, President Ford dropped his request for $330 million additional aid for Cambodia in anticipation of that country's imminent collapse.

With American aid withdrawn, morale plummeted in Cambodia. Satsukhan drafted his peace offer to Peking while the military situation worsened by the hour.

When no word was received from Sihanouk by April 17 he agreed to establish a government in exile, although remaining somewhere in Cambodia. All helicopters were out on missions so it was impossible that day to evacuate the government. He decided instead to resist to the death in Phnom Penh. Then a cable arrived from Peking that Sihanouk had rejected his peace proposal, branding the seven members of the Supreme Committee as chief traitors, in addition to the other seven who had taken power in 1970.

Upon availability of a few helicopters Sutsakhan, his family and some members of his government departed. They stopped first in Thailand, making the last part of their journey in darkness to U-Tapao in an American transport. They arrived weary from grief, lack of sleep and fear. During the trip they had been sad and silent, each lost to his or her own thoughts, and barely aware of what they had just experienced. Their arrival at U-Tapao marked the end of the nightmare for a few individuals but the start of a worse fate for millions of other Cambodians.

With the fall of Cambodia an ancient civilization died at the hands of a cynical communist dictatorship. While his plane hovered over the western plains of his country, Sutsakhan had realized that it was not a question only of a little country, submerged under a murderous rule, but of world totalitarianism that was engulfing new territories in its march toward world domination. In his mind was a question whether the people of the world would stand still and simply watch genocide committed against one poor, defenseless nation after another and do nothing at all? He found it difficult not to become bitter when their only reaction was to offer condolences.

CHAPTER 39

"Don't Curse the Darkness.
Light a Candle."

THE UNITED STATES PAID A HEAVY PRICE FOR ITS INVOLVEMENT IN Indochina. The toll in dead and missing reached 58,132 as 3.7 million Americans, including 7,500 women, served there and 47,428 died in combat while the rest died of disease, air and vehicle accidents and friendly fire. Of the latter, a shocking 15 percent or 8,700 personnel may have been accidentally killed by their own troops due to inadequate training and poor officer supervision. Those suffering combat wounds requiring hospitalization totaled 143,329 while over 150,000 others were wounded but did not require such care. Among those wounded 6,655 lost limbs. There were 93,250 deserters, but 20,000 had served a full term in Indochina before they deserted. The Veterans Administration cites many causes for their desertion, including family and personality problems that were not handled properly by their units' officers, and some men were encouraged to desert by their friends.

Only a third of the United States' 27 million men of draft age served at all and only 13.7 percent went to Southeast Asia. Men of the National Guard and the Reserves numbered 1,040,000 but only 15,000 were sent to Indochina while the remainder were never mobilized. In 1968 and 1970, 28,000 more college-trained men entered these organizations than enlisted or were inducted into all of the active services. Such action was taken primarily to avoid the draft.

The Selective Service Administration deferred men for occupational and agricultural reasons, because they were students or had family dependents. Each board relied upon local conditions to determine which registrants should be deferred. Deferments for graduate students were phased out in 1968 and for undergraduates in 1971. In both cases, however, students kept their deferments as long as they were justified. In addition, during the 1960s fathers were deferred regardless of their hardship situation. Reserve and senior level students who had enrolled in Reserve Officer Training Corps were not drafted if they agreed to accept a commission and fulfilled their service obligations. Conscientious objectors were assigned civilian service in lieu of military service. The system was unfair and undemocratic, but it was created by a political decision made at the highest level of the government to reduce protests to the war.

The armed forces of the United States reached a peak strength of 549,500 in Southeast Asia while its allies contributed another 62,400 combat personnel. The military forces of the Republic of Vietnam reached a total in excess of one million, but this figure included regulars and members of the militia.

It was a costly war in terms of money with the United States spending approximately $141 billion of which $23.7 billion was in aid to South Vietnam. All but $1.8 billion of this aid was given free to the South Vietnamese government.

On the battlefield, America's armed forces were unbeatable and Vietcong and North Vietnamese Army units suffered terrible losses. Although a true figure is impossible to determine, the communist dead probably reached a total of one million, and possibly more. There is no precise record of those wounded, or the number of civilians on both sides who were killed in the war, but a figure of four million dead and wounded Vietnamese appears realistic—roughly 10 percent of their combined populations. For South Vietnam, the military death toll was considerably less—approximately 240,000. But this figure also may be conservative.

United States losses in military hardware were extremely high including 3,695 helicopters, 4,783 aircraft and untold quantities of other war materiel that seriously degraded the nation's combat effectiveness for years to come.

Despite incredible losses in men and materiel, the North Vietnamese emerged victorious. They did so because their leaders refused to admit defeat and inspired their soldiers to fight on, often against impossible odds.

The communist victory was not due entirely to their perseverance. American Army commanders must accept part of the blame. The cautious and methodical General Westmoreland lacked the bold, imaginative leadership qualities that were so vitally needed in his position. All too often his search and destroy operations merely drove the communists into sanctuaries in Cambodia and Laos where he could not attack them. With total command of the air, vertical envelopment deep into the rear of enemy positions would have been more productive, or huge pincer moves to the borders of Cambodia and Laos would have swept enemy units towards advancing American and South Vietnamese troops where they could have been destroyed. Both are old methods of waging offensive war that have long since proved their effectiveness. Westmoreland used such tactics too timidly and in a limited way and not in the grand style of a General Dwight D. Eisenhower, Omar N. Bradley or George S. Patton—to name just a few resourceful generals of other wars.

The American Army's so-called strategy of flexible response was prepared by civilian analysts and political scientists from the academic world while Army generals like Westmoreland too often abrogated their responsibilities to devise a workable strategy to achieve political ends advocated by their presidents. It is too simplistic to blame a president for failure of a particular strategy. A president does not formulate military proposals but decides on the strategy recommended to him by his military and civilian advisers. In the case of President Johnson, he decided against mobilization of the country to fight the war. This was a serious error because he involved the United States in a major war without first committing the American people. The highest officials of the military service should have laid their careers on the line to tell him he was wrong. Only General LeMay did so. He warned Kennedy and Johnson that their actions violated all the rules of war but they refused to listen. Kennedy told intimates that "LeMay is a fine combat soldier, but we don't want him doing any planning for the future." As a result, LeMay's advice was ignored and amateurs were permitted to run the war, and the United States and its allies lost a lot of soldiers, sailors and airmen unnecessarily.

Since the war ended, Westmoreland has complained bitterly about restraints placed upon him and his command. These complaints would have more validity if he had made them at the time. After all, the first duty of a field commander is to take care of his troops. Now he has no reason to complain because he knew the guidelines imposed upon his command and accepted them. If he felt strongly about them, he should have resigned, and his resignation might have changed the situation for the new commander.

A story made the rounds after President Nixon assumed the presidency in 1969 that all pertinent data about the war in Southeast Asia was fed into a Pentagon computer. It was asked, "When will we win?"

The computer replied. "You won in 1964!"

This was typical of much of the thinking during this period. It was unacceptable to think that, in the long run, the most powerful nation on earth could be defeated by a backward nation like North Vietnam. Computers are helpful tools but they cannot analyze the character of a nation's will. The American government's failure to get the backing of its people for the war effort produced a vulnerability that the North Vietnamese skillfully exploited.

Early in his presidency Lyndon Johnson understood this fact. He said that President Truman's one mistake in going to the defense of South Korea in 1950 had been his failure to ask Congress for an expression of its backing. "He could have had it easily," Johnson said, "and it would have strengthened his hand. I made up my mind not to repeat that error."

Unfortunately for the United States, Johnson did repeat Truman's error. In August, 1964, after the Gulf of Tonkin incident, he could have had a congressional declaration of war. Instead, he asked the Congress for a resolution empowering him to take all necessary measures to repel an armed attack against the forces of the United States and to prevent further aggression. The Congress voted overwhelmingly for it. At the time Johnson did not think he needed a war declaration. Later, when he needed support, he could not have gotten it.

Although General Westmoreland criticized Johnson after the war for not seeking a war declaration, there is no evidence that either he or any other top military officer pressed him to take such action.

Anti-militarism was not unique to the war in Indochina. Former Army Chief of Staff General Fred C. Weyand says of the war-time Army, "If we cannot be loved, we can be trusted and respected." The Army failed to be either loved or respected and it was the fault of many of its own commanders who did not have the courage of their convictions.

The decision to grant draft deferments to students caused unnecessary problems. These deferments, plus the decision not to seek a declaration of war or to mobilize the nation's reserve forces, were part of a deliberate presidential policy not to arouse the emotions of the American people against the war. Therefore, the true nature of the war was concealed from the American people at a time when television for the first time was bringing the realities of war into the living rooms of the American people. To them the war in Southeast Asia was symbolized by a little girl running down the road seared by napalm. This was a familiar part of war in Europe and Asia during World War II, but there were no television cameras then to bring the terrible realities of war into American homes in living color. War is never humane, and it cannot be made to look so.

The news media made mistakes in reporting the war, and in some cases their stories parroted communist propaganda. However, most reporting was honest, relating what had been seen at first hand. The media should not be blamed for America's political failures. Newsmen reported the true nature of the war in all its ugliness and horror. It was the horror and ugliness, not the reporting, that turned the American people against the war.

War is death and destruction on a mass scale and the American way of war is particularly violent because of the massive use of artillery and bombs to spare the lives of American service men and women. North Vietnam did not have such firepower so they had to expend their men and suffered enormous casualties in comparison to the numbers involved.

By law, the chairman of the Joint Chiefs of Staff is the president's chief military adviser. During this war, whoever was chairman hardly ever demanded to see the president, or vice versa. By default, therefore, most military advisers allowed strategy to be dominated by civilian analysts with unfortunate results. After World War II, most of these analysts believed there was no need for a conventional military establishment because massive nuclear retaliation would prevent wars. Two wars have been fought since then without nuclear weapons and without adequate conventional weapons.

The words of Confederate General Thomas J. "Stonewall" Jackson a hundred years earlier can be applied to the war in Indochina: "Never take counsel of your fears." He did not mean that one should not fear war but that one's fears should not dominate one's thinking and result in paralysis of thoughts and deeds that only increase the hazard. In the Indochina war there was too much fear of what the Soviet Union and the People's Republic of China might do. Both China and the Soviet Union bluffed the United States throughout the war, constantly harping about the dangers of United States involvement. As a result, American strategic thinking became paralyzed. There is no evidence that China ever intended to intervene with her armed forces. Actually, there is evidence that Mao Tse-tung refused to go along with the Soviet Union on joint military action. The Chinese leader evidently feared—and rightly so—that Russian leaders were trying to involve his country in a war with the United States over Vietnam. They had done so during the Korean War and more than a million Chinese soldiers had died, but not one Russian soldier.

Most wars have had limited national objectives and there is nothing wrong with such a philosophy if there is the determination by the American people to achieve those limited objectives. This happened during the Korean War and South Korea has remained free ever since.

But memories of China's reaction when North Korea was overrun by United Nations troops in 1950 haunted the White House during the Indochina war years. America's fear of war with China protected North Vietnam from invasion more surely than any Army she could have fielded in her defense. A unified intelligence-gathering system might have dispelled such fears, but one was never established.

A career State Department Foreign Service officer, Norman Hannah, with long experience in Southeast Asia wrote in 1975, "In South Vietnam we responded mainly to Hanoi's simulated insurgency rather than to its real, but controlled aggression, as a bull charges the toreador's cape, not the toreador." Instead, the United States adopted a defensive strategy that had failed so many times before. Westmoreland believed his strategy would eventually achieve success. The United States was fighting for time rather than space, and time ran out along with the patience of the American people. Actually, the United States never had a real strategy to force North Vietnam to stop its aggression.

That aggression proved costly. General Giap admitted the loss of 500,000 men in fighting just between 1965 and 1968. By 1970, 80 percent of the fighting in the South was carried out by regular North Vietnamese Army troops because the Vietcong had been decimated in earlier battles.

In strategic terms the United States merely reacted to communist strategy. The North Vietnamese established the kind of war they wanted to fight and the Americans played their game instead of constantly carrying the war to them by every means possible. All too often the true nature of the war confused the defense establishment and resulted in arguments over tactics and strategy. Each president had a view, the Joint Chiefs another and the field commander still another.

The communist National Liberation Front was not an autonomous organization with a life of its own. It was a controlled group that the North Vietnamese communist party used to mobilize the people in the South to accomplish its ends, and to garner international sympathy and support.

The real losers in the 1968 Tet offensive were the communists who surfaced in the South to lead the attacks and were destroyed. Just as the Russians eliminated their Polish competitors with the Warsaw uprising in World War II, the North Vietnamese eliminated their southern competitors in 1968. By this action they insured that the South would eventually be dominated not by South Vietnamese communists but by North Vietnamese communists.

The establishment of a China sanctuary—the entire country was off-limits to the armed forces of the United States—made sound strategic sense in avoiding a major war against a formidable adversary. But the sanctuaries in Laos and Cambodia made no sense at all. The myth of their neutrality gave North Vietnam an immense tactical and strategic advantage that plagued the United States armed forces throughout the war.

During the McNamara era, the United States devised a purely defensive strategy and even Westmoreland's search and destroy operations were defensive because they were withdrawn. His concept of a war of attrition against an Asian foe was ill-advised and doomed to fail. Decisive offensive actions, where each territory was gained and held, including consistent strategic bombing of the North, would have ended the war and saved Indochina from communism. The strategy of a "slow squeeze" to give the United States the option of escalating or reducing the pressure at any point in time failed miserably to end the communist aggression.

The Joint Chiefs repeatedly denounced such strategy, as did Admiral Sharp, particularly in regard to bombing that they wanted applied fast and hard to achieve maximum impact with minimum losses. They believed that to start lightly and escalate slowly "would be like pulling a tooth bit-by-bit rather than all at once and getting it over with." The intelligence community agreed with them but President Johnson overrode them, going along with McNamara's theory of "gradual response." Instead, a policy of strategic defense was adopted, and Westmoreland was given responsibility to "wear the enemy down."

Instead of a multi-layered command structure, there should have been a supreme ground commander in Vietnam with total control of all forces, and responsible directly to the Joint Chiefs. This command should have included South Vietnam's armed forces despite the possibility of wounding South Vietnam's sensibilities. Westmoreland should have fought for such authority instead of trying to be such a good soldier. General Eisenhower threatened to resign twice as Supreme Allied Commander in Europe during World War II when others tried to whittle away at his authority. Westmoreland complained after the war about his lack of authority, but he should have done so during the war.

Although Admiral Sharp was overall commander, Westmoreland ran the ground war with little or no interference from the Commander-in-Chief, Pacific. In a sense Sharp was not acting as a true commander-in-chief who dominated all combat operations. Even though Westmoreland always kept Sharp advised, and never tried to undercut him, the Commander-in-Chief, Pacific, for the most part let Westmoreland run the ground war as he saw fit.

In this war, no military commander ever threatened to resign to back up his views. Napoleon spelled it out years earlier that military advisers should tender their resignations rather than be the instrument of their army's downfall. In the Indochina war, by failing to press their military advice, top officers permitted the United States to pursue a strategic policy that was faulted from the start.

Army Colonel Harry G. Summers, Jr., Chief of the Negotiations

Division of the Four-Party Military Team, met in Hanoi April 25, 1975, with North Vietnamese Army Major Huyen. "You should not feel badly," Huyen said. "You have done more than enough. . . . more than enough."

Despite his mortification to be told the truth in the capital of his one-time enemy, Summers had to admit the truth of the major's statement. He realized that one of the reasons why the United States had failed in South Vietnam was due to the fact that his country had attempted to do too much. Instead of concentrating its efforts towards repelling external aggression as the United States had done in Korea, the United States had taken upon itself the task of nation building. This was an error that Americans had not made in Korea. Although the situation in South Korea was far worse in June, 1950, with their government in disorderly retreat, their economy destroyed and their social fabric torn to shreds, the United States did not intervene but left the resolution of its internal problems to the Republic of Korea's government.

In Vietnam, American power was sometimes used with arrogance and with total disregard for that nation's sensibilities. The worst case was Diem's overthrow, plotted by a president of the United States and that nation's ambassador, but there were many others. Some Americans considered that, as the self-appointed world's policeman, the American way of life must be forced upon a centuries-old society that did not understand it, or desire such a drastic change in their social, political and economic customs. The Kennedy administration in particular tried to force so-called liberal reforms on the South Vietnamese government and even used intimidation and subversion in their over-zealousness to force the Diem government to accept reforms that they considered necessary. This dictatorial manner contributed greatly to South Vietnam's eventual collapse because it started the breakup of South Vietnam's society that, with all its faults, was based largely on the expression of a free people trying desperately to forge a nation under almost impossible conditions, and to govern themselves without outside interference. There would have been no war in the mid-1950s if the South Vietnamese and their leaders had been willing to forsake freedom and knuckle under to totalitarianism. Millions demonstrated by their actions that they preferred death to slavery.

North Vietnam was aided materially by the Soviet Union and the People's Republic of China, but her men and women did the fighting. Unlike the United States, North Vietnam's allies provided massive military and economic aid, but they did not participate in the fighting. They tried to keep out of sight whereas Americans were always too visible and tried to do everything for the South Vietnamese.

Colonel Summers, an American member of the Four-Party Military Team, met in Hanoi in April, 1975, with Colonel Tu, chief of the North

Vietnamese delegation. He told him, "You know you never defeated us on the battlefield."

"That may be so," Tu replied, "but it is also irrelevant."

Americans contributed to some of the atrocities in Indochina, as they have done in every war, and the free world's press exposed them. It was correct for them to do so but they should have given similar coverage to Vietcong and North Vietnamese atrocities. The world was shocked by the My Lai massacre of March, 1968, but few people have ever heard of Cai Be where the Vietcong murdered forty wives and children of local military men, or Dak Son where they incinerated two hundred and fifty Montagnards—mostly women and children—with flame throwers. There were countless other instances of excessive brutality.

American anti-war activists spoke out against the breaching of dams and dikes in North Vietnam assuming such destruction would cause starvation. What they never bothered to investigate was that the tops of the dikes were many yards wide and were almost impossible to breach with bombs. Attacks against dikes were not carried out because their breaching would have had minimal value. Actually, nature did more to breach the dikes during the annual floods than any kind of bombing could have accomplished.

A great many people in Canada opposed the war but it is little known that up to fifteen thousand Canadian volunteers enlisted in the American armed forces and fifty-six were killed. They included fifty Mohawk Indians from the Caughnawaga Indian Reservation near Montreal. While American veterans have their problems, these Canadians cannot claim health, education or survivor's benefits unless they live in the United States. They are truly the forgotten Vietnam veterans.

In the final analysis the United States won all the battles in Southeast Asia but lost the war. In the process, the United States was temporarily disunited and its fellow citizens set against each other in a way that is unique in the nation's history.

It is always easy, after the fact, to point out the substantial faults that were committed by some of America's leaders, including some military operations that have not been understood due to past emphasis on shortcomings of the nation's political leaders. Although many Americans made a moral judgment against the war they have now come to recognize the decency, valor and commitment of those men and women who fought in Southeast Asia.

No greater tribute can be paid to the men of the United States Air Force and Navy who flew in combat in Southeast Asia than the words of retired Rear Admiral James D. Ramage who served as chief of staff of Carrier Task Force 77, deputy chief of staff for operations and plans on the Pacific Fleet

Staff, and as commander of Carrier Division 7 in the Gulf of Tonkin during a time period encompassing seven years. An operational commander throughout most of his Navy career dating back to World War II's earliest days, Ramage was also a superb pilot. Long after the war he said, "There is a tendency to look back at the big one—World War II—as the greatest period in air combat history. In my opinion, the air crews flying from the carriers of Task Force 77, and those of the Seventh Air Force in Thailand who operated in North Vietnam, faced a greater challenge than tactical aviation's air crews have ever faced. There were a few limited exceptions such as the carrier crews at the Battle of Midway, and I am aware of similar instances in the experiences of Army Air Forces. But the air defenses of North Vietnam were permitted to develop into a very effective system. This was the first time that American air personnel encountered surface-to-air missiles, and the combination of anti-aircraft artillery, automatic weapons and small arms was formidable. This combination of missiles and guns presented an entirely new problem. MIGs were not a serious threat, but they had to be considered in each strike into the northern areas.

"While I can speak only from personal knowledge of Navy operations, the experience is probably shared by Seventh Air Force air crews. There was no surprise possible, and because of the highly restrictive rules of engagement imposed by Washington there was very little flexibility in our attack options. More pervasive was the daily monotony of doing the same thing. Also, there was the certainty that risks were not worth the value of assigned targets.

"Many Navy air crew members had over 300 missions over North Vietnam. The carriers would remain in the Gulf of Tonkin from thirty to eighty days operating around the clock with only infrequent standdowns. During World War II, carriers would have a few days of intensive operations followed by a rest period in some Pacific anchorage where air crews could rest and prepare for the next campaign. During the Korean War a carrier generally flew three out of four days in the Sea of Japan.

"During my six years of close connection with strike operations in the Gulf of Tonkin I was unaware of a single case of refusal to carry out the assigned mission. With all of our problems, morale remained high. This is a tribute to the quality of personnel, their training, dedication and the leadership of the strike commanders. They were incredible."

The war in Southeast Asia could have been successfully resolved, and in less than three years, if major decisions had been made early in the United States' involvement. As it was the nation fought an indecisive war, first with advisers dating back to late 1945, that lasted a total of twenty-one years, seven of which included the use of combat American troops, airmen and sailors. The ending could have been far different, and much sooner, if the full might of America's airpower and seapower had been unleashed once it was clear that the North Vietnamese were bent upon domination of the free and independent nations of South Vietnam, Laos and Cambodia. There was no need for American combat troops except in the role of advisers.

Secretary of Defense McNamara's plan for graduated response to North Vietnamese aggression was doomed from the start. It was a "no-win" position that resolved nothing either politically or militarily.

Once the United States was definitely committed to take military action in Vietnam, air and naval power should have been used against North Vietnam from the start of its involvement to destroy North Vietnam's will and resources to continue its aggression in the South. Attacks against military targets of a strategic nature would soon have brought North Vietnam to a state of economic collapse. When President Nixon unleashed air and seapower in December, 1972—a step long advocated by the Joint Chiefs of Staff—the North Vietnamese quickly returned to the peace table after an eleven-day blitz that destroyed most of North Vietnam's industry and lines of communication. These attacks precipitated the start of a total economic breakdown. The fear expressed throughout the war that such attacks against North Vietnam would run the risk of involving China and the Soviet Union proved false. When the chips were down these communist countries were, to use a favorite Chinese expression, "paper tigers." The mining of Haiphong Harbor, and other port cities, brought international supplies from other nations to a halt, and it was accomplished with no casualties to either side, with less than forty mines dropped in a few minutes.

The North Vietnamese would have succumbed quickly—or at least have renounced their attempts to conquer the South—if the United States had blocked North Vietnam's ports early in the United States' involvement (a measure condoned by international law in wartime) and had placed a South Vietnamese infantry division across the Ho Chi Minh Trail to block it in all countries through which it passed including both Vietnams, Laos and Cambodia. Westmoreland proposed such an action but he wanted to use an American division. Bombing the trail was a costly and useless way to close it. Airpower was used to bomb jungles on the theory that the Vietcong and the North Vietnamese feared heavy bombers more than anything else. Such a misuse of airpower by trying to kill coolies carrying a couple of artillery shells through an impenetrable jungle instead of destroying them and other military supplies in their factories, warehouses or on their docks is almost incredible. A total of more than seven million tons of bombs was dropped during the war by the United States and its allies—mostly on jungle hideaways. By comparison, only 147,000 tons of bombs were used to destroy Japan in World War II prior to the dropping of two atomic bombs. Airpower advocates have always insisted upon hitting military targets at the source of the supply line instead of along its routes to the front. Such operations in Southeast Asia were a costly and ineffective way of waging air warfare.

Kissinger and Le Duc Tho were awarded the Nobel Peace Prize for drafting the so-called peace agreement, which made a mockery of a just peace. North Vietnam's delegate to the peace talks at least had the graciousness to turn it down when it was originally offered to him. Kissinger tried to return the award after South Vietnam's fall in 1975 but the Nobel committee refused to accept it.

The war was lost on the home front when most Americans became outraged by the constant exposure of a seemingly endless war in their newspapers and on their television sets. They became resigned to the fact that there was no evident prospect of an honorable conclusion acceptable to all parties.

Anti-war activists had little impact on the war's outcome, except to prolong the war's agony. They were noisy, often violent, but the war ended because the majority of the American people were fed up with it. By the mid-1980s, the liberalism of the war years had turned to a strong conservatism throughout the United States as Americans took a more mature view of their country and its past actions. A better understanding of those years can be acquired if one accepts at face value the words of an old Chinese proverb, "Don't curse the darkness. Light a candle."

PART IV

THE FINAL COLLAPSE

CHAPTER 40

Ceasefire Violations

THE PARIS PEACE AGREEMENT SIGNED JANUARY 27, 1973, WAS FORCED upon President Thieu and he had to accept its terms. It proved to be South Vietnam's death warrant because Thieu still refused to take responsibility for his country's survival. He continued to believe that the United States would fight his country's battles if the North Vietnamese renewed the war. Under the ceasefire terms both sides were permitted to hold the territory they occupied at the time of the signing, but they could not add to the area under their control. All fighting was to cease while the governments of South and North Vietnam negotiated for a permanent end to the war. The agreement specified that neither side could increase the level of armaments in South Vietnam. The North Vietnamese agreed that the United States would be permitted one-for-one replacement of military items for South Vietnam, and the United States abided strictly by that agreement. In one important paragraph the United States and North Vietnam agreed to report to an International Commission on Control and Supervision. Actually, the government of South Vietnam permitted on-site inspection, but the government of North Vietnam did not. The agreement was a farce, permitting thousands of North Vietnamese Army troops to remain in South Vietnam after the ceasefire, in addition to 50,000 Vietcong. The agreement further called for the complete withdrawal of allied troops and their air force that had maintained a precarious balance of power.

President Nixon said of the agreement, "The most important thing was not to talk about peace, but to get peace and to get the right kind of peace; this we have done. Now that an honorable agreement has been acheived, let us be proud that America did not settle for a peace that would have betrayed our allies—that would have ended the war for us, but would have continued the war for the 50 million people of Indochina."

Of course that is just what happened, and Nixon and Kissinger must have known there was no honor in a ceasefire that tied the hands of the South Vietnamese without further hindrance from that country's so-called allies.

In a news conference the day following the signing, Special Assistant to the President for National Security Affairs Dr. Henry A. Kissinger tried to clarify the issue about the number of North Vietnamese troops in the South. "Our estimate is approximately one hundred and forty-five thousand." He added that there was nothing in the agreement that established the right of North Vietnam to be in the South. "The North Vietnamese have never claimed that they have a right to have troops in the South." He concluded that the North Vietnamese armed forces, over a period of time, would be subject to considerable reduction.

He was wrong, and he should have known it. Intelligence estimates that were readily available to Kissinger and the president had established that there were at least thirteen division headquarters in the South and seventy-five regiments. These intelligence estimates stated there were probably 160,000 North Vietnamese troops in the South—an estimate that proved too low—supplied and backed by secure bases in the North and in Laos.

The agreement, extolled by Kissinger and President Nixon, set forces in motion that later led directly to South Vietnam's collapse. Withdrawal of United States support—actually South Vietnam did not even receive all the assistance it was entitled to under the agreement—proved catastrophic. South Vietnam's logistical and training bases, and their lines of communication, proved vulnerable to infiltration, sabotage and hit-and-run attacks. The Paris agreement provided that the United States would stop all military activities against the Democratic Republic of Vietnam and it lived up to its pledge, but the North Vietnamese did not. In the coming months the United States did nothing to counteract increasingly bold communist attacks as more and more forces from North Vietnam invaded the South. The United States still retained forces in Thailand and the South China Sea and it could have resumed strong air attacks that might initially have made a difference in the outcome. In the long run, South Vietnam's leaders were totally responsible for their country's survival—not the United States which had already sacrificed too much—but they were not equal to their grave responsibilities.

The 1972 communist offensive had dramatically brought to the surface the basic weakness of the Vietnamization process. Without United States airpower, the Republic of Vietnam could not have held An Loc, defended Kontum or reoccupied Quang Tri. Most of the areas taken over by the

North Vietnamese during the 1972 spring offensive were lost for good, and the nation's chances of remaining free were reduced.

While American aid to South Vietnam was sharply curtailed after the ceasefire, Soviet Russia and the People's Republic of China continued to provide massive military and economic support. It is now known that North Vietnam received a record 3.8 million tons of supplies during 1973, an amount 50 percent greater than it received in 1972. It was even 10 percent higher than the previous record set in 1971. This trend continued throughout 1974 when more than 3.85 million tons were received. Tragically, the American-arranged ceasefire had made no provision to stop such a flow of military supplies.

Again, in violation of the ceasefire, the North Vietnamese stepped up their efforts to encourage desertion and disaffection in the South. Territorial troops—those most prone to desert—were primary targets. Communist efforts failed and the number of territorial troops actually increased during 1973 while regular members of the armed forces declined in number.

By far the largest enemy-controlled population in South Vietnam was located in northern and western Quang Tri Province. It totalled approximately one hundred and eighty thousand. Many of them were Montagnards—tough mountain people who had fled to Laos earlier in the war but who had now returned to their homes after the ceasefire.

Despite the ceasefire there was sporadic fighting in early February, 1973, that cost North Vietnam more than 5,000 killed with little alteration in the tactical situation. By February 9, only twenty-three of more than four hundred hamlets that the North Vietnamese had attacked were still under their control. The North Vietnamese failed because their local forces were too limited to be decisive, and because the South Vietnamese armed forces fought superbly. The communists, in breaking down their local forces into small groups with too many simultaneous attacks, made a strategic mistake that cost them heavily. In contrast, the South Vietnam armed forces reacted solidly against each threatened area. With the military balance about even between the two sides, American observers believed that South Vietnam's armed forces could hold their own with the present communist strength in the South.

Prior to the ceasefire, it had been North Vietnam's strategy to capture as much populated area as possible so that the International Commission for Control and Supervision would turn over these areas to North Vietnam. Its success hinged on local communist forces gaining access to areas and winning over the population through propaganda, kidnaping of area leaders and often their assassination. This major pre-ceasefire campaign was called "land grab" by the South Vietnamese. It was instigated in conjunction with North Vietnam's political offensive that was focused on world opinion against South Vietnam's civilians and members of its armed forces. Simultaneously, Hanoi's leadership instituted a strong propaganda campaign directed at its own people in the North. "Land grab" failed in South Vietnam, but the North Vietnamese were highly successful with their propaganda in the rest of the world. Their line fell on receptive ears almost everywhere in the Western world, and many United States citizens were at least acquiescent supporters of the communist party line. Basically, North Vietnam and the communist nations that supported her goals argued that the North Vietnamese were observing the terms of the ceasefire despite constant, aggressive violations by those in the South. Of course the opposite was true. North Vietnam explained its military operations by saying they were initiated only to punish "the Thieu puppets and to promote peace." It was not until North Vietnam's armed forces conquered Phuoc Long Province in December, 1974, that their credibility came into question.

Once the North Vietnamese were convinced, despite their provocative acts against the South, that the United States would maintain its neutrality despite anything that they did, the stage was set for the takeover and the communists prepared for the final phase of their long war.

One of the many incongruities of the so-called "peace with honor" agreement signed by Kissinger on behalf of President Nixon and the United States was contained in Article 7. It stated that there would be no introduction of troops, military advisers, personnel or armaments and munitions except as periodic replacement for those that were destroyed, damaged, worn out, or used up after the ceasefire. Such replacements were limited to a piece-by-piece basis. The agreement applied only to the United States and allied countries and it did not include military assistance provided to North Vietnam by the Soviet Union and the People's Republic of China. Therefore, after the ceasefire men and munitions continued to flow into North Vietnam.

Kissinger tried to explain the specific prohibition against the United States without any comparable restriction against the communist countries. In a January 24, 1973, press conference he said, "It is not inconceivable that the agreement will not in all respects be lived up to. In that case, adding another clause that will not be lived up to, specifically requiring it, would not change the situation." This was an understatement of the problem, and not entirely true because he should have known from past experience that the communists would never give up their goal of Vietnam unification. Therefore, while the North Vietnamese ignored the agreement, the United States lived up to the letter of its provisions and, in some cases, did not even replace all of the expended arms and equipment used up by the South Vietnamese armed forces.

The agreement permitted the partition of Vietnam much like the accords that were reached in 1954. In his press conference, Kissinger said, "The provisions of the agreement with respect to infiltration, with respect to replacement, with respect to any of the military provisions, would have made no sense whatsoever if there was not some demarcation line defining where South Vietnam began." Actually, the true demarcation line was 18.6 miles south of the 17th parallel on the Thach Han River where South Vietnam's Marines held to the rubble of Quang Tri City.

North Vietnam maintained the fiction of the so-called demilitarized zone by locating a customs post on the south bank of the Ben Hai River. The most extensive logistics base in South Vietnam was constructed by the North Vietnamese through Dong Ha and west along Highway 9 to Khe Sanh near the Laotian border. Dong Ha became the major North Vietnamese port of entry for military supplies to the South. Traffic across the demilitarized zone soon surpassed pre-ceasefire levels.

North Vietnam had established the Ho Chi Minh Trail in southern Laos and eastern Cambodia earlier in the war as its main logistical corridor to South Vietnam. When the ceasefire was signed in January, 1973, there were about seventy thousand North Vietnamese regular troops in Laos mainly along the trail, while another thirty thousand were in Cambodia.

When asked at the press conference about communist troops in these countries, Kissinger replied, "There is a flat prohibition against the use of the base areas in Laos and Cambodia, or infiltration into South Vietnam." He said there was a requirement that all foreign troops be withdrawn from Laos and Cambodia and that it had been agreed with North Vietnam that their troops were foreign. "It is our firm expectation that within a short period there will be a formal ceasefire in Laos which in turn will lead to a withdrawal of all foreign forces from Laos and, of course, to the end of the use of Laos as a corridor of infiltration."

Such naïveté on Kissinger's part is difficult to understand. The withdrawal, of course, never took place, and the North Vietnamese had no intention of doing so. Not only did they not withdraw their troops from Laos and Cambodia but they increased their presence in southern Laos. With North Vietnam's record of violating agreements in 1954 and 1962, Kissinger's statement borders on the incredible.

Within two years after North Vietnam agreed to a ceasefire in early 1973 it shifted sizable units from Laos into South Vietnam as it developed the Route 14 corridor south from Khe Sanh. Her leaders transferred the 968th Infantry Division from Laos into the Kontum-Pleiku area in the central part of South Vietnam. Not only was the route of the Ho Chi Minh Trail kept constantly in use, but some macadam roads and concrete culverts and bridges were built to facilitate infiltration. By the end of 1973, over 75,000 replacements had entered South Vietnam—mostly through Laos. Although United States officials were concerned by these flagrant breaches of the ceasefire agreement, they did nothing to oppose them except talk about them. South Vietnam's armed forces were helpless to oppose moves because they were already spread too thin.

The International Commission of Control and Supervision that was established to detect and investigate violations, control the entry of communist troops and supplies to the South and to supervise the ceasefire, was composed of four members including Canada, Indonesia, Hungary and Poland. Two of them—Poland and Hungary were not impartial. After three Canadian members of the commission were detained by the North Vietnamese in 1973 and suffered hardships and casualties, the Canadian government became so disenchanted with the commission's failure to man North Vietnam's entry points that it resigned from the commission May 29, saying, "Canada had come to Vietnam to help supervise a ceasefire, but instead it was observing a war." Iran was selected to replace Canada, and that nation tried to give some balance to the commission but found it impossible to do so.

In the United States, anti-war sentiment in Congress was so strong that President Nixon's administration was forced to strictly abide by the terms of the agreement, although it was openly flouted by the North Vietnamese.

Definite patterns developed in 1973. North Vietnam initiated four division-size attacks—all serious violations of the ceasefire agreement—to secure strategically advantageous positions that could later provide points of entry for war supplies. Meanwhile, North Vietnam continued to consolidate new bases and the number of incidents of military activity increased by a third over the previous year. In northern Quang Tri Province and western Thua Thien Province, South Vietnam's armed forces had to use artillery sparingly because of a shortage of shells, and airpower was not used at all in the defense of military outposts and lines of communication along the coast. Most planes were grounded due to a shortage of fuel, ammunition and bombs.

Both sides developed strong positions around Kontum City in South Vietnam's central section, and South Vietnamese armed forces fought to deny the communists access to II Corps' coastal lowlands.

III Corps was the scene of constant harassment of outlying hamlets with the North Vietnamese concentrating their troops against Ton Le Chon. In other areas, isolated South Vietnamese troops deep in communist-controlled northern Tay Ninh Province faced regular attacks.

The heaviest action in IV Corps in the summer of 1973 was concentrated in the Seven Mountains area of Chau Doc Province where South Vietnamese Rangers fought to destroy the remaining elements of North Vietnam's 1st Division in its mountain stronghold. This campaign proceeded slowly and at great cost to both sides. There was also heavy combat near the Hong Ngu region along the border where the Mekong River enters South Vietnam from Cambodia.

The most difficult problem that the North Vietnamese faced was to restore their infrastructure and network of bases to their pre-1968 levels. Just to maintain their expeditionary force required a major logistical effort. Therefore, during 1973 they expanded their network of supply bases and hard-surfaced the roads along the old Ho Chi Minh Trail in Laos for all-weather use. Once this work was completed truck convoys—often totaling more than 200 vehicles—brought men, weapons and war materiel into South Vietnam.

The following year the intricate road system that made up the old Ho Chi Minh Trail was enlarged and extended southward. Its north-south axis, formerly located primarily in Laos and Cambodia, was augmented by routes in South Vietnamese territory. This Truong Son corridor by now extended for nearly 600 miles from the 17th parallel to the northern edge of Tay Ninh Province, with lateral routes linking the corridor to the Trail and some of the coastal areas. These routes were not all-weather because pontoon bridges had to replace wooden structures that were destroyed by high water and floods during the rainy season.

The North Vietnamese expanded their control of areas in the South, and all of South Vietnam's remote highland bases and outposts that might interfere with their plans were systematically overwhelmed. Roads off the north-south axis were then built toward the eastern coastal plains. The communists built an enormous network of fuel storage areas that were supplied by pipelines and pumping facilities. Some light and medium-size airfields were reconditioned, and storage areas were constructed at key points.

Officials of the South Vietnamese government watched this buildup and takeover of her outposts with dismay. Her generals knew that these preparations were aimed at supporting a general offensive that could be sustained for at least eighteen months. It was believed that with this new network the North Vietnamese had reduced the time needed to bring new people and supplies from the North to the South from four months to three weeks.

South Vietnam's armed forces were able to contain most of North Vietnam's land grab during 1973, but remote outposts could not be defended despite President Thieu's insistence that they be held. He was advised that to attempt to hold all remote outposts a substantial number of troops would have to be sacrificed who could be used more effectively elsewhere.

Officials of South Vietnam's government still hoped that North Vietnam would abide by at least some parts of the Paris agreement. It now became the reluctant policy of Thieu's government to consider the abandonment of certain land areas in order that the most populated areas could be held. This meant turning over to the communists a sizable portion of their nation, and Thieu continued to cling stubbornly to a policy of keeping all the nation's territory intact, and to maintain control over all of its population even if it meant sustaining high casualties in trying to wrest occupied areas from the North Vietnamese.

It was a difficult decision, and one that President Thieu never came to grips with until it was too late. Instead, he ordered that the armed forces modernize in every way possible, particularly in logistics, firepower and mobility. Meanwhile, he ordered the armed forces to continue to assist in national pacification and to take part in projects to consolidate the military territorial structure at the village level with the farmland reclamation and resettlement program. These steps were geared to achieve South Vietnam's goal of self-defense, self-management and self-sufficiency.

To maintain a level of 1.1 million men, 200,000 to 240,000 new recruits for the armed services were required each year. Manpower available from the draft of men eighteen to thirty-nine only brought in 100,000 to 150,000 men so there was a yearly deficit of at least 100,000. Meanwhile, the desertion rate of 1.5 to 2 percent per month remained high. As a result, the armed forces lost up to one-fourth of their total strength each year. There was extensive draft dodging. Few military-age men were receptive to communist propaganda, but they deserted so they could return to their villages to be with their families.

One of many problems soon became apparent after the Americans went home. The most crucial involved motor vehicles. More than 4,000 that were transferred to the South Vietnamese by the United States and its allies remained unserviceable because of a lack of spare parts.

In combat, the South Vietnamese Air Force now faced heavy anti-aircraft fire, posing a grave threat to its planes as guns were brought into the South. The SA-7 hand-held missile posed a dramatic threat and during the first six months after the ceasefire there were eight successful firings out of twenty-two against South Vietnamese planes. In addition, heavy guns and tanks kept infiltrating the South, including 140 new 122 mm. and 130 mm. guns and 250 new tanks.

During attempts to relieve the siege of Ton Le Chon in III Corps near the Cambodian border, countermeasures against SA-7 missiles were successful in reducing hits on South Vietnamese airplanes to one out of three firings. When the SA-7 was fired it emitted a distinctive flash that often could be seen from the air. The flash was followed by smoke and vapor trails. South Vietnamese aircraft attacked in pairs in order that one or the other might see the missile after it was launched and take or direct evasive action. Several countermeasures were tried. High-energy flares sometimes were tossed out of the aircraft, or ejected mechanically. Frequently these flares caused the missile's heat-seeking mechanism to lock on so that the missile would burst near the flare without harm to the aircraft. Helicopter crews watched closely for these missiles, and their vehicles used special methods to reduce infrared emissions that attracted the missiles. The UH-1 had a hot spot on its fuselage below its main rotor. This area was shielded and the hot exhaust diverted upward by means of a piece of elbow piping attached to the tail pipe. These missiles forced the South Vietnamese Air Force to eliminate large formations and to confine their activities to higher altitudes.

CHAPTER 41

Battles for Key Terrain

WHILE THE RING WAS DRAWN TIGHTER AROUND TON LE CHON, AND North Vietnamese armed forces prepared to assault Trung Nghia in Kontum Province, they continued heavy attacks against Hong Ngu by troops based in Cambodia.

Meanwhile, diplomats returned to Paris to seek a real ceasefire and a lasting peace. South Vietnamese officials referred to these deliberations as "Ceasefire II." After the meeting, the four signatories to the original agreement issued a communique calling upon themselves to observe the provisions of the January ceasefire agreement. Nothing else was achieved, although there was a temporary lull in fighting in South Vietnam.

Before skeptical newsmen Kissinger called the renewed peace efforts in Paris a consolidation of the original agreement. "I am not naive enough to pretend to you that the mere fact of having again agreed to certain words in itself guarantees peace; but I will also say that since all parties have worked so seriously for the past three weeks, we have every hope that they will match this effort with performance and therefore there is fresh hope, and we hope a new spirit, in the implementation of the agreement, which in itself is maintained."

When Graham A. Martin became the new United States ambassador in Saigon, South Vietnam's government officials gained a measure of hope that United States support would continue. At that time there were signs of a North Vietnamese military buildup in the South, although intelligence sources could detect few signs that a major offensive was in the offing. Thieu and his cabinet did not expect a full attack in 1973, but they expected that North Vietnam would wait until near the end of President Nixon's second term before taking any precipitate action.

Thieu had no way of knowing, however, that Nixon would be forced to resign as United States president a year later after accepting responsibility for the Watergate break-in and its cover up.

A North Vietnamese offensive in mid-1973 actually was out of the question because North Vietnam had to rebuild its southern armies. Then, too, in the summer of 1973, communist soldiers and their leaders were badly demoralized by a seemingly endless war that still had to be fought. While Nixon remained in office the North Vietnamese knew they faced a formidable opponent who would not hesitate to take firm action against a full invasion of South Vietnam. They were well aware that Nixon had said following the ceasefire that he would work with the Congress in order to take appropriate action if North Vietnam mounted an offensive that jeopardized the stability of Indochina and that he had threatened to overturn the settlements reached "after so much sacrifice by so many for so long."

Vice President Spiro Agnew's resignation in disgrace in the fall of 1973, and the knowledge of Nixon's growing involvement with the Watergate scandal precluded any possibility that the president could work with Congress and take any decisive action.

South Vietnam's 44th Regiment, 23rd Division, was driven out of Trung Nghia by a tank/infantry assault June 8, 1973, but the South Vietnamese immediately attempted to retake this key position west of Kontum. Casualties mounted on both sides as successive attempts failed to dislodge the North Vietnamese who were not only deeply entrenched, but also enjoyed the advantage of observation from the heights of Ngoc Bay Mountain. The 44th gained only a few yards after several days of combat, but they were unable to move farther despite the employment of massive artillery barrages and air strikes.

Lieutenant General Nguyen Van Toan was determined to retake this strategic site and he decided to try an approach from the south against the positions at Plei Djo Drap, directly across the Dak Bla River from Trung Nghia. Such an attack, he believed, would strike the communist defenses on their flank and force them to withdraw. He directed that the 23rd Division be reinforced by Rangers, and attack north from their base at Plei Mrong.

The southwest monsoon, now in full force over the western highlands of Pleiku and Kontum Provinces, allowed the North Vietnamese to maneuver in daylight due to bad weather conditions that reduced air strikes to a minimum.

The South Vietnamese regiments made their final assault September 1 after heavy losses were suffered by both sides. The North Vietnamese suffered so severely that they were forced to withdraw. Some units, due to sickness, were down to 60 percent of their strength. Total North Vietnam combat losses were around 30 percent.

One of the few impediments to the steady growth of North Vietnam's logistical corridor throughout the length of the western highlands was the South Vietnamese camp at Plei Djereng that was called Le Minh. It was manned by the 80th Ranger Border Defense Battalion. This position, astride Route 613, blocked the free movement from the communist-controlled Plei Trap Valley into North Vietnam's base at Duc Co and east to Pleiku. This camp had long been a strategic enemy objective and, in violent action, the camp was overrun by the North Vietnamese. Thieu was so incensed by the loss that he rebuked Lieutenant General Toan for not reacting to advance warnings of the attack and taking steps to reinforce his command or at least provide adequate artillery support for the defenders. General Toan had earlier gained a reputation for aggressiveness, and after this loss he did employ his troops with skill.

Toan now set out to retake the camp and, in the process, to destroy North Vietnam's 320th Division. The battle lines changed little during the summer of 1973 despite bloody exchanges. Eleven months later Toan was relieved of his command. Thieu never forgave him for the loss of the strategic camp at Plei Djereng.

Events in III Corps' Quang Duc Province close to the Cambodian border were more successful for the South Vietnamese. In this province the North Vietnamese had long capitalized on their ability to concentrate overwhelming forces against lightly defended South Vietnamese areas. South Vietnam's armed forces were employed here with considerable skill, particularly in the use of rapid air deployment to key areas under attack. With good air support for ground troops, and strong artillery fire, the South Vietnamese defeated the North Vietnamese. They were so successful that the communists were denied use of Highway 14 through Quang Duc City, and their lines of communication in the border region around the Tuy Duc crossroads were subjected to permanent harrassment. The successes of South Vietnam's armed forces in this region proved again that if they were given sufficient ammunition and fuel, strong maintenance support for their equipment, and were properly led that they could overcome the traditional advantages of an attacker.

During the last half of 1973 North Vietnam devoted its major efforts towards rebuilding and expanding its armed forces in the South. The intense fighting that occurred from Kontum to Quang Duc was due mainly to North Vietnam's need to expand its logistical system in the South.

Communist sappers dealt South Vietnam a severe blow in December when they destroyed nine and a quarter million gallons of fuel at Nha Be.

This first year of fighting on their own had been costly to South

Vietnam's manpower. They had lost twelve thousand men on the battle-fields but the North Vietnamese had lost far more—an estimated forty-five thousand. With a combined population of 42 million people, such a loss was heavy. When equivalent figures between the United States and the combined Vietnams are adjusted to their respective populations and com-pared to the 250,000 Americans who died in World War II, the losses in this one year of so-called peace surpassed the American loss in that earlier war.

By the anniversary of the first ceasefire in January, 1974, South Viet-nam's regular forces controlled the major population areas and the impor-tant lines of communication. North Vietnam, meanwhile, continued to recover and rebuild its southern units with a constant flow of replace-ments.

Morale of the territorials in I Corps, who lived closest to the demilita-rized zone and therefore bore the brunt of consistent communist attacks, suffered a drastic decline. Not only were territorial troops in almost daily combat, but economic conditions were so poor that there was a slow decline in the number of people under South Vietnamese control.

Fighting in the northern and central provinces rose and fell as each side fought for key terrain, while the war in the Mekong Delta became primarily a contest for the rice harvest. The communists relied upon this region for 90 percent of their rice and it was taken from farmers with or without their consent. For South Vietnam's armed forces the rice war forced them to tie up sizable contingents of soldiers to prevent shipment of rice to delta base areas and then to collection points in Cambodia where it was shipped to communist units in II and III Corps. Large numbers of communists therefore fought to control rice-producing hamlets and to protect their requisitioning parties. Boats were used to transport the rice so the war was fought largely on canals and rivers. The battle for rice was bitter because it was the basic food staple that was needed by both sides. In September, 1973, a rice shortage developed in Saigon because alternate floods and drought in the region had reduced plantings. Wherever the communists were based they lived off rice taken from the countryside. In Cambodia they took so much rice from farmers that a shortage developed throughout this neighboring country.

South Vietnamese armed forces were spread so thin throughout the South that there was a steady erosion of government influence not only in the delta but throughout the country. In Saigon, this was not so readily apparent because the economy was growing with many prosperous-looking shops and restaurants. The dense, noisy traffic in Saigon's streets gave the appearance of prosperity. Inflation was growing almost uncontrolled, however, and members of the armed services and their families suffered the most because of their low pay. In the previous two years, rice harvests had been so poor that rice had to be imported. United States-aid dollars, along with the currency of most other countries, had declined in value as worldwide inflation kept increasing at an alarming rate. Many staples in South Vietnam rose in price more than 200 percent above their 1972 prices. The South Vietnamese military, including the officers, could not survive on their low pay once inflation rose to peak levels.

These factors led to low morale in the armed forces. One unit was so demoralized that when the communists attacked in the Song Bo corridor west of Hué December 15, 1973, the 3rd Infantry Company of the 1st Division fled in panic after sustaining only light casualties, despite the efforts of Colonel Hoang Mao. Such demoralization was happening all too frequently because these soldiers had been fighting more or less continuously all fall. This was a typical instance of poorly trained draftees whose morale had suffered a crippling loss.

Worsening economic conditions even affected the elite Airborne Division whose volunteers lost their high spirit. All too often the problem was acute because of the desperate economic conditions of their families. Morale was a problem among the officers as well. A full colonel received the equivalent in American currency of $80.00 a month after twenty years of service. Some enlisted men resorted to selling equipment and ammunition to the communists.

Ranger forces were reorganized in September, 1973, to provide South Vietnam's armed forces with a small strategic reserve that could be used quickly to react against communist infiltrations in the first three corps areas. Rangers were established in twenty-seven forward defense bases, mostly along the Laotian and Cambodian borders. Each base was assigned a minimum of one battalion. Before this new concept was adopted only six border posts were occupied by Rangers. All other posts were either inaccessible or in enemy hands. In addition, one Ranger group was kept in reserve to reinforce or rescue a threatened or besieged Ranger base.

North of the demilitarized zone the communists were prepared to resume the offensive in the South. North Vietnam's strategic reserves were being reconstituted with most of its fighting elements concentrated in Thanh Hoa Province between Hanoi and Vinh.

Government officials in Saigon knew that, for the present, there was a rough parity of military power deployed in the South, but it was a precarious balance. The South Vietnamese did not have a single division in reserve. Top officers warned that they would be forced to give up territory and population centers if the North Vietnamese made a full-scale attack.

The communists had the advantage of being able to concentrate their forces on one objective, and they had six full-strength infantry divisions with adequate artillery, tanks and ammunition to use in an attack at a decisive moment. In addition, the North Vietnamese had improved their roads from the North to the South and, in the absence of United States strategic airpower, the communists could deploy overwhelming forces to the sector of their choice without fear of hindrance.

The problems of South Vietnam's government were compounded by the fact that United States military assistance was funded by the three American services unlike earlier military assistance that had been funded separately by the United States Congress. With money coming directly from the United States military establishment, funds had to be weighed against the needs of America's own armed forces. For fiscal year 1974, this amount was budgeted by the Defense Department at $1.1 billion, but the Senate reduced the amount to $650 million. The House funded a different amount, and a figure of $900 million was established in conference committee. This amount was for all of Indochina, and not just for South Vietnam whose share actually was $813 million.

The United States Army, anticipating this drastic reduction by Congress, cut off all operational and maintance funds for South Vietnam. General Murray, who headed the Defense Attaché Office in Saigon, once he was apprised of this action, told Ambassador Graham Martin that he should advise Lieutenant General Dong Van Khuyen, commanding general of South Vietnam's Logistics Command, of the United States Army's action so he could take immediate action in South Vietnam to conserve supplies. Martin refused to pass the word along, saying it would be politically unsettling. For four months, therefore, the South Vietnamese armed forces used supplies at a normal rate instead of conserving them. Supplies normally were on a four month order-to-ship schedule. Therefore by April, 1974, the supply line from the United States had dried up and the South Vietnamese armed forces faced a crisis of major proportions. After South Vietnam officials were advised of the problem, they took immediate corrective action, but it was too late. Their logistics system never recovered.

United States and South Vietnamese officials in Saigon proposed a budget of military aid of $1.45 billion for fiscal 1975. When Congress began to debate the matter this figure was reduced to $1.136 billion, the lowest amount considered necessary to meet the minimum operational requirements for the South Vietnamese armed forces. Under such a restricted budget, one-for-one losses as approved by the ceasefire agreement could not be replaced, requiring severe controls on equipment usage and the use of ammunition. General Murray addressed the problem candidly, saying that these restraints would permit the armed forces of South Vietnam to defend their country only against the level of enemy activities at present in South Vietnam. He said such an amount would help to counter country-wide attacks against the South's defense position, but that it would be totally inadequate to help counter a sustained major offensive. Any further reductions, he said, would have a disastrous effect on South Vietnam's capabilities and morale, and enhance the enemy's potential. Further, he warned that a reduction of military assistance to a level of $750 million would be disastrous. With such an amount, he said, no investment program (equipment buys) could be supported at all. He stated that critical operational requirements for fuel, ammunition, spare parts, medical and communications supplies could not be met under such a budget. He claimed that the construction program would have to be eliminated, flying hours for the South Vietnamese Air Force reduced, and training and maintenance budgets slashed to the bone. He spelled out in unmistakable terms the effects of a $750 million military assistance budget saying, "It would cause South Vietnam to abandon large segments of the country and weaken possibilities and probabilities of a negotiated settlement."

Congress passed a final bill for all of Indochina that totalled $1 billion, and the president signed it August 5. The House and Senate approved for South Vietnam only $700 million for funding in fiscal year 1975. This amount covered all shipping costs, certain undelivered 1973 and 1974 items and commitments, and it paid for operation of the United States office in Saigon. In effect, only $500 million was left to meet the operational requirements of South Vietnam's armed forces, or two-thirds of what General Murray had specified was needed to permit South Vietnam's armed forces to defend themselves.

General Murray left Saigon in August, 1974, when his assignment was terminated, and he returned home to retire. He had fought long and hard for justice for South Vietnam. Before his departure he did what he could to get as much out of the limited budget as possible. Through no fault of his own he achieved only small success.

Major General Ira Hunt temporarily replaced Murray in Saigon until Major General Homer Smith could take over as Murray's permanent replacement.

The Vietnamese Air Force could expect only 30 percent of its requirements or $160 million under the new budget, and the South Vietnamese Navy only $9 million. With the operational budget reduced, only 55 percent of available transportation could be fueled. As a result, any tactical movement of vehicles had to be approved by corps commanders. Bandages and surgical dressings had to be washed and reused to save money, as well as the re-use of surgical equipment such as syringes and needles. Air Force squadrons were reduced from 66 to 56, and there was no replacement for the 162 aircraft destroyed in operations or accidents. Even worse, 224 aircraft were placed in storage because there were no funds to maintain and fly them. The Navy was forced to inactivate twenty-one of its forty-four riverine units for the same reason.

As South Vietnam approached the eve of its final battles for survival, budget-conscious members of the United States Congress effectively reduced the beleaguered country to a state bordering on impotence. That they fought so well in the months ahead is a tribute to the dedication of the average South Vietnamese fighting man.

Critical decisions were made by each side in 1974 about ending the war in Indochina. In Washington, government officials continued to hope for a negotiated peace. The communists in Hanoi had no such intentions. The United States Congress took the most damaging action against South Vietnam by reducing military assistance to a level well below that needed to maintain operational efficiency of her armed forces. Such action seriously undermined the will of the South Vietnamese people to continue their sacrifices and to maintain an effective resistance to increased communist infiltrations.

President Nixon's resignation in August, 1974, convinced North Vietnamese government officials that the time was ripe to make their final move against South Vietnam. With decreasing support for South Vietnam by the Congress of the United States, communist leaders in Hanoi decided that 1975 would be the year of the major battles to achieve victory.

In October, 1973, the American Defense Attaché Office in Saigon had listed three likely courses that the communists might follow to achieve their goal of conquering the South. The first possibility involved recognition of a North Vietnamese government by South Vietnam as a government-within-a-government to compete with it in an economic and political struggle. Secondly, it was thought that the North Vietnamese might start a limited military offensive that South Vietnam's government and armed forces could not handle. The third, and most realistic, appraisal was that the North Vietnamese might start a major military offensive to cause the immediate collapse of the South Vietnamese government and its armed forces.

Officials of the Defense Attaché Office were convinced that North Vietnam would base its final decision for 1974 operations primarily on its expectation of Soviet Russia and People's Republic of China economic and military support, and the fact that the United States probably would not react militarily to an escalation of the war. American analysts had no way of knowing how much assistance and/or influence the Soviets and Chinese would exert on the North Vietnamese.

The continued North Vietnamese buildup in the South appeared to indicate to the Americans that a major military move was in the offing, but members of the Defense Attaché Office reached the conclusion that North Vietnam was not ready for a major decisive offensive in 1974 despite its heavy infiltration of men and supplies in the South. American officials believed that North Vietnam would start a phased offensive to create conditions beyond the capacity of South Vietnam's armed forces to counteract. It was also anticipated by these American officials that North Vietnam's military buildup would continue for a later decisive invasion.

Hanoi's leaders had met in the early spring of 1974 to study resolutions at the Lao Dong Party Central Committee's 21st Plenum. Security was so tight that little information reached the South about the discussions at these meetings. It is interesting, in retrospect, to note that most of the strategic concepts promulgated at this conference paralleled the views of the Defense Attaché Office in Saigon.

The architect for the final offensive in the South was Senior General Van Tien Dung. He told the Central Committee that the path of revolution in the South should be the path of revolutionary violence. "No matter what the situation, we must firmly grasp the opportunity and the strategic offensive line."

Early in March, 1974, the Central Military Party Committee went into session to study the party's Central Committee resolution that the war in the South might be resolved in various transitional stages, and that it could achieve success only through violence with the support of political and military forces. "If the war resumes on a large scale, a revolutionary war will be waged to win total victory. The southern resolution must firmly grasp the concept of strategic offensive. We must resolutely counterattack and attack the enemy, and we must firmly maintain and develop our active position in all respects." At the time, such comments were secret, and bore no resemblance whatsoever to the party line their supporters were given throughout the world. Some of these supporters, particularly in the United States, would have been shocked.

The Central Party Committee approved these recommendations and orders went out to the corps areas to start training in preparation for offensive preparations of the expeditionary army.

South Vietnam's armed forces in IV Corps had only been successful in countering North Vietnamese attacks in the delta region, and in the border areas of Svay Rieng Province in Cambodia. In III Corps, although

South Vietnam's armed forces eventually ejected units of the North Vietnamese Army from the Iron Triangle, this costly success was largely overshadowed by the critical loss later of Phuoc Long Province. All remaining outposts had fallen to the North Vietnamese in the Highlands to the north except for a protective screen around Hué and Da Nang. Even around these cities defenses were not strong enough to withstand concerted attacks.

Cambodia's Svay Rieng Province was sixty miles long and sixteen miles wide at its neck where it thrust into Vietnam's rich delta region, ending in what was known as the Parrot's Beak thirty miles west of Saigon. Although the Cambodian government maintained a garrison at the provincial capital, it did so only at the sufferance of the North Vietnamese Army that controlled the rest of the province. Hostile Cambodians were not considered a serious threat to the North Vietnamese so they were largely ignored.

South Vietnam's armed forces attacked a strategic North Vietnamese Army base known as Tri Phap February 12, 1974, and thwarted the North Vietnamese Army's attempt to sever Saigon from the delta at My Tho. As a result of this attack, North Vietnam's 5th Division was prevented from establishing a base from which to extend its operations southward into Dinh Tuong Province and westward toward Saigon through Long An. When the North Vietnamese were denied this approach, the 5th Division concentrated between an area called the Elephant's Foot and another area known as Angel's Wing in Cambodia (their names described their shape) and threatened South Vietnam's district headquarters at Moc Hoa. More seriously, the 5th Division prepared to occupy the narrow strip of marshland between the Svay Rieng Province's border and the Vam Co Tay River. This river was the last defensible location between the Cambodian border and Saigon thirty miles distant. If the North Vietnamese had been successful, Tay Ninh Province to the north would have fallen since the seizure of the vital road junction at Go Dau Ha would have ended all land and water communications between Saigon and the province capital.

South Vietnamese forces made a daring armored thrust into Cambodia in late April, meeting North Vietnam's 5th Division in combat. The communist division's defeat was so decisive that it was never again able to threaten seriously the South Vietnamese in this sector.

In spite of their great victory, the South Vietnamese were unable to prevent the North Vietnamese from continuing their strategic raids against the crucial defense perimeter of bases north of Saigon. The first to fall was the relatively unimportant outpost at Chi Linh.

Constraints on ammunition and fuel forced the South Vietnamese to reduce flying hours again, and South Vietnam had to cancel new offensives. In the future, although their armed forces frequently reacted strongly to local threats within supporting distances of major bases, outlying threats were beyond their capability. The decline that began to develop early in 1974 soon proved to be irreversible.

South Vietnam's 5th Division, based at Lai Khe, twenty-five miles north of the capital, now was assigned to defend Saigon. This was the last strongly held position with an uninterrupted connection to Saigon.

CHAPTER 42

Fall of Phuoc Long

THE IRON TRIANGLE, BOUNDED ON THE NORTH BY JUNGLE AND THE overgrown rubber plantations of Long Nguyen, was enclosed on the west by the Saigon River, and on the east by the smaller but unfordable Thi Tinh River. The latter joined the Saigon River near Phu Hoa at the southern apex of the triangle, seven miles from Phu Cuong, the capital of Binh Duong Province. It was an important industrial and farming center. The terrain within the triangle was flat and featureless, and covered by dense brush and undergrowth. The clearings, especially in the northern part, were thick with elephant grass, higher than a man's head. The ground was scarred by countless bomb and shell craters so motor vehicles found it almost impossible to travel except over the narrow, dirt roads. Even tracked vehicles had difficulty traversing this area. Underground there was a vast network of tunnels, most of which were now abandoned and caved in. Earlier in the war the territory had been the scene of numerous battles. To defend the northern part of the triangle the South Vietnamese had a weak string of three outposts.

On the triangle's western flank the South Vietnamese had some semi-fixed positions north of Cu Chi manned by the 25th Division, plus some regional forces. Constant sweeps were made through this area to detect and drive back infiltrators.

Opposite Rach Bap in the Ho Bo Woods, the North Vietnamese resisted incursions but the Saigon River was a formidable obstacle for the South Vietnamese to overcome. Then, too, the 25th Division's lack of resources limited the influence they could exert within the triangle.

South Vietnam was stronger in the Ben Cat District east of the Thi Tinh boundary of the triangle, but only a road with a small bridge incapable of handling heavy vehicles connected the district town and the triangle hamlet of An Dien.

North Vietnamese Army units continued to make strategic raids in this area, but they paid a heavy price. However, in the deep forests of northern Tay Ninh, Binh Long and Phuoc Long Provinces the communists continued to build a large combat capability by stockpiling weapons, ammunition, fuel and supplies. While replacement soldiers from North Vietnam were brought into the area and put through intensive training courses, their engineers built hospitals and improved the area's roads and bridges.

While the buildup was underway in these provinces near the Cambodian border, the North Vietnamese 5th, 7th and 9th Divisions were pressing forward against South Vietnam's outer line of defenses around Saigon and threatening to systematically reduce them.

The North Vietnamese also tried to eliminate isolated South Vietnamese outposts in the Central Highlands so they could move into the coastal lowlands. Heavy fighting persisted in this vast region from the Darlac high plateau to the narrow coastal plains of Quang Nam.

By the spring of 1974, South Vietnam still maintained two district outposts deep in the highlands of Quang Tin Province in the north but they controlled only shallow perimeters around the towns of Tien Phuoc and Hau Duc. Thus the South Vietnamese continued to hang on to these areas but only with a tenuous hold on their lines of communication. The sparse population in these northern areas made it difficult to recruit sufficient territorials to help the regular forces in defending the region.

Strategic raids by communist soldiers in the vast region below the Hai Van Pass northwest of Da Nang helped to place their forces in an excellent position to begin a major offensive south of the demilitarized zone. The communists suffered heavy losses but South Vietnam's armed forces were severely depleted of experienced leaders and soldiers in heavy fighting. Those who replaced the battle-hardened troops were not well trained, or in sufficient numbers to bring their battalions up to strength. On the other hand North Vietnamese replacements were plentiful and they were moved into the area without interference. It was evident to South Vietnam's generals that North Vietnam's command organization, logistics and communications were rapidly expanding and proving themselves. The North Vietnamese 3rd Corps, in particular, emerged as a well-trained outfit now that it had a successful campaign behind it. The corps had moved to the edge of the narrow coastal plain in I Corps and was within artillery range of nearly every major South Vietnamese installation and population center. Similar progress was made north of Hai Van Pass.

Throughout the early months of 1974 the North Vietnamese Army maintained constant pressure against South Vietnam's armed forces north of Hai Van Pass by concentrating on the Airborne Division and the 1st

Infantry Division entrenched west and south of Hué. For the time being, North Vietnam did little to disturb the balance of power in the northernmost province. Her leaders knew that they faced three South Vietnamese Marine brigades in Quang Tri Province, and they did not want to invite retaliation against their huge logistical complex around Dong Ha that was being built for the contemplated full-scale invasion. There were some skirmishes for high ground south of Phu Bai which had the only major airfield serving Hué. The South Vietnamese 1st Infantry Division was responsible for protecting the airfield and Highway 1 that passed through the narrow defile in the Phu Loc District, and the vital Ta Trach corridor to Hué.

Lieutenant General Ngo Quang Truong was able to hold the communist's main forces at bay when they did attack Hué, but the ring soon closed on the Imperial City. Reinforced North Vietnamese battalions—equipped with new weapons and fresh replacements from the North—engaged in close combat with South Vietnamese outposts along the length of the front. Behind these battalions new formations of tanks were assembled, and large supply installations were constructed, heavily protected by anti-aircraft guns and connected by newly improved roads.

The situation in the northern part of South Vietnam was ominous, but one of the most tragic events of the war was unfolding in Phuoc Long Province in the South, although at first this was not apparent.

General Van Ten Dung, North Vietnam's senior general, was not entirely truthful when he told the Central Military Party Committee and the General Staff that between April and October, 1974, the North Vietnamese Army had stepped up its offensive actions and had won great victories from Thua Tien to Saigon. Actually, North Vietnamese Army units were stalemated at the extreme ends of the long battlefield in Thua Tien and also around Saigon. It had overrun isolated bases in the Central Highlands and had succeeded in penetrating to the edge of Quang Nam Province's lowlands although they had suffered grievous losses. General Dung described the battle for the district capital of Thuong Duc by claiming that South Vietnamese forces had been destroyed in a test of strength against some of the best of South Vietnam's armed forces. He said that South Vietnam had sent a whole division of paratroopers into the area to launch repeated counter attacks in a bid to recapture a sub-sector of Thuong Duc's district capital. General Dung told the Central Military Party Committee that his forces had decimated the ranks of the South Vietnamese and forced them to give up. He conceded, however, that the South Vietnamese eventually did win a victory at Thuong Duc, along with some smaller victories in the Highlands.

The North Vietnamese General Staff now called for an even bolder

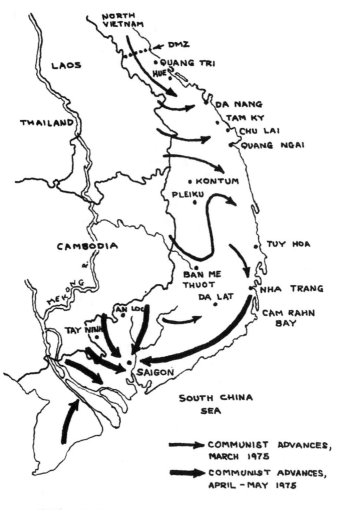

THE FINAL DAYS

Final days of the republic of South Vietnam. *(Drawn by Master Sergeant Bradley A. Spencer, M.C., Ret.)*

strategy. The Central Military Party Committee was advised that the combat capability of their mobile regular troops was superior to that of the enemy. The General Staff said that the war had reached its final stage and that the balance of forces had changed in North Vietnam's favor. Both the military committee and the General Staff reached agreement that such superiority should be exploited. It was agreed that, in the future, North Vietnam's armed forces would no longer attack only to destroy South Vietnam's armed forces, but would combine this objective with attacks to "liberate" populated areas. In effect, this would move the fighting out of the jungles and mountains into the lowlands. Planners advised the military committee that "the reduction of United States aid made it impossible for the puppet troops to carry out their combat plan and build up their forces, and the South Vietnamese were forced to fight a poor man's war." The North Vietnamese estimate that South Vietnam's firepower had been decreased by nearly 60 percent due to bomb and ammunition shortages was remarkably accurate. This knowledge is not surprising because the debate in the United States Congress about reductions in military assistance to South Vietnam's "mobility had been reduced by half due to lack of aircraft, vehicles and fuel" gave the North Vietnamese invaluable information for their own military operations.

North Vietnam's Politburo and Central Military Committee met again in October to consider the General Staff's assessments and recommendations. Their opinion of South Vietnam's capability was unanimous. It was agreed that the "puppet" troops were militarily, politically and economically weakening every day while North Vietnam's forces were stronger than those in the South. There was no question in the minds of the communist leaders that the United States was facing mounting difficulties both at home and in the world, and that its potential for aiding the "puppets" was rapidly declining. North Vietnam's leaders believed that the chain of mutual support bases that had been created in the South, and their reserve forces, had strengthened their capacity to mount a full-scale invasion. They also were convinced that their strategic and political systems in South Vietnam were also improving. Lastly, they were convinced that the movement to demand peace, plus the efforts in the South to overthrow Thieu's government, was gaining momentum in many cities.

In regard to the United States, North Vietnam's leaders were well informed about the rise of anti-war sentiment, and not only among the political activists. There was agreement that after signing the Paris Accord, and the withdrawal of American troops from Vietnam, the United States would face even greater embarrassment with the fall of South Vietnam. They knew, for example, of the internal fights within the Ford administration, and the absolute rejection by most political leaders in both parties of any resumption of active support for resuming military activities in Indochina. They had followed the Watergate scandal with glee, correctly estimating that it had seriously eroded confidence in the Republican Party throughout the nation. The resignation of President Nixon August 8, 1974, had been greeted by North Vietnam's leaders with great satisfaction. He had been viewed as an extremely reactionary president. The economic recession in the United States, with its mounting inflation, serious unemployment and the oil crisis were all considered by Hanoi's leaders as mitigating against any return to military participation by the United States. North Vietnam's leaders were aware that relations between the United States and its allies were at a low ebb, and many countries who were dependent upon the United States were now seeking to escape its control in the conduct of their foreign affairs. Most important of all, and of greatest satisfaction to North Vietnam's government leaders, was the fact that the United States had decreased its aid to the Saigon regime.

Le Duan, first secretary of North Vietnam's communist party, spoke the views of many at the conference by saying that having withdrawn militarily from the South, the United States would hardly jump back in. "No matter how it might intervene, the United States would be unable to save the Saigon administration from collapse." As the first, and most crucial, test of this assessment, Phuoc Long was selected as the battleground to test United States reaction.

III Corps had been the scene of several battles during the summer and fall of 1974 but little new territory changed hands. The divisional battles in Binh Duong, Tay Ninh and Bien Hoa Provinces had caused thousands of casualties but all positions, except those on the Tay Ninh-Cambodia frontier, were retaken by South Vietnam's armed forces.

South Vietnam made strong efforts during the year to retake important areas and population centers that had been occupied by the communists. Losses were high, and now South Vietnam's armed forces were overextended. Meanwhile, the North Vietnamese continued to commit units of ever-increasing size and to expand their logistical systems along the South Vietnamese side of the Laotian and Cambodian borders.

North Vietnam had been unable during 1973 and 1974 to occupy any provincial capital in South Vietnam. It had tried to take Kontum and Tay Ninh. Now, its generals turned to Phuoc Long, the northernmost capital of III Corps, and prepared to attack it with two infantry divisions augmented by an infantry regiment, and supported by a tank regiment, an anti-aircraft regiment, a field artillery regiment and several engineer assault units.

The city of Phuoc Long is thirty-seven air miles northeast of Saigon.

The province was bounded on the north by Cambodia and consisted of four districts. At the time, there were 30,000 people in the city—mostly Montagnards—who worked on the rubber plantations and in lumbering. The terrain is mountainous and covered by dense jungle that denied air observation. Phuoc Long City was linked to Saigon by Inter-provincial Route 1A and National Route 14. The latter also connected Phuoc Long with Quang Duc and Ban Me Thuot to the northeast. The Song Be airfield had asphalt runways and could handle cargo planes as large as C-130s. Phuoc Long was normally supplied by trucks via 1A and 14. The city was defended by five Regional Force battalions numbering 4,500 men and 1,000 members of the Popular Forces who had fought at An Loc.

Phuoc Long Province was far outside Saigon's defenses, so its importance to South Vietnam was primarily political. As long as it remained in their control they could claim possession of all province capitals. On the other hand, the presence of South Vietnamese bases deep inside otherwise North Vietnamese-controlled territory was totally unacceptable to the communists.

During late November and early December of 1974 Phuoc Long Province remained relatively tranquil with only sporadic attacks. The communists ended that quiet period by striking Don Luan December 13 with simultaneous assaults on Duc Phone and New Bo Duc. The battle ranged around Song Be airfield and New Bo Duc where the South Vietnamese 341st Regional Forces Battalion beat back successive assaults. Four days later, however, the South Vietnamese lost an airstrip, and the positions in the northern part of the province started to fall to the North Vietnamese. Phuoc Long City now faced a crisis with the loss of so many surrounding strong points, plus the increasingly strong enemy pressure in Tay Ninh Province, adjoining Cambodia. Lieutenant General Du Quoc Dong was faced with no suitable options. He had to stop communist advances toward Tay Ninh, and also hold Binh Tuy Province on the east coast. Despite his limited number of troops, General Dong sent a battalion by helicopter from Lai Khe to the beleaguered men at Song Be airfield. As this 2nd Battalion, 7th Infantry Regiment of South Vietnam's 5th Division reached Song Be, General Dong met December 23 with Lieutenant General Dong Van Quang, President Thieu's national security adviser. He told him that III Corps needed at least part of I Corps' Airborne Division to save Phuoc Long. Thieu rejected Dong's request, telling him that the Airborne Division was not available, and that it could not be moved south in time anyway. The president promised Dong that his command would receive priority on air and logistical suport, but that he had to fight with the troops available.

December 26 the North Vietnamese 7th Division, with the assistance of heavy artillery fire in advance and diversionary attacks, moved against South Vietnamese positions in and around Phu Giao, and overran Don Luan south of Phuoc Long City. Refugees fled, crowding into Song Be airfield that was now isolated.

The South Vietnamese tried to supply the garrison and its refugees by air drop in early January, 1975, but none of the supplies reached the defenders. In a series of sharp battles against Song Be, the North Vietnamese lost sixteen tanks but immediately rushed ten more towards the airfield. General Dong now dispatched two companies of his best troops from the 81st Airborne Rangers into the battle. These highly trained volunteers were normally used in commando operations.

Photographic planes spotted seven 37-mm. anti-aircraft guns around Song Be January 6, but continuous surveillance could not be maintained by the South Vietnamese because their flying time for the month had already been used up.

North Vietnamese sapper squads now moved in with tanks, mopping up bypassed positions and establishing strong points around the city of Phuoc Long. Despite the fact that recoilless rifles fired by the South Vietnamese either destroyed or damaged some communist tanks, most escaped because the ranges were often so short that the missiles did not have time to arm themselves and bounced harmlessly off tank hulls. The communists, aware of the destructiveness of these recoilless rifles, had welded extra armor plating on the sides of their tanks, and their crews were kept buttoned up so grenades could not be dropped through their hatches.

North Vietnamese artillery, increasing to 300 rounds per day by January 3, was devastating. Structures, bunkers and trenches collapsed, and casualties mounted. It was not long before South Vietnamese artillery guns were out of action, destroyed by fire from communist tanks, recoilless rifles and 130-mm. guns. The province chief, deciding that his forces could no longer endure without artillery support and adequate communications, ordered a withdrawal January 6, 1975, from the city of Phuoc Long. The retreat was made under constant enemy fire. It was the first province capital to fall since the ceasefire.

An airborne trooper who had fought at An Loc said of the fight, "Enemy troops were not so good and so courageous as we might have thought. There were simply too many of them. The enemy's artillery fire was fierce and many times more accurate than it had been during the battle of An Loc. Enemy tanks had something new and strange. Our M-72 rockets were unable to knock them out. We hit them. They stopped for a while but then moved on. Our air support was not very effective. The planes flew too high. If only we could have had B-52s like we did at An Loc!"

The capture of Phuoc Long gave North Vietnam an extended control over a large area. Three of the communist base areas were now linked together in a continuous arc from the Cambodian border across northern III Corps with access routes toward Ham Tan on the coast. Psychologically and politically the loss of Phuoc Long came as a shock to South Vietnam government officials and members of the armed forces. The apparent total indifference with which the United States and other non-communist nations regarded this loss reinforced the doubts of the viability of the Paris Ceasefire Agreement held by the people of South Vietnam. There was little hope left that the United States would punish North Vietnam for their continued violations of the agreement.

Phuoc Long was not merely a military victory for the North Vietnamese. They had gained a psychological and political victory of the greatest importance. It was their first big step toward military conquest of South Vietnam. They now believed they could boldly proceed with conquest without fear of any military reaction from the United States.

Not many civilians and soldiers survived the retreat. Small groups of Montagnards trekked through the jungles to Quang Duc, while approximately 200 Rangers, members of the 7th Infantry Division and territorials were rescued by air. The province chief was crippled by wounds, and he was never heard from again. A few other commanders survived and reached a South Vietnamese outpost at Bu Binh on Highway 14 in Quang Duc Province. South Vietnamese losses were heavy. Of the 5,400 officers and men of the 7th Infantry, the Airborne Rangers and the territorials who were committed to the battle, less than 850 survived. Only eighty-five members of the Rangers came out alive. Civilian casualties were exceptionally high. Before the battle there had been 30,000 in the area but only a tenth of that number survived. Province and village officials who were captured were summarily executed. Although the battle occurred during the dry, northeast monsoon season, heavy rain drenched Saigon and the rest of the region. One official said with sadness, "Even the gods are weeping on Phuoc Long."

CHAPTER 43

Ban Me Thuot Falls

THE LOSS OF PHUOC LONG PROVINCE WAS THE MOST FLAGRANT BREACH of the ceasefire agreement that had yet occurred. In anticipation of the loss, the United States Department of State had said January 3, 1975, that the offensive "belies Hanoi's claims that it is the United States and South Vietnam who are violating the 1973 Paris truce agreements and standing in the way of peace."

The so-called Provisional Revolutionary Government of Vietnam rejected the accusation, and North Vietnam's Communist Party newspaper claimed that the offensive was a "legitimate right of riposte" in defense of the Paris agreement.

The United States State Department issued an official protest dated January 11. It was delivered to the non-Vietnamese participants at the International Commission of Control and Supervision. It stated that when the agreement was concluded two years earlier—January 28, 1973—and the Act of the International Conference on Vietnam was signed at Paris, March 2, it was the United States' hope that it would provide a framework under which the Vietnamese people could make their own political choices and resolve their problems in an atmosphere of peace. It said that such hope was clearly frustrated by the flagrant violations of the agreement, citing the buildup of North Vietnam's main-force army in the South by sending over 400 new vehicles, as well as greatly increasing their artillery and anti-aircraft weapons. It was further pointed out that North Vietnam had improved its military logistics system throughout Laos, Cambodia and the demilitarized zone as well as in South Vietnam by expanding its armament stockpiles. The United States charged that North Vietnam had refused to deploy teams to oversee the ceasefire, had failed to pay its share of the expenses of the control commission, and had failed to resolve and honor the American men missing in action. Further, the State Department condemned North Vietnam's failure to maintain negotiations with the Republic of Vietnam, saying that it had gradually increased its military pressure against South Vietnam by overrunning Phuoc Long Province and engaging in military activities against eleven district towns that clearly and unequivocally were held by South Vietnam at the time of the ceasefire. In conclusion, the State Department urged the Democratic Republic of Vietnam to halt its military offensive and to join the Republic of Vietnam in re-establishing stability and seeking a political solution to their differences.

North Vietnam's officials responded by accusing the United States of making reconnnaissance flights over South Vietnam to assist the Saigon administration in intensifying its bombing and land-grabbing operations against Provisional Government-controlled areas. In response, the United States said these flights were the result of extreme North Vietnamese provocations. Actually, these photoreconnaissance flights by American aircraft were of some value to units of the South Vietnamese armed forces, but they were rarely used for targeting by the South's planes and artillery. Reconnaissance over Laos actually had stopped June 4, 1974.

General Van Tien Dung, in analyzing the United States reaction to the capture of Phuoc Long, told the Politburo in Hanoi during its sessions between December 18 and January 8, 1975, that he was convinced that the United States would not again participate in the Vietnamese war. He urged members to exploit South Vietnam's weaknesses which, he said, "herald a new opportunity for us . . . to fully exploit this great opportunity we have to conduct large-scale annihilating battles to destroy and disintegrate the enemy on a large scale." Members of the Politburo agreed and details for a spring offensive were refined at this midwinter conference.

North Vietnam's leadership was heartened by the fact that President Gerald R. Ford made no mention of Vietnam in his State of the Union message to Congress January 15. They were even more encouraged six days later when Ford said at a press conference that he could foresee no circumstances in which the United States might actively re-enter the war.

Although South Vietnam's armed forces were successful in fighting off North Vietnam's main Army forces in most of the central and northern delta region, security in the southern provinces continued to deteriorate. Territorial soldiers were not competent to deal with the threat posed by experienced North Vietnamese regular soldiers, and there were insufficient numbers of South Vietnamese regular army units. In addition, South Vietnam's delta naval units had been reduced from forty-four to twenty-one due to budgetary limitations. With their forces cut more than in half, riverine units no longer could provide adequate security on major canals.

In addition, another security problem arose in the northern part of the delta in mid-February that was to have tragic overtones. The collapse of Cambodia's armed forces caused thousands to seek refuge in Chau Doc Province where more than 7,000 people, including at least 500 military men, streamed across the border.

The American embassy, and the Defense Attaché Office, kept reporting the true state of affairs in South Vietnam to Washington, saying there were no doubts but that the North Vietnamese were preparing for a major offensive.

Some members of Congress came to South Vietnam to see for themselves. Senator Sam Nunn, a member of the Armed Services Committee, spent two days in Saigon in mid-January. He was given detailed briefings and returned to the United States convinced that military aid reductions had seriously weakened South Vietnam's armed forces. Representative Leo J. Ryan, who had made a similar visit in December, had reached the same conclusion.

President Ford requested an additional appropriation of $522 million for Vietnam and Cambodia January 28, of which $300 million would go directly to South Vietnam.

The Senate and the House then sent a joint bipartisan group to Saigon to report on the appropriateness of the president's request. They were given candid briefings, and offered trips to any place they wished to visit. Congresswoman Bella Abzug insisted upon seeing and talking to "political prisoners," and her request was granted. Even she was unsure of just what a "political prisoner" was and South Vietnam officials were unsure themselves. At the time the desperate, war-torn nation had imprisoned many outright enemies of the state and, quite possibly, some were incarcerated solely because of their opposition to the present regime. Tours of the battlefields were also arranged, and fact sheets that underlined the seriousness of South Vietnam's military position were issued to members of Congress. South Vietnam's leaders stressed that the infiltration from the North continued to grow and that they expected it would be especially heavy during the next few months. They said that more than half as many replacements were expected to arrive from the North into South Vietnam during the first three months of 1975 as had arrived during all of 1973. Thieu's briefers claimed that, since the ceasefire, 200,000 North Vietnamese replacements had moved south, a clear sign that an offensive was in the offing. They further stressed that the North Vietnamese Army now had twice as many tanks in South Vietnam as they had, or a total of 700 versus their 352. Finally, they told the congressmen that the North Vietnamese had built a complex logistical system in South Vietnam stockpiled with enough supplies to support a major offensive for more than a year. For the first time in the war Thieu's staffers stressed that South Vietnam was in a militarily inferior position.

The bipartisan congressional delegation was told that the North Vietnamese Expeditionary Army's force was less than half the size of South Vietnam's combat forces, but that North Vietnam made up the difference by maintaining secure garrisons in North Vietnam where more than 70,000 men were available for immediate deployment to the battle fronts. North Vietnam's Army also had the advantage of surprise, the congressmen were advised, and the ability to mass overwhelming force at a given point. South Vietnam's briefers said their country was at a disadvantage because it was unable to move sufficient reserves to a threatened area even though it had advance warning of an attack. It was stated that defense of populated areas, with thousands of bridges and hundreds of miles of highways to guard, left South Vietnam with insufficient forces to meet countrywide threats. With no reserves, they said, deep or prolonged North Vietnamese offensive operations could not be countered effectively.

The Defense Attaché Office in Saigon presented its 1975 threat assessment, concluding with the statement that a significant upsurge in combat in the northern part of South Vietnam could be expected as poor weather gradually abated in late February and March with a resumption of major attacks in II Corps once the communists completed their preparations. Congressmen were advised that the war in the delta region was expected to remain at the recent intensified levels of combat, indicating that communist attacks were part of an ambitious move to conquer the South.

Two days after the congressional group departed from South Vietnam the North Vietnamese Army launched its final offensive, severing Highway 19 between the Highlands and the coast in the northern part of II Corps.

All-out attacks were planned by General Van Tien Dung who had strongly recommended them January 8, 1975, two days after Phuoc Long Province fell to the communists. At that time Comrade Le Duan summed up the feelings of the Politburo and the General Staff when he said, "The situation is now clear to everybody. We are now determined to fulfill the two-year plan." In calling for a strategic strike in 1975, Le Duan said that military pressure must be brought closer to Saigon, and as many enemy main-force units as possible must be annihilated. In the Mekong Delta Le Duan called for military pressure to be brought against My Tho. "We have agreed that this year the attack on the Central Highlands will begin." He pointed to the map behind him. "Attacks must be unleashed toward Ban Me Thuot and Tuy Hoa. The Fifth Region will have to form a liberated area from Binh Dinh Province northward, and in the Tri Thien area forces will have to control an area from Hué to Da Nang."

He was interrupted by a question as to where the main battlefield would be established. After a detailed discussion of South Vietnam's military strength and the relative strategic value of each region, the conferees agreed unanimously with the General Staff's plan that the Central Highlands would be the main battlefield.

It is interesting to note that North Vietnam's leaders did not at first expect total victory in 1975. The country-wide offensive they had approved was not expected to be decisive until 1976.

Le Duc Tho entered the conference room just before discussion began on selection of the main objective. The conferees learned later that the Political Bureau was troubled because an attack on Ban Me Thuot had not been clearly outlined in the combat plan. Tho was sent to assure that the military committee understood the importance that the Political Bureau attached to such an attack. Once Le Duc Tho was briefed, he became an enthusiastic supporter. He told the conference, "We must definitely raise the problem of liberating Ban Me Thuot and Duc Lap. It would be absurd if, with almost five divisions in the Central Highlands, that we could not attack Ban Me Thuot."

General Vo Nguyen Giap, secretary of the Central Military Party Committee, concluded the conference by establishing the areas and targets for the offensive, and the campaign objectives and orders for employing the army units. He also suggested the fighting methods that should be applied, stressing the principles of force, secrecy and surprise. Giap also advised that it was necessary to deceive the enemy into concentrating their forces in areas north of the Central Highlands.

General Vu Lang was assigned as commander and he left the conference at the request of Le Duan and Le Duc Tho to go to the Ban Me Thuot area with special cadres to assess the situation. Prior to his departure, he told General Tran Van Tra, "This time I will fight in the Central Highlands until the rainy season. Then I will go to Nam Bo to join you in studying the battlefield situation and making preparations for military activities in the 1975–1976 dry season."

The conference adjourned January 9 and the Central Military Party Committee prepared plans to support the conference's resolution. Ban Me Thuot was selected as the army's first objective, and the main effort of its Central Highlands campaign.

The 320th, 10th and 968th North Vietnamese Divisions had long experience in the Highlands, and now they were reinforced by the 316th Division.

General Van Tien Dung was given responsibility for capturing Ban Me Thuot. He planned to use the element of surprise, enhanced by strong diversionary attacks on Kontum and Pleiku to achieve his objective. Once surprise was achieved, he expected to concentrate his forces against Ban Me Thuot to prevent South Vietnam from reinforcing their units.

Major General Pham Van Phu, who had commanded South Vietnam's 1st Infantry Division, replaced Lieutenant General Nguyen Van Toan as commander of the II Corps in December, 1974. President Thieu had reluctantly ordered the change, although believing that Toan was a competent field commander, because of charges of corruption against Toan by Vice President Tran Van Hoang. Toan was re-assigned as chief of armor and February 5, 1975, he was assigned to command III Corps replacing General Dong who had resigned a month earlier. This change of command in II Corps contributed to the later collapse of that area.

The communists prepared for their next major campaign with more confidence, encouraged by the United States' continued hands-off attitude.

The North Vietnamese 320th Division based near Pleiku was reported moving south toward the Darlac plateau by the end of January. Although South Vietnam's II Corps headquarters was alerted by the move, no significant action was taken other than daily aerial attacks against communist truck convoys.

North Vietnamese convoys during February were sighted almost daily moving south in great numbers along the western border routes. Toward the end of the month, the South Vietnamese Air Force inflicted immense destruction during repeated attacks on these convoys.

South Vietnamese intelligence sources reported that the North Vietnamese 316th, 312th and 341st Divisions were moving south, but their destinations were unknown. The 316th concealed its movement toward Ban Me Thuot by cautiously approaching from lower Laos. It was not until March 5 that the South Vietnamese learned from captured documents that an engineering regiment of the F-10 Division had moved from Kontum towards Ban Me Thuot. From other fragmentary bits of information it appeared to some South Vietnamese officers that the North Vietnamese were preparing for a major offensive and that Ban Me Thuot was the target.

What the South Vietnamese did not know was that the North Vietnamese first planned to cut National Routes 14, 19 and 21 to sever the two highland provinces from II Corps' lowlands, and preclude any South Vietnamese reinforcements in the area. The 320th Division was ordered to take up positions north of Ban Me Thuot and to neutralize all outposts on Route 14 as well as the Phuong Duc Airfield. The F-10 Division would then spearhead the main attack from the southwest into the city along Route 14. The North Vietnamese imposed strict security precautions to keep their plans secret.

South Vietnam's II Corps intelligence officer Colonel Trinh Tieu correctly assessed the situation as early as mid-February. His commander, General Phu, disagreed. Therefore, the disposition of South Vietnam's forces reflected Phu's belief that Pleiku—Route 19's western terminal—was the target and not Ban Me Thuot. General Phu deployed his entire 23rd Division in the Pleiku area, leaving the defense of Ban Me Thuot to a Ranger group and units of the Provincial Regional Forces and Popular Forces who were composed mostly of Montagnards.

Once Phu was alerted that the North Vietnamese 320th Division was moving toward Ban Me Thuot at the beginning of March, he compounded his error in judgment by sending only a headquarters detachment and a regiment back to Ban Me Thuot.

While those North Vietnamese divisions converged on their initial objectives in Darlac and Quang Duc provinces for a later assault on Ban Me Thuot, the opening guns sounded along Route 19, lifeline to the Highlands, during the early hours of March 4. Simultaneous attacks were also launched to close the highway from the Mang Yang Pass in Pleiku Province to Binh Dinh Province.

Phu was confused when the communists also attacked along Route 21—the other major road to the Highlands—that ran to Ban Me Thuot and blocked it to Nha Trang on the coast. Phu's error in failing to realize North Vietnam's true objective was just what the North Vietnamese had hoped it would be.

Colonel Tien continued to disagree with General Phu's assessment of the situation, insisting that Ban Me Thuot would be the principal objective. He based his conviction on indications that elements of the North Vietnamese 10th and 320th Division had shifted south, or had at least conducted reconnaissance in Quang Duc and Darlac Provinces. He advised General Phu that, in his opinion, the attacks in Kontum and Pleiku Provinces in the north, and on Route 19, were diversionary, designed primarily to hold major South Vietnamese units in place in Binh Dinh, Kontum and Pleiku Provinces.

General Phu continued to disagree with his intelligence chief's assessment, insisting that Pleiku was the major objective. He based his views on the weight of the current enemy attacks against the 44th South Vietnamese Infantry Division in the Thanh An district of Pleiku Province, and against the Rangers north of Kontum. He said there were only two regiments protecting the western approaches to Pleiku, and he refused to weaken this front to reinforce Ban Me Thuot where no significant action had yet taken place. His preconceived and inflexible opinion convinced him that the North Vietnamese would strike Pleiku and Kontum, the usual objectives of North Vietnam's main efforts in the past.

The North Vietnamese 10th Division launched simultaneous attacks throughout Quang Duc Province (southwest of Ban Me Thuot) on March 9. Rangers at Kien Duc repulsed the assault, and the territorials held at Duc Lap. South of there, at the Dak Song crossroads, heavy artillery bombardment and infantry assaults drove South Vietnam's 2nd Battalion of the 53rd Infantry Regiment from its defenses. By noon, their position was overrun.

General Phu, despite protestations by his intelligence officer Colonel Tien, continued to insist that Pleiku would become the main battlefield and that his forces there had to receive immediate reinforcement. He asked the Joint General Staff for an additional Ranger group, but he was turned down. There were few reserves, and threats to Saigon and Tay Ninh were mounting daily.

Phu now ordered the transfer by air of the 72nd and 96th Ranger Battalions, 21st Ranger Group, from the Chu Pao Pass and Kontum to Buon Ho, twenty-five miles northeast of Ban Me Thuot. He also ordered the 4th Reconnaissance Company at Ban Don to return to Ban Me Thuot.

At first all assaults were repulsed by the South Vietnamese on the various fronts with heavy communist losses, although the units at Kien Duc were later overrun.

In Binh Dinh Province east of Kontum, Brigadier General Phan Dinh Niem, who commanded the 22nd Division and some Rangers, fought off strong communist attacks. The North Vietnamese sent a heavy rocket barrage against Pleiku airfields that caused extensive damage. Now a steady stream of traffic moved south through the Chu Pao Pass as the population of Kontum fled the daily rocket attacks, and the imminent threat of its fall. Lines at the Air Vietnam terminal at Kontum flowed into the streets as residents sought to buy tickets to Pleiku and points south. Highway 14 was closed to traffic March 10 in southern Pleiku Province by enemy attacks on territorial outposts in the mountains close to the boundary of Darlac Province.

Major elements of the 320th North Vietnamese Division penetrated Ban Me Thuot's outskirts March 10. Five of their tanks were quickly destroyed or disabled, but fierce fighting continued in the city's streets. General Phu's attempt to fly two battalions from Ban Do to the city were thwarted by heavy enemy small arms fire so they were diverted to Buon Ho twenty-two miles to the northeast. The airfield there came under attack and eight South Vietnamese aircraft were destroyed on the ground, and only three damaged helicopters were able to fly out. That night the North

Vietnamese had a firm hold on the center of Ban Me Thuot although South Vietnamese units still held positions east, west and south of the city. There was continued fighting the following day marked by extensive use of communist flamethrowers. While pockets of resistance continued to hold out, the province chief Colonel Nguyen Cong Luat was captured.

As the North Vietnamese consolidated their gains in Ban Me Thuot, the battle for Phuong Duc airfield continued to the east of the city.

South Vietnam's Joint General Staff, fully aware of the critical nature of the battles in the Highlands, agreed to send its last major reserve, the 7th Ranger Group, from Saigon to replace the 44th Infantry Regiment east of Pleiku so it could be released to join a counterattack in Darlac Province to regain Ban Me Thuot. The situation at Pleiku rapidly deteriorated, however, and the South Vietnamese were forced to retreat and the move of the 7th was cancelled.

At Phuoc An, troops of the 44th and 45th Regiments were assembled to make a counterattack. This was the last base for a drive to retake Ban Me Thuot. It also was a way station for the civilian population fleeing the fighting. Some of the new troops met their dependents here and both disappeared into the streaming flow of refugees.

March 14, General Phu assigned the task force assembled at Phuoc An to Brigadier General Le Trung Tuong, commander of the 23rd Division. Tuong was ordered to attack to the west along Route 21 and to link up with the tenacious defenders at Phuong Duc airfield. Chaos quickly enveloped members of his task force, however, and Phuoc An was overrun four days later by the North Vietnamese F-10 Division. Only one battalion and the 44th's regimental headquarters were moved out because of a lack of airlift. Any hope now of re-capturing Ban Me Thuot was gone, although President Thieu did not immediately concede to this realistic viewpoint.

CHAPTER 44

Exodus from the Highlands

THE LOSS OF BAN ME THUOT RESULTED PRIMARILY FROM GENERAL PHU'S failure to send a sufficient force to defend the city before the attack began. The North Vietnamese achieved tactical surprise by committing three divisions and their supporting tanks and artillery almost without detection. When Phu ignored his intelligence chief's recommendations he created a situation that was bound to end in disaster after the North Vietnamese 320th and F-10 Divisions headed towards Ban Me Thuot. Instead, Phu deployed the bulk of his forces in the Pleiku-Kontum area and left the defense of Ban Me Thuot to regional and popular forces who were not equipped to fight against North Vietnamese regulars.

The North Vietnamese had a golden opportunity to achieve surprise when they concealed the movements of their major forces, and they made the most of it.

After General Phu announced that all organized resistance was at an end inside Ban Me Thuot, survivors were moved by helicopter to points east of the city.

This disastrous turn of events turned out to be the turning point in the war. Although Thieu considered it important to retake Ban Me Thuot, he believed he had to sacrifice Kontum and Pleiku.

Some members of the Joint General Staff had long thought that South Vietnam's armed forces would stand a better chance of containing the North Vietnamese Army if the territory to be held was reduced in size. Such a proposal until now was politically impossible because of President Thieu's intransigence.

With the imminent loss of Ban Me Thuot, Thieu began to change his mind. He invited Prime Minister Tran Thien Khiem, and his assistant for security affairs, Lieutenant General Dang Van Quang, to join him and General Cao Van Vien, chairman of the Joint General Staff, to a working breakfast at the palace March 11—the day after Ban Me Thuot was attacked. After food was served Thieu took out a small-scale map of South Vietnam and began to discuss the military situation. Matter-of-factly, he said, "Given our present strength and capabilities, we certainly cannot hold and defend all the territory we want." He said that he believed that the armed forces should be redeployed to hold and defend only those populous and flourishing areas that were most important. On the map he outlined those areas he considered most important. Quang and Vien noted that they encompassed all of III and IV Corps plus their territorial waters. The president stressed that those few areas that were still under communist control in these regions should be re-occupied at all costs. Thieu explained that these regions contained the nation's most important resources of rice, rubber and manufacturing plants, and were the most populous and prosperous. He called this land the nation's untouchable heartland—the irreducible national stronghold. It included Saigon, its surrounding provinces, and the Mekong Delta.

Thieu turned back to the map and they noted that he lost some of his assurance when he looked at I and II Corps. "In the Central Highlands," indicating the area by a sweeping motion of his hand, "the Ban Me Thuot area is more important than Kontum and Pleiku taken together because of its economic and demographic preponderance." He stressed that II Corps' coastal provinces were equally important because they bordered on the potentially rich continental shelf.

As to I Corps, he said, it is a matter of "hold what we can." He sketched his idea of the land to be held by drawing a series of phase lines cutting across the width of I Corps at different locations on the coastline from the north downward. "If we are strong enough," he said, "we can hold the territory up to Hué and Da Nang. If not, then we can re-deploy farther south to Chu Lai or even Tuy Hoa. This way," he emphasized, "we can hold the most important part of our national territory with a chance of surviving and prospering as a nation."

A momentous decision was reached, although all of its ramifications were not clear. There were wide-ranging problems of a military nature, and General Vien spoke up. He agreed that this redeployment was necessary, saying that he had embraced such an idea for some time. The senior military adviser said he had kept the matter to himself because he had believed it was improper to make such a proposal. First off, he said, such a redeployment had conflicted with the prevailing national policy, and second, if he had made such a suggestion it might well have been interpreted as an indication of defeatism.

He refrained from saying that, in his private view, he believed it was too late for a successful redeployment of such a magnitude. He also believed that President Thieu had already reached a decision, and that he would not appreciate unfavorable comments from him. He believed that Thieu, as commander-in-chief, had the sole prerogative and responsibility for dictating control of the war. General Vien knew that Thieu's proposal was the most logical at this stage because the military situation in South Vietnam was deteriorating. But he listened to Thieu and wondered why the president had taken so long to reach such a decision. Possibly the president had hesitated in hopes that the United States would intervene with its armed forces. Nixon had promised such a decision, but he was no longer president of the United States.

Thieu should have had no illusions about America's hands-off attitude towards the war. Despite North Vietnam's escalation of the war in the past two years the United States had taken no military action. Certainly the negative aspects of the last congressional visit to South Vietnam should have convinced Thieu that the United States Congress would not authorize a return to military intervention. It had repeatedly shown that it was in no mood to intervene.

President Thieu's redeployment plan came too late to achieve success. It should have been done in mid-1974, or at the very latest when President Nixon resigned. Thieu and many other South Vietnam government officials believed that Nixon was the only American official with the moral obligation to enforce the ceasefire. They believed he was the only one in the United States who was bold enough to take forceful action. If the redeployment decision had been made earlier, South Vietnam would have been far better off with a reduced but more tightly controlled country. With Ban Me Thuot about to be lost during this conference, it was too late. Conversely, if redeployment was not attempted, Vien was convinced that South Vietnam might be saved. He reasoned later that North Vietnamese officials would have thought twice before pressing on with another offensive of the same scale in II Corps. In that region there was still the 22nd Division and the equivalent of two other combat divisions, plus two air divisions and sufficient logistical support to continue fighting through the dry season. Vien believed that without the redeployment the North Vietnamese would not have succeeded in gaining much headway in I Corps. He was realistic enough to understand that the military situation would have dragged on as before, possibly more precariously in the face of dwindling military aid and difficulties in reconstituting a general reserve. Although he did not say so at the meeting with Thieu he was privately convinced that the military situation would not deteriorate as rapidly as it did if the redeployment was not attempted.

Vien's unexpressed views at this breakfast conference were based partly on his belief that the North Vietnamese would have tried to pressure them for a coalition, and President Thieu might have been inclined to accept it. Vien believed at the time that such a coalition would have merely postponed the inevitable loss of his country to the North Vietnamese. The communists would have sought more military victories, he believed, to gain still more political concessions. Vien was pessimistic that South Vietnam could resist such pressure without massive help from the United States, particularly airpower. Actually, South Vietnam's armed forces would have run out of fuel and ammunition by June, and that would have been the end of hostilities regardless of any steps that were taken in the interim.

Two days after this meeting to discuss redeployment at Independence Palace President Thieu asked to see II Corps Commander Pham Van Phu.

The president said he would meet him in Pleiku but Phu said this was too dangerous for the president and he suggested Cam Ranh instead.

They met March 14 in a handsome building on top of a sand hill erected by the United States in 1966 to accommodate President Johnson when he stopped there to visit American troops. With Thieu and Phu were Prime Minister Khiem, and Generals Quang and Vien. Thieu first wanted to talk about plans to save Pleiku.

General Phu gave his estimate of the situation in II Corps. He said all major axes of communication, including National Routes 14, 19 and 21, had been cut by the enemy, and that traffic was about at a standstill. The most important route—19—was cut, he said, across the width of the country. It served as a link between Pleiku and the coastal city of Qui Nhon. Phu said the North Vietnamese 3rd Division blocked Route 19 at Binh Khe, and the South Vietnamese 22nd Division and its four regiments under Brigadier General Niem had tried unsuccessfully to dislodge the communists. He said another North Vietnamese regiment was poised at Le Trung in the east within striking distance of Pleiku and that the city was under intense artillery fire and was threatened by ground attacks.

Thieu asked Phu directly if it was possible to retake Ban Me Thuot, but Phu refused to commit himself, saying only that there was "fierce fighting in the area."

Thieu turned to General Vien. "What reserve forces can be mustered?"

Vien shrugged helplessly, knowing the question was rhetorical. Thieu already knew the answer. There were none available.

They all knew they were faced with the final showdown. The only major reserve units, the Airborne and the Marine Divisions, had been committed to I Corps since 1972. Before the attack on Ban Me Thuot the president, apparently for political reasons, had decided to reassign the Airborne to the Saigon area. The newly created and combat ready 468th Marine Brigade, plus a Ranger group, had been assigned to replace it. The

Ranger group order later was countermanded by Thieu due to the changing situation. The first Airborne Brigade, set to leave March 3 by sealift for Saigon, had received orders March 17 to debark instead at Nha Trang and proceed to Khanh Duong on National Route 21 in an emergency move to stop the communist advance towards the coast after Ban Me Thuot was lost. In fierce combat, the 2nd Airborne Brigade had been decimated, and it never returned to Saigon.

Now, when reserves were most needed, there were none for General Phu. It appeared that President Thieu, knowing the futility of seeking reserves that did not exist, tried to justify the decision he had reached earlier at Independence Palace. He walked to a map and discussed the new strategy that he had revealed earlier. With hand gestures Thieu pointed out the vital areas that Phu was supposed to hold. He said that Ban Me Thuot was more important than Pleiku and Kontum put together, so he ordered Phu to redeploy his II Corps forces and to reoccupy Ban Me Thuot at all costs. In closing, he asked Phu how he planned to redeploy his troops and which routes he would use to reach Ban Me Thuot.

Phu stood up, saying that National Route 19 from Pleiku eastward to the coast was impassable. "My best division, the 22nd, has been unable to break through at Binh Khe." He said that National Route 14, connecting Pleiku to Ban Me Thuot on a north-south axis, was also blocked at Thuan Man, north of Ban Me Thuot. He described this route as extremely difficult to clear. He said he planned, therefore, to use Interprovincial Route 7B. This was a secondary route that, branching off National 14 twenty miles south of Pleiku, ran southeasterly through Hau Bon toward Tuy Hoa on the coast. He described 7B as a road that had long been neglected and out of use. He admitted that except for a usable short stretch from 14 to Hau Bon, no one seemed to know its condition. Phu said one of the major bridges across the Song Ba River had been destroyed beyond repair, and that the road's terminal stretch west of Tuy Hoa was unusable because of extensive mining by Korean forces a few years earlier. General Phu stressed that his operations would benefit from tactical surprise, and he requested that the Joint General Staff provide river-crossing facilities. General Vien agreed to do so.

Vien was concerned because the movement of a corps-size column of troops, equipment and vehicles along a largely unknown road 160 miles through mountains and jungles was a hazardous undertaking of great magnitude. He cautioned Phu that surprise would only be achieved if the movement was swift and unimpeded. Vien reminded him that the North Vietnamese had sprung some of their bloodiest ambushes against the French Union Forces during the 1946–1954 war in this area. He told Phu that he foresaw difficulties and hazards in such an operation, and that strict security measures would be needed. "You must be organized to afford protection for the lead element of your column, and its rear element, as well as for troops in between. You must have adequate and appropriate signal communications plus air cover and close air support."

Before the conference ended Phu pleaded with Thieu that his subordinate, Colonel Pham Van Tat who commanded the Ranger forces in the region, be promoted to brigadier general. Vien listened to this request and was appalled by it. He did not know Tat but he was aware that the colonel had no special credits on his combat record. He expressed his concern to Thieu, and the president did not immediately make up his mind. He finally agreed reluctantly to Tat's promotion and General Phu placed him in command of the redeployed forces, calling him his most trusted subordinate.

Phu's deputies, Brigadier Generals Tran Van Cam and Le Van Than, were shunted aside and were not given any responsibilities for the redeployment except that Cam was assigned the vague job of supervising the total effort.

Although the Joint General Staff had had little authority in the past, from now on its influence was reduced to zero. President Thieu worked directly with his field commanders.

General Phu was ordered to withdraw from the Highlands, and hopefully surprise the enemy by doing so.

That same day North Vietnamese sappers blew up Pleiku's ammunition storage complex, including 1,400 scarce rounds of 105 mm. howitzer shells.

Thieu accepted Phu's basic plan to use Interprovince Route 7B to recover his Kontum/Pleiku forces, and assemble them in Khanh Hoah Province before fighting back along Route 21 to Ban Me Thuot. The president returned to Saigon, and Phu went back to his headquarters.

Earlier troop deployments to the Ban Me Thuot area had weakened security in Pleiku, and General Phu ordered evacuation of all nonessential military personnel and their dependents from both Kontum and Pleiku. The general now moved his headquarters to Nha Trang on the coast, and surprisingly replaced the captured Darlac province chief with his intelligence officer Colonel Trinh Tieu whose estimate of the North Vietnamese offensive he had rejected.

Since redeployment out of the highlands to regroup II Corps' battered forces to try and stop the North Vietnamese Army from advancing on Route 21 at Khanh Duong was conceived in secrecy, no word was passed to the province chiefs of Kontum, Pleiku and Phu Bon. March 17 orders were given to three Ranger groups in Kontum late at night to fall back to Pleiku. Only then did Kontum's province chief Colonel Phan Dinh Hung learn about the redeployment. He departed in haste, but he was killed in an ambush.

The first convoy now moved out of Pleiku as planned. No sooner was the last truck dispatched than news of the movement reached the city's residents. They quickly began to leave by every mode of transportation—even on foot—taking whatever belongings they could carry. They were joined later by refugees from Kontum and with the evacuating troops they formed a long line of people and vehicles flowing along Route 7B, a track overgrown by brush, whose fords were not repaired, and whose important bridges were out. The exodus from the Highlands had begun.

To help clear the way, General Phu ordered the 20th Engineer Group to precede the others. In the rear, to act as guards, were five groups of Ranger battalions from Kontum and Pleiku Provinces, along with one tank company. They were ordered to leave Pleiku March 19 and to make the trip in four days.

The evacuation proceeded without serious incidents during the first two days. By March 18, officials of II Corps reached Hau Bon in Phu Bon Province where a command post was established. It was in this area that all the convoys of the last three days came together, and there was a huge mass of refugees. Further advance to the coast, still 100 miles away, proved impossible because the engineers had not completed a pontoon bridge across the Ea Pa River farther down the road.

North Vietnamese troops, caught at first by surprise by the sudden pullout, struck back at night, presumably with local units who had been ordered to intercept the stalled column. They began shelling and mounted savage ground attacks. The Hau Bon airstrip, less than a mile from II Corps' command post, was overrun. Fighting continued into late evening of the next day—March 19. Wounded soldiers and refugees milled about. Civilian refugees, in particular, died by the thousands. There was no control in the town. Some unruly Montagnard Regional and Popular Forces began looting, or broke ranks and ran away creating a chaotic condition among both troops and refugees. With the situation growing increasingly serious General Phu ordered Colonel Dong, commander of the 2nd Armored Brigade, to take command.

The withdrawal ended in complete failure. Almost all the units withdrawn from the Kontum-Pleiku area were disrupted. Colonel Le Khan Ly, the II Corps chief of staff, estimated that 5,000 out of 20,000 logistical and support troops were retrieved. About 900 of the five Ranger groups involved in the withdrawal reported to II Corps headquarters at Nha Trang. The 34th Ranger Battalion, later called the "block destruction heroes" by grateful refugees, lost over 50 percent of its men. The battalion was retained at Tuy Hoa for defense of the city.

A retreat is the most difficult of all military maneuvers. It requires detailed planning and strong leadership at all echelons. Redeployment, however, is not a retreat but a scheduled movement of organized convoys with self-defense capabilities. In this instance it was impeded by refugees and civilian vehicles plus the poor condition of the road and the inadequate river-crossing facilities.

The North Vietnamese 320th Division did not learn of the redeployment at first so surprise was achieved. If other conditions had been right, General Vien later claimed, the South Vietnamese would never have been caught. When one considers General Phu's limited abilities, this is a viewpoint that could be disputed.

The price of secrecy came high. Colonel Le Khac Ly, II Corps' chief of staff, was never told of the move in advance. The commander of the 231st Direct Support Group in Pleiku said later, "I didn't know anything about redeployment orders. Only when an artillery unit nearby hastily assembled its men, equipment and dependents and loaded them on trucks was I told by its commander, 'We're leaving town. Withdrawal orders. You'd better hurry.'"

The Direct Support Group commander ordered his men to load some equipment and to follow the artillery convoy. He had no time to destroy anything. He did not even report his move to the 2nd Logistics Command because the withdrawal was supposed to be kept secret.

II Corps Commander Phu's trust in some of his subordinates to carry out orders was not justified. The entire withdrawal lacked unified and effective control. Each general looked after his own troops, without concern for anyone else's men, and the army as a whole. Overall control of the movement was exercised by II Corps' chief of staff, but only up to Hau Bon, although he was not actually given that responsibility.

The province chiefs of Phu Bon and Phu Yen failed to provide road security and protection, and they proved unable to control elements of their regional and popular forces. The outcome might have been different if Route 7B had been properly protected, and river-crossing facilities had been provided. General Phu's excessive preoccupation with secrecy precluded pre-arranged moves such as road repairs that would have appeared normal. Such road rehabilitation had been long contemplated by the Joint General Staff, and included mine clearing on the terminal stretch from Cung Son to Tuy Hoa.

There was total failure of leadership at all levels. The troops were not briefed, and discipline was not enforced. The soldiers were not even ordered to destroy communist road blocks that proved to be a major obstacle to their survival. The rout of Phu's army was of massive and strategic proportions, and at least 7 percent of his troop strength was lost.

March 24 the 42nd South Vietnamese Infantry Division pulled back along Route 19, and the 41st Infantry Division assumed the defense of Binh Khe. That same day the North Vietnamese began their assault. Two South Vietnamese regiments—the 41st and 42nd—did not wait for reinforcements but attacked eastward toward Qui Nhon March 27, taking over 400 territorials with them. These territorials had been flown out of the An Khe area the day before by helicopter. As regiments dug in for defense of Qui Nhon, orders arrived from Saigon to evacuate what remained of the 22nd Division. All agreed that II Corps was virtually lost to South Vietnam.

The North Vietnamese attacked Phu Cat Air Base northeast of Qui Nhon March 31, and South Vietnamese pilots managed to fly out thirty-two aircraft, but fifty others were either disabled or destroyed.

The following day 27,000 troops of the 22nd Division and Binh Dinh territorial soldiers boarded Navy craft at Qui Nhon and sailed for Vung Tau on the coast southeast of Saigon. Enemy tanks and infantry troops were soon moving through the streets of Qui Nhon.

The 23rd South Vietnamese Division had been decisively defeated earlier by North Vietnamese General Dung's 10th Division when it had tried to counterattack from Phuoc An in Darlac Province. The survivors of this division and civilians who escaped from the province now streamed eastward across the plateau along Route 21. Military units were assembled at Khanh Duong, the last district on the high plains before the highway twists through the Deo Cao Pass to the coastal hills and lowlands of Khanh Hoa Province. This pass was the obvious place to make a defensive stand to protect Nha Trang on the coast where II Corps was headquartered, along with Navy and Air Force headquarters.

The chaos at Nha Trang as the North Vietnamese poised to attack the city reached the impossible stage for authorities to control. Police and local defense forces disappeared into the tide of humanity flowing south. Prisoners broke out of jails and created havoc throughout the city by shooting haphazardly with seized weapons.

Despite Joint General Staff orders to organize the defense of the air base in coordination with air force and naval units, General Phu fled by plane without providing instructions for his staff or his base commander. He was admitted to Cong Hoa General Hospital in Saigon April 4. It was quickly apparent that he was no longer mentally fit to command. Actually, there was little left of his II Corps to command. Those who survived were evacuated from Nha Trang, and by April 18 the entire territory of II Corps was in enemy hands.

CHAPTER 45

Americans Flee Nha Trang

PRIOR TO ITS FALL, 60,000 REFUGEES STRAGGLED INTO NHA TRANG ON the coast almost due east of Ban Me Thuot. Tragically, at least 100,000 others were stranded in western Phu Yen Province without food, water or medical assistance. The withdrawal was the most poorly executed of any in the war, and it ended tragically for South Vietnam.

The North Vietnamese 320th Division set out in hot pursuit of the fleeing mob of soldiers and civilians and by March 31 they had Tuy Hoa under fire about forty-five miles north of Nha Trang.

The North Vietnamese command had conducted its campaign in the Central Highlands with great skill and precision. It had been directed from the start with Ban Me Thuot as the central focus of the campaign while communist armies attacked the three northern provinces—Quang Tri, Thua Thien and Quang Nam. At first, the South Vietnamese had held their own, but they soon found it impossible to resist overwhelming forces skillfully employed.

On March 12, General Truong at Da Nang had received orders from the Joint General Staff to pull the Airborne Division out of the line, and send it south. He had forwarded a strong protest to General Vien, but President Thieu had personally ordered the move so that it could participate in the offensive to retake Ban Me Thuot. Vien promised to send the 468th Marine Brigade and a Ranger group to replace the division if it was at all possible. Such a replacement could not be made and Truong pulled the Marine Division out of Quang Tri and northern Thua Thien Province and shifted it south to cover the Phu Loc District and Da Nang.

Truong had flown to Saigon March 13 to participate in a secret meeting with Thieu, Prime Minister Khiem and General Vien. There he learned about the decision to evacuate the Highlands and he was ordered to prepare a plan for eventual evacuation of I Corps. He was given permission

655

to delay the departure of the 1st Airborne Brigade to March 18, and the remainder of the division's departure to March 31. Thieu advised the general that the rest of the region must be sacrificed although it was important to hold Da Nang. The president said he would send the 468th Marine Brigade north to help defend Da Nang as soon as the Airborne Division arrived in Saigon. He insisted that this division was vital to the defense of III and IV Corps without which the Republic of Vietnam could not survive.

Bad news came in after the meeting that North Vietnamese attacks in southwestern Quang Tri Province had overrun strongpoints on the western flank. During the meeting, Lieutenant General Lam Quang Thi, I Corps' commander, said that all combat forces would be pulled back to Quang Nam and that Da Nang would be defended by the 1st and 3rd Divisions and the Marine Division while the 2nd Division was held in reserve. Each knew that once the Marines started to leave Quang Tri there would be a mass civilian exodus, and they tried to prepare for it.

Prime Minister Khiem flew to Da Nang March 18, realizing quickly that drastic measures were needed to adjust the country's defenses to conform to the new strategy for defense of the South only. The exodus from Pleiku and Kontum was underway, but other calamitous events were set in motion. The military goal was to hold a smaller South Vietnam with a northern frontier anchored at Ban Me Thuot—at present in enemy hands—but such a strategy required the salvaging of most of the nation's military strength that now was under attack from Phu Bon to Quang Tri in the northern provinces.

In the South, Tri Tam north of Saigon fell, and the North Vietnamese Army offensive was gaining momentum in Tay Ninh, Long Khanh and Binh Tay Provinces. The prime minister came to Da Nang for several reasons: one was to assess the impact of the loss of the Airborne Division that had been sent south to bolster the defenses around Saigon. With the loss of one of its strongest divisions, I Corps faced a rapidly deteriorating situation. In discussions with General Truong, the prime minister sought advice on what to tell President Thieu upon his return to Saigon as to what part of his region could be defended with available forces. He made it clear to the general that he could not hope to obtain additional troops, and that the earlier promised Marine Brigade would remain to defend the capital. Meanwhile, the 3rd Airborne Brigade had been diverted at Nha Trang and sent to block the North Vietnamese advance on Khanh Duong, with the rest of the division proceeding to Saigon. Prime Minister Khiem did promise Truong to send a staff to Da Nang, representing all interested ministries, to assist in handling the monumental refugee problem that was developing in the region.

Five province chiefs and the mayor of Da Nang briefed the prime minister during his visit. The mayor told him that morale was very low, and that many families had already left for Saigon. He said that lack of United States support at this critical time was deeply felt by his people. Quang Nam's province chief, Colonel Pham Van Chung, said troop morale was good, but that people were worried about the departure of the Airborne Division. The prime minister was told that the territorial troops had all but given up, and that they were deserting in large numbers. Many units, he learned, were below half strength.

Furious battles were also underway in Darlac Province close to the Cambodian border in the center of South Vietnam as three North Vietnamese divisions attacked South Vietnam's out-manned and out-gunned 23rd Division.

Meanwhile, in Binh Dinh Province along the eastern coast the 22nd Division under Brigadier General Phan Dinh Niem fought to break the hold that North Vietnam's 3rd Division had on terrain controlling Highway 19 through An Khe Pass. Niem's soldiers and guns, along with South Vietnam's Air Force, did inflict heavy losses on the communists. At first, Niem had expected that the heavy losses incurred by North Vietnam's 3rd Division would force it to withdraw. What Niem had not foreseen, however, was the turn of events in the rest of II Corps where the North Vietnamese were rapidly gaining ground. South Vietnamese losses in the north had made the gallant performance of his division in Binh Dinh Province futile through no fault of their own.

Initially the 3rd North Vietnamese Division had succeeded in driving the territorials of Niem's division back from their positions overlooking An Khe Pass and guarding the bridges. In some cases, the territorials withdrew without putting up much of a fight. By the time that General Niem had sufficient battalions in position to make a counterattack, North Vietnamese units had exploited their early gains by concentrating major elements of three 3rd Division regiments, along with sappers, artillery batteries and supporting units at the mouth of the Vinh Tanh valley between An Khe Pass and Binh Khe.

On March 10, when the 320th North Vietnamese Division entered Ban Me Thuot more than a hundred miles to the southwest, General Niem had three of his four regiments committed to An Nhon where Highway 19 leaves Highway 1, at the eastern end of the An Khe Pass. His men fought tenaciously to keep from being driven from the field. Later, as Niem's men drove off repeated heavy attacks by five communist battalions, four successive commanders of the 2nd Battalion were killed. The situation deteriorated rapidly and by March 17, with only two regiments available and no reserves, Niem decided he could not open An Khe Pass and he ordered his battalions to hold in place. Although several thousand civilians and several hundred territorial troops at An Khe were cut off from Qui Nhon on the coast, there was no longer any compelling military reason to pursue the attack. The exodus from the Highlands was already underway along the jungle track known as Route 7B.

The North Vietnamese controlled the pass westward by March 19, almost to the outskirts of An Khe. Three days later the 5th North Vietnamese Battalion was inside An Khe and all South Vietnamese resistance ended. Meanwhile, more than 5,000 people were struggling south over rural roads and trails trying to escape from Qui Nhon on the coast. Any attempt to re-occupy Ban Me Thuot was out of the question because II Corps no longer had any worthwhile combat troops. As a result, North Vietnamese troops took over Kontum and Pleiku without a fight. The communist leadership was elated, and ordered their army to move ahead with all speed. They knew that only the South Vietnamese 3rd Airborne Brigade at Khanh Duong faced them in their drive to the coast.

Rumors spread throughout South Vietnam that territorial concessions would have to be made to the North Vietnamese. These rumors unleashed an uncontrollable surge of refugees who tried to leave all provinces in II Corps. The same concern was expressed in I Corps to the north. I Corps' people now joined refugees from the Central Highlands and dispirited troops streamed south along the coast. They overwhelmed facilities in Phan Rang and Phan Thiet before hurrying on towards Saigon. Even in the capital confidence in the government was at a low level, and members of the underground came into the open to voice their antigovernment feelings. Demonstrators demanded that President Thieu be replaced, and anti-American sentiment rose to a fever pitch. Officials ordered the arrest of a number of agitators March 27. Some people still hoped for a miracle.

After Prime Minister Khiem returned to Saigon General Truong followed him the next day. In a meeting with Thieu, the general told the president, "We have only one choice. We had better act before it is too late." He recommended that I Corps' troops be withdrawn towards Hué, Chu Lai and Da Nang to take advantage of existing fortifications in these cities, particularly those in the hilly terrain around Hué. The general told the president that he had heard unconfirmed reports that the Marine Division was scheduled for redeployment to III Corps. If this occurred, he said, it would have a profound effect on his plan, and he asked Thieu what decision had been reached about the division's deployment.

Thieu's position was difficult. He had ordered the redeployment from the Central Highlands, and it had turned into a rout. Worst of all, he knew, was the psychological impact the debacle was having on the civilian population. His whole plan to regroup the armed forces into a smaller and more defensible area was not working out. Still, he continued to procrastinate and he did not give his field commander the straight answer he sought. Truong was advised to hold whatever territory he could with the forces available and that, he said, included the Marine Division.

Truong was somewhat encouraged because the withdrawal decision for I Corps had been temporarily set aside.

Thieu agreed to speak to the South Vietnamese people on television, hoping to calm their worst fears, and to let them know that Hué would be defended at all costs.

Truong returned March 19 and stopped the evacuation of Hué even though the communists were attacking the outermost line at the Thach Han River, artillery shells were striking inside the Citadel and Highway 1 was clogged with southbound traffic and thousands of refugees.

It was obvious to Truong that an all-out offensive for I Corps had begun. This river line had been peaceful for two years.

North Vietnamese attacks continued all along the northern front, and the official count of refugees in Da Nang, based upon police registrations, totaled 121,000 by the night of March 23. The United States Consul General gave a more realistic appraisal of 400,000. The necessities to sustain life were rapidly disappearing, and the following day the government began to move refugees south by every available boat and ship. Thousands made it safely, but many did not. Fortunately, North Vietnamese attacks in Quang Nam Province were blunted by the 3rd South Vietnamese Division and territorial troops. As a result, the security of Da Nang was temporarily improved.

The situation worsened when unauthorized withdrawals started from My Chanh, and territorial troops refused to stop at delaying positions. Panic broke out and a general rout resulted in headlong flight by troops and civilians alike. I Corps officers tried to rally their troops at the Bo River, but mass desertions frustrated their efforts. The soldiers now were more concerned for the safety of their families in Hué than they were of the enemy.

Da Nang was close to panic, and refugees jammed the streets.

On March 24, Truong ordered the evacuation of all troops defending Hué. He told his officers that all forces north and west of Hué should assemble at Tan My, Hué's port northeast of the city, across the narrow channel to Phu Thuan and then march southwest down Vinh Loc Island. He instructed them to cross at the mouth of the Dam Cau Hai Bay on a pontoon bridge that would be constructed by engineers and proceed along the beach to Highway 1 where they would go through Hai Van Pass and proceed on to Da Nang. Inasmuch as no trucks, tanks or heavy guns could make the march, he ordered that they be destroyed or disabled. He instructed the commanding general of the 1st Division to protect the column by blocking the Phu Thu district to prevent the communists from interfering with the withdrawal.

Those still left in Hué now streamed out in panic towards Tan My to take any boat or ship out of Thua Thien Province.

Just as the withdrawal was getting underway, General Truong was visited by officers from the Joint General Staff who directed him to release the Marine Division immediately for the defense of Saigon. He told them that he could not defend Da Nang without the Marines, and he objected strongly to its removal. Joint General Staff officials suggested that Chu Lai, fifty miles to the southeast of Da Nang, should be given up and the 2nd Division sent to Da Nang. Truong reluctantly issued the order, but he still claimed that Da Nang could not be held without the Marine Division. He knew that by the time the remnants of the 1st and 2nd Divisions were recovered, neither division would be of much help in the defense of Da Nang.

The sealift from Chu Lai began after dark March 25 on LSTs (Landing Ships, Tanks) that were sent from Saigon.

An embattled column of soldiers and refugees meanwhile struggled north on Highway 1 from Quang Ngai City toward Chu Lai. Dead and wounded littered the road—a scene reminiscent of the carnage in Quang Tri on this same highway during the 1972 offensive. Once the Chu Lai sealift started, panic engulfed the soldiers who fought for places on the first boats. It was some time before order was restored and 7,000 soldiers embarked for Da Nang.

Although the 3rd South Vietnamese Division still held the Dai Loc and Duc Duc districts, chaos continued to reign by March 26 in Da Nang. With morale at rock-bottom, soldiers deserted their units to save their families. Officials lost control of the population as two million people surged through the streets trying to locate their families and escape with them to the south. Police deserted their posts, and those who remained were unable to control mobs of armed soldiers who roamed the streets. There were even instances of shooting between the soldiers and police.

North of Da Nang the withdrawal from Thua Thien Province was orderly at first as the 258th Marine Brigade linked up with the 914th Regional Forces Group on Vinh Loc Island and crossed the narrow channel to Loc Tri in the Phu Loc District. Unfortunately, the bridge that was supposed to be installed by engineers never arrived. Engineering boats were evidently commandered by other military units seeking to escape. The withdrawing forces managed to cross by using local fishing boats.

General Truong flew over Vinh Loc Island, noting with dismay that the only disciplined units apparently were Marines. The rest were fleeing like a frightened mob.

The 147th Marine Brigade was unable to leave Tan My until March 26 due to heavy seas. The following day the 258th Brigade's Marine Battalion holding the Phu Gia Pass—a short, twisting road about twelve miles east of the Phu Loc District—came under attack. With the communists approaching Hai Van Pass from the north, and Vietnamese navy boats breaking down faster than they could be repaired, General Truong stopped the sea movement of people and equipment from Hué. Now that he was unable to reinforce Da Nang with adequate strength from the 2nd Infantry Division, the general concentrated on recovering elements of the Marine Division at Da Nang.

South Vietnamese planes destroyed four enemy tanks attacking an outer support base March 27 and, when the North Vietnamese broke off their attack, the 3rd Division's battalions held their positions. It was evident to Truong, however, that the men of the division would be unable to contain North Vietnamese attacks in the outlying districts of Quang Nam Province around Da Nang. The general ordered a withdrawal to a shorter line within artillery range of the center of the city. However, attempts to hold that line also failed as large numbers of 3rd Division soldiers deserted to save their families.

With defeat imminent, Truong shipped all his remaining organized forces—mostly Marines—out of Da Nang to Saigon. He, and most of his staff, were the last of the military to leave. Some members of the staff, including the general, had to swim through the surf to the rescuing fleet of boats.

Da Nang, last bastion of South Vietnam's I Corps, was in North Vietnamese hands by nightful March 30.

The 22nd Division had initially held firm at Binh Khe on National Route 19 after the Highlands was evacuated, and at Tam Quan in the northern Binh Dinh Province on the coast. The fighting became a fierce seesaw battle against the North Vietnamese Army's 3rd Division in the foothills of the Binh Khe district west of Qui Nhon. Each hill, each stretch of road changed hands as both sides fought desperately. With the outcome undecided, and communist losses heavy, North Vietnamese reinforcements arrived. The 95B Regiment now joined the battle after it was freed from its blocking mission at Le Trung. The regiment had moved east and joined 3rd Division troops. The pressure against the South Vietnamese increased but the 41st and 42nd Regiments clung stubbornly to their defenses. Additional communist reinforcements came south from

Quang Ngai and began to attack the South Vietnamese in force at Tam Quan March 25. Still the gallant South Vietnamese held on, forced back March 30 only by overwhelming forces.

The Nha Trang-Ninh Hoa area was the last vital concentration of South Vietnamese forces in II Corps. Without its control any effort to recapture the Highlands was impossible. If this area could be held the North Vietnamese might be prevented from moving down Highway 1 to Saigon.

Brigadier General Tran Van Cam was given command of the 3rd Airborne Brigade, the 40th Infantry Division, the 34th Ranger Battalion and the region's territorial troops to defend Khanh Hoa Province around Da Nang. Before Cam could move his headquarters from Phu Yen Province to the north where he had been controlling the eastern end of Route 7B while the exodus from the northern provinces was underway, the 10th North Vietnamese Division attacked his 3rd Airborne Brigade on March 30 in the Deo Cao Pass. Despite bitter resistance, the Airborne Brigade collapsed under the weight of savage attacks, forcing a rapid withdrawal of all South Vietnamese troops. The brigade fought well, but it lost three-quarters of its men.

The North Vietnamese 10th Division pursued the fleeing South Vietnamese units so closely that the American Consul General and his staff in Nha Trang had to flee to Saigon by aircraft. April 2 North Vietnamese tanks entered the city.

The momentum of the North Vietnamese Army was so great that defense of Cam Ranh proved unfeasible, and the Joint General Staff authorized its evacuation.

CHAPTER 46

The Final Stand

THE NORTH VIETNAMESE ARMY NOW COORDINATED ITS OFFENSIVE countrywide as a ring of North Vietnamese divisions tightened around III Corps, and American military assistance slowed to a trickle. Members of the United States House of Representatives voted March 12 189 to 49 in favor of a resolution opposing additional military aid for either Cambodia or Vietnam before the end of the fiscal year. The following day the House Foreign Affairs Committee rejected a compromise proposal that would have provided some additional aid. President Ford again urged the Congress to provide more assistance, saying it was essential to South Vietnam's survival, and that its decision to withdraw from the Highlands was due to Congress's lack of interest in their fate.

President Thieu met with United States Ambassador Graham Martin and asked him whether his resignation would affect the possibility of more aid from Congress.

Martin replied, "It might have changed some votes several months ago, but your resignation now would not change enough votes to affect the outcome." The ambassador added that Thieu's resignation in exchange for more aid "was a bargain whose day had passed, if indeed it had ever existed."

The United States Congress should not be faulted in this instance, particularly in blaming it for the loss of the Central Highlands. South Vietnam's predicament was caused by II Corps commander's failure to accept his intelligence officer's estimate that Ban Me Thuot was North Vietnam's primary target and General Phu's failure to fight with the forces available to him. When Phu followed this critical mistake in judgment with two others—inadequate planning and execution of the counterattack from Phuoc An, and a mismanaged withdrawal down Route 7B—

he started the entire nation on a downhill slide that not even the valor of thousands of loyal officers and men could reverse. Like an unplugged hole in a dike, the flow of North Vietnamese armed forces started with a trickle and soon became an uncontrollable flood.

South Vietnam's problems increased in the United States as word spread via the news media that she lacked the will to fight. Some officers and men did fail in their duty to their country, but the majority fought tenaciously to overcome the invaders. There were countless instances of bravery by units and soldiers, and awesome examples of valor in combat even in the face of overwhelming enemy firepower and superior numbers of men. Fifty-two South Vietnamese battalion commanders died during the war. Unfortunately, the American people were not told the truth about this phase of the developing story of disaster gripping a land for whom so many Americans and their allies had paid the supreme sacrifice.

President Ford, almost alone among America's politicians, repeatedly sought permission from the Congress to help its one-time ally. He sent General Frederick C. Weyand, the Army's Chief of Staff, and the last senior American commander in Vietnam, to Saigon to give him a personal assessment. The general arrived March 27 and met with Ambassador Martin and Major General Homer D. Smith, Jr., the head of the Defense Attaché Office. They were briefed by President Thieu and General Vien who told them that a United States commitment to Vietnam was essential if the nation was to survive. It was already too late. The military effort would have had to include as a bare minimum the use of American airpower against the North Vietnamese Army in the field, its bases, and lines of communication in the South. Colonel William E. Le Gro, an officer with an outstanding record during Vietnam's American war years, and now a senior staff officer with the Defense Attaché Office, gave Weyand a written summary of his assessment as of March 31. In it Le Gro said that with abundant resupply and a great deal of luck, the South Vietnamese could conduct a successful defense of what remained of resistance in III and IV Corps, but that it was extremely doubtful the South Vietnamese could withstand an offensive involving the commitment of three additional communist divisions in III Corps without United States strategic air support, and that defeat of South Vietnam's armed forces in the region was tantamount to defeat of all of South Vietnam's armed forces. Le Gro said that South Vietnam was almost certain to fall within three to six months, or possibly sooner.

Other assessments of South Vietnam's survival prospects were even gloomier. Most knowledgeable military men gave her thirty days at the most.

It was unfortunate that in Washington it was believed South Vietnam's reverses had not involved much fighting. Secretary of Defense Schlesinger said April 2 that there was very little major fighting. He compounded the error by saying April 6, "It is plain that the great offensive is a phrase that probably should be in quotation marks. What we have had here is a partial collapse of South Vietnamese forces so that there has been little major fighting since the battle of Ban Me Thuot, and that was an exception in itself."

The head of the Defense Attaché Office in Saigon knew that these statements were not true. He sent messages to CINCPAC and other agencies, saying, "On the contrary, there was heavy fighting all along the coastal plain and in the foothills from south of Phu Bai to Khang Duong in Khanh Hoa Province.

Meanwhile, he wrote that in the hills south of Phu Bai, the 1st South Vietnamese Division had repelled numerous heavy attacks by two divisions, and even gained some lost positions before it was finally ordered to withdraw after its northern flank was exposed.

In Phu Loc District, just north of the Hai Van Pass on Route 1, Smith said that an overpowering attack by up to two regiments of North Vietnam's 325th Division had forced outnumbered South Vietnamese defenders from their positions and severed their lines of communication. In no way, he said, could these attacks be described as "little fighting."

He stated that in the An Khe region along Highway 19 in Binh Dinh Province South Vietnam's 22nd Division had defended its sector with great perseverance despite heavy North Vietnamese attacks. Outflanked, out-gunned and eventually cut off he said the 22nd Division fought its way back to the beaches and was eventually evacuated after a long and costly battle.

Along Highway 21 the fight at Khanh Duong was a battle of major proportions, Smith said. The North Vietnamese 10th Division used three and possibly four infantry regiments before South Vietnamese defenses were overcome. He said the 3rd Airborne Brigade was reduced to only 600 men by the time it was able to fight its way out of encirclement and regroup near Phan Rang.

Smith concluded his message respectfully recommending that the Chairman of the Joint Chiefs of Staff acquaint the Secretary of Defense with these facts so that an accurate representation of what had occurred might be presented to the American people. "There is a great offensive underway."

Few American politicians cared that the bloody struggle continued as the South Vietnamese assembled its few remaining forces from its defeated regions and reorganized for a final stand.

As the front lines contracted, stiff South Vietnamese resistance and strong local counterattacks in Tay Ninh, Binh Duong, Binh Long and Long Khanh Provinces caused the North Vietnamese Army to pull back and regroup. During the first week of April, therefore, a relative calm descended on the battlefields, time that the South Vietnamese used to reorganize their shattered units trickling in from the north. Hurriedly, South Vietnam's military leaders redeployed their forces to meet the certain resumption of attacks.

South Vietnam's Joint General Staff was so shocked by the necessity of withdrawing their armed forces from the northern regions that they failed to plan properly and to reorganize decimated units for the final showdown. While shattered units fled to the temporary safety of South Vietnam's southern ports, military officers attempted to obtain reliable reports about them. They were in such a state of shock that sensible activity was impossible. There were enormous personal and family tragedies to deal with, and many of the top South Vietnamese military men were too dazed to cope with the deteriorating situation. The American Defense Attaché Office tried to prod the Joint General Staff into action before it was too late. Colonel Edward Pelosky, chief of the office's Army Division, took the lead in encouraging the Central Logistics Command to develop a plan. The command's chief, Lieutenant General Dong Van Khuyen, and the chief of staff approved a plan March 27 for the reconstitution of units from I and II Corps, including requirements for replacement vehicles, weapons and supplies. However, General Khuyen was unable to secure information about personnel strengths and unit dispositions from other sections so the plan was unworkable.

The Defense Attaché Office reprogrammed whatever unused American funds were still available, but again lack of up-to-the-minute data was crucial. Meanwhile, the evacuation of the northern regions continued and no suitable plan to reorganize military units was ever devised.

Approximately forty thousand South Vietnamese troops had escaped capture in I and II Corps by April 1, and they had reported for reassignment in camps in III Corps. In many divisions the officer corps had been decimated and morale was low. The 22nd Division, whose resistance to the North Vietnamese at Binh Dinh was one of the war's most remarkable feats of determination, courage and leadership, was in better shape than the others. However, it had lost most of its equipment and the division arrived in the South with only a skeleton organization. It was deployed to Long An Province, southwest of Saigon, on April 12.

A critical battle was shaping up in Long An as the 5th North Vietnamese Division moved from Svay Rieng Province in Cambodia and launched a strong attack near Tan An. Long An's territorial troops fought well, and they temporarily held off the North Vietnamese after they were reinforced by the 17th Division's 12th Infantry Regiment.

North Vietnamese Army units in Bien Hoa Province, meanwhile, northeast of the capital, and in Tay Ninh, near the Cambodian border and northwest of Saigon, kept the pressure on during the first two weeks of April.

A major battle was now taking shape at Xuan Loc on Highway 1 east of Saigon. South Vietnamese military men fought so well that the North Vietnamese high command was forced to sacrifice its own units to destroy irreplaceable South Vietnamese forces. While savage battles continued for Xuan Loc, III Corps moved its divisions to the west to prepare for the expected assault against Saigon.

After the first North Vietnamese assault against Xuan Loc was thrown back, the 341st North Vietnamese Division began a second assault April 9 against the 18th South Vietnamese Division. Infantry and tanks were held back until 4,000 artillery shells were fired at the defenders in one of the war's heaviest pre-attack bombardments. North Vietnamese tanks then moved in while infantrymen on both sides fought a fierce hand-to-hand battle in the streets of Xuan Loc that lasted until dusk. By then the North Vietnamese division was forced to retreat from the city, their ranks decimated in the fighting with members of the 18th Division's 43rd Infantry Regiment. The 52nd Infantry Regiment, meanwhile, retained its hold on Route 20 to the north of the city.

North Vietnam's high command issued orders that Xuan Loc must be taken and the 341st Division tried the following day, but they were repulsed again by the South Vietnamese.

Heavy fighting continued in the provinces around Saigon as General Smith reported to CINCPAC headquarters and to Washington that the South Vietnamese were putting up a determiend and so far successful battle for the strategic city of Xuan Loc.

Smith wired the chairman of the Joint Chiefs of Staff April 3, "We have a victory in the making. In the battle for Long Khanh the armed forces of South Vietnam have shown unmistakeably their determination, their will and courage to fight even though the odds are heavily weighted against them. Although the battle may have passed only through Phase 1, we can say without question that the South Vietnamese have won Round 1." He described the battle for control of the vital road junction, where Highways 1 and 20 meet in the provincial capital of Xuan Loc, as one in which the South Vietnamese held their ground. In conclusion, he said he had nothing but praise for the valor and aggressiveness of the South Vietnamese, particularly Long Khanh's regional forces. He said that the battle indicated that these soldiers, adequately equipped and properly led, were, man-for-man, vastly superior to their adversaries. He concluded that the battle for Xuan Loc appears to settle the question for the time being "will the South Vietnames armed forces fight?"

For the South Vietnamese, with the communists threatening their capital, it was now a fight to the death. During this difficult period, re-supply missions flown by the South Vietnamese Air Force demonstrated the high courage of its flight-crew members.

The North Vietnamese resumed the Xuan Loc assault April 13 but, despite strong attacks and reinforcement of their forces, they were unable to crack the South Vietnamese defenses.

While the battle continued on the vital eastern approaches at Xuan Loc, the Joint General Staff ordered its III Corps Headquarters to bolster Saigon's inner defenses. Most of these defenses were manned by territorial troops, with a few regular formations—some of which had only recently been reconstituted.

The eastern and southeastern approaches to Saigon were anchored at Long Binh by a brigade of Marines, and, for a time, the Marines held firm.

Communist troop concentrations and logistical bases were now largely exposed and excellent targets for mass destruction weapons. The Viet-namese requested that the American government provide them with 15,000-pound so-called "daisy-cutter" bombs, and they were approved for immediate shipment. The first bombs arrived in mid-April. A total of twenty-seven was authorized within a week's time along with American training specialists. These men taught the Vietnamese how to strap the bombs to their aircraft but an American pilot, who was approved to fly the first plane, never arrived. With the need to start using the bombs daily becoming more acute, a skilled Vietnamese pilot went up with the first bomb attached to a C-130 cargo plane. This flight had to be aborted due to a technical failure and its return to base, with the bomb still attached, caused anxious moments.

The first bomb was dropped on the North Vietnamese northwest of Xuan Loc. The provincial city was rocked as if by an earthquake, and reportedly the 341st Division Headquarters was wiped out. The South Vietnamese fighting for Xuan Loc were jubilant, believing that the B-52s had returned. Others thought that the explosion had been caused by an atomic bomb. North Vietnamese officials immediately condemned South Vietnam and the United States for using mass-destruction weapons.

Only a few missions were flown with the big bombs because of the fuel shortage.

Throughout the first two weeks of April the South Vietnamese had been barraged by appeals from North Vietnam's so-called "liberation" radio to rise against the Thieu regime, but the calls were largely ignored.

On the western front, Long An territorials and the 12th South Vietnamese Infantry Division still held at Tan An. They maintained their defense even when North Vietnamese artillery moved in close to Saigon April 18 and blasted Phu Lam with rockets. This attack was only a few miles south of Tan Son Nhut airport and near the headquarters of the American Defense Attaché Office. Now Saigon was seriously threatened for the first time because the communists were attempting to sever Route 4 near Binh Chanh. If this attack was successful, the 7th and 9th South Vietnamese Divisions would be prevented from moving up to the capital on Route 4 to assist in its defense. Also, the city would be vulnerable to sappers and terrorists moving up from Binh Chanh who could infiltrate through Phu Lam to Tan Son Nhut airport and Saigon.

While the South Vietnamese continued to hold the line near Tan An, the 5th North Vietnamese Division was forced to pull back, unable to breach the stout defenses. The 5th's leaders called for reinforcements and waited for their arrival before they tried again.

Far to the east and north of Saigon the final battles for Ninh Thuan and Binh Thuan Provinces were being fought. Although the North Vietnamese were repulsed at first, they tried again with even stronger forces and this time forced the South Vietnamese to withdraw. Binh Thuan Province held out for two more days, but Phan Thiet fell April 18. In the battle in this province some of South Vietnam's best territorial troops fought determined battles until they were forced to retreat in the face of overwhelming odds.

The final decisive battle was being fought at Xuan Loc sixty-two miles away. After a week of the toughest, most continuous combat experienced since the North Vietnamese offensive began, the 18th South Vietnamese Division was forced to retreat from Xuan Loc and fight its way back toward Bien Hoa. Armored tank forces on Route 1 also had to pull back after half their equipment was destroyed, and the 6th North Vietnamese Division moved north of Route 1 toward Trang Bom.

The South Vietnamese moved along Route 1 in a general withdrawal until April 20 by which time there were no organized forces east of Trang Bom. The 1st Airborne Brigade, meanwhile, frustrated in its attack toward Xuan Loc, withdrew through the plantations and jungles toward Ban Ria in Phuoc Tuy Province where it remained to help defend Saigon.

Between April 20 and 26 there was an uneasy quiet over the battlefields while the North Vietnamese conducted reconnaissance sweeps, and prepared for their final drive. There were now sixteen North Vietnamese Divisions in III Corps poised for a three-pronged attack on Saigon.

The American Defense Attaché Office at Tan Son Nhut had prudently established an evacuation control center April 1, and began to send non-essential American civilian employees home three days later. The full-scale evacuation of its personnel, dependents and Vietnamese civilian employees began April 20.

As North Vietnam's army moved southward along the coast, President Thieu sent a detachment of elite South Vietnamese troops to guard his native village outside the coastal city of Phan Rang. To Thieu's dismay, the lightly manned garrison at Phan Rang mutinied as three North Vietnamese divisions approached. The Marines and Rangers whom Thieu had sent to guard his village were among his staunchest and best supporters. He was equally upset by news that the North Vietnamese drove bulldozers over the Thieu family's ancestral burying ground and plowed its tombs into the earth. The news so shocked the president that he went to the palace's bomb shelter and sat alone in despair for twenty-four hours.

Upon hearing of the president's condition, Saigon's regional commander Lieutenant General Nguyen Van Toan helicoptered to the capital the next day to pick up Chief of Staff General Cao Van Vien. They flew to the palace to meet a nervous and white-faced Thieu. Toan's words were blunt, "Monsieur le President, la guerre est finis."

Thieu should have been the strong leader that his country needed. He was the son of a humble fisherman, and a graduate of the French military academy at Dalta. A convert to Catholicism, he had fought with the French colonial army against the communists. After he became president, however, he used his office to provide draft deferments to the rich, the influential and the educated sons of his friends. Officers frequently were promoted to the rank of general more as a political plum for their support than for their ability.

With the forlorn hope that the North Vietnamese might stop their offensive and negotiate a settlement providing for some South Vietnam representation, President Thieu resigned April 21. He charged there was collusion between officials of the United States government and those in the communist governments in reaching agreement at the Paris peace talks. He stated that the United States had sold out South Vietnam to the communists. "I had courage enough to tell that to Kissinger at the time," Thieu said, adding that Nixon had exerted undue pressure on him to sign the agreement.

In assessing the state of South Vietnam's armed forces he said that the loss of small bases led to the loss of larger ones. He said that the North Vietnamese, by invading the South in strength, had tested United States resolve and that the United States had remained silent despite communist provocations. The United States did not dare to react, he said, and they have asked us to do an impossible thing. I have therefore told them that you have asked us to do something that you failed to do with half a million powerful troops and skilled commanders and with nearly 300 billions in expenditures over six long years. "If I do not say that you were defeated by the Communists in Vietnam, I must modestly say that you did not win either. . . . Also you have let our combatants die under a hail of bullets. This is an inhumane act by an inhuman ally. The Americans fought a war here without success and went home," he said with bitterness. "There was a promise that if the Communists intruded and invaded again, there would be a reaction. But there has been no reaction," he said. "What does this amount to? This amounts to a breach of promise, injustice, lack of responsibility and inhumanity toward an ally who has suffered continuously—the shirking of responsibility on the part of a great power."

Thieu's bitterness at the time is understandable, but he bore a large part of the responsibility for the fall of his country through his inept leadership, although he never admitted his own failings.

Credibility for some of Thieu's charges was established when a former South Vietnamese official released two letters that were written in November, 1972, and in January, 1973, in which President Nixon promised that the United States would "take swift and severe retaliatory action" and "would respond with full force" if Hanoi violated the Paris ceasefire agreement. These words were far stronger than Nixon had said publicly in 1973 that the United States "will not tolerate violations of the agreement." And, they were more concise than his pledge to "react vigorously." Now, of course, Nixon was no longer president.

Thieu's resignation had no discernible effect on the North Vietnamese whose successes on the battlefields, and the absence of any prospect of United States military support, left no basis for further negotiation. In effect, South Vietnam's politicians had no bargaining power left.

With the end near, an official of the North Vietnamese government called the last days of the South Vietnamese regime the "dance of the puppets."

Thieu's successor, Vice President Tran Van Huong was lame and ill. The seventy-one-year-old Huong had served briefly as premier in the mid-1960s but he had been ousted by a military coup because of his poor administration of the country.

The North Vietnamese resumed their attacks April 26, focusing on Bien Hoa east of Saigon. Two air bases received heavy artillery fire as North Vietnamese divisions moved on Route 1 toward Bien Hoa. The communists moved forward with confidence, crossing Route 15 south of Long Binh and isolated the southern coast city of Vung Tau. The Defense

Attaché Office's plans for large-scale evacuation through this port had to be abandoned.

North Vietnamese Army units in Long An and Hau Nghia Provinces renewed their efforts to dislodge the stubborn South Vietnamese defenders in the west.

Thieu's successor tried to form a new government that might be acceptable to the North Vietnamese for negotiating a settlement, but he was proclaimed unacceptable and Huong had to admit defeat April 27. He resigned and was succeeded by General Duong Van "Big" Minh—so named because he was six feet tall and weighed over 200 pounds—who now openly boasted of his contacts with the North Vietnamese in past years. A neutralist Buddhist, he had long advocated a conciliatory policy towards them. Any hope that the fifty-nine-year-old Minh may have had that his contacts might help him or South Vietnam were quickly dispelled. The communists soon demonstrated that they had nothing but contempt for him. Such futile political machinations were irrelevent in the face of the reality of continued communist victories.

A flight of A-37s, piloted by South Vietnamese pilots who were forced to serve the communists, bombed Tan Son Nhut on the evening of April 28. A number of aircraft were destroyed on the ground. The bombing was more damaging psychologically than the material damage caused by the attack. Most Saigon residents thought it was an attempted coup d'état. This was the first time aircraft had been used against the South Vietnamese and it was ironic that the planes were flown under duress by South Vietnamese Air Force pilots.

The following day Tan Son Nhut came under heavy bombardment by the North Vietnamese who used guns and rockets. Aircraft storage areas and runways were hit by artillery shells, while rockets landed in the Defense Attaché Office's compound. The end clearly was in sight.

With Cu Chi on Route 1 under attack less than twenty miles to the northwest of Saigon, and North Vietnamese sappers and infantry units in Vo Gap just north of Tan Son Nhut, Ambassador Martin knew that the time had come for the few remaining Americans to leave the country. At dawn, April 30, the American evacuation was completed and Duong Van Minh surrendered the country to the North Vietnamese.

North Vietnam's expeditionary force, although no longer supported by an effective southern guerrilla force, and badly battered by the battles in the first part of 1972, had embarked on an intensive program of reorganization. Their victory was a remarkable achievement but it must be understood that it was accomplished without serious interference. The United States had withdrawn its military forces after the ceasefire, leaving

South Vietnam without the airpower to attack North Vietnam's rear logistical areas and its new lines of communications.

Although South Vietnam had built up its defensive military capability, and was growing steadily stronger in combat effectiveness, it lacked a true offensive capability to strike at the heart of North Vietnam's strength in the North. This was done deliberately by the United States to force the South Vietnamese to restrict the war to the South.

During the last two years of the war, South Vietnam's leaders adopted an aggressive defense that strengthened its influence and improved its security in the populated regions of the country. Without regard to the terms of the ceasefire, North Vietnam directed its operations towards the defeat of pacification. Although their plan failed, the North Vietnamese Army was able to eliminate isolated government outposts, most of which interferred to some degree with the communist plan for developing sparsely populated regions and protecting their logistical system in the South in support of its growing expeditionary army. Despite notable gains in the southern regions, such as in the Seven Mountains of Chau Duc in Tri Phap and Svay Rieng Province in Cambodia, South Vietnam's defenses were restricted to major population centers.

As outposts were routinely overrun by the North Vietnamese, the South Vietnamese Army gained in one respect. It now had shorter frontlines with fewer demands on their limited logistical and tactical resources. Still, South Vietnam's overall military resources were so limited due to the reduction in American aid, that they were never able to build up sufficient reserves to meet all contingencies. North Vietnamese Army units took full advantage of the situation by increasing their hold on the countryside outside of South Vietnam's cities, and used with great skill their ability to remain on the offensive, and to bring overwhelming force against strategic objectives. A typical instance was the battle for Ban Me Thuot.

South Vietnam's collapse was predictable. Although its leaders blamed the United States, they had only themselves to blame.

For the United States the war did not end with the evacuation of South Vietnam. Khmer Rouge gunboats seized the American ship *Mayaguez* seventy miles off Cambodia's east coast May 12. This unprovoked seizure shocked the American people. It was an arrogant act, and one that implied that the United States lacked the will or the ability to act decisively in even minor incidents.

American patrol pilots spotted the *Mayaguez* the next day as it was towed by its captors towards the mainland. By firing across its bows in harassing attacks, the planes tried to force the Cambodians to release the ship. Later, an Air Force pilot prepared to fire at a fishing trawler but he thought he spotted Americans on board. He reported the incident and was advised not to attack. Appearance of American planes had forced the Cambodians to abandon the *Mayaguez* and attempt to take its thirty-nine crew members to Sihanoukville.

Tactical aircraft sank five Cambodian boats May 14 and damaged a number of others although the trawler with its American prisoners reached shore.

When diplomatic efforts failed, the United States Defense Department was ordered by President Ford to seize the *Mayaguez* and recover its crew.

The following day 230 Marines in helicopters equipped with armor plating and rapid-firing miniguns landed on Koh Tang to search for the ship's crew thought to be on this island. The helicopters were hit by heavy fire and three were shot down. Intelligence officers had predicted there were only twenty old people on the island. Instead there were approximately 300 Cambodians with automatic weapons who were well dug in.

Meanwhile, the destroyer escort *Harold E. Holt* was sent to seize the *Mayaguez*. But the boarding party found the ship abandoned and took possession.

An hour after the boarding, the destroyer *Robert L. Wilson* spotted a small boat coming from the mainland with its crew waving white flags. The thirty-nine crew members of the *Mayaguez* were picked up and returned to their ship.

Meanwhile, the Marines were in serious trouble on Koh Tang because they had been dispersed in three isolated groups due to the heavy fire during landing operations. After Marine reinforcements arrived the three groups were reunited and were ordered to withdraw.

During these actions, twenty-five fighter-bombers from the Coral Sea bombed Ream airport and destroyed seventeen Cambodian aircraft on the ground. Then a second wave bombed the railroad yards and an oil refinery at Sihanoukville.

With the Marines fighting desperately on Koh Tang and Cambodian fire driving off helicopters trying to rescue the wounded, a C-130 from Thailand dropped a 15,000-pound bomb where the Cambodians were hiding. This bombing was followed with attacks by Navy planes from the Coral Sea.

After extensive bombardment the pressure on the Marines eased and it was decided to withdraw them that night. With communist defenses leveled, the eastern side of the island had an unearthly glow from the fires as they silently left. On the west side all was dark except for the intermittent blinking of a Marine strobe light—abandoned on the beach by the departing Marines.

The *Mayaguez* incident was mishandled from the start, compounded by

Admiral Noel Gayler's actions as Commander-in-Chief, Pacific, who personally gave orders to those on the scene instead of going through proper channels. Failure of his command's intelligence officers to assess the true situation on Koh Tang caused unnecessary casualties. What should have been a routine operation resulted in five dead, sixteen missing and more than seventy wounded Americans.

Despite derogatory comments in the United States and in many other countries about the fighting abilities of the South Vietnamese, when they are compared unit-for-unit, man-for-man with their counterparts from North Vietnam they proved themselves superior. What was lacking was inspired leadership at the top among civilian and military leaders. South Vietnam's leaders had long since lost the confidence of the American people because they did not make the same sacrifices as the men in the field. Such self-sacrifice was crucial to American support, and reforms should have been initiated long before 1973, but South Vietnam's leaders failed to do so.

General Vien, chairman of the Joint General Staff, believes that with South Vietnam's advantageous military position following the 1968 Tet offensive in which the North Vietnamese were beaten that the war could have been won if forceful actions by his country's leaders had been taken with large-scale counterattacks. He is rightly critical of the Joint General Staff (including himself) because it permitted President Thieu to make the important decisions on the war's conduct despite the fact that the organization was created for the opposite purpose.

Some Westerners, including many Americans, gained the impression that North Vietnam's leaders were morally superior to those in the South, and their control of the people in the Democratic Republic of Vietnam had a grass-roots foundation. Such was not the case. North Vietnam was, and the whole country now is, a controlled communist dictatorship. Despite war-time controls, the former Republic of Vietnam's citizens for the most part enjoyed the rule of law, and went about their affairs without undue government interference.

Perhaps the major reason for South Vietnam's failure to preserve its identity as a free nation was that no national leader of strength and stature emerged during the war years who was committed to personal sacrifice. What was needed was a man who could get tough with inept or corrupt subordinates, and who could rally support in time of stress. Perhaps if members of the younger generation had had the opportunity to develop a strong leader the outcome would have been different, but none emerged to institute the internal reforms that were so desperately needed.

Out of the present dissatisfaction with communist rule such a leader, or leaders, may emerge to overthrow their oppressors. Such a move must come from within, and without outside support; otherwise it, too, shall fail.

Epilogue

THERE WERE SOME PEOPLE DURING THE WAR WHO ACCUSED THE
United States of interfering in civil wars in Southeast Asia. If the United
States would only leave this tortured land, they said, the wars would end.
In the intervening years since 1975 there has been no United States
military presence throughout this part of the world, but there is still no
peace.

Guerrillas under Communist Party Chairman Pol Pot took over Cambodia April 17, 1975, and soon launched a reign of terror resulting in the
deaths of at least two million people. Pol Pot's bizarre scheme to purify
this nation of eight million people by returning it to its rural origins, free
of outside influence, defies rationality. In ordering the capital of Phnom
Penh to be evacuated he sent most of its people to their deaths in the
countryside where they were used as forced labor.

The horror ended for some December 25, 1978, when 170,000 Vietnamese Army troops invaded Cambodia and established a pro-Vietnamese
government under President Heng Samrin, a former Khmer Rouge official.

The last Vietnamese were withdrawn September 30, 1989, although
they had failed to destroy the Khmer Rouge and its guerrilla partners.

In 1989, guerrillas of the Khmer People's National Liberation Front led
by former Premier Son Sann, and two other loosely allied Cambodian
factions, were still trying to oust Heng Samrin's government in Phnom
Penh. The Khmer Front has joined forces with the communist Khmer
Rouge that governed Cambodia so brutally from 1975 until Pol Pot's
ouster from office by the North Vietnamese, and the Moulinake. The
latter are loyal to Cambodia's deposed head of state, Prince Norodom
Sihanouk.

Although Pol Pot is vilified as the personification of every evil carried
out by his subordinates, his Khmer Rouge represents the largest force in
the coalition.

The Vietnamese officially unified their own country July 2, 1976, and proclaimed it the Socialist Republic of Vietnam with its capital at Hanoi.

Laos has also been under Vietnam's control since the Pathet Lao seized its capital Vientiane in August, 1975. Now the Vietnamese communists have achieved their long-standing goal of domination of their neighbors.

Since 1975 more than a million Vietnamese have fled their country, with a majority coming to the United States, while more than 50,000 have died trying to escape. Millions more would follow if they could get out. For those with money escape can be arranged by paying a substantial bribe.

Conditions inside Vietnam are repressive and appalling since the communists gained control. There are bribes for almost everything, including shipments from the Soviet Union and its satellite countries. Goods may not be landed without paying off port authorities. In Hanoi, its buildings are decaying and nothing new has been built since the war ended. With the nation getting ever deeper into debt, the Soviets realize they will never be repaid and they have refused additional credit beyond what they are already paying—possibly the equivalent of two billion dollars a year. There is insufficient food to feed the people although communist leaders are enjoying the fruits of victory by living in relative luxury compared to the rest of the people. In a country that formerly grew two rice crops a year, only one crop has been grown in the post-war years and that is of poor quality. This is due to a shortage of fertilizer formerly supplied by the United States. Vietnam's factories are either idle or run so inefficiently that they are a constant drain on the economy.

Politically, the situation for the Socialist Republic of Vietnam has changed drastically for the worse. Its one-time ally, the People's Republic of China, is now a bitter enemy, and there are constant border skirmishes between their respective armed forces. China, once an enemy of the United States, is now a friend. There is also growing concern in China about Vietnam's aspirations in Southeast Asia, and a major conflict between the two nations cannot be ruled out.

Much of Vietnam's problem lies in its inability to get along with the rest of the world due to warlike acts that have alienated her from countries that might otherwise help her out of her economic and political quagmire. To protect herself from supposed enemies, and to complete her political goals, Vietnam has more than a million men under arms—the fifth largest armed forces in the world. For a nation with only a fraction of the United States' gross national product, such a military establishment cannot be maintained indefinitely.

Fears by South Vietnam officials and military officers that they would meet an uncertain fate if they remained in their country following collapse of its armed forces have been justified. Re-education camps were set up first near Can Tho and up to 200,000 former members were incarcerated. Some were beaten, tortured, or worked to death clearing forests and building new camps. Many died of disease. The situation became so appalling that the communist government in 1982 instituted regular inspection of camp conditions.

In September, 1984, the United States offered to accept 10,000 political prisoners over a three-year period. Vietnamese leaders insisted the United States must take all those whom they describe as "criminals" but the American government refused to take them on such a basis. Fidel Castro's unloading of Cuban criminals on the United States during the Jimmy Carter presidency was still too fresh in the minds of the Reagan administration.

Political prisoners were charged with national treason but the camps also hold former intellectuals, Buddhists and Christian clergymen and ethnic Chinese. The latter have been driven out by the tens of thousands. Some senior military officers were executed but the communist government decided against a major bloodletting. Intellectuals are of greatest concern to the communists because they fear the return of well-educated people to society. The Vietnamese government claims that a million people were incarcerated right after the war ended but most were freed after short-term indoctrination courses. There have been many re-arrests and at least 200,000 have spent more than a year in camps, with about 40,000 incarcerated for longer terms.

Anti-war activists, who loudly trumpeted alleged war crimes of the United States against the Vietnamese people, have been largely silent about communist crimes against the people of Southeast Asia. They like to express their beliefs—although only among themselves now that most Americans oppose their radicalism—that their activities helped to force an end to the war. Now they find it difficult to accept any blame for actions that helped the communists to gain control of Southeast Asia and resulted in the deaths of more than two million Cambodians, and untold hundreds of thousands of Laotians and South Vietnamese. Few activists are willing to accept any responsibility although they are indirectly involved whether they like it or not.

The majority of Americans who took part in anti-war demonstrations were duped by modern Pied Pipers who frequently played a communist tune that was not recognized as such. Their aversion to the war is understandable, and in most cases they expressed deep-felt beliefs. For others, who were led into intemperate acts by those whom they should have distrusted, nothing can condone their excesses.

After the war the Veterans Administration hired pollster Louis Harris and Associates to conduct surveys among the American people and veterans of that era. A number of myths and misconceptions were revealed. Most veterans did not enter the armed forces through the draft, even in the Army where more than half enlisted. Minority veterans were not overrepresented. But surveys revealed they were more likely to serve in Southeast Asia and to be involved in heavy combat than other veterans, but the difference was not large. Almost half of all veterans who served during the war were sent to Indochina, and most were exposed to moderate to heavy combat.

Men who had not completed high school were three times more likely to participate in heavy combat than those who had completed college. Those who were younger than twenty when they entered the combat theater were twice as likely as those thirty-five and over to be exposed to heavy combat.

Surveys revealed that pride rather than shame is the most common characteristic among veterans. They are proud that they served, and 66 percent would serve again if their service was needed. However, a significant minority—especially young men with heavy combat experience—are bitter about their military service and would not fight again.

Veterans of this war believed that their reception upon returning home was not on a par with veterans of earlier wars. There are differences between these veterans and those of World War II and Korea in their respective receptions by close friends and family. However, the most significant difference lies in the reception given to Indochina war veterans by people of their own age who did not serve. Nearly three-quarters of the veterans of earlier wars feel people their own age gave them a very friendly reception, compared to less than half of the veterans from Southeast Asia.

The surveys concluded that a majority of the American people and 82 percent of Indochina veterans place responsibility for the unsuccessful war on the shoulders of their political leaders in Washington. Most veterans are convinced American troops lost the war by failure of the political will rather than any failure of arms. Three-quarters of these veterans also believe that political leaders in Washington misled the American people about the war's prosecution. It is interesting to note that in these surveys the American people say they believe the war was a mistake, but they do not hold the men who fought in Indochina responsible for the war. In general, most people have a positive view of the veterans. Actually, their feelings are on a par with veterans of earlier wars. As for the veterans themselves, they resent those who demonstrated against the war or left the country to avoid the draft.

Like veterans of all wars some Indochina veterans have found it difficult to get a job—a situation particularly acute for minorities. They resent having their education disrupted, and for some there has been a lack of direction in their lives.

The news media's reporting of the war was considered by both the public and the veterans as fairly realistic, but they both disagree whether this was good or bad for the country.

Other reviews of attitudes in the post-war years have shown that young men who did not serve their country now are among the nation's most vocal adherents of a military draft. Such an attitude strikes the Indochina veterans with wry amusement, knowing how incongruous it is for anyone to favor a draft once you are too old for it.

A belated recognition of the valor of the men and women of this era was given November 11, 1982, when a veterans memorial was unveiled in Washington, D.C. It is a good start to the long healing process that is necessary to bind up the nation's wounds.

Records for 1983 show there were 65,530 patients in Veterans Administration Medical Centers, including 10,893 or 16.6 percent of the total from the war in Indochina. Of this number, 3,694 were being treated for psychosis—a lasting mental derangement that is characterized by defective or lost contact with reality. Another 3,707 were undergoing psychiatric treatment for mental, emotional or behavioral disorders. When the total number of veterans who served in Southeast Asia is considered—3.7 million men and women—this is not an unusually high number.

Another lingering problem associated with the war is the chemical dioxin. This by-product of Agent Orange has caused concern because animal studies have shown it to be toxic to certain species, with the possibility of ill effects on humans.

President Ronald Reagan signed a new law October 24, 1984, that will provide some understanding assistance to veterans exposed to this chemical. They can now get a Veterans Aministration examination if they are concerned about dioxin's ill effects. The Veterans Dioxin and Radiation Exposure Compensation Standards Act requires that the Veterans Administration develop regulations to specify the circumstances under which certain diseases will be considered service-connected if they were suffered by veterans who served in Indochina and may have been exposed to Agent Orange, and those exposed to radiation during the American occupation of Hiroshima and Nagasaki in World War II and the atomic tests after that war. The law requires that regulations must be established for veterans who have developed cancers of some soft-tissue organs such as tendons, fat and muscles plus conditions that affect the liver and skin. One of the latter, chloracne, is a skin disorder that may be severe. These illnesses have been suffered by some veterans. In addition, the bill authorizes interim payments to veterans disabled by such illnesses suffered within a year after their departure from Southeast Asia.

A condition known as delayed stressed syndrome has afflicted some veterans. This is a new name for an old affliction that American veterans of all wars have experienced. In the final analysis, it is a battle that each must fight on his own.

Little has been written about the problems of those who spoke out and acted against America's involvement in the war in Indochina. There have been such protesters in all wars and World War II was no exception, but most of those men and women were a different breed from their Vietnam counterparts. Lew Ayres, one of the stars of "All Quiet on the Western Front" about World War I, refused to be drafted for World War II. His action temporarily destroyed his career, but when war was forced upon the nation he volunteered to serve as a medical corpsman—a dangerous, non-rifle-carrying job of taking care of the wounded on the fields of battle. He was decorated for bravery as a non-combatant, and resumed his acting career after the war. Another medical corpsman, Private Desmond Doss, was equally opposed to serving as a combat soldier, but he was honored with the nation's highest award, the Medal of Honor, for service as a corpsman above and beyond the call of duty. For some of those who opposed the war in Indochina, the intervening years have created a doubt whether they were motivated solely out of a deep conviction against the war, or whether their actions were governed by cowardice. In the long run, that doubt will become as deadly as a communist bullet.

For those who served honorably in Indochina, this is one problem they have never had to face—nor will they ever have to do so.

Bibliography

Ballard, Jack S. *Development and Employment of Fixed-Wing Gunships, 1962–1972.* Office of Air Force History, United States Air Force, Washington, D.C., 1982.

Buckingham, William A. Jr. *Operation Ranch Hand: The Air Force and Herbicides in Southeast Asia, 1961–1971.* Government Printing Office, Washington, D.C., 1983.

Butterfield, Fox.; E. W. Kenworthy; Neil Sheehan; and Hedrick Smith. *The Pentagon Papers as Published by the New York Times.* Quandrangle Books, New York, 1971.

Collins, Brig. Gen. James Lawton, Jr. *The Development and Training of the South Vietnamese Army, 1950–1972.* Department of the Army, Washington, D.C., 1975.

Devanter, Lynda Van, with Christopher Morgan. *The Story of an Army Nurse,* Beaufort Books, New York, 1983.

Eckhardt, Maj. Gen. George S. *Command and Control: 1950–1969.* Department of the Army, Washington, D.C., 1974.

Fall, Bernard B. *Last Reflections on a War.* Doubleday, New York, 1967.

Ford, Gerald R. *A Time to Heal: The Autobiography of Gerald R. Ford.* Harper & Row and the Reader's Digest Association, New York, 1979.

Fulton, Gen. William B. *River Operations, 1966–1969.* Department of the Army, Washington, D.C., 1973.

Futrell, Robert F. *The United States Air Force in Southeast Asia: The Advisory Years to 1965.* Office of Air Force History, Washington, D.C., 1981.

Goldman, Nancy Loring, ed. *Female Soldiers: Combatants or Non-combatants.* Greenwood Press, Westport, 1982.

Gropman, Lt. Col. Alan L. *Airpower and the Airlift Evacuation of Kham Duc.* Airpower Research Institute, Air War College, Maxwell Air Force Base, Alabama, 1979.

Herrington, Stuart A. *Peace with Honor? An American Reports on Vietnam, 1973–1975.* Presidio Press, Novato, CA, 1983.

Hersh, Seymour M. *The Price of Power: Kissinger in the Nixon White House.* Summit Books, New York, 1983.

Hilgenberg, Lt. Col. John F., and Lt. Col. Arthur E. Laehr. *Last Flight from Saigon.* U.S. Government Printing Office, Washington, D.C., 1978.

Hinh, Maj. Gen. Nguyen Duy, and Brig. Gen. Tran Dinh Tho. *The South Vietnamese Society.* U.S. Army Center of Military History, Washington, D.C., 1983.

Holm, Maj. Gen. Jeanne, Ret. *Women in the Military: An Unfinished Revolution.* Presidio Press, Novato, CA., 1982.

Johnson, Lyndon Baines. *The Vantage Point: Perspectives of the Presidency, 1963–1969.* Holt, Rinehart and Winston, New York, 1971.

Kelly, Col. Francis J. *U.S. Army Special Forces, 1961–1971.* Department of the Army, Washington, D.C., 1973.

Kendrick, Alexander. *The Wound Within: America in the Vietnam Years, 1945–1974.* Little Brown and Company, Boston, 1974.

Kissinger, Henry. *The White House Years.* Little Brown and Company, Boston, 1979.

Kissinger, Henry. *Years of Upheaval.* Little, Brown and Company, Boston, 1982.

Ky, Nguyen Cao. *Twenty Years and Twenty Days.* Stein and Day, New York, 1976.

Larsen, Lt. Gen. Stanley Robert, and Brig. Gen. James Lawton Collins, Jr. *Allied Participation in Vietnam.* Government Printing Office, Washington, D.C., 1980.

Lavalle, Maj. A.J.C., ed. *Airpower and the 1972 Spring Invasion.* United States Air Force, Maxwell Air Force Base, Alabama, 1976.

Lavalle, Maj. A.J.C., ed. *The Tale of Two Bridges and the Battle for the Skies over North Vietnam.* Government Printing Office, Washington, D.C., 1980.

Lavalle, Maj. A.J.C., ed. *The Vietnamese Air Force, 1951–1975, An Analysis of Its Role in Combat, and Fourteen Hours at Koh Tang.* U.S. Government Printing Office, Washington, D.C., 1973.

Le Gro, Col. William E. *Vietnam from Cease-fire to Capitulation.* U.S. Army Center of Military History, Washington, D.C., 1981.

Lung, Col. Hoang Ngoc. *The General Offensive of 1968–69.* U.S. Army Center of Military History, Washington, D.C., 1983.

MacPherson, Myra. *Long Time Passing: Vietnam and the Haunted Generation.* Doubleday, New York, 1984.

McCarthy, Brig. Gen. James R., and Lt. Col. George B. Allison. *Line-*

backer II: A View from the Rock. Airpower Research Institute, Air War College, Maxwell Air Force Base, Alabama, 1979.

McChristian, Maj. Gen. Joseph A. *The Role of Military Intelligence: 1965–1967.* Department of the Army, Washington, D.C., 1974.

Momyer, Gen. William W. *Airpower in Three Wars.* Department of the Air Force, Washington, D.C., 1978.

Nixon, Richard. *The Memoirs of Richard Nixon.* Grosset and Dunlap, New York, 1978.

Pearson, Lt. Gen. Willard. *The War in the Northern Provinces: 1966–1968.* Department of the Army, Washington, D.C., 1975.

Rogers, Lt. Gen. Bernard William. *Cedar Falls-Junction City: A Turning Point.* Department of the Army, Washington, D.C., 1974.

Salisbury, Harrison E., ed. *Vietnam Reconsidered: Lessons from a War.* Harper & Row, New York, 1984.

Schneider, Maj. Donald K. *Air Force Heroes in Vietnam.* Airpower Research Institute, Air War College, Maxwell Air Force Base, Alabama, 1979.

Sharp, Adm. U.S.G. *Strategy for Defeat.* Presidio Press, Novato, CA, 1978.

Shore, Capt. Moyers S., II, USMC. *The Battle for Khe Sanh.* History and Museums Division, Headquarters, Marine Corps, Washington, D.C., 1967.

Shulimson, Jack, and Maj. Charles M. Johnson, USMC. *U.S. Marines in Vietnam: The Landing and the Buildup, 1965.* History and Museums Division, Headquarters, Marine Corps, Washington, D.C., 1978.

Shulimson, Jack. *U.S. Marines in Vietnam: An Expanding War.* History and Museums Division, Headquarters, Marine Corps, Washington, D.C., 1982.

Starry, Gen. Donn A. *Mounted Combat in Vietnam.* Department of the Army, Washington, D.C., 1973.

Stockdale, Jim and Sybil. *In Love & War: The story of a family's ordeal and sacrifice during the Vietnam years.* Harper & Row, New York, 1984.

Summers, Col. Harry G., Jr. *On Strategy: The Vietnam War in Context.* Strategic Studies Institute, U.S. Army War College, Carlisle Barracks, PA, 1981.

Sutsakhan, Lt. Gen. Sak. *The Khmer Republic at War and the Final Collapse.* U.S. Army Center of Military History, Washington, D.C., 1983.

Taylor, Maj. Gen. Leonard B. *Financial Management of the Vietnam Conflict: 1962–1972.* Department of the Army, Washington, D.C., 1974.

Tho, Brig. Gen. Tran Dinh. *The Cambodian Incursion.* U.S. Army Center of Military History, Washington, D.C., 1983.

Tolson, Lt. Gen. John J. *Airmobility 1961–1971.* Department of the Army, Washington, D.C., 1973.

Truong, Lt. Gen. Ngo Quang. *The Easter Offensive of 1972.* U.S. Army Center of Military History, Washington, D.C., 1983.

Vien, Gen. Cao Van and Lt. Gen. Dong Van Khuyen. *Reflections on the Vietnam War.* U.S. Army Center of Military History, Washington, D.C., 1983.

Index

Abrams, General Creighton, 356, 397, 404, 422, 418, 437, 440, 444, 465, 467, 470, 486, 527

Abzug, Representative Bella, 637

Acheson, Dean, 17–19, 22

Adams, Private First Class Billy, 237, 256, 258

Agent Orange, 465–467, 469–473, 681

Agent White, 466–468

Agnew, Vice President Spiro T., 429, 447, 536, 580, 584 (resignation of), 614, 617

Ai Mo Warehouse, 556

Air America, xxv–xxii, xxxv

Airborne Rangers, 633

Aircraft:
  A-1 Skyraider, xxx, 223, 224, 226, 231, 234, 291, 292, 308, 309, 350, 367, 368, 423, 404
  A-4 Skyhawk, 161, 179, 234, 249, 292, 320, 345, 351, 525
  A-6 Intruder, 188, 296, 301, 311, 320, 398, 503
  A-37, xlvi, 485
  AC-47, 239, 431–433
  AC-119, 432, 457
  AC-130, 432
  AH-1G Huey Cobra, 357
  B-26, 20, 61
  B-29 Superfortress, 28, 29, 546
  B-52 Stratofortress, 156, 163, 200, 204, 277, 282, 334, 381, 403, 409, 411, 412, 434, 444, 448, 459, 486, 502, 512, 513, 515, 517–519, 523, 524, 527, 528, 543, 545–547, 549, 550, 553–557, 560–562, 564, 565, 568, 569, 579, 581, 668
  B-57, 149
  Caribou, 143
  C-5, xxv
  C-47, xxix, 61, 150, 151
  C-123 Provider, 73, 89, 408, 413, 414

C-130 Hercules, xix, xx, xxi, xxvii, 151, 244, 366, 408, 431, 524, 631, 688, 674

CH-53, xxxviii

C-141, 565

EC-121, 452, 548

F-4 Phantom, 170, 181, 187, 496

F6F Hellcat, 20

F8F Bearcat, 20

F-8, 273

F-105, 163, 170, 304, 306, 307, 309, 323

F-111, 57

HH-3E, 366–368

KC-135, 549

MIGS, 187, 188, 207, 287, 304, 308, 309, 311, 312, 316, 318, 321, 323, 360, 361, 429, 487, 497–500, 547, 548, 555, 563, 566–568, 570, 598

O-1, xlvi, xlvii

OV-10 Bronco, 503–505

T-28, 61

T-29, 79

TFX, 55, 95

U-2, 122

UH-1, xxv, 226, 611

U-lH, xxxiv

UH-34, 226

Albert, Carl, 584

Alger, Major Richard, 354

All Quiet on the Western Front, 682

Alpert, Richard, 80

Alvarez, Lieutenant Commander Everett, 579

Amundson, Major Vernon, 565

Anderson, Admiral George, 56, 95, 97, 167

Anderson, R.B. (ship), 503, 549

An Dien, 625

Angel's Wing, 454, 456, 459, 622

Anh, Nguyen, 4, 5

An Hoa, 286, 354, 430

An Khe, 188, 217, 514, 657, 653, 658, 666
An Ky Peninsula, 196
An Lac, 220, 485
An Loc, 501, 505, 507, 511, 514, 521–525,
    527–530, 533, 534, 604, 632
Annamite Mountains, 34, 178, 209, 237, 379
An Nhon, 657
Anonsen, Major Charles E., 426, 457
Anthis, General Rollin H., 67, 82, 124, 131
Ap Bac, 81–83
Ap Bau Dang, 213, 340
Ap Cha Do, 340
Apollo, 11, 484
Army Special Forces, 52, 53
Arnold, Lieutenant Commander Robert, 345–
    352, 481
A Shaw Valley, 221–223, 226, 227, 238, 409,
    430, 475, 489, 562
Ashley, Major Clifford, 550, 552
Associated States of Indochina, 20
Associated States of Vietnam, 28
Atlantic Charter, 11
Atlantic Fleet, 48
Auriol, President Vincent, 17
Ayres, Lew, 682

Ba, Colonel Ly Tong, 516–519
Babylift, xxv
Back Mai Storage area, 560
Ba Gia, 181, 194
Bac Giang, 287
Ball, George W., 65, 66, 90, 92
Ban Ban, 457
Ban Do, 642
Ban Me Thuot, 89, 390, 513, 515, 631, 635,
    638, 639, 640 (fall of), 641–647, 649, 650,
    655, 656, 658, 663, 673
Ban Ria, 669
Bao Lac, 302
Baragan Peninsula, 196
Bardshar, Vice Admiral Fred, 481, 482
Barrow, Colonel R. H., 430
Barnum, Jr., Lieutenant Harvey C., 204
Bartley, Capt. John F., 89
Batangan, Peninsula, 282
Ba Thu, 459
Bat Lake, 429
Batson, Lieutenant J.E.D., 187
Battalions:
    1st South Vietnamese
    1st North Vietnamese
    1st Reconnaissance, 205, 286
    3rd Marine Tank, 211
    3rd Reconnaissance, 189, 277
    3rd South Vietnamese Ranger, 181, 189
    5th Marine Battalion, 271
    8th Airborne, 392

C-10 Sapper, 391
39th South Vietnamese Ranger, 181
60th Vietcong, 195
70th Vietcong, 199
79th Australian Signal Troop, 185
80th Vietcong, 195
808th North Vietnamese, 264
Ba Hambang, 456
Battle of Midway, 598
Bau Long, 335
Ba Xueyman Province, 68
Bay of Pigs, 48, 57, 111, 114
Bell, Major Kenneth, 305, 306
Ben Cat, 153, 327, 332, 625
Bender, Lieutenant Colonel John A., 340
Ben Hai River, 353, 607
Bennett, Jr., Dr. Ivan L., 468, 504, 505
Bennett, Captain Steve, 503
Ben Suc, 329, 330–332
Ben Thuy, 248
Bernasconi, Lieutenant Colonel, 560
Bettie, Lance Corporal, 280
Bien Hoa, 43, 75, 89, 149, 151, 181, 184,
    185, 188, 306, 331, 336, 389, 392, 432,
    513, 520, 630, 661, 669, 671
Bien Yien No, 279
Binh Chanh, 669
Binh Dinh Province, 188, 192, 215, 230, 515,
    516, 519, 637, 641, 642, 653, 657, 661,
    666
Binh Duong Province, 625, 630, 666
Binh Gia, 155, 156
Binh Hoa, 578
Binh Khe, 648, 649, 657, 661
Binh Long Province, 335, 336, 457, 459, 460,
    520, 521, 626, 656
Binh Tay Province, 656
Binh Thuan, 669
Binh Thuy, xiv, 631
Binh Xuyen, 39
Binns, Lance Corporal Ricardo, 226, 268
Black Panthers, 463
Blair, IV, Captain John D., 222, 226
Blume, Private First Class, Larry, 257
Bodley, Lieutenant Colonel, Charles H., 196,
    198
Bollaert, Emile, 16
Bong Song, 220, 575
Bon Homme, Richard (carrier), 360
Borchgrave, Arnaud de, 537, 540
Bo River, 659
Borodin, Mikhail, 7
Brigades:
    1st South Vietnamese Airborne, 523–525,
        529, 649, 656, 669
    1st Cavalry Brigade, 220
    Marine Expeditionary, 173, 177

New Zealand Army Corps, 185
2nd Marine Brigade, 185
2nd Korean Marine, 215, 282, 358
2nd South Vietnamese Airborne, 516, 649
2nd South Vietnamese Armored, 651
3rd South Vietnamese Airborne, 457, 656, 658, 662, 665
9th U.S. Marine Amphibious, 502
14th South Vietnamese Marine, 492, 493
147th South Vietnamese Marine, 394, 488, 491, 502, 661
173rd Airborne, 165, 185, 188, 212, 215, 336, 337
258th, 661
468th Marine, 648, 655, 656
Breznev, Leonid, 487
Brower, Captain Ralph, 366, 367
Brown, General George S., 432
Brown, Dr. Harold, 55, 56, 432
Brown, Lance Corporal James, 274
Brown, Specialist Fourth Class, 192
Brown, Captain Michael, 503–505
Bruce, Ambassador David K.E., 463, 464, 470, 478
Brust, David E., 222
Bu Binh, 633
Buddhists, 6, 85, 87–93, 101, 102, 109, 110, 144, 217, 229, 230, 232, 235, 238, 264, 281, 282, 374, 393, 677
Buford, Wallace, 27
Buis, Major Dale, 43
Bundy, McGeorge, 128, 143, 152, 153, 160, 161, 163, 176, 182, 192, 206
Bundy, William, 143
Bunker, Ambassador Ellsworth, 312, 377, 434, 470, 471, 536, 538, 541, 583
Buon Ho, 642
Burke, Admiral Arleigh, 95, 96
Butler, Lieutenant Stephen, 270
By Prang, 445, 454

Cabel, General Charles Pearre, 48
Calley, Jr., Lieutenant William 476
Ca Lu, 407, 409, 418
Ca Mau Peninsula, 128, 209
Cam La, 199
Cam Lo, 264, 277
Campbell, Jesse W., 414
Camp Bon Song, 192
Camp Carroll, 380, 490, 491
Cam Ne, 191, 192
Cam Pha, 247, 319, 320, 359
Cam, Brigadier General Tran Van, 650, 662
Canadian volunteers (participation by), 597
Cam Ranh Bay, 176, 185, 356, 514, 648, 662
Can Be, 597
Can, Major General Huynh Van, 233

Can Lo Party, 98
Can Tho, xxxiii, xlii, xlv, 389, 578, 679
Cao Dai, 38, 39, 53, 111, 233–235
Cape Ca Mau, 532, 533
Card, (ferry), 128
Carey, Brigadier General, xxxvii, xl
Carl, Brigadier General Marion E., 222, 223
Carmody, Captain Martin D., 245, 247
Carmody, Captain Neil, xli
Carpenter, Major Kenneth, 432, 433
Carrier Division 7, 598
Carter, Jimmy, President, 679
Case, Major Thomas F., 244, 245
Castries, Brigadier General Christian de, 24, 27, 30
Castro, Fidel, 48, 114, 115, 679
Cedar Falls, 329
Central Highlands, 31, 34, 53, 71, 158, 159, 183, 188, 197, 209, 210, 219, 237, 302, 371, 415, 433, 483, 513–515, 520, 626, 638, 639, 643, 646, 650, 655, 658, 662
Central Intelligence Agency, xxii, xliii, 47, 49, 77, 84, 92, 99, 113, 114, 127, 313, 453, 477, 508
Chae, Major General Nyung Shin, 217, 218
Chase, Captain Gregory, xxi
Chaisson, Colonel John R., 231–233
Chau Doc Province, 609, 637
Chau, Phan Boi, 5
Chiang Kai-shek, 10, 94
Chi Linh, 622
Chin, Luong Dinh, 30
Cholon, 100, 103, 107, 108, 392, 520
Chon Thanh, 522, 528
Chool, Brigadier General Le Bong 282
Chou En-lai, 32, 69, 453, 484, 507, 581
Chu Pao Pass, 642
Chuan, General, 227, 230, 231
Chu Lai, 178–181, 193, 194, 198, 211, 223, 228, 230, 261, 262, 264, 265, 267, 272, 274, 279, 282, 286, 296, 302, 404, 425, 430, 646, 658, 660
Chung, Colonel Pham Van, 657
Chu Pao Pass, 519
Churchill, Winston, 29, 32
CINCPAC Plan, 32–59, 65
Civil Guards, 40, 44, 50, 51, 56, 58, 76, 77, 85, 133, 134
Civilian Irregular Defense Group, 52, 187, 453, 457
Clancy, Captain Roger E., 458
Clanton, Captain Norman C., 244
Clark Air Force Base, xx, xxviii, xxix, xxxvii, 579
Clark, Ramsay, 535
Clay, Staff Sergeant Eugene L., 367
Cleeff, Major Jay, 413

Clifford, Clark, li, 399, 400, 426, 423
Cobb, Colonel William W., 131
Cochin China, 7, 9, 10, 13, 17
Coldby, Major Dwain A., 281
Cole, Lieutenant Colonel Daryl, 411
Coleman, Lieutenant Richard, xxviii, xxix, xxxvii
Collins, Colonel Edward J., 339
Collins, General J. Lawton, 37
Collins, Major General William R., 179
Colson, Charles, 509
Columbia Broadcasting System, 313
Colvin, John, 320
COMPANIES:
  93rd Helicopter, 82
Conein, Lucien, 92, 104
Conlee, Lieutenant Colonel William, 560, 569
Co, Nguyen Huu, 111
Confucius, 6
Conner, Lieutenant Colonel Hendsley, 549, 551, 552
Connor, Master Sergeant Kenneth, 551
Con Son, xxxii–xxxv
Constellation, (carrier), 139, 351
Con Thanh, 523
Con Thien, 322, 357, 380, 381
Cook, Staff Sergeant Fred J., 428
Coontz (ship), 287
Coral Sea (carrier), 674
Corps
  I, xxiii, 166, 178, 180, 183, 184, 189, 194, 197, 212, 215, 218–220, 227–229, 232, 235, 236, 238, 245, 251, 261, 263, 264, 281, 284, 285, 287, 295–297, 306, 357, 358, 377, 379, 384, 390, 398, 410, 422, 430, 433, 489, 491, 492, 495, 501, 503, 510–513, 515, 516, 522, 531, 534, 577, 582, 616, 626, 631, 646, 648, 655, 656, 658, 659, 661, 666
  II, 145, 152, 161, 183, 184, 188, 192, 220, 230, 282, 295, 365, 395, 445–463, 485, 502, 513, 518, 552, 577, 608, 616, 638, 640, 641, 646–648, 659–653, 657, 658, 662, 666
  III, 152, 188, 215, 359, 365, 389, 390, 392, 415, 434, 445, 457–461, 513, 520–522, 529, 531, 611, 615, 621, 630–632, 646, 657, 658, 662–664, 666–669
  3rd North Vietnames, 626
  IV, Xlii, 81, 82, 93, 100, 144, 152, 165, 183, 233, 358, 359, 384, 404, 445, 457, 458, 460, 501, 511, 522, 530, 531, 609, 621, 646, 656, 664
  XVIII Airborne, 123
  XXIV, 430
Cox, Archibald, 584
Craner, Leiutenant Colonel Robert, 369

Cricket (Airborne Command and Control Plane) xxxix, xIiv
Critz, Lieutenant Colonel Richard L. 425, 426, 430, 431
Cua Viet River, 277, 285, 490–492, 510
C. Turner Joy, (ship), 139, 140
Cua Viet Naval Base, 577
Cua Viet River, 397, 512
Cuba, invasion of, 48
Cu Chi, 331, 392, 625
Cundiff, Captain Brian H. 342
Cung Son, 652
Cu, Nguyen Huu, xlvii
Cunningham, Lieutenant Randall H., 500
Cunningham, Sergeant William, 252, 253, 254, 257, 258
Cushman, Jr., Lieutenant General Robert E., 381–383, 407, 411, 418

Dabney, Captain William H., 406, 407

Dai, Emperor Bao, 8, 11, 16–18, 20, 33, 35, 38–40, 520
Cai Co Viet, 4
Dai Loc District, 660
Dak Bla River, 517, 614
Da Krong River, 430
Dak To, 366, 375, 514, 516, 519
Dak Seang, 454
Dak Son, 597, 642
Daley, Mayor Richard, 423
Da Lat, xxxii, 34, 235, 513
Dam Cau Hai Bay, 659
Da Nang, xxii, xxiii, 5, 61, 89, 134, 138, 160, 165, 166, 174, 178, 179, 189, 193, 198, 205, 211, 222, 230–236, 243, 244, 251, 257, 262, 284, 296, 366, 367, 381, 413, 414, 416, 430, 433, 481, 488, 501, 504, 513, 578, 622, 639, 646, 655–662
Da Nang River, 178
Dang, Hai, xlviii, xlix
Dang, Phat, xlviii–l
Dang, Phi, xlviii
Dao Phu Quoc, xlviii
Dao, Tran Hung, 4
d'Argenlieu, Admiral Thierry, 13
Darlac Plateau, 34, 513, 626
Darlac Province, 641, 643, 650, 657
Darling, Lieutenant Marshall, 272, 274
Dat, Colonel Le Duc, 514, 515
Da, General Trieu, 4
Dau Tieng, 331
David, Jr., Dr. Edward E., 469
Davis, Captain Paris D., 192
Davis, Brigadier General Raymond G., 160, 193
Day, Major George E., 353

Dean, John, 582, 583
Deane, Brigadier General John R., 331, 336
Debellevue, Captain Charles, 498–500
Decker, General George H., 50
Defense Attaché Office (Cambodia), 462
Defense Attaché Office, xxi, xxiii, xxv, xxvii, xxviii, xxx, xxxi, xxx–xl, xli, xliii, xlvii, 578, 618, 620, 621, 638, 664–666, 670–672
de Gaulle, Charles, 44, 46, 58, 94, 95, 124
Deilke, Lieutenant Richard W., 273
Delayed Stress Syndrome, 682
Democratic National Committee Headquarters (break-in), 507, 509
Denton, Captain, Jeremiah P., 579
Deo Cao Pass, 653, 662
De Puy, Brigadier General William E., 220, 330
Dethlefsen, Captain Marlyn Hans, 305, 306
Dewey Canyon, 430
Dewey, Lieutenant Colonel A. Peter, 13
Di An, 185
Diefenbach, Captain Brent, 568
Diem, Bui, xlii, 180, 218, 281, 364, 477, 596
Diem, Ngo Dinh, 35–39, 40, 42–44, 46, 50–52, 58, 60, 62–65, 67–70, 73–76, 78, 83–85, 87, 89–95, 97–106, 108–113, 115, 119, 120, 122, 124, 130, 131, 158, 159, 233
Diem, Pham Thi, 310, 365, 393
Dien Bien Phu, 31, 45, 209, 231, 373, 379, 383, 405, 409
Di Linh, 302
Dillon, C. Douglas, 28
Dinh, Emperor Kah Khai, 7, 8, 232, 233
Dinh, Colonel Pham Van, 490
Dirksen, Senator Everett M., 202
Divisions:
   Airborne South Vietnamese, 461, 510, 511, 512, 617, 626, 631, 648, 655, 657
   Air Cavalry, 459
   Capital Infantry (Korean), 185
   1st Air South Vietnamese, xxxii
   1st Cavalry Airmobile, 188, 190, 197, 215, 357, 384, 395, 409, 457, 459
   1st Khmer, 587
   1st Marine, 205, 219, 221, 231, 261, 264, 268, 282, 286, 296, 301
   1st South Vietnamese Infantry, 186, 188, 212, 327, 330, 331, 343, 358, 392, 393, 395, 397, 433, 453, 490, 502, 512, 617, 626, 627, 656, 660, 665
   Korean Capital Division, 217
   2nd Air, xxxii, 70m 80, 82, 124, 131, 150, 151, 230
   2nd South Vietnamese Infantry, 199, 235, 285, 489, 513, 519, 656, 660
   2nd North Vietnamese, 286, 354, 514, 577

3rd Infantry Division, 485, 533, 560, 660
3rd North Vietnamese, 648, 657, 661
3rd South Vietnamese, 166, 168, 179, 180, 189, 194, 204, 231, 296, 395, 430, 489, 490, 491–494, 500, 510, 512, 513, 515, 516, 659
4th Marine Division, 156
5th North Vietnamese, 475, 521, 523, 527, 529, 622, 626, 666, 669
5th South Vietnamese, 459, 529, 623, 631
5th Marine Division, 205, 422
Marine Division, (South Vietnamese), 648, 656, 659–661
6th North Vietnamese, 669
7th North Vietnamese, 522, 523, 627, 529, 626, 631, 633
7th South Vietnamese, 81, 210, 365
9th Korean Division, 217
9th South Vietnamese, 336, 359, 457
9th Vietcong, 156, 157, 284, 327, 339, 340, 343, 391, 420, 456, 459, 521, 523, 524, 527, 529
10th North Vietnamese, 339, 640, 642, 653, 662, 665
11th Armored Cavalry, 213, 330, 331, 333, 337, 343, 457, 459
17th North Vietnamese, 667
18th South Vietnamese, 529, 67, 669
21st South Vietnamese, 122, 354, 522, 523, 528–530
22nd South Vietnamese, 461, 485, 514, 519, 642, 648, 649, 653, 657, 661, 665, 666
23rd South Vietnamese, 390, 461, 515, 516, 614, 643, 653, 657
25th Infantry, 313, 330, 331, 333, 337, 343, 342
25th South Vietnamese, 521, 529, 625
34th South Vietnamese Infantry, 662
40th South Vietnamese Infantry, 662
41st Infantry Division, 653
42nd South Vietnamese Infantry, 653
44th South Vietnamese, 641
53rd South Vietnamese Infantry, 642
81st Airborne Rangers, 525, 528, 530, 632
101st Airborne, 433, 475
136th North Vietnamese, 488
304th North Vietnamese, 379, 383, 490, 501, 510
308th South Vietnamese, 490, 501
312th North Vietnamese, 510, 640
316th North Vietnamese, 339
320th North Vietnamese, 339, 516, 519, 615, 640–642, 652, 655
324B North Vietnamese, 263, 279, 489, 501
325C North Vietnamese, 322, 379, 665
341st North Vietnamese, 640, 667
342B North Vietnamese, 512

620th North Vietnamese, 261, 286
711th North Vietnamese, 513
868th North Vietnamese, 339, 607
Dixie Station, 163, 176
Dobrynin, Anatoly, 198, 444, 445, 464, 507, 539, 582
Don, Major General Tran Van, 90, 92, 99, 101–103, 106, 108
Dong, Colonel, 651
Dong, Lieutenant General Du Quoc, 459, 631, 632
Dong Ha, 277, 279, 281, 284, 285, 380, 381, 322, 397, 409, 490–492, 577, 607, 627
Dong, Pham Von, 6, 8, 45, 144, 184, 537, 540, 580
Dong Hoi, 161, 162, 238, 423
Dong, Tam, 359
Dong Tri Mountain, 379
Don Loan, 631, 632
Donlon, Captain Roger H.C., 134
Doremus, Lieutenant Commander Robert, 187
Do, Tran Van, 39
Doss, Private Desmond, 682
Dow Chemical Company, 466
Do Xa, 261, 285, 286
Dragon's Jaw Bridge, 403
Drande, Specialist Fifth Class Hardey, 265, 266
Driscoll, Lieutenant, Willie, 500
Drummond, Captain David, 560
Duan, Le, 639
Dubois, W. E. B., 146
DuBridge, Dr. Lee A., 465, 466, 468
Durbrow, Ambassador Eldridge, 42, 45, 47
Duc Co., 427, 615
Duc Lap, 445, 454, 639
Duc, Nguyen, Phu, 542
Duc, Emperor Te, 5
Duc Tho, 580
Dulinsky, Sergeant Barbara J., 306
Dulles, John Foster, 22, 28–30
Dung, Mac Dang, 4
Dung, General Van Tien, 621, 627, 636, 638, 640, 653
Duong Phuong Bridge, 169
Dykes, Lance Corporal Joe, 254
Dzu, Lieutenant General Ngo, 514, 515
Dzu, Truong Dinh, 373

Ea Pa River, 651
Eaves, Captain Steven, 498
Eden, Sir Anthony, 28, 30
Edmondson, Lieutenant William, 244
Edney, Lieutenant Commander Leon A., 351
Eglin Air Force Base, 61, 244
Eighth Air Force, 545, 547, 561
Eighth Route Army (Communist Chinese), 10
Eisenhower, President Dwight D., 22, 25, 28–

30, 33, 35, 36, 41, 46, 47, 66, 80, 158, 202, 416
Ellsberg, Edward, 477, 478
Ely, General Paul H. R., 31, 37, 39
English, Brigadier General Lowell E., 277, 285, 297
Enterprise (carrier), 398, 481
Eppinger, Major Dale L., 427
Erlichman, John, 477
Ervin, Senator Sam, 582
Esau, Captain Richard, 355
Evacuation Control Center, xxiii, xi
Evacuation Processing Center, xxx, xxxv

Falck, Major Louis, 564
Far East Air Force, 25, 29
Feezel, Lieutenant Tom, 499
Felt, Admiral Harry D., 46, 53, 58, 60, 62, 66, 70, 78, 82, 83, 84, 102, 107, 131, 132, 135
Field Force I, 217
Field Force II, 213, 327, 329, 330, 335, 339, 392, 460
Fields, General, 219, 230, 285, 286, 305
Fisher, Major Bernard F., 223–226
Fishbook, 456, 457, 459
"Five O'Clock Follies," 289, 503
Fleet Marine Pacific, 174, 199
Fleming, Lieutenant James F., 427, 428
Flying Tigers Airlines, xxix, xxxii
Flynn, Colonel John F., 554
Fonda, Jane, 1, 535
Fontana, Major General Paul J., 179
Ford, President Gerald R., xxi, xxx, xlv, li, lii, 1, 369, 472, 553, 584, 586, 588, 629, 636, 663, 664, 674
Forrestal (carrier), 363, 364
Foster, Jr., Dr. John S., 466
Foster, Commander Wynne E., 249
Francis, Major William, 567
Freedman, Technical Sergeant Morton, 412, 413
French Foreign Legion, 14, 27
Fulbright, Senator J. William, 51, 142, 474

Garcia, Lance Corporal Guadalupe, 280
Gavin, Major General James M., 29, 30
Gaylor, Admiral Noel, xxvi, xxxi, xlii, 675
General Dynamics, 56, 57, 95
Geneva Accords, 128, 541, 574
Geneva Protocol, 468
Gia Dinh, 329, 392
Giai, Brigadier General Vu Van, 489–494, 503, 516
Gia Lam River, 398, 559
Gia Linh, 380
Gia Long Palace, 99
Giao Chi Province, 4
Giap, General Vu Nguyen, 6, 8, 10, 13, 14, 16,

31, 24, 27, 45, 243, 365, 370, 372, 374, 435, 594, 639
Gibbs, Sergeant James, 254
Gilpatric, Roswell, 57, 58, 64, 71, 73, 74
Gilroy, Captain Kevin, 305, 306
Go Dau Ha, 622
Gia Linh, 322
Goldwater, Senator Barry, 152
Gonzales, Major Leonard, 427, 428
Goodpaster, General, 437
Goodsell, William J., 270
Gorsline, Captain Samuel, 289
Gracey, General Douglas, 12
Graham, Captain James A., 354, 355, 356
Greathouse, Lieutenant Commander E. A., 187
Green Berets, xxxii, 380, 426, 428
Green, Gunnery Sergeant John S., 355, 356
Greene, Jr., General Wallace M., 129, 144, 152, 168, 178
Gregory, Dick, 448
Grimsley, Colonel James A., 331
Grinder, Joe, 559
Grippen, Technical Sergeant Spencer, 568
Groups:
  7th South Vietnamese Ranger, 643
  Air Group 12, 179, 425, 430
  20th South Vietnamese Engineer, 651
  21st South Vietnamese Ranger Group, 642
  33rd Tactical, 89
  34th Tactical, 89
  231st South Vietnamese Direct Support, 652
  559th Group, 43
  959th Group, 42
Gromyko, Andrei, 443
Grubbs, Staff Sergeant Manson, 414
Gulf of Tonkin, 139, 142, 144, 156–163, 245, 352, 503, 563, 566, 584, 579, 592, 598

Hague, Captain Dennis, 224
Hai Duong Province, 310
Haig, Lieutenant Colonel Alexander M., 331, 340–342; General, 539, 542, 575
Hai Nguyen, 310
Hai Van Pass, 34, 174, 238, 262, 296, 488, 501, 513, 626, 659, 661, 665
Haldeman, H. R., 506
Ham Tan, 632
Hao Lo Prison, 369
Hancock, (carrier), 287, 482
Han Duc, 286
Han Dynasty, 4
Hanecak, Captain Richard, 161, 162
Hannah, Norman, 594
Hanoi Hannah, 409
Hanoi "Hilton", 324
Harkins, Lieutenant General Paul D., 67, 70,

79, 80, 87, 88, 93, 94, 98, 100, 102, 105, 107, 121, 172, 129–131
Harold E. Holt, (ship), 674
Harriman, Averell, 124, 414
Harris, Louis, 679
Harrison, Lieutenant Randolph C., 426
Hart, Captain John, 252, 283
Hartman, Lieutenant, (j.g.) Charles W., 187, 188
Hartman, Lieutenant Commander Richard, 351
Ha Sac Province, 310
Hastings, Sergeant Peter, 253, 257
Hastings, Lieutenant Richard, 139
Ha Tien City, 532
Hau Bon Airstrip, 649, 651, 652
Hau Duc, 626
Hau Nghia, 520, 673
Hawkins, Colonel Gains B., 313
Hay, Jr., Major General John H., 336, 339, 342
Hayden, Tom, 1, 80
Healey, Brigadier General Michael D., 519
Heath, Donald H., 20, 37
Hee, President Park Chung, 217, 218
Henderson, Brigadier General Melvin D., 199, 200
Heng, Cheng, 452, 475
Hensley, Major Dale, xxxii
Herbicides, 73–76, 78, 79, 208, 465, 466, 467, 468, 470–473
Herrick, Captain John J., 138, 140
Hersey, Lieutenant General Lewis B., 202, 203
Hien Giang River, 490
Hiep Duc, 198, 199, 261, 286, 354
Hiep, Brigadier General Phan Hos, 489
Hilgartner, Lieutenant Colonel Peter, 355
Hilgenbert, Lieutenant Colonel John E., xxviii, xxx, xxxi, xxiv, xxxvii, xxxviii, xxxix, xli
Hill 558, 379
Hill 861, 379, 383
Hill 881, 379
Hill 881S, 383, 406, 407
Hill, Lieutenant Richard A., 341
Hilliard, David, 448
Hilsman, Roger, 124
Hilton, Lieutenant Colonel June H., 385
Hinh, General Nguyen Van, 38
Hinh, Brigadier General Nguyen Duy, 503
Hitler, Adolf, 9, 10
Hoa Hao, 38, 39, 53, 111
Hoa Lac, 318, 547
Hoang, Tran Van, 640
Hoa Loa Prison, 553, 561, 568
Ho Bo Woods, 331, 625
Ho Chi Minh, 3, 6, 7, 13, 14, 15, 17, 18–21, 25, 30, 31, 35, 39, 42, 68, 79, 113, 119, 223, 239, 241, 300, 301, 306, 322, 372, 379, 389, 409, 441, 443, 447

Ho Chi Minh Trail, 123, 125, 197, 208, 243, 284, 301, 431, 448, 475, 482, 582, 583, 599, 608, 609
Hock, Nguyen Thai, 5
Hoi An, 232, 266, 268
Holmes, Corpsman Billie Don, 266, 268, 273
Hon Gai, 141, 310, 320, 359
Hong Ngu, 609, 613
Hon Me, 130
Hon Ngu, 138
Hoover, J. Edgar, 463
Hope, Bob, 570
Houghton, Colonel Kenneth J., 354, 356
House, Lieutenant Colonel Charles A., 226, 227
House Judiciary Committee (votes for impeachment of Nixon), 585
Howard, Staff Sergeant Jimmie L., 261, 265, 266–268, 260, 269–271, 272, 273, 275
Hué, 6–8, 34, 87, 94, 221, 229, 230, 232, 235, 238, 262, 264, 384, 393, 395, 397, 399, 403, 430, 433, 489, 490, 492, 494, 495, 501, 502, 504, 514, 534, 617, 622, 639, 646, 658, 660, 661
Humphrey, Hubert H., 371, 423, 429
Hung, Brigadier General Le Van, 529
Hung, Pham, 399
Hung, Colonel Phan Dinh, 650
Hung, Colonel Ton That, 515
Hunt, Howard, 509
Hunt, Major General Ira, 619
Huong River, 397
Huong, Tran Van, 156, 671
Huyen, Major, 596
Hunh, Major Thu, xxxiii
Hyland, Vice Admiral John J., 314, 316
Hymel, Lieutenant Robert, 568

Ia Drang Valley, 197, 215
Independence, (carrier), 48, 188
Independence Palace, 371, 391, 522, 649
International Commission of Control and Supervision, 40, 82, 95, 145, 608
Iron Hand, 345, 346
Iron Triangle, 327, 329, 330–332, 398, 333–335, 343, 360, 520, 622, 625

Jackson, Lieutenant Colonel Joe H., 413, 414
Jackson, Lieutenant Colonel Mallard, 355
Jackson, General Thomas J., 593
Jaworski, Leon, 585
Jenkins, Jr., Captain Harry T., 579
Jennotte, Jr., Colonel Alfred J., 413, 414
Johnson, Captain, 308, 309
Johnson, Lieutenant, Clinton B., 187, 188
Johnson, General Harold K., 168, 212, 549, 561
Johnson, President Lyndon B., 51, 52, (Assumes office of Presidency) 114, 115, 119–123, 125–128, 130–133, 139, 141, 142, 144, 146, 149, 150, 152–168, 174, 288, 292, 296, 300, 301, 182–184, 190, 191, 197, 201–203, 206, 207, 213, 220, 221, 235, 262, 282, 283, 306, 309, 312, 313, 317, 319, 321, 355, 361, 373, 393, 400, 401–403, 420, 442, 448, 477, 482, 507, 570, 584, 592, 595, 648
Johnson, Sergeant Paul R., 428
Johnson, Admiral Roy, 291
Joint Chiefs of Staff, 19, 28, 30, 31, 36, 37, 39, 40, 44, 48, 59, 60, 61, 64, 70, 71, 74, 77, 78, 84, 88, 89, 100, 107, 119, 121–123, 125, 126, 127, 129, 130, 133, 140, 144, 145, 147, 149, 152, 158, 163, 165, 166, 168, 169, 173, 181–183, 207, 215, 216, 264, 285, 294, 296, 299, 303, 307, 315, 317, 319, 383, 400, 401, 429, 441, 465, 467, 469, 470, 476, 477, 481, 488, 505, 506, 519, 545, 546, 543, 593, 595, 599, 665
Joint General Staff, 88, 90, 91, 93, 103, 108, 283, 389, 390, 391, 393, 456, 502, 503, 539, 643, 645, 649, 650, 652, 653, 655, 660, 662, 666, 668, 675
Jones, Captain George A., 342, 424, 425
Jones, Captain Ronald C., 457
Jones, Captain Vera M., 384
Jones, III, Lieutenant Colonel William A., 423
Junction City, 327, 329, 335, 336, 338, 339, 343

Kadena Air Base, 549, 565
Karch, Brigadier General Frederick J., 160, 165, 166, 177, 178
Katum, 336
Kearsarge, (carrier), 139
Kelly, Colonel Joseph E., 196
Kennedy, President John F., 62–64, 66–67, 69, 70, 74–77, 78–81, 87, 88, 80, 91–93, 95, 96, 98, 100, 102–104, 107–111, 114 (death of) 115, 119, 120, 132, 167, 443, 448, 477, 596
Kennedy, Robert F., 67, 216, 443
Kent State University, (students killed at), 462
Kep Airfield, 249, 311, 312, 318, 547
Kep Marshalling Yards, 167, 247, 422, 563
Kham Duc Special Forces Camp, 410–413, 419
Khanh Duong, 550, 649, 653, 656, 665
Khanh Hoa Province, 650, 662, 665
Khanh, General Nguyen, 111, 124, 125, 126, 129, 132, 133, 137, 141, 144, 153, 154, 164, 165
Khe Sanh, 228, 238, 263, 281, 284, 285, 322, 357, 357, 366, 375, 379–38s, 395, 405, 407, 409, 410, 411, 418, 419, 490, 607

Khe Tre, 133, 134
Khiem, Tran Thien, 94, 143, 648, 655, 656, 658
Khmer Issarak, 112
Khmer Rouge, xxvi, 538, 581, 673, 677
Khmer Serei, 113
Khoi, Lieutenant Colonel Nguyen Ngoc, 93
Khuyen, Lieutenant General Don Van, 618
Khyteb, Lieutenant General Dong Van, 666
Kien Duc, 642
Kien Long, 128
Kien Phong Province, 43
Kien Kuong Province, 457
Kim, Major General, LeVan, 99, 100, 107, 124
King, Colonel Benjamin H., 61
King, Captain Hubert, 224
King No Railroad and Storage Plant, 554, 558, 559
Kissinger, Dr. Henry, 445–448, 455, 463, 468, 469, 471, 473, 474, 476–478, 484, 486, 487, 505, 507, 535–540, 542, 543, 573–578, 580–582, 600, 604, 606, 607, 613, 670
Kitty Hawk, (carrier), 245, 247, 248, 311, 398, 399
Klingman, Glenn C., 466
Klinker, Captain Mary T., xxv
Koh Tang, 674, 675
Kompong Cham, 456, 459
Kompong Song, 141, 454
Kompong Spean River, 457
Kompong Trach, 458, 459, 530
Kontum, 34, 74, 173, 188, 215, 366, 485, 496, 501, 511, 513–520, 533, 534, 604, 607, 608, 614, 615, 630, 640–642, 645, 646, 649–651, 656, 658
Korat, 170
Korth, Navy Secretary, 96
Kosoglow, Private First Class Joseph, 267
Koster, Major General Samuel, 411
Kosygin, Aleksei N., 160, 161, 300, 301, 321, 453
Krogh, Egil, 478
Krulak, Major General Victor, 88, 174, 178, 179, 199, 205, 219, 220, 281
Krushchev, Nikita, 44, 45, 47, 58, 59, 78, 160
Kuala Lumpur, xlix
Kutushev, Konstantin, 487
Ky, Nguyen Cao, xxix, xxxiii, 99, 111, 131, 132, 153, 165, 181, 218, 221, 227, 229–235, 238, 282, 365, 373, 458, 480
Kyle, Major General Wood B., 279, 281
Ky Phu, 391
Kzu, Lieutenant General Ngu, 459

Laehr, Lieutenant Colonel Arthur E., xxviii, xxxi, xl, xli, xlvi

Lai Khe, 336, 369, 523, 528, 623, 631
Laird, Melvin, 466, 467, 470, 479, 483, 486
Lam, Lieutenant General Hoang Xuan, 199, 235, 236, 262, 264, 383, 475, 489, 490, 491, 493, 501, 575
Lam, Tran Van, 586
Lan, Colonel Bui The, 502
Lane, Lieutenant Sharon A., 404
Lang, General Vu, 639
La Nga, 357
Lang Dang Railroad Yards, 570
Languirand, Master Sergeant Leo, 559
Lang Vei, 379, 314, 407, 410
Lanigan, Colonel John P., 380
Laniel, Joseph, 28, 32
Lansdale, Colonel Edward G., 33, 57, 174
Lao Dong Party, 21, 43, 45, 68, 327, 621
La Porte, Roger, 203
La Vang, 301, 511
Leary, Timothy, 80
Lebar, Major Thomas, 554, 555, 564–566
Le Duan, 630, 658
Le Duc To, 441, 448, 455
Le, Captain Kong, 44
Lee Captain Lee L., 233
Le Duc Tho, 473
Le Gro, Colonel William E., 664
LeMay, General Curtis E., 47, 48, 56, 57, 59, 60, 61, 63, 66, 67, 75, 77, 84, 97, 98, 123, 127, 129–131, 144, 150, 151, 152, 156, 167, 216, 500
Lemnitzer, General Lyman, 47, 51
Le My, 179, 180
Leonard, Sergeant Mathew, 338
Le Quang Tung, 100
Le Trung, 661
Levitow, Airman First Class John C., 432
Lewis, Corporal Raymond, 253, 254, 256, 257
Linebacker I, 506, 545
Linebacker II, 545, 546
Linh, Emperior Dinh Bo, 4
Lin Piao, Defense Minister, 196
Loan, Colonel Ngoc, 232, 234
Loc Chao, 141
Locher, Captain Roger C., 498–500
Loc Ninh, 366, 375, 520, 522, 523, 525
Lodge, Henry Cabot, 90–93, 97–100, 102, 103, 106, 109, 111, 129, 197, 190, 207, 220, 312, 358
Lodge, Major Robert, 498, 500
Lo Go, 335
Long An, 358, 666, 669, 672
Long Beach, (ship), 163
Long Binh, xliv, 385, 392, 432, 520, 668, 671
Long, Emperor Gia, 393
Long Khanh, 656, 666, 667
Long Nguyen, 343, 625

Long Son, 320
Lopez, Jr., Staff Sergeant Adolfo, 458
Lownds, Colonel David H., 282, 381, 383, 407, 408
Luat, Colonel Nguyen Cong, 643
Lucas, Captain Jon, 224
Ludwig, Lieutenant Colonel Verle E., 191
Lundie, Staff Sergeant James, 412, 413
Ly, Colonel Le Khan, 651, 652
Lycée Quôc Hoc, 6

MacArthur, General Douglas, 21, 49, (dismissal of), 81
MacDonald, Admiral David, 294, 295
McCain, Admiral John S., 418, 429, 465–468, 471
McCarthy, Eugene, 444, 548, 549
McCarthy, Colonel James R., 547, 553–555, 564–568
McCarthy, Senator Joseph, 114
McChristian, Major General Joseph A., 313, 329
McClelland, Senator John L., 57, 96
McClelland, Major Paul, 426
McCone, John A., 127, 176
McConnell, General John P., 167, 168, 216, 401
McGovern, Senator George, 537, 541
McGovern, Captain James, 27
McChord, James, 509
McCutcheon, Major General Keith B., 179, 180
McGart, General Lionel C., 66
McGee, Senator Gale W., 203
McGinty, III, Staff Sergeant John H., 278
McLaughlin, Brigadier General John N., 413
McNamara, Robert S., 47, 48, 49, 50, 53, 55, 57, 59, 60, 62, 64, 65, 67, 69, 70, 72, 74, 75, 78–81, 83, 84, 87–89, 90, 93, 95, 140, 141, 143, 145, 150, 152, 162, 167, 170, 176–178, 190, 197, 205, 206, 209, 216, 221, 249–251, 252, 283, 288, 294, 296, 299, 307, 309, 314–321, 357, 359, 360, 361, 393, 399, 419, 477, 513, 594, 595, 599
Ma Da River, 89
Maddox, (ship), 138–140
Madison, Thomas, 308
Maggie's Drawers, 407
Mai Loc, 491
Mai, Nguyen Van, 405
Makins, Roger M., 28
Malik, Yakov, 453
Mallano, Captain Arthur, xix–xxi
Man, Dr. Nguyen Van, 230
Mang Ca, 393, 395, 397
Mang Yang Pass, 31, 641

Mansfield, Senator Mike, lii, 84, 114, 121, 474, 476, 586
Mao, Colonel Hoang, 617
Mao Tse-tung, 3, 7, 8–10, 17, 21, 196, 295, 373, 473, 484, 581, 593
Marcos, President Ferdinand, xxvi, 217
Maris, Captain Louis, 268
Markillie, Hospitalman 3rd Class John, 272
Markle, Lieutenant John, 498–500
Marks, Colonel Sydney M., 331, 338
Marshall, Captain Carl, 75
Marshall, George C., 15
Martin, Ambassador Graham, xxi, xxiii, xxvi, xxx, xxxi, xxxviii, xlii, xliii, xlv, 613, 618, 663, 664
Martin Corporal, John, 253
Martin, Graham, 583
Mathews, Lieutenant Owen S., 406
Massion, Colonel John, xliii
Mayaguez (attack against), 673, 674
Mayall, Lieutenant, 560
Maysey, Sergeant Larry W., 367
Medal of Honor, 134, 160, 195, 204, 226, 279, 303, 306, 309, 338, 356, 360, 414, 425, 433, 505, 652
Meeks, Captain Paul A., 423–425
Mekong Delta, 34, 42, 62, 68, 81, 151, 209, 215, 358, 401, 458, 523, 530, 531, 616, 638, 646
Mekong River, 33, 183, 309, 359, 456, 460, 609
Melville, Corporal, 272, 273
Mendenhall, Joseph, 88
Messer, Captain Michael, 497, 500
Meyer, General John C., 545, 557–569
Meyer, Lieutenant Ronald, 272
Mickler, Colonel Earl, xxx
Midway, (carrier), xxix, xxxiii, xlvi, xlvii, xxxiv, xlix, 187
Milacek, Captain Alan D., 457, 458
Military Assistance Advisory Group, (Cambodia), 38
Military Assistance Command, 67, 70, 78, 80, 83, 89, 98, 100, 124, 126, 127, 129, 131, 132, 135, 143, 155, 182, 184, 188, 190, 211–213, 227, 242, 262, 281, 285, 290, 298, 306, 311, 390, 395, 407, 417, 456, 465, 480, 509, 578
Military Sealift Command, xxvi, xlii
Mendes-France, Pierre, 32
Menzer, Lieutenant Edward H., 273
Miller, Captain David, 427
Minh, President Duong Van, xlvi, xlvii, 97–105, 107, 108, 111, 120, 121, 124, 131, 143, 480, 523
Minh, Lieutenant General Nguyen Van, 522, 529

Minh, Lieutenant General Tran Van, xxxi, 101, 335
Mitchell, Lieutenant Colonel John F., 383
Mitchell, Lieutenant Colonel Richard, xxxi, xxxii
Mobile Riverine Force, 359, 401
Noc Hoa, 622
Modrzejewski, Captain Robert J., 278, 279
Mohawk Indians, (participation by), 597
Mohrhardt, Commander Robair, 139, 141
Molotov, Vyascheslav, 32
Momyer, General William W., 309, 314, 316, 398, 402
Mongolardi, Peter, 161, 162
Montagnards, 53, 61, 145, 302, 471, 513, 587, 605, 631, 632, 641, 651
Moore, Airman First Class Albert, 563
Moore, Major General Joseph H., 124, 131, 32, 140, 140, 151
Moore, Colonel Harold G., 220
Moore, Rear Admiral R. B., 139
Moorer, Admiral Thomas H., 132, 139, 140, 293, 429, 467, 470, 476, 505, 507, 545, 547, 557
Moratorium, 442, 444
Morgan, Staff Sergeant David, 192
Morgan, Thomas E., 142
Morrison, Norman, 203
Morse, Senator Wayne, 201
Moser, Lieutenant Richard E., 270
Moulinake, 677
Mount McKinley (ship), 165
Moutet, Marius, 13
Mo Vat, 520
Moynihan, Patrick, 444
Mow, Commander Douglas, 346, 348
Mu Gia Pass, 429
Murray, Major General John E., 578, 618, 619
Mus, Paul, 15
Murville, Maurice Couvé de, 18'
Muskie, Senator Edmund, 429
Mutual Defense Assistance Act, 17, 20
Muir, Colonel Joseph E., 196
My Chanh, 495, 501, 502, 509, 534, 659
Myers, Major Clifford, 550, 552
Myers, Major Dafford W., 224, 225
My Lai, 476, 597
My Tho River, 622, 638
My Tho, 622, 638
My Thuy, 502

Nakhon Phanom Air Force Base, 423, 425
Nam Dinh, 248
Nam Dong, 133, 134, 373, 374
Nam-Nghi, Emperor, 6
Nam Phong, 553
Namsach District, 535

Na Phuoc, 320
Napoleon, 595
NaSon, 24
Nash, Technical Sergeant Albert A., 458
National Liberation Front, 95, 130, 145, 156, 202, 238, 301, 327, 375, 395, 396, 426, 435, 438, 580, 594
National Security Council, xxx, 19, 37, 41, 71, 74, 87, 92, 125, 127, 128, 152, 437, 505
Navarre, General Henri-Eugène, 2–25, 29, 31, 37
Neak Luong, 460, 587
Nelson, Lieutenant Colonel Robert B., 410
New Bo Duc, 631
Newport News (ship), 503
Ngai Province, 357
Ngan Valley, 277
Ngo Dynasty, 4
Ngo, Major General Nguyen, 101
Ngoc Tavark, 410
Ngo Trang, 516
Nguu, Lieutenant Colonel, xx, xvii
Nguyen Hue (codename), 488
Nha Be, 359, 615
Nha Trang, xxxii, 61, 70, 217, 222, 390, 513, 571, 649–653, 655, 656, 622
Nhieu, Ai, xxvii
Nhieu, Cuong, xxvii
Nhu, Madame, 87, 90, 105, 108, 110
Nhu, Ngo Dinh, 35, 45, 84, 85, 87, 90–95, 98, 100, 102, 103, 105–109, 119
Nhuan, Pham Xuan, 264
Nhut, Brigadier General Tran Van, 513, 528, 577
Niem, Brigadier General Phan Dinh, 519, 642, 648, 657
Nihn Binh, 289, 290
Ninh Thuan, 669
Ninth Expeditionary Force, 179, 165
Nixon, Richard M., lii, 46, 49, 168, 300, 312, 429, 430, 438, 441–449, 451, 452, 455, 462–465, 468–471, 474, 476–480, 482, 486, 505–507, 509, 534–538, 540–545, 547, 553, 558, 673–576, 579, 581–586, (resignation of) 599, 603, 604, 606, 608, 613, 614, 620, 630, 647, 670, 671
Nixon Doctrine, 440, 446
Nobel, Colonel John D. 179
Nobel Peace Prize, 600
Nol, General Lon, 452–456, 459, 461, 462, 465, 474, 475, 538, 575, 581, 583, 586–568
Nolting, Frderick W., 47, 58, 60, 84, 89, 90, 92, 98
Non, Lon, 475
North Atlantic Treaty Organization, 17, 18, 22
Nosavan, Phoumi, 44, 46, 47

Nui Loc Son, 198, 199, 204
Nui Vu, 286
Nungs, 134
Nunn, Senator Sam, 637

O'Brien, Captain Brent C., 147
O'Brien, William C., xxviii
O'Connor, Colonel Thomas J., 198
O'Daniel, Lieutenant General John W., 23, 37
O'Donnell, Lieutenant General Emmett, 50, 78
O'Malley, Corporal Robert E., 194, 195
O'Neill, Major James E., 89
Operation Ranch Hand, 76
Oriskany, (carrier) 145, 249, 346, 352, 363, 415, 481, 482
O'Rourke, Lieutenant Thomas J., 279, 280
Ostrozny, Captain N. J., 546
Oswald, Lee Harvey, 113
Outlaw, Rear Admiral E. C., 161
Ovnand, Chester, 43
Owen, Sergeant Ellis C., 432, 433

Packard, David, 465, 467, 471
Pacific Air Force, 50, 66, 78, 94, 87, 135, 150
Pacific Fleet, 41, 132, 135, 139, 205, 291
Page, Commander Lou, 187
Palmer, Jr., Lieutenant General Bruce, 339
Pan American Airways, 564, 565
Pao, General Vang, 468
Parrish, Major Richard, 559
Parrott's Beak, 456, 497, 520, 622
Passman, Representative Otto, 87
Pathet Lao, 43, 47, 50, 80, 112, 143, 448, 678
Patrol Base Cat Sroc Con Trang, 339
Patton, General George S., 70
Paul Doumer Bridge, 167, 168, 170, 323, 496, 497, 500
Paul, Lance Corporal Joe C., 195
Payne, Corporal Jerry, 256, 258
Peelle, Morris A., 415, 416
Pelosky, Colonel Edward, 666
Pentagon Papers, 477, 478
People's Army Magazine, 371
People's Self-Defense Corps, 439
Perkins, Hospitalman 3rd Class, Robert E., 253
Pfeiffer, Professor, E.W., 208
Phan Rang, 658, 665, 670
Phan Khac Suu, 144
Phan Thiet, 658, 669
Phnom Penh, 83, 166, 405, 452, 453, 455, 456, 458, 460, 462, 465, 538, 581, 585, 587, 588, 677
Phouc Duc, 354
Phouma, Prince Souvanna, 42, 44, 59, 448, 582
Phu Bai, 174, 189, 178, 221, 222, 227, 228, 231, 243, 262, 384, 395, 488, 504, 627, 643, 645, 665

Phu Bon, 650, 651, 656
Phu Can, 287
Phu Cat Air Base, 653
Phu Cui, 248
Phu Cuong, 332, 625
Phu Ciao, 632
Phu Hoa Dong, 331, 625
Phu Lam, 669
Phu Loc, 627, 648, 660, 661, 665
Phu Lei, 141, 213, 331
Phu, Major General Pham Van, 640, 642, 648, 652, 662
Phu, General Tran, 8, 502
Phu Thu District, 660
Phu Tuan, 659
Phu Yen Province, 143, 655, 662
Phuc Yen, 318, 323, 361, 547
Phung, Phan Dinh, 5
Phuoc An, 643, 653, 663
Phuoc Ha Valley, 200, 204
Phuoc Loan City, 632
Phuoc Long, 375, 606, 622, 625, 626, 630, 631, 633, 635, 636, 638
Phuoc Thanh Province, 60
Phuoc Tuy Province, 669
Phuoc Vinh, 60
Phuong Duc Airfield, 640, 643
Phuoc Long, 460
Phy Yen Airfield, 141
Phy Yen Province, 652
Plain of Jars, 448, 468
Plain of Reeds, 43, 81, 129, 210
Platt, Brigadier General Jonas M., 200
Plei Djereng, 615
Pleiku, xxiii, 44, 161, 164, 173, 188, 215, 219, 224, 226, 505, 513–515, 517, 519, 607, 614, 640–646, 649–652, 656, 658
Plei Mai, 197
Plei Mrong, 614
Plei Trap Valley, 615
Plet Djox Drap, 614
Plummer, Staff Sergeant Howard C., 254, 256
Polei Kleng, 516
Pope Paul, 300
Popular Forces, 206, 230, 279, 280, 285, 358, 417, 428, 523, 641, 651
Port Walut, 320
Pot, Pol, 454, 677
Potsdam Conference, 11
Pratt, Captain William, 239
Prek Lok, 337, 339
Program Evaluation Office, (Laos), 38
Provisional Revolutionary Government, 435, 452, 522–524, 529, 635
Pulau Bidong Island, xlix
Puong, Nguyen Thanh, 39

Quang, Lieutenant General Dang Van, xliii, 509, 522, 631, 645, 646, 648

Quang Duc, 454, 615, 631, 633, 641, 642

Quang Khe, 141

Quan Loi, 336, 339

Quang Nam, 180, 261, 626, 627, 655–657, 659, 661

Quang Ngai Province, 153, 178, 180, 184, 185, 199, 205, 262, 282, 469, 513, 519, 660, 662

Qui Nhon, 163, 164, 185–188, 189, 217, 219, 390, 513, 514, 648, 653, 658, 661

Quang Ninh, 310

Quang Thich Tri, 232

Quang Tin, 178, 261, 262, 469, 539, 626

Quang Tri City, 489, 491, (fall of) 501, 563

Quang Tri Combat Base, 492, 493, 505, 509, 510–519, 531, 533, 534, 577, 604, 607

Quang Tri Province, 34, 221, 235, 237, 238, 262–264, 281, 285, 379, 380, 382, 384, 395, 405, 410, 430, 493, 494, 503, 509, 510, 531, 532, 605, 608, 627, 655, 656, 660

Quat, Dr. Phan Huy, 165, 180

Que Son Valley, 198, 199, 261, 262, 285, 286, 354, 513

Quill, Captain Chris, 559

Quoc, Nguyen Ai, (Ho Chi Minh) 7

Raborn, Vice Admiral William F., 176

Rach Bap, 625

Radford, Admiral Arthur W., 28, 30

Raio Quan River, 379

Ramage, Captain James D., 247, 248, 289, 290, 481, 482, Rear Admiral, 597, 598

Ranch Hand, 208, 470, 472

Ranger, (carrier), 482

Reagan, Ronald, 1

Ready, Captain Peggy E., 237

Reasoner, Lieutenant Frank S., 189

Redic, Lance Corporal Terry, 272

Redmon, Captain Donald, 567

Red River, 21, 31, 33, 169, 304, 307, 322, 360, 398, 499

Reed, Lieutenant Philip, 273

Reed, Sergeant 1st Class, Donald, 265, 266

Reedy, Rear Admiral James, 245, 248

Regiments:
    1st Marine, 193, 200, 240, 409
    1st Vietcong, 181, 198, 199
    2nd Infantry, 339, 341
    3rd Marine, 196, 233, 284, 380, 381
    3rd North Vietnamese, 286
    Fourth Marine, 195, 196
    5th Marine, 354
    6th Infantry, 457
    7th South Vietnamese, 330

7th Marine, 194, 196, 200, 279

8th Cavalry, 357

9th Regiment, 191, 231, 251, 383, 430

12th Marine, 179

12th Infantry, 340

16th Infantry, 337

18th North Vietnamese, 220

20th Infantry, 340

22nd Infantry, 340

26th Marine, 381, 406, 408, 410

28th Infantry, 340

31st Infantry, 457

32nd, 528

47th, South Vietnamese, 215

51st South Vietnamese, 512

64th North Vietnamese, 518

77th Artillery, 340

95th, North Vietnamese, 215, 228

101st North Vietnamese, 340

272nd North Vietnamese, 339, 340

273rd, 340

325C North Vietnamese, 380

Regional Forces, 50, 133, 182, 192, 198, 199, 295, 358, 417, 428, 523, 631, 641, 651, 660

Reinburg, Specialist First Class, 193

Rembers, Major Richard T., 244

Republic of Korea Division, 182

Reston, James, 59, 477

Rew, Colonel Thomas F., 547, 550

Richardson, Rear Admiral David C., 288, 291–294, 297, 298

Richardson, John H., 84, 295

Ricketts, Admiral Claude V., 96

Ridgway, General Matthew B., 29, 30

Riley, Corporal Leland, 280, 281

Riojas, Sergeant Frank, 271, 274

Risner, Colonel Robinson, 170–172, 579

Ritchie, Captain Steven, 498–500

River of Perfume, 395

Rivers, Representative Mendel L., 202

Roberts, Major General Elvy B., 459

Robertson, Major Glenn, 564

Robert L. Wilson, (ship), 474

Robinson, Jr., Captain William F., 75

Rock Pile, 238, 281, 380

Rogers (ship), 287

Rogers, William, 437, 443

Rolling Thunder, 157, 159, 168, 206, 245, 296, 314, 315

Rome Plow, 333, 334

Roosevelt, President Franklin D., 11

Rosson, Major General William B., 302

Rostow, Dr. Walt W., 61, 62–64, 66, 67, 73, 124, 149

Roth, Corporal Samuel, 274

Route 1, 34, 178, 217, 221, 231, 238, 261,

262, 286, 384, 457, 459, 560, 492–494, 496, 510, 513, 515, 520, 587, 627, 631, 659, 660, 662, 665, 667, 669, 671
Route 4, 34, 336, 531, 669
Route 4 (Cambodia), 575
Route 5, 456
Route 7B, 649, 652, 663
Route 9, 238, 379, 382, 407, 409, 475
Route 13, 335, 339, 522, 528
Route 14, 34, 188, 410, 513, 516, 517, 519, 607, 640–642, 648, 649
Route 15, 75
Route 19, 217, 513, 514, 638, 640, 61, 648, 649, 653, 657
Route 20, 34, 513, 667
Route 21, 513, 640, 643, 648–650, 665
Route 137, 423
Route 244
Route 246, 337, 339
Route 547, 238
Route 548, 430
Royal Australian Air Force, 143
Rusk, Dean, 48, 82, 89, 93, 94, 97, 98, 99, 101, 102, 105, 107, 111, 113, 128, 143, 152, 168, 176, 197, 198, 231, 430
Russel, Captain James A., 457
Russell, Admiral James A., 457
Russell, Admiral James S., 55, 56, 363–365
Rutledge, Captain Howard, 553
Ryan, Representative Leo J., 637

Safer, Morley, 191, 192
Samrin, President Heng, 677
Sa Hynh, 577
Saigon River, xxv, xxvi, 128, 327, 329, 331, 625
Saint Francis Xavier, 103
Sa Ky River, 196
SALT Agreement, 507
SAM (missile), 294, 304–308, 311, 318, 323, 345, 346, 349, 360, 363, 429, 497, 546–548, 550, 554–558, 560–564, 567–570, 579
Sananikone, Phoui, 42
Sann, Premier San, 677
SA-7 (missile), xxii, xxxv, 488, 503, 523, 610, 611
Savio, Mario, 146
Schell, Airman First Class Kenneth, 467
Schlesinger, James, li, 655
Schurr, Lieutenant Colonel Harry W., 323
Scott, Senator Hugh, 586
Scott, Captain Rolland A., 556, 557
Seaborn, James B., 130, 145
Seaman, Major General Jonathan O., 212, 213, 327, 329, 333, 334–337
Self-Defense Force, 40, 50, 58, 60

Senate Armed Services Committee, 218, 251, 637
Senate Foreign Relations Committee, 51, 469
Senate Select Committee, 582
The Seven Mountains, 34, 673
Seventh Air Force, xxii, 163, 230, 245, 247, 283, 314, 384, 432, 486, 495, 547, 598
Seventh Fleet, xxvi, xxxvi, xliii, xlvi, 160, 173, 188, 196, 289, 290, 292, 314
Sharp, Admiral U.S. G., 132, 135, 149, 152, 165, 173, 177, 178, 186, 188, 189, 197, 208, 215, 216, 219, 245, 250, 283, 288, 295, 296, 303, 309, 314–318, 322, 359–361, 409, 418, 429, 506, 507, 595
Shaughnessy, Jr., John F., 89
Sigholtz, Lieutenant Colonel Robert H., 336
Sihanouk, Norodom, 23, 41, 42, 111–113, 126, 144, 145, 156, 157, 434, 435, 440, 452–454, 460, 581, 588, 677
Sihanoukville, 360, 474
Sijan, Captain Lance P., 369
Simmons, Colonel Edwin, 251
Simpson, Lieutenant Colonel William C., 333, 341
Smart, General Jacob E., 94, 97, 98
Smith, Captain Gerald W., 397
Smith, Major General Homer D., xxiii, xxx–xxxii, xxxv, xxxvii, xl, xli, 619, 664, 665, 667
Smith, Lieutenant John, 187
Snyder, Lieutenant Ray G., 191
Song Ba, 649
Song Be Airfield, 631
Song Be Valley, 357, 632
Song Bo corridor, 617
Song Ma River, 170, 244, 496, 497
Song Ngan River, 277
Song Thu Bon, 198
SonTay Prison, 481, 482
Sotello, Lance Corporal David, 272
Southeast Asia Treaty Organization, 36, 46, 49, 71, 127, 128, 154, 183
Special Forces, 60, 124, 132, 133, 134, 197, 212, 223, 228, 263, 268, 285, 335, 339, 343, 354, 366, 384, 407, 426
Special Investigating Subcommittee, xxxviii
Spencer, Master Sergeant Bradley, 193, 240, 241, 243
Spock, Dr. Benjamin, 203, 204, 443
Sproul Hall, 146
Squadrons:
  1st Air Commando, 89
  12th Special Operations, 468
  VA-23, 415
  VA-25, 187
  VA-35, 398
  VF-51, 139, 141

60th Bombardment, 546
67th Tactical Fighter, 170
VA-75, 398
VA-97, 481
VA-163, 249, 346
VA-164, 145
469th Tactical Fighter, 324
486th Bombardment, 550
VMFA-531, 181
4400th Combat Crew Training, (Jungle Jim), 61–63, 66, 77
Staley, Dr. Eugene, 60
Stalin, Joseph, 8, 9, 10, 44, 45
Stannard, Lieutenant Colonel John E., 357
Stay, Private First Class Michael, 253
Stegelin, Lieutenant Forest, 551, 552
Stennis, Senator John C., 318
Sterlin, Thomas, 308
Stilwell, Lieutenant General Richard G., 102, 430
Stockdale, Commander James B., 139–141, 579
Stocker, Major William, 548, 549, 563, 564, 567
Strait, Captain James, 565
Strategic Air Command, 545, 546, 556–570
Strategic Hamlet Program, 180
Stratton, Lieutenant Colonel Ray E., 494, 496
Stratton, Commander Richard, l, li
Students for a Democratic Society, 1, 80, 202
Stump, Admiral Felix B., 41
Sullivan, Captain Howard, 265
Sullivan, Captain Joseph, 279
Sullivan, Sergeant Joseph, 279
Sullivan, Lieutenant Colonel, 267
Sullivan, William H., 208, 286
Summers, Jr., Colonel Harry G., 595, 596
Sun Yat-Sen, 8
Suoi Da, 337
Suoi Tre, 340
Support Patrol Base Cat Stroc Con Trang, 340
Sûreté Générale, 9
Sutsakhan Lieutenant General, Sak, 586–588
Svay Rieng Province, 457, 459, 622, 666, 673
Sweeney, Jr., General Walter G., 151
Symington, Senator Stuart, 251, 320, 366

Tactical Air Force, 61, 74, 80, 150, 151, 163, 444, 495
Tag Quang Tu Pagoda, 396
Tai Nguyen Thermal Power Plant, 556
Takhli, 305
Tam Ky, 198, 286
Tam Quang, 661, 662
Tan An, 666, 669
Tan Canh, 514, 516, 519
Tan Khai, 529

Tan My, 659–661
Tan Son Nhut, xix–xxi, xxv, xxvii, xxviii, xxx, xxxi–xxxvi, xxxix–xli, xliii, xliv, xlvi, 70, 89, 100, 102, 143, 385, 389, 391–393, 577, 669, 670
Tan Trac, 11
Task Force 77, 139, 144, 163, 196, 247, 289, 361, 402, 481, 597, 598
Task Force Deane, 331, 332
Tassigny, General Jean de Lattre de, 22
Tat, Colonel Pham Van, 650
Ta Trach, 627
Tau O, 523, 528, 529
Tay Loch Airfield, 395, 396
Tay Ninh Province, 284, 327, 460, 520, 521, 522, 609, 622, 626, 630, 661, 642, 656, 666
Taylor, Captain Dennis, xxv
Taylor, Master Sergeant, xxxvii
Taylor, Major General Leonard B., 251
Taylor, General Maxwell D., 61–67, 69, 77, 88, 98, 102, 103, 107, 121, 126, 129, 132, 133, 136–138, 143, 145, 149, 152–165, 174, 176, 178, 182–185, 188, 190, 212, 477
Terry, Captain Ronald W., 151
Tet Offensive, 216, 313, 340, 343, 389, 401, 403, 404, 405, 409, 416, 417, 420–422, 439, 495, 594, 675
Thach Hab River, 492, 493, 510, 607, 659
Thach Tru, 199
Thai Nguyen Marshalling Yards, 422, 563
Thai Nguyen Steel Mill, 305
Than, Colonel Le Van, 650
Thang Bien, 354
Thang, Ton Duc, 45
Thanh An District, 641
Thanh Binh, 199, 286
Thanh Dien Forestry Preserve, 329, 331, 333, 334
Thanh, General, 365, 370
Thanh Hoa, 169, 170, 177, 244, 289, 617
Thanh Hoa Bridge, 168, 170, 171, 290, 323, 496, 497
Thanh, Nguyen That (original name of Ho Chim Minh), 6, 369
Thanh Quit Bridge, 231
Thanh, Son Ngoc, 113
The, General Trinh Minh, 39
Thi, Lieutenant General Lan Quang, 181, 189, 231, 238, 261, 264, 327, 330, 331, 333, 625, 656
Thieu, Nguyen Van, 165, 166, 178, 179, 195, 198, 200, 211, 218, 227, 229, 230, 232, 233, 236, 365, 373, 377, 389, 390, 391, 414, 415, 417, 420, 421, 430, 437, 439, 456, 458, 460, 470, 475, 476, 480, 483,

493, 501, 503, 515, 518, 522, 529, 533,
534, 536–538, 540, 574, 580–582, 585,
603, 610, 613, 613, 615, 629, 631, 637,
638, 640, 641, 643, 645, 647–650, 655,
656, 663, 664, 658, 669–671, 675
Tho, Le Duc, 474, 476, 478, 484, 486, 505,
536, 539–543, 573, 574, 576, 581, 583,
600, 639
Thua Thien Province, 34, 221, 237, 238, 262,
263, 479, 501, 510, 512, 608, 621, 665,
660
Thud Ridge, 304, 323, 559
Thuong Duc, 627
Ticonderoga (carrier), 138, 139–141
Tien, Colonel, 642
Tieu, Colonel, 650
Tin Phuoc, 626
III Amphibious Force, 174, 181, 188, 189,
197, 199, 200, 219, 227, 232, 262, 264,
285, 286, 297, 356, 381, 384, 398, 411
Thompson, Charles, 171, 172
Thompson, Sir Robert G. K., 66, 68, 84
Thirteenth Air Force, 70, 80
Thomas, Lieutenant Ronald, 567
Thorsness, Major Leo K., 307–309
312th Evacuation Hospital, 403
Throckmorton, Lieutenant General, John L.,
165
Thua Man, 649
Tiensha Peninsula, 233, 234
Tinh Hoi Pagoda, 234, 235
Thuan, Brigadier General Quoc, 330
Thuc, Archbishop, 98
Thurmond, Senator, 400
Timmes, Major General Charles T., 67
Toan, Lieutenant General Nguyen Van, 515,
517, 519, 615, 640, 670
Ton Le Chan Base, 521, 608, 611, 613
Throckmorton, Lieutenant General John L., 131
Thu, Nguyen Chang, 111
Thuy, Xuan, 415, 438, 439, 441, 447, 474,
478, 536, 541
Tra, General Tran Van, 371, 639
Trammel, Captain James, 550, 551
Trang Bom, 669
Tran, Loan, xxxii
Tran, Major Tanh, xxxii–xxv, 1
Tran, Van Huong, 144
Trapnell, General Thomas H., 31
Trejo, Technical Sergeant Edward M., 414
Tri, General Do Cao, 365, 458
Tri Phapp, 622, 673
Tri Tam, 656
Tri Tien, 639
Tri Quang, 101, 102, 107, 282
Truman, President Harry S., lii, 13, 17–21,
312, 400, 592, 609

Trung, Emperor Quang, 488
Trung, Ly Bon, 4
Trung Nghia, 614
Trung, Trieu An, 4
Truong, Brig. Gen. Ngo Quang, 365, 395,
396, 501–503, 655, 656, 658, 660, 661
Tu, Colonel, 597
Tuong, Brigadier General Le Trung, 643
Turner, Captain James, 568
Tuy Duc, 615
Tuy Hoa, 215, 514, 638, 646, 649, 651, 652,
655
Twentieth Air Force, 506, 546
Twining, General Nathan F., 29
Ty, General Le Van, 39

Ulm, Captain Donald S., 337, 338
Union (Codename), 354
Union II (Codename), 354
Union of Associated States, 37
United Nations, 21, 94, 129, 203, 208, 453,
593
Uong Bi, 207
U-Tapao, xxix, 546–548, 553, 560, 561, 563,
564, 570, 571, 578, 588
U Thant, 94, 95, 454
Utter, Lieutenant Colonel Leon N., 200

Vale, Lieutenant Colonel Sumner A., 278
Vam Co Tay River, 622
Van, Nguyen Thi, 310
Vann, John Paul, 514, 516, 577, 519
Veterans Administration, 589, 679, 681
Veterans Dioxin and Radiation Exposure Com-
prensation Standards Act, 681
Veterans Memorial, 681
Veth, Rear Admiral Kenneth L., 397
Vasdias, Lieutenant Richard A., 222
Vazquez, Captain Francisco, 223
Vessey, Jr., Lieutenant Colonel John W., 340
Vickers, Captain Gary, 551
Victory, Lance Corporal, Ralph Glober, 267,
268
Vidaurie, Private First Class, 254
Vien, General Cao Van, 390, 393, 509, 522,
539, 646–649, 652, 655, 664, 670, 675
Vientiane, 154, 199, 678
Vinh, 138, 141, 248, 293, 546
Vinh Loc Island, 659, 661
Vinh Long, xlviii, 617
Vo Dinh, 516
Voice of America, 91, 99
Vojvodich, Wing Commander Mele, 555
Volet, Colonel Leonard, 425
Vote, Captain Gary V., 302, 303
Vung Tau, xxv, xxvi, xxxix, xlii, 75, 184, 392,
653, 671

Vung Tau Charter, 124, 185, 359

Walt, Major General Lewis W., 179, 180, 189, 192, 194–196, 199, 200, 205, 206, 217, 218, 225, 230, 232–236, 262, 264, 279, 281, 283, 284–286, 296
War Powers Resolution, 584
Waugh, Master Sergeant Billy, 192, 193
Weathermen, 463
Wessel, Captain Lawrence, xxi
West, Jr., General Arthur L., 208
Westmoreland, General William C., 123, 124, 129, 131, 133, 135, 141, 150, 155–161, 164–166, 175, 176, 178–182, 186, 188– 190, 192, 195, 197, 199, 200, 205, 208, 210–214, 217, 219–221, 227, 228, 230, 236–238, 262, 263, 281–284, 297, 301, 306, 307, 311, 313, 314, 317, 327, 329, 335, 343, 356, 359, 370, 377, 379, 381– 385, 390, 393, 396, 397, 403, 434, 592, 595, 599
Weyand, Major General Frederick C., 213, 330, 336, 592, 664
Weyland, General Otto P., 25
Wheeler, General Earle G., 83, 123, 128, 140, 143, 144, 150, 182, 288, 314, 317, 319, 429, 437, 467
White, General Thomas, 47
Wickwire, Lieutenant Colonel Peter A., 284
Wilbanks, Captain Hilliard, A., 302, 303
Wild Weasels, 304, 323, 497, 555
Williams, Lieutenant General Samuel T., 40
Wilson, J. Harold, 154
Wings:
    1st Marine Aircraft, 179, 380

8th Tactical Fighter, 323, 497
43rd Strategic, 553, 563
62nd South Vietnamese, xxxii
72nd Strategic, 547
303rd Consolidated Aircraft Maintenance, 546
307th Strategic, 546, 547, 561
315th Air Commando, 413
355th Tactical Fighter, 323
388th Tactical Fighter, 323, 555
Women's Army Corps, 237, 385
Wonson, 506, 507
Wood, Captain Anthony, xxxvi, xxxvii
Wood, Lieutenant Barry, 351
Wood, Captain Robert, 293
World War I, 8, 682
World War II, 3, 11, 13, 20, 48, 52, 70, 73, 121, 131, 162, 175, 208, 209, 219, 298, 314, 365, 412, 414, 422, 497, 506, 546, 556, 573, 593, 594, 598, 600, 616, 680, 682
Wulzen, Rear Admiral B. W., 166

Xavier, Lieutenant Augustus M., 223
Xuan Loc, 330, 667–669
Xuan, General Mai Huu, 103, 307, 308
Xuan, Nguyen Van, 38

Yankee Station, 160, 163, 188, 292, 298, 398
Yen Vien Railroad Yards, 497, 556
Yeu, Colonel Dam Quang, 231–232
Young, Captain Gerald O., 366–369
Yuill, Lieutenant Colonel, 560
Y Uong-Bi, 248

Zacharais, Commander Jerrold, 398, 399

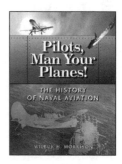
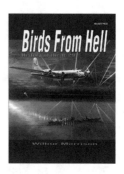

The Parrot's Beak

U.S. Operations in Cambodia

by Paul B. Morgan

By the author of *K-9 Soldiers: Vietnam and After,* Morgan's latest book divulges secret insertion techniques and information about Nixon's secret war that the government still refuses to acknowledge.

ISBN: 1-55571-543-5   200 pages, paperback: $14.95

Regret to Inform You

Experiences of Families Who Lost A Family Member in Vietnam

by Norman Berg

How do you cope with the knowledge that a loved one is missing in action, remains not recovered? Thirty years later, real people still wait for the war in Vietnam to end—to know what happened to their loved ones. *Regret to Inform You* provides a glimpse of the human strength and persistence needed to survive the maze of government bureaucracy, miscommunication, and inconclusive evidence. Eight families relate their stories as only they can.

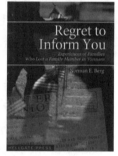

ISBN: 1-55571-509-5   168 pages, paperback: $16.95

Coast Guard Action in Vietnam

Stories of Those Who Served

by Paul Scotti

Written by the author of *Seaports: Ships, Piers, and People* and *Police Divers,* this well-crafted lively and engaging history will rejuvenate one's pride in the American military with its little-known details of the Coast Guard's involvement in Vietnam. The fact that they were in Vietnam at all is a surprise to many. What they were doing there will be an even bigger surprise!

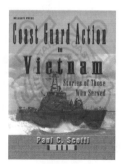

ISBN: 1-55571-528-1   250 pages, paperback: $17.95

Project Omega

Eye of the Beast

by James E. Acre

"CNN tried its level best to dishonor the reputation of the brave men of Special Operations Group.... Acre's beautifully written and accurate portrayal of some of the actions of that noble unit will allow the reader to see how these daring young men made accomplishing the impossible routine and to also set the record straight."

– David Hackworth, Author of *About Face* and H*azardous Duty*

ISBN: 1-55571-511-7   228 pages, paperback: $13.95

Honor & Sacrifice

The Montagnards of Ba Cat, Vietnam

by Anthony J. Blondell

Special Forces (Green Beret) A-Team member, Anthony Blondell, tells an action-packed story of the exploitation of the Montagnards, and what happens when the South Vietnamese government not only backs out of a nearly completed, $5,000-per-day Special Forces mission, but tries to sabotage it to keep from paying.

ISBN: 1-55571-533-8   250 pages, hardcover: $21.95

After the Storm

A Vietnam Veteran's Reflection

by Paul Drew

Even after 25 years, the scars of the Vietnam War are still felt by those who were involved. *After the Storm: A Vietnam Veteran's Reflection* is more than a war story. It concerns itself with the mood of the nation during the war years, and covers the author's intellectual and psychological evolution as he questions the political and military decisions that resulted in nearly 60,000 American deaths.

ISBN: 1-55571-500-1   132 pages, paperback: $14.95

K-9 Soldiers

Vietnam and After

by Paul B. Morgan

A retired U.S. Army officer, former Green Beret, Customs K-9 and Security Specialist, Paul B. Morgan, has written *K-9 Soldiers*. In his book, Morgan relates twenty-four brave stories from his lifetime of working with man's best friend in combat and on the streets. They are the stories of dogs and their handlers who work behind the scenes when a disaster strikes, a child is lost, or some bad guy tries to outrun the cops.

ISBN: 1-55571-495-1   196 pages, paperback: $13.95

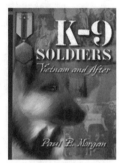

How It Was

A Vietnam Story

by John Patrick O'Hara

How it Was is not a blow-by-blow record, but a shoebox of memories presented as they flashed inside the mind of a Vet trying to come to terms with what he had seen and done during his tour. It is a non-traditional, thought-provoking journey into a war-torn mind.

ISBN: 1-55571-516-8   125 pages, Paperback: $12.95

Rockets Like Rain

A Year in Vietnam

by Dale Reich

Ten men from the little town of Oconomowoc, Wisconsin, were killed in the Vietnam War; Dale Reich survived. He wants his hometown heroes and the war that took them to be remembered. This is the story of his year as an American infantryman in Vietnam—365 unforgettable days that took Dale 30 years to finally write about.

ISBN: 1-55571-615-6   185 pages, paperback, $15.95